BIOMARKERS IN CANCER DETECTION AND MONITORING OF THERAPEUTICS

BIOMARKERS IN CANCER DETECTION AND MONITORING OF THERAPEUTICS

Volume 1: Discovery and Technologies

Edited by

R.C. SOBTI
Biotechnology, Panjab University, Chandigarh, India

AWTAR KRISHAN GANJU
Department of Pathology, University of Miami Medical School, Miami, FL, United States

AASTHA SOBTI
Department of Immunotechnology, University of Lund, Lund, Sweden

ELSEVIER

ACADEMIC PRESS
An imprint of Elsevier

Academic Press is an imprint of Elsevier
125 London Wall, London EC2Y 5AS, United Kingdom
525 B Street, Suite 1650, San Diego, CA 92101, United States
50 Hampshire Street, 5th Floor, Cambridge, MA 02139, United States
The Boulevard, Langford Lane, Kidlington, Oxford OX5 1GB, United Kingdom

Notices
Knowledge and best practice in this field are constantly changing. As new research and experience broaden our understanding, changes in research methods, professional practices, or medical treatment may become necessary.

Practitioners and researchers must always rely on their own experience and knowledge in evaluating and using any information, methods, compounds, or experiments described herein. In using such information or methods they should be mindful of their own safety and the safety of others, including parties for whom they have a professional responsibility.

To the fullest extent of the law, neither the Publisher nor the authors, contributors, or editors, assume any liability for any injury and/or damage to persons or property as a matter of products liability, negligence or otherwise, or from any use or operation of any methods, products, instructions, or ideas contained in the material herein.

ISBN 978-0-323-95116-6

For information on all Academic Press publications
visit our website at https://www.elsevier.com/books-and-journals

Publisher: Stacy Masucci
Acquisitions Editor: Rafael E. Teixeira
Editorial Project Manager: Matthew Mapes
Production Project Manager: Sajana Devasi P K
Cover Designer: Vicky Pearson Esser

Typeset by STRAIVE, India

Working together
to grow libraries in
developing countries

www.elsevier.com • www.bookaid.org

Contents

11. Viral miRNAs role as diagnostic, prognostic biomarkers for cancer and infectious diseases   **199**

Sneha Kumari, Abhishek Pandeya, Raj Kumar Khalko, Ulkarsha,
R.C. Sobti, and Sunil Babu Gosipatala

12. Pharmacogenomics and oncology: A therapeutic approach for cancer treatment   **223**

Neetu Saini, Monika Kadian, and Anil Kumar

Contributors

Eman R. Abd Elhaliem
Physiology Division, Zoology Department, Faculty of Science, Beni-Suef University, Beni-Suef, Egypt

Mohamed Abd-Elbaset
Faculty of Pharmacy, El Saleheya El Gadida University, El Sharqia, Egypt

Shyam Aggarwal
Department of Molecular Oncology, Sir Ganga Ram Hospital, New Delhi, India

Noha A. Ahmed
Physiology Division, Zoology Department, Faculty of Science, Beni-Suef University, Beni-Suef, Egypt

Osama M. Ahmed
Physiology Division, Zoology Department, Faculty of Science, Beni-Suef University, Beni-Suef, Egypt

Seema Bansal
Department of Pharmacology, Postgraduate Institute of Medical Education and Research, Chandigarh, India

Sudha Bansal
Department of Pharmaceutical Sciences, Guru Jambeshwar University of Science and Technology, Hissar, India

Gitika Batra
Department of Neurology; Department of Pharmacology, Postgraduate Institute of Medical Education and Research, Chandigarh, India

Puneet Bhardwaj
Department of Zoology, Panjab University, Chandigarh, India

Anmol Bhatia
Department of Biotechnology, Thapar Institute of Engineering and Technology, Patiala, India

Ramila Bisht
Centre for Social Medicine and Community Health, Jawaharlal Nehru University, New Delhi, India

Sudeep Bose
Amity Institute of Biotechnology, Amity University Uttar Pradesh, Noida, India

Mani Chopra
Department of Zoology, Panjab University, Chandigarh, India

Gajendra Choudhary
Department of Pharmacology, Postgraduate Institute of Medical Education and Research, Chandigarh, India

Neha Dhir
Department of Pharmacology, Postgraduate Institute of Medical Education and Research, Chandigarh, India

Asit Ranjan Ghosh
Microbial Molecular Biology Laboratory, Department of Integrative Biology, School of BioSciences and Technology, Vellore Institute of Technology (VIT), Vellore, India

Rajwant K. Gill
Freelancer Scientist, Vancouver, BC, Canada

Sikander S. Gill
Freelancer Scientist, Vancouver, BC, Canada

Sunil Babu Gosipatala
Department of Biotechnology, Babasaheb Bhimrao Ambedkar University, Lucknow, India

Ashish Jain
Department of Pharmacology, Postgraduate Institute of Medical Education and Research, Chandigarh, India

Shweta Jain
Department of Pharmacology, Postgraduate Institute of Medical Education and Research, Chandigarh, India

Rupa Joshi
Department of Pharmacology, Postgraduate Institute of Medical Education and Research, Chandigarh, India

Monika Kadian
Pharmacology Division, University Institute of Pharmaceutical Sciences (UIPS), UGC Centre of Advanced Study, Panjab University, Chandigarh, India

Gurjeet Kaur
Department of Pharmacology, Postgraduate Institute of Medical Education and Research, Chandigarh, India

Hardeep Kaur
Department of Pharmacology, Postgraduate Institute of Medical Education and Research, Chandigarh, India

Raj Kumar Khalko
Department of Biotechnology, Babasaheb Bhimrao Ambedkar University, Lucknow, India

Anurag Kuhad
UIPS, Panjab University, Chandigarh, India

Anil Kumar
University Institute of Pharmaceutical Sciences, Panjab University, Chandigarh, India

Subodh Kumar
UIPS, Panjab University; Department of Pharmacology, Postgraduate Institute of Medical Education and Research, Chandigarh, India

Sneha Kumari
Department of Biotechnology, Babasaheb Bhimrao Ambedkar University, Lucknow, India

Satyabrata Kundu
Department of Pharmacology, ISF College of Pharmacy, Moga, Punjab, India

Anjoy Majhi
Department of Chemistry, Presidency College, Kolkata, India

Deepti Malik
Department of Biochemistry, All India Institute of Medical Sciences, Bilaspur, India

Gladson David Masih
Department of Pharmacology, Postgraduate Institute of Medical Education and Research, Chandigarh, India

Bikash Medhi
Department of Pharmacology, Postgraduate Institute of Medical Education and Research, Chandigarh, India

Sweety Mehra
Department of Zoology, Panjab University, Chandigarh, India

Shaveta Menon
Centre for Public Health and Healthcare Administration, Eternal University, Baru Sahib, Himachal Pradesh, India

Madhusmita Mishra
Amity Institute of Biotechnology, Amity University Uttar Pradesh, Noida, India

Shivani Arora Mittal
Department of Research, Sir Ganga Ram Hospital, New Delhi, India

Abhishek Pandeya
Department of Biotechnology, Babasaheb Bhimrao Ambedkar University, Lucknow, India

Sandip Paul
Department of Chemistry, Presidency University; Department of Chemistry, Bhawanipur Education Society, Kolkata, India

Praisy K. Prabha
Department of Pharmacology, Postgraduate Institute of Medical Education and Research, Chandigarh, India

Manisha Prajapat
Department of Pharmacology, Postgraduate Institute of Medical Education and Research, Chandigarh, India

Ajay Prakash
Department of Pharmacology, Postgraduate Institute of Medical Education and Research, Chandigarh, India

Peeyush Prasad
Department of Research, Sir Ganga Ram Hospital, New Delhi, India

Neetu Saini
Dolphin PG College of Science and Agriculture, Chunni Kalan, Punjab, India

Pinki Saha Sardar
Department of Chemistry, Bhawanipur Education Society, Kolkata, India

Amit Raj Sharma
Department of Pharmacology, Post Graduate Institute of Medical Education and Research, Chandigarh, India

Anuradha Sharma
Department of Zoology, Panjab University, Chandigarh, India

Indu Sharma
Department of Zoology, Panjab University, Chandigarh, India

Madhu Sharma
Department of Zoology, Panjab University, Chandigarh, India

Saurabh Sharma
Department of Pharmacology, Postgraduate Institute of Medical Education and Research, Chandigarh, India

Siddharth Sharma
Department of Biotechnology, Thapar Institute of Engineering and Technology, Patiala, India

Ashutosh Singh
Department of Pharmacology, Postgraduate Institute of Medical Education and Research, Chandigarh, India

Rahul Soloman Singh
Department of Pharmacology, Postgraduate Institute of Medical Education and Research, Chandigarh, India

Shamsher Singh
Department of Pharmacology, ISF College of Pharmacy, Moga, Punjab, India

Shweta Sinha
Post Graduate Institute of Medical Education and Research, Chandigarh, India

R.C. Sobti
Department of Biotechnology, Panjab University, Chandigarh, India

Shriyansh Srivastava
Department of Pharmacology, ISF College of Pharmacy, Moga, Punjab, India

Benjamin Suroy
Department of Pharmacology, Postgraduate Institute of Medical Education and Research, Chandigarh, India

Nida Taimoor
Amity Institute of Biotechnology, Amity University Uttar Pradesh, Noida, India

Shiva Tushir
Department of Pharmacy, Panipat Institute of Engineering and Technology (PIET), Samalkha, Panipat, Haryana, India

Bulbul Tyagi
Amity Institute of Biotechnology, Amity University Uttar Pradesh, Noida, India

Ulkarsha
Department of Biotechnology, Babasaheb Bhimrao Ambedkar University, Lucknow, India

Monu Yadav
Department of Pharmacy, School of Medical & Allied Sciences, GD Goenka University, Gurgaon, India

Preface

Cancer is one of the most formidable health challenges, resulting in recurrence and poor survival. The complex nature of cancer cells evades early detection, and their extreme complexity impedes effective early diagnosis and treatment. Detection and monitoring of specific tumor marker expression is of diagnostic, prognostic, and therapeutic value. These molecular footprints have the potential to revolutionize our understanding of cancer detection and therapeutics.

Cancer biomarkers provide insights into the possible origin, stage, and aggressiveness of a tumor. Biomarker testing holds the key to unlocking a new era in personalized medicine where disease prevention, diagnosis, and treatment are tailored to the expression of specific genes and proteins. It has the potential to transform cancer diagnosis and management, steering in an era of personalized and targeted therapeutics that can improve treatment outcomes.

Cancer biomarkers cover a wide spectrum of biochemical components, including nucleic acids, proteins, sugars, cellular metabolites, and genetic and cytokinetic parameters. The study of biomarkers facilitates diagnosis, risk assessment, and prognosis, as well as predictions regarding treatment effectiveness, toxicity, and recurrence.

This book *Biomarkers in Cancer* delves into the complexities of cancer biomarkers, exploring the diverse techniques and methods available for their study.

Volume 1 is an introduction to the problem and various efforts for the study and use of different biomarkers in cancer diagnosis and treatment, whereas Volume 2 deals with applications of biomarker research.

R.C. Sobti and Aastha Sobti are thankful to Dr. Vipin Sobti, Er. Aditi, Er. Vineet, Er. Ankit, and Irene for their full support in preparing the book.

R.C.S. acknowledges Indian National Science Academy, New Delhi, for providing a platform as Senior Scientist to continue the academic pursuits.

Editors
R.C. Sobti
Awtar Krishan
Aastha Sobti

CHAPTER ONE

Milestones in cancer research

Anmol Bhatia[a], Siddharth Sharma[a], and R.C. Sobti[b]
[a]Department of Biotechnology, Thapar Institute of Engineering and Technology, Patiala, India
[b]Department of Biotechnology, Panjab University, Chandigarh, India

1. Introduction

Immeasurable advancements have been made over the last few decades in the field of cancer research. This has been mainly possible because of the unfolded new technologies that successfully aid research in cancer. It has been a while that cancer has been identified and established to be a chronic disease and is a complex disease involving changes in multiple genes (Hanahan and Weinberg, 2011). According to the World Health Organization (WHO), one of the main principles of cancer prevention is early screening. Improved early cancer screening could prevent one-third of cancers from developing to extreme stages, ultimately improving the survival rate (Ngoma, 2006). The past few decades have brought about many collective, rather distinct breakthrough advancements in the field of Cancer Biology. Considering the current time to be the post-Human Genome Project (HGP) era, the scientists in the field of Cancer Biology have begun to consider the root of carcinogenesis, i.e., the molecular mechanisms on the genome level (Stratton, 2011).

There have been various landmark findings helping achieve the advancements in cancer research. To begin with, it's the finding of aberrant chromosomal patterns in DNA methylation and its formation and expression in cancer—next, the establishment of tumor virology by discovering the Rous sarcoma virus (RSV) in 1901. The knowledge of cancer development due to viruses has been expanding since then. The cascade of cancer metastasis is the ultimate reason for cancer morbidity and has a complex advance. Lung cancer is the reason for most cancer-related deaths worldwide causes frequent malignant neoplasms in the body. Tobacco smoking is one of the primary triggers for the spread of lung cancer. Next, chromosomal translocations, protein phosphorylation, and suppressed apoptosis are the most frequent reasons for oncogenesis. Significant research on the tumor microenvironment has been reported to bring out possible treatment options in various cancers. Also, the immune system plays an active role in tumor formation inside the human body. Lastly, in this chapter, possible blocks in the current cancer research and its way out have been briefly mentioned.

Biomarkers in Cancer Detection and Monitoring of Therapeutics
https://doi.org/10.1016/B978-0-323-95116-6.00008-6

2. Landmark researches

2.1 Aberrant chromatin

One of the most significant types of research in Cancer Biology has been about the epigenetic changes being carried out during carcinogenesis. Epigenetics is defined as the changes in the arrangement and expression of genes without any alterations in the primary DNA sequence. These alterations are heritable and pass down during somatic cell replication. Cancer is considered to be an epigenetic disease rather than genetic. There are majorly two epigenetic processes that are studied during tumorigenesis. One is DNA hypermethylation, and the other is the changes in DNA packaging components. These processes are linked to each other and modify epigenetic regulation of transcription participating in tumorigenesis (Feinberg et al., 2006; Herman and Baylin, 2003; Jones and Laird, 1999).

The process of DNA methylation occurs when the methyl group is transferred from the donor substrate S-adenosyl methionine to the C5 position of the cytosines, also known as CpG dinucleotides, with the help of DNA methyltransferase (DNMT) enzymes. Throughout evolution, delamination has been observed throughout the genome and successive thymidine repair of these cytosines (CpG). Eventually, there has been a noticeable dip in the CpG dinucleotides within the normal cells of the human genome. The CpG sites have been conserved that reside in the 5′ end of about 50% of human genes (Bird, 2002).

Various hypermethylated genes have been reported concerning human cancers, and about half of them are related to the familial types of cancer. A few of the hypermethylated genes in nonfamilial cancers are E-cadherin, LKB1, Rb, VHL, BRCA-1, APC, MLH1, p16INKA, etc. There is a selective loss of a gene function. Hypermethylation can be seen in a particular tumor type (Baylin and Herman, 2000).

2.2 Rous sarcoma virus

There has been a diverse range of carcinogens (cancer-causing agents) such as chemical carcinogens (smoke from tobacco, aflatoxin), radiations (ultraviolet, X-rays), etc. In addition to the most commonly known carcinogens, viruses are capable of causing cancers and are widely known as "tumor viruses" or "Oncoviruses." About 15% of cancer caused in humans is caused by viruses. For example, cervical carcinoma, which is prevalent in women across the globe, is caused by an infection from the human papillomavirus virus (HPV). Tumor viruses have been in research ever since the 1980s. The ultimate discoveries of oncogenes and tumor suppressor genes have been made due to the investigation of tumor viruses. Tumor viruses were first found in mice, and their related were found in humans later. These viruses can progress tumor formation and transformation (Howley

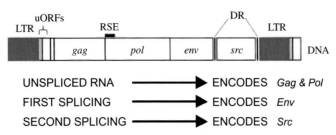

Fig. 1 The RSV genome.

and Livingston, 2009). The first-ever oncovirus was discovered in 1908 by Drs. Ellerman and Bang in chickens. It was an avian retrovirus and was known to cause leukemia in chickens. This finding wasn't treated as a milestone back then because leukemia wasn't regarded as cancer. A few years later, in 1911, Peyton Rous discovered a sarcoma-inducing virus in chickens. The virus was named after its discoverer and was called Rous sarcoma virus (RSV) (Rous, 1911).

RSV is an avian retrovirus initially isolated from a common fowl with two copies of capped and polyadenylated positive RNA strands (Beemon et al., 1974; Furuichi et al., 1975). The retrovirus genome (genomic RNA) is reverse transcribed into a complementary DNA copy upon entering the host cell. This DNA is then carefully integrated into the host cell chromosomal DNA with the assistance of a retroviral integrase enzyme. This forms a provirus that carries out the next course of action for the expression of the gene with the help of RNA polymerase II and Ribosomal machinery (Coffin et al., 1997). As shown in Fig. 1, RSV contains three upstream open reading frames (uORFs): gag, *pol, env,* and *src.* These are expressed from the DNA of the provirus into three RNA isoforms. Gag and pol are individually described as polyproteins and then are cleaved to form functional polypeptides. Gag encodes for the structural elements of the viral capsid, whereas Pol helps encode for reverse transcriptase and integrase (Coffin et al., 1997). The first RNA splicing leads to the expression of env, which forms glycoproteins that cover the retro lipid bilayer on the outside. It aids in facilitating cell entry by interacting with the cell surface receptors. Upon second RNA splicing, src is expressed. Various point mutations in the src and C-terminal substitution causes downregulation inside the host cell (Coffin et al., 1981; Martin, 2004; Petersen et al., 1984; Petersen and Hackett, 1985).

2.3 Cancer metastasis

The mortality related to cancer can be linked to metastasis in the primary tumor. When a primary tumor metastases, it spreads the cancer cells to distant surroundings and organs in the body (1–8). In 2011, it was reported that the metastasis of the primary tumor causes about 90% of cancer-related deaths worldwide (9). The series of metastasis begins with cancer cells detaching from the primary tumor and invading the body's circulatory and lymphatic system, escaping the immune responses along the way and ultimately coloniz-ing and proliferating in different regions of the body (7,12,13). The metastatic cascade can broadly be categorized into two phases: (i) physical translocation and (ii) colonization (Chaffer and Weinberg, 2011). For the physical translocation of cancer cells from the primary tumor to the dissemination site, the cells must first acquire the potential to migrate and invade. These cell attributes enable it to merge within lymphatic and blood vessels traveling toward distant sites within the body. The only indication of the meta-static spread of cancer cells is their presence in the draining lymph nodes. A break-off point is established from these lymph nodes, from which further metastasis is triggered (Joyce and Pollard, 2009).

The chromosomal instability is the m stair toward the invasion of the cancer cells (Lambert et al., 2017). The fluctuation in the chromosomes is the result of the ongoing mistakes prevalent during the segregation of chromosomes in mitosis. This further causes the breach of the micronuclei exposing the genomic DNA into the cytoplasm. Upon this, the cytosolic DNA-sensing pathways such as cyclic GMP-AMP synthase get acti-vated (Bakhoum et al., 2018). The epigenetic changes such as aging, disruptions in the circadian rhythm, signals from the extracellular matrix, etc., aid in the invasion and metastasis (Fares et al., 2020).

2.4 Smoking: A cause of lung cancer

Lung cancer is the most rapidly growing malignant neoplasm within men and the cause of the most extensive cancer-related deaths worldwide (Siegel et al., 2015). According to a study conducted in 2012 by GLBOCAN, about 1,242,000 new lung cancer cases have been reported among men constituting 17% of all cancers excluding nonmelanoma skin cancer. And about 583,000 new cases of lung cancer have been reported in women, con-stituting 9% of all cancers (Ferlay et al., 2013). The middle and the low-income countries include about 58% of all the cases worldwide (Foreman et al., 2014). As mentioned ear-lier, lung cancer is the most significant cause of cancer-related deaths, accounting for approximately 19% of all cancer deaths (Ferlay et al., 2012). The prevalence of lung can-cer is lower in people aged <40 compared to age groups ranging from 75 to 80 years in most populations (Malvezzi et al., 2013).

Cigarette smoking is the primary cause of all major histological types of lung cancer—routine smoking sources for 30% of all cancer-related deaths (WHO, 1997). Not only lung cancer but tobacco smoking is one of the root causes of other cancers. These include oral, laryngeal, oropharyngeal, hypopharyngeal, and esophageal cancers (International Agency for Research on Cancer, 1986). It has also been linked with other body cancers such as liver, colon, stomach, cervix, nose, and myeloid leukemia (Doll, 1996; Chao et al., 2000).

According to the assessments carried out by the International Agency of Research on cancer, bout 4000 chemicals have been pinned down in cigarette smoke, with more than

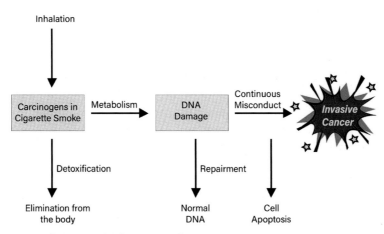

Fig. 2 Factors contributing to the formation of an invasive cancer.

60 of them have been established as lung cancer carcinogens. A carcinogen is a cancer-causing agent and can be chemical, physical, or biological (Hoffmann et al., 2001). Although present in small quantities of about 5–200 ng per cigarette, these carcinogens comprise the most potent carcinogens—polycyclic aromatic hydrocarbons (PAHs), aromatic amines, and N-nitrosamines. Other volatile carcinogens such as benzene and butadiene are present in 10–1000 μg per cigarette. The most critical carcinogens linked to the onset of lung cancer are benzopyrene and nitrosamine 4-(methylnitrosamino)-1-(3-pyridyl)-1-butanone (nicotine-derived nitrosamine ketone) (Hecht, 1999). Nicotine in cigarette smoke, by and large, cannot be considered a carcinogen. It, although occasionally induce tumor formation under special conditions of hyperoxia. Nicotine is the fundamental cause of smoking addiction (Schuller et al., 1995).

One of the most effective ways comprises the prevention of cigarette smoking altogether. For those who are routine smokers, possible termination practices should be followed. These practices have shown a significant pay-off in the later years of the 20th century (American Cancer Society, 2001). However, lower than 20% of cigarette smokers are subject to developing lung cancer (International Agency for Research on Cancer, 1986). As depicted in Fig. 2, multiple factors can give lung cancer susceptibility in cigarette smokers. These include the carcinogenic scale of uptake, detoxification, metabolism, DNA repair frequency, ability, cell apoptosis, impact on genes involved in signal transduction pathway, and cell cycle (Hecht et al., 2000; Perera, 1997).

2.5 Chromosomal translocations in cancer

Chromosomal abnormalities such as chromosomal translocations are the predominant genetic alteration in oncogenesis. Furthermore, it also points toward the phenotype of the tumor and the clinical outcome. In 1060, two scientists, Nowell and Hungerford, observed chronic myeloid leukemia (CML) and the Philadelphia chromosome. Later, it was caused by translocation between chromosome numbers 9 and 22 (Nowell and Hungerford, 1960; Rowley, 1973). A similar chromosomal translocation was reported simultaneously linked to acute myelogenous leukemia. This was caused due to reciprocal rearrangement of chromosomes 8 and 21 (Rowley and Potter, 1976). Many similar observations helped to conclude the association of genetics with cancer.

Chromosomal translocations can be defined as chromosomal rearrangements within a genome. This involves the swapping of certain parts of two nonhomologous chromosomes. These translocations are generally classified into two categories reciprocal and nonreciprocal. Reciprocal translocations occur when there is an exchange between the chromosomal segments, whereas nonreciprocal translocation occurs between two acrocentric chromosomes with a fusion of their centromeric region. This leads to the loss of short arms and depletion in chromosomal numbers (Kirsch, 1933).

Translocations can elicit the juxtaposition of the coding region of a gene close to the active promoter or enhancer of the other gene giving rise to the overexpression of the first gene. An instance of this situation is that of IgH–BCL2 and IgH–MYC translocations. BCL2 and MYC are the overexpressed target genes because of their proximity to genes encoding for immunoglobulin heavy chains known to be expressed in B cells (Rabbitts, 1991). Another instance is that of the BCL6 gene rearranged to adjoin the promoter elements of multiple genes. This constitutes the diffusion of large B cell lymphoma (Korsmeyer, 1992). Also, translocations of TMPRSS2–ETS have been recently observed in prostate cancers (Kumar-Sinha et al., 2008).

Another consequence of chromosomal translocation is the emergence of a unique chimeric gene. The *t*(9;22) translocation leads to the modulation of the ABL gene located on chromosome number 9 by the gene promoter of BCR situated on chromosome number 22 because of the formation of a unique chimaera of an mRNA and protein. Another such chimeric gene formation has been found in the case of EWS in Ewing's sarcoma case and ETV6–NTRK3 in breast carcinomas (Rowley, 1973, 2001).

Overall, chromosomal translocations have been successfully evaluated as one of the causes of various kinds of cancer tumor progression.

2.6 Suppressed apoptosis

In the last few decades, one of the milestones in cancer research has been the advances in comprehending the links between malignancy and cancer genetics. The chief development has been the discovery of the association between apoptosis and the genes controlling it with the malignant phenotype (Lowe and Lin, 2000). At first, apoptosis was defined by its morphology, and the characteristics such as shrinkage of the cell, blebbing of the cell membrane, fragmentation of the nucleus, and chromatin condensation were taken into consideration (Kerr et al., 1972, 1994; Wyllie et al., 1980).

Tumorigenesis and the resistance to treatments partly depend on the suppression of apoptosis. The first-ever tumor suppressor gene linked to apoptosis has been p53. Mutation of the p53 gene has been seen to be prevalent among cancer patients with advanced tumor stages and a below-par patient prognosis (Wallace-Brodeur and Lowe, 1999). By the end of the 20th century, p53 was officially accepted as the gene involved in seizing the cell cycle and keeping up with genomic integrity post DNA damage. However, overexpression of p53 can give rise to apoptotic cell death in the case of the myeloid leukemia cell line suggesting its role in cell survival (Yonish-Rouach et al., 1991). A study conducted in p53 knockout mice helped conclude that the p53 was essential for radiation-induced cell death in the thymus but however not required in case of cell death induced by glucocorticoids or any other apoptotic stimulant (Lowe et al., 1993; Clarke et al., 1993). Therefore, it's only logical to deduce that p53's role in apoptosis is indirectly linked to DNA damage and is specific to stimulation and tissue, i.e., radiation and thymocytes, respectively. A piece of additional information about p53 states the mutation of several upstream and downstream components of the p53 pathway such as Mdm-2, ARF, and Bax which are mutated in malignant tumors (Wallace-Brodeur and Lowe, 1999).

Apoptosis is triggered during tumor progression by various external factors such as depletion in the growth or survival factors, radiations, hypoxia, and misses in cell-matrix interactions. Some internal factors such as DNA damage, telomere malfunctioning, and inappropriate signals also contribute to the onset of apoptosis. Many forms of cellular stress activate p53 that promotes apoptosis with the help of Bax, a proapoptotic molecule (Yin et al., 1997; McCurrach et al., 1997; Miyashita and Reed, 1995). Few of the triggers also contribute to the antiapoptotic signals such as IGF-1, which promotes cell survival (Kauffmann and Earnshaw, 2000).

2.7 Context dependence of carcinomas

The growth and the spread of tumors highly depend on the tumor microenvironment (TME) further influencing the treatment outcomes. TME is the environment surrounding the tumor. This may include blood vessels, circulating immune cells, and signaling molecules in the close vicinity. In the tumor microenvironment, the immune system's complement cascade has a major role. The complement system can act as per killing the tumor, or aiding the inflammation locally, or reinforcing the tumor progression by hindering the T-cell responses (Roumenina et al., 2019).

The malignant cells interact with the surrounding reactive nontransformed host cells releasing soluble mediators into the TME (Fridman et al., 2017). TME also often consists of the components of the complement system which are produced by the tumor and infiltrating cells (Merle et al., 2015a, b). Complement cascade has a major role in innate immune defense against foreign antigens and maintains the homeostasis of the human body. The complement system is composed of about more than 50 plasma components released by the liver into the blood circulation. Some of these plasma components are expressed on the cell membrane of various cell types and these components interact with one another contained in extracellular space (Merle et al., 2015a, b). Various studies covered over the past decade have reported the presence of complementary proteins in the TME (Reis et al., 2018).

In cancer, the relationship between the complement and the carcinomas is diverse. It can either cause antitumor defense or promote tumor progression. The practicality and purpose of the complement proteins in the TME help determine the tumor's fate (Roumenina et al., 2019).

2.8 Protein phosphorylation in cancer

Protein phosphorylation is a crucial regulatory mechanism of a cell as it aids in the activation/deactivation of various enzymes and receptors via phosphorylation and dephosphorylation. It is also one of the most important posttranslational modifications (PTM) (Li et al., 2013; Sacco et al., 2012). The process of protein phosphorylation is reversible and is assisted by enzymes called protein kinases. During the phosphorylation, a phosphate group is attached to the polar R group of amino acids making its confirmation to change from hydrophobic apolar to hydrophilic polar (Alberts et al., 2007). The phosphate group attached comes with a great interactive capacity. It's mainly due to the presence of Phosphorous. The phosphorous has five outer electrons that are able to form five covalent bonds and has an intrinsic high solubility in water (Hunter, 2009).

As mentioned earlier, phosphorylation is one of the most crucial PTM conducting the regulation of various biological processes and overexpression of kinases. Mutations in the regulatory pathways may lead to aberrations in the kinase signaling. This is what is mainly responsible for the tumorigenesis of multiple tumors (Harsha and Pandey, 2010; Hanahan and Weinberg, 2011; Hynes and MacDonald, 2009).

Cancer is not just a disease arising from genetic mutations but also epigenetic changes (Vogelstein and Kinzler, 2004; Petricoin et al., 2002; Jones and Baylin, 2002) which gives rise to the dysregulation of signal transduction pathways further abrupting the normal cellular mechanism (Hanahan and Weinberg, 2000).

Kinases target various important regulatory proteins responsible for gene expression. In general, their overexpression or malfunction can be detected in various diseases including cancer. Upon phosphorylation, with the addition of the phosphate group to a protein by kinase, a modification within the protein can occur which can be used as a switch. For instance, in chronic myeloid leukemia, a chromosomal translocation gives rise to a unique kinase that remains active at all times. The process monitored by this kinase is always switched on leading to the proliferation of the tumor cells (Murphree and Benedict, 1984).

2.9 The immune system in cancer

The human immune system is highly capable and is accountable for recognizing foreign bodies and eliciting a response against them. It can also efficiently differentiate between self and nonself cells. The human immune system is largely consisting of white blood cells and organs such as the spleen, thymus, tonsils, lymph nodes, lymph vessels and, bone marrow. They work in harmony to terminate threats and sustain the body's homeostasis (Abbott and Ustoyev, 2019).

The immune system comes into play against tumor cells. The tumor cells are genetically unstable with their DNA altering the protein products continuously. Due to this, the tumor cells are recognized as an antigen by the adaptive immune system. With that, an inflammatory response is elicited and a series of different cytokines are released. In case of a passable immune response, tumor cells can be efficiently banished otherwise an equilibrium stage is reached between the tumor proliferation and the immune components. Sooner or later, the tumor cells clone further and escape the immune surveillance by the virtue of high genetic instability forming clinically recognizable neoplasms (Dunn et al., 2004).

After the initial few stages of tumor development, CD8+ T cells and NK cells work on eliminating cancer cells with the most immunogenicity (Teng et al., 2015). In the initial stages, there are tumor cells that are less immunogenic and are not detected by the immune cells. Once the tumor develops into a neoplasmic stage and can be clinically detected, the inflammatory cells help define the further condition/fate of the tumor. To give an instance, the prognosis of many solid cancer tumors can be associated with the high amounts of tumor-infiltrated T cells (Clemente et al., 1996; Oldford et al., 2006; Dieu-Nosjean et al., 2008). In another instance, high amounts of tumor-infiltrated macrophages can be associated with a substandard prognosis (Mantovani et al., 2002; Zhang et al., 2012).

Tumor cells have developed an escape mechanism. Despite the onset of cytotoxic T-cell response and action of NK cells, the immune system falls short of preventing tumor cells to evade. The tumor cells divert the immune surveillance by releasing immunosuppressants like cytokines, prostaglandins, and vascular endothelial growth factors. Malignant cells also could elude immune surveillance by altering the expression of the MHC. They may also activate induced cell death to escape the immune effector cells (Loose and Van de Wiele, 2009).

2.10 Circumventing the blocks: Cancer drug resistance

Normally, a cancerous tumor is framed with genetically and phenotypically heterogeneous clones. Similarly, a drug-resistant tumor is composed of drug-resistant clones with a diverse range of modes of action. The drug resistance by the tumor is caused due to various combined factors leading to cell growth or death. A drug-resistant cancer growth never seizes its evolution under the influence of drug treatment and forms newer clones with better resistance to chemotherapeutic drugs. Therefore, the concept and the process of drug resistance are continuous and complex (Vogelstein and Kinzler, 2004).

Resistance to chemotherapeutic drugs is the most challenging obstacle in the field of cancer treatment and cancer research. According to an estimation reported in a scientific study, maximum cancer deaths occur due to the failure of chemotherapy as tumors grow resistant after successive exposure to chemotherapeutic drugs (Goldman, 2003). The variety of factors that give rise to drug resistance includes cellular malfunctions such as blocked apoptosis, the reduced influx of the drugs, activation of DNA repair decreased accumulation and increased efflux of the drugs, mutation of the drug targets, etc. (Gottesman et al., 2002). The most involved and extensively studied mechanism is the overexpression of the drug efflux transporters like P-glycoprotein (MDR-1/P-gp/ABCB1), multidrug resistance-related protein (MRP-1/ABCC1), and breast cancer resistance protein (BCRP/MXR/ABCP/ABCG2), which are all ATP-binding cassettes (Gottesman et al., 2002).

In order to circumvent this block in cancer research and cancer treatment, a potential and novel resistant mechanism needs to be devised. They must help predict the prognosis and the eventual chemotherapeutic drug resistance in association with genomic and proteomic technologies (Garraway and Jänne, 2012). One such approach includes microRNAs (miRNAs). MiRNAs are small noncoding RNAs that cause posttranscriptional modification of the target genes by intercommunicating with specific sequences in their 3′ untranslated regions (3′ UTR). In a few studies, it has been found that the alterations in the miRNA give rise to anticancer drug resistance. The miRNAs level in biological samples can be linked to the patient's response to chemotherapy as a prognostic biomarker (Kenneth, 2013).

3. Summary

Over the past few decades cancer research has been in a blooming stage. As discussed in the above sections, there have been major breakthrough researches acting as the steps toward bringing about better cancer management and high thorough-put diagnosis along with the treatment options. The rapid growth in the latest techniques is helping to put forward the solutions to the previously considered blocks in the field of cancer biology. Few of such blocks include chemotherapy drug resistance and lack of early screening. With rigorous research ability, cancer biology is moving forward toward developing better and more promising mechanisms to overcome such limitations.

References

Abbott, M., Ustoyev, Y., 2019. Cancer and immune system: the history and background of immunotherapy. Semin. Oncol. Nurs. 35, 150923.

Alberts, B., Johnson, A., Lewis, J., Raff, M., Roberts, K., Walter, P., 2007. In: Anderson, M., Granum, S. (Eds.), Molecular Biology of the Cell, fifth ed. Garland Science, New York, NY, p. 1752007.

American Cancer Society, 2001. Tobacco use. In: American Cancer Society (Ed.), Cancer Facts & Figures. American Cancer Society, Atlanta, GA, pp. 4–5.

Bakhoum, S.F., et al., 2018. Chromosomal instability drives metastasis through a cytosolic DNA response. Nature 553 (7689), 467–472. https://doi.org/10.1038/nature25432.

Baylin, S.B., Herman, J.G., 2000. DNA hypermethylation in tumorigenesis: epigenetics joins genetics. Trends Genet. 16, 168–174.

Beemon, K., Duesberg, P., Vogt, P., 1974. Evidence for crossing-over between avian tumor viruses based on analysis of viral RNAs. Proc. Natl. Acad. Sci. U. S. A. 71, 4254–4258.

Bird, A., 2002. DNA methylation patterns and epigenetic memory. Genes Dev. 16, 6–21.

Chaffer, C.L., Weinberg, R.A., 2011. A perspective on cancer cell metastasis. Science 331, 1559–1564.

Chao, A., Thun, M.J., Jacobs, E.J., et al., 2000. Cigarette smoking and colorectal cancer mortality in the cancer prevention study II. J. Natl. Cancer Inst. 92, 1888–1896.

Clarke, A.R., Purdie, C.A., Harrison, D.J., Morris, R.G., Bird, C.C., Hooper, M.L., Wyllie, A.H., 1993. Thymocyte apoptosis induced by p53-dependent and independent pathways. Nature 362, 849–852.

Clemente, C.G., Meihm Jr., M.C., Bufalino, R., Zurrida, S., Collini, P., Cascinelli, N., 1996. Prognostic value of tumor-infiltrating lymphocytes in the vertical growth phase of primary cutaneous melanoma. Cancer 77, 1303–1310.

Coffin, J.M., Varmus, H.E., Bishop, J.M., Essex, M., Hardy Jr., W.D., Martin, G.S., Rosenberg, N.E., Scolnick, E.M., Weinberg, R.A., Vogt, P.K., 1981. Proposal for naming host cell-derived inserts in retrovirus genomes. J. Virol. 40, 953–957.

Coffin, J.M., Hughes, S.H., Varmus, H.E., 1997. Retroviruses. Cold Spring Harbor Laboratory Press, Cold Spring Harbor, NY.

Dieu-Nosjean, M.C., Antoine, M., Danel, C., Heudes, D., Wislez, M., Poulot, V., Rabbe, N., Laurans, L., Tartour, E., de Chaisemartin, L., et al., 2008. Long-term survival for patients with nonsmall-cell lung cancer with intratumoral lymphoid structures. J. Clin. Oncol. 26, 4410–4417.

Doll, R., 1996. Cancers are weakly related to smoking. BMJ 52, 35–49.

Dunn, G.P., Old, L.J., Schreiber, R.D., 2004. The three Es of cancer immunoediting. Annu. Rev. Immunol. 22, 329.

Fares, J., Fares, M.Y., Khachfe, H.H., et al., 2020. Molecular principles of metastasis: a hallmark of cancer revisited. Signal Transduct. Target. Ther. 5, 28.

Feinberg, A.P., Ohlsson, R., Henikoff, S., 2006. The epigenetic progenitor origin of human cancer. Nat. Rev. Genet. 7, 21–33.

Ferlay, J., Soerjomataram, I., Dikshit, R., et al., 2012. Cancer incidence and mortality worldwide: sources, methods and major patterns in GLOBOCAN 2012. Int. J. Cancer 136, E359–E386.

Ferlay, J., Soerjomataram, I., Ervik, M., et al., 2013. GLOBOCAN 2012 v1.0. In: Cancer Incidence and Mortality Worldwide: IARC CancerBase no. 11. IARC, Lyon.

Foreman, D., Bray, F., Brewster, D.H., et al., 2014. Cancer Incidence in Five Continents. Volume X International Agency for Research on Cancer, Lyon.

Fridman, W.H., Zitvogel, L., Sautes-Fridman, C., Kroemer, G., 2017. The immune contexture in cancer prognosis and treatment. Nat. Rev. Clin. Oncol. 14, 717–734.

Furuichi, Y., Shatkin, A.J., Stavnezer, E., Bishop, J.M., 1975. Blocked, methylated $5'$-terminal sequence in avian sarcoma virus RNA. Nature 257, 618–620.

Garraway, L.A., Jänne, P.A., 2012. Circumventing cancer drug resistance in the era of personalized medicine. Cancer Discov. 2 (3), 214–226.

Goldman, B., 2003. Multidrug resistance: can new drugs help chemotherapy score against cancer? J. Natl. Cancer Inst. 95, 255–257.

Gottesman, M.M., et al., 2002. Multidrug resistance in cancer: role of ATP-dependent transporters. Nat. Rev. Cancer 2 (1), 48–58.

Hanahan, D., Weinberg, R.A., 2000. The hallmarks of cancer. Cell 100, 57–70.

Hanahan, D., Weinberg, R.A., 2011. Hallmarks of cancer: the next generation. Cell 144, 646–674.

Harsha, H.C., Pandey, A., 2010. Phosphoproteomics in cancer. Mol. Oncol. 4, 482–495.

Hecht, S.S., 1999. Tobacco smoke carcinogens and lung cancer. J. Natl. Cancer Inst. 91, 1194–1210.

Hecht, S.S., Hochalter, J.B., Villalta, P.W., Murphy, S.E., 2000. 2′-Hydroxylation of nicotine by cytochrome P450 2A6 and human liver microsomes: formation of a lung carcinogenic precursor. Proc. Natl. Acad. Sci. U. S. A. 97, 12493–12497.

Herman, J.G., Baylin, S.B., 2003. Gene silencing in cancer in association with promoter hypermethylation. N. Engl. J. Med. 349, 2042–2054.

Hoffmann, D., Hoffmann, I., El Bayoumy, K., 2001. The less harmful cigarette: a controversial issue. A tribute to Ernst L Wynder. Chem. Res. Toxicol. 14, 767–790.

Howley, P.M., Livingston, D.M., 2009. Small DNA tumor viruses: large contributors to biomedical sciences. Virology 384 (2), 256259.

Hunter, T., 2009. Why nature chose phosphate to modify proteins. Philos. Trans. R. Soc. Lond. Ser. B Biol. Sci. 367, 2513–2516.

Hynes, N.E., MacDonald, G., 2009. ErbB receptors and signaling pathways in cancer. Curr. Opin. Cell Biol. 21, 177–184.

International Agency for Research on Cancer, 1986. Tobacco Smoking. IARC Monographs on the Evaluation of the Carcinogenic Risk of Chemicals to Humans. vol. 38 IARC, Lyon, pp. 127–135.

Jones, P.A., Baylin, S.B., 2002. The fundamental role of epigenetic events in cancer. Nat. Rev. Genet. 3, 415–428.

Jones, P.A., Laird, P.W., 1999. Cancer epigenetics comes of age. Nat. Genet. 21, 163–167.

Joyce, J.A., Pollard, J.W., 2009. Nat. Rev. Cancer 9, 239.

Kauffmann, S.H., Earnshaw, W.C., 2000. Induction of apoptosis by cancer chemotherapy. Exp. Cell Res, 256 (1), 12 19.

Kenneth, K.W., 2013. MicroRNA: a prognostic biomarker and a possible druggable target for circumventing multidrug resistance in cancer chemotherapy. J. Biomed. Sci. 20 (1), 1–19.

Kerr, J.F., Wyllie, A.H., Currie, A.R., 1972. Apoptosis: a basic biological phenomenon with wide-ranging implications in tissue kinetics. Br. J. Cancer 26, 239–257.

Kerr, J.F.R., Winterford, C.M., Harmon, B.V., 1994. Apoptosis—its significance in cancer and cancer therapy. Cancer 73, 2013–2026 (Published erratum appears in Cancer (1994) 73, 3108).

Kirsch, I.R., 1933. The Causes and Consequences of Chromosomal Translocations. CRC Press.

Korsmeyer, S.J., 1992. Chromosomal translocations in lymphoid malignancies reveal novel proto-oncogenes. Annu. Rev. Immunol. 10, 785–807.

Kumar-Sinha, C., Tomlins, S.A., Chinnaiyan, A.M., 2008. Recurrent gene fusions in prostate cancer. Nat. Rev. Cancer 8 (7), 497–511.

Lambert, A.W., Pattabiraman, D.R., Weinberg, R.A., 2017. Emerging biological principles of metastasis. Cell 168 (4), 670–691. https://doi.org/10.1016/j.cell.2016.11.037.

Li, X., Wilmanns, M., Thornton, J., Köhn, M., 2013. Elucidating human phosphatase-substrate networks. Sci. Signal. 6, rs102013.

Loose, D., Van de Wiele, C., 2009. The immune system and cancer. Cancer Biother. Radiopharm. 24 (3), 369–376.

Lowe, S.W., Lin, A.W., 2000. Apoptosis in cancer. Carcinogenesis 21 (3), 485–495.

Lowe, S.W., Schmitt, E.M., Smith, S.W., Osborne, B.A., Jacks, T., 1993. p53 is required for radiation-induced apoptosis in mouse thymocytes. Nature 362, 847–849.

Malvezzi, M., Bosetti, C., Rosso, T., et al., 2013. Lung cancer mortality in European men: trends and predictions. Lung Cancer 80, 138–145.

Mantovani, A., Sozzani, S., Locati, M., Allavena, P., Sica, A., 2002. Macrophage polarization: tumor-associated macrophages as a paradigm for polarized M2 mononuclear phagocytes. Trends Immunol. 23, 549–555.

Martin, G.S., 2004. The road to Src. Oncogene 23, 7910–7917.

McCurrach, M.E., Connor, T.M., Knudson, C.M., Korsmeyer, S.J., Lowe, S.W., 1997. Bax-deficiency promotes drug resistance and oncogenic transformation by attenuating p53-dependent apoptosis. Proc. Natl. Acad. Sci. U. S. A. 94, 2345–2349.

Merle, N.S., Church, S.E., Fremeaux-Bacchi, V., Roumenina, L.T., 2015a. Complement system part I—molecular mechanisms of activation and regulation. Front. Immunol. 6, 262.

Merle, N.S., Noe, R., Halbwachs-Mecarelli, L., Fremeaux-Bacchi, V., Roumenina, L.T., 2015b. Complement system part II: role in immunity. Front. Immunol. 6, 257.

Miyashita, T., Reed, J.C., 1995. Tumor suppressor p53 is a direct transcriptional activator of the human *bax* gene. Cell 80, 293–299.

Murphree, A.L., Benedict, W.F., 1984. Retinoblastoma: clues to human oncogenesis. Science 223, 1028–1033.

Ngoma, T., 2006. World Health Organization cancer priorities in developing countries. Ann. Oncol. 17, viii9–viii14.

Nowell, P.C., Hungerford, D.A., 1960. A minute chromosome in human chronic granulocytic leukemia. Science 132, 1497.

Oldford, S.A., Robb, J.D., Codner, D., Gadag, V., Watson, P.H., Drover, S., 2006. Tumor cell expression of HLA-DM associates with a Th1 profile and predicts improved survival in breast carcinoma patients. Int. Immunol. 18, 1591–1602.

Perera, F.P., 1997. Environment and Cancer: who are susceptible? Science 278, 1068–1073.

Petersen, R.B., Hackett, P.B., 1985. Characterization of ribosome binding on Rous sarcoma virus RNA in vitro. J. Virol. 56, 683–690.

Petersen, R.B., Hensel, C.H., Hackett, P.B., 1984. Identification of a ribosome-binding site for a leader peptide encoded by Rous sarcoma virus RNA. J. Virol. 51, 722–729.

Petricoin, E.F., Zoon, K.C., Kohn, E.C., Barrett, J.C., Liotta, L.A., 2002. Clinical proteomics: translating benchside promise into bedside reality. Nat. Rev. Drug Discov. 1, 683–695.

Rabbitts, T.H., 1991. Translocations, master genes and differences between the origins of acute and chronic leukemias. Cell 67 (1991), 641–644.

Reis, E.S., Mastellos, D.C., Ricklin, D., Mantovani, A., Lambris, J.D., 2018. Complement in cancer: untangling an intricate relationship. Nat. Rev. Immunol. 18, 5–18.

Roumenina, L.T., Daugan, M.V., Petitprez, F., Sautès-Fridman, C., Fridman, W.H., 2019. Context-dependent roles of complement in cancer. Nat. Rev. Cancer 19 (12), 698–715.

Rous, P., 1911. A sarcoma of the fowl transmissible by an agent separable from the tumor cells. J. Exp. Med. 13, 397–411.

Rowley, J.D., 1973. A new consistent chromosomal abnormality in chronicmyelogenous leukaemia identified by quinacrine fluorescence and Giemsa staining. Nature 243, 290–293.

Rowley, J.D., 2001. Chromosomal translocations; dangerous liaisons revisited. Nat. Rev. Cancer 1, 245–250.

Rowley, J.D., Potter, D., 1976. Chromosomal banding patterns in acute nonlymphocytic leukemia. Blood 47 (5), 705–721.

Sacco, F., Perfetto, L., Castagnoli, L., Cesareni, G., 2012. The human phosphatase interactome: an intricate family portrait. FEBS Lett. 586, 2732–2739.

Schuller, H.M., McGavin, M.D., Orloff, M., et al., 1995. Simultaneous exposure to nicotine and hyperoxia causes tumors in hamsters. Lab. Investig. 73, 448–456.

Siegel, R.L., Miller, K.D., Jemal, A., 2015. Cancer statistics. CA Cancer J. Clin. 65, 5–29.

Stratton, M.R., 2011. Exploring the genomes of cancer cells: progress and promise. Science 331, 1553–1558.

Teng, M.W., Galon, J., Fridman, W.H., Smyth, M.J., 2015. From mice to humans: developments in cancer immunoediting. J. Clin. Invest. 125, 3338–3346.

Vogelstein, B., Kinzler, K.W., 2004. Cancer genes and the pathways they control. Nat. Med. 10, 789–799.

Wallace-Brodeur, R.R., Lowe, S.W., 1999. Clinical implications of *p53* mutations. Cell. Mol. Life Sci. 55, 64–75.

WHO, 1997. Tobacco or Health: A Global Status Report. WHO, Geneva, pp. 10–48.

Wyllie, A.H., Kerr, J.F., Currie, A.R., 1980. Cell death: the significance of apoptosis. Int. Rev. Cytol. 68, 251–306.

Yin, C., Knudson, C.M., Korsmeyer, S.J., Van Dyke, T., 1997. Bax suppresses tumorigenesis and stimulates apoptosis *in vivo*. Nature 385, 637–640.

Yonish-Rouach, E., Resnitzky, D., Lotem, J., Sachs, L., Kimchi, A., Oren, M., 1991. Wild-type p53 induces apoptosis of myeloid leukemic cells that is inhibited by interleukin-6. Nature 352, 345–347.

Zhang, Q.W., Liu, L., Gong, C.Y., Shi, H.S., Zeng, Y.H., Wang, X.Z., Zhao, Y.W., Wei, Y.Q., 2012. Prognostic significance of tumor-associated macrophages in solid tumor: a meta-analysis of the literature. PLoS One 7, e50946.

CHAPTER TWO

Cancer burden: Epidemiology, racial, and geographical disparities

Shaveta Menon[a] and Ramila Bisht[b]
[a]Centre for Public Health and Healthcare Administration, Eternal University, Baru Sahib, Himachal Pradesh, India
[b]Centre for Social Medicine and Community Health, Jawaharlal Nehru University, New Delhi, India

1. Introduction

Noncommunicable diseases (NCDs) account for 71% of all deaths globally and 77% of these deaths are in the low- and middle-income countries (LMICs). After cardiovascular diseases, cancers account for most of the deaths contributed by NCDs, making it an important public health issue (WHO, 2021). Between 2012 and 2018, cancer cases have increased in all countries for whom data is available from the population-based registries. This rise in the number of cases of cancer globally can be attributed to an increase in the life expectancy of the population and epidemiological as well as demographic transitions (Ferlay et al., 2019). The burden of NCDs, cancers included, offsets the burden of communicable diseases in nearly every country and is projected to grow in the coming decades. This growing urgency due to the NCDs has led to the adoption of Sustainable Development Goals' target 3.4 which aims to reduce the mortality from NCDs by one-third by the year 2030 (The Lancet, 2020).

This burden is especially of concern in LMICs as they are in the process of economic transition leading to greater mechanization of labor, cultural transitions in the role of women, and penetration and exposure to international markets. As a result, the various risk factors such as tobacco use, obesity, physical inactivity and reproductive patterns which already existed in high-income countries (HICs) are becoming common in the LMICs (Torre et al., 2016). This increasing magnitude of the disease is also followed by the change in the profile of various types of cancer. The causes of cancers that were infection-related or attributed to poverty are now being replaced by those cancers which are most prevalent in the HICs. Despite this, the differing profiles of cancer that exist in individual countries and among regions mark the geographic variations and persistence of local risk factors among the populations. It is also marked by the phases of social and economic transitions in the individual countries or regions, which is evident by the differences in the rates of cancers of the cervix, stomach, and liver, which are associated with infection at the opposite ends of the human development spectrum (Bray and

Biomarkers in Cancer Detection and Monitoring of Therapeutics
https://doi.org/10.1016/B978-0-323-95116-6.00007-4

Soerjomataram, 2015). However, the impact of cancer on individuals, communities, and populations poses a major threat to development in less developed countries due to lack of services, education, and poverty which is in turn responsible for mortality and morbidity from the disease (Sloan and Gelband, 2007).

This chapter aims to detail and address these variations in cancer globally within the geographical and racial boundaries and to critically analyze the reasons for these differentials. According to World Bank, countries are globally classified as low income, lower middle income, upper middle income, and high income based on GNI per capita. These low- and middle-income economies are usually referred to as developing economies, and upper and high-income economies are referred to as developed countries. For this chapter, we will be using these terminologies interchangeably (Gbadamosi, n.d.).

2. Global burden of cancer

In the year 2018, 18.1 million new cases of cancer were detected and 9.6 million deaths from cancer were reported in the same year. One in the six deaths globally is caused by cancer (Ferlay et al., 2019) and it is believed that one in five people will develop cancer before they reach 75 years of age. Globally, in 2018, lung cancer was the most frequently diagnosed cancer (11.6%) followed by breast (11.6%) and colorectal cancer. Lung cancer is also the leading cause of death from cancer (18.4% of total deaths) followed by colorectal (9.2%) and stomach cancer (8.2%) (Fig. 1). Out of these most cancers are responsible for 60% to 70% of cancer incidence and mortality (Fig. 2). The global burden of cancer when differentiated by gender in 2018 showed that frequently diagnosed cancer

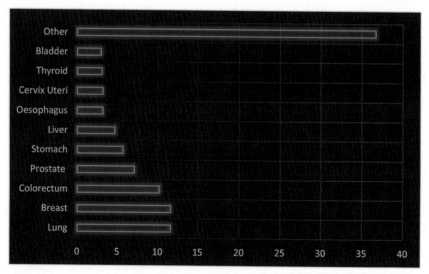

Fig. 1 Incidence of cancer in 2018. (*Source: WHO, 2020. WHO Report on cancer Setting Priorities, Investing Wisely and Providing Care for all. World Health Organisation, Geneva, p. 26.*)

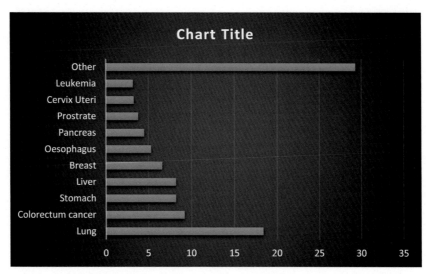

Fig. 2 Mortality due to cancer in 2018. *(Source: WHO, 2020. WHO Report on cancer Setting Priorities, Investing Wisely and Providing Care for all. World Health Organisation, Geneva, p. 26.)*

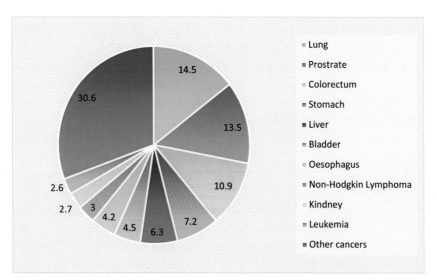

Fig. 3 Percentage of incident cases in men in 2018. *(Source: WHO, 2020. WHO Report on cancer Setting Priorities, Investing Wisely and Providing Care for all. World Health Organisation, Geneva, p. 25.)*

in men was lung cancer, followed by cancer of the prostate and colorectal cancer (WHO, 2020) (Fig. 3). As far as females are concerned, the most frequently diagnosed cancer in women in 2018 was breast cancer followed by colorectal cancer and cancer of the lung (Fig. 4). The overall burden of cancer in females is higher in HICs as compared to LMICs. However, the mortality rates due to cancer are higher in LMICs as compared to HICs largely due to inadequate access to early detection and treatment (Torre et al., 2017).

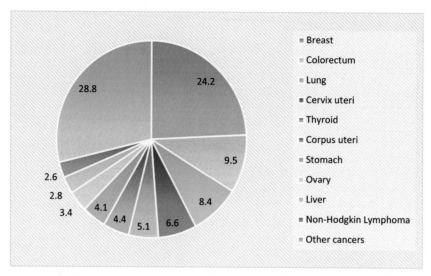

Fig. 4 Percentage of incident cases in women in 2018. *(Source: WHO, 2020. WHO Report on cancer Setting Priorities, Investing Wisely and Providing Care for all. World Health Organisation, Geneva, p. 25.)*

An epidemiological transition that has occurred in the last six decades has led to a decrease in the infectious diseases burden and an increase in NCDs including cancer. The reason for this epidemiological shift has been the development of vaccines, improvements in sanitary conditions, and, the discovery of antibiotics. Also, the changes in the various risk factors associated with cancer have led to trends in the types of cancer. To illustrate, the impact of the tobacco epidemic on the incidence of lung cancer in countries with high and low HDI (Human Development Index) has been differential (WHO, 2020) The estimated new cases of cancer in the developed countries have been projected to decrease from 44% in 2008 to 19% in 2030, whereas in developing countries, they are projected to increase from 56% in 2008 to 81% (Williams et al., 2016).

The disparities in cancer at the global level have moved beyond the macroeconomic analysis which involves the assessment of socioeconomic status or national income. The recent concept of establishing these inequalities against the division of developing and developed has been now superseded by Human Development Index (HDI). HDI is a composite measure of access to education, a long and healthy life, and a decent standard of living which are based on mean and expected years of schooling, life expectancy, and gross national income per capita respectively (UNDP, 2015). There has been a strong correlation between the magnitude of overall cancer rates and HDI, the overall cancer has been increasing with the increase in human development (Fidler et al., 2016). However, in terms of the profile of cancer, the distribution of cancers is different with cancers caused due to infections and poverty dominating in countries with low HDI (cervical and liver cancer) whereas breast, colorectal, prostate, and lung cancer dominate in countries

Table 1 Estimated numbers of new cases from 2020 to 2040 in both sexes (0–85 years).

Populations	Estimated number of new cases in 2020	Estimated number of new cases in 2040	Change (%)
Low HDI	650,423	1,274,930	96
Medium HDI	2,326,749	3,832,586	64.7
High HDI	7,371,321	11,511,711	56.2
Very High HDI	8,934,818	11,812,586	32.2

Source: Computed from IARC., 2020. Cancer Tomorrow. World Health Organisation. Available from: https://gco.iarc.fr/tomorrow/en/dataviz/bubbles?sexes=0&mode=population. Retrieved 21 October 2021.

with high HDI (Plummer et al., 2016). Apart from the profile of cancer, the future incidence burden means new cases of cancer will be proportionately greater in countries with low HDI. The countries with low and medium HDI are expected to see an increase in the burden of incident cases of cancers to 96% and 64.7% respectively in both the sexes and age group of 0–85 years from 2020 to 2040 (Table 1).

3. Social class disparities in cancer

The inequalities in the cancer are not only restricted to the physical nature of the disease but it is also lived differently. There are variations at the national and the sub-national levels on understandings and beliefs about cancer. These inequalities exist in symptom presentation, access to timely diagnosis, and treatment of cancer. In all these, the cancer outcome is, therefore, dependent on knowledge and beliefs which are determined by the socioeconomic status (SES) of the population (McCutchan et al., 2015). Social inequalities form an important component of the differences observed in cancer rates within and across the countries. To reiterate what has been said earlier is that the differences between HICs and LMICs are available but the data on the social inequalities in cancer is difficult to obtain (Marmot, 2019).

The indigenous population, people living in poverty, and ethnic minority groups are the ones who experience different cancer incidence as well as survival rates as compared to privileged groups in both HICs and LMICs (Singh and Jemal, 2017; Sarfati, 2019). The magnitude of association with social factors is most often greater than the traditional risk factors for cancer (Teng et al., 2016). The explanation for this phenomenon is that the risk factors tend to be more prevalent in the members of the disadvantaged groups. Various factors such as environmental, (availability of tobacco, alcohol, and healthy food), cultural, economic, and psychosocial factors (such as lack of social support, stress due to material hardships, and lack of control over one's life) create complex and multifaceted reasons for cancer disparities (Mackenbach et al., 2008).

In LMICs it was found that the studies which were based on individual socioeconomic status, data reported the greatest inequalities in the cancers related to smoking and infections related to cancers of the liver, stomach, and cervix. On the contrary, colorectal cancer and breast cancer do not show any clear association with socioeconomic status in LMICs. Also, a lower education level is related to higher incidence and mortality of oral cancer and lung cancer in LMICs (de Vries et al., 2015; Dikshit et al., 2012). Significantly, in some LMICs, the types of cooking methods which also have an association with SES contribute to lung cancer (Hosgood et al., 2011; Jia et al., 2018). Approximately 85% of the global burden of cervical cancer occurs in LMICs which is attributed to 12% of all cancers in women (Girianelli et al., 2014; Oguntoke, 2014) especially those in the rural areas (Cavalini and de Leon, 2008) and in areas of low SES which have highest incidence and mortality rates for cervical cancer (Girianelli et al., 2014).

4. Racial disparities in cancer

Within the developed and the developing countries, there are differences in the incidence and mortalities due to cancers among the population of different races and ethnicities. The disparities in the between different population groups can also be explained due to access to healthcare, cultural barriers, diet, and exposure to various pathogens and carcinogens (Wallace et al., 2011; Nguyen et al., 2020). For example, the disparities in liver cancer are present across the United States in various racial and ethnic groups. This cancer affects American Indians, American Asians, and Hispanic Americans more than African Americans and European Americans. American Indians have the lowest 5-year survival across all types of cancers and also experience increased rates for many malignancies. On the contrary, Hispanic and Asian Americans have lower cancer rates than other US populations (Trinh et al., 2015). Also, among Hispanics, infection is diagnosed at a later stage than in European Americans (Islami et al., 2017). African Americans disproportionately bear the burden of cancer and experience the highest mortality from cancers of breast, lung, prostate, and GI than other groups of populations (Wallace et al., 2011; DeSantis et al., 2019).

Several reports advocate that South Asians (those with ancestry in India, Pakistan, Sri Lanka, and Bangladesh) may have a lower risk of cancer than other racial-ethnic groups (Goggins and Wong, 2009 as cited in Tran et al., 2018). A study on the incidence of cancer confirmed that South Asians are at a lower risk of cancer as compared to other racial and ethnic groups in the United States (Tran et al., 2016 as cited in Tran et al., 2018). Another study on cancer incidence among South Asians in the UK, United States, Singapore, and India reported lower cancer incidence in Indians and highest among the whites in the United States (Rastogi et al., 2008). When compared with the non-South Asian first-generation immigrants in England and Wales, the cancer rates in South Asian immigrants were half as in other immigrant groups (Mangtani et al., 2010). Important research based on a long-term study on South Asian migrants to England from 1986 to 2004 revealed that the overall age-adjusted incidence of cancer in South Asians was half of Non-South Asians but it rose over time (Maringe et al., 2013).

However, later it was reported that the survival advantage of the South Asians for some cancer types tended to narrow, it remained present for lung, liver, and colorectal cancers in men (Maringe et al., 2015). Although the explanations for these disparities have been speculative, an interplay of genetic and environmental factors can be seen as a possible elucidation for the same. The dietary patterns of vegetarianism and also the use of spices like turmeric and other food additives are other reasons for the decreased incidence of cancer in the South Asian population when compared to the white population (Sinha et al., 2003). The disparities in the between different population groups can also be explained due to access to healthcare, cultural barriers, diet, and exposure to various pathogens and carcinogens (Wallace et al., 2011; Nguyen et al., 2020) which will be detailed in the subsequent sections.

5. Risk factors for cancer

Many epidemiological studies have explained biological and social factors responsible for racial or ethnic differences in the incidence, morbidity, and mortality of cancer (Collins et al., 2002; Smedley et al., 2001), and they speculate that unmeasured cultural factors may be better indicators for these differences. Culture is the "core, fundamental, dynamic, responsive, adaptive and relatively coherent organizing system of life designed to ensure the survival and well-being of its members." Through different beliefs, values, and lifestyles the cultural group manipulates the food as well as the environment around them. It also outlines suitable emotional reactions and behavior responses to disease and how the social network provides safety and social support. Therefore, diet, marriage, social rules, as well as means of livelihood that influence the gene expression, health status, and disease, are largely culturally prescribed and proscribed (Bronfenbrenner and Ceci, 1994). Every population has a culture that has a specific set of traits and characteristics including advantages and disadvantages in health. This therefore partly explains why site-specific and overall incidence rates of cancers differ across cultural groups in the United States and internationally (American Cancer Society, 2008). However, cancer rates change for immigrants as they adopt the culture and lifestyle practices of their host country and this change usually occurs within one generation (Nelson, 2006) and is usually associated with lifestyle (Kagawa-Singer et al., 2010).

Approximately 30% of the cancers throughout the globe can be prevented by modifying the predominant risk factors (Danaei et al., 2005) most of which are related to lifestyle. Smoking and dietary patterns play an important role in reducing the burden of cancer in HICs and LMICs (Ezzati et al., 2005). Tobacco smoking contributes to around 70% of deaths due to lung cancer and 42% of cancers of the esophagus and oral cavity.

During the period from 1990 to 2010, in countries that had higher resources for curbing tobacco use, the cancers related to smoking decreased. On the contrary, in countries that were in the process of transition, cancer deaths due to smoking increased from 12% to 14% (Lim et al., 2012). The prevalence of smoking in HICs has decreased for many decades, and in LMIC, it is stable or showing limited signs of decline (Ng et al., 2014).

Bacterial, viral, or parasitic infections are responsible for around 16.1% of cases of human malignancies throughout the globe (Fig. 5). This fraction is higher in LMICs than in the HICs. Hepatitis B and C virus, *Helicobacter pylori*, and human papilloma virus (HPV) is responsible for liver, gastric and cervical cancers. The cancers due to chronic infections are more prevalent in LMICs; for example, these cancers range from 1 in 3 in Sub-Saharan Africa to 1 in 30 in New Zealand and Australia and 1 in 25 in North America (Harper et al., 2004; Herrero et al., 2013). The four most important infections which cause cancer throughout the globe are *Helicobacter pylori,* HPV, hepatitis B virus (HBV), and hepatitis C virus (HCV). Worldwide the infections due to HBV and HCV infections cause 56% and 20% of the liver deaths respectively. However, these proportions vary geographically with HBV major cause of liver cancer in less developed countries (2/3 of the cases) and HCV in more developed regions (44%) (Jemal et al., 2019).

Excess consumption of Alcohol is also an important risk factor for the cancers of the oral cavity, larynx, oral cavity, and pharynx as well as breast, liver, and colorectum (IARC, 2010). Approximately 4% of the cancers globally are attributed to the intake of alcohol (Boffetta et al., 2006) with similar distribution in the HICs and LMICs (Rehm and Shield, 2013). Interestingly, the global consumption of alcohol has been

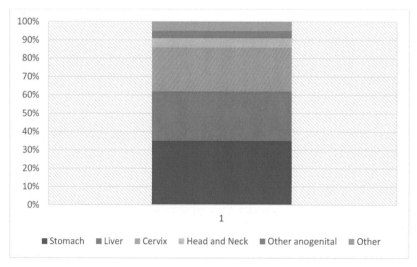

Fig. 5 *Most common infection attributable cancers worldwide. (Source: Jemal, A., Torre, L., Soerjomataram, I., Bray, F., 2019. The Cancer Atlas. American Cancer Society, Atlanta, p. 22.)*

stable in recent decades. There has been a small decrease in the countries where it was historically high (for example, Europe) and a small increase in countries where the consumption had been relatively low (for example, South East Asia) (Shield et al., 2013). As far as diet is concerned, around 15% of all deaths due to cancer are related to unhealthy diets which include consumption of red meat, processed meat, and sodium as well as low intake of fruits and vegetables (Lim et al., 2012). In a recent development cruciform vegetables have been found to offer protection against lung cancer and possibly cancers of the gastrointestinal tract (Moy et al., 2008). The traditional Chinese diet consists of a large proportion of vegetables, especially cruciform vegetables. There are pieces of evidence that provide a protective effect of Green Tea in the development of cancer (Moy et al., 2008; Yuan et al., 2007). The Mediterranean diet involves increased uptake of vegetables, fruits, and nuts and dietary patterns where olive oil is used rather than saturated oils and fats, more fish and less meat, and sourdough bread that is rich in antioxidants and micronutrients such as vitamin E and C (Simopoulos, 2001; Levi et al., 2004). However, the research is still inconclusive about the dietary patterns and the comprehensive review of diet-related risks and cancers points out increased risk due to consumption of red meat but still has less evidence to prove the consumption of fruits and vegetables in reducing the risks (WCRF and AICR, 2007).

6. Reasons for disparities in cancer

The disparities in the cancers mentioned above are an agglomerate of various factors which play differentially in the developed and developing world. These factors include healthcare, governmental policies, and the physical environment in the nations which are responsible for collectively shaping the healthcare and health outcomes (Williams et al., 2016). The access to healthcare as mentioned earlier for disadvantaged groups has been created by the geographical and political divisions within and outside the countries. This section provides a detailed account of the structural issues in the health system and physical environment within and across countries.

6.1 Health system settings

As mentioned earlier in the LMICs, risk factors such as tobacco consumption, alcohol use, sedentary behavior, infectious agents, and pollution are responsible for increasing incidence of cancer cases. Sadly, when LMICs contribute to the majority of cancer cases, they lack the resources to address the challenges of cancer. While 80% of the cancer cases globally occur in the LMICs, less than 5% of the global spending is on health (Ginsburg et al., 2012). This problem is intensified by various structural discrepancies of lack of political will and poverty leading to a lack of access to quality healthcare in cancer control programs (Gupta et al., 2014). In a study, it was found that most of the countries that have policies related to cancer control, strategies, or action plans were HICs or upper middle-income countries. Only 22% of the LICs had national cancer registries in comparison with 75% of the HICs. In addition, 31% of the LICs had a national plan for cancer control as compared to 79% of the HICs. This difference in the presence of cancer registries among countries is related to the income of the country as well as the mean per capita expenditure on health. Therefore, without the presence of data from population-based registries, the estimation of the burden of cancer in LMIC is limited (Siddiqui and Zafar, 2018).

Population-based cancer registries (PBCRs) are considered gold standards for providing information on the incidence of cancer in a defined population. PBRCs are instrumental in identifying the possible causes of cancer in the community and accessing the impact of cancer control activities (Bray et al., 2014). Compared to 80% of North America, 1% of Africa, 4% of Asia, and 4% of South and Central America have population-based data sufficient to be included in the cancer registries (IARC, 2008). There are many challenges with the cancer registration in developing countries which include a lack of accurate records of death and population data, problems due to political and economic instability, and issues related to cultural norms, and mobile populations (Valsecchi and Staliarova, 2008 as cited in Tervonen et al., 2017). Therefore, data needs to be collected from multiple sources such as death certificates, laboratories, and hospitals for registering all cases of cancer (Bray et al., 2015).

There are poorly developed communications between different stakeholders, an absence of networks in healthcare, and an inability to uniquely identify the individuals, which complicates the process of data collection (Valsecchi and Staliarova, 2008 as cited in Tervonen et al., 2017). Moreover, underestimation of deaths due to cancer is common when there is a lack of access to basic health services, especially in the rural areas (Jedy-Agba et al., 2015). As the registration of cancer involves considerable costs, low-resource countries consider regional registries which collect data on subnational samples (Bray et al., 2015). This lack of data makes it difficult for the government to allocate appropriate resources or measure how specific interventions are performing (Siddiqui and Zafar, 2018).

The developing countries are already struggling with the dual burden of communicable and noncommunicable diseases. Cancer which was once seen as a burden of the developed world has now become a death sentence in the developing world due to absence of the health care services and access to cancer drugs. As far as radiology services are concerned there is an extreme limitation of human resources, physical resources, and equipment in the developing world. To reiterate, due to the presence of limited data in developing countries, there is little information available on the capacity of cancer prevention, screening, and treatment services (Hanna and Kangole, 2010). It is assumed that human capacity for these services is limited in developing countries and public awareness and government health programs are largely geared toward communicable diseases (Pezzatini et al., 2007).

The medical structure in the developing countries has been historically designed to manage communicable diseases, child and maternal health as well as nutritional deficiencies. The lack of resources in addressing cancer along its continuum is responsible for increased mortality due to cancer in the developing world. For example, given the burden of cancer in the developing world, the supply of radiation machines is inadequate to meet the demands (Barton et al., 2006 as cited in Hanna and Kangole, 2010). Although the developing is home to 85% of the world's population, only 40% of the world's radiotherapy facilities are available to them (Salminen et al., 2005). Also, the diagnosis and treatment are not planned rationally where the technology and infrastructure are not related to strategies of early detection. This causes excessive reliance on procedures that are costly and only the wealthy can afford (WHO, 2008) leading to increased mortality. Also, in LMICs the majority of the population cannot pay for the treatment of cancer; hence the diagnosis of cancer does little but contributes to the malicious cycle of poverty (Bray et al., 2014).

6.2 Environmental settings

Air pollution is seen as a major public health risk factor globally. Although air pollution has declined in HICs in the past 25 years, it is on increase in the LMICs, which is a threat to public health and development in these regions. One of the major reasons for this gap is that the governments in HICs have implemented air quality management programs. However, the poor in the LMICs still rely on solid fuels for cooking and heating (Boogaard et al., 2019). Approximately, 3.8 million deaths across the globe were attributed to Household Air Pollution in 2016, almost all of which were concentrated in the LMICs. Apart from lung cancer, the diseases attributed to air pollution are chronic obstructive pulmonary disease (COPD), acute lower respiratory infections (ALRI), and ischemic heart diseases. Noncommunicable diseases amount to around 73% of these deaths, lung cancer being one of them (WHO, 2018).

The pollution might vary within or between the countries or has a rural–urban divide, its effect is expected to be greater in the developed world due to economic transitions and development resulting in massive levels of air pollution. This growth in the less developed countries results in the expansion of the slum area where the poor population lives in overcrowded and unsanitary conditions. As mentioned earlier the socioeconomically deprived population is at higher risk of morbidity and mortality due to lesser access to health services, compromised nutrition, and other factors (O'Neill et al., 2003). Thus, air pollution can worsen the already deplorable health conditions in less developed countries.

In addition, the neighborhood and the built environment play a significant role in the way the health of the population is shaped. The built environment consists of man-made physical attributes such as walkability, recreation, health promotion resources, and amenities that are undesirable which in turn influence the health behavior of the individuals

(Jackson, 2003). Given that the built environment can affect health outcomes through access to resources, material deprivation, and health behaviors, they are also likely to influence cancer across the continuum, cancer risk, diagnosis, treatment, survival, and mortality (Lynch and Rebbeck, 2013) in the LMICs.

7. Response to the burden of cancer

The answers to the growing burden of cancer in the developing world are many and it is significant to formulate the policies which lead to optimal response (Baltussen, 2006). With the shrinking budgets for health, the government has to confront difficult choices when facing current problems in health. As already mentioned, by 2030 the world is expected to see 70% of its cancer cases in the developing world (American Cancer Society, 2011 as cited in Moten et al., 2014). Although it has been estimated that 0.1% of the total expenditure on health should be directed to health services and policy research in LMICs, the amount spent is 0.007% of the total health expenditure (Gonzalez Block and Mills, 2003). There has been increasing interest in strengthening the research capacity in the developing world in the last decade (Chandiwana and Ornbjerg, 2003). However, the research on cancer in developing countries is difficult, and the major problem is that the diagnosis of cancer is relatively expensive and is not available to all the inhabitants of the developing world. The statistics which are available for the incidence and mortality of cancer are incomplete, of dubious validity, and biased in their representation of geographical regions, social class, and other factors which affect the access to diagnostic services (Siemiatycki, 2002). There remains massive underinvestment in the health concerns of the developing countries as compared to the developed countries and the gap is still widening (Mellstedt, 2006).

Although this direct access to oncological services will remain a challenge in the developing world, the current initiatives in the health systems in these countries can be implemented cost-effectively. The strengthening of the primary health infrastructure so that it is responsive to the prevention and early detection of cancers. Moreover, an increase in the number of community health workers combined with access to early detection of cancer cases will result in improved health outcomes. Along with building the health infrastructure, the potential for developing novel therapeutic techniques needs to be exploited in developing countries. While conventional medicine is unapproachable to patients in the developing countries due to its dependence on laboratory facilities, technology, and highly trained medical professionals, nanomedicine relies mainly on the prevention and early management of the disease bypassing the need for the specialized medical expertise and expensive laboratory equipment (Moten et al., 2012). To reduce the incidence of cancer, especially in the developing world particular attention should be paid to preventable cancers. To make it possible along with the reconstruction of health infrastructure and training of health professionals, financial resources should be expanded for the prevention and treatment of cancer (Moten et al., 2014).

8. Conclusion

The epidemiological transitions in the developed and developing world have been instrumental in changing the disease profile in the nations, cancer being one of them. Although developed countries have robust health systems which are more responsive to cancer prevention, detection, and treatment, the developing world is still struggling with providing basic health needs to the population at large. The social and racial disparities in the HICs, as well as LMICs, are present along the continuum of cancer. The response of health infrastructure, as well as maintenance of cancer data, play a significant part in addressing the burden. Also, a large proportion of cancers can be prevented by adopting measures such as tobacco control, adopting healthy lifestyles, vaccinations, and early detection. To curb the increasing burden of cancer, efforts are required by the governments, especially in the developing world where attention should be paid to reconstructing the health systems, financing the cancer research, and training the health professionals to make use of the latest technology for early detection of cancer.

Cancer Scenario in India

As far as India is concerned it exhibits heterogeneity for cancer. Tobacco related cancers contribute to 27.1% of the total cancer burden in the country. Also, local cultural factors and lifestyle choices have contributed to the heterogeneity and difference in cancer patterns in India. The most common sites for cancer are lung, mouth, esophagus stomach, and nasopharynx in men. Cancer of lung is the most leading site in the metropolitan cities and southern region while mouth cancer was most common in the western and central regions of India. Lung cancer and oral cancers are the most common cancers among males in Indian subcontinent (ICMR, 2020). Cancer of breast and of cervix are most common cancers in Indian women with the highest burden being observed in metropolitan cities. There is an increase in the incidence of breast cancer while cancer of cervix is on decline. Presently, breast cancer and cancer of cervix are the leading sites for women in India and pose an important public health problem (Takiar, 2018). In the North Eastern (NE) regions, cancer of stomach, esophagus and nasopharynx are the leading sites which is different from rest of India. An important mention is that the NE region lacks required infrastructure as far as human resources and treatment facilities (Ngaihte et al., 2019). The projected incidence for cancer in 2020 was higher for females (712,758) than for males (679,421), and for 2025, it is 806,218 in females and 763,575 in males. The projected burden of incidence at the national level for population was 98.7 per 100,000 population. NRCP has estimated a higher incidence for cancer at all sites as compared to IARC and GLOBOCON for the year 2018 (Mathur et al., 2021).

References

American Cancer Society, 2008. Cancer Facts and Figures 2008. American Cancer Society, Atlanta, GA.

Baltussen, R., 2006. Priority setting of public spending in developing countries: do not try to do everything for everybody. Health Policy 78 (2–3), 149–156. https://doi.org/10.1016/j.healthpol.2005.10.006.

Boffetta, P., Hashibe, M., Veccchia, C., Zantoski, W., Rehm, J., 2006. The burden of cancer attributable to alcohol drinking. Int. J. Cancer 119 (4), 884–887. https://doi.org/10.1002/Ijc.21903.

Boogaard, H., Walker, K., Cohen, A.J., 2019. Air pollution: the emergence of a global health risk factor. Int. Health 11, 417–421. https://doi.org/10.1093/inthealth/ihz078.

Bray, F., Soerjomataram, I., 2015. The changing global burden of cancer: transitions in human development and implications for cancer prevention and control. In: Gelband, H., Jha, P., Sankaranarayanan, R., Horton, S. (Eds.), Disease Control Priorities. World Bank, Washington, pp. 23–44.

Bray, F., Znaor, A., Cueva, P., Korir, A., Swaminathan, R., Parki, D.M., 2014. Planning and Developing Population-Based cancer Registration in Low- and Middle-Income Settings. IARC, Technical Publication 43. WHO, Geneva.

Bray, F., Znaor, A., Cueva, P., Korir, A., Swaminathan, R., Ullrich, A., Parkin, D.M., 2015. Planning and Developing Population-Based Cancer Registration in Low- and Middle-Income Settings. IARC Technical Publication no. 43. International Agency for Research on Cancer, Lyon.

Bronfenbrenner, U., Ceci, S.J., 1994. Nature-nurture reconceptualized in developmental perspective: a bioecologic model. Psychol. Rev. 101 (4), 568–586. https://doi.org/10.1037/0033-295x.101.4.568.

Cavalini, L.T., de Leon, A.C., 2008. Morbidity and mortality in Brazilian municipalities: a multilevel study of the association between socioeconomic and healthcare indicators. Int. J. Epidemiol. 37 (4), 775–783. https://doi.org/10.1093/ije/dyn088 (PMID:18503078).

Chandiwana, S., Ornbjerg, N., 2003. Review of north-south and south-south cooperation and conditions necessary to sustain research capability in developing countries. J. Health Popul. Nutr. 21, 288–297.

Collins, K.S., Hughes, D.L., Doty, M.M., Ives, B.L., Edwards, J.N., Tenny, K., 2002. Diverse Communities, Common Concerns: Assessing Healthcare Quality for Minority Americans. The Commonwealth Fund, New York.

Danaei, G., Hoorn, S.V., Lopez, A.D., Murray, C.J., Ezzati, M., 2005. Causes of Cancer in the world: comparative risk assessment of nine behavioural and environmental risk factors. Lancet 366 (9499), 1784–1793.

de Vries, E., Arroyave, I., Pardo, C., 2015. Time trends in inequalities in premature cancer mortality by educational level in Colombia, 1998–2007. J. Epidemiol. Community Health 69 (5), 408–415. https://doi.org/10.1136/jech-2014-204650.

DeSantis, C.E., Miller, K.D., Sauer, A.G., Jemal, A., Siegel, R., 2019. Cancer statistics for African Americans. CA Cancer J. Clin. 69 (3), 211–233.

Dikshit, R., Gupta, P.C., Ramasundarahettige, C., Gajalakshmi, V., Aleksandrowicz, L., Badwe, R., Million Death Study Collaborators, 2012. Cancer mortality in India: a nationally representative survey. Lancet 379 (9828), 1807–1816. https://doi.org/10.1016/S0140-6736(12)60358-4.

Ezzati, M., Henley, S.J., Lopez, A.D., Thun, M.J., 2005. Role of smoking in global and regional cancer epidemiology: current patterns and data needs. Int. J. Cancer 116 (6), 963–971. https://doi.org/10.1002/Ijc.21100.

Ferlay, J., Ervik, M., Colombet, M., Mery, L., Pineros, M., et al., 2019. Global Cancer Observatory: Cancer Today. Lyon International Agency for Research on Cancer.

Fidler, M.M., Soerjomataram, I., Bray, F., 2016. A global view on cancer incidence and national levels of the human development index. Int. J. Cancer 139, 2436–2446. https://doi.org/10.1002/ijc.30382.

Gbadamosi, A., n.d. Understanding the Developed/Developing Country Taxonomy. Available from: Understanding the Developed/Developineg Country Taxonomy, A4ID.

Ginsburg, O.M., Hanna, T.P., Vandenberg, T., Joy, A.A., Clemons, M., Game, M., et al., 2012. The global cancer epidemic: opportunities for Canada in low-and middle-income countries. Can. Med. Assoc. J. 184 (15), 1699–1704.

Girianelli, V.R., Gamarra, C.J., Azevedo e Silva, G., 2014. Disparities in cervical and breast cancer mortality in Brazil. Rev. Saude Publica 48 (3), 459–467.

Gonzalez Block, M.A., Mills, A., 2003. Assessing capacity for health policy and systems research in low- and middle-income countries. Health Res. Policy Syst. 1 (1), 1.

Gupta, S., Rivera-Luna, R., Ribeiro, R.C., Howard, S.C., 2014. Pediatric oncology as the next global child health priority: the need for national childhood cancer strategies in low-and middle income countries. PLoS Med. 11 (6), e1001656.

Hanna, T.P., Kangole, A.C.T., 2010. Cancer control in developing countries: using health data and health services research to measure and improve access, quality and efficiency. BMC Int. Health Hum. Rights 10, 24. http://www.biomedcentral.com/1472-698X/10/24.

Harper, D.M., Franco, E.L., Wheeler, C., Ferris, D.G., Jenkins, D., Schuind, A., et al., 2004. Efficacy of a bivalent L1 virus-like particle vaccine in prevention of infection with human papillomavirus types 16 and 18 in young women: a randomised controlled trial. Lancet 364 (9447), 1757–1765. https://doi.org/10.1016/S0140-6736(04)17398-4.

Herrero, R., Quint, M., Hildesheim, A., Gonzalez, P., Struijk, L., Katki, H.A., 2013. Reduced prevalence of oral human papillomavirus (HPV) 4 years after bivalent HPV vaccination in a randomized clinical trial in Costa Rica. PLoS One 8 (7), e68329. https://doi.org/10.1371/journal.pone.0068329.

Hosgood 3rd, H.D., Wei, H., Sapkota, A., Choudhury, I., Bruce, N., Smith, K.R., Rothman, N., Lan, Q., 2011. Household coal use and lung cancer: systematic review and meta-analysis of case-control studies, with an emphasis on geographic variation. Int. J. Epidemiol. 40 (3), 719–728.

IARC, 2008. In: Cancer Incidence in Five Continents. vol. IX. IARC Scientific Publications, France.

IARC, 2010. Alcohol Consumption and Ethyl Carbamate. Monographs on the Evaluation of Carcinogenic Risks to Humans. International Agency for Research on Cancer, Lyon, France.

ICMR, 2020. Report of National Cancer Registry Programme 2020. ICMR-National Centre for Disease Informatics and Research, Bengaluru.

Islami, F., Miller, K.D., Siegel, R.L., Fedewa, S.A., Wards, E.M., Jemal, A., 2017. Disparities in liver cancer occurrence in the United States by race/ethnicity and state. CA Cancer J. Clin. 67, 273–289.

Jackson, R.J., 2003. The impact of the built environment on health: an emerging field. Am. J. Public Health 93 (9), 1382–1384.

Jedy-Agba, E.E., Oga, E.A., Odutola, M., Abdullahi, Y.M., Popoola, A., Achara, P., Adebamowo, C.A., 2015. Developing national cancer registration in developing countries – case study of the Nigerian National System of cancer registries. Front. Public Health 3, 186.

Jemal, A., Torre, L., Soerjomataram, I., Bray, F., 2019. The Cancer Atlas, third ed. The American Cancer Society, Atlanta, GA.

Jia, P.L., Zhang, C., Yu, J.J., Xu, C., Tang, L., Sun, X., 2018. The risk of lung cancer among cooking adults: a meta-analysis of 23 observational studies. J. Cancer Res. Clin. Oncol. 144 (2), 229–240. https://doi.org/10.1007/s00432-017-2547-7. 29164315.

Kagawa-Singer, M., Dadia, A.V., Yu, M.C., Surbone, A., 2010. Cancer, culture and health disparities time to chart a new course. CA Cancer J. Clin. 60 (1), 12–39.

Levi, F., Lucchini, F., Negri, E., La Vecchia, C., 2004. Trends in mortality from major concerns in the European Union, including acceding countries, in 2004. Cancer 101 (12), 2843–2850.

Lim, S.S., Vos, T., Flaxman, A.D., Danaei, G., Shibuya, K., Memish, Z.A., 2012. A comparative risk assessment of burden of disease and injury attributable to 67 risk factors and risk factor clusters in 21 regions, 1990–2010: a systematic analysis for the global burden of disease study 2010. Lancet 80 (9859), 2224–2260. https://doi.org/10.1016/S0140-6736(12)61766-8.

Lynch, S.M., Rebbeck, T.R., 2013. Bridging the gap between biologic, individual, and macroenvironmental factors in cancer: a multilevel approach. Cancer Epidemiol. Biomark. Prev. 22 (4), 485–495.

Mackenbach, J.P., Stirbu, I., Roskam, A.-J.R., Schaap, M.M., Menvielle, G., Leinsalu, M., Kunst, A.E., European Union Working Group on Socioeconomic Inequalities in Health, 2008. Socioeconomic inequalities in health in 22 European countries. N. Engl. J. Med. 358 (23), 2468–2481.

Mangtani, P., Maringe, C., Rachet, B., Coleman, M.P., dos Santos, S.I., 2010. Cancer mortality in ethnic south Asian migrants in England and Wales (1993-2003): patterns in the overall population and in first and subsequent generations. Br. J. Cancer 102, 1438–1443. https://doi.org/10.1038/sj.bjc.6605645.

Maringe, C., Mangtani, P., Coleman, M.P., Rachet, B., 2015. Cancer survival differences between South Asians and non-South Asians of England in 1986–2004, accounting for age at diagnosis and deprivation. Br. J. Cancer 113 (1), 173–181.

Maringe, C., Mangtani, P., Rachet, B., Leon, D.A., Coleman, M.P., dos Santos Silva, I., 2013. Cancer incidence in South Asian migrants to England, 1986–2004: unraveling ethnic from socioeconomic differentials. Int. J. Cancer 132 (8), 1886–1894.

Marmot, M., 2019. Social inequalities, global public health and cancer. In: Vaccarella, S., Lorter Tieulant, J., Saracci, R., Conway, D.I., Straif, K., Wild, C.P. (Eds.), Reducing Social Inequalities in Cancer: Evidence and Priorities for Research. World Health Organisation, Geneva, pp. 7–12.

Mathur, P., Sathiskumar, K., Chaturvedi, M., Das, P., Sudharshan, K., Santhappan, S., Roselind, F.S., 2021. Cancer statistics, 2020: Report from National Cancer Registry Programme, India. JCO Glob. Oncol. 6, 1063–1075. https://doi.org/10.1200/GO.20.00122.

McCutchan, G.M., Wood, F., Edwards, A., Richards, R., Brain, K.E., 2015. Influences of cancer symptom knowledge, beliefs and barriers on cancer symptom presentation in relation to socioeconomic deprivation: a systematic review. BMC Cancer 15 (1), 1000. https://doi.org/10.1186/s12885-015-1972-8.

Mellstedt, H., 2006. Cancer initiatives in developing countries. Ann. Oncol. 17 (8), viii24–viii31. https://doi.org/10.1093/annonc/mdl984.

Moten, A., Schafer, D., Montgomery, E., 2012. A prescription for health inequity: building public health infrastructure in resource–poor settings. J. Glob. Health 2, 020302. https://doi.org/10.7189/jogh.02.020302.

Moten, A., Schafer, D., Ferrari, M., 2014. Redefining global health priorities: improving cancer care in developing settings. J. Glob. Health 4 (1), 010304. https://doi.org/10.7189/jogh.04.010304.

Moy, K.A., Yuan, J.-M., Chung, F.-L., Den Berg, D.V., Wang, R., Gao, Y.-T., Yu, M.C., 2008. Urinary total isothiocyanates and colorectal cancer: a prospective study of men in Shanghai, China. Cancer Epidemiol. Biomark. Prev. 17 (6), 1354–1359.

NCD Countdown 2030 Collaborators, 2020. NCD countdown 2030:pathways to achieving sustainable development goals target 3.4. Lancet 396, 918–934. doi:10.1016/.

Nelson, N., 2006. Migrant studies aid the search for factors linked to breast cancer risk. J. Natl. Cancer Inst. 98 (7), 436–438.

Ng, M., Freeman, M.K., Fleming, T.D., Robinson, M., Dwyer-Lindgren, L., Gakidaou, E., 2014. Smoking prevalence and cigarette consumption in 187 countries, 1980–2012. J. Am. Med. Assoc. 311 (2), 183–192. https://doi.org/10.1001/Jama.2013.284692.

Ngaihte, P., Zomawia, E., Kaushik, I., 2019. Cancer in the NorthEast India: where we are and what needs to be done? Indian J. Public Health 63, 251–253. https://doi.org/10.4103/ijph.IJPH_323_18.

Nguyen, V.K., Kahana, A., Heidit, J., Polemi, K., Kvasnicka, J., Colacino, J.A., 2020. A comprehensive analysis of racial disparities in chemical biomarker concentrations in United States women, 1999–2014. Environ. Int. 137, 105496. https://doi.org/10.1016/j.envint.2020.105496.

Oguntoke, O., 2014. Spatial and socio-demographic disparities of cancer morbidity in Nigeria: patterns and factors. Malays. J. Soc. Space 10 (1), 25–35.

O'Neill, M.S., Jerrett, M., Kawachi, I., Levy, J.I., Cohen, A.J., Gouveia, N., Schwartz, J., 2003. Health, wealth, and air pollution: advancing theory and methods. Environ. Health Perspect. 111 (16), 1861. https://doi.org/10.1289/ehp.6334.

Pezzatini, M., Marino, G., Conte, S., Catracchia, V., 2007. Oncology: a forgotten territory in Africa. Ann. Oncol. 18 (12), 2046–2047.

Plummer, M., de Martel, C., Vignat, J., Ferlay, J., Bray, F., Franceschi, S., et al., 2016. Global burden of cancers attributable to infections in 2012: a synthetic analysis. Lancet Glob. Health 4, e609–e616. https://doi.org/10.1016/S2214-109X(16)30143-7.

Rastogi, T., Devesa, S., Mangtani, P., Mathew, A., Cooper, N., Kao, R., Sinha, R., 2008. Cancer incidence rates among South Asians in four geographic regions: India, Singapore, UK and US. Int. J. Epidemiol. 37 (1), 147–160. https://doi.org/10.1093/ije/dym219.

Rehm, J., Shield, K.D., 2013. Global alcohol-attributable deaths from cancer, liver cirrhosis, and injury in 2010. Alcohol Res. 35 (2), 174–183.

Salminen, E., Izewsk, J., Andre, P., 2005. IAEA's role in the global management of cancer-focus on upgrading radiotherapy services. Acta Oncol. 44, 816–824.

Sarfati, D., 2019. Why social inequalities matter in the cancer continuum. In: Vaccarella, S., Lorter Tieulant, J., Saracci, R., Conway, D.I., Straif, K., Wild, C.P. (Eds.), Reducing Social Inequalities in Cancer: Evidence and Priorities for Research. World Health Organisation, Geneva, pp. 15–24.

Shield, K.D., Rylett, M., Gmel, G., Kehoe-Chan, T.A., Rehm, J., 2013. Global alcohol exposure estimates by country, territory and region for 2005: a contribution to the comparative risk assessment for the 2010 global burden of disease study. Addiction 108 (5), 912–922. https://doi.org/10.1111/Add.12112.

Siddiqui, A., Zafar, S.N., 2018. Global availability of cancer registry data. J. Glob. Oncol., 1–3. https://doi.org/10.1200/JGO.18.00116.

Siemiatycki, J., 2002. Commentary: epidemiology on the side of the angels. Int. J. Epidemiol. 31, 1027–1029.

Simopoulos, A., 2001. The Mediterranean diets: what is so special about the diet of Greece? The scientific evidence. J. Nutr. 131 (11 Suppl), 3065S–3073S.

Singh, G.K., Jemal, A., 2017. Socioeconomic and racial/ethnic disparities in cancer mortality, incidence, and survival in the United States, 1950-2014: over six decades of changing patterns and widening inequalities. J. Environ. Public Health 2017, 2819372. https://doi.org/10.1155/2017/2819372. 28408935.

Sinha, R., Anderson, D.E., Mcdonald, S.S., Greenwald, P., 2003. Cancer risk and diet in India. J. Postgrad. Med. 49 (3), 222–228.

Sloan, F.A., Gelband, H., 2007. Cancer Control Opportunities in Low-and Middle-Income Countries. National Academies Press, Washington DC.

Smedley, B.D., Stith, A.Y., Nelson, A.R. (Eds.), 2001. Unequal Treatment Confronting Racial and Ethnic Disparities in Healthcare. The National Academic Press, Washington.

Takiar, R., 2018. Status of breast and cervix cancer in selected registries of India. Ann. Womens Health 2 (1), 1012. Available from: Status of Breast and Cervix Cancer in Selected Registries of India (remedypublications.com). Retrieved: 24 October 2021.

Teng, A.M., Atkinson, J., Disney, G., Wilson, N., Sarfati, D., McLeod, M., Blakely, T., 2016. Ethnic inequalities in cancer incidence and mortality: census-linked cohort studies with 87 million years of person-time follow-up. BMC Cancer 16 (1), 755. https://doi.org/10.1186/s12885-016-2781-4.

Tervonen, H.E., Bray, F., Folaiki, S., Rodder, D., 2017. Cancer registration in low and middle income countries -the case of Pacific Islands. Eur. J. Cancer Care 26, e12650. https://doi.org/10.1111/ecc.12650.

Torre, L.A., Siegal, R.L., Ward, E.M., Jemal, A., 2016. Global cancer incidence and mortality rates and trends-an update. Cancer Epidemiol. Biomark. Prev. 25 (1), 16–27. https://doi.org/10.1158/1055-9965.EPI-15-0578.

Torre, L.A., Islami, F., Siegel, R.L., Ward, E.M., Jemal, A., 2017. Global cancer in women: burden and trends. Cancer Epidemiol. Biomark. Prev. 26 (4), 444–457.

Tran, H.N., Udaltsova, N., Li, Y., Klatsky, A.L., 2018. Low cancer risk of south Asians: a brief report. Perm. J. 22, 17–095.

Trinh, Q.D., Ngyuen, P.L., Leow, J.J., Dalela, D., Chao, G.F., Mahal, B.A., Aizer, A.A., 2015. Cancer-specific mortality of Asian Americans diagnosed with cancer: a nationwide population-based assessment. J. Natl. Cancer Inst. 107. https://doi.org/10.1093/jnci/djv054.

United Nations Development Programme, 2015. Human Development Report 2015. pp. 1–10. Available from: 2015_human_development_report.pdf (undp.org). (Accessed 7 October 2021).

Wallace, T.A., Martin, D.N., Ambs, S., 2011. Interactions among genes, tumor biology and the environment in cancer health disparities: examining the evidence on a national and global scale. Carcinogenesis 32 (8), 1107–1121.

WCRF (World Cancer Research Fund) and AICR (American Institute for Cancer Research), 2007. Food, Nutrition, Physical Activity, and the Prevention of Cancer: A Global Perspective. WCRF and AICR, Washington, DC.

WHO, 2008. Cancer Control Knowledge into Action: WHO Guide for Effective Programs. WHO, Geneva.

WHO, 2018. Burden of diseases from Household Air Pollution for 2016. Available from: Microsoft Word –
    HAP_BoD_results_May2018_final.docx (who.int) (Accessed 4 October 2021).

WHO, 2020. WHO Report on cancer Setting Priorities, Investing Wisely and Providing Care for all. World
    Health Organisation, Geneva.

WHO, 2021. Non Communicable diseases. Available from: Noncommunicable diseases (who.int)
    (Accessed 28 September 2021).

Williams, F., Zoellner, N., Hovmand, P.S., 2016. Understanding global cancer disparities: the role of social
    determinants from system dynamics perspective. Transdiscipl. J. Eng. Sci. 7, 1–13.

Yuan, J.M., Gao, Y.-T., Yang, C.S., Yu, M.C., 2007. Urinary biomarkers of tea polyphenols and risk of
    colorectal cancer in the Shanghai cohort study. Int. J. Cancer 120, 1344–1350.

CHAPTER THREE

Technological evolution in cancer diagnosis and therapeutics

Madhusmita Mishra, Bulbul Tyagi, Nida Taimoor, and Sudeep Bose
Amity Institute of Biotechnology, Amity University Uttar Pradesh, Noida, India

Abbreviations

CAR-T	cellular therapy
Cas 9	caspases 9
CD80 and CD86	cluster of differentiation 80 and 86
cDNA	cell-free DNA
CEA	carcinoembryonic antigen
CGH	comparative genomic hybridization
CRISPR	clustered regularly interspaced short palindromic repeats
CSF	cerebrospinal fluid
CTCs	circulating tumor cells
CTLA-4	cytotoxic T lymphocyte-associated antigen
EGFR	epidermal growth factor receptor
ER	endoplasmic reticulum
FDA	US Food Drug and Administration
FISH	fluorescence in situ hybridization
GnRH	gonadotropin-releasing hormone
HepG2	liver hepatocellular carcinoma
HER2	human epidermal growth factor receptor 2
LH	luteinizing hormone
LOD	limit of detection
MMP	matrix metalloproteinase
MRI	magnetic resonance imaging
MUC1	mucin 1
NPs	nanoparticles
PD-L1	programmed cell death ligand-1
PSA	prostate-specific antigen
PTX	paclitaxel
SLNs	solid lipid nanoparticles
SPIONs	superparamagnetic iron oxide NPs

Biomarkers in Cancer Detection and Monitoring of Therapeutics
https://doi.org/10.1016/B978-0-323-95116-6.00018-9

1. Introduction

Cancer is a dreadful disease yet surfacing with limited therapeutic options despite immense breakthroughs in medical science and technology. Metastasis and its recurrence are responsible for a significant number of fatal outcomes, even though the exact mechanisms are still elusive (Gallaher et al., 2018). The mechanism of the development of cancerous cells is depicted in Fig. 1. Cancer is usually assumed to be caused by mutations of several genes. DNA methylation, histone modifications, and RNA-mediated silencing are all important processes for the steady transmission of gene activity states from one cell generation to the next (Feinberg et al., 2006). Any of these three separate and mutually supportive epigenetic pathways can be disrupted, leading to abnormal gene expression and cancer development as well as other "epigenetic illnesses" (Egger et al., 2004). Since abnormal protein expression in cancer has been documented for decades, the revelation of proteomic cancer biomarkers has a lot of significance in cancer diagnosis and therapy in the past. Alpha-fetoprotein, PSA, thyroglobulin, leptin, prolactin, Her-2/neu, and troponin I are some of the FDA-approved cancer biomarkers (Polanski and Anderson, 2007).

Early detection of the tumor is an effective approach to treat the said condition and improve the patient's quality of life. However, most patients have local proliferation and metastasis at the time of diagnosis, and only a few patients are eligible for surgery. Surgery, chemotherapy, and radiation therapy are preferred treatments for these patients (Fig. 2). Chemotherapeutic medications can harm the patient's body since they affect all rapidly dividing cells, including healthy cells (Padhi et al., 2020a). Drug resistance, which is a key

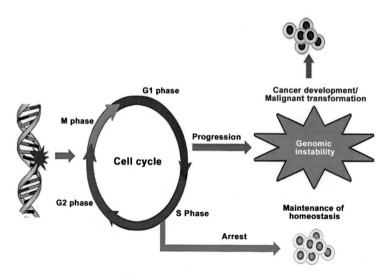

Fig. 1 Mechanism of cancer development.

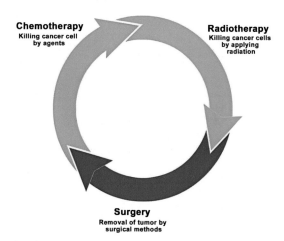

Fig. 2 Gold standard of cancer treatment.

issue with chemotherapy, occurs when cancer cells that were previously inhibited by chemotherapeutics gain resistance to it. Decreased drug absorption and rampant drug efflux are known to be the leading reasons. Traditional chemotherapeutic method limitations include dosage selection complexity, paucity of selectivity, faster drug metabolism, and primarily severe adverse effects (Mondal et al., 2014).

As a result, new approaches for diagnosing and treating tumors that directly target malignant cells while avoiding normal cells would be ideal candidates (Vasir and Labhasetwar, 2007). Treatment modalities such as surgery, radiation therapy, and the use of chemotherapy are among cancer treatments that are presently available. Over the last decade, a better comprehension of the tumor microenvironment has contributed to the growth of new cancer therapeutics. The use of imaging in diagnostics has aided the advancement of this field. It enables the assessment of the biodistribution and pharmacokinetics of newly developed drug delivery systems in a noninvasive manner, permitting to choice of the best drug choices. The advancement in imaging, biopsy, and different molecular techniques has enabled clinicians and researchers to efficiently map the tumors.

Therapy has proven to showcase a pertinent role in the clinical investigation of cancer, and it is widely known to have an impact on the effectiveness of all chemotherapeutics, with clinical efficiency and translation of therapeutic systems being particularly impacted (Hare et al., 2017).

Therapies targeted to specific genes, prediction and treatment, drug delivery, biomarker tracing, targeted drug delivery, and molecular imaging are just a few of the anticipated outcomes of nanotechnology in diagnosis and treatment modality for cancer (Behera et al., 2020). Nanotechnology has been employed in the generation of nanomaterials that are exploited for molecular cancer diagnostics (Fig. 3) (Patnaik et al., 2021). The advent of biomarkers, a type of molecular diagnostic based on

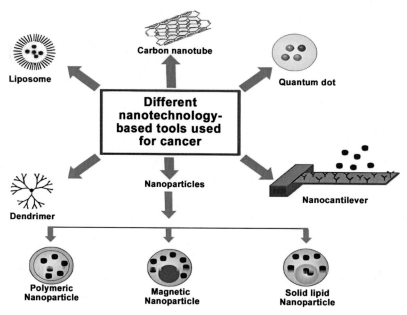

Fig. 3 Nanotools for cancer therapy.

nanotechnology, helps in the accurate and swift diagnosis of cancers (Tran et al., 2017). The emergence of nanocarriers, for example, can provide accurate malignant tissue targeting with minimum adverse effects (Padhi et al., 2020a,b). Nanomaterials can easily bypass cell barriers due to their biological attribute (Khuroo et al., 2014).

As a result, multiple research works have explored various types of nanotools, with the premise that combining these nanocarriers in the cancer therapy framework can strike the right balance between enhancing efficacy and minimizing drug toxicity (Padhi et al., 2021). The present chapter emphasizes the advancements in diagnostic and therapeutic strategies that can enhance the efficacy of cancer treatment.

2. Cancer diagnosis

The insufficient delivery of essential clinical details about diverse cancer kinds and stages limits the widespread usage of conventional imaging systems (Kim et al., 2010). As a result, obtaining a complete assessment of the illness state on which to base optimal therapy is challenging (Akhter et al., 2013).

Nanotechnology usage in the diagnosis and detection of cancer has gotten a lot of interest, and numerous nano-based strategies are now being used for molecular imaging. The said domain has recently added significance in cancer research and detection owing to its advantages, which include smaller size, strong biocompatibility, and a higher atomic number. Nanoparticles employed in cancer research have some differential attributes that best fit them for broad usages. Chemotherapeutic drugs and biomolecules can be combined with nanoparticles to identify extremely intricate tumors and can be effective for cancer cell identification and screening (Singh, 2019).

2.1 Nanotechnology-mediated cancer diagnostics

In cancer diagnosis, biopsies of tumor specimens with nanoparticles have made it possible to spot tumors in their early stages. The monitoring of exponential spread in lung cancer can be confirmed by generating immune SPIONs that may have suitable applications in imaging and targeted cancer cell lines (Wan et al., 2016). SPIONs have been proven in the latest research works to have high specificity and no known adverse effects, rendering them appropriate basic components for imaging usages (Jafari et al., 2015). Rand and coworkers discovered that the clumps of hepatic tumor cells in the gold nanocarriers were considerably superior to those detected in the control group, as measured by X-ray imaging. The technology enabled the detection of cancers in the body, which may have crucial implications for early diagnosis (Shrivas et al., 2018). The production of silver-rich quantum dots using a sulfur source allows for visualization in a wide IR range (Zhang et al., 2020).

Another method is to employ nano-enabled strategies to develop chip-based microfluidics devices for immunoscreening or studying tumor cell characteristics (Jokerst et al., 2009). Magnetic powder imaging has also been employed and has demonstrated a higher level of sensitivity and resolution in cancerous tissues (Garrigue et al., 2018).

2.2 Molecular techniques for cancer diagnostics

For many periods, traditional histopathology predicated on morphological assessment has been the gold standard diagnostic approach. Enzyme histochemistry and electron microscopy were used to enhance the main microanatomic assessment to incorporate biochemical and subcellular ultrastructural aspects (Bhardwaj, 2005). Immunohistochemistry, cytogenetics, DNA ploidy analysis, and molecular genetic assays have lately been included in the list of useful adjuncts to light microscopy in cancer detection. Antisera and monoclonal antibodies tailored against specific protein sequences of tumors are used in immunohistochemistry, an established technique for detecting them. It is especially critical in undifferentiated tumors including lymphoid malignancies. Estrogen, progesterone, and HER2 neu receptor status have been determined using immunohistochemistry.

Malignant cells commonly have chromosomal abnormalities, which are generally indicative of a certain tumor type. Different forms of chromosomal abnormalities exist (Marcucci Guido et al., 2005). Fluorescence in situ hybridization (FISH) is a technique that can be used on interphase cells. As a result, it is more sensitive than traditional cytogenetics. CGH stands for comparative genomic hybridization and is a recently documented approach for detecting chromosomal gains and losses in the genomic complement. These newly advanced procedures seem to be more promising. Microarray, a relatively newer technology, allows for the evaluation of differential expression of a certain gene complement in various histomorphological types and grades of a tumor (Dabritz et al., 2005).

2.3 Advancement in biopsy

Strategies targeting liquid biopsies as a marginally invasive option to tissue-based cancer diagnosis methodologies are often constrained by irregular distribution of tumor mass. The samples obtained from a patient contain tumor-derived mutational, epigenetic, and transcriptomic characteristics, laying the groundwork for generating useful diagnostic biomarkers from these samples (Zhang, 2021). Even though radiographic imaging and serological markers are regarded as the "gold standard" in clinical cases, they have associated drawbacks, including poor sensitivity and specificity (Watanabe et al., 2021).

The use of circulating tumor cells (CTCs) and cell-free DNA (cfDNA) in liquid biopsies has enormous potential in diagnosing, monitoring, and treating various malignancies (Rhim et al., 2012). In the realm of targeted medicine, liquid biopsy offers a potential way to detect molecular abnormalities in malignancies. The use of cfDNA analysis to identify specific genetic variants has been successfully adopted in therapeutic contexts. CTC counting is challenging because of the lack of CTC recovery along with the growing demand for distinguishing molecular changes (Sanger et al., 2011).

Quantification of CTCs can be employed in the clinical setting for early tumor detection in patients who are at higher risk for encountering lung cancer and for sequential surveillance of its responsiveness to chemotherapy, with a decrease in CTC numbers indicating treatment success. Immunochemical examination of CTCs can be used to assess the expression of proteins including HER2 and PD-L1. CTC single-cell sequencing could reveal potentially targetable genomic changes like somatic mutations and chromosomal abnormalities. Patient-derived xenografts were established by transferring CTCs into an animal model, allowing researchers to analyze tumor pathogenesis and responsiveness to various therapies (Pantel and Speicher, 2016).

Liquid biopsies, as opposed to traditional tumor biopsies, provide a better way of measuring heterogeneous tumor populations to assign probabilities and thereby offer better possibilities for its treatment. By identifying ctDNA with standard blood indicators to boost sensitivity, liquid biopsies can augment established approaches in detecting gynecological malignancies (Maron et al., 2019; Wang et al., 2018).

2.4 Radiomics and pathomics

These are the exciting new spheres that utilize quantitative imaging features from radiology and pathology screens as therapeutic and prognostic predictors of illness progression (Aerts, 2016). Radiomics relates to the measurement of characteristics of tumors based on medical image analysis (Grove et al., 2015). While pathomics depends heavily on the emergence and analysis of tissue images of higher resolution (Fuchs and Buhmann, 2011), several research works have focused on developing unique image processing approaches to expand insights through quantitative assessment and disease categorization (Lewis et al., 2014).

2.5 Biomarker and biosensors

Despite recent technical improvements, delayed diagnosis and dismal prognosis are the chief causes of cancer patients' poor survival rates. Due to their reliance on the phenotypic features of tumor, traditional procedures such as magnetic resonance imaging, biopsies, and ultrasound are ineffective for initial stage cancer identification (Altintas and Tothill, 2013). Cancer is a cascaded disease condition with a diverse combination of genetic and epigenetic alterations that disrupt cellular signaling and lead to tumorigenic aggressiveness and transition (Padhi et al., 2018). Biomarkers are components that undergo significant changes during cancer and have significant therapeutic implications. Prognostic, predictive, and diagnostic biomarkers include proteins, isoenzymes, nucleic acids, metabolites, and hormones (Sankara et al., 2007). Biomarkers are typically found in bodily fluids such as urine, serum, CSF, or blood, but they can also be found in tumor cells.

The utilization of biomarkers, which will direct physicians at every phase of disease care, is likely to be critical in the advent of cancer management. Cancer biomarkers can be exploited to accurately assess and regulate the illness at various stages. They can be used to estimate a variety of outcomes during the period of an illness, including early identification, prognosis, and relapse (Harris and Lohr, 2002). Technological improvements in genomic and proteomic technologies, such as gene array technology, enhanced two-dimensional gel electrophoresis, and novel mass spectrometric methodologies, paired with advances in bioinformatics tools, demonstrate excellent potential in achieving the requirement for the exploration of a bunch of diverse sensitive and precise biomarkers (Hristova and Chan, 2019). A list of potential cancer biomarkers for cancer is enlisted in Table 1.

However, the conventional techniques have some added restrictions. As a result, novel, cost-effective ways for monitoring cancer biomarkers are urgently needed. Various types of biosensors were developed throughout the last decade; the major being electrochemical, optical, and mass-sensitive biomarkers for identifying cancer biomarkers (Hasan et al., 2021). Their advantages include flexibility of use, higher sensitivity, lower detection limit, and outstanding performance and specificity.

Wang et al. reported a POC adaptable magnetic-controllable electrochemical-based biosensor with great sensitivity, which enabled an early-stage oral cancer biomarker (miR) diagnosis with a higher recovery rate (93%) and a lower LOD (Wang et al., 2013). Another group of researchers implied the use of a biosensor that can trace CEA

Table 1 List of potential cancer biomarkers.

Biomarker	Cancer type	Clinical usage	Reference
Calcitonin	Thyroid	Diagnosis, monitor treatment, and predict cancer recurrence	Bao et al. (1998)
Carcinoembryonic antigen (CEA)	Numerous cancers such as colorectal, lung, breast, liver, pancreatic, thyroid, and bladder	Determine recurrence as well as monitor treatment efficacy	Yilmaz et al. (2001)
MMP inhibitors	Prostate, breast	Prognosis	Tuck and Chambers (2001)
Interleukin-6 soluble receptor and transforming growth factor 1	Prostate	Cancer prediction	Kattan et al. (2003)
Myc and A1B1	Hepatocellular carcinoma	Determines cancer prognosis	Rhodes et al. (2004)
E-cadherin	Prostate	Determines the risk associated with cancer recurrence after surgery	Rhodes et al. (2004)
β-2 microglobulin (β-2M)	Multiple myeloma and lymphomas	Determines cancer prognosis	Avilés et al. (1996)
Caspase-3	Gastric carcinoma	Determines cancer prognosis	Isobe et al. (2004)
D-dimer	Colorectal carcinoma	Determines cancer prognosis	Blackwell et al. (2004)
Type I collagen (ICTP)	Ovarian cancer	Predicts the aggressiveness of cancer	Santala et al. (2004)
BRCA1 or BRCA2 gene	Breast cancer	Predicts the risk of developing cancer	Miki et al. (1994)
β-15, antizyme, antizyme inhibitor and collagen XXIII	Prostate cancer	Diagnosis of cancer	Bao et al. (1996)

and EGFR. AuNPs layer deposition on which antibodies were immobilized to detect CEA and EGFR biomarker boosted the signal amplification of interdigitated electrode (Altintas et al., 2014). Mathew et al. designed an electrochemical immunosensor that accurately detected prostate tumor-derived extracellular vesicles (Mathew et al., 2020). A disposable electrochemical sensor was reported to detect MUC1 in human serum (Rauf et al., 2018). Another group developed an extremely sensitive immunochemical aptasensor for identifying stomach cancer-derived exosomes (Huang et al., 2019). Yang et al. (2018) demonstrated an effective Au nanoparticle amended Au electrode-based biosensor for detecting HER2 in humans. Lin and his team employed magnetic graphene oxide to immobilize Avastin as a biorecognition element on an Au electrode to identify malignant vascular endothelial growth factors (Lin et al., 2015).

2.6 Other omics-based technologies

Multiomics-based advanced analytic methodologies at various cellular function domains, such as genomes, epigenomes, transcriptomes, proteomes, metabolomes, and microbiomes, provide unrivaled opportunities to study the underpinning pathophysiology of cancer (Fig. 4) (Menyhárt and Győrffy, 2021).

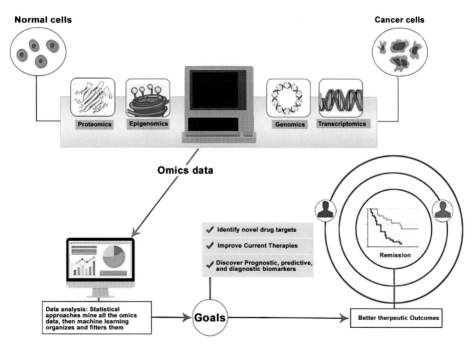

Fig. 4 Omics based platforms for cancer diagnosis.

Proteomics explicates the specific proteins and posttranslational alterations occurring in the cell and gives details about the proteome's organization (Uzozie and Aebersold, 2018). Proteomics may improve patient segregation; new quantitative proteomics has further allowed classification of early-stage hepatocellular carcinomas (Jiang et al., 2019).

Metabolomics refers to the study of metabolites in a biological fluid, cell, or tissue at a given time and has become more important in precision medicine, specifically in the finding of cancer biomarkers. The metabolome not only gives a direct assessment of physiological alterations but also permits conclusions regarding upstream variations. The discovery of important oncometabolite was made possible by metabolomic profiling of cancer cells, which could be a noninvasive method for distinguishing malignant tissue or tumor subtypes (Yang et al., 2013).

Microbiomics is a new field that studies microbial populations that colonize our bodies. The ineffectiveness of PD1 blockage in melanoma has long been associated with an abnormal gut flora (Matson et al., 2018). The findings imply that sustaining a healthy commensal microbiome influences antitumor immunity; nevertheless, the microbial presence linked to immune checkpoint blockade susceptibility differed between several investigations.

Pharmacogenetics, or the research of how genes impact drug response, enables physicians to categorize patients into those who are more likely to adhere to therapy or those who are more likely to encounter toxicity (Patel et al., 2014).

The transcriptome profile can be thought of as a portrait of the current cell state, and hence, its examination offers insights on genome plasticity, gene expression control, and alterations of individual transcripts in addition to genetic alterations (Cieślik and Chinnaiyan, 2018).

3. Cancer therapy
3.1 Nanotechnology-mediated cancer therapy

Lack of selectivity, cytotoxicity to nearby healthy cells, shorter circulation times, limited solubility profile, substantial resistance to an array of chemotherapeutics, and stem-like cell proliferation are all concerns with current chemotherapy. Nanomaterial-based chemotherapy and targeted therapy are being employed in cancer treatment to alleviate these drawbacks (Kundu et al., 2022). One of the key advantages of drug entrapped nanocarriers over native drugs is the ability for targeted delivery to tumor tissues (Padhi et al., 2022). Targeted delivery using nanoparticles has made huge accomplishments in recent times. Targeted delivery is a concept that seeks for exact targeting of specific cancer cells, which can be accomplished through passive or active targeting. Passive targeting makes use of leaky vasculature in tumor tissues that enables a larger quantity of nanocarriers to assemble at the desired tumor sites while active targeting is achieved by anchoring of ligands specific to over-expressed receptors on the surface of cancer cells (Fig. 5) (Behera et al., 2020).

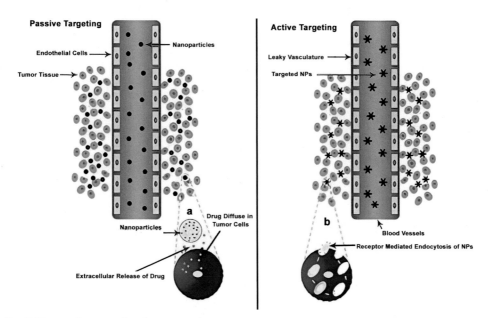

Fig. 5 Targeted approaches for cancer therapy.

The various nanotools that are explored for the treatment of cancer are listed in Table 2.

These nanosystems are worth mentioning, as are some new nanoparticles that are now being investigated at the preclinical level; in addition, many nanosystems are in the pipeline. SLNs, for instance, have been shown to provide greater drug stability and protracted release than other systems; however, because of their higher crystallinity, entrapment efficiency is often noted to be lower (Padhi et al., 2020a, b).

According to a recent study, lipid nanoparticles have been implemented in combating glioblastoma (Grillone et al., 2015). Dendrimers are exceptionally applicable to a wide spectrum of applications due to their easy fabrication design. In vivo tumor model, dendrimers entrapped with a chemotherapeutics termed as doxorubicin, for example, have been demonstrated to produce antiangiogenic effects (Al-Jamal et al., 2013).

Combination chemotherapy, also known as anticancer polychemotherapy, has marked a significant milestone in the treatment of cancers as it delivers better therapeutic success than single chemotherapeutic drugs (Padhi et al., 2021). Combination therapy, in contrast, is known to be effective or cytotoxic to cancerous cells with a high dosage of each drug. Additionally, it ensures a broader spectrum of drug interactions with cancer cells with various genetic aberrations (Lilenbaum et al., 2005).

3.2 Immunotherapy

Due to an improved understanding of the immune system, cancer immunotherapy is now the most appealing option to all standard therapies. With a single vaccine shot,

Table 2 Nanotools for cancer therapy.

Nanocarriers	Types	Chemotherapeutic drug	Therapeutic effect	Reference
Nanoparticles	Polymeric	Alantolactone Erlotinib	Significant cancer cell apoptosis and anticancer effect	Bao et al. (2021)
		Trastuzumab modified docetaxel	Increased cytotoxicity in HER2-positive BT474 cells	Zhang et al. (2019)
		Paclitaxel	Drug delivery efficiency was highly improved compared with free PTX	Le Broc-Ryckewaert et al. (2013)
	Extracellular vesicle	Doxorubicin	Superior cytotoxicity was noted, and it prevented drug retention in the heart	Hadla et al. (2016)
		Aminoethyl anisamide-polyethylene glycol conjugated exosome entrapping paclitaxel	Enhanced therapeutic efficacy in a mouse model of pulmonary metastases was demonstrated.	Kim et al. (2018)
		miRNA-497	The tumor growth, as well as the expression of related genes, were both inhibited	Jeong et al. (2020)
Lipid-based	Liposome	Vincristine Sulfate	No dose-limiting neurotoxicity was noted	Shah et al. (2016)
		Cytarabine and Daunorubicin	Notable longer survival rates were observed	Lancet et al. (2018)
		Lipovaxin-MM	Formulation was well-tolerated without clinically significant toxicity profile	Gargett et al. (2018)
	Nanoemulsion	Spirulina polysaccharides and PTX	Enhancement in antitumor effect was noted	Du et al. (2020)
		Temozolomide, rapamycin, and bevacizumab	Increased cytotoxicity against melanoma cells was reported along with improved suppression of tumor recurrence, migration, and angiogenesis	Dianzani et al. (2020)
Carbon nanomaterials	Carbon nanotubes	Doxorubicin	Superior cytotoxicity in HepG2 tumor cells were observed	Gu et al. (2011)
	Carbon quantum dots	Doxorubicin	At pH 5.0, 80% coxorubicin load was released, with a significantly improved antitumor efficacy	Zhou et al. (2013)
	Reduced graphene oxide	Methotrexate	Improvement of therapeutic activity was observed when evaluated on MCF-7 as compared to free drug	Jafarizad et al. (2017)
	Fullerene	Gd@C82 (OH)22	Several Proangiogenic factors were noted to be downregulated in mice model	Meng et al. (2010)

cancer can be prevented and eradicated with minimal intrusiveness. It is a type of cancer treatment that boosts and improves the immune system's antitumor reaction (Yan et al., 2020). Immune checkpoint inhibitors are intended to reactivate anticancer immune responses by disrupting coinhibitory signaling pathways and promoting immune-mediated cell elimination (Seidel et al., 2018).

Ipilimumab, a human IgG1 antibody, was the first immune checkpoint inhibitor to be approved in 2011 which binds to CTLA-4, a membrane protein found in regulatory T cells. The tumor microenvironment promotes CTLA-4 overexpression, which adheres to the antigen–presenting cells' activating proteins CD80 and CD86, prohibiting them from interacting with the specific receptor (Zitvogel et al., 2013). Pembrolizumab and nivolumab are anti-PD-1 human IgG4 antibodies (Vokes et al., 2018).

These are frequently used in conjunction with one another or with other chemotherapeutics to make the therapy as successful as feasible and to extend the patients' overall survival. When compared to monotherapy, combinatorial therapy has demonstrated a longer-lasting effect (Mahoney et al., 2015). These drugs have transformed the therapy of an array of incurable cancers, extending patients' lives and preventing future metastases.

3.3 Gene therapy

Gene therapy has attracted much attention for the amelioration of a variety of disorders (Pucci et al., 2019). RNA interference (RNAi) is a relatively new technology that has proven to be effective in both fundamental research and medicinal translation. siRNAs are known to silence specific genes (Elbashir et al., 2001). Since cancer is caused by specific molecular pathways, siRNAs can be deliberately tailored to block specific targets involved in cellular proliferation and metastatic spread (Vita and Henriksson, 2006). As naked siRNAs cannot cross cell membranes, various delivery techniques are now being investigated for efficient targeting (Xu and Wang, 2015). For siRNA loading, the use of lipid-based nanocarriers has achieved wide attention. Negatively charged nucleic acids engage with cationic liposomes and can be efficiently transfected via electrostatic interactions (Sarisozen et al., 2015).

A theranostic agent containing siRNA along with survivin entrapped in lipid-based nanocarrier has been designed for sequential localization inside tumor cells using entrapped MR agents and fluorophores, as well as decrease of proliferation in vivo (Kenny et al., 2011). Neutral liposomes have shown high therapeutic efficacy in gynecological malignancy when evaluated in vivo models (Gray et al., 2008). To enhance their stability during circulation in the biological environment and cellular absorption, siRNAs can be attached to peptides, antibodies, and aptamers (Jeong et al., 2009). Nanocarriers have significantly improved the stability, pharmacokinetics, and biodistribution aspects of siRNAs, as well as the targeting specificity (Gallas et al., 2013).

Despite the many accomplishments, some aspects remain unanswered, making the practical translation of siRNA-based strategy extremely difficult. More research into regulated release to only reach certain targets, as well as the development of the finest personalized therapy for cancer patients, will be critical in the future years.

3.4 Hormonal therapy

It is used to treat malignancies that are hormone-sensitive or hormone-dependent in their progression. In some cases of ovarian cancer, estrogen receptors have been discovered to be overexpressed. LH blockers, antiandrogens, and inhibitors of GnRH have all been used to reduce serum testosterone levels in prostate cancer patients (Pham et al., 2015). Tamoxifen has become the gold standard in breast cancer hormonal therapy (Heldermon and Ellis, 2006). US Food and Drug Administration has not approved toremifene for adjunct therapy. Fulvestrant, on the other hand, is an ER antagonist with a stronger affinity for ER receptors than tamoxifen. Fulvestrant's overall response was noted to be similar to that of tamoxifen

3.5 Molecular radiotherapy

Radiopharmaceutical therapy is a unique therapeutic modality for cancer treatment that has numerous benefits over the current treatments. The radiation is distributed systemically or locoregionally, similar to chemotherapeutic or biologically focused therapies, rather than from outside the body, as is the case with radiotherapy (Sgouros et al., 2020). The cytotoxic radiation is conveyed explicitly to cancer cells or tumor microenvironment, or more commonly, through delivery carriers that either specifically binds to intracellular targets or accrue through a wide range of physiological processes unique to neoplasia, allowing for a tailored therapeutic approach. It is significantly less reliant on comprehending signaling pathways and generating drugs that disrupt the hypothesized cancer phenotype-driving route than biologic therapies (Lin et al., 2019). Further, Table 3 represents a list of commercially available radiopharmaceuticals or the ones in the development phase.

3.6 Magnetic hyperthermia

When superparamagnetic or ferromagnetic nanoparticles are activated by an alternating magnetic field, they produce heat. SPIONs are the most studied nanoparticle-based systems (Hervault and Thanh, 2014). Heat is produced owing to the orientation of magnetic specificities of the particles under the influence of the magnetic field, and consecutive relaxation cycles during which heat is released back when the magnetic field is withdrawn and the magnetization of the particles reverts to the ground state (Dennis and Ivkov, 2013). SPIONs can also be employed as MRI contrast agents to guarantee that they are accurately positioned upon activation, as magnetic hyperthermia can impact any area of the body. The particles can be encapsulated in biocompatible polymers and/or lipids

Table 3 Radiopharmaceuticals that are commercially available/in development phase.

Radiopharmaceutical	Therapeutic indication	Status	Reference
^{131}I radioiodine	Thyroid cancer	Commercialized	Benua et al. (1962)
^{177}Lu-labeled CTT-1403	Prostate cancer	Under development	Meyer et al. (1989)
(^{153}Sm)CycloSam	Osteosarcoma	Under development	Simon et al. (2011)
^{90}Y-loaded resin microspheres	Hepatic cancer	Commercialized	Lewandowski et al. (2011)
Radium-223 chloride	Bone cancer	Commercialized	Tombal et al. (2019)
^{177}Lu-labeled DOTATATE	Neuroendocrine tumors	Commercialized	Strosberg et al. (2017)
^{177}Lu-labeled DOTA-JR11	Neuroendocrine tumors	Under development	Fani et al. (2017)
^{227}Th-labeled aCD22-TTC[a]	Lymphoma	Under development	Grant et al. (2018)
(^{131}I)mIBG	Adrenergic tumor receptors	Commercialized	Schoot et al. (2013)

and complexed with specific ligands to provide targeting capabilities (Giustini et al., 2010). A formulation referred to as Nanotherm has received FDA approval to treat glioblastoma (Sanchez et al., 2011). SPIONs have also been reported to encase lipid nanostructures with a chemotherapeutic agent for cancer treatment (Grillone et al., 2015).

3.7 Other techniques

Several clinical trials for new medications and therapeutic techniques for the treatment of hematological and solid cancers are in the pipeline. Significant findings were achieved in the field of cellular therapy, with the deployment of so-called CAR-T cell therapy, which prompted the approval of axicabtagene, ciloleucel, and tisagenlecleucel (Grupp, 2018). Many research groups are working on new treatment techniques based on genome editing with CRISPR/Cas9 technology to fix genetic abnormalities that contribute to cancer transformation (Zhan et al., 2018). Furthermore, several research institutions have been generating therapeutic anticancer vaccines based on the unique characteristics of the tumor (Falzone et al., 2018).

4. Conclusion

The spatially coordinated architecture and interconnections of cancer therapies and Nanotechnology will open up new insights on cancer progression and may lead to betterment in the efficacy of current therapies. Nanomaterials have helped to improve cancer detection and treatment through their better pharmacokinetic and pharmacodynamic properties. When compared to traditional chemotherapy and radiation therapy, the targeted delivery of drugs via NPs has shown therapeutic potential in improving cancer treatment efficacy. Given the limitations of nanotechnology, additional progress must be made to optimize drug delivery, maximize efficacy, and minimize drawbacks.

Immunotherapy, gene therapy, hormonal therapy, molecular radiation, and magnetic hyperthermia are some of the most effective cancer treatments available till now. Hormonal therapies include many side effects as compared to other therapies for example: Selective estrogen receptor modulators, such as tamoxifen, are the gold standard in the treatment of breast cancer, however, they are linked to an increased risk of endometrial abnormalities such as endometrial polyps' hyperplasia, carcinoma, and sarcomas, as well as thromboembolic events. Hyperthermia is also an efficient treatment that can improve the outcomes of radiation and chemotherapy by modulating numerous cellular processes and causing cell death. One disadvantage is that it is less specific for cancerous cells than for healthy tissue. Future hyperthermia research should concentrate on various hyperthermia enhancers that should be tested in conjunction with magnetic hyperthermia with the ultimate goal of clinical practicality.

Despite the significant advances achieved in the field of cancer therapeutics, it is still in its infancy, with numerous problems and roadblocks to overcome. Target therapies are more selective, less harmful to healthy cells, have accurate response biomarkers, and have considerably greater response rates than conventional treatments. As a result, combining nanotechnology with other cancer medicines can yield more effective results with increased efficacy, ultimately assisting us in overcoming the negative effects of the therapies alone. Therefore, such advancements will bolster the clinical success of cancer-targeted therapeutics in the coming years.

References

Aerts, H.J., 2016. The potential of radiomic-based phenotyping in precision medicine: a review. JAMA Oncol. 2 (12), 1636–1642.

Akhter, S., Ahmad, I., Ahmad, M.Z., Ramazani, F., Singh, A., Rahman, Z., et al., 2013. Nanomedicines as cancer therapeutics: current status. Curr. Cancer Drug Targets 13, 362–378.

Al-Jamal, K.T., Rubio, N., Buddle, J., et al., 2013. Cationic poly-l-lysine dendrimer complexes doxorubicin and delays tumor growth in vitro and in vivo. ACS Nano 7 (3), 1905–1917.

Altintas, Z., Tothill, I., 2013. Biomarkers and biosensors for the early diagnosis of lung cancer. Sensors Actuators B Chem. 188, 988–998.

Altintas, Z., Kallempudi, S.S., Gurbuz, Y., 2014. Gold nanoparticle modified capacitive sensor platform for multiple marker detection. Talanta 118, 270–276.

Avilés, A., Huerta-Guzmán, J., Delgado, S., Fernández, A., Díaz-Maqueo, J.C., 1996. Improved outcome in solitary bone plasmacytomata with combined therapy. Hematol. Oncol. 14, 111–117.

Bao, L., Loda, M., Janmey, P.A., Stewart, R., Anand-Apte, B., Zetter, B.R., 1996. Thymosin β15: a novel regulator of tumor cell motility upregulated in metastatic prostate cancer. Nat. Med. 2 (12), 1322–1328.

Bao, L., Loda, M., Zetter, B.R., 1998. Thymosin β15 expression in tumor cell lines with varying metastatic potential. Clin. Exp. Metastasis 16 (3), 227–233.

Bao, S., Zheng, H., Ye, J., Huang, H., Zhou, B., Yao, Q., Lin, G., Zhang, H., Kou, L., Chen, R., 2021. Dual targeting EGFR and STAT3 with Erlotinib and Alantolactone co-loaded PLGA nanoparticles for pancreatic cancer treatment. Front. Pharmacol. 12, 625084.

Behera, A., Mittu, B., Padhi, S., Patra, N., Singh, J., 2020. Bimetallic nanoparticles: green synthesis, applications, and future perspectives. In: Abd-Elsalam, K. (Ed.), Multifunctional Hybrid Nanomaterials for Sustainable Agri-food and Ecosystems. Elsevier, pp. 639–682.

Benua, R.S., Rawson, R.W., Sonenberg, M., Cicale, N.R., 1962. Relation of radioiodine dosimetry to results and complications in treatment of metastatic thyroid cancer. Am. J. Roentgenol. Radium Therapy, Nucl. Med. 87, 171–182.

Bhardwaj, S., 2005. Adenovirus mediated growth factor gene transfer to periadventitial space. Effects on angiogenesis and intimal hyperplasia (Adenovirusvälitteinen kasvutekijägeeninsiirto verisuonen seinämään. Vaikutukset verisuonten kasvuun ja seinämän paksuuntumiseen). Kuopion Yliopisto.

Blackwell, K., Hurwitz, H., Lieberman, G., et al., 2004. Circulating D-dimer levels are better predictors of overall survival and disease progression than carcinoembryonic antigen levels in patients with metastatic colorectal carcinoma. Cancer 101 (1), 77–82.

Cieślik, M., Chinnaiyan, A.M., 2018. Cancer transcriptome profiling at the juncture of clinical translation. Nat. Rev. Genet. 19 (2), 93–109.

Dabritz, J., Hanfler, J., Preston, R., Stieler, J., Oettle, H., 2005. Detection of Ki-ras mutations in tissue and plasma samples of patients with pancreatic cancer using PNA-mediated PCR clamping and hybridisation probes. Br. J. Cancer 92, 405–412.

Dennis, C.L., Ivkov, R., 2013. Physics of heat generation using magnetic nanoparticles for hyperthermia. Int. J. Hyperth. 29 (8), 715–729.

Dianzani, C., Monge, C., Miglio, G., Serpe, L., Martina, K., Cangemi, L., Ferraris, C., Mioletti, S., Osella, S., Gigliotti, C.L., Boggio, E., 2020. Nanoemulsions as delivery systems for poly-chemotherapy aiming at melanoma treatment. Cancers 12, 1198.

Du, M., Yang, Z., Lu, W., Wang, B., Wang, Q., Chen, Z., Chen, L., Han, S., Cai, T., Cai, Y., 2020. Design and development of spirulina polysaccharide-loaded nanoemulsions with improved the antitumor effects of paclitaxel. J. Microencapsul. 37 (6), 403–412.

Egger, G., Liang, G., Aparicio, A., Jones, P.A., 2004. Epigenetics in human disease and prospects for epigenetic therapy. Nature 429, 457–463.

Elbashir, S.M., Harborth, J., Lendeckel, W., et al., 2001. Duplexes of 21-nucleotide RNAs mediate RNA interference in cultured mammalian cells. Nature 411 (6836), 494–498.

Falzone, L., Salomone, S., Libra, M., 2018. Evolution of cancer pharmacological treatments at the turn of the third millennium. Front. Pharmacol. 9, 1300.

Fani, M., Nicolas, G.P., Wild, D., 2017. Somatostatin receptor antagonists for imaging and therapy. J. Nucl. Med. 58, 61S–66S (Trial that demonstrates the greater tumour uptake and absorbed dose with somatostatin receptor antagonists compared with agonists).

Feinberg, A.P., Ohlsson, R., Henikoff, S., 2006. The epigenetic progenitor origin of human cancer. Nat. Rev. 7, 21–33.

Fuchs, T.J., Buhmann, J.M., 2011. Computational pathology: challenges and promises for tissue analysis. Comput. Med. Imaging Graph. 35 (7–8), 515–530.

Gallaher, J.A., Enriquez-Navas, P.M., Luddy, K.A., Gatenby, R.A., Anderson, A.R.A., 2018. Spatial heterogeneity and evolutionary dynamics modulate time to recurrence in continuous and adaptive cancer therapies. Cancer Res. 78 (8), 2127–2139.

Gallas, A., Alexander, C., Davies, M.C., et al., 2013. Chemistry and formulations for siRNA therapeutics. Chem. Soc. Rev. 42 (20), 7983–7997.

Gargett, T., Abbas, M.N., Rolan, P., Price, J.D., Gosling, K.M., Ferrante, A., et al., 2018. Phase I trial of Lipovaxin-MM, a novel dendritic cell-targeted liposomal vaccine for malignant melanoma. Cancer Immunol. Immunother. 67, 1461–1472.

Garrigue, P., Tang, J., Ding, L., Bouhlel, A., Tintaru, A., Laurini, E., et al., 2018. Self-assembling supramolecular dendrimer nanosystem for PET imaging of tumors. Proc. Natl. Acad. Sci. U. S. A. 115, 11454–11459.

Giustini, A.J., Petryk, A.A., Cassim, S.M., et al., 2010. Magnetic nanoparticle hyperthermia in cancer treatment. Nano Life 1 (1n02), 17–32.

Grant, D., et al., 2018. Pharmacokinetics and dosimetry of BAY 1862864, an alpha-emitting targeted thorium conjugate (CD22-TTC) in the Cynomolgus monkey. Eur. J. Nucl. Med. Mol. Imaging 45, S124.

Gray, M.J., Van Buren, G., Dallas, N.A., et al., 2008. Therapeutic targeting of neuropilin-2 on colorectal carcinoma cells implanted in the murine liver. J. Natl. Cancer Inst. 100 (2), 109–120.

Grillone, A., Riva, E.R., Mondini, A., et al., 2015. Active targeting of sorafenib: preparation, characterization, and in vitro testing of drug-loaded magnetic solid lipid nanoparticles. Adv. Healthc. Mater. 4 (11), 1681–1690.

Grove, O., Berglund, A.E., Schabath, M.B., Aerts, H.J., Dekker, A., Wang, H., Velazquez, E.R., Lambin, P., Gu, Y., Balagurunathan, Y., Eikman, E., Gatenby, R.A., Eschrich, S., Gillies, R.J., 2015. Quantitative computed tomographic descriptors associate tumor shape complexity and intratumor heterogeneity with prognosis in lung adenocarcinoma. PLoS One 10 (3), e0118261.

Grupp, S., 2018. Beginning the CAR T cell therapy revolution in the US and EU. Curr. Res. Transl. Med. 66, 62–64.

Gu, Y.J., Cheng, J., Jin, J., Cheng, S.H., Wong, W.T., 2011. Development and evaluation of pH-responsive single-walled carbon nanotube-doxorubicin complexes in cancer cells. Int. J. Nanomedicine 6, 2889.

Hadla, M., Palazzolo, S., Corona, G., Caligiuri, I., Canzonieri, V., Toffoli, G., Rizzolio, F., 2016. Exosomes increase the therapeutic index of doxorubicin in breast and ovarian cancer mouse models. Nanomedicine (London) 11 (18), 2431–2441.

Hare, J.I., Lammers, T., Ashford, M.B., Puri, S., Storm, G., Barry, S.T., 2017. Challenges and strategies in anti-cancer nanomedicine development: an industry perspective. Adv. Drug Deliv. Rev. 108, 25–38.

Harris, R., Lohr, K.N., 2002. Screening for prostate cancer: an update of the evidence for the U.S. Preventive Service Task Force. Ann. Intern. Med. 137, 917–929.

Hasan, M.R., Ahommed, M.S., Daizy, M., Bacchu, M.S., Ali, M.R., Al-Mamun, M.R., Aly Saad Aly, M., Khan, M.Z.H., Hossain, S.I., 2021. Recent development in electrochemical biosensors for cancer biomarkers detection. Biosens. Bioelectron. 8, 100075.

Heldermon, C., Ellis, M., 2006. Endocrine therapy for breast cancer. Update Cancer Ther. 1, 285–297.

Hervault, A., Thanh, N.T.K., 2014. Magnetic nanoparticle-based therapeutic agents for thermo-chemotherapy treatment of cancer. Nanoscale 6 (20), 11553–11573.

Hristova, V.A., Chan, D.W., 2019. Cancer biomarker discovery and translation: proteomics and beyond. Expert Rev. Proteomics 16 (2), 93–103.

Huang, R., He, L., Xia, Y., Xu, H., Liu, C., Xie, H., Wang, S., Peng, L., Liu, Y., Liu, Y., He, N., Li, Z., 2019. A sensitive aptasensor based on a hemin/Gquadruplex-assisted signal amplification strategy for electrochemical detection of gastric cancer exosomes. Small 15, 1–7.

Isobe, N., Onodera, H., Mori, A., et al., 2004. Caspase-3 expression in human gastric carcinoma and its clinical significance. Oncology 66 (3), 201–209.

Jafari, A., Salouti, M., Shayesteh, S.F., Heidari, Z., Rajabi, A.B., Boustani, K., et al., 2015. Synthesis and characterization of Bombesin-superparamagnetic iron oxide nanoparticles as a targeted contrast agent for imaging of breast cancer using MRI. Nanotechnology 26, 075101.

Jafarizad, A., Aghanejad, A., Sevim, M., Metin, N., Barar, J., Omidi, Y., Ekinci, D., 2017. Gold nanoparticles and reduced graphene oxide-gold nanoparticle composite materials as covalent drug delivery systems for breast cancer treatment. ChemistrySelect 2 (23), 6663–6672.

Jeong, J.H., Mok, H., Oh, Y.K., et al., 2009. SiRNA conjugate delivery systems. Bioconjug. Chem. 20 (1), 5–14.

Jeong, K., Yu, Y.J., You, J.Y., Rhee, W.J., Kim, J.A., 2020. Exosome-mediated microRNA-497 delivery for anti-cancer therapy in a microfluidic 3D lung cancer model. Lab Chip 20 (3), 548.

Jiang, Y., Sun, A., Zhao, Y., Ying, W., Sun, H., Yang, X., et al., 2019. Proteomics identifies new therapeutic targets of early-stage hepatocellular carcinoma. Nature 567 (7747), 257 (Cancer transcriptome profiling at the juncture of clinical translation).

Jokerst, J.V., Raamanathan, A., Christodoulides, N., Floriano, P.N., Pollard, A.A., Simmons, G.W., et al., 2009. Nano-bio-chips for high performance multiplexed protein detection: determinations of cancer biomarkers in serum and saliva using quantum dot bioconjugate labels. Biosens. Bioelectron. 24, 3622–3629.

Kattan, M.W., Shariat, S.F., Andrews, B., et al., 2003. The addition of interleukin-6 soluble receptor and transforming growth factor beta1 improves a preoperative nomogram for predicting biochemical progression in patients with clinically localized prostate cancer. J. Clin. Oncol. 21 (19), 3573–3579.

Kenny, G.D., Kamaly, N., Kalber, T.L., et al., 2011. Novel multifunctional nanoparticle mediates siRNA tumour delivery, visualisation and therapeutic tumour reduction in vivo. J. Control. Release 149 (2), 111–116.

Khuroo, T., Verma, D., Talegaonkar, S., Padhi, S., Panda, A., Iqbal, Z., 2014. Topotecan–tamoxifen duple PLGA polymeric nanoparticles: investigation of in vitro, in vivo and cellular uptake potential. Int. J. Pharm. 473, 384–394. https://doi.org/10.1016/j.ijpharm.2014.07.022.

Kim, D., Jeong, Y.Y., Jon, S., 2010. A drug-loaded aptamer? Gold nanoparticle bioconjugate for combined CT imaging and therapy of prostate cancer. ACS Nano 4, 3689–3696.

Kim, M.S., Haney, M.J., Zhao, Y., Yuan, D., Deygen, I., Klyachko, N.L., Kabanov, A.V., Batrakova, E.V., 2018. Engineering macrophage-derived exosomes for targeted paclitaxel delivery to pulmonary metastases: in vitro and in vivo evaluations. Nanomedicine 14 (1), 195–204.

Kundu, A., Padhi, S., Behera, A., Hasnain, M.S., Nayak, A.K., 2022. Tumor targeting strategies by chitosan-based nanocarriers. In: Chitosan in Biomedical Applications. Academic Press, pp. 163–188.

Lancet, J.E., Uy, G.L., Cortes, J.E., Newell, L.F., Lin, T.L., Ritchie, E.K., et al., 2018. CPX-351 (cytarabine and daunorubicin) liposome for injection versus conventional Cytarabine plus Daunorubicin in older patients with newly diagnosed secondary acute myeloid leukemia. J. Clin. Oncol. Off. J. Am. Soc. Clin. Oncol. 36, 2684–2692.

Le Broc-Ryckewaert, D., Carpentier, R., Lipka, E., Daher, S., Vaccher, C., Betbeder, D., Furman, C., 2013. Development of innovative paclitaxel-loaded small PLGA nanoparticles: study of their antiproliferative activity and their molecular interactions on prostatic cancer cells. Int. J. Pharm. 454 (2), 712–719.

Lewandowski, R.J., Geschwind, J.-F., Liapi, E., Salem, R., 2011. Transcatheter intraarterial therapies: rationale and overview. Radiology 259, 641–657.

Lewis Jr., J.S., Ali, S., Luo, J., Thorstad, W.L., Madabhushi, A., 2014. A quantitative histomorphometric classifier (QuHbIC) identifies aggressive versus indolent p16-positive oropharyngeal squamous cell carcinoma. Am. J. Surg. Pathol. 38 (1), 128–137.

Lilenbaum, R.C., Herndon, J.E.I.I., List, M.A., Desch, C., Watson, D.M., Miller, A., et al., 2005. Single-agent versus combination chemotherapy in advanced non- small-cell lung cancer: the cancer and leukemia group B (study 9730). J. Clin. Oncol. 23, 190–196.

Lin, C.W., Wei, K.C., Liao, S.S., Huang, C.Y., Sun, C.L., Wu, P.J., Lu, Y.J., Yang, H.W., Ma, C.C.M., 2015. A reusable magnetic graphene oxide-modified biosensor for vascular endothelial growth factor detection in cancer diagnosis. Biosens. Bioelectron. 67, 431–437.

Lin, A., et al., 2019. Off-target toxicity is a common mechanism of action of cancer drugs undergoing clinical trials. Sci. Transl. Med. 11, eaaw8412.

Mahoney, K.M., Rennert, P.D., Freeman, G.J., 2015. Combination cancer immunotherapy and new immunomodulatory targets. Nat. Rev. Drug Discov. 14, 561–584. https://doi.org/10.1038/nrd4591.

Marcucci Guido, A., Mrozek Krzysztof, A., Bloomfield, C.D., 2005. Molecular heterogeneity and prognostic biomarkers in adults with acute myeloid leukemia and normal cytogenetics. Curr. Opin. Hematol. 12 (1), 68–75.

Maron, S.B., Chase, L.M., Lomnicki, S., Kochanny, S., Moore, K.L., Joshi, S.S., et al., 2019. Circulating tumor DNA sequencing analysis of gastroesophageal adenocarcinoma. Clin. Cancer Res. 25, 7098–7112.

Mathew, D.G., Beekman, P., Lemay, S.G., Zuilhof, H., Le Gac, S., Van Der Wiel, W.G., 2020. Electrochemical detection of tumor-derived extracellular vesicles on nanointerdigitated electrodes. Nano Lett. 20, 820–828.

Matson, V., Fessler, J., Bao, R., 2018. The commensal microbiome is associated with anti-PD-1 efficacy in metastatic melanoma patients. Science 359, 104–108.

Meng, H., Xing, G., Sun, B., Zhao, F., Lei, H., Li, W., Song, Y., Chen, Z., Yuan, H., Wang, X., Long, J., 2010. Potent angiogenesis inhibition by the particulate form of fullerene derivatives. ACS Nano 4, 2773–2783.

Menyhárt, O., Győrffy, B., 2021. Multi-omics approaches in cancer research with applications in tumor subtyping, prognosis, and diagnosis. Comput. Struct. Biotechnol. J. 19, 949–960.

Meyer, K.L., Schwendner, S.W., Counsell, R.E., 1989. Potential tumor or organ-imaging agents. 30. Radioiodinated phospholipid ethers. J. Med. Chem. 32, 2142–2147.

Miki, Y., Swensen, J., Shattuck-Eidens, D., et al., 1994. A strong candidate for the breast and ovarian cancer susceptibility gene BRCA1. Science 266, 66–71 (Identification of BRCA1).

Mondal, J., Panigrahi, A.K., Khuda-Bukhsh, A.R., 2014. Conventional chemotherapy: problems and scope for combined therapies with certain herbal products and dietary supplements. Austin J. Mol. Cell. Biol. 1, 10.

Padhi, S., Kapoor, R., Verma, D., Panda, A., Iqbal, Z., 2018. Formulation and optimization of topotecan nanoparticles: in vitro characterization, cytotoxicity, cellular uptake and pharmacokinetic outcomes. J. Photochem. Photobiol. B Biol. 183, 222–232. https://doi.org/10.1016/j.jphotobiol.2018.04.022.

Padhi, S., Behera, A., Saneja, A., 2020a. Nanotechnology based targeting strategies for the delivery of camptothecin. In: Panda Amulya, K., Lichtfouse, E. (Eds.), Pharmaceutical Technology for Natural Products Delivery, Impact of Nanotechnology. Springer Nature, Switzerland, pp. 243–272.

Padhi, S., Nayak, A., Behera, A., 2020b. Type II diabetes mellitus: a review on recent drug based therapeutics. Biomed. Pharmacother. 131, 110708. https://doi.org/10.1016/j.biopha.2020.110708.

Padhi, S., Dash, M., Behera, A., 2021. Nanophytochemicals for the treatment of type II diabetes mellitus: a review. Environ. Chem. Lett. 19, 4349–4373.

Padhi, S., Behera, A., Hasnain, M.S., Nayak, A.K., 2022. Chitosan-Based Drug Delivery Systems in Cancer Therapeutics. Academic Press, pp. 159–193.

Pantel, K., Speicher, M.R., 2016. The biology of circulating tumor cells. Oncogene 35, 1216–1224.

Patel, J.N., Mandock, K., McLeod, H.L., 2014. Clinically relevant cancer biomarkers and pharmacogenetic assays. J. Oncol. Pharm. Pract. 20 (1), 65–72.

Patnaik, S., Gorain, B., Padhi, S., Choudhury, H., Gabr, G., Md, S., et al., 2021. Recent update of toxicity aspects of nanoparticulate systems for drug delivery. Eur. J. Pharm. Biopharm. 161, 100–119. https://doi.org/10.1016/j.ejpb.2021.02.010.

Pham, T., Martin, C.S., Li, H., Richard, D.J., Emden, M.C., Richard, K., 2015. Advances in hormonal therapies for hormone naive and castration—resistant prostate cancers with or without previous chemotherapy. Exp. Hematol. Oncol. 5, 1–11.

Polanski, M., Anderson, N.L., 2007. A list of candidate cancer biomarkers for targeted proteomics. Biomark. Insights 1, 1–48.

Pucci, C., Martinelli, C., Ciofani, G., 2019. Innovative approaches for cancer treatment: current perspectives and new challenges. Ecancermedicalscience 13, 961. https://doi.org/10.3332/ecancer.2019.961.

Rauf, S., Mishra, G.K., Azhar, J., Mishra, R.K., Goud, K.Y., Nawaz, M.A.H., Marty, J.L., Hayat, A., 2018. Carboxylic group riched graphene oxide based disposable electrochemical immunosensor for cancer biomarker detection. Anal. Biochem. 545, 13–19.

Rhim, A.D., Mirek, E.T., Aiello, N.M., Maitra, A., Bailey, J.M., McAllister, F., Reichert, M., Beatty, G.L., Rustgi, A.K., Vonderheide, R.H., Leach, S.D., Stanger, B.Z., 2012. Emt and dissemination precede pancreatic tumor formation. Cell 148, 349–361.

Rhodes, D.R., Yu, J., Shanker, K., et al., 2004. ONCOMINE: a cancer microarray database and integrated data-mining platform. Neoplasia 6 (1), 1–6.

Sanchez, C., Belleville, P., Popall, M., et al., 2011. Applications of advanced hybrid organic- inorganic nanomaterials: from laboratory to market. Chem. Soc. Rev. 40 (2), 696–753.

Sanger, N., Effenberger, K.E., Riethdorf, S., Van Haasteren, V., Gauwerky, J., Wiegratz, I., Strebhardt, K., Kaufmann, M., Pantel, K., 2011. Disseminated tumor cells in the bone marrow of patients with ductal carcinoma in situ. Int. J. Cancer 129, 2522–2526.

Sankara, V.S.P.K., Jayanthi, A., Das, A.B., et al., 2007. Recent advances in biosensor development for the detection of cancer biomarkers. Biosens. Bioelectron. 91 (15), 15–23.

Santala, M., Risteli, J., Kauppila, A., 2004. Comparison of carboxyterminal telopeptide of type I collagen (ICTP) and CA 125 as predictors of prognosis in ovarian cancer. Anticancer Res. 24, 1057–1062.

Sarisozen, C., Salzano, G., Torchilin, V.P., 2015. Recent advances in siRNA delivery. Biomol. Concepts 6 (5–6), 321–341.

Schoot, R.A., et al., 2013. The role of 131I-metaiodobenzylguanidine (MIBG) therapy in unresectable and compromising localised neuroblastoma. Eur. J. Nucl. Med. Mol. Imaging 40, 1516–1522.

Seidel, J.A., Otsuka, A., Kabashima, K., 2018. Anti-PD-1 and anti-CTLA-4 therapies in cancer: mechanisms of action, efficacy, and limitations. Front. Oncol. 8, 86.

Sgouros, G., Bodei, L., McDevitt, M.R., et al., 2020. Radiopharmaceutical therapy in cancer: clinical advances and challenges. Nat. Rev. Drug Discov. 19, 589–608.

Shah, N.N., Merchant, M.S., Cole, D.E., Jayaprakash, N., Bernstein, D., Delbrook, C., et al., 2016. Vincristine sulfate liposomes injection (VSLI, Marqibo®): results from a phase I study in children, adolescents, and young adults with refractory solid tumors or Leukemias. Pediatr. Blood Cancer 63, 997–1005.

Shrivas, K., Nirmalkar, N., Thakur, S.S., Deb, M.K., Shinde, S.S., Shankar, R., 2018. Sucrose capped gold nanoparticles as a plasmonic chemical sensor based on non-covalent interactions: application for selective detection of vitamins B(1) and B(6) in brown and white rice food samples. Food Chem. 250, 14–21.

Simon, J.J., et al., 2011. Preclinical evaluation of Sm-153-DOTMP as a therapeutic bone-seeking radiopharmaceutical. J. Nucl. Med. 52, 1751.

Singh, R., 2019. Nanotechnology based therapeutic application in cancer diagnosis and therapy. 3 Biotech 9, 415.

Strosberg, J., et al., 2017. Phase 3 trial of Lu-177-dotatate for midgut neuroendocrine tumors. N. Engl. J. Med. 376, 125–135.

Tombal, B.F., et al., 2019. Decreased fracture rate by mandating bone-protecting agents in the EORTC 1333/PEACE III trial comparing enzalutamide and Ra223 versus enzalutamide alone: an interim safety analysis. J. Clin. Oncol. 37, 5007.

Tran, S., Degiovanni, P.J., Piel, B., Rai, P.J.C., 2017. Cancer nanomedicine: a review of recent success in drug delivery. Clin Transl Med 6, 44.

Tuck, A.B., Chambers, A.F., 2001. The role of osteopontin in breast cancer: clinical and experimental studies. J. Mammary Gland Biol. Neoplasia 6, 419–429.

Uzozie, A.C., Aebersold, R., 2018. Advancing translational research and precision medicine with targeted proteomics. J. Proteome 189, 1–10.

Vasir, J.K., Labhasetwar, V., 2007. Biodegradable nanoparticles for cytosolic delivery of therapeutics. Adv. Drug Deliv. Rev. 59 (8), 718–728.

Vita, M., Henriksson, M., 2006. The Myc oncoprotein as a therapeutic target for human cancer. Semin. Cancer Biol. 16 (4), 318–330.

Vokes, E.E., Ready, N., Felip, E., Horn, L., Burgio, M.A., Antonia, S.J., et al., 2018. Nivolumab versus docetaxel in previously treated advanced non-small-cell lung cancer (CheckMate 017 and CheckMate 057): 3-year update and outcomes in patients with liver metastases. Ann. Oncol. 29, 959–965. https://doi.org/10.1093/annonc/mdy041.

Wan, X., Song, Y., Song, N., Li, J., Yang, L., Li, Y., et al., 2016. The preliminary study of immune superparamagnetic iron oxide nanoparticles for the detection of lung cancer in magnetic resonance imaging. Carbohydr. Res. 419, 33–40.

Wang, Z.W., Zhang, J., Guo, Y., Wu, X.Y., Yang, W.J., Xu, L.J., Chen, J.H., Fu, F.F., 2013. A novel electrically magnetic-controllable electrochemical biosensor for the ultra sensitive and specific detection of attomolar level oral cancer-related microRNA. Biosens. Bioelectron. 45, 108–113.

Wang, Y., Li, L., Douville, C., Cohen, J.D., Yen, T.T., Kinde, I., et al., 2018. Evaluation of liquid from the Papanicolaou test and other liquid biopsies for the detection of endometrial and ovarian cancers. Sci. Transl. Med. 10, eaap8793.

Watanabe, K., Nakamura, Y., Low, S.K., 2021 Sep. Clinical implementation and current advancement of blood liquid biopsy in cancer. J. Hum. Genet. 66 (9), 909–926.

Xu, C.F., Wang, J., 2015. Delivery systems for siRNA drug development in cancer therapy. Asian J. Pharm. Sci. 10 (1), 1–12. https://doi.org/10.1016/j.ajps.2014.08.011.

Yan, S., Luo, Z., Li, Z., Wang, Y., Tao, J., Gong, C., Liu, X., 2020. Improving cancer immunotherapy outcomes using biomaterials. Angew. Chem. Int. Ed. Eng. 59 (40), 17332–17343.

Yang, M., Soga, T., Pollard, P.J., 2013. Oncometabolites: linking altered metabolism with cancer. J. Clin. Invest. 123 (9), 3652–3658.

Yang, S., You, M., Zhang, F., Wang, Q., He, P., 2018. A sensitive electrochemical aptasensing platform based on exonuclease recycling amplification and host-guest recognition for detection of breast cancer biomarker HER2. Sens. Actuators B Chem. 258, 796–802.

Yilmaz, A., Ece, F., Bayramgurler, B., Akkaya, E., Baran, R., 2001. The value of ca-125 in the evaluation of tuberculosis activity. Respir. Med. 95, 666–669.

Zhan, T., Rindtorff, N., Betge, J., Ebert, M.P., Boutros, M., 2018. CRISPR/Cas9 for cancer research and therapy. Semin. Cancer Biol. https://doi.org/10.1016/j.semcancer.2018.04.001.

Zhang, W., 2021. Advances in cancer early diagnosis with liquid biopsy-based approaches. J. Cancer Metastasis Treat. 7, 22.

Zhang, X., Liu, J., Li, X., Li, F., Lee, R.J., Sun, F., Li, Y., Liu, Z., Teng, L., 2019. Trastuzumab- coated nanoparticles loaded with docetaxel for breast cancer therapy. Dose-Response 17 (3). 1559325819872583.

Zhang, Y., Yang, H., An, X., Wang, Z., Yang, X., Yu, M., et al., 2020. Controlled synthesis of Ag(2) Te@Ag(2) S core-shell quantum dots with enhanced and tunable fluorescence in the second near-infrared window. Small 16, e2001003.

Zhou, L., Li, Z., Liu, Z., Ren, J., Qu, X., 2013. Luminescent carbon dot-gated nanovehicles for pH-triggered intracellular controlled release and imaging. Langmuir 29 (21), 6396–6403.

Zitvogel, L., Galluzzi, L., Smyth, M.J., Kroemer, G., 2013. Mechanism of action of conventional and targeted anticancer therapies: reinstating immunosurveillance. Immunity 39, 74–88.

CHAPTER FOUR

How does time speak about cancer, its diagnosis, treatments, and challenges?

Asit Ranjan Ghosh

Microbial Molecular Biology Laboratory, Department of Integrative Biology, School of BioSciences and Technology, Vellore Institute of Technology (VIT), Vellore, India

1. Introduction

"Time and tide wait for none."

With the evolution of intelligence, human society has been in constant utilization of it for better and comfortable survived life. Time has always given us challenges, but human intelligence and development of science has brought challenges under control. With the discovery of cell, as a functional living unit of life, in the beginning of the modern science, we came across to know many more lessons about it. Somatic cells in human system are in trillions with an odd 215 different types of presentations constitute several tissues, organs, systems, and the whole human body. Architectures of cells are different in many ways and their behavior, number, life span as well. Cells mostly follow social livelihood and develop an orchestrated system. However, this harmonious environment is challenged with de-establishment of the programmed lifeline and difficulties are mounted. Disciplined cells become rebellious and cause a manifestation, cancer.

Cancer is defined as an uncontrolled growth of cells. It is difficult to figure out the possible timeline when it was observed first. As with the evolution of several life forms, so with the access of indiscipline in cells and cancer formation must be an obvious process from days of yore. The understanding of cancer biology draws its existence since ancient times. There are several evidences found in fossilized bones, mummies in Egypt and in oldest texts. Right from the time of Hippocrates (460–370 BC), "Father of Medicine," Celsus (50–28 BC), and Galen (130–200 AD), the concept of cancer or tumor was in infancy with a little importance in medicine. After a long time, during the period of Renaissance (15th AD onward), scientific intervention started with the works of William Harvey (1628) and Giovanni Morgagni (1761) to understand the role of surgery in autopsy discovering many physiological processes including tumor. Later, John Hunter (1728–1793) gave suggestion for removal of operable tumor surgically to stop movement or/and invasion to other tissue to save life https://www.cancer.org/cancer/cancer-basics/history-of-cancer/what-is-cancer.html. And in the 19th century, Rudolf Virchow (1850s) envisaged the cellular pathology of cancer using micro-scope (https://www.cancer.org/cancer/cancer-basics/history-of-cancer/what-is-cancer.html).

The objective of this review is to outline the sequential medical/ clinical/biological/cellular research journey in understanding cancer biology better and better till date with special emphasis on last 100 years.

2. What causes cancer?

Answer was not known, what really cause to develop cancer. This question became the driving force to renew knowledge to know cancer better.

One time, cancer was believed to be the curse and as a God's act. Overcoming the time and situation, medical practitioners understood the physiological process and devel-opment of cancer through a journey of hundreds of years, to place cancer as a deadly disease. Actual understanding came into existence during the 19th century. There is also a long history supported by sustainable theories to know cancer better. A line sketch is drawn here to follow the journey.

Since the time of Hippocrates (460–370 BC), the status of human health was explained by fluid systems, called *humors*, composed of blood, phlegm, yellow bile and black bile. Human health remains healthy if all are in balance and unhealthy when any one of them are high or less. If the black bile was more, then it was considered to be a case of cancer. This theory was known as "*Humoral Theory*" and was popular till the beginning of Renaissance. However, this well accepted and long-time prevailed theory got overtaken by the proposition of "*Contagious Theory*" or "*Infectious Diseases Theory*" by Dutch physicians, Zacutus Lusitani (1575–1642) and Nicholas Tupl (1593–1674), explain cancer was the result of contact as observed in breast cancer episodes in families or households. This continued for over a century. Later, Stahl and Hoffman (1720), introduced a new theory, known as, "*Lymph Theory*," which explained cancer was a fermented and degenerated Lymph with varying density, acidity and alkalinity and was fostered by John Hunter (1728–1793). Renewal of theories remains the lifeline of understanding cancer better. To this direction, German pathologist, Johannes Muller (1838) nullified "*Lymph Theory*," and introduced "*Blastema Theory*," with an explanation that the composition of cancer is of cells, budding cellular elements (blastema) between normal tissues, and not because of lymph. This theory got momentum with the contri-bution of his scholar, Rudolph Virchow (1821–1902) who proposed "all the cells are produced from cells" (*Omnis cellula e cellula*) and theorized "*Chronic Irritation Theory*" (Kuiper, 2010). Virchow and John Huges Bennet of England independently described leukemia in some patients where there was abnormal increase in white blood cells (WBC) in 1845 (Kampen, 2012). This theory demonstrated the chronic irritation was the cause of cancer and that spread like liquid. This was later on modified by Karl

Thiersch (1860s) with a proposition that cancer spread not through liquid. Besides these theories, there was a theory where trauma was found as a cause of cancer and was known as *"Trauma Theory"* between late 1800 and 1920. Therefore, journey to know about tumor or/and cancer moved from ancient Egypt to Greece, Rome, Scotland, Holland, Germany, England for several millennia.

3. New knowledge about cause of cancer

As the medical history on cancer moved since ancient Egypt till the beginning of the 20th century, with parallel development of all branches of knowledge domains, a considerable foundation was established to know about cell biology, biochemistry, microbiology, molecular biology, genetics, immunology, physiology, animal study, physics, chemistry, mathematics and also cancer. If we look back, then we see the terminologies like carcinogens, oncogenes, tumor suppressor gene, anesthesia, etc. gave modern shape in understanding cancer.

3.1 Carcinogens

Carcinogens are those substances have the ability of causing cancer. Concept of carcinogens though is now known among common people. However, development of this understanding took long time. Available evidence suggests the concept started growing since the 18th century. During 1765, John Hill, a clinician of London could probably recognize tobacco as a carcinogen, for the first time (https://www.cancer.org/cancer/cancer-basics/history-of-cancer/what-is-cancer.html), and later on in 1775, English surgeon Percival Pott reported scrotum cancer with chimney sweeps. In between time, there was much more understanding developed in medical microbiology with the contributions of Louis Pasteur and Robert Koch. Etiologies of infectious diseases were believed to be the possible cause of cancer. In 1911, Francis Peyton Rous, an American pathologist found that the cell-free filtrate of a tumor (sarcoma) from a chick when was transferred to a normal chick developed tumor in the normal. The cell filtrate contained a type of cancer, which was named after him, Rous virus. This seminal work made a foundation of cancer causes due to certain viral infection. In 1913, Johannes Fibiger observed development of cancer in esophagus and stomach in experimental rats with the introduction of a cockroach borne nematode worm *Spiroptera carcinoma*. One breakthrough happened in 1915 when Japanese scientists, Katsusabura Yamagiwa and Kochi Ichikawa persistently irritated the inner skins of ears of 10 experimental rabbits with coal tar painting for 4 years and got a result of cancer development (carcinoma). The work of Yamagiwa and Ichikawa was influenced by Virchow's hypothesis on tissue irritation or injury as a cause of cancer in one hand and previous observations on chimney sweeps and coal distillation. They also could describe the steps in cancer progression (Lipsick, 2021). However, Yamagiwa and Ichikawa were not sure whether coal tar as a whole or its particular ingredient caused carcinoma. In 1921, Bruno Block found carcinogenic properties in the chemical composition of coal tar. Thus in the following years, benzanthracene was found a potential carcinogen from coal tar.

With the invention of X-rays by Wilhelm Roentgen in 1895, it was applied in medical imaging for bones, however, was found as a potent carcinogen in 1902. In the beginning, carcinogenic property of X-ray exposure was thought in the line of persistent irritation or tissue injury. But the works of Morgan and Muller on model organisms, maize (*Zea mays*) and fruit fly (*Drosophila melanogaster*) (1927) brought the concept of mutation by the exposure of X-ray and demonstrated presentations of different phenotypes and genotypes during 1920. In between time there was World War II where atom bombs were exploded in Hiroshima and Nagasaki (August 1945) and had exposure of radioactive substances, Uranium caused cancer among survivors. Other than carcinogenic, mutagenic properties of X-ray, and radiation due to radioactive substances, ultraviolet (UV) radiation was also used experimentally for remedial against a skin cancer (*Xeroderma pigmentosum*) in 1968 (Lipsick, 2021).

World Health Organization (WHO) was founded in 1948 as a dedicated society of United Nations to look after international public health. One of the wings of WHO, the International Agency for Research on Cancer (IARC) was established to identify cancer causes. It developed system to classify different objects, natural or man-made products for the role of cancer causing potential in humans or/ and animals. During 1971, IARC identified over 900 agents and published them after due categorization. On the basis of scientific evidences, IARC categorized these carcinogens into five groups (Groups 1, 2A, 2B, 3, and 4). Group 1 substances are considered to be the most potential carcinogens where smoking, alcoholic beverages exposure to radiation and even processed meat are kept together (https://www.compoundchem.com/2015/10/26/carcinogens/) while substances listed under Group 4 is not truly classifiable as carcinogens for humans/animals.

3.2 Chemical carcinogens
Tobacco
Tobacco smoking is one of the earliest practices from ancient times. It was introduced and got popularized in Europe and colonized America and Asia during the 17th century. Later the deadliest artifact, tobacco smokes was considered as the major cause of lung cancer in Germany, as early as 1920 (Proctor, 2012). Proctor (2012) reviewed and found the nexus of cigarette smoking and lung cancer epidemic during the 1940s and 1950s, while popularization of smoking started at the end of the 19th century (Proctor, 2012). Tobacco, and its products, is a single such carcinogen that can cause multiple types of cancers including cancers of lung, nostrils, larynx, pharynx, esophagus, stomach, liver, pancreas, bladder, ureter, kidney, and cervix and may cause myeloid leukemia (Hecht, 2003). No less than 60 carcinogens from its smoke and 16 from unburned tobacco have

been reported. Many of the products are either DNA adducts, or protein adducts. Tobacco-produced nitrosamines, polycyclic aromatic hydrocarbons and aromatic amines, majorly derived from nicotine play key role in carcinogenesis (Hecht, 2003).

In 2010, Centers for Disease Control and Prevention (CDC) of US Department of Health and Human Services published a seminal report of 727 pages on, "How tobacco smoke causes disease: the biology and behavioral basis for smoking–attributable diseases." It describes how different carcinogens from tobacco promote carcinogenesis to cancer (CDC, 2010).

Coal tar

Coal tar is now known as a potential source of carcinogens which contains polycyclic aromatic hydrocarbons like benzene, naphthalene, anthracene, phenanthrene, and many other harmful compounds, forms DNA adducts and induces tumor at the inhalation, oral, and dermal exposure routes. It is also produced from tobacco smoking. Regular exposure increases the risk of cancer as evidenced from occupational and animal studies (Moustafa et al., 2015). As early as 1665, coal tar was discovered and was found useful for treatment purposes for dermatitis, psoriasis and later on as a source ingredient for synthetic dyes during 1800–1850 AD. However, it is considered as Group 1 carcinogen (IARC). As described before, Yamagiwa and Ichikawa were the pioneer in working with coal tar and showed the tumor formation on repeated use for years. However, they were not sure about its composition and the ingredient(s) caused carcinoma. Later on in the 1920s, benzanthracene was found a potential carcinogen from coal tar.

Benzene

Benzene is a volatile colorless inflammable compound with sweat odor, produced from modern human activities (occupational health hazards) including forest fires. However, Benzene can induce cancer in humans was known during the 1920s and conclusive report came from animal study only in 1979. It causes chromosomal aberrations and thus induces blood related cancers like leukemia, myeloma and lymphoma. Environmental Protection Agency (EPA) of USA has classified it as a known human carcinogen for all routes of exposure (Huff, 2007).

Hydrocarbons

Polycyclic aromatic hydrocarbons (PAH) are outcome of tobacco smoke, industrial smokes, forest fires, and coal distillations and were known during 1775, from Percival Pott's seminal work on chimney sweeps' cancer (Brookes and Duncan, 1971). Only during 1925 and with last 55 years of research shows PAH with its proven role in DNA binding, inducing mutations in oncogenes results in tumor formation (Baird et al., 2005).

Arsenic

Arsenic is a natural environmental contaminant in water, food, air, and soil and thus it remains a concern for human and animal health since olden days. Once known, "King of poisons" or/and "Poison of kings," Arsenic received reputation for killings of several personalities either with an intention of removal of rivalry and/or politically during the mid-18th century. It is notoriously associated with death of Napoleon Bonaparte in 1851 (Hughes et al., 2011). A nice display of timeline of some historic events in the toxicology of Arsenic has been depicted and reviewed by Hughes et al. (2011). It is described that Thomas Fowler (1736–1801) introduced Fowler's solution in 1786 for the treatment of fever and later on was used in civil war, treatment of leukemia, and renewed application as a pesticide in recent times. In 1887, Hutchison proposed it as human skin carcinogen. About 8 years later, Tseng et al. (1968) reported skin cancer among arsenic-exposed Taiwanese population. Later on, an arsenic compound (dimethylarsinic acid) showed tumorigenic potential in four rat organs (1995) and urinary bladder (1998), while role of inorganic arsenic as a complete carcinogen in adult mice on exposure was reported in 2010 (Hughes et al., 2011).

Asbestos

Ever-growing industrialization has brought prosperity in economy in one hand and polluted the environment with harmful, deleterious, carcinogenic dust particles including asbestos on the other hand, during beginning of the 20th century. Once known "magic"/ "indispensable" mineral, asbestos were in multiple applications because of its unique features in withstanding high temperature, insulation, malleable, Asbestos as a cause of human cancer was discovered in 1924 in Britain and was reported in British Medical Journal. Association with asbestos and lung cancer was presumed since 1930–1940; however, scientific observation came during the 1960s (Batrip, 2004).

3.3 Viruses

In general, infections were considered as one of the most important causes of cancer. This constitutes 12% of total cancers and among them seven viruses is found predominant (White et al., 2014). These are Epstein–Barr virus (EBV), human papillomavirus (HPV), human T-cell lymphotropic virus (HTLV), hepatitis C virus (HCV), Kaposi's sarcoma herpesvirus, and Merkel cell polyomavirus. The pace of research in establishing etiological role of several human cancers was even slow during the 1990s. In between time, discovery of viral life cycles, transduction, proto-oncogenes, oncogenes, tumor suppressor gene, knowledge about in vitro cell culture, etc. brought speed in research in understanding of viral role in tumorigenesis. Interestingly, most human virus transmissions are either asymptomatic or mildly symptomatic but do not lead to neoplasia.

Between the 1930s and 1950s, nonhuman viruses were discovered with a link to cancer development. Viral isolates from keratinous carcinoma from a rabbit (Shope papillomavirus), from mammary gland of a milking mother mouse (mouse mammary tumor virus), mouse leukemia virus and mouse polyomavirus were discovered with a possible conclusion of causing likely tumors in human.

Rous sarcoma virus (RSV)

As depicted above that the association of virus and human cancer came to know since the seminal work by Rous (1911) who could demonstrate that a transferred filterable component of sarcoma caused tumor in a normal chick. We now know that transferred component induced (transduced) a gene (*v-src*) by a retrovirus, honored after FP Rous as Rous sarcoma virus (RSV) which got revealed during the 1970s and 1980s (White et al., 2014). FP Rous was honored with the Noble Prize in 1966 for his contribution. The bacteria-free cell-filtrate of breast tumor of a chicken when was transferred to a normal chicken and induced breast tumor among recipients, gave a way of relooking of the genes (DNA). The reviewed works originated the concept of oncogene (a normal gene which function normally gets mutated) which has the ability of developing tumor.

Epstein–Barr virus (EBV)

The first human viruses those caused human tumors were discovered during the 1960s and 1970s studying Burkitt's lymphoma with the help of electron microscope. It is EBV which is also known as human herpesvirus 4 (HHV4), a double-stranded DNA herpesvirus and was reported in 1964 for the first time (REF). It is found a causal agent of several other cancers, nasopharyngeal carcinoma, most lymphoproliferative disorders, some Hodgkin's disease, some non-Hodgkin's lymphoma and some gastrointestinal lymphoma (Moore and Chang, 2010). Though EBV is lymphotropic but can also infect epithelial cells as its primary site of replication.

Hepatitis B virus (HBV)

Hepatitis is an inflammatory disease of liver because of HBV infection, popularly known as jaundice. Since the 1940s, jaundice was known as a serum-borne infection. It is a single-stranded and double stranded hepadnavirus causes some hepatocellular carcinoma. It was discovered and reported in 1965. However, association with HBV and cancer got revealed from series of epidemiological researches and then in 1981, we came to know HBV's role in causing hepatocellular carcinoma (HCC).

Human T-lymphotropic virus-1 (HTLV-1)

It is a positive-strand, single-stranded RNA retrovirus, causes adult T-cell leukemia. It was discovered and reported for the first time in 1980. This observation happened during the 1970s among a cluster of leukemia patients in south west Japan followed by isolation, and sequencing which revealed it identical to human T-cell leukemia virus type 1, isolated from a T-cell line and was reported by RC Gallo in 1980. It was the first known human retrovirus. It was found in association with sexual behavior globally. And later on was found transmission might happened also by blood transfusion, contaminated needles, and breastfeeding. Noble Prize was awarded to Francois Barre'-Sinoussi and Luc Montagnier for the discovery of HIV in 2008 which does not cause cancer directly but indirectly immunosuppress host for developing malignancy.

High-risk human papillomaviruses (HPV) 16 and HPV 18 (some other α-HPV types are carcinogenic)

These are double-stranded papillomavirus are associated with most cervical cancer, penile cancer and some other anogenital and head and neck cancers and were discovered and reported during 1983–1984. Globally, HPV infections and linked cancers are more than 50% in females in comparison to only 5% in males. Anticancer vaccines, Cervarix and Gardasil, against HPV16 and HPV 18 have been developed to prevent resultant cancers (White et al., 2014). Noble Prize was awarded to Harald zur Hausen for the discovery of HPV in 2008.

Hepatitis C virus (HCV)

It is a positive-strand, single-stranded RNA flavivirus and is causal agent of some hepatocellular and some lymphomas. It was reported in 1989. It is a non-A non-B viral particle cause infection worldwide lead to liver damage and cirrhosis and was found an indirect cancer causing agent in humans.

Kaposi's sarcoma herpesvirus (KSHV)

It causes Kaposi's sarcoma (KS)—a rare skin tumor which was reported in 1872 by Moritz Kaposi. However, with the advent of AIDS during the 1980s, association of KS like symptoms came into being. Later on, it was found to be caused by human herpesvirus 8 (HHV-8) and was discovered and reported in 1994. It also causes primary effusion lymphoma and some multicentric Castleman's disease. It is thus alternatively also known as human herpesvirus 8 (HHV8).

Merkel cell polyomavirus (MCV)

It is a double-stranded DNA polyomavirus which causes most Merkel cell carcinoma and was reported in 2008. It is the only proven oncogenic virus among human polyomaviruses. Though it is a rare type of cancer, neuroectodermal tumor is very aggressive, and immunosuppression induces its tumorigenesis.

Some key discoveries and events in tumorigenic virus research
    1898: Experiments on virus transmission of rabbit myxomatosis
    1908: First demonstration of cell-free transmission of avian viral leukemia
    1909: Rous carries out virus transmission experiments for avian sarcoma

1933: Identification of papillomavirus in rabbit papillomas

1936: Description of mouse mammary tumor virus

1951: Discovery of murine leukemia retrovirus

1953: Discovery of murine polyomavirus

1962: Adenovirus and SV40 are shown to induce tumors in rodents

1964: Discovery of first human tumor virus: EBV described in Burkitt's lymphoma cell lines

1965: HBV described as cause of hepatitis

1966: Noble Prize awarded to FP Rous

1967: EBV immortalization of primary lymphocytes

1970: Description of reverse transcription and retroviruses

1975: Noble Prize awarded to Temin, Baltimore and Dulbecco

1976: Cellular origin of *SRC* oncogene described; Noble Prize awarded to Blumberg

1979: Discovery of p53 associated with SV40 T antigen

1980: Discovery of HTLV-I

1981: HBV linked to hepatocellular carcinoma (HCC); Approval of first "anticancer vaccine" against HCC; Initial description of AIDS and related cancer like Kaposi's sarcoma and non-Hodgkin's lymphomas

1983: Discovery of high-risk HPV types in cervical cancer; Initial descriptions of HIV

1984: EBV genome sequenced

1988: Tumor virus targeting of retinoblastoma protein and p53

1989: Discovery and cloning of Hepatitis C virus; Noble Prizes awarded to Bishop and Varmus

1990: Epidemiology of Kaposi's sarcoma (KS) hints to virus

1992: Description of herpesvirus homologues to cellular oncogenes

1994: Discovery of Kaposi's sarcoma herpesvirus (KSHV) in KS

1995: Isolation of KSHV in primary effusion lymphoma cells

2006: FDA approved HPV VLP-based preventive vaccine

2008: Noble Prizes awarded to Zur Hausen, Barre'-Sinoussi, and Montagnier

Several intriguing thoughts got evolved over the period of time, one of them being the concept of direct and indirect involvement of pathogens including viruses, bacteria and parasites as cancer causing agents. Direct carcinogens are those which express viral oncogenes and contribute directly to cancer formation (HPV, MCV, EBV, and KSHV) while indirect agents cause or influence carcinogenesis through chronic infection and inflammation like HBV, HCV, HTLV-I and *Helicobacter pylori* (Moore and Chang, 2010).

3.4 Environmental radiations

The concept of environmental causes including radiations for increased cancer risk was not understood till 1927. It was first recognized by Herman Joseph Muller in 1927. Then another 50 years took to establish the fact that several environmental radiations could be the cause of many types of cancers. In 1977, four scientists, Higginson, Muir, Doll, and Peto explained the evidences gathered from several studies including epidemiological data on migrants, geographical variations with allied risks over time and found that 80% of all cancers are caused by environmental factors.

As described before, a breakthrough discovery of X-rays or Rontgen rays brought a great facility in medical history with its discovery in 1895. WC Rontgen was the inaugural Noble Prize recipient in 1901 for his discovery. Rontgen's wife, Anna Berthe herself exposed her fingers to X-rays and experienced its deleterious effects. Dose-dependent treatment and/or exposure were not known during those days, hence increase of cancer risk was observed. This was identified by American geneticist, HJ Muller in 1927 and was awarded Noble Prize in 1946 for his contribution. Evidences got accrued when studies carried out with atom bomb survivors (with leukemia, multiple myeloma, cancers in thyroid, bladder, breast, lung, ovary, colon, stomach, liver, skin) during World War II, people exposed during Chernobyl nuclear accident (thyroid cancer, leukemia) and people exposed to high levels of radiation at work, like in uranium mine.

Ultraviolet (UV) radiation

This electromagnetic radiation is originated from sun and man-made like tanning beds and welding torches. It is a type of radiation that falls between high-frequency radiation like X-rays and Gamma rays and low frequency radiation like radio waves. Based on energy/frequency, UV rays are of three different types: UVA rays, with least energy can cause cells to age and damage DNA indirectly and thus is the cause of some skin cancers (basal cell and squamous cell cancer). UVB with more energy than UVA but lower than UVC, can directly damage DNA of skin cells resulting most skin cancers (Melanoma). UVC with highest energy among UVs is not a risk factor for cancer and are produced from man-made sources like mercury lamp, wielding torch, UV sanitizing bulb for surface sterilization. According to IARC, solar radiation is carcinogenic to humans.

3.5 Medical radiations

To treat cancer, radiation therapy has also a long record of enhancing several other cancers than what for it was treated.

Studies showed the higher risk of leukemia, thyroid cancer, and early onset of breast cancer among treated groups. However, development of cancer may be figured out at the elapse of 5 to 15 years. Over the period of time, more accurate methodologies and instrumentation have been brought to use radiation therapy more appropriately for the benefit of cancer treatment.

3.6 Medication causes

To treat benign conditions, radiation therapy was used before and those are the medical evidences demonstrate the increase of cancer risk. However, radiation therapy is a now the key medication widely to treat cancer.

1. *Peptic ulcer:* studies showed patients treated with 15 Gy radiation for the treatment of peptic ulcers caused to increase higher risk of cancers of stomach and pancreas.
2. *Ringworm of the scalp:* Several other studies showed that radiation treatment to eradicate fungus, *Tinea capitis* from scalp increased the risk of cancer of scalp's basal cell.
3. *Ankylosing spondylitis:* To treat patients with such autoimmune disease, injectable radium increased higher risk of cancers (bone sarcoma with cancers of breast, liver, kidney, bladder, etc.) among them.

3.7 Life style factors

The history behind the fact that lifestyle of an individual could be a contributing factor for cancer was not known since recent times. More aptly, the claim of bad lifestyle and cancer association is also not much evidence based. However, the concept has been grown on types of habits and conditions like, smoking, alcoholism, malnutrition, pollution, noise, radiation, obesity, infections and even psychological stress may influence many different types of cancers.

3.8 Mutagens

There remained confusion between carcinogen and mutagen. As the timeline moves, X-rays were considered both as carcinogen and mutagen during the 1950s. Carcinogens cause or directly increase the cases of cancer while mutagens change the codon (DNA), bring genetic changes and thus may or may not cause cancer. Though it is now known that more than 90% of carcinogens are mutagens. However, the argument continued for long time, especially with benzo(*a*)pyrene. Later on, in 1960, James and Miller found that the compound inhibited the carcinogenesis in carcinogen-treated rats with the development of a DNA adduct. Then this and several other series of works enabled to discover the role of P450 protein in xenotoxicity and genotoxicity. In 1973, Ames and coworkers figured out that many carcinogens were truly mutagens with the introduction of his popularly known "Ames test" (Ames et al., 1973).

4. Animal models and chemical carcinogenesis

Animal models play always an essential role in understanding any sort of diseases, its mechanism, and prophylaxis. Similarly, several animal models were developed and have been developing to elucidate different aspects of cancer. Though we consider its limitation, but animal study remains an inevitable part of life sciences. In cancer research, primarily two major approaches are followed animal models of chemical carcinogenesis: (1) to know the etiology and carcinogenicity and (2) to find the mechanisms of prevention which may facilitate early detection. As it is understood that cancer is resulted from genetic mutation and environmental exposures, so experimental models are there to elucidate this hypothesis. Beyond the classical toxicity tests and dysfunction of multiorgans damage, leading to cancer using mouse models, new sets of mouse models have been introduced those are genetically engineered mouse models (GEMMs). As described before the work of Yamagiwa and Ichikawa, (1918) used rabbits to prove that irritation in ear lobes caused to develop malignant epidermal tumors, by the continuous application of coal tar for 4 years. Later on in 1930, several polycyclic aromatic hydrocarbons induced tumors in mice. In 1935, Sasaki and Yoshida experimentally got success in inducing liver cancer in rats by feeding an azo dye (o-amidoazotoluene), commonly used in dye industry. Followed by Kinosita, (1938), induced liver cancer using 4-dimethyl-aminazobenzene, and 2-acetylaminofluorene–exposed rats developed bladder and other cancer in 1941 (Kemp, 2015). During 1950 and 1975, Japanese patients were exposed to a sedative drug, ethyl carbamate (urethane), which was later on proved as a potent carcinogen using mouse. The use of carcinogen to induce cancer in animal is long which obviously help to understand carcinogen and mutagens better. It is true that the exposure of all environmental factors including radiations and carcinogenesis have been understood well with animal study.

Eventually several carcinogen bioassays were developed and were modified from time to time. In 1964, an important observation came from the work carried out by Brookes and Lawley that the carcinogen binds to DNA and thus the concept of mutagen got sharpened. Oncologists systematically learnt that cancer is the outcome of interaction between genotype and environment (Kemp, 2015). Genetically engineered models gave scientific evidences to correlate between exposed carcinogens or radiations and associated genes. This paved the way of discovery of p53 tumor suppressor gene using p53 knockout mice. Likely was the discovery of cyclin dependent kinase inhibitor p27 and associated cancer in human. As per the records, the National Cancer Institute, USA introduced animal testing programs to detect potential carcinogens and related safety level in the 1970s. Followed by the activity was redefined and refined by the initiative of National Toxicology Program, 2011. As a result, a summarized Handbook of Carcinogenic Potency and Genotoxicity Database including over 5000 experimental data on 1298 chemical agents supported by more than 1000 research articles and 400 Technical Reports were published (Kemp, 2015).

5. History of cancer treatment

As per literature, the early known treatment with diagnosed cancer came into existence during the early 20th century. Nowadays, cancer is treated majorly alone or in combination of chemotherapy, surgery and radiation. Besides, novel treatment systems have been facilitated the process of cancer treatment that is with Immunotherapy, Nano-structured therapeutics, targeted therapy like gene therapy.

5.1 Chemotherapy

The term "chemotherapy" was coined by German Scientist, Paul Ehrlich in treating diseases with chemical compounds as early as the 1930s. Experience with the exposure of mustard gas and decrease in leukocytes among soldiers of World War II (1939–1945) became useful for the treatment of lymphomas for the first time by Gilman in 1943. Subsequently, alkylating synthetic compounds like cyclophosphamide and chlorambucil were used to treat cancer. With the synthesis of folate antagonists like aminopterin and amethopterin and further formulated to a drug in 1948, methotrexate became extremely useful in the treatment of child leukemia (Arruebo et al., 2011). In 1951, Elion and Hitchings developed antileukemia drugs, 6-thioguanine and 6-mercaptopurine followed by development of an antitumor drug, 5-fluorouracil (5-FU) by Heidelberger, which is found to be an important chemotherapeutic to treat colorectal cancer, head and neck cancer. During the 1950s, corticosteroids were also designed to treat cancers. In 1955, Cancer Chemotherapy National Service Centre, USA, was established to qualify the compounds for the treatment of cancers. As a result, stories of success in this field came into existence. The first cured case was of choriocarcinoma using chemotherapy reported in 1958. Followed by discovery of alkaloids as anticancer drugs like vinblastine (from *Vinca rosea*) and ibenzmethyzin for treatment of leukemia and Hodgkin's disease during the 1960s and cure of advanced Hodgkin's disease using combination therapy with nitrogen mustard, vincristine, methotrexate, and prednisone brought confidence in cancer treatment in the 1970s (Moxley et al., 1967). Success was there in treating patients with advanced diffuse large B-cell lymphoma by using same combinations of drugs replacing nitrogen mustard with cyclophosphamide only in 1975 (Arruebo et al., 2011). In 1978, more success achieved treating cancer patients with cisplatin, bleomycin, and vinblastine and gathered experiences that different drugs have had different mode of action at different phases of cell cycle. Such a combination therapy is in use for treatment of breast cancer since the 1970s is CMF (cytoxan, methotrexate, and 5-fluorouracil). Later on, about three decades ago, targeted therapy came into practice with the development of drug delivery system (like liposomal therapy) and with immunoglobulin and nano-structured molecules.

5.2 Surgery

At the end of the 19th century and beginning of the 20th century was the dawn of cancer treatment by surgery. The first radical mastectomy was performed by Halsted in 1890 and subsequently got declined with the innovation of least radical surgery. However, the first radical suprapubic prostatectomy performed by Young in 1904, Wertheim performed radical hysterectomy in 1906 and in 1908, Miles carried out the first nonradical abdominoperineal resection, followed by lobectomy in 1912. In modern times, surgery is carried out by more and more noninvasive techniques like laparoscopic colectomy, videothoracoscopy, radiofrequency ablation, use of cyber knife, sentinel-node removal for breast-conserving surgery, laryngoscope laser surgery in early laryngeal cancer, or/and introduction of robotics for the removal of cancer from prostate and kidney (Arruebo et al., 2011).

5.3 Radiation

As described before, radiation science and technology was started with contributions of Becquerel, Rontgen and Marie Curie during the end of the 19th century and beginning of the 20th century. However, radiation could be used as cancer therapy came to practice in 1960 when Ginzton and Kaplan used rotational linac (linear accelerator) radiotherapy for deep tissues without damaging much skin. In recent past, computer enabled three-dimensional X-ray therapy was introduced, called intensity modulated radiation therapy (IMRT) with computed Tomography (CT). More recent developments happened with the use of proton or helium ions and four-dimensional conformal radiotherapy: image guided radiation therapy (IGRT) and Image-guided adaptive radiation therapy (IGART). Another novel approach is the radiogenic therapy where cytotoxic agents are induced to control cancer. Again targeted radiotherapy was introduced using isotopes, Iodine-125 and Indium-111 to specific receptor bound cells so as to avoid damages to healthy cells (Arruebo et al., 2011).

5.4 Immunotherapy

Use of components (antibody, cytokines, dendritic cells, etc.) in immune system is found useful in the management of several diseases like infection, allergy, autoimmune disorders and cancers and is called Immunotherapy. It has higher potentials of therapeutic values like highly specific, efficacious, less toxic, and better tolerant and targeted. In 1890, von Behring and Kitasato described antibody production in serum in an immunized animal with toxoids. The serum of the immunized animal gave protection against infectious diseases like diphtheria and tetanus, and is known as "Serum Therapy." Later on, it was revealed the major immune component is the antibody of serum therapy offered protection against those diseases. In 1972, Porter and Edelman received Noble Prize for their work on structural elucidation of an antibody. In 1975, Cesar Milstein and George Kohler discovered technique of monoclonal antibody production (hybridoma technology), followed by its first application as antitumoral drug in 1981, then designing of chimeric antibodies in 1984, designing of humanized antibodies in 1986, development of transgenic mice carrying human immunoglobulin genes and production of large number of antitumoral antibodies, engineered antibodies. This pace is on to enhance the best way of treatment for cancer. Table 1 displays major monoclonal antibodies (mAbs) got approved by FDA and in use as anticancer immunotherapy.

Table 1 Major FDA (Food and Drug Administration) approved anticancer monoclonal antibodies (mAbs) for immunotherapy.

Antibody	Company	Target	Indication	Source	Approval
Abciximab (ReoPro)	Eli Lilly & Co	Platelet glycoprotein, GPIIb/IIIa	High risk angioplasty	Chimeric Fab fragment	FDA (1994)
Arcitumomab (CEA-Scan)	Immunomedics Inc.	Carcinoembryonic antigen	Detection of tumors	Mouse Ig fragment-^{99m}Tc	FDA (1996)
Basiliximab (Simulect)	Novartis Pharmaceutical Corp.	CD25	Prevent rejection in organ transplantation	Chimeric	FDA (1998)
Alemtuzumab (Campath-1H)	Genzyme	CD52	Chronic lymphocytic leukemia, T-cell lymphoma	Humanized	FDA (2001)
Adalimumab (Humira)	Abott Laboratories	TNFα	Rheumatoid arthritis, psoriasis, Crohn's disease	Human	FDA (2002)
Bevacizumab (Avastin)	Genentech Inc./ Roche	VEGF-A	Cancer, age related macular degeneration	Humanized	FDA (2004)
Panitumumab (Vectibix)	Amgen/Abgenix	EGFR	Metastatic colorectal carcinoma	Human	FDA (2006)
Eculizumab (Soliris)	Alexion Pharmaceuticals	C5 complement factor	Paroxysmal nocturnal hemoglobinuria	Humanized	FDA (2007)
Canakinumab (Ilaris)	Novartis Pharmaceutical Corp.	IL-1β	Cryopyrin-associated periodic syndromes	Human	FDA (2009)
Atlizumab (RoActemra)	Hoffman-la Roche	IL-6 receptor	Rheumatoid arthritis	Humanized	FDA (2010)
Belimumab (Benlysta)	Human Genome Sciences GSK	BAFF (B cell activation factor)	Systemic lupus erythematosus	Human	FDA (2011)
Ipilimumab (Yervoy)	Bristol-Myers Squibb.	CD152 (CTLA-4)	Activator of the immune system	Human	FDA (2011)

5.5 Therapy using nanotechnology

Apart from chemotherapy, radiation therapy and surgery, many more therapeutics are in practice which include angiogenesis inhibition therapy, biologics-based therapy (interferons, interleukins, colony-stimulating factors, transcription factors, mAbs, vaccines, gene therapy and nonspecific immunomodulating agents), transplantations (bone marrow, blood stem cells), laser therapy, hypothermia, photodynamic therapy, and targeted cancer therapy. One more addition has brought accuracy and novelty in cancer treatment, that is nanoscale and nanostructure-based therapy. The optimistic view of this ever-growing and promising therapeutics is that several of its products already got clinically approved for treatment and diagnosis and several hundreds of products are in different phases of clinical trials. Some of such marketed products with (i) the property of improved drug solubility and bioavailability like DaunoXome (Daunorubicin liposomal—for advanced Kaposi's sarcoma), Onco TCS (Vincristine liposomal, for cancer of breast, testes, HIV-associated Kaposi's sarcoma, Hodgkin's disease), and Neulasta/PEG filgrastim (polymer–protein conjugate, prevention of chemotherapy-associated neutropenia); (ii) controlled drug release like BrachySil, Gliadel; (iii) in vivo diagnosis like Resovist, Feridex/Endorem are few to mention. Several thousands of peer-reviewed scientific publications are also getting poured every year.

5.6 Treatment beyond the limit

Recently several more new technologies are in practice and progress to prevent, diagnose and cure cancer. The journey started with the evolution of Next-Generation sequencing (NGS) and Immunotherapy (Scott et al., 2012; Li et al., 2021). If the status of *RAS* gene is diagnosed as wild type in a colorectal cancer patient using NGS, then an anti-EGFR antibody, like cetuximab or panitumumab can be used for treatment. Largely noninvasive technique like liquid biopsy has enhanced the treatment and diagnostic method as with novel devices and drugs. Nowadays, surgery is done with the help of robotics. New drugs like checkpoint inhibitors, T-cell transfer therapy are in practice (Bharadwaj, 2005; Atlihan-Gundogdu et al., 2020). Besides, Immunotherapy, new areas are evolved in cancer research: exosomes, microsomes, and organoids. The science of exosome is very novel and unique. It is a nanoscale (50–150 nm) cellular component, originates from cell membrane and may carry biomolecules like, microRNAs, mRNAs and proteins and thus is used as a cargo for targeted drug delivery. As exosomes are secreted by cells so they can modulate the microenvironment and prevent cancer progression and diagnosis (Ando et al., 2021; Li et al., 2021). Microbiome, on the other hand maintains the physiological homeostasis in collaboration with human cell system. Number, volume, and type of microbiota in the human are unique for good health. Change in condition of microbiota leads to dysbiosis and which in turn may lead to certain cancer. Thus, Microbiome becomes a tool of cancer diagnosis and therapy during last 10 years. An organoid is a synthetic 3-D structure produced in vitro, a miniaturized and simplified version of an organ with a property of self-renewal and differentiation. With this unique quality, organoids are in use in cancer research since 2010 (Ando et al., 2021).

6. Major breakthroughs in cancer research

A summary of Table 2 displays the innovations and developments occurred in cancer research since last century. It is obvious that cancer is still a life threatening disease however survival rate with value added life extension and precision therapies, vaccines brought lot of hopes to conquer cancer in recent future.

Table 2 Chronological major events in cancer research during 1903–2020.

Year	Major events in cancer research during 1903–2020	Reference
1903	Marie Curie discovered radioactive elements radium and polonium and coined the word "radioactivity" in 1898 and was the beginning of successful application of radiation therapy using radioactive elements for different cancers	https://www.cancer.gov/research/progress/250-years-milestones
1911	Discovery of Rous sarcoma virus to cause cancer in chickens	https://www.cancer.gov/research/progress/250-years-milestones
1915	Application of coal tar onto rabbit to induce cancer came as an experimental outcome	https://www.cancer.gov/research/progress/250-years-milestones
1928	Pap Smear test was introduced as a tool for early detection of cervical cancer	https://www.cancer.gov/research/progress/250-years-milestones
1937	The National Cancer Institute (NCI), USA was established	https://www.cancer.gov/research/progress/250-years-milestones
1941	Hormone Therapy was introduced to regress testicular cancer by removal of testicles and/or administering estrogens	https://www.cancer.gov/research/progress/250-years-milestones
1947	First-ever remission of pediatric leukemia using a drug, aminopterin, an antimetabolite	Faber et al. (1948)
1949	First chemotherapy drug got approved by FDA, was nitrogen mustard for the treatment of Hodgkin lymphoma	Goodman et al. (1946)
1958	Combination therapy came into practice for leukemia with dosing and scheduling	Frei et al. (1958)
1965	Chemotherapy, MOPP (Mechlorethamine, vincristine, procarbazine, and prednisone) to treat patients with advanced Hodgkin lymphoma and was found 50% of patients got cured	DeVita and Chu (2008)

Continued

Table 2 Chronological major events in cancer research during 1903–2020—cont'd

Year	Major events in cancer research during 1903–2020	Reference
1971	National Cancer Act became law	https://www.cancer.gov/research/progress/250-years-milestones
	Introduction of Fecal Occult Blood Test (FOBT) for detection of Colorectal cancer	Greegor (1967)
1974	Introduction of Computed Tomography (CT) scan brought enhancement in getting clearer images and guiding radiation and other treatments	https://www.cancer.gov/research/progress/250-years-milestones
1975	First adjuvant chemotherapy introduced and thus enhanced the cure rates in early stage breast cancer	Jamieson and Ludbrook (1977)
1977	New combination chemotherapy (Cisplatin, Vinblastin, and Bleomycin) showed 70% cure in testicular cancer and was approved by FDA in 1978.	Einhorn and Donohue (1977)
	Mammography became the regular and increasing practice in screening breast cancer and gave a guidance for proper treatment	https://www.cancer.gov/research/progress/250-years-milestones
1981	First Cancer vaccine was introduced to prevent liver cancer due to HBV infection	https://www.asco.org/research-guidelines/cancer-progress-timeline
1982	Restricted surgery brought relief among patients with rectal cancer, called mesorectal excision	https://www.asco.org/research-guidelines/cancer-progress-timeline
1986	Early detection of prostate cancer was made possible by introduction of PSA (prostate-specific antigens) test	Seidman et al. (1992)
	Tamoxifen was introduced to reduce breast cancer recurrence following breast cancer surgery	Baum et al. (1983)
	Global guidelines, issued by WHO to help proper pain management for cancer patients	https://www.asco.org/research-guidelines/cancer-progress-timeline
1988	Benzene was discovered to cause blood cancers	Rinsky et al. (1987)
1989	FDA-approved RBC (Epoetin alfa) and WBC (Filgrastim) boosting drugs reduced infections and improved cancer treatment	https://www.asco.org/research-guidelines/cancer-progress-timeline
1990	Laparoscopic surgery was introduced which minimized pain, recovery time for many cancers, kidney, prostate, and colorectal cancer	McDougall et al. (1993)
	Integration of computer and medicine improved radiation therapy by innovating 3-D radiation treatment plans	McShan et al. (1990)

Table 2 Chronological major events in cancer research during 1903–2020—cont'd

Year	Major events in cancer research during 1903–2020	Reference
1993	Increasing risk of Melanoma was connected with sun exposure	https://www.asco.org/research-guidelines/cancer-progress-timeline
	FDA approved Taxanes family drugs (Taxol) came into practice for the treatment of ovarian and breast cancer	McGuire et al. (1996)
1994	BRCA 1 Tumor suppressor gene got cloned	https://www.cancer.gov/research/progress/250-years-milestones
1995	BRCA 2 Tumor suppressor gene got cloned	https://www.cancer.gov/research/progress/250-years-milestones
1997	First ever FDA approved targeted drug, Rituximab, an mAB for the treatment of B-cell non-Hodgkin lymphoma	McLaughlin et al. (1998)
1998	New radiotherapy (Intensity Modulated Radiation Therapy—IMRT) was introduced for precise targeting tumors close to vital organs	Fraass et al. (1999)
1999	FDA approved first targeted antibreast cancer drug, trastuzumab (Herceptin) was introduced	Slamon et al. (2001)
2000	Household radon exposure was found linked to lung cancer	Greenland et al. (1999)
2001	An approved drug, Imatinib for myelogenous leukemia was found effective against a rare abdominal tumor, gastrointestinal stromal tumor (GIST). Imatinib blocks the growth signal, c-Kit for tumor growth	Demetri et al. (2002)
2003	Human Genome project result announced mapping of human genome	Collins et al. (2003)
	Obesity was discovered as an etiology of many cancers	Calle et al. (2003)
	FDA approved first targeted drugs (gefitinib and erlotinib) for lung cancer which bind to EGFR and delay the survival of patients	Thatcher et al. (2005)
2004	First antiangiogenic drug, a new generation drug, Bevacizumab got FDA approval for the treatment of colorectal cancer, followed by used for the treatment of other cancer like advance lung, ovary, kidney and certain brain tumors	Hurwitz et al. (2004)
2005	FDA approved two targeted drugs (etuximab and panitumumab) for advanced colon cancer	Karapetis et al. (2008)

Continued

Table 2 Chronological major events in cancer research during 1903–2020—cont'd

Year	Major events in cancer research during 1903–2020	Reference
2006	FDA approved first vaccine (Gardasil) against HPV16 and HPV 18 to prevent cervical cancer	Garland et al. (2007)
2010	FDA approved first human cancer treatment vaccine (sipuleucel-T) for the treatment of metastatic prostate cancer	Anassi and Ndefo (2011)
	First drug (Ipilimumab) showed improved survival of patients with melanoma	Hodi et al. (2010)
2013	Chimeric antigen receptor-modified T-cell (CAR-T) therapy was introduced to treat childhood leukemia	Timmers et al. (2019)
2014	Four new drugs (obinutuzumab, ofatumumab, idelalisib, and ibrutinib) got FDA approval and brought improved changes in chronic lymphocytic leukemia (CLL)	Goede et al. (2014)
2016	Pembrolizumab was introduced to extend survival of patients of non–small cell lung cancer (NSCLC)	Reck et al. (2016)
2017	First gene therapy for B-cell acute lymphoblastic leukemia (ALL), Tisagenlecleucel was introduced	Grupp et al. (2016)
2018	Patients with BRCA-mutated ovarian cancer received maintenance therapy with Poly (ADP-ribose) polymerase or PARP inhibitors, olaparib following surgery and chemotherapy and thus could lower 70% risk of disease progression	Moore et al. (2018)
	First effective treatment evolved for Anaplastic Thyroid cancer in nearly 50 years. The combination of trametinib (Mekinist) and dabrafenib (Tafinlar) got approved for patients	Subbiah et al. (2018)
	Combined Immunotherapy lengthens survival for Renal cell carcinoma. Nivolumab, a programmed cell death 1(PD-1) check point inhibitor antibody while ipilimumab, an anticytotoxic T lymphocyte-associated antigen 4 (CTLA-4) antibody. Combined therapy gave survival benefit to patients	Motzer et al. (2018)
	A 21-gene-based test (Oncotype DX) predicts risk of recurrence and guides adjuvant therapy for women with certain Breast cancer	Sparano et al. (2018)

Table 2 Chronological major events in cancer research during 1903–2020—cont'd

Year	Major events in cancer research during 1903–2020	Reference
	Atezolizumab, the first approved immunotherapy for metastatic triple-negative Breast cancer	Schmid et al. (2018)
	Less toxic treatment regimen of methotrexate resulted highest cure rates pediatric patients with T-cell acute lymphoblastic leukemia (T-ALL)	Winter et al. (2018)
	Major advance in the treatment of small cell lung cancer (SCLC) using FDA approved combined immunotherapy (atezolizumab) and chemotherapy (carboplatin)	Horn et al. (2018)
2019	The first vaccine for human papillomavirus (HPV) was in practice since 2006 but analysis approved the drop in incidence rate in high-risk HPV 16 and 18 by 83% among females age of 13 to 19 years 66% in 20 to 24 age group of young women in 2019	Drolet et al. (2019)
	Combination of checkpoint inhibitor (CDK4/6 inhibitor, ribociclib) and hormone improved survival in young women with certain types of Breast cancer.	Im et al. (2019)
	Good news came for patients with slow growing forms of Non-Hodgkin's lymphoma while FDA approved the first chemotherapy –free combination therapy (Lenalidomide and rituximab)	Leonard et al. (2019)
2020	Luspatercept, a first-in-class drug introduced to support anemic patient due to myelodysplastic syndromes to increase the red blood cell count	Fenaux et al. (2020)
	International Pan-cancer analysis of more than 2600 whole genomes from 38 types of cancer revealed changes from normal tissue to identify and specify treatment modalities	ICGC/TCGA Pan-Cancer Analysis of Whole Genomes Consortium (2020)

7. Cancer in India since antiquity

As India, a member country of oldest civilizations keeps its marks on understanding of cancer dates back to about 2500 years. However, paleoepidemiological studies on carcasses of Indus civilization did not reveal occurrence of cancer. The oldest literatures are evident of comprehensive understanding about tumor during ancient times when

Ayurveda and Siddha methods of treatment were prevalent. Singhal (1983) published a report from Banaras Hindu University, India depicting the knowledge of surgery and cancer. This report is mostly based on the works carried out by Susrut (6th or 7th century BCE), Father of Surgery and presented in treatise, Samhita, an asset in Ayurveda. His work has been translated in English in the form of Encyclopedia, comprising 5000 pages and 12 volumes.

Susruta Samhita has six cantos: I—Sutra-sthana, II—Nidana-sthana, III—Sarira-sthana, IV—Cikitsa-sthana, V—Kalpa-sthana, and VI—Uttara-tantra. All these works depicts and demonstrates particularly or generally about the concept of cancer and surgery. By definition, body falls ill when there are imbalances among *Dosaas* or "defects" in Ayurveda; vata, pitta, and kapha. Besides, rakta (blood), mamsa (tissue), and meda (fat) are also associated. Pathologically, tumor is to be designated as "*Arbuda* or *Granthi* or *Gulmo*" or lumps which may be produced at any part of the body and was predicted to be produced by swelling of mamsa which in turn may be circular, fixed, slightly painful, big and/or broad, slow growing and nonsuppurate (Singhal, 1983).

The philosophy of health, body and mind was known during ancient times in India with the evidence of three Ayurvedic classic scriptures, "Brihat Troyi": Agnivesh or/and Charaka Samhita, Sushrut Samhita, and Astanga Hridaya (Muthu, 1913). Prognosis, diagnosis, surgery and treatment of diseases were known to Vedic era (c.5000 BCE), long before the Greek Physician, Hippocrates (c.460–c.379 BCE), honored as the Father of Medicine. During those days, wine was used as an anesthetic to do surgery. While Ayurveda was the practice in northern part of India, then Siddha system was in use in south India. However, very few literature and scriptures are found during mediaeval part of India in medicine in general and cancer-like disease in particular.

Knowledge about cancer and cancer-like diseases came to know in India with the arrival of Europeans during the 16th century and with the discovery of flora, fauna and diseases and obviously with the arrival of European physicians (D'Cruz, 1991). Post-colonization era visualized significant growth in understanding different diseases including cancer in India. Williams (1908) described that prevalence of malignant tumors are less in India than Europe. However, cause of cancer and their relative nomenclatures were unique among study groups. Because of the use of kangri pot (kangri cancer), use of betel nut and/or tobacco for chewing and keeping in the buccal cavity (cheek cancer), poor penile hygiene (penile cancer), use of dhoti around the waist tied tightly (dhoti cancer) and may more. However, all forms of so called cancers got subsided over the period except betel nut and tobacco association (Smith and Mallath, 2019).

Along with other diseases, diagnosis of cancer and cancer-like diseases were elusive and thus real figure of its prevalence was not known till the beginning of the 20th century. A meticulous study was conducted in 1927 and found Breast cancer was common followed by uterine cancer, skin cancer and stomach cancer (Megaw and Gupta, 1927). By the same time, it was revealed that cancer was mostly associated with older subjects (above 50 years) than younger Indian population. A study was conducted between 1917 and 1932 and revealed that women were found more prone to cancer than men (Nath and Grewal, 1935, 1939). Cancer research in India is currently guided by the International societies and national centers like National Centre for Disease Informatics, and Research, and National Cancer Registry Programme (Singh et al., 2018).

8. Conclusion

The road map for cancer research and to eradicate the menace of the disease is near to clear. Meaningfully, lot of development happened for last decades with discovery of several therapy systems, biomarkers, technological innovations, NGS, syphoning more budgets (Zugazagoita et al., 2016). In recent time, cancer research approaches with majorly fulfilling two goals: oncogene driven and immune-oncology to reduce sufferings, extend survival periods, prevention from further advancement by vaccination and combination therapy, early diagnosis with precision. Still road does not find its end, yet in progress.

Acknowledgment

Author appreciates the support rendered by the VIT Management for bringing novelty in research. There is no conflict of interest.

References

Ames, B.N., Durstone, W.E., Yamasaki, E., et al., 1973. Carcinogens are mutagens: a simple test system combining liver homogenates for activation and bacteria for detection. Proc. Natl. Acad. Sci. 70, 2281–2285. https://doi.org/10.1073/pnas.70.8.228.

Anassi, E., Ndefo, U.A., 2011. Sipuleucel-T (provenge) injection: the first immunotherapy agent (vaccine) for hormone-refractory prostate cancer. P T. 36 (4), 197–202. 21572775. PMC3086121.

Ando, K., Hu, O., Kasagi, H., et al., 2021. Recent developments in cancer research: expectations for a new remedy. AGSurg 5 (4), 419–426. https://doi.org/10.1002/ags3.12440.

Arruebo, M., Vilaboa, N., Sáez-Gutierrez, B., et al., 2011. Assessment of the evolution of cancer treatment therapies. Cancer 3 (3), 3279–3330. https://doi.org/10.3390/cancers3033279. 24212956. PMC3759197.

Atlihan-Gundogdu, E., Ilem-Ozdemir, D., Ekinci, M., et al., 2020. Recent developments in cancer therapy and diagnosis. J. Pharm. Investig. 50, 349–361. https://doi.org/10.1007/s40005-020-00473-0.

Baird, W.M., Hooven, L.A., Mahadevan, B., 2005. Carcinogenic polycyclic aromatic hydrocarbon-DNA adducts and mechanism of action. Environ. Mol. Mutagen. 45 (2–3), 106–114. https://doi.org/10.1002/em.20095.

Bartrip, P.W.J., 2004. History of asbestos related disease. Postgrad. Med. J. 80, 72–76.

Baum, M., Brinkley, D.M., Dossett, J.A., et al., 1983. Improved survival amongst patients treated with adjuvant tamoxifen after mastectomy for early breast cancer. Lancet 322 (8347), 450. https://doi.org/10.1016/S0140-6736(83)90406-3.

Bhardwaj, J.R., 2005. Recent advances in diagnosis of cancer. Med. J. Armed Forces India 61 (2), 112–114. https://doi.org/10.1016/S0377-1237(05)80002-4. 27407728. PMC4923002.

Brookes, P., Duncan, M., 1971. Carcinogenic hydrocarbons and human cells in culture. Nature 234, 40–43. https://doi.org/10.1038/234040a0.

Calle, E.E., Rodriguez, C., Walker-Thurmond, K., et al., 2003. Overweight, obesity, and mortality from cancer in a prospectively studied cohort of U.S. adults. N. Engl. J. Med. 348 (17), 1625–1638. https://doi.org/10.1056/NEJMoa021423. 12711737.

Centers for Disease Control and Prevention (US); National Center for Chronic Disease Prevention and Health Promotion (US); Office on Smoking and Health (US), 2010. How Tobacco Smoke Causes Disease: The Biology and Behavioral Basis for Smoking-Attributable Disease: A Report of the Surgeon General. Centers for Disease Control and Prevention (US), Atlanta, GA. 5, Cancer. Available from: https://www.ncbi.nlm.nih.gov/books/NBK53010/.

Collins, F.S., Green, E.D., Guttmacher, A.E., et al., 2003. US National Human Genome Research Institute. A vision for the future of genomics research. Nature 422 (6934), 835–847. https://doi.org/10.1038/nature01626 (Epub 2003 Apr 14) 12695777.

D'Cruz, I.A., 1991. Garcia da Orta in Goa: pioneering tropical medicine. BMJ 303, 1593–1594.

Demetri, G.D., von Mehren, M., Blanke, C.D., et al., 2002. Efficacy and safety of imatinib mesylate in advanced gastrointestinal stromal tumors. N. Engl. J. Med. 347 (7), 472–480. https://doi.org/10.1056/NEJMoa020461. 12181401.

DeVita Jr., V.T., Chu, E., 2008. A history of cancer chemotherapy. Cancer Res. 68 (21), 8643–8653. https://doi.org/10.1158/0008-5472.CAN-07-6611. 18974103.

Drolet, M., Bénard, É., Pérez, N., et al., 2019. HPV vaccination impact study group. Population-level impact and herd effects following the introduction of human papillomavirus vaccination programmes: updated systematic review and meta-analysis. Lancet 394 (10197), 497–509. https://doi.org/10.1016/S0140-6736(19)30298-3 (Epub 2019 Jun 26) 31255301. PMC7316527.

Einhorn, L.H., Donohue, J., 1977. Cis-diamminedichloroplatinum, vinblastine and bleomycin combination chemotherapy in disseminated testicular cancer. Ann. Intern. Med. 87, 293–298.

Faber, S., Diamond, L.K., Mercer, R.D., et al., 1948. Temporary remissions in acute leukemia in children produced by folic acid antagonist, 4-aminopteroyl-glutamic acid (Aminopterin). N. Engl. J. Med. 238, 787–793.

Fenaux, P., Platzbecker, U., Mufti, G.J., et al., 2020. Luspatercept in patients with lower-risk myelodysplastic syndromes. N. Eng. J. Med. 382 (2), 140–151. https://doi.org/10.1056/NEJMoa1908892.

Fraass, B.A., Kessler, M.L., McShan, D.L., et al., 1999. Optimization and clinical use of multisegment intensity-modulated radiation therapy for high-dose conformal therapy. Semin. Radiat. Oncol. 9 (1), 60–77. https://doi.org/10.1016/s1053-4296(99)80055-1. 10196399.

Frei 3rd, E., Holland, J.F., Schneiderman, M.A., et al., 1958. A comparative study of two regimens of combination chemotherapy in acute leukemia. Blood 13 (12), 1126–1148. 13596417.

Garland, S.M., Hernandez-Avila, M., Wheeler, C.M., et al., 2007. Females united to unilaterally reduce Endo/Ectocervical disease (FUTURE) I investigators. Quadrivalent vaccine against human papillomavirus to prevent anogenital diseases. N. Engl. J. Med. 356 (19), 1928–1943. https://doi.org/10.1056/NEJMoa061760. 17494926.

Goede, V., Fischer, K., Busch, R., et al., 2014. Obinutuzumab plus chlorambucil in patients with CLL and coexisting conditions. N. Engl. J. Med. 370 (12), 1101–1110. https://doi.org/10.1056/NEJMoa1313984 (Epub 2014 Jan 8) 24401022.

Goodman, L.S., Wintrobe, M.M., Dameshek, W., et al., 1946. Nitrogen mustard therapy: use of methyl-Bis(Beta-Chloroethyl)amine hydrochloride and Tris(Beta-Chloroethyl)amine hydrochloride for Hodgkin's disease, lymphosarcoma, leukemia and certain allied and miscellaneous disorders. JAMA 132 (3), 126–132. https://doi.org/10.1001/jama.1946.02870380008004.

Greegor, D.H., 1967. Diagnosis of large-bowel Cancer in the asymptomatic patient. JAMA 201 (12), 943–945. https://doi.org/10.1001/jama.1967.03130120051012.

Greenland, P., Daviglus, M.L., Dyer, A.R., et al., 1999. Resting heart rate is a risk factor for cardiovascular and noncardiovascular mortality: the Chicago heart association detection project in industry. Am. J. Epidemiol. 149 (9), 853–862. https://doi.org/10.1093/oxfordjournals.aje.a009901. 10221322.

Grupp, S.A., Laetsch, T.W., Buechner, J., et al., 2016. Analysis of a global registration trial of the efficacy and safety of CTL019 in pediatric and young adults with relapsed/refractory acute lymphoblastic leukemia (ALL). Blood 128 (22), 221. https://doi.org/10.1182/blood.V128.22.221.221.

Hecht, S.S., 2003. Tobacco carcinogens, their biomarkers and tobacco-induced cancer. Nat. Rev. Cancer 3 (10), 733–744. https://doi.org/10.1038/nrc1190.

Hodi, F.S., O'Day, S.J., McDermott, D.F., et al., 2010. Improved survival with ipilimumab in patients with metastatic melanoma. N. Engl. J. Med. 363 (8), 711–723. https://doi.org/10.1056/NEJMoa1003466. 20525992. PMC3549297. (Epub 2010 Jun 5. Erratum in: N Engl J Med. 2010 Sep 23;363(13):1290).

Horn, L., Mansfield, A.S., Szczęsna, A., et al., 2018. IMpower133 study group. First-line atezolizumab plus chemotherapy in extensive-stage small-cell lung cancer. N. Engl. J. Med. 379 (23), 2220–2229. https:// doi.org/10.1056/NEJMoa1809064. Epub 2018 Sep 25 30280641.

Huff, J., 2007. Benzene-induced cancers: abridged history and occupational health impact. Int. J. Occup. Environ. Health 13 (2), 213–221. https://doi.org/10.1179/oeh.2007.13.2.213. 17718179. PMC3363002.

Hughes, M.F., Beck, B.D., Chen, Y., et al., 2011. Arsenic exposure and toxicology: a historical perspective. Toxicol. Sci. 123 (2), 305–332. https://doi.org/10.1093/toxsci/kfr184.

Hurwitz, H., Fehrenbacher, L., Novotny, W., et al., 2004. Bevacizumab plus irinotecan, fluorouracil, and leucovorin for metastatic colorectal cancer. N. Engl. J. Med. 350 (23), 2335–2342. https://doi.org/ 10.1056/NEJMoa032691. 15175435.

ICGC/TCGA Pan-Cancer Analysis of Whole Genomes Consortium, 2020. Pan-cancer analysis of whole genomes. Nature 578 (7793), 82–93. https://doi.org/10.1038/s41586-020-1969-6. 32025007. PMC7025898. (Epub 2020 Feb 5).

Im, S.A., Lu, Y.S., Bardia, A., et al., 2019. Overall survival with ribociclib plus endocrine therapy in breast cancer. N. Engl. J. Med. 381 (4), 307–316. https://doi.org/10.1056/NEJMoa1903765 (Epub 2019 Jun 4) 31166679.

Jamieson, G.G., Ludbrook, J., 1977. Adjuvant chemotherapy for cancer: a point of view. Arch. Surg. 112 (2), 119–120. https://doi.org/10.1001/archsurg.1977.01370020013001.

Kampen, K.R., 2012. The discovery and early understanding of leukemia. Leuk. Res. 36 (1), 6–13. https:// doi.org/10.1016/j.leukres.2011.09.028.

Karapetis, C.S., Khambata-Ford, S., Jonker, D.J., et al., 2008. K-ras mutations and benefit from cetuximab in advanced colorectal cancer. N. Engl. J. Med. 359 (17), 1757–1765. https://doi.org/10.1056/ NEJMoa0804385. 18946061.

Kemp, C.J., 2015. Animal models of chemical carcinogenesis: driving breakthroughs in cancer research for 100 years. Cold Spring Harb Protoc 2015 (10), 865–874. https://doi.org/10.1101/pdb.top069906. 26430259. PMC4949043.

Kinosita, R., 1938. Research on the carcinogenesis of the various chemical substances. Gann 30, 423–426.

Kuiper, K., 2010. The Britanica guide to theories and ideas that changed the modern world. Britanica Educational Publications in Association with Rosen Educational Services, New York, NY, p. 28. ISBN 978-1-61530-029-7.

Leonard, J.P., Trneny, M., Izutsu, K., et al., 2019. AUGMENT trial investigators. AUGMENT: a phase III study of Lenalidomide plus rituximab versus placebo plus rituximab in relapsed or refractory indolent lymphoma. J. Clin. Oncol. 37 (14), 1188–1199. https://doi.org/10.1200/JCO.19.00010. 30897038. PMC7035866. (Epub 2019 Mar 21).

Li, H., Li, Z.S., Pascale, C., et al., 2021. Editorial: new technologies in cancer diagnostics and therapeutics. Front. Pharmacol. 12, 1–3. https://doi.org/10.3389/fphar.2021.760833.

Lipsick, J., 2021. A history of cancer research: carcinogens and mutagens. Cold Spring Harb. Perspect. Med. 11, a035857. https://doi.org/10.1101/cshperspect.a035857.

McDougall, E.M., Clayman, R.V., Anderson, K., 1993. Laparoscopic wedge resection of a renal tumor: initial experience. J. Laparoendosc. Surg. 3 (6), 577–581. https://doi.org/10.1089/lps.1993.3.577. 8111112.

McGuire, W.P., Hoskins, W.J., Brady, M.F., et al., 1996. Cyclophosphamide and cisplatin versus paclitaxel and cisplatin: a phase III randomized trial in patients with suboptimal stage III/IV ovarian cancer (from the gynecologic oncology group). Semin. Oncol. 23 (5 Suppl 12), 40–47. 8941409.

McLaughlin, P., Grillo-López, A.J., Link, B.K., et al., 1998. Rituximab chimeric anti-CD20 monoclonal antibody therapy for relapsed indolent lymphoma: half of patients respond to a four-dose treatment program. J. Clin. Oncol. 16 (8), 2825–2833. https://doi.org/10.1200/JCO.1998.16.8.2825. 9704735.

McShan, D.L., Fraass, B.A., Lichter, A.S., 1990. Full integration of the beam's eye view concept into computerized treatment planning. Int. J. Radiat. Oncol. Biol. Phys. 18 (6), 1485–1494. https://doi.org/10.1016/0360-3016(90)90325-e. 2370198.

Megaw, J.W.D., Gupta, J.C., 1927. The geographical distribution of some of the diseases of India. Ind. Med. Gaz. 62, 299–313.

Moore, P.S., Chang, Y., 2010. Why do viruses cause cancer? Highlights of the first century of human tumour virology. Nat. Rev. Cancer 10 (12), 878–889. https://doi.org/10.1038/nrc2961. 21102637. PMC3718018. (Epub 2010 Nov 24).

Moore, K., Colombo, N., Scambia, G., et al., 2018. Maintenance Olaparib in patients with newly diagnosed advanced ovarian cancer. N. Engl. J. Med. 379 (26), 2495–2505. https://doi.org/10.1056/NEJMoa1810858 (Epub 2018 Oct 21) 30345884.

Motzer, R.J., Tannir, N.M., McDermott, D.F., et al., 2018. CheckMate 214 investigators. Nivolumab plus Ipilimumab versus Sunitinib in advanced renal-cell carcinoma. N. Engl. J. Med. 378 (14), 1277–1290. https://doi.org/10.1056/NEJMoa1712126 (Epub 2018 Mar 21) 29562145. PMC5972549.

Moustafa, G.A., Xanthopoulou, E., Riza, E., et al., 2015. Skin disease after occupational dermal exposure to coal tar: a review of the scientific literature. Int. J. Dermatol. 54 (8), 868–879. https://doi.org/10.1111/ijd.12903].

Moxley, J.H., DeVita, V.T., Brace, K., et al., 1967. Intensive combination chemotherapy and X-irradiation in Hodgkin's disease. Cancer Res. 27, 1258–1263.

Muthu, C., 1913. A short review of the history of ancient Hindu medicine. Proc. R. Soc. Med. 6, 177–190.

Nath, V., Grewal, K.S., 1935. Cancer in India. Indian J. Med. Res. 23, 149–190.

Nath, V., Grewal, K.S., 1939. Cancer in India. Indian J. Med. Res. 26, 785–832.

Proctor, R.N., 2012. The history of the discovery of the cigarette-lung cancer link: evidentiary traditions, corporate denial, global toll. Tob. Control. 21 (2), 87–91. https://doi.org/10.1136/tobaccocontrol-2011-050338 (Erratum in: Tob. Control. 2013 Jan;22(1):62) 22345227.

Reck, M., Rodríguez-Abreu, D., Robinson, A.G., et al., 2016. Keynote-024 investigators. Pembrolizumab versus chemotherapy for PD-L1-positive non-small-cell lung cancer. N. Engl. J. Med. 375 (19), 1823–1833. https://doi.org/10.1056/NEJMoa1606774. 27718847. (Epub 2016 Oct 8).

Rinsky, R.A., Smith, A.B., Hornung, R., et al., 1987. Benzene and leukemia. An epidemiologic risk assessment. N. Engl. J. Med. 316 (17), 1044–1050. https://doi.org/10.1056/NEJM198704233161702. 3561457.

Rous, P., 1911. A sarcoma of the fowl transmissible by an agent separable from the tumor cells. J. Exp. Med. 13 (4), 397–411. https://doi.org/10.1084/jem.13.4.397.

Schmid, P., Adams, S., Rugo, H.S., et al., 2018. Atezolizumab and Nab-Paclitaxel in advanced triple-negative breast cancer. N. Engl. J. Med. 379 (22), 2108–2121. https://doi.org/10.1056/NEJMoa1809615. Epub 2018 Oct 20 30345906.

Scott, A.M., Allison, J.P., Wolchok, J.D., 2012. Monoclonal antibodies in cancer therapy. Cancer Immun. 12, 14 (Epub 2012 May 1) 22896759. PMC3380347.

Seidman, A.D., Scher, H.I., Petrylak, D., et al., 1992. Estramustine and vinblastine: use of prostate specific antigen as a clinical trial endpoint for hormone refractory prostatic cancer. J. Urol. 147, 931–934.

Singh, M., Prasad, C.P., Singh, T.D., et al., 2018. Cancer research in India: challenges & opportunities. Indian J. Med. Res. 148 (4), 362–365. https://doi.org/10.4103/ijmr.IJMR_1711_18. 30665997. PMC6362726.

Singhal, G., 1983. Cancer in ancient Indian surgery. Anc. Sci. Life 2, 137–140.

Slamon, D.J., Leyland-Jones, B., Shak, S., et al., 2001. Use of chemotherapy plus a monoclonal antibody against HER2 for metastatic breast cancer that overexpresses HER2. N. Engl. J. Med. 344 (11), 783–792. https://doi.org/10.1056/NEJM200103153441101. 11248153.

Smith, R.D., Mallath, M.K., 2019. History of the growing burden of cancer in India: from antiquity to the 21st century. JCO Glob. Oncol., 1–15. https://doi.org/10.1200/JGO.19.00048.

Sparano, J.A., Gray, R.J., Makower, D.F., et al., 2018. Adjuvant chemotherapy guided by a 21-gene expression assay in breast cancer. N. Engl. J. Med. 379 (2), 111–121. https://doi.org/10.1056/NEJMoa1804710 (Epub 2018 Jun 3) 29860917. PMC6172658.

Subbiah, V., Kreitman, R.J., Wainberg, Z.A., et al., 2018. Dabrafenib and Trametinib treatment in patients with locally advanced or metastatic BRAF V600-mutant Anaplastic thyroid cancer. J. Clin. Oncol. 36 (1), 7–13. https://doi.org/10.1200/JCO.2017.73.6785 (Epub 2017 Oct 26) 29072975. PMC5791845.

Thatcher, N., Chang, A., Parikh, P., et al., 2005. Gefitinib plus best supportive care in previously treated patients with refractory advanced non-small-cell lung cancer: results from a randomised, placebo-controlled, multicentre study (Iressa survival evaluation in lung Cancer). Lancet 366 (9496), 1527–1537. https://doi.org/10.1016/S0140-6736(05)67625-8. 16257339.

Timmers, M., Roex, G., Wang, Y., et al., 2019. Chimeric antigen receptor-modified T cell therapy in multiple myeloma: beyond B cell maturation antigen. Front. Immunol. 10, 1613. https://doi.org/10.3389/fimmu.2019.01613. 31379824. PMC6646459.

Tseng, W.P., Chu, H.M., How, S.W., et al., 1968. Prevalence of skin cancer in an endemic area of chronic arsenicism in Taiwan. J. Natl. Cancer Inst. 40, 453–463.

White, M.K., Pagano, J.S., Khalili, K., 2014. Viruses and human cancers: a long road of discovery of molecular paradigms. Clin. Microbiol. Rev. 27 (3), 463–481. https://doi.org/10.1128/CMR.00124-13.

Winter, S.S., Dunsmore, K.P., Devidas, M., et al., 2018. Improved survival for children and young adults with T-lineage acute lymphoblastic leukemia: results from the children's oncology group AALL0434 Methotrexate randomization. J. Clin. Oncol. 36 (29), 2926–2934. https://doi.org/10.1200/JCO.2018.77.7250. 30138085. PMC6366301. (Epub 2018 Aug 23. Erratum in: J Clin Oncol. 2019 Mar 20;37(9):761.).

Yamagiwa, K., Ichikawa, K., 1918. Experimental study of the pathogenesis of carcinoma. J. Cancer Res. 3 (1), 1–29.

Zugazagoitia, J., Guedes, C., Ponce, S., et al., 2016. Current challenges in cancer treatment. Clin. Ther. 38 (7), 1551–1566. https://doi.org/10.1016/j.clinthera.2016.03.026 (Epub 2016 May 2) 27158009.

CHAPTER FIVE

Role of artificial intelligence in cancer diagnostics and therapeutics

Rahul Soloman Singh, Gladson David Masih, Rupa Joshi, Saurabh Sharma, Ashutosh Singh, and Bikash Medhi
Department of Pharmacology, Postgraduate Institute of Medical Education and Research, Chandigarh, India

1. Introduction

Alan Turing was the first to propose that computers be used to emulate intelligent behavior and critical reasoning. Dr. John McCarthy defines a machine's capability in the term of AI (artificial intelligence) to do a task that is commonly associated with human competence and was codified in the 1950s. AI gave rise to machine learning, which is the capability of an algorithm to learn data and execute tasks without explicit programming. Deep learning is an emerging recent machine learning method that can find patterns in unstructured, unprocessed data. AI is affecting every area in a tangible way, and its past time to grasp its progression in order to plan future development strategies specifically in health science. In oncology, AI is currently opening up new crucial areas for the better management of cancer patients. As more multidimensional data is generated in routine care such as patient's symptoms, history, tumor pathology, medical imaging, AI can assist doctors in forming a personalized perspective of a patient by affecting clinical decisions. Additionally, these datasets are constantly changing during a patient's journey. The number of published, steeply AI algorithms are still in the early stages of clinical translation. Many countries have shifted to value-based healthcare system as the worldwide cancer incidence rises and the high sensitivity of cancer care becomes more prominent. The evidence of AI's potential utility in cancer has been presented in this section.

2. Artificial intelligence in cancer diagnostics

Clinical decision-making and outcomes are influenced by the timing of cancer detection, the precision of cancer diagnosis, and tumor staging. AI has made substantial contributions to this vital field of cancer in just a few years, with the added advantages of scalability and automation, it may potentially match the performance of human specialist (Bhinder et al., 2021).

Biomarkers in Cancer Detection and Monitoring of Therapeutics
https://doi.org/10.1016/B978-0-323-95116-6.00015-3

2.1 Artificial intelligence in radiographic

In cancer diagnostics, interventional oncologists play a key role. Early diagnosis is critical for influencing outcomes, hence image analysis is critical (Suzuki, 2014). As digitized radiographic images and digital clinical information are widely available, radiology is one of the important medical sectors with AI using machine learning applications (Hosny et al., 2018). The AI application like artificial neural network (ANN) and convolutional neural network (CNN) can assess hundreds of digitized radiographic images, arrange them by differentiating attributes, and output them based on pathologic anomalies (Hosny et al., 2018). This digital radiography images may be related to clinical stored information in electronic medical records to assist with cancer identification, diagnosis, and therapy. By prescreening images for diagnostic criteria and classifying them by severity, AI might assist radiologists work more efficiently. (Hosny et al., 2018). Computer-aided detection (CAD) in mammography is among the most extensively employed applications of machine learning in cancer screening (Masud et al., 2019). Several studies have evaluated the identification of lesions using machine learning algorithms to that of radiologists (Aggarwal et al., 2021). In 2019, He et al. found a reduction in recall frequencies in 5147 patients with BIRADS 4 lesions using an AI-based deep-learning algorithm that included mammography images and clinical records with fairly good outcomes (100% sensitivity and 74% specificity, AUC = 0.93, Hamamoto et al., 2020).

2.2 Artificial intelligence in digital pathology

The final diagnosis of a lesion is pathological diagnosis, which plays a significant role in deciding the treatment plan and efficacy of treatment. However, pathologists are in low supply in the developed nations along with and other nondeveloping nations throughout the world, posing an issue for sustaining quality of healthcare services in each country (Coudray et al., 2018; Metter et al., 2019). In these situations, disease diagnosis employing AI research and development are essential.

Pathologists have depended on microscopic examination of stained cells and tissues for many years. Technological and AI breakthroughs will improve pathology, reducing labor-intensive microscopic work, increasing efficiency, and preserving quality for improved clinical treatment. By standardizing processes and incorporating AI into digital pathology, clinicians can evaluate pictures for correct interpretation and eliminate subjectivity. Larger-scale image viewing and more consistent color information are also possible with digital pathology. For diagnosis, prognosis, and therapy, this strategy allows for the effective identification of unique markers connected to disease-specific biomarkers (Bera et al., 2019; Niazi et al., 2019).

There seems to be no uncertainty that adopting AI as diagnosis is one option to compensate for scarcity of pathologists, and AI-assisted pathological diagnosis will become more frequent in clinical practice in the future (Steiner et al., 2021).

In 2018, Coudray et al. (Coudray et al., 2018) reported an intriguing discovery using AI technology for pathological diagnosis. He developed a large number of digitally recorded pathological glass slide specimens images in high-definition (also referred to Virtual Slides) for histological categorization lung cancer (adenocarcinoma and squamous cell carcinoma) and normal lung using the deep learning system called Inception V3. The finding showed that tissue classification has a significant level of precision of 0.97 AUC (Coudray et al., 2018). Importantly, these genes mutations (STK11, EGFR, FAT1, SETBP1, KRAS, and TP53) could be successfully diagnosed from pathological virtual slide images using the constructed AI analysis method (AUC: 0.733–0.856). These findings show that adopting AI to analyses pathological virtual slide images might lead to more accurate lung cancer tissue classification and genetic mutation prediction (Hamamoto et al., 2020).

2.3 Artificial intelligence in endoscopy

Artificial intelligence (AI) technologies have a lot of promise for gastroenterology practice and research because of their rapid development (Hamamoto et al., 2020). Endoscopic identification of early malignant tumors has already been successfully used with AI-guided image interpretation (Hann and Meining, 2021). Convolutional neural networks (CNNs), a kind of deep learning technology, have the capability to revolutionize gastrointestinal endoscopy, such as colonoscopy, EGD (esophagogastroduodenoscopy), and CE (capsule endoscopy) (Min et al., 2019). For cancer detection, assessment of cancer invasion, pathological diagnostic prediction, and *Helicobacter pylori* infection prediction are the key aims of AI in EGD (Wu et al., 2019; Sarker, 2021). Automated identification of bleeding spots, ulcers, tumors, and numerous small intestinal illnesses is being researched in the field of CE. The use of artificial intelligence in colonoscopy has mostly been limited to numerous patient-based prospective studies on the automated detection and classification of colon polyps (Wu et al., 2019; Sarker, 2021). In addition, there has been current study on inflammatory bowel illness. Due to the retrospective approach employing still images, most AI investigations in the field of GI endoscopy are still in the preclinical phases (Wu et al., 2019). In order to grow in this field, video-based prospective research is essential. AI may continue to expand, and it will shortly be employed in clinical therapy on a regular basis (Yamada et al., 2019; Okagawa et al., 2021).

One of the previous studies used transfer learning of pretrained convolutional neural networks (CNNs) based on the PyTorch platform to develop deep learning models that categorize the invasion depth (mucosa-confined vs submucosa-invaded) of gastric neoplasms using endoscopic images (Wu et al., 2019; Sarker, 2021). The accuracy of the external assessment was 77.3%. Developing a deep learning model, on the other hand, takes time, and elevated performance is required before some models can be used in real-world clinical settings (Sarker, 2021).

Professional endoscopists, who could detect and classify lesions while operating an endoscope and analyzing endoscopic images in general, are not required to perform as well as the recently developed deep learning based models in GI endoscopic assessment (Wu et al., 2019). The major portion of AI systems employed in endoscopy are designed to assist with closely specified tasks like lesion detection (CADe) or characterization (computer-aided diagnosis, CADx) (Sumiyama et al., 2021; Bang et al., 2021; Jia and Meng, 2016). CADe initially developed to detect suspicious areas on an endoscopic image with aberrant results, CADx, on the other hand, provides qualitative information about a specific area of interest, such as a histopathological examination, cancer invading degree, even mucosa proinflammatory status. Each model must be developed using images labeled with critical clinical information (Wu et al., 2019; Yamada et al., 2019; Jin et al., 2022).

2.4 Food and Drug administration (FDA) approved artificial intelligence devices with examples

The Food and Drug Administration (FDA) has authorized almost 15 AI devices aimed particularly toward clinical oncology. Each of these devices has a particular function and uses a single data stream at a single cancer care point (Table 1).

Table 1 FDA approved AI devices.

S. No.	Product name	Company	FDA approval number	Year	Description
1.	Origin Test Kit-FFPE	Pathwork Diagnostics	K092967	2010	Formalin-fixed, paraffin-embedded samples are used in the ML technique to help in the diagnosis of difficult-to-diagnose malignancies
2.	AmCAD-US	AmCad BioMed Corporation	K162574	2017	Backscattered signal ultrasound image data visualization and quantification software
3.	DM-Density	Densitas	K170540	2018	Mammography for breast density
4.	Arterys Oncology DL	Arterys	K173542	2018	An AI-based diagnostic imaging tool that analyses and records lesions and nodules in MRI and CT images automatically

Table 1 FDA approved AI devices—cont'd

S. No.	Product name	Company	FDA approval number	Year	Description
5.	Arterys MICA	Arterys	K182034	2018	CT and MRI scans are used to diagnose liver and lung cancer
6.	SubtlePET	Subtle Medical	K182336	2018	During the acquisition step of the radiology workflow, an AI-powered tool improves images
7.	ProFound AI Software V2.1	iCAD	K191994	2018	Mammography for breast density
8.	AiCE	Canon Medical Systems Corporation	K183046	2019	In a single rotation, visualize the cross-sectional volumes of entire body
9.	Deep Learning Image Reconstruction	GE Medical Systems	K183202	2019	CT image reconstruction system based on deep learning
10.	cmTriage	CureMetrix	K183285	2019	A mammography triage software based on artificial intelligence
11.	Koios DS for Breast	Koios Medical	K190442	2019	For identifying lesions on captured medical images and classifying it
12.	RayCare 2.3	RaySearch Laboratories	K191384	2019	A system for cancer care and follow-up that includes workflow, scheduling, and clinical data management
13.	Transpara	ScreenPoint Medical	K192287	2019	Mammogram workflow
14.	QuantX	Quantitative Insights	DEN170022	2020	Radiological software for cancer-suspicious lesions
15.	Genius AI Detection	Hologic	K201019	2020	A software tool for detecting any anomalies in breast tomosynthesis images

3. Artificial intelligence in cancer drug therapy

The objective of drug discovery is to find molecules which may modulate the activity of identified molecular targets. The traditional Computer-Aided Drug Design Methods (CADD) methods rely on a "Lock-And-Key" theory as a starting point of in silico drug discovery. The protein acts as a lock while the goal of the drug discovery is to find a key which can fit into the receptor pocket and modulate the functioning of target protein. The recent development of Deep Learning has opened new avenues in to application in the prediction of putative drugs targets and small molecule. This can be accomplished by analyzing the complex pattern of molecular data such as to extract, process, and extrapolate the information. This section will provide numerous instance of the utility of AI in cancer drug therapy.

3.1 Artificial intelligence in drug targets

A drug target is a protein that is inherently connected to a certain disease and might be targeted by a drug to have a therapeutic effect. AI platform can be employed to identify putative cancer targets. One class support vector machine is an AI-based method that correlates gene expression and protein interaction networks with clinical data to identify new treatment options in liver cancer (Tong et al., 2019). For predicting putative drug targets in the pathogenesis of breast cancer, deep learning used different cancer databases like cancer genome interpreter, PharmGKB, and The Cancer Genome Atlas (TCGA) to identify the proteins linked to the disease (Tamborero et al., 2018; Klein et al., 2001; López-Cortés et al., 2020, 2018; Ding et al., 2018). Another machine learning approach ECLIPSE employs DepMap platform (Consortium of hundreds of screened loss of function datasets) to predict various drug targets for cancer (Gilvary et al., 2019).

3.2 Artificial intelligence in drug discovery

There are two methods of virtual drug screening employed in drug discovery—ligand based and protein structure based. Structure based screening related AI algorithm are based on nonparametric scoring functions like RF score, ANN-based NN score, and SVM-based ID score. Existing experimental data used to find the causal relation between protein ligand free energy and features vector provides potential ligands. RF-based software found to be promising in predicting the protein–ligand docking parameters at large scale using istar platform (Li et al., 2014, 2015; Ballester et al., 2014). Behler-Parinello symmetry function, an integration of AI technology with computational chemistry is used for developing high dimensional neuronal network to evaluate numerous atoms. But the approach has several issues for instance solvation for Schrodinger equation (Mills et al., 2017), classification of chemical trajectory data (Carpenter et al., 2018), elevated virtual screening to detect novel compounds (Mannodi-Kanakkithodi et al., 2016), heterogeneous catalysts (Ma et al., 2015), and band gap prediction (Pilania et al., 2017).

In drug discovery, AI can predict 3D structure of the protein from their amino acid sequence (Shi et al., 2020; Callaway, 2020). A virtual kinome profiler, a computational platform, presents different representations of the durggable kinome and enhance the drug discovery process (Ravikumar et al., 2019). An ensemble support vector machine (eSVM) algorithm facilitated kinome specific activity prediction of >151 K compounds for drug repositioning and potential lead. Experimental biochemical assay validation demonstrated 1.5 times increase in precision.

Reinforcement learning allows integrative feedback, along with recurrent neural network. The approach generated celecoxib analogs (Olivecrona et al., 2017). Reinforcement learning along with graph convolutional approach used for specific property, yields novel compounds with high accuracy (You et al., 2018). Random forest model trained with preclinical data and support vector machine predict drug toxicity and adverse events and ADME properties (Shen et al., 2010).

3.3 Artificial intelligence in drug repurposing

Identification of a new indication of an existing drug beyond its existing therapeutic use is termed as drug repurposing. It is a speedy, cost-effective, and secure approach of drug discovery. The availability of enriched transcriptional data sets, such as LINCS (Library of Integrated Network-based Cellular Signatures), allowed AI to be used to speed up the drug development process (Subramanian et al., 2017). Using the given LINCS dataset along with other datasets, one of the study identified potential repurpose candidate drug that can inhibit the cancer causing gene expression (Mokou et al., 2020; Chen et al., 2017; Mastrogamvraki and Zaravinos, 2020). AI models such as NCI-60, PRISM, and GDSC use cell viability assay datasets to predict the drug efficacy based on their somatic mutation profile (Yang et al., 2013; Corsello et al., 2020; Shoemaker, 2006). PREDICT, a computational pipeline can integrate drug and disease similarity to predict the novel indications of existing drugs (Gottlieb et al., 2011).

In multilabel learning algorithm, the new therapeutic indication of old drug was determined along with identification of new drugs for known target protein (Mei and Zhang, 2019). Each drug was treated as a class label, and its protein target was considered as class-specific training data in the logistic regression model. Cross validation showed that about 85% of known drug targets were predicted correctly for at least one drug, and nearly 87% of drug target interactions (DTIs) were correctly predicted. The information provided bypass the need of drug chemical structure information and target protein information. Furthermore, the iDrug method involves a cross network embedding approach for drug repositioning and DTI integration, resulting in improved prediction accuracy by combining drug-target-disease data on a single platform. (Chen et al., 2020).

3.4 Artificial intelligence for drug interaction prediction

Use of drug target space deconvolution approach to train the machine learning algorithm about the ligand-protein molecular structure, guide the in silico predictions (Daina et al., 2019; Mervin et al., 2018). Several deep learning models are available for predicting the DTI which can be used for virtual screening. Some of the available tools are DeepDTA (https://doi.org/10.1093/bioinformatics/bty593), DeepConv-DTI (Lee et al., 2019), and graphDTA (Nguyen et al., 2021). Further, several encoders may be used for representing drug SMILES in a machine readable format. These include Morgan, Pubchem, Daylight, RDKit, convolutional neural networks (CNN), transformer, message-passing neural network (MPNN), etc. The generated drug representation may be fed into an AI algorithm for optimal prediction of DTI (Huang et al., 2020).

Convolutional network model uses graph convolutional approach to provide inputs in the form of characteristics of each DTI and to classify negative and positive interactions (Zhao et al., 2021).

3.5 Artificial intelligence in drug therapy

Drug activity is influenced by cancer cell genomic heterogeneity. The response of anti-cancer medications can be predicted using a random forest model that is particular to the mutation state of the malignant cell. (Sherbet et al., 2018). AI improve efficacy and tolerance of chemotherapy for instance CURATE. The effective dose of Zen 3694 and Enzalutamide was identified by AI (AI based platform). (Pantuck et al., 2018). Signature multivariate analysis (SIGMA), a computational tool can predict patients of breast cancer who can be benefitted with poly ADP-ribose polymerase (PARP) inhibitors therapy (Gulhan et al., 2019). Dorman et al. (2016) developed a machine learning approach that can predict breast cancer treatment tolerance. In Radiotherapy, AI can help in planning radiation regimen for treatment and target areas comparable to radiologist (Fiorino et al., 2020; Lou et al., 2019; Meyer et al., 2018). 3DCNN can delineate nasopharyngeal carcinomas (Lin et al., 2019). Radiomics combined with deep learning can evaluate treatment response in bladder cancer (Cha et al., 2017). AI platform predicted the effect of PD1 inhibitor in advanced solid tumors (Sun et al., 2018). AI method based on HLA mass spectroscopy database can identify cancer neoantigen thereby improve cancer immunotherapy (Bulik-Sullivan et al., 2018). One AI-based approach can identify high-risk lesions that are likely to become cancerous, eliminating unnecessary surgery (Bahl et al., 2018). A deep learning approach based on CDSS can extract and assess huge clinical data retrospectively and guide suitable cancer treatment (Printz, 2017). IBM Watson for oncology support, another AI based program developed for precision and personalized medicine, can precisely determine an approach to treatment for breast (Somashekhar et al., 2018), gastric (Tian et al., 2020) and nonsmall lung cancer in concordance to oncologist.

3.6 Artificial intelligence in drug response

A regression based classifier was built by input of data of treated genomic, transcriptomics and clinical features of advanced melanoma patients to predict PD-1 inhibitors resistance (Liu et al., 2019). To evaluate or predict the response of check point immunotherapies in cancer, XG-Boost based cancer profiler was trained by the input of large cohort data of matched genomic and transcriptomic profile in patient treated with checkpoint inhibitors (Litchfield et al., 2021). Convolutional neural network (CNN), an advanced approach of AI was trained and tested using naïve histopathological slides and clinical characteristics considerably predicted the response of advanced melanoma patients to checkpoint immunotherapy (Johannet et al., 2021). CNN significantly predicted the cancer patient's survival based on pretreatment CT scans (Lou et al., 2019; Kim et al., 2020). CNN applied to hematoxylin and eosin (HE)–stained whole slide image and considerably predicted the prognosis of patient undergoing chemotherapy or radiotherapy in colorectal cancer (Skrede et al., 2020). In one study, ensemble of 6 algorithms was trained on treatment specific features by using CT scans in non–small cell lung cancer patients. The model successfully predicted patient's sensitivity toward chemotherapy and immunotherapies (Dercle et al., 2020). CNN was trained using data from PET and MRI images of both treated and chemotherapy-treated breast cancer patients in one of the methods. In comparison to traditional methods, the study revealed remarkable prediction accuracy (Choi et al., 2020). Both cancer genome atlas (TCGA) and the CCLE database were utilized in one study to train three deep neural networks (DNN) to predict existing and novel targeted therapy for cancer treatment (Sakellaropoulos et al., 2019). A visible neural network is referred to as a "drug cell" that predicted the efficacy of 17,000 compounds using chemical information and biological information (Cortés-Ciriano et al., 2016).

NCI dream drug sensitivity prediction challenge showed high predictive performance of machine learning algorithms when trained with omics data and drug response profile of 53 human breast cancer cell lines (Costello et al., 2014). The treatment prognosis in response to drug therapy may be predicted using an AI system trained on high throughput screening data (Fig. 1).

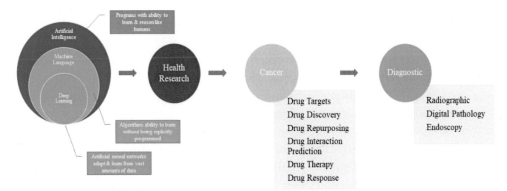

Fig. 1 Artificial intelligence in cancer.

4. Limitations to artificial intelligence in cancer diagnostics and therapeutics

As discussed, AI being a boom for cancer diagnostics and therapeutics had greatly progressed in last decade. However, there are several limitations to employ AI in cancer research (Cheung and Rubin, 2021).

Large quality data plays a vital role in cancer research. Data analysis and interpretation directly depends upon good quality large datasets. Generally, large data from multiple centers can be obtained from large databases like TCGA and NELSON trials etc. In contrast to other many cancer types where these types of databases are not available, it is difficult to create appropriate datasets from collaborative institutes.

Moreover, little data from any solitary institute could not be used over all populations. High quality image is the key component for detection, segmentation and analysis of features of cancer cells. This is critical in instances when heterogeneous data has been acquired from numerous sources, because most AI research needs image segmentation and annotation, which is a time-consuming and arduous task. As a result, to improve interrater reliability, automated or semiautomatic segmentation techniques should be implemented.

Another crucial point to be considered in AI research is the validity and feasibility of the results in the real clinical scenario. There are chances of high false positive results of cancer detection in early CAD solutions in actual clinical settings (Giganti et al., 2020).

As we know, AI requires large set of clinical data and images from multiple centers for its implementation, thus there are various ethical and legal issues regarding the ownership of the data and right to use it commercially (Rigby, 2019). Although consent from the patient is sufficient for collection of data in most of the settings, however, collection of the retrospective data from the patient seems to be cumbersome in many cases as the consent of the patient was not taken at the time of scan. Additionally, in some cases the retrospective de-identification of the imaging data also becomes difficult. Another ethical issue can be the exacerbation of the existing healthcare disparities both in research and implementation. Therefore, proper documentation regarding the legal and ethical issues should be obtained from everyone involved in the study, i.e., patients, researchers, institutions and governing agencies, etc. (Geis et al., 2019).

The analysis of such a large dataset and its deployment in normal clinical settings with cancer diagnosis and treatment is a huge issue for AI. Skilled bioinformatics and large servers are required for vast data management and interpretation. During diagnosis, it is burdensome to categorize data of numerous variants and interpret its clinical relevance for management of cancer patients. In the case of BRCA genes for breast cancer, p53 and PTEN for prostate cancer, KRAS for pancreatic cancer, and ERBB2 for lung cancer, extremely positive findings have been found. Despite its extensive coverage, increased sensitivity, and reduced prices, it is unable to identify vast genomic rearrangements and potentially pathogenic mutations (Kaur et al., 2022). Then, whole genome sequencing is the alternative but it is associated with high cost. The complicated data analysis and vast computational burden further limits its use (Dlamini et al., 2020). In the current scenario, cost is the main issue in AI systems as they are largely dependent on the fast processing of huge data with expert computational staff and systems. The staff should be well trained and updated with the advanced intended requirements with regular training sessions (Kelly et al., 2019).

5. Future prospective of artificial intelligence in cancer management

Although AI has been utilized in the health care sector from last so many years, still its role is evolving to overcome its limitation and barriers to be considered as boom in healthcare facilities. Therefore, utilization of next-generation sequencing (NGS) and precision oncology with AI will increase the sensitivity, efficacy and reduce the cost of the system. It can act as revolutionary process to transform the future of cancer management from diagnosis to therapeutic treatment options. Moreover, the advanced AI technology is required in future for omic analysis like epigenomics and genomics. Additionally, highly developed AI systems are the prerequisite for its use in drug discovery. Computational biology integrated with AI could potentially change the drug discovery system for cancer precision medicine (Nagarajan et al., 2019).

Furthermore, there is great need of building confidence in the healthcare system in AI for its entry into the real clinical scenario. As a result, the development and implementation of systematic and practical AI model risk assessment tools is critical. Additional research in deep learning models should be readily performed. Advancement in seminal research perhaps an important way to predict the risk factors for cancer. Smart phone or other electronic gadgets can have sensors to collect data from every patient and help in empowerment of the AI system for precision diagnosis. These systems could be useful for remote monitoring of cancer patients in routine practices. In addition, AI systems integrated with electronic health records and genetic predisposition in combination with environmental and lifestyle modifications would assess the possible risk of cancer in normally healthy individuals and can also personalize the early intervention for its management (Nagarajan et al., 2019).

Considering its pros and cons, the future prospects of AI should be planned as the combination of both AI and humans to get an excellence in cancer management by emphasizing on diagnosis and treatment as well.

References

Aggarwal, R., Sounderajah, V., Martin, G., Ting, D.S.W., Karthikesalingam, A., King, D., Ashrafian, H., Darzi, A., 2021. Diagnostic accuracy of deep learning in medical imaging: a systematic review and meta-analysis. npj Digit. Med. 4, 65.

Bahl, M., Barzilay, R., Yedidia, A.B., Locascio, N.J., Yu, L., Lehman, C.D., 2018. High-risk breast lesions: a machine learning model to predict pathologic upgrade and reduce unnecessary surgical excision. Radiology 286, 810–818.

Ballester, P.J., Schreyer, A., Blundell, T.L., 2014. Does a more precise chemical description of protein–ligand complexes lead to more accurate prediction of binding affinity? J. Chem. Inf. Model. 54, 944–955.

Bang, C.S., Lim, H., Jeong, H.M., Hwang, S.H., 2021. Use of endoscopic images in the prediction of submucosal invasion of gastric neoplasms: automated deep learning model development and usability study. J. Med. Internet Res. 23, e25167.

Bera, K., Schalper, K.A., Rimm, D.L., Velcheti, V., Madabhushi, A., 2019. Artificial intelligence in digital pathology—new tools for diagnosis and precision oncology. Nat. Rev. Clin. Oncol. 16, 703–715.

Bhinder, B., Gilvary, C., Madhukar, N.S., Elemento, O., 2021. Artificial intelligence in cancer research and precision medicine. Cancer Discov. 11, 900–915.

Bulik-Sullivan, B., Busby, J., Palmer, C.D., et al., 2018. Deep learning using tumor HLA peptide mass spectrometry datasets improves neoantigen identification. Nat. Biotechnol. https://doi.org/10.1038/nbt.4313.

Callaway, E., 2020. "It will change everything": DeepMind's AI makes gigantic leap in solving protein structures. Nature 588, 203–204.

Carpenter, B.K., Ezra, G.S., Farantos, S.C., Kramer, Z.C., Wiggins, S., 2018. Empirical classification of trajectory data: an opportunity for the use of machine learning in molecular dynamics. J. Phys. Chem. B 122, 3230–3241.

Cha, K.H., Hadjiiski, L., Chan, H.-P., Weizer, A.Z., Alva, A., Cohan, R.H., Caoili, E.M., Paramagul, C., Samala, R.K., 2017. Bladder cancer treatment response assessment in CT using radiomics with deep-learning. Sci. Rep. 7, 8738.

Chen, B., Ma, L., Paik, H., Sirota, M., Wei, W., Chua, M.-S., So, S., Butte, A.J., 2017. Reversal of cancer gene expression correlates with drug efficacy and reveals therapeutic targets. Nat. Commun. 8, 16022.

Chen, H., Cheng, F., Li, J., 2020. iDrug: integration of drug repositioning and drug-target prediction via cross-network embedding. PLoS Comput. Biol. 16, e1008040.

Cheung, H.M.C., Rubin, D., 2021. Challenges and opportunities for artificial intelligence in oncological imaging. Clin. Radiol. 76, 728–736.

Choi, J.H., Kim, H.-A., Kim, W., et al., 2020. Early prediction of neoadjuvant chemotherapy response for advanced breast cancer using PET/MRI image deep learning. Sci. Rep. 10, 21149.

Corsello, S.M., Nagari, R.T., Spangler, R.D., et al., 2020. Discovering the anti-cancer potential of non-oncology drugs by systematic viability profiling. Nat. Cancer 1, 235–248.

Cortés-Ciriano, I., van Westen, G.J.P., Bouvier, G., Nilges, M., Overington, J.P., Bender, A., Malliavin, T.E., 2016. Improved large-scale prediction of growth inhibition patterns using the NCI60 cancer cell line panel. Bioinformatics 32, 85–95.

Costello, J.C., Heiser, L.M., Georgii, E., et al., 2014. A community effort to assess and improve drug sensitivity prediction algorithms. Nat. Biotechnol. 32, 1202–1212.

Coudray, N., Ocampo, P.S., Sakellaropoulos, T., Narula, N., Snuderl, M., Fenyö, D., Moreira, A.L., Razavian, N., Tsirigos, A., 2018. Classification and mutation prediction from non-small cell lung cancer histopathology images using deep learning. Nat. Med. 24, 1559–1567.

Daina, A., Michielin, O., Zoete, V., 2019. SwissTargetPrediction: updated data and new features for efficient prediction of protein targets of small molecules. Nucleic Acids Res. 47, W357–W364.

Dercle, L., Fronheiser, M., Lu, L., et al., 2020. Identification of non-small cell lung cancer sensitive to systemic cancer therapies using radiomics. Clin. Cancer Res. 26, 2151–2162.

Ding, L., Bailey, M.H., Porta-Pardo, E., et al., 2018. Perspective on oncogenic processes at the end of the beginning of cancer genomics. Cell 173, 305–320.e10.

Dlamini, Z., Francies, F.Z., Hull, R., Marima, R., 2020. Artificial intelligence (AI) and big data in cancer and precision oncology. Comput. Struct. Biotechnol. J. 18, 2300–2311.

Dorman, S.N., Baranova, K., Knoll, J.H.M., Urquhart, B.L., Mariani, G., Carcangiu, M.L., Rogan, P.K., 2016. Genomic signatures for paclitaxel and gemcitabine resistance in breast cancer derived by machine learning. Mol. Oncol. 10, 85–100.

Fiorino, C., Guckemberger, M., Schwarz, M., van der Heide, U.A., Heijmen, B., 2020. Technology-driven research for radiotherapy innovation. Mol. Oncol. 14, 1500–1513.

Geis, J.R., Brady, A.P., Wu, C.C., et al., 2019. Ethics of artificial intelligence in radiology: summary of the joint European and north American multisociety statement. J. Am. Coll. Radiol. 16, 1516–1521.

Giganti, F., Allen, C., Emberton, M., Moore, C.M., Kasivisvanathan, V., 2020. Prostate imaging quality (PI-QUAL): a new quality control scoring system for multiparametric magnetic resonance imaging of the prostate from the PRECISION trial. Eur. Urol. Oncol. 3, 615–619.

Gilvary, C., Madhukar, N.S., Gayvert, K., Foronda, M., Perez, A., Leslie, C.S., Dow, L., Pandey, G., Elemento, O., 2019. A machine learning approach predicts essential genes and pharmacological targets in cancer. bioRxiv, 692277.

Gottlieb, A., Stein, G.Y., Ruppin, E., Sharan, R., 2011. PREDICT: a method for inferring novel drug indications with application to personalized medicine. Mol. Syst. Biol. 7, 496.

Gulhan, D.C., Lee, J.J.-K., Melloni, G.E.M., Cortés-Ciriano, I., Park, P.J., 2019. Detecting the mutational signature of homologous recombination deficiency in clinical samples. Nat. Genet. 51, 912–919.

Hamamoto, R., Suvarna, K., Yamada, M., et al., 2020. Application of artificial intelligence technology in oncology: towards the establishment of precision medicine. Cancers (Basel) 12, 3532.

Hann, A., Meining, A., 2021. Artificial Intelligence in Endoscopy. Visc Med 37, 471–475.

Hosny, A., Parmar, C., Quackenbush, J., Schwartz, L.H., Aerts, H.J.W.L., 2018. Artificial intelligence in radiology. Nat. Rev. Cancer 18, 500–510.

Huang, K., Fu, T., Glass, L.M., Zitnik, M., Xiao, C., Sun, J., 2020. DeepPurpose: a deep learning library for drug-target interaction prediction. Bioinformatics 36, 5545–5547.

Jia, X., Meng, M.Q.-H., 2016. A deep convolutional neural network for bleeding detection in wireless capsule endoscopy images. In: 2016 38th Annual International Conference of the IEEE Engineering in Medicine and Biology Society (EMBC). IEEE, pp. 639–642.

Jin, Z., Gan, T., Wang, P., Fu, Z., Zhang, C., Yan, Q., Zheng, X., Liang, X., Ye, X., 2022. Deep learning for gastroscopic images: computer-aided techniques for clinicians. Biomed. Eng. Online 21, 12.

Johannet, P., Coudray, N., Donnelly, D.M., et al., 2021. Using machine learning algorithms to predict immunotherapy response in patients with advanced melanoma. Clin. Cancer Res. 27, 131–140.

Kaur, G., Bhadada, S.K., Santra, M., Pal, R., Sarma, P., Sachdeva, N., Dhiman, V., Dahiya, D., Saikia, U.N., Chakraborty, A., Sood, A., Prakash, M., Behera, A., Rao, S.D., 2022. Multilevel annotation of germline MEN1 variants of synonymous, nonsynonymous, and uncertain significance in Indian patients with sporadic primary hyperparathyroidism. J. Bone Miner. Res. 37 (10), 1860–1875. https://doi.org/10.1002/jbmr.4653.

Kelly, C.J., Karthikesalingam, A., Suleyman, M., Corrado, G., King, D., 2019. Key challenges for delivering clinical impact with artificial intelligence. BMC Med. 17, 195.

Kim, H., Goo, J.M., Lee, K.H., Kim, Y.T., Park, C.M., 2020. Preoperative CT-based deep learning model for predicting disease-free survival in patients with lung adenocarcinomas. Radiology 296, 216–224.

Klein, T.E., Chang, J.T., Cho, M.K., et al., 2001. Integrating genotype and phenotype information: an overview of the PharmGKB project. Pharmacogenetics research network and knowledge base. Pharmacogenomics J. 1, 167–170.

Lee, I., Keum, J., Nam, H., 2019. DeepConv-DTI: prediction of drug-target interactions via deep learning with convolution on protein sequences. PLoS Comput. Biol. 15, e1007129.

Li, H., Leung, K.-S., Ballester, P.J., Wong, M.-H., 2014. Istar: a web platform for large-scale protein-ligand docking. PLoS One 9, e85678.

Li, H., Leung, K.-S., Wong, M.-H., Ballester, P.J., 2015. Improving AutoDock Vina using random Forest: the growing accuracy of binding affinity prediction by the effective exploitation of larger data sets. Mol. Inf. 34, 115–126.

Lin, L., Dou, Q., Jin, Y.-M., et al., 2019. Deep learning for automated contouring of primary tumor volumes by MRI for nasopharyngeal carcinoma. Radiology 291, 677–686.

Litchfield, K., Reading, J.L., Puttick, C., et al., 2021. Meta-analysis of tumor- and T cell-intrinsic mechanisms of sensitization to checkpoint inhibition. Cell 184, 596–614.e14.

Liu, D., Schilling, B., Liu, D., et al., 2019. Integrative molecular and clinical modeling of clinical outcomes to PD1 blockade in patients with metastatic melanoma. Nat. Med. 25, 1916–1927.

López-Cortés, A., Paz-Y-Miño, C., Cabrera-Andrade, A., Barigye, S.J., Munteanu, C.R., González-Díaz, H., Pazos, A., Pérez-Castillo, Y., Tejera, E., 2018. Gene prioritization, communality analysis, networking and metabolic integrated pathway to better understand breast cancer pathogenesis. Sci. Rep. 8, 16679.

López-Cortés, A., Cabrera-Andrade, A., Vázquez-Naya, J.M., Pazos, A., Gonzáles-Díaz, H., Paz-y-Miño, C., Guerrero, S., Pérez-Castillo, Y., Tejera, E., Munteanu, C.R., 2020. Prediction of breast cancer proteins involved in immunotherapy, metastasis, and RNA-binding using molecular descriptors and artificial neural networks. Sci. Rep. 10, 8515.

Lou, B., Doken, S., Zhuang, T., Wingerter, D., Gidwani, M., Mistry, N., Ladic, L., Kamen, A., Abazeed, M.E., 2019. An image-based deep learning framework for individualizing radiotherapy dose. Lancet Digit. Health 1, e136–e147.

Ma, X., Li, Z., Achenie, L.E.K., Xin, H., 2015. Machine-learning-augmented chemisorption model for CO2 electroreduction catalyst screening. J. Phys. Chem. Lett. 6, 3528–3533.

Mannodi-Kanakkithodi, A., Pilania, G., Huan, T.D., Lookman, T., Ramprasad, R., 2016. Machine learning strategy for accelerated design of polymer dielectrics. Sci. Rep. 6, 20952.

Mastrogamvraki, N., Zaravinos, A., 2020. Signatures of co-deregulated genes and their transcriptional regulators in colorectal cancer. npj Syst. Biol. Appl. 6, 23.

Masud, R., Al-Rei, M., Lokker, C., 2019. Computer-aided detection for breast cancer screening in clinical settings: scoping review. JMIR Med. Inform. 7, e12660.

Mei, S., Zhang, K., 2019. A multi-label learning framework for drug repurposing. Pharmaceutics. https://doi.org/10.3390/pharmaceutics11090466.

Mervin, L.H., Bulusu, K.C., Kalash, L., Afzal, A.M., Svensson, F., Firth, M.A., Barrett, I., Engkvist, O., Bender, A., 2018. Orthologue chemical space and its influence on target prediction. Bioinformatics 34, 72–79.

Metter, D.M., Colgan, T.J., Leung, S.T., Timmons, C.F., Park, J.Y., 2019. Trends in the US and Canadian pathologist workforces from 2007 to 2017. JAMA Netw. Open 2, e194337.

Meyer, P., Noblet, V., Mazzara, C., Lallement, A., 2018. Survey on deep learning for radiotherapy. Comput. Biol. Med. 98, 126–146.

Mills, K., Spanner, M., Tamblyn, I., 2017. Deep learning and the Schrödinger equation. Phys. Rev. A 96, 042113.

Min, J.K., Kwak, M.S., Cha, J.M., 2019. Overview of deep learning in gastrointestinal endoscopy. Gut Liver 13, 388–393.

Mokou, M., Lygirou, V., Angelioudaki, I., et al., 2020. A novel pipeline for drug repurposing for bladder cancer based on patients' omics signatures. Cancers (Basel). https://doi.org/10.3390/cancers12123519.

Nagarajan, N., Yapp, E.K.Y., Le, N.Q.K., Kamaraj, B., Al-Subaie, A.M., Yeh, H.Y., 2019. Application of computational biology and artificial intelligence technologies in cancer precision drug discovery. Biomed. Res. Int. 2019, 1–15.

Nguyen, T., Le, H., Quinn, T.P., Nguyen, T., Le, T.D., Venkatesh, S., 2021. GraphDTA: predicting drug target binding affinity with graph neural networks. Bioinformatics 37, 1140–1147.

Niazi, M.K.K., Parwani, A.V., Gurcan, M.N., 2019. Digital pathology and artificial intelligence. Lancet Oncol. 20, e253–e261.

Okagawa, Y., Abe, S., Yamada, M., Oda, I., Saito, Y., 2021. Artificial intelligence in endoscopy. Dig. Dis. Sci. https://doi.org/10.1007/s10620-021-07086-z.

Olivecrona, M., Blaschke, T., Engkvist, O., Chen, H., 2017. Molecular de-novo design through deep reinforcement learning. J. Cheminform. 9, 48.

Pantuck, A.J., Lee, D.-K., Kee, T., et al., 2018. Modulating BET bromodomain inhibitor ZEN-3694 and enzalutamide combination dosing in a metastatic prostate cancer patient using CURATE.AI, an artificial intelligence platform. Adv. Ther. 1, 1800104.

Pilania, G., Gubernatis, J.E., Lookman, T., 2017. Multi-fidelity machine learning models for accurate bandgap predictions of solids. Comput. Mater. Sci. 129, 156–163.

Printz, C., 2017. Artificial intelligence platform for oncology could assist in treatment decisions. Cancer 123, 905.

Ravikumar, B., Timonen, S., Alam, Z., Parri, E., Wennerberg, K., Aittokallio, T., 2019. Chemogenomic analysis of the Druggable Kinome and its application to repositioning and lead identification studies. Cell Chem. Biol. 26, 1608–1622.e6.

Rigby, M.J., 2019. Ethical dimensions of using artificial intelligence in health care. AMA J. Ethics 21, 121–124.

Sakellaropoulos, T., Vougas, K., Narang, S., et al., 2019. A deep learning framework for predicting response to therapy in cancer. Cell Rep. 29, 3367–3373.e4.

Sarker, I.H., 2021. Deep learning: a comprehensive overview on techniques, taxonomy, applications and research directions. SN Comput. Sci. 2, 420.

Shen, J., Cheng, F., Xu, Y., Li, W., Tang, Y., 2010. Estimation of ADME properties with substructure pattern recognition. J. Chem. Inf. Model. 50, 1034–1041.

Sherbet, G.V., Woo, W.L., Dlay, S., 2018. Application of artificial intelligence-based technology in cancer management: a commentary on the deployment of artificial neural networks. Anticancer Res. 38, 6607–6613.

Shi, Y., Zhang, X., Mu, K., Peng, C., Zhu, Z., Wang, X., Yang, Y., Xu, Z., Zhu, W., 2020. D3Targets-2019-nCoV: a webserver for predicting drug targets and for multi-target and multi-site based virtual screening against COVID-19. Acta Pharm. Sin. B 10, 1239–1248.

Shoemaker, R.H., 2006. The NCI60 human tumour cell line anticancer drug screen. Nat. Rev. Cancer 6, 813–823.

Skrede, O.-J., De Raedt, S., Kleppe, A., et al., 2020. Deep learning for prediction of colorectal cancer outcome: a discovery and validation study. Lancet 395, 350–360.

Somashekhar, S.P., Sepúlveda, M.-J., Puglielli, S., et al., 2018. Watson for oncology and breast cancer treatment recommendations: agreement with an expert multidisciplinary tumor board. Ann. Oncol. 29, 418–423.

Steiner, D.F., Chen, P.-H.C., Mermel, C.H., 2021. Closing the translation gap: AI applications in digital pathology. Biochim. Biophys. Acta, Rev. Cancer 1875, 188452.

Subramanian, A., Narayan, R., Corsello, S.M., et al., 2017. A next generation connectivity map: L1000 platform and the first 1,000,000 profiles. Cell 171, 1437–1452.e17.

Sumiyama, K., Futakuchi, T., Kamba, S., Matsui, H., Tamai, N., 2021. Artificial intelligence in endoscopy: present and future perspectives. Dig. Endosc. 33, 218–230.

Sun, R., Limkin, E.J., Vakalopoulou, M., et al., 2018. A radiomics approach to assess tumour-infiltrating CD8 cells and response to anti-PD-1 or anti-PD-L1 immunotherapy: an imaging biomarker, retrospective multicohort study. Lancet Oncol. 19, 1180–1191.

Suzuki, K., 2014. Pixel-based machine learning in computer-aided diagnosis of lung and colon cancer. In: Machine Learning in Healthcare Informatics. Springer, pp. 81–112.

Tamborero, D., Rubio-Perez, C., Deu-Pons, J., et al., 2018. Cancer genome interpreter annotates the biological and clinical relevance of tumor alterations. Genome Med. 10, 25.

Tian, Y., Liu, X., Wang, Z., et al., 2020. Concordance between Watson for oncology and a multidisciplinary clinical decision-making team for gastric cancer and the prognostic implications: retrospective study. J. Med. Internet Res. 22, e14122.

Tong, Z., Zhou, Y., Wang, J., 2019. Identifying potential drug targets in hepatocellular carcinoma based on network analysis and one-class support vector machine. Sci. Rep. 9, 10442.

Wu, L., Zhou, W., Wan, X., et al., 2019. A deep neural network improves endoscopic detection of early gastric cancer without blind spots. Endoscopy 51, 522–531.

Yamada, M., Saito, Y., Imaoka, H., et al., 2019. Development of a real-time endoscopic image diagnosis support system using deep learning technology in colonoscopy. Sci. Rep. 9, 14465.

Yang, W., Soares, J., Greninger, P., et al., 2013. Genomics of drug sensitivity in cancer (GDSC): a resource for therapeutic biomarker discovery in cancer cells. Nucleic Acids Res. 41, D955–D961.

You, J., Liu, B., Ying, R., Pande, V., Leskovec, J., 2018. Graph Convolutional Policy Network for Goal-Directed Molecular Graph Generation., https://doi.org/10.48550/arXiv.1806.02473.

Zhao, T., Hu, Y., Valsdottir, L.R., Zang, T., Peng, J., 2021. Identifying drug-target interactions based on graph convolutional network and deep neural network. Brief. Bioinform. 22, 2141–2150.

CHAPTER SIX

Addressing the diagnosis and therapeutics of malignant tumor cells

Anjoy Majhi[a], Sandip Paul[a,b], and Pinki Saha Sardar[b]
[a]Department of Chemistry, Presidency College, Kolkata, India
[b]Department of Chemistry, Bhawanipur Education Society, Kolkata, India

1. Introduction

"Cancer" is the widespread term in the Medical Sciences and is a condition that occurs when biological alterations promote unregulated growth and division of cell. Some cancers promote rapid cell proliferation, while others cause cells to divide and develop more slowly. Certain types of cancers result the visible growths called tumors, while others like leukemia do not. The majority of the cells in the body have distinct functions and span. While cell death may appear to be a negative phenomenon, it is actually a natural and helpful process known as apoptosis. A cell receives the commands to die so that the body can replace it with a better-functioning cell. Cancerous cells are missing the components that command them to cease proliferating and die. Cancerous cells may emerge in one location and then move to other parts of the body via lymph nodes. These are clumps of immunological cells that can be found all over the body. Cancerous cells can create tumors, immune system impairment, and other alterations those prohibit the body from operating normally.

Over the last few decades, a plenty of information on the molecular action has emerged on cancer in human cells. Cancer may cause the death of about a quarter of the people in the developed world. The uncontrolled growth of aberrant cells, which is the precursor to cancer, may be treated more efficiently in order to early detection of malignant cancer cells. Typically, cancer is treated as a worldwide disease, and tumors are viewed as a collection of cells. As a result, a thorough knowledge about the functional activity of the cells is essential for developing accurate and effective treatments. Tumors become extremely heterogeneous as the transmission cancer cells, resulting in a mixed population of cells with a variety of biological characteristics and therapeutic responses. This variability may be seen at both the spatial and temporal level, and the significant element in the establishment of resistance phenotypes is aided by a selection pressure applied during drug administration (Jack and Shaw, 2018). Numerous anticancer targets

Biomarkers in Cancer Detection and Monitoring of Therapeutics
https://doi.org/10.1016/B978-0-323-95116-6.00010-4

have emerged as a result of better understanding of signaling networks that regulate cellular growth, cell cycle, and programmed cell death. Cancer could be able to demonstrate that how the convergence of different fields of investigation can lead to big breakthroughs.

Many cancer patients are diagnosed by emergency appearance, which is linked to poorer clinical and patient-reported outcomes than individuals who are diagnosed voluntarily or through screening. Reducing the proportion of cancer patients classified as emergencies is thus desirable; yet, the best way to achieve this goal is unknown due to the interaction of several tumor, patient, and health-care factors, often in combination. The majority of cancer patients are diagnosed after the onset of symptoms, and many of them go to emergency with life-threatening symptoms of their undiagnosed malignancy (Bottle et al., 2012). Patients who are diagnosed with cancer after an emergency appearance had worse clinical and patient-reported outcomes than those who are diagnosed with cancer after a nonemergency appearance or through a screening program. The utilization of curative treatments is less common, there are well-established correlations between emergency appearance and poor survival, and patients have a worse quality of life and experience than those diagnosed with cancer through other channels. Evidence from patients with a variety of common and uncommon solid tumors, such as colorectal, esophageal, and lung cancers, shows that individuals who present as an emergency are less likely to be treated with a curative purpose than patients who are discovered by elective means (McArdle and Hole, 2004). After controlling for socio demographic and tumor-specific characteristics, most importantly, the cancer stage at diagnosis, the link remains (Palser et al., 2013). Part of this link can be explained by differences in tumor stage at diagnosis; nevertheless, even after adjusting for tumor stage at diagnosis, emergency appearance continue to be independently predictive of poorer survival than elective presentations (Comber et al., 2016). Patients' outcomes are anticipated to improve if the number of patients identified with cancer through emergency appearance is reduced. However, progress toward reaching this goal is difficult due to the complicated pathways that contribute to such measures, which frequently involve tumor-related, patient-related, and health-care-related aspects in combination.

Nanomedicine provides a broad range of biocompatible and biodegradable systems that can administer traditional chemotherapeutic medicines in vivo, enhancing bioavailability and concentration near tumor tissues while also improving release profile (Martinelli et al., 2019). Nanoparticles can be used for a variety of purposes, from diagnostic to therapy (Martinelli et al., 2019). Extracellular vesicles (EVs), which are involved in cancer formation, microenvironment change, and metastatic progression, have recently been studied as effective drug delivery vehicles (Kumar et al., 2016). Due to the antiproliferative and proapoptotic qualities, natural antioxidants and a variety of phytochemicals have lately been offered as anticancer adjuvant therapy (Chikara et al., 2018). Targeted therapy is a type of cancer treatment that focuses on a single place, such as tumor vasculature or intracellular organelles, while leaving the rest of the body unharmed. This greatly improves the treatment's specificity, lowering its disadvantages (Bazak et al., 2015). There are so many process of cancer therapeutics and all these tactics, when combined, will be able to deliver the finest individualized therapies for cancer patients, emphasizing the importance of merging several disciplines to achieve the greatest results.

2. Tumor-related factors; tumor stage at diagnosis

Tumor stage at diagnosis is a function of both tumor biology (defined as the tumor's intrinsic malignant potential during oncogenesis) and tumor development throughout time (and, consequently, an indirect function of time to diagnosis). Cancer patients who were diagnosed as an emergency are more likely to have advanced-stage malignancies at the time of diagnosis, according to several reports. According to a report on the routes to diagnosis of 10 different types of cancer in England from 2012 to 2013, 30% of patients who appeared with cancer as an emergency were later diagnosed with stage IV cancers, compared to 17% and 14% of those diagnosed through a fast-track ("2-week wait") and nonurgent ("non-2-week wait") referral, respectively (National Cancer Intelligence Network, 2016). According to the same source (National Cancer Intelligence Network, 2016), the proportion of patients who appeared with cancer as an emergency and were diagnosed with stage IV disease varies significantly among the 10 cancers studied, ranging from 18% and 20% for melanoma and prostate cancer, respectively, to 44% and 45% for lung and ovarian cancer, respectively.

3. Tumor subtype and location

The majority of the information on how tumor location and subtype are linked to emergency appearance comes from a few common cancers such as colorectal, lung, breast, and gastric cancers. Patients with malignancies of the brain or central nervous system, pancreatic, lung, stomach, cancer of unclear source, acute leukemia, or multiple myeloma frequently report frequencies of >30%. On the other hand, 10% of all patients with melanoma, breast, and oropharyngeal, oral, uterine, testicular, or prostate cancer present as an emergency. These large differences in the proportions of patients classified as emergency point to a link between the "symptom signature" (or diagnostic difficulties) of certain malignancies and the reported proportions of patients diagnosed as emergencies (Hamilton, 2012). Cancers in which the majority of patients present with visible or palpable signs or symptoms (such as melanoma and breast cancer) have a low proportion of emergency appearance, whereas cancers in which the majority of patients present with nonspecific symptoms have a high proportion of emergency appearance (such as pancreatic cancer or multiple myeloma, when stomach or musculoskeletal pain are the most common symptoms). The availability and scope of primary-care testing for other malignancies, as well as the fact that some tumors show few symptoms before a dramatic event leading to the emergency appearance (as an initial indication of certain types of brain cancer, such as seizure), are critical considerations (such as leukemia, which is frequently identified following a complete blood count). Aside from general differences in the frequency of cancer diagnosis as an emergency by major organ site, differences in the incidences of emergency presentation by tumor location or subtype have also been described for a small number of cancers, such as colorectal, colon, gastroesophageal, and rectal cancers, as well as acute and chronic types of leukemia.

In general, the findings show that patients diagnosed with cancer as an emergency are more likely to have aggressive tumor subtypes. Patients with high-grade colorectal malignancies (poorly differentiated, undifferentiated, or anaplastic) were found to present as an emergency at a higher rate than those with low-grade (well-differentiated or moderately well-differentiated) colorectal cancers.

4. Prior consultations and usage of health-care services

Estimation of the potential for preventing the detection of cancer as an emergency situation, consistent with our previous theoretical framing, needs consideration of whether or not patients had previously presented, and if so, what symptoms they presented with. According to data from a major data source in England, almost 30% of emergency appearances are caused by primary-care physicians referring patients directly to hospital services (National Cancer Intelligence Network, 2013). Similarly, research from three small primary-care studies suggests that up to 20% of cancer patients who visit their general practitioner are referred as an emergency (Barrett and Hamilton, 2008). An investigation plan and/or referral has been created for some patients, but an emergency situation occurs during the time between the referral and the scheduled investigation or specialist assessment. The majority of individuals who have cancer as an emergency had consultations within the preceding 12 months of diagnosis. This percentage is comparable to or somewhat lower than that of patients who were diagnosed with cancer voluntarily (Sheringham et al., 2014). Another study compared for emergency and nonemergency cases with cancer of the colon or rectal tract found that between 30 days and 12 months before diagnosis, 97% of both emergency and nonemergency cases had past consultations for any reason (Renzi et al., 2016). However, only around half of all such visits were for relevant symptoms among individuals who presented as an emergency, but the proportion for nonemergency presenters was much higher (Renzi et al., 2016). Prior consultations can reduce the probability of a diagnosis of cancer as an emergency in individuals compared to that of later diagnosed with cancer, as seen in patients with colorectal cancer who had at least one before primary care visit in the 2–12 months prior to diagnosis against those who did not (Sikka, 2010).

5. Preceding symptomatic presentations

Identifying symptoms linked to a higher probability of a subsequent cancer diagnosis as an emergency may aid in the identification of patient groups for whom emergency appearance could be avoided. Evidence of earlier symptoms has only been found in patients who have been observed in either primary or secondary care, despite the fact that a significant number of emergency cases may have sought no help from any health-care practitioner prior to their emergency diagnosis. To avoid confounding of prior probable cancer symptoms with those directly generating the emergency presenting measure, data on earlier symptoms should be excluded from the period immediately preceding the emergency appearance.

The majority of the current empirical evidence of links between past symptoms and diagnosis as an emergency situation concerns patients with colorectal cancer. Patients with colorectal cancers who have been identified via emergency shows are much more likely than the ones identified electively to have formerly visible their medical doctor with stomach ache or to have had constipation or weight loss (Sheringham et al., 2014). Emergency appearance, are less likely to have sought medical advice due to rectal bleeding, gastrointestinal changes, or anemia (Sheringham et al., 2014; Renzi et al., 2016). There is some evidence, however it is confined to colorectal cancer patients (primarily treated at a single center), that patients who present with symptoms that have a lower cancer predictive value are more likely to be identified as emergencies (Sheringham et al., 2014; Renzi et al., 2016). Results, lowering the referral threshold for suspected cancer may reduce the number of emergency cases, but it will also result in a higher proportion of individuals without cancer being referred. The patients with malignancies other than colon or rectal cancer, evidence on the clinical consequences of prior symptoms is essential, as well as a clear distinction between earlier symptoms and those that precipitate the emergency appearance measures.

6. Health-care factors

The majority of cancer patients are initially treated by nonspecialist doctors. Examining the efficacy of primary-care institutions (quantitative research analyzing practice-level features and emergency appearance, for example, or qualitative studies involving analysis of important aspect), as well as the implications of various screening criteria and degrees of compliance, can reveal possibly reversible aspects that contribute to cancer emergency diagnoses. The majority of the evidence is based on studies that looked at relationships between general practice characteristics (activity or performance) and cancer emergency diagnosis.

7. Patient factors

Part of the link between sociodemographic patient characteristics and the chance of appearance of the emergency cancer could be due to disease-related factors including age, tumor kind, or anatomical differences between men and women. However, some of these disparities could be due to sociocultural influences on patients' help-seeking behaviors or health-care disparities. Understanding how overall sociodemographic inequalities differ for different cancers may reveal the potential mechanisms behind such behavioral differences; an understanding of these inequalities is thus particularly useful in efforts to design targeted interventions with the goal of reducing the frequency of cancer diagnosis as an emergency presentation.

8. Age of the patient

Patients with most cancers at both excessive of the age spectrum (the youngest and oldest patients) are much more likely than the middle of the age spectrum to be recognized as emergencies. In general, older age is linked to a higher likelihood of a cancer emergency diagnosis, with this risk being especially significant in people over the age of 80 (Sheringham et al., 2014; Renzi et al., 2016). Patients over the age of 85 in England, for example, are 2.5 times more likely than those aged 65–74 to arrive as an emergency for all gender specific malignancies (Abel et al., 2015). Similarly, people with colorectal cancer who are 90 years old have a threefold higher risk of developing the disease than those who are 70 years old (Wallace et al., 2014).

Significant differences in this association by cancer site can be disguised when evaluating the overall influence of a patient's age on the risk of diagnosis of cancer as an emergency across all malignancies. For certain forms of cancer, there is a stronger link between growing (adult) age and an increased likelihood of emergency diagnosis. In case of acute lymphocytic leukemia a negative association is observed between the age and diagnosis of cancer as an emergency exists, i.e., a lowering risk of a diagnosis of cancer as an emergency appearance is observed with increasing the age (Abel et al., 2015). As a result, cancer-age interactions are likely to reflect disease-specific variables.

With the exception of two peer-reviewed studies and two online reports, most investigations evaluating the association between age and cancer diagnosis as an emergency have omitted patients under the age of 25 (Brookes et al., 2012; McPhail et al., 2013). About 54% of all cancer patients aged 0–14 are diagnosed as emergency (Brookes et al., 2012). Patients in-between the age of 0–14 years were more likely to be diagnosed as an emergency than those of aged 15–24 years (54% vs 26%). In case of 0–14-year-old patients leukemias and CNS tumors were the most likely to be diagnosed as an emergency, with 69% and 57% (National Cancer Intelligence Network, 2013). When all cancer sites are evaluated together, differences in the likelihood of emergency appearance by sex are minor compared to differences in age (Abel et al., 2015). In several studies, women were found to have a higher likelihood of receiving a cancer diagnosis as an emergency appearance than men (Renzi et al., 2016; Sikka, 2010; Wallace et al., 2014). A few other studies found no link between sex and the likelihood of a cancer emergency diagnosis (Sheringham et al., 2014; Gunnarsson et al., 2013). The magnitude of sex-related disparities in emergency appearance, varies significantly by cancer. Women with bladder cancer, in particular, have a significantly higher probability of being diagnosed as an emergency disappearance than men with bladder cancer (Abel et al., 2015).

9. Breast cancer

Very little primary care evidence required to guide general physician (GP) in their referrals of women with breast complaints for such an important and emotive malignancy. Breast signs and symptoms account for nearly 3% of woman consultations in primary care. Breast soreness and masses are the most commonly reported complaints, with the 25- to 44-age range being the most affected (Eberl et al., 2008). Nipple discharge or alterations in the skin of the breast are far less common (Newton et al., 1999). In general, 8% of women who report a breast lump to primary care are later diagnosed with cancer. As one might assume, this figure is greatly dependent on age, with the incidence of breast cancer 15 times higher in women aged 45–64 than in those under 25 (Eberl et al., 2008). Thus, a breast lump has an estimated risk of cancer of 0.5% in people under the age of 25, assuming the probability ratios are identical across all ages, which is usually the case in cancer diagnostic investigations (Hamilton et al., 2009a). Only about 2% of women with nipple problems have cancer. Indeed, because such a small percentage of women with this symptom have an underlying cancer, it is unclear that nipple bleeding (which usually shows duct ectasia) warrants such prominence in referral guidelines. Breast pain, on the other hand, is a symptom that has a very minimal risk. GPs must rely on their clinical skills to spot worrisome lumps in younger women, yet many women will be referred as the only way to provide enough reassurance. Inflammatory breast cancer is more common in younger women (which accounts for around 5% of all breast cancers). The main symptoms are breast swelling, redness, and warmth, as the name implies.

10. Lung cancer

When a person is diagnosed with lung cancer, they often become nihilistic, even fatalistic. The analysis is normally poor, and plenty of humans query how a lot is to be received from early diagnosis. Some patients may share this nihilism, which stems from shame over a self-inflicted condition (Corner et al., 2006). By the time of symptoms are recognized, the cancer has progressed to the point where therapy is no longer possible. Furthermore, lung cancer symptoms are typically nonspecific, it might be difficult to determine that cancer is the cause, even if the patient appears early (Weller and Campbell, 2006). Due to these characteristics, only 20% of UK lung cancer patients are suitable for surgical resection; only 17% of those who undergo surgery actually do so, and only half of those who do survive for 5 years (Read et al., 2006; Devbhandari et al., 2007).

Sputum cytology, which has a low sensitivity, and conventional chest X-ray screening are both ineffective. The UK Lung-SEARCH experiment is currently investigating annual cytology in smokers with chronic obstructive lung disease, supplemented with computer-assisted image analysis (Hamilton, 2010). As the symptoms can go unnoticed for a long time before being reported to a doctor, attempts have been undertaken to raise symptom awareness and, as a result, earlier presentation (Hamilton, 2010). Although audits imply a moderate effect in terms of early staging with an associated rise in respectability, such programs are difficult to research. Patients in Doncaster, UK, were encouraged to report coughs to their doctors as part of a campaign, and following this effort, the percentage of malignancies discovered in stages I or II increased from 11% to 19% (Hamilton, 2010).

Lung cancer is easier to diagnose than most other cancers in one way: the principal diagnostic (a chest X-ray) is widely available, moderately inexpensive, and very accurate. Approximately one out of every five chest X-rays required by primary care is for the study of probable lung cancer (Hamilton, 2010).

11. Prostate cancer

There is some skepticism about the value of early detection of prostate cancer, similar to that of lung cancer, but from a different perspective. To put it bluntly, early detection of lung cancer is pointless because the patient will die anyway; early detection of prostate cancer is pointless because the patient will survive anyway. Prostate cancer nihilism is largely due to screening trials. Recent research on prostate cancer screening have found no indication of a mortality advantage (Schroder et al., 2009). Treatment of tiny malignancies results in a slight increase in mortality, but at the expense of potential problems such as incontinence (Hamilton, 2010). Larger tumors and sickness that has spread, are treated with far less controversy (Syrigos, 2001). The larger the tumor, the more probable it is to cause symptoms. For primary care, this simplifies the clinical dilemma. Given the benefits of treating symptomatic prostate cancer, it is reasonable to suspect prostate cancer when a man exhibits symptoms of the lower urinary tract. On the other hand Lower urinary tract symptoms, imply that the prostate gland is enlarging, but they don't indicate whether it's benign or cancerous (Hamilton et al., 2006). The majority of typical lower urinary tract symptoms have roughly a 3% positive predictive value for prostate cancer (Hamilton et al., 2006). Thus, rectal examination and testing of prostate specific antigen (PSA) should be part of clinical therapy for males with lower urinary tract symptoms (Issa et al., 2006). Urologists may select patients for biopsy based on the rate at which PSA rises or the level of free PSA (Hamilton, 2010).

12. Ovarian cancer

A number of primary care studies have lately shed light on this challenging cancer. It's now obvious that the label "silent killer" is incorrect. Symptoms are common, according to all primary care studies, and are frequently reported to doctors. It's a "noisy killer," to put it that way. The issue is that the noise is generic, with initial symptoms including weariness, stomach pain, and urine frequency (Hamilton, 2010). Even though it is not included in current guidelines, abdominal distension has a rather significant risk of cancer, with a positive predictive value of 2.5% (Hamilton et al., 2009b). One issue appears to be that doctors, understandably, either don't think about ovarian cancer when patients present with such symptoms or believe it is so unlikely that no examination or investigation is necessary. Therefore, ovarian cancer is commonly overlooked by general practitioners. In reality, general practitioners are probably no worse (or no better) in diagnosing ovarian cancer than they are at diagnosing any other internal malignancy (Hamilton, 2010). Ultrasound, preferably trans-vaginally, is a better test for diagnosis of ovarian cancer (Hamilton, 2010). This has been well examined in screening studies and has shown to be effective.

13. Other cancers

Due to the relative rarity, few additional malignancies have been studied in primary care. As a result, referral decisions must be made based on the GP's experience, which must be combined with intuition, with intuition being the most essential factor. Only a few studies have been conducted, however they mostly support current therapeutic practice. The risk of esophageal cancer with dysphagia is 5.7% in males and 2.4% in women, while the risk of urinary tract malignancy with hematuria is 7.4% and 3.4%, respectively, indicating that further research is necessary (Jones et al., 2007). Similarly, general practitioners appear to be adept at determining which patients with enlarged cervical lymph nodes have cancer and which do not (Allhiser et al., 1981). In general, only around 2% of cervical lymphadenopathy seen in primary care is cancerous (Fijten and Blijham, 1988). The likelihood of a brain tumor occurring in conjunction with a headache is 1 in 1000, bolstering the argument that screening people with usual headache is unnecessary (Hamilton and Kernick, 2007).

14. Biomarkers; imaging technique

Individuals who are most likely to benefit from molecularly focused therapy require molecular diagnostics. Target inhibition proof of concept and dosage schedule optimization will both required for molecular biomarkers (Workman, 2003). Biomarkers are employed in scientific studies to make them more intelligent and informative, as well as to make decision-making more reasonable and effective (Sawyers, 2003).

Due to the good solubility, high specificity, simple manufacturing process, and high fluorescence intensity, fluorescent probes are exceptionally capable of demonstrating bio-sensing and bioimaging (Paul et al., 2017, 2019). Therefore, the direct viewing and dynamic information provided by the process, studies on the design, synthesis, and development of fluorescent probes are currently have drawn an attraction of a lot of interest in biological and clinical research (Paul et al., 2017, 2019). Fluorescent probes can attach to a specific receptor in a cell, causing a significant shift in the wavelength of the produced light as well as the fluorescence intensity.

In the last two decades, fluorescence imaging has received a lot of attention for its ability to detect a wide range of cancerous cells. With the use of high-resolution, high-contrast images, the fluorescence imaging approach offers clinicians a better way to diagnose and treat cancer patients. In the field of healthcare, molecular imaging plays a vital role in making accurate diagnoses of disorders inside the body. The numerous types of imaging techniques to consider for current study include magnetic resonance imaging (MRI), ultrasound, tomography, gamma scintigraphy, optical imaging, and so on (Jenkins et al., 2016).

15. Nanomedicine

Nanoparticles having 1 to 1000 nm in size, which is very small system with unusual physicochemical features due to their small size and high surface-to-volume ratio (Tinkle et al., 2014). In cancer medicine, biocompatible nanoparticles are utilized to address some of the drawbacks of traditional therapies, such as low specificity and bioavailability of medicines or contrast agents (Martinelli et al., 2019). Therefore, encapsulating active drugs in nanoparticles will improve their solubility/biocompatibility, stability in body fluids, and tumor vasculature retention time (Gerlowski and Jain, 1986). Nanoparticles can also be made to be highly selective for a certain target and to respond to a specific stimuli in order to release the medicine in a regulated manner (Shi et al., 2017; Sinha, 2006).

Inorganic nanoparticles are frequently utilized as diagnostic contrast agents. Quantum dots are minuscule light-emitting semiconductor nanocrystals with unique electrical and optical properties that make them extremely luminous, photobleach resistant, and sensitive for detection and imaging (Matea et al., 2017). They have potential for theranostic uses when combined with active substances (Matea et al., 2017). Because of their interaction with magnetic fields, superparamagnetic iron oxide nanoparticles (SPIONs) are commonly used as contrast agents in magnetic resonance imaging (MRI) (Leiner et al., 2005). Magnetic hyperthermia has also been researched with SPIONs, and a formulation of iron oxide coated with aminosilane known as Nanotherm has previously been certified for the treatment of glioblastoma (Sanchez et al., 2011). The visual and electrical features of gold nanoparticles, as well as their low toxicity, have piqued curiosity (Sun et al., 2014). The Food and Drug Administration (FDA) approved a nanoshell comprised of a silica core and a gold shell coated with PEG (polyethylene glycol) in 2012, and it was commercialized as Auro Shell (Nanospectra) for the treatment of breast cancer using photodynamic therapy (Kim and Jeong, 2017). Organic nanoparticles are mostly utilized as medication delivery vehicles. Phospholipids are found in both liposomes and micelles, but their morphology differs. Liposomes are spherical particles with at least one lipid bilayer that have a structure similar to cell membranes. They're most commonly utilized to encapsulate hydrophilic pharmaceuticals in their aqueous cores, but hydrophobic medications can also be encapsulated in the bilayer or chemically bonded to the particles. Micelles, on the other hand, have a hydrophobic core that allows them to encapsulate hydrophobic medicines (Narang et al., 2007).

16. Extracellular vesicles (EV) for cancer diagnosis and therapy

Based on their biogenesis, EVs are divided into two groups. Exosomes are small vesicles with a typical size of 50–1300 nm that originate from endosomes in physiological and pathological conditions and are released by a fusion of multivesicular bodies (MVBs) to the cell membrane, whereas shed microvesicles (sMVs) are small vesicles with a typical size of 50–1300 nm that are found in almost any extracellular bodily fluid and are responsible for the exchange of molecular materials between cells (Vlassov et al., 2012; Witwer et al., 2013). Exosomes have a role in cancer formation and dissemination, bidirectional communication between tumor cells and surrounding tissues, and the creation of the milieu required for the establishment of a premetastatic niche and metastatic progression (Suetsugu et al., 2013; Raimondo et al., 2015). As a result, circulating vesicles are important in the diagnosis, prognosis, and follow-up of cancer patients. Exosomes are used as diagnostic tools, but they can also be extracted and used as anticancer vaccinations or nanoscale medication carriers in cancer treatment. One of the most pressing concerns in cancer diagnosis nowadays is the early detection of biomarkers using noninvasive approaches. Obtaining a large amount of data before and throughout tumor therapy should enable cancer progression and therapeutic regimen efficacy to be monitored. Indicators for personalized therapy have included liquid biopsies to detect circulating tumor cells, RNAs, DNAs, and exosomes (Siravegna et al., 2017). Many challenges surrounding exosome clinical translation remain unresolved, the majority of which are related to the development of preclinical methodologies for exosome separation, quantification, storage, and standard drug loading protocols. To characterize their postisolation half-life and perform conventional content studies, it is becoming increasingly important to discriminate between cancer and healthy blood cell–derived vesicles.

17. Natural antioxidants in cancer therapy

Every day, the human body is subjected to a variety of exogenous insults, including ultraviolet (UV) rays, air pollution, and tobacco smoke, all of which result in the production of reactive species, particularly oxidants and free radicals, which are responsible for the onset of a variety of diseases, including cancer. These molecules can be created in the clinic as a result of drug treatment, but they can also be produced spontaneously inside our cells and tissues during normal physiological aerobic activities by mitochondria, peroxisomes, and macrophage metabolism. Our bodies' preventive capabilities against these chemicals are sometimes insufficient to counteract the massive damage they cause. Despite the benefits of employing natural medications, their practical implementation is problematic due to their low bioavailability and/or toxicity.

Curcumin is a polyphenolic molecule isolated from turmeric (*Curcuma longa*) that has antiinflammatory, antioxidant, chemopreventive, and therapeutic properties (Kocaadam and Şanlier, 2017). At effective therapeutic levels, it has been demonstrated to have cytotoxic effects in a variety of tumors, including brain, lung, leukemia, pancreatic, and hepatocellular carcinoma, with no deleterious effects in normal cells (Pucci et al., 2019). Berberine is an alkaloid found in a variety of plants, including Berberis. It has recently been shown to be effective against a variety of tumors and to act as a chemopreventive drug by altering a variety of signaling pathways (Pucci et al., 2019). Because it is poorly soluble in water, like curcumin, a variety of nanotechnological approaches have been developed to assist it cross cell membranes (Pucci et al., 2019). By attaching to cellular receptors and interfering with a range of signaling pathways, quercetin, polyphenolic flavonoid found in fruits and vegetables, has been demonstrated to be effective in the treatment of a variety of tumors, including lung, prostate, liver, colon, and breast cancers (Pucci et al., 2019). It has been proven to be efficacious in the presence of chemotherapeutic drugs (Pucci et al., 2019).

18. Targeted therapy and immunotherapy

The low specificity of chemotherapeutic medicines for cancer cells is one of the key difficulties of conventional cancer therapy. In fact, most medications have severe side effects because they act on both healthy and sick organs. Researchers are working hard to figure out how to target only the targeted site. Due to the increased permeability and retention impact, nanoparticles have sparked a lot of attention because of their tendency to accumulate more in tumor tissues. The small size of nanoparticles, as well as the leaky vasculature and poor lymphatic drainage of neoplastic tissues, are used in this passive targeting method (Bazak et al., 2015). Passive targeting, is difficult to manage and can result in multidrug resistance (MDR) (Barua and Mitragotri, 2014). Active targeting, enhances tumor cell uptake by focusing on overexpressed receptors on the cells. Nanoparticles can be functionalized with ligands that have a high degree of selectivity in binding to certain cells or subcellular sites (Bazak et al., 2015). To combat ovarian and endometrial malignancies, many nanocarriers have been functionalized with folic acid (Senol et al., 2015). Small peptides and proteins of various types are also efficient in active targeting. Angiopep-2 is a peptide that has sparked a lot of interest for its potential use in the treatment of brain cancer (Demeule et al., 2008). The gastrin-releasing peptide receptor, which is overexpressed on the cell surface of prostate, breast, ovarian, pancreatic, and colorectal cancer cells, was targeted by the bombesin peptide attached to poly(lactic-co-glycolic acid) (PLGA) nanoparticles loaded with docetaxel (Kulhari et al., 2014).

In recent times antibodies are the most commonly used active targeting ligands. When attached to a medication or nanoparticle, antibodies can be employed as immunoconjugates, or they can be used naked also. The main purpose is to target a specific antigen that is overexpressed in cancer cells. Antibodies that bind to the human epidermal growth factor receptor 2 (HER2), the epidermal growth factor receptor (EGFR), the transferrin receptor (TfR), and the prostate-specific membrane antigen (PSMA) are utilized for this purpose (Bazak et al., 2015). Rapamycin-PLGA nanoparticles coupled to EGFR antibody showed increased cellular uptake and apoptotic activity in human breast cancer cells (MCF-7) (Acharya et al., 2009).

Adoptive cell transfer (ACT) is a method of immunotherapy that involves collecting T-lymphocytes (T-cells) with the strongest anticancer activity straight from the patient's blood, growing them ex vivo, and reinfusing them back into the patient (Rosenberg et al., 2008). In vitro, autologous T-cells can be genetically modified to express a chimeric antigen receptor (CAR), making them more selective toward antigens found on cancer cells (McCune, 2018). Different CARs can be engineered to target certain tumor antigens. Despite these encouraging findings, substantial work is still being done to better understand the long-term consequences of CAR T-cell therapy and their fate within tumors, as well as to improve CAR T-cell expansion methods.

19. Gene therapy for cancer treatment

Gene therapy entails inserting a healthy copy of a faulty gene into the genome in order to treat a specific condition. A retroviral vector was used to transfer the adenosine deaminase (ADA) gene to T cells in patients with severe combined immunodeficiency for the first time in 1990 (Rosenberg et al., 1990). Further study revealed that gene therapy might be used to cure a variety of human uncommon and chronic diseases, as well as, most significantly, cancer. One strategy involved delivering the thymidine kinase (TK) gene, then administering the prodrug ganciclovir to trigger its expression and induce particular cytotoxicity (Freeman et al., 1993). In recent decades, many vectors encoding the p53 tumor suppressor gene have been tried for clinical uses. In head and neck squamous cell cancer, Gendicine, a recombinant adenovirus containing wild-type p53, had a comparable outcome, producing total disease regression when paired with radiation (Raty et al., 2010). Despite significant advances, there are still certain hurdles to overcome when it comes to gene therapy, such as determining the appropriate settings for optimal expression levels and selecting the best delivery mechanism to unambiguously target cancer cells. Gene therapy has a number of limitations, including genomic integration, limited efficacy in some patient subgroups, and a significant risk of being neutralized by the immune system (Pucci et al., 2019).

20. Conclusion

Cancer is most commonly diagnosed, or at least suspected, in primary care. It's also where the majority of presymptomatic risk assessment happens, such as compiling a family history and paying attention to modifiable risk factors like smoking or obesity. The impact of tumor-related, patient-related, and healthcare-related factors has all been investigated; however, more research is needed to determine the exact contributions of these factors and the mechanisms that can be targeted by interventions to reduce the proportion of cancer patients diagnosed as emergencies. Almost every day in clinical practice, cancer is mentioned as a possibility. In recent years, cancer research has made significant progress toward more effective, precise, and less intrusive cancer treatments. Nano-medicine combined with targeted therapy improves the bio-distribution of new or already tested chemotherapeutic medicines around the specific tissue to be treated, additional strategies like gene therapy, immunotherapy, and others provide cancer patients with new options. The uncontrolled growth of aberrant cells, which is a precursor to cancer, may be more effectively treated in order to detect malignant cancer cells earlier. Tumors are considered as a collection of cells, and cancer is treated as a single, global disease. Almost every day in clinical practice, cancer is mentioned as a possibility. Cancer research has made great progress in recent years toward more effective, accurate, and minimally invasive cancer treatments. Now a day, the percentage of survival from cancer increased much. There are numerous cancer treatment processes, and when all of them are integrated, they can provide the best customized therapy for cancer patients, highlighting the need of combining several disciplines to produce the best results.

Acknowledgment

Authors acknowledge Science and Engineering Research Board (SERB), New Delhi, for research grant ref. no. EEQ/2019/000194. Authors are also extremely appreciative to Presidency University, Kolkata, India, for providing laboratory facilities.

References

Abel, G., Shelton, J., Johnson, S., Brookes, L.E., Lyratzopoulos, G., 2015. Cancer-specific variation in emergency presentation by sex, age and deprivation across 27 common and rarer cancers. Br. J. Cancer 112, S129–S136.

Acharya, S., Dilnawaz, F., Sahoo, S.K., 2009. Targeted epidermal growth factor receptor nanoparticle bioconjugates for breast cancer therapy. Biomaterials 30 (29), 5737–5750.

Allhiser, J.N., McKnight, T.A., Shank, J.C., 1981. Lymphadenopathy in a family practice. J. Fam. Pract. 12, 27–32.

Barrett, J., Hamilton, W., 2008. Pathways to the diagnosis of lung cancer in the UK: a cohort study. BMC Fam. Pract. 9, 31. https://doi.org/10.1186/1471-2296-9-31.

Barua, S., Mitragotri, S., 2014. Challenges associated with penetration of nanoparticles across cell and tissue barriers: a review of current status and future prospects. Nano Today 9 (2), 223–243.

Bazak, R., Houri, M., Achy, S.E., Kamel, S., Refaat, T., 2015. Cancer active targeting by nanoparticles: a comprehensive review of literature. J. Cancer Res. Clin. Oncol. 141 (5), 769–784.

Bottle, A., Tsang, C., Parsons, C., Majeed, A., Soljak, M., Aylin, P., 2012. Association between patient and general practice characteristics and unplanned first-time admissions for cancer: observational study. Br. J. Cancer 107, 1213–1219.

Brookes, L.E., McPhail, S., Ives, A., Greenslade, M., Shelton, J., Hiom, S., Richards, M., 2012. Routes to diagnosis for cancer– determining the patient journey using multiple routine data sets. Br. J. Cancer 107, 1220–1226.

Chikara, S., Nagaprashantha, L.D., Singhal, J., Horne, D., Awasthi, S., Singhal, S.S., 2018. Oxidative stress and dietary phytochemicals: role in cancer chemoprevention and treatment. Cancer Lett. 413, 122–134.

Comber, H., Sharp, L., Cancela, M.C., Haase, T., Johnson, H., Pratschke, J., 2016. Causes and outcomes of emergency presentation of rectal cancer. Int. J. Cancer 139, 1031–1039.

Corner, J., Hopkinson, J., Roffe, L., 2006. Experience of health changes and reasons for delay in seeking care: a UK study of the months prior to the diagnosis of lung cancer. Soc. Sci. Med. 62, 1381–1391.

Demeule, M., Currie, J.C., Bertrand, Y., Ché, C., Nguyen, T., Régina, A., Gabathuler, R., Castaigne, J.P., Béliveau, R., 2008. Involvement of the low-density lipoprotein receptor-related protein in the transcytosis of the brain delivery vector Angiopep-2. J. Neurochem. 106 (4), 1534–1544.

Devbhandari, M.P., Yang, S.S., Quennell, P., Krysiak, P., Shah, R., Jones, M.T., 2007. Lung cancer resection rate in south Manchester: is it comparable to international standards? Results of a prospective tracking study. Interact. Cardiovasc. Thorac. Surg. 6, 712–714.

Eberl, M.M., Phillips, R.L., Lamberts, H., Okkes, I., Mahoney, M.C., 2008. Characterizing breast symptoms in family practice. Ann. Fam. Med. 6, 528–533.

Fijten, G.H., Blijham, G.H., 1988. Unexplained lymphadenopathy in family practice. An evaluation of the probability of malignant causes and the effectiveness of physicians' workup. J. Fam. Pract. 27, 373–376.

Freeman, S.M., Abboud, C., Whartenby, K.A., Packman, C.H., Koeplin, D.S., Moolten, F.L., Abraham, G.N., 1993. The "bystander effect": tumor regression when a fraction of the tumor mass is genetically modified. Cancer Res. 53 (21), 5274–5283.

Gerlowski, L.E., Jain, R.K., 1986. Microvascular permeability of normal and neoplastic tissues. Microvasc. Res. 31 (3), 288–305.

Gunnarsson, H., Ekholm, A., Olsson, L.I., 2013. Emergency presentation and socioeconomic status in colon cancer. Eur. J. Surg. Oncol. 39, 831–836.

Hamilton, W., 2010. Cancer diagnosis in primary care. Br. J. Gen. Pract. 60, 121–128.

Hamilton, W., 2012. Emergency admissions of cancer as a marker of diagnostic delay. Br. J. Cancer 107, 1205–1206.

Hamilton, W., Kernick, D., 2007. Clinical features of primary brain tumours: a case-control study using electronic primary care records. Br. J. Gen. Pract. 57, 695–699.

Hamilton, W., Sharp, D., Peters, T.J., Round, A., 2006. Clinical features of prostate cancer before diagnosis: a population-based case-control study. Br. J. Gen. Pract. 56, 756–782.

Hamilton, W., Lancashire, R., Sharp, D., Peters, T.J., Cheng, K.k., Marshall, T., 2009a. The risk of colorectal cancer with symptoms at different ages and between the sexes: a case-control study. BMC Med. 7, 17. https://doi.org/10.1186/1741-7015-7-17.

Hamilton, W., Peters, T.J., Bankhead, C., Sharp, D., 2009b. Risk of ovarian cancer in women with symptoms in primary care: population based case-control study. BMJ 339, b2719. https://doi.org/10.1136/bmj.b2998.

Issa, M.M., Zasada, W., Ward, K., Hall, J.A., Petros, J.A., Ritenour, C.W.M., Goodman, M., Kleinbaum, D., Mandel, J., Marshall, F.F., 2006. The value of digital rectal examination as a predictor of prostate cancer diagnosis among United States Veterans referred for prostate biopsy. Cancer Detect. Prev. 30, 269–275.

Jack, I.D., Shaw, A.T., 2018. Tumour heterogeneity and resistance to cancer therapies. Nat. Rev. Clin. Oncol. 15 (2), 81–94.

Jenkins, R., Burdette, M.K., Foulger, S.H., 2016. Mini-review: fluorescence imaging in cancer cells using dye-doped nanoparticles. RSC Adv. 6, 65459–65474.

Jones, R., Latinovic, R., Charlton, J., Gulliford, M.C., 2007. Alarm symptoms in early diagnosis of cancer in primary care: cohort study using general practice research database. BMJ 334, 1040. https://doi.org/10.1136/bmj.39171.637106.AE.

Kim, E.M., Jeong, H.J., 2017. Current status and future direction of nanomedicine: focus on advanced biological and medical applications. Nucl. Med. Mol. Imaging 51 (2), 106–117.

Kocaadam, B., Şanlier, N., 2017. Curcumin, an active component of turmeric (Curcuma longa), and its effects on health. Crit. Rev. Food Sci. Nutr. 57 (13), 2889–2895.

Kulhari, H., Pooja, D., Shrivastava, S., Naidu, V.G.M., Sistla, R., 2014. Peptide conjugated polymeric nanoparticles as a carrier for targeted delivery of docetaxel. Colloids Surf. B Biointerfaces 117, 166–173.

Kumar, B., Garcia, M., Murakami, J.L., Chen, C.C., 2016. Exosome-mediated microenvironment dysregulation in leukemia. Biochim. Biophys. Acta 1863 (3), 464–470.

Leiner, T., Gerretsen, S., Botnar, R., Lutgens, E., Cappendijk, V., Kooi, E., Engelshoven, J.V., 2005. Magnetic resonance imaging of atherosclerosis. Eur. Radiol. 15 (6), 1087–1099.

Martinelli, C., Pucci, C., Ciofani, G., 2019. Nanostructured carriers as innovative tools for cancer diagnosis and therapy. APL Bioeng. 3 (1), 011502-1–011502-13.

Matea, C.T., Mocan, T., Tabaran, F., Pop, T., Mosteanu, O., Puia, C., Iancu, C., Mocan, L., 2017. Quantum dots in imaging, drug delivery and sensor applications. Int. J. Nanomedicine 12, 5421–5431.

McArdle, C.S., Hole, D.J., 2004. Emergency presentation of colorectal cancer is associated with poor 5-year survival. Br. J. Surg. 91, 605–609.

McCune, J.S., 2018. Rapid advances in immunotherapy to treat cancer. Clin. Pharmacol. Ther. 103 (4), 540–544.

McPhail, S., Brookes, L.E., Shelton, J., Ives, A., Greenslade, M., Vernon, S., Morris, E.J.A., Richards, M., 2013. Emergency presentation of cancer and short-term mortality. Br. J. Cancer 109, 2027–2034.

Narang, A.S., Delmarre, D., Gao, D., 2007. Stable drug encapsulation in micelles and microemulsions. Int. J. Pharm. 345 (1–2), 9–25.

National Cancer Intelligence Network, 2013. Routes to Diagnosis: Exploring Emergency Presentations. Public Health England.

National Cancer Intelligence Network, 2016. Routes to Diagnosis of Cancer by Stage, 2012–2013. Public Health England.

Newton, P., Hannay, D.R., Laver, R., 1999. The presentation and management of female breast symptoms in general practice in Sheffield. Fam. Pract. 16, 360–365.

Palser, T.R., Cromwell, D.A., Hardwick, R.H., Riley, S.A., Greenaway, K., van der Meulen, J.H.P., 2013. Impact of route to diagnosis on treatment intent and 1-year survival in patients diagnosed with oesophagogastric cancer in England: a prospective cohort study. BMJ Open 3, e002129. https://doi.org/10.1136/bmjopen-2012-002129.

Paul, S., Sepay, N., Sarkar, S., Roy, P., Dasgupta, S., Sardar, P.S., Majhi, A., 2017. Interaction of serum albumins with fluorescent ligand 4-azido coumarin: spectroscopic analysis and molecular docking studies. New J. Chem. 41, 15392–15404.

Paul, S., Roy, P., Sardar, P.S., Majhi, A., 2019. Design, synthesis, and biophysical studies of novel 1,2,3-triazole- based quinoline and coumarin compounds. ACS Omega 4, 7213–7230.

Pucci, C., Martinelli, C., Ciofani, G., 2019. Innovative approaches for cancer treatment: current perspectives and new challenges. Ecancermedicalscience 13, 961. https://doi.org/10.3332/ecancer.2019.961.

Raimondo, S., Saieva, L., Corrado, C., Fontana, S., Flugy, A., Rizzo, A., Leo, G.D., Alessandro, R., 2015. Chronic myeloid leukemia-derived exosomes promote tumor growth through an autocrine mechanism. Cell Commun. Signal 13, 8. https://doi.org/10.1186/s12964-015-0086-x.

Raty, J., Pikkarainen, J., Wirth, T., Ylä-Herttuala, S., 2010. Gene therapy: the first approved gene-based medicines, molecular mechanisms and clinical indications. Curr. Mol. Pharmacol. 1 (1), 13–23.

Read, C., Janes, S., George, J., Spiro, S., 2006. Early lung cancer: screening and detection. Prim. Care Respir. J. 15, 332–336.

Renzi, C., Lyratzopoulos, G., Card, T., Chu, T.P.C., Macleod, U., Rachet, B., 2016. Do colorectal cancer patients diagnosed as an emergency differ from non-emergency patients in their consultation patterns and symptoms? A longitudinal data-linkage study in England. Br. J. Cancer 115, 866–875.

Rosenberg, S.A., Aebersold, P., Cornetta, K., Kasid, A., Morgan, R.A., Moen, R., Karson, E.M., Lotze, M.-T., Yang, J.C., Topalian, S.L., 1990. Gene transfer into humans–immunotherapy of patients with advanced melanoma, using tumor-infiltrating lymphocytes modified by retroviral gene transduction. N. Engl. J. Med. 323 (9), 570–578.

Rosenberg, S.A., Restifo, N.P., Yang, J.C., Morgan, R.A., Dudley, M.E., 2008. Adoptive cell transfer: a clinical path to effective cancer immunotherapy. Nat. Rev. Cancer 8 (4), 299–308.

Sanchez, C., Belleville, P., Popall, M., Nicole, L., 2011. Applications of advanced hybrid organic-inorganic nanomaterials: from laboratory to market. Chem. Soc. Rev. 40 (2), 696–753.

Sawyers, C.L., 2003. Opportunities and challenges in the development of kinase inhibitor therapy for cancer. Genes Dev. 17, 2998–3010.

Schroder, F.H., Hugosson, J., Roobol, M.J., 2009. Screening and prostate cancer mortality in a randomized European study. N. Engl. J. Med. 360, 1320–1328.

Senol, S., Ceyran, A.B., Aydin, A., Zemheri, E., Ozkanli, S., Kösemetin, D., Sehitoglu, I., Akalin, I., 2015. Folate receptor α expression and significance in endometrioid endometrium carcinoma and endometrial hyperplasia. Int. J. Clin. Exp. Pathol. 8 (5), 5633–5641.

Sheringham, J.R., Georghiou, T., Chitnis, X.A., Bardsley, M., 2014. Comparing primary and secondary health-care use between diagnostic routes before a colorectal cancer diagnosis: cohort study using linked data. Br. J. Cancer 111, 1490–1499.

Shi, J., Kantoff, P.W., Wooster, R., Farokhzad, O.C., 2017. Cancer nanomedicine: progress, challenges and opportunities. Nat. Rev. Cancer 17 (1), 20–37.

Sikka, V., 2010. Cancer diagnosis and outcomes in Michigan emergency departments vs other settings. Ann. Emerg. Med. 56, S92. https://doi.org/10.1016/j.annemergmed.2010.06.328.

Sinha, R., 2006. Nanotechnology in cancer therapeutics: bioconjugated nanoparticles for drug delivery. Mol. Cancer Ther. 5 (8), 1909–1917.

Siravegna, G., Marsoni, S., Siena, S., Bardelli, A., 2017. Integrating liquid biopsies into the management of cancer. Nat. Rev. Clin. Oncol. 14 (9), 531–548.

Suetsugu, A., Honma, K., Saji, S., Moriwaki, H., Ochiya, T., Hoffman, R.M., 2013. Imaging exosome transfer from breast cancer cells to stroma at metastatic sites in orthotopic nude-mouse models. Adv. Drug Deliv. Rev. 65 (3), 383–390.

Sun, T., Zhang, Y.S., Pang, B., Hyun, D.C., Yang, M., Xia, Y., 2014. Engineered nanoparticles for drug delivery in cancer therapy. Angew. Chem. Int. Ed. Engl. 53 (46), 12320–12464.

Syrigos, K., 2001. Prostate Cancer. Oxford University Press, Oxford.

Tinkle, S., Mcneil, S.E., Mühlebach, S., Bawa, R., Borchard, G., Barenholz, Y.C., Tamarkin, L., Desai, N., 2014. Nanomedicines: addressing the scientific and regulatory gap. Ann. N. Y. Acad. Sci. 1313, 35–56.

Vlassov, A.V., Magdaleno, S., Setterquist, R., et al., 2012. Exosomes: current knowledge of their composition, biological functions, and diagnostic and therapeutic potentials. Biochim. Biophys. Acta 1820 (7), 940–948.

Wallace, D., Walker, K., Kuryba, A., Finan, P., Scott, N., van der Meulen, J., 2014. Identifying patients at risk of emergency admission for colorectal cancer. Br. J. Cancer 111, 577–580.

Weller, D., Campbell, C., 2006. Early lung cancer detection: the role of primary care. Prim. Care Respir. J. 15, 323–325.

Witwer, K.W., Buzas, E.I., Bemis, L.T., et al., 2013. Standardization of sample collection, isolation and analysis methods in extracellular vesicle research. J. Extracell. Vesicles 2, 20360. https://doi.org/10.3402/jev.v2i0.20360.

Workman, P., 2003. How much gets there and what does it do?: the need for better pharmacokinetic and pharmacodynamic endpoints in contemporary drug discovery and development. Curr. Pharm. Des. 9, 891–902.

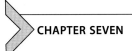

CHAPTER SEVEN

Insights into genetic predisposition of somatic cancers

Amit Raj Sharma[a], Benjamin Suroy[a], Shweta Sinha[b], Gitika Batra[a], Ashish Jain[a], Neha Dhir[a], Ashutosh Singh[a], Rahul Soloman Singh[a], Manisha Prajapat[a], Ajay Prakash[a], and Bikash Medhi[a]

[a]Department of Pharmacology, Post Graduate Institute of Medical Education and Research, Chandigarh, India
[b]Post Graduate Institute of Medical Education and Research, Chandigarh, India

1. Introduction

Cancer is a multicondition disease caused by a variety of cell types. Specifically, one form of cancer may present in a variety of ways. Precisely, one type of cancer might exhibit different types of manifestations. Multiple subtypes of cancer can be identified using different molecular and histological investigations as well as cancer-specific mutations, which can result in a variety of clinical outcomes. The discovery of new cancer subtypes could aid in identifying patients with similar clinical pathology or therapy responses. Breast cancer, for example, is categorized into four basic subtypes based on molecular changes such as hormone receptor expression and HER2, as well as tumor grade. These diverse subtypes of breast cancer have varied prognosis profiles and respond to hormone treatment in different way (Kuijjer et al., 2018; Vijg and Dong, 2020; García-Nieto et al., 2019). Even while these classifications would be utilized to control patient therapy, they represent a variety of smaller groups. Since the beginning of large-scale genomic experiments, the cancer subtype has been recognized in a range of cancers utilizing microRNA and mRNA expression levels, nucleotide alteration, methylation data, and combinational multiple omics datasets but few investigations have subtyped treatment on somatic mutations. The somatic mutations impacted tumor genetics, which may aid tumor progression. The clinical criteria for a particular type of cancer can be decided based on single-gene changes. In addition, mutational profiling is used in clinical practice significantly more frequently than other omics techniques. As a result, categorization based on variation patterns might be especially useful in determining subgroups of patients are more likely to react to particular treatment regimens. Cancer is a hereditary illness caused by mutations in genes that regulate cell functions, particularly cell divisions and growth. In the micro-evolutionary mechanism of neoplasia, the formation of a varied

Biomarkers in Cancer Detection and Monitoring of Therapeutics
https://doi.org/10.1016/B978-0-323-95116-6.00021-9

mutational landscape in normal tissue under stressful conditions is a critical element. Several genes contain the instructions for producing proteins, which aid in important biological processes. The proliferation stimulator proteins stimulate the production of a protein that causes cells to grow and divide rapidly, allowing them to evade normal growth limits and become cancerous. Recent studies have discovered a wide range of "driver" mutations linked to tumors with varying degrees of clonal expansion in noncancerous tissue biopsies, including Barrett's esophagus, colorectal epithelial cells, sun-exposed eyelid epidermis, and liver, implying a precancerous landscape for proliferation and differentiation that starts with genetic changes (Kuijjer et al., 2018; Vijg and Dong, 2020; García-Nieto et al., 2019; Hong et al., 2022; Fiala and Diamandis, 2020; Kakiuchi and Ogawa, 2021). Individuals who have a high mutation rate are more likely to acquire cancer.

Many inherited cancer predisposed genes (CPGs), which are genes with gained germline variants that confer relatively high risks, are significant components of repairing processes for damaged DNA, like BRCA1 and BRCA2 in homologous recombination, supporting this notion (García-Nieto et al., 2019; Fiala and Diamandis, 2020; Kakiuchi and Ogawa, 2021; Capellini et al., 2021).

CPGs were discovered in pedigrees enriched for hereditary (germline) cancer cases and huge sets of noninherited (somatic) cancer cases thanks to advances in sequencing technology. Approximately 5%–15% of cancer cases are carriers of pathogenic polymorphism within CPGs, according to these large sample sets. Several newly discovered CPGs, on the other hand, do not appear to play a central role in these two fundamental predisposition processes. Metabolism, rRNA processing, and protein translation are all affected by these CPGs (García-Nieto et al., 2019; Hong et al., 2022; Fiala and Diamandis, 2020; Kakiuchi and Ogawa, 2021; Capellini et al., 2021).

Majorly, cancers are classified into two classes which are as follows.

2. Germline cancers

Hereditary mutations, also known as germline mutations, are passed down from parents to children. Inherited germline mutations play a critical role in cancer susceptibility and risk. This type of cancer is caused by genetic alterations in germ cells inherited from parents. Germline modifications are seen in every cell of the progeny and raise the risk of diseases such as familial melanoma, breast cancer caused by p53 mutations for various cancers, BRCA1 or BRCA2 gene mutations, and several others. Germline tumors are extremely fatal and nearly untreatable, whereas cancers caused by somatic mutations might be treated using a variety of approaches, including classical, traditional, or advanced methods of medical sciences (Kakiuchi and Ogawa, 2021; Capellini et al., 2021; Abascal et al., 2021; Moore et al., 2021). This chapter focuses solely on somatic mutations and cancer propensity.

3. Somatic cancers

Cancer-causing genetic changes might be acquired throughout one's lifetime as a result of errors made during cell division or exposure to carcinogenic substances that damage the DNA, including certain components in tobacco, and radiation, like ultraviolet rays of the sun. Genetic changes occur after developed somatic modifications.

The deposition of confirmed somatic mutations (sMs) with epigenetic alterations over a person's lifetime, which might be exacerbated by environmental parameters in a variety of tissues, has been associated with higher cancer risk in the elderly. According to extended research on cancer genome sequencing exhibit, several malignancies have highly frequent sMs in classical oncogenes, tumor suppressor genes (including p53, PIK3CA, and others), as well as several other individually uncommon sMs in other genes (Vijg and Dong, 2020; Abascal et al., 2021; Moore et al., 2021; The Genetics of Cancer, 2022).

High penetrance (cancer susceptibility) genes are caused by genetic mutations that carry a very high risk of cancer. These mutations are known as high penetrance (neoplastic predisposition) genes because they act as Mendelian dominants. These include (i) genes required for genome stability (e.g., BLM, ATM, BRCA2, XPA, MSH2, FANCA), (ii) tumor suppressors (e.g., p53, VHL, APC, MEN1, GPC3, CDKN2A), and (iii) oncogenes (e.g., KIT, RET, MET, PDGFRA). There are already several dozens of known high penetrance genes. They may or may not be a tumor (site) specific (e.g., BRCA2 and p53, respectively). Furthermore, several clinical facts suggest that cancer predisposition could run in families quite softly, leading to the concept of low penetrance (cancer susceptibility) genes (Kaur et al., 2022; Luzzatto, 2011).

There are many different types of DNA modifications, and some of them modify a single nucleotide of DNA. Likely, one nucleotide is substituted by other or can be missing entirely. Conformational changes, strand duplications, and deletions are mostly examples involved in additional large-scale DNA alterations. The changes are also not found in the DNA sequence. Epigenetic alterations might occur after chemical (like alkaloids, EtBr, etc.) addition or removal of DNA. These modifications might alter the gene expressions (Gibney and Nolan, 2010). Cancer cells have more generous genetic changes than normal cells. Each person's cancer has its own set of genetic alterations. These kinds of changes might be the result of cancer instead of the cause. As the advancement of cancers, more changes are likely to occur. Even within the same tumor, cancer cells may have different genetic changes.

There is the number of cell divisions required to evolve from a single-cell zygote to a mature organism, while somatic mutations occur during the developmental process of an organism. A mutation that occurs during development is passed down to all descendent cells, resulting in genetic mosaicism. Genetic mosaicism is invariably caused by developmental mutations. It's possible that cells with somatic mutations during development are susceptible to cancer. Diseases that arise from a few genetically changed cells, such as cancer, may impact global genetic mosaicism. Furthermore, differences in the level of genetic mutations set at a young age might account for much of the diversity in cancer risk across individuals. It also implies several neurodegenerations diseases, like amyotrophic lateral sclerosis (ALS), etc. (Risques and Kennedy, 2018).

Until recently, practically all data on de novo mutagenesis in healthy tissues were collected through the use of reporter genes that might be used to select for mutations. All investigations have found a significant and frequently tissue-specific increase in somatic mutations as people get older. Nevertheless, while such mutational reporter models are valuable, they have the major limitation of not reflecting the entire mammalian genome. As a result, they make it impossible to acquire quantitative mutational data loads over the genome. As a result of significant advancements in next-generation sequencing in recent years, help to understand of the prevalence and kinds of genetic variations in human tissues throughout aging has vastly improved. All information about SMs in animal and human tissues, was collected in less than 5-years. Their deposition related to aging was already gathered in the earlier half-century. As a result, it's time to talk about how to turn the technological advances that have resulted in a plethora of datasets related to in vivo SMs to explore the mechanism of their likely causative association with age-related cell cognitive dysfunction and enduring illness. The current state of the field in terms of technological advancements has permitted this progress and then gone over the mechanisms. It might lead to cellular damage during aging and disease from spontaneous somatic mutations (Vijg and Dong, 2020).

In males mutational loss of chromosome Y (LOY) during aging is the most thoroughly investigated aging chromosomal deformity that arises in genome sMs, which was first reported in the beginning of the 1970s by investigating human's bone marrow leucocytes metaphases and widely proved with more technological advancements. A reduced richness of DNA in Y chromosome with a specified edge value, such as 10% or more of afflicted cells, is termed LOY. LOY was discovered to impact between 2.5% of males at age 40 and 43.6% of men at age 70 in the latest report of 205,011 men from the Biobank UK, made most frequent de novo SMs across the period. The small life time, a greater cancer risk by the smoking, diabetes, immunological deficiencies, cardiovascular disease, Alzheimer's disease, and other aging disorders have all been linked to LOY frequency (Vijg and Dong, 2020).

LOY is the only one of several postzygotic mutations, despite being the most prevalent. Genome mosaicism was discovered at the subchromosomal level of blood's genome after the advent of whole genome sequencing technology roughly 10 years back. For example, copy number variants (CNVs) mutations were discovered around 0.5% in young population and 2%–3% in geriatric population utilizing SNP arrays. Clonal hematopoiesis is a universal outline of genomic variations discovered with the development of next-generation sequencing of whole genome, gene of interest or complete exomes. More recently, ultradeep sequencing was done for different human tissues revealing that somatic mutations resulting in genomic mutations are not limited to the blood but are a common occurrence. RNA sequence alignment of healthy tissue by using genotype-tissue expression (GTEx) data groups along with normalization by using 30 control tissue types of people have revealed the clonal spread of somatic mutations. The findings show an expected rise in mutations with age, a link between the several gene variations and tissue-specific growth, and the improvement of cancer stimulatory genomic changes (Yizhak et al., 2019; Yokoyama et al., 2019).

The quantitative examination of SMs sequences in single cell type propagated in vitro is highly instructive, but it has one major drawback in progenitor cell's de novo mutations. Furthermore, by definition method only find mutations in the precursor cells, which have small genetic variability compared to specialized cells. A recent comparison of liver stem cells from human and completely developed hepatocytes revealed that the latter had a roughly twofold greater average mutation frequency. Due to the position of the mutation in the mechanism of cellular differentiation are displayed considerably more cell-to-cell heterogeneity in mutation occurrences of fully matured cells (Brazhnik et al., 2020).

Further, somatic clonal proliferation of a single cells sequencing data has revealed insertions and deletions (INDELs) and single-nucleotide variants (SNVs). SNVs might lead to functional modifications besides nonsynonymous SNVs in coding regions of proteins. As a result, mutations are relatively common in normal cells. Small INDELs, which are approximately one base pair long, can be discovered using the exact method as SNVs. The incidence in somatic cells is approximately one-tenth of SNVs. Genome structural variants (SVs) like insertions, deletions, inversions, rearrangements (chromosomal translocations), and retrotransposition, telomere repeats loss at the end of chromosomes are very harmful to the cell. The SVs can change gene-regulatory sequences by their size range from a few bp to an entire chromosome, efficiently impacting on functions of the cell (King and Wilson, 1975). CNVs, SVs, and retrotranspositions have single-cell sequencing data and the occurrence of a few events per cell. There is no other data in the case of large size of DNA estimating correct SV percentages from whole-genome sequencing data remains a technical challenge. For example, large genomic rearrangements might be occurred with tissues aging, like the heart and liver of mice, as well as cells of mice and humans in FISH. Significantly, it was recently demonstrated that additionally resilient double-strand break (DSB) repair of DNA developed in tandem with lifespan in 18 species of the rodent with varying longevity (Vijg and Dong, 2020).

4. Identifying somatic mutations

Every cancer cell can develop its pattern of altered genes. Each person's cancer and even its small section might have unique features of cancer. It has ramifications for diagnosis, prognosis, and responsiveness to treatment. Researchers can establish a precise genetic fingerprint of the tumor and identify major tumor subtypes by looking for recurring somatic mutations (Stratton et al., 2009). The comprehensive detection of tumor-specific SMs needs whole-genome sequencing with a minimum of $30\times$ sequencing range of each cancerous and healthy genome, with matched reads in the range of 100–250 bp in size, relying upon an instrument, cost, capacity, and analytical experience. However, sample preparation, tumor, healthy sample coverage, and read lengths differ from project to project. Furthermore, the many ways employed to determine all somatic single-base mutations (SSM), insertion/deletion mutations (SIM), and structural changes demonstrate the variety in approaches to identifying differences between tumor and normal genome. With the unknown effects of different channel elements and parameters on the quality of cells, comparing mutation cells across tumors is difficult. The development of benchmark data sets and analysis techniques in variant annotation on standard genomes concentrated on SSM identification from exome sequencing. On the other hand, cancer has concentrated on exome sequencing to detect SSM. The Cancer Genome Atlas' exome data has been used to benchmark mutation calling, which has expanded concerns regarding prejudiced conclusions and highlighted the necessity for standard datasets (Alioto et al., 2015; Wang et al., 2020).

5. Next-generation sequencing (NGS) in mutation detection

Next-generation sequencing (NGS) or massive parallel sequencing has revolutionized the field of oncology. With NGS, complete genome can be sequenced without any prior knowledge of the genome. This advanced technology can be applied for detecting the genomic, transcriptomic and epigenomic alternations in cancer. Small insertions or deletions, mutations, CNVs, and SVs that can be discovered through DNA sequencing have all been found as risk modifiers. RNA-sequencing can be used to find spliceogenic variations, gene fusions, and differential expression. NGS can also be used to evaluate somatic mutation analysis, pharmacogenetics, and liquid biopsy. To summarize, isolated DNA fragments from biological samples to be sequenced are attached to an array, and DNA polymerase successively inserts tagged nucleotides, with each nucleotide integration caught by a high-resolution camera. With the help of computer program, a contiguous DNA sequence is generated and compared with normal samples for alteration identification.

The volume and quality of DNA or RNA collected are crucial for generating correct data for a definitive diagnosis, as it affects future sequencing quality and ultimate outcomes. Although fresh-frozen (FF) tissue is ideal, collecting enough tissue from patients for all of the experiments required might be difficult. The majority of anatomical specimens are formalin-fixed (4% formaldehyde) and paraffin-embedded (FFPE). On the other hand, formalin cross-links both DNA fragments and causes chemical changes, resulting in more errors than utilizing frozen specimens. Liquid biopsies are used in standard pathological diagnosis that is based on circulating tumor cells (CTCs). Apoptotic cells release circulating tumor DNA (ctDNA), which can be detected in the bloodstream. Furthermore, because RNA has a lower stability than DNA, RNA-based assays are demanding to perform with CTCs. However, RNA species can be kept in extracellular vesicles and stored information concerning tumor recurrence. Overall, genotyping of germline and somatic DNA mutations from tumor tissues or liquid biopsies, as well as RNA studies, can significantly improve patient care, but the application of next-generation sequencing (NGS) is still being investigated (Grada and Weinbrecht, 2013).

References

Abascal, F., Harvey, L.M., Mitchell, E., Lawson, A.R., Lensing, S.V., Ellis, P., Russell, A.J., Alcantara, R.E., Baez-Ortega, A., Wang, Y., Kwa, E.J., 2021. Somatic mutation landscapes at single-molecule resolution. Nature 593 (7859), 405–410.

Alioto, T.S., Buchhalter, I., Derdak, S., Hutter, B., Eldridge, M.D., Hovig, E., Heisler, L.E., Beck, T.A., Simpson, J.T., Tonon, L., Sertier, A.S., Patch, A.M., Jäger, N., Ginsbach, P., Drews, R., Paramasivam, N., Kabbe, R., Chotewutmontri, S., Diessl, N., Previti, C., Gut, I.G., 2015. A comprehensive assessment of somatic mutation detection in cancer using whole-genome sequencing. Nat. Commun. 6, 10001.

Brazhnik, K., Sun, S., Alani, O., Kinkhabwala, M., Wolkoff, A.W., Maslov, A.Y., Dong, X., Vijg, J., 2020. Single-cell analysis reveals different age-related somatic mutation profiles between stem and differentiated cells in human liver. Sci. Adv. 6, eaax2659.

Capellini, A., Williams, M., Onel, K., Huang, K.L., 2021. The functional hallmarks of cancer predisposition genes. Cancer Manag. Res. 13, 4351.

Fiala, C., Diamandis, E.P., 2020. Mutations in normal tissues—some diagnostic and clinical implications. BMC Med. 18 (1), 1–9.

García-Nieto, P.E., Morrison, A.J., Fraser, H.B., 2019. The somatic mutation landscape of the human body. Genome Biol. 20 (1), 1–20.

Gibney, E.R., Nolan, C.M., 2010. Epigenetics and gene expression. Heredity 105 (1), 4–13.

Grada, A., Weinbrecht, K., 2013. Next-generation sequencing: methodology and application. J. Invest. Dermatol. 133 (8), e11.

Hong, Y., Zhang, D., Zhou, X., Chen, A., Abliz, A., Bai, J., Wang, L., Hu, Q., Gong, K., Guan, X., Liu, M., 2022. Common postzygotic mutational signatures in healthy adult tissues related to embryonic hypoxia. Genom. Proteom. Bioinform. 20 (1), 177–191.

Kakiuchi, N., Ogawa, S., 2021. Clonal expansion in non-cancer tissues. Nat. Rev. Cancer 21 (4), 239–256.

Kaur, G., Bhadada, S.K., Santra, M., Pal, R., Sarma, P., Sachdeva, N., Dhiman, V., Dahiya, D., Saikia, U.N., Chakraborty, A., Sood, A., Prakash, M., Behera, A., Rao, S.D., 2022. Multilevel annotation of germline MEN1 variants of synonymous, nonsynonymous, and uncertain significance in Indian patients with sporadic primary hyperparathyroidism. J. Bone Miner. Res. 37 (10), 1860–1875. https://doi.org/10.1002/jbmr.4653.

King, M.C., Wilson, A.C., 1975. Evolution at two levels in humans and chimpanzees. Science 188, 107–116.

Kuijjer, M.L., Paulson, J.N., Salzman, P., Ding, W., Quackenbush, J., 2018. Cancer subtype identification using somatic mutation data. Br. J. Cancer 118 (11), 1492–1501.

Luzzatto, L., 2011. Erratum to: somatic mutations in cancer development. Environ. Health 10 (1), 1–8.

Moore, L., Cagan, A., Coorens, T.H., Neville, M.D., Sanghvi, R., Sanders, M.A., Oliver, T.R., Leongamornlert, D., Ellis, P., Noorani, A., Mitchell, T.J., 2021. The mutational landscape of human somatic and germline cells. Nature 597 (7876), 381–386.

Risques, R.A., Kennedy, S.R., 2018. Aging and the rise of somatic cancer-associated mutations in normal tissues. PLoS Genet. 14 (1), e1007108.

Stratton, M.R., Campbell, P.J., Futreal, P.A., 2009. The cancer genome. Nature 458 (7239), 719–724.

Anon., 2022. The Genetics of Cancer. https://www.cancer.gov/about-cancer/causes-prevention/genetics. (accessed 28.03.22).

Vijg, J., Dong, X., 2020. Pathogenic mechanisms of somatic mutation and genome mosaicism in aging. Cell 182 (1), 12–23.

Wang, M., Luo, W., Jones, K., Bian, X., Williams, R., Higson, H., Wu, D., Hicks, B., Yeager, M., Zhu, B., 2020. SomaticCombiner: improving the performance of somatic variant calling based on evaluation tests and a consensus approach. Sci. Rep. 10 (1), 12898.

Yizhak, K., Aguet, F., Kim, J., Hess, J.M., Kübler, K., Grimsby, J., Frazer, R., Zhang, H., Haradhvala, N.J., Rosebrock, D., et al., 2019. RNA sequence analysis reveals macroscopic somatic clonal expansion across normal tissues. Science 364, eaaw0726.

Yokoyama, A., Kakiuchi, N., Yoshizato, T., Nannya, Y., Suzuki, H., Takeuchi, Y., Shiozawa, Y., Sato, Y., Aoki, K., Kim, S.K., et al., 2019. Age-related remodelling of oesophageal epithelia by mutated cancer drivers. Nature 565, 312–317.

CHAPTER EIGHT

The use of tumor markers in prognosis of cancer and strategies to prevent cancer predisposition and progress

Osama M. Ahmed[a], Mohamed Abd-Elbaset[b], Noha A. Ahmed[a], and Eman R. Abd Elhaliem[a]
[a]Physiology Division, Zoology Department, Faculty of Science, Beni-Suef University, Beni-Suef, Egypt
[b]Faculty of Pharmacy, El Saleheya El Gadida University, El Sharqia, Egypt

1. Introduction

Cancer is a generic term for a large group of disorders that can influence any part of the body. Other terms used are malignant tumors and neoplasms. One describing feature of cancer is the rapid creation of abnormal cells that grow elsewhere their usual boundaries, and which can then attack adjacent parts of the body and spread to other organs, the end process is referred to as metastases. As a matter of fact, metastases are the main reason of death from cancer (de Martel et al., 2012; World Health Organization, WHO, 2022).

Globally, cancer is the leading cause of deaths in developed countries and the second leading cause of deaths in developing countries, where the cancer burden is rising. Estimates for 2008 pointed to 12.7 million cancer cases and 7.6 million cancer deaths worldwide (Jemal et al., 2011; Bray et al., 2013). In 2020, nearly 10 million deaths were accounted as a result of cancer (Ferlay et al., 2020; WHO, 2022). The most common in 2020 (in terms of new cases of cancer) were breast (2.26 million cases), lung (2.21 million cases), colon and rectum (1.93 million cases), prostate (1.41 million cases), skin (non-melanoma) (1.20 million cases), and stomach (1.09 million cases) (WHO, 2022).

The prognosis of cancer is crucial not only to avoid the risks of cancer onset and progress but also to develop strategies for cancer prevention. Only 5%–10% of all cancer cases can be attributed to genetic defects, and the remaining 90%–95% have their roots in the environmental factors and bad lifestyle which include cigarette smoking, diet (fried foods, red meat), alcohol, sun exposure, environmental pollutants, infections, stress, obesity, and physical inactivity. The evidence indicates that of all cancer-related deaths, almost 25%–30% are due to tobacco smoking, as many as 30%–35% are related to diet, about 13% or more are due to infections, and the remaining percentage are due to other factors like radiation, stress, physical activity, environmental pollutants etc. (Lichtenstein et al., 2000; Irigaray et al., 2007; Anand et al., 2008; González-Marrón et al., 2019; de Martel et al., 2020).

Cancer risk assessment and laboratory prognosis tests are very important for cancer early detection as well as to provide accurate counseling on cancer risk reduction and cancer prevention strategies (e.g., smoking cessation, lifestyle modifications, dietary changes, use of chemopreventive agents). Cancer risk assessment is an individualized evaluation of a patient's risk for cancer based on a variety of both intrinsic and extrinsic factors and starts with a detailed history which includes thorough past medical (such as hormone use), obstetric/gynecologic and surgical histories, level of physical activity, environmental exposures, history of tobacco smoking, alcohol use, and documentation of recent age-appropriate screening tests, or lack thereof. The family history is a critical part of cancer risk assessment and includes at least a three-generation pedigree, particularly if a hereditary cancer syndrome is suspected (Mahon, 2000; WHO, 2022).

Between 30% and 50% of cancers can currently be prevented by avoiding risk factors and implementing existing evidence-based prevention strategies. The cancer morbidity and mortality can also be minimized through early detection of cancer, prognosis and appropriate treatment and care of patients who develop cancer. Many cancers have a high chance of cure if early diagnosed and treated appropriately (WHO, 2022).

In conduction with the previous literature, this review sheds light on the tumor biomarkers used for prognosis of different types of cancer and describes strategies that can be applied to reduce cancer risks and to prevent cancer onset and progress.

2. The use of tumor markers in prognosis of cancer

Prognosis of any ailments means the estimate of the likely course and outcome of the disease. Prognosis of cancers usually means the estimate of success with treatment and chances of recovery. There are several factors that affect the prognosis of a cancer including type of cancer, location of cancer, stage of the cancer, cancer grade, patient age, general health conditions, and responses to treatment (Mandal, 2019).

Once cancer is diagnosed, the next step in the clinical management has to be taken by the clinician, that is to evaluate the prognosis for this patient or in other words to estimate the likely progression of the cancer and the aggressiveness that it may exhibit (recurrence likelihood, progression and/or chance for metastasis despite adjuvant therapy). The current practice for prognosis assessment is based on radiological (computed tomography [CT] scan, magnetic resonance imaging [MRI]) and pathological (TNM, lymphovascular, perineural, and venous invasion) criteria. In fact, TNM staging remains the strongest prognostic tool (Edge and Compton, 2010). The TNM staging system (based on a combination of tumor size or depth (T), lymph node spread (N), and presence or absence of metastasis (M)) provides a basis for prediction of survival, choice of initial treatment, stratification of patients in clinical trials, accurate communication among healthcare providers, and uniform reporting of the end result of cancer management (Ludwig and Weinstein, 2005).

However, the prognostic tools mentioned above do not provide clear evidence on which of these cancer cases are more prone to relapse, give metastasis or are proven to be resistant to chemotherapy. Thus, much effort has been made for the evaluation of the potential of several molecules and gene alterations to serve as prognostic biomarkers.

2.1 Tumor markers in prognosis

By definition, a biomarker is an objective measure such as, a gene, a protein, enzyme, or hormone that can reflect the entire spectrum of the ailment from the earliest features to the end stages. Reliable biomarkers are of great clinical significance in expecting cancer occurrence/recurrence, anticipating its detection at an asymptomatic stages, supporting the radiological diagnosis, stratifying patients for prognosis and proper therapy, and measuring the response to treatment (Trevisani et al., 2019).

The tumor markers are most useful if utilized not only as confirmatory tests for clinical diagnosis, but also as a part of follow-up assessment, and assessment of prognosis. The sequential estimation of a tumor marker level during the follow-up period and the chronology of the pattern obtained could then be correlated with the response in the patient to tumor therapy or as an indicator of recurrence (Virji et al., 1988).

Cancer cells or other body cells in response to tumor development secrete or release a subset of biomarkers into tissues and different biological body fluids. The body fluids' biomarkers can be investigated and evaluated in succession with noninvasive or slightly invasive means, whereas tissues-derived ones need invasive techniques like biopsies (Hussein et al., 2018).

In only few tumors, serum tumor marker levels currently utilized as a part of routine clinical follow-up studies or as a regular guide to therapeutic decisions. In addition, the markers are usually followed individually rather than used as a selected panel of tumor-derived and tumor-associated markers. The pattern of current tumor marker use is related to the empirical information about a marker, the perceived ease of interpretation of the laboratory result in the clinical setting, and a reliance on other factors to judge the course of the disease.

Prognostic biomarkers in colorectal cancer

Carcinoembryonic antigen (CEA) was first isolated from human colorectal cancer (CRC) tissue in 1965 by Gold and Freedman. CEA can become elevated in a number of pathologies. The most common clinical use is surveillance for recurrence of CRC. Moreover, CEA used as a prognostic biomarker in patients with CRC, in follow-up after CRC resection, and the management of patients with raised CEA and no history of CRC

Table 1 Summary of some commonly used significant biomarkers in cancer prognosis.

Significant biomarker	Associated cancers	Potential clinical use	References
CEA	Colorectal cancer, gastric cancer, lung cancer, breast cancer.	Prognosis	Hall et al. (2019), Uehara et al. (2008)
CA 19-9	Colorectal cancer, pancreatic cancer, gastric cancer	Prognosis	Yu et al. (2022)
AFP	Hepatocellular carcinoma	Prognosis	Virji et al. (1988), Personeni et al. (2012)
IL-17 and IL-17RE	Hepatocellular carcinoma	Prognosis	Liao et al. (2013)
PSA	Prostatic cancer	Prognosis	Sardana et al. (2008)
Ki-67	Prostatic cancer	Prognosis	Bjartell et al. (2011)
CA 15-3		Prognosis	Uehara et al. (2008)
HER2/neu	Breast cancer	Prognosis	Nicolini et al. (2018)
uPA/PAI-1	Breast cancer	Prognosis	Nicolini et al. (2018)
CYFRA21-1	Lung adenocarcinoma	Prognosis	Chen et al. (2021)
CA-125	Lung adenocarcinoma, ovarian cancer	Prognosis	Chen et al. (2021), Muinao et al. (2018)
CA-199	Lung squamous cell carcinoma	Prognosis	Chen et al. (2021)
HE4	Ovarian cancer	Prognosis	Montagnana et al. (2011)
Mesothelin	Ovarian cancer	Prognosis	Montagnana et al. (2011)
KLK4	Ovarian cancer	Prognosis	Montagnana et al. (2011)

(Hall et al., 2019). CEA is the only marker that has been recommended by the ASCO (2006) update of recommendations for the management of CRC patients (Table 1).

Preoperative CEA levels have a bearing on prognosis, since they correlate with the Dukes' grading of colon cancer, with stages progressing from A2 to D showing increases in 25%–80% of patients. Well-differentiated colon cancers produce CEA, but poorly differentiated tumors lack CEA (Virji et al., 1988).

CEA and carbohydrate antigen 19-9 (CA19-9), have been used to determine prognosis and monitor the therapeutic effects of treatments. The level of CEA may be increased in gastric carcinoma, lung carcinoma, and especially colorectal carcinoma, while CA19-9 is used mainly as a specific marker for pancreatic cancer (Yu et al., 2022).

CA 19-9 is a documented marker with prognostic value for CRC. It is shown that cases with increased CA 19-9 present more frequently metastases thus making it a marker of poor prognosis. Similarly, a recent study with stage IV CRC proved that the preoperative serum CA 19-9 level can be a promising marker of tumor recurrence and prognosis in cases submitted to curative resection (Yu et al., 2022).

Lymphopenia is associated with impaired cell-mediated immunity, while neutrophilia is associated with systemic inflammation. The neutrophil-to-lymphocyte ratio (NLR) was first studied as a marker for immune responses to various stressful conditions other studies found potential for NLR as a prognostic marker for pancreatic cancer, gastric cancer, and hepatocellular carcinoma (Oh and Joo, 2020).

A higher circulating free DNA (cfDNA) concentration is reportedly related to significantly shorter overall survival (OS) in CRC patients. Furthermore, CRC patients with higher cfDNA levels showed a higher risk of recurrence and shorter OS (Oh and Joo, 2020).

Circulating exosomal miRNAs may be associated with CRC staging and severity, which are considered as potential biomarkers of a poor prognosis. miR-203 expression increased significantly in a TNM stage-dependent manner and that its high expression was associated with increased aggressiveness and pathological tumor progression, including lymph node metastasis, venous invasion, distant metastasis, and advanced TNM staging in patients with CRC, as validated by qRT-PCR (Alves dos Santos et al., 2020).

Prognostic biomarkers in hepatocellular carcinoma (HCC)

Despite the plethora of biomarkers proposed for hepatocellular carcinoma, the first one identified, α-fetoprotein (AFP), remains the most utilized. Moreover, the prognostic usefulness of AFP in patients undergoing both curative and palliative treatment of HCC is evidenced. AFP levels decline rapidly following surgical resection of HCC (Virji et al., 1988) Also, a decrease in serum AFP in patients treated with sorafenib for advanced HCC is reported (Personeni et al., 2012) (Table 1).

High expression of IL-17 and IL-17RE associated with poor survival and increased recurrence of HCC patients (Liao et al., 2013).

Prognostic biomarkers in gastric cancer (GC)

The neutrophil-to-lymphocyte ratio is an important prognostic indicator of gastric cancer. Current researchers not only believe that gastric cancer patients with higher nucleotide-binding domain leucine-rich repeat proteins or NOD-like receptors (NLRs) have a poorer prognosis but also indicate to a certain extent that the incidence of complications after surgery, such as anastomotic leakage, has increased. The NLR has been adopted for prognostic evaluation in many cancers, as well as PLR (the platelet-to-lymphocyte ratio) and LMR (lymphocyte-to-monocyte ratio) (Yu et al., 2022).

CA 19-9 is one of the most common tumor biomarkers of stomach cancer, and positivity is frequently linked to tumor stage, poor prognosis, recurrence and metastasis (Yu et al., 2022) (Table 1).

The prognosis of GC patients with low levels of CA19-9 before surgery was significantly better than that of patients with high levels. Moreover, the NLR and CA19-9 represent not only simple changes in several indicators but also the balance of tumor and antitumor status in the body. When this balance is broken, tumor promotion is prioritized, leading to a poor prognosis.

Prognostic biomarkers in prostatic cancer

PSA (prostate-specific antigen) is considered both the best tumor marker available for any cancer and a marker with many shortcomings. PSA was originally used for monitoring PC patients and was subsequently implemented for screening. PSA is currently used as a marker for diagnosis, but PSA values are now be in recognized as representing the relative degree of risk for PC. Measurement of total PSA levels have been shown to be useful as a prognostic tool, with high preoperative values being associated with advanced disease and a poor clinical outcome (Sardana et al., 2008) (Table 1).

The Ki-67 protein is well known and widely used to evaluate the tumor proliferation rate and numerous studies have shown Ki-67 to be a prognostic marker in prostate cancer patients treated by radical prostatectomy, radiotherapy or androgen deprivation therapy (ADT) (Bjartell et al., 2011).

Human kallikrein-related peptidase 2 (KLK2) is a secreted serine protease from the same gene family as PSA. KLK2 increases during progression and therefore may have use as a PC biomarker. KLK2 also provided improved independent prognostic information compared with PSA regarding the risk of biochemical recurrence in men with PSA values of 10 g/L (Sardana et al., 2008).

Tumor-associated trypsin inhibitor (TATI), which is alternatively called pancreatic secretory trypsin inhibitor (PSTI) or serine protease inhibitor Kazal type 1 (SPINK1), is expressed in various normal and malignant tissues, and is known as a prognostic tumor marker. TATI was first shown to be overexpressed in high-grade prostate cancer and later, outlier expression of SPINK1, the gene coding for the TATI protein was identified exclusively in a subset of ETS rearrangement-negative cancers (approximately 10% of total cases). A series of in vitro and in vivo experiments revealed SPINK1/TATI to be associated with prostate cancer aggressiveness and with invasive growth in a prostate cancer cell line (22RV1) with outlier expression. It was thus shown that SPINK1 outlier expression defines an aggressive molecular subtype of prostate cancer (approximately 10% of cases) not attributable to known gene fusion events. The potential role of SPINK1 expression as a prognostic biomarker was recently demonstrated (Bjartell et al., 2011).

Prognostic biomarkers in breast cancer

Determining prognosis can best be addressed with a combination of traditional clinico-pathological prognostic factors, biomarkers such as HER2/neu and specific multigene genes tests. Among the best validated prognostic multigene tests are uPA/PAI1, Oncotype DX, and MammaPrint. Oncotype DX and MammaPrint, may be used for predicting outcome and aiding adjunct therapy decision making in patients with ER-positive, HER2-negative breast cancers that are either lymph node-negative or node positive (1–3 metastatic nodes), while uPA/PAI-1 may be similarly used in ER-positive, lymph node-negative patients (Nicolini et al., 2018) (Table 1).

A number of tumor markers (e.g., carcinoembryonic antigen [CEA] and carbohydrate antigen 15-3 (CA 15-3) are used clinically in the treatment of breast cancer, but the sensitivity of these markers is low, so that they are not useful as screening tools. However, abnormally elevated levels of tumor markers prior to surgery in a patient with primary breast cancer suggest the presence of undetectable metastatic foci, and this is a negative prognostic factor (Uehara et al., 2008).

Prognostic biomarkers in lung cancer

Serum tumor markers CEA, CYFRA21-1, a fragment of cytokeratin subunit, and CA-125 are associated with worse prognosis in advanced nonsmall-cell lung cancer (NSCLC) (Cedrés et al., 2011). The preoperative serum CEA, CYFRA21-1, and CA-125 were independent prognostic factors for lung adenocarcinoma (ADC) while elevated preoperative serum CA-199 was associated with poorer prognosis in lung squamous cell carcinoma (SCC) (Chen et al., 2021) (Table 1).

Prognostic biomarkers in epithelial ovarian cancer

CA-125 is the most studied serum biomarker for screening of epithelial ovarian cancer (EOC). A serum concentration of CA-125 >35 U/mL is indicative of potential malignancies. The increased levels may precede clinical detection by more than a year. Persistently elevation of CA-125 had inferior prognosis. The level of CA-125 is also used in monitoring of recurrence of disease; postoperative serum of CA-125 >65 U/mL is associated with worse 5 years survival (Muinao et al., 2018).

Human epididymis 4 (HE4) as tumor marker for EOC has received authorization from FDA to monitor disease progression or recurrence of disease (Montagnana et al., 2011).

Mesothelin is a surface glycoprotein on mesothelial cells lining the peritoneum, pleura and pericardium. Cancer cells with high mesothelin are involved in metastasis. Raised levels denote poor overall survival in patients following optimal debulking surgery or with advanced stage (Muinao et al., 2018).

Kallikrein are overexpressed in ovarian cancer at mRNA and/or protein level. KLK4 is related to progression of ovarian cancer predominantly in late stage of serious ovarian carcinomas and with KLK5/6 produce poor outcome (Muinao et al., 2018) (Table 1).

3. Strategies to prevent cancer predisposition and progress

Cancer is the cause of approximately 90,000 deaths and 12,000 new cases annually in the world. It is hard to assess the validity of individual etiological factors, but it can be concluded that interaction of various risk factors has the largest contribution to the cancer development. Environmental, exogenous and endogenous factors, as well as individual factors, including genetic predisposition, which contribute to the development and progress of cancer (Schulz et al., 2008; Crowe et al., 2013; WHO, 2022).

Cancer is a leading cause of deaths in the United States after heart disorders. In 2018, it is determined that ~1.7 million cancers will be diagnosed in men and women, with a corresponding 609,000 deaths cancer-related deaths (Siegel et al., 2018).

Prevention is defined as "the protection of health by personal and community-wide efforts" (Miller et al., 2008). These efforts are achieved by describing the burden of cancer, identifying its causes, and evaluating and implementing cancer prevention interventions (Stewart et al., 2016).

Cancer control aims to reduce the burden and suffering from cancer by preventing exposure to cancer risk factors, early detection, effective treatment and relief of symptoms and pain from incurable advanced cancers. A combination of various approaches involving education, awareness, advocacy, legislation, vaccination, screening, early diagnosis and treatment is used to prevent the occurrence of and suffering and death from cancer. Both screening and prevention can reduce mortality from many cancers. Screening detects abnormalities before they are clinically evident, permitting for intervention either before cancer develops or at an early stage, when treatment is most often effective. Prevention strategies focus on modifying environmental and lifestyle risk factors that promote cancer. Despite a robust knowledge of what factors decrease cancer risk, implementation of cancer prevention lags (Colditz et al., 2012; WHO, 2009; Emmons and Colditz, 2017).

3.1 Cancer prevention

In 2008, an estimated 1,437,180 new cases of cancer are expected to be diagnosed in the United States, and 565,650 are not expected to survive. Two-thirds of these cancer deaths will be related to tobacco use, poor nutrition, physical inactivity, and obesity (American Cancer Society, ACS, 2008). Globally, the number of cancer deaths is expected to rise to 11.5 million in 2030. Up to 40% of all cancer deaths can be avoided by reducing tobacco use, improving diets and physical activity, lowering alcohol consumption, eliminating workplace carcinogens and immunizing against hepatitis B virus and the human papillomavirus (WHO, 2007). Additionally, more than 1 million new cases of skin cancer are expected to be diagnosed this year, and many could be prevented by avoiding overexposure to the sun. Cancers related to viral and/or bacterial infections, such as the hepatitis B virus, human papillomavirus (HPV), HIV, and Helicobacter, also can be prevented through changes in lifestyle and use of vaccines or antibiotics (ACS, 2006; de Martel et al., 2020; WHO, 2022).

Strategies for cancer prevention

Cancer can be decreased and controlled by applying evidence-based strategies for cancer prevention, primary detection of cancer and managing of patients with cancer (de Martel et al., 2012; PATO/WHO, 2022).

Despite improvements in the treatment of various common cancers, a large cancer burden remains, providing a growing incentive to address this problem by a preventive approach. Although eliminating exposure to carcinogens, such as tobacco, is a well-established approach to prevention, active intervention with agents that are expected to reduce the risk of cancer is becoming increasingly accepted (Lippman and Hawk, 2009) and (Greenwald and Dunn, 2009).

Therefore, cancer prevention requires smoking cessation, increased ingestion of fruits and vegetables, moderate use of alcohol, caloric restriction, exercise, avoidance of direct exposure to sunlight, minimal meat consumption, use of whole grains, use of vaccinations, and regular check-ups. In this review, we present evidence that inflammation is the link between the agents/factors that cause cancer and the agents that prevent it. In addition, we provide evidence that cancer is a preventable disease that requires major lifestyle changes (Anand et al., 2008).

There is overwhelming evidence that lifestyle impacts cancer risk and that positive, population-wide changes can significantly reduce the cancer burden (Institute of Medicine US and National Research Council US National Cancer Policy, 2003). Current epidemiologic evidence relates behavioral factors to a variety of malignancies, including the most common cancers diagnosed in the developed world (lung, colorectal, prostate, and breast cancer) (Ezzati et al., 2002).

Cancer can be decreased and controlled by applying evidence-based strategies for cancer prevention, primary detection of cancer and managing of patients with cancer (de Martel et al., 2012).

Primary cancer prevention

Cancer preventions are achieved through primary, secondary, and tertiary methods (Fig. 1). The primary cancer prevention is attained via 2 mechanisms: the promotion of health and wellness and reduction of risks known to contribute to cancer development (ONS, 2002). Primary prevention methods aim to reverse or inhibit the carcinogenic process through modifications in a patient's diet or environment or through pharmacologic mechanisms (Turini and DuBois, 2002). Primary prevention includes for examples smoking cessation interventions and chemoprophylaxis in women at high risk for breast cancer.

Secondary cancer prevention

The secondary cancer prevention methods include screening and early detection. In general, screening for cancer refers to checking for the occurrence of disease in populations at

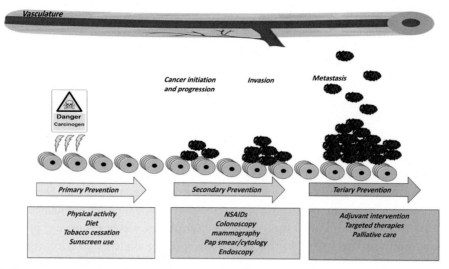

Fig. 1 Because cancer preventive techniques may be effective throughout the course of cancer initiation and progress, they can be used at any time during the disease's development. Changes in physical activity or diet, as well as the cessation of cigarette use and the use of sunscreen, are all primary preventative approaches that may help to lessen the harmful effects of exposures in cancer initiation. Secondary prevention methods, such as cancer screening or the use of nonsteroidal anti-inflammatory medicines (NSAIDs), help discover precancerous lesions early and slow cancer progression. Chemotherapy or targeted therapy are examples of tertiary preventive measures that can be used to protect a localized cancer from spreading or metastasizing (Loomans-Kropp and Umar, 2019).

risk, and early detection is defined as testing for cancer when no symptoms are present (Oncology Nursing Society, ONS, 2002). The secondary preventions seek to detect cancer at the earliest possible stage, when the diseases are most likely to be successfully treated.

Tertiary cancer prevention

Tertiary cancer prevention is used when the individuals have already been diagnosed with a malignancy but are now candidates for screening and early detection of secondary malignancies (ONS, 2002).

Precision cancer prevention

A substantial number of research studies have been devoted to investigating the pathways involved in cancer initiation, progression, and metastasis, and identifying biomarkers that are associated with these mechanisms for clinical utility. The term "biomarker," however, is broad and encompasses multiple biological features or molecules, such as imaging or radiomic alterations, DNA alterations, expression of different RNA types, and metabolomic and proteomic changes. Regardless of the biomarker type, the ideal biomarker should be: (1) directly associated with the disease of interest, (2) be involved in at least one part of the cancer spectrum, (3) provide high sensitivity and specificity, (4) have relatively noninvasive detection, and (5) have reasonable cost benefit ratios (Kohler et al., 2011).

Although the success of individual biomarkers has been limited, the progress has been made in the application of biomarker panels for the early detection and precision treatment of several tumors, such as breast tumor and melanoma. The American Society for Clinical Oncology (ASCO) recommended tumor-typing for estrogen receptor (ER), progesterone receptor (PR), and human epidermal growth factor receptor 2 (HER2) in breast biopsies. The information obtained from this tumor-typing can then be used to inform interceptive options, such as tamoxifen for ER-positive cancers, trastuzumab for HER2-positive cancers, or the needs for additional genetic analyses (Denduluri et al., 2016; Krop et al., 2017).

Similar tiered methods can be utilized in the early detection of melanoma harboring BRAF-V600E mutations. Approximately 50% of melanoma has a mutation in BRAF which results in the constitutive activation of the Ras/Raf/MEK pathway. Of these, over 90% of the BRAF mutations are a missense mutations resulting in the substitution of valine for glutamic acid at codon 600 (Ascierto et al., 2012).

Early detection of melanomas and tumor-typing for the BRAF-V600E mutation can then identify therapeutic options, such as treatment with vemurafenib or dabrafenib which specifically target the activating mutation (Morris and Kopetz, 2013).

Cancer prevention and antioxidants

Antioxidants

The first definition of antioxidant was proposed by Halliwell et al. in 1992 as "any substance that, is present in low concentrations compared to oxidizable substrates (carbohydrates, lipids, proteins or nucleic acids), significantly delays, suppress or inhibits the oxidation of the mentioned substrates" (Halliwell et al., 1992). Later on, other definitions of antioxidant were proposed, such as "any substance that prevents, delays or eliminates oxidative damage of a target molecule" (Halliwell and Gutteridge, 1990) or "any substance that can eliminate reactive oxygen species (ROS) directly or indirectly, acting as a regulator of the antioxidant defense system, or inhibiting the production of those species" (Khlebnikov et al., 2007).

Antioxidants defense

Antioxidants can be classified into three lines of defense according to their mechanisms of actions. The first group includes antioxidants that prevent the formation of new free radicals. It is a very heterogeneous group which includes enzymes such as superoxide dismutase (SOD), catalase (CAT), and glutathione peroxidase (GPX); proteins that bind metals such as ferritin and ceruloplasmin; and minerals such as Se, Cu, and Zn. The second line includes antioxidants that are responsible for capturing free radicals, and thus they prevent oxidative chain reactions. Those antioxidants are formed by the glutathione enzyme, albumin, vitamins C and E, carotenoids, and flavonoids. The third line of defense includes antioxidant enzymes that repair the damage caused by free radicals to biomolecules, such as lipases, proteases, DNA repair enzymes, transferases, and methionine-sulfoxide reductases (Shetti et al., 2009; Irshad and Chaudhuri 2002; Sindhi et al., 2013). Most exogenous antioxidants are produced by vegetables. Therefore, they are often called phytochemicals, although this is a concept which refers to any chemical compound derived from plants (El Gharras, 2009).

If ROS-generating agents combine with ROS inhibitors (e.g., glutathione [GSH], thioredoxin [TRX], or SOD), can reduce the power of cancer cells to adapt to either agent. Even while various antioxidant proteins and regulators are upregulated in cancers they can be usefully targeted to cause antitumor influences, and it will be essential to discover the processes and redox regulation properties which are enriched in tumor cells and subsequently use them as clinically relevant therapeutic targets (Glasauer and Chandel, 2014).

The role of antioxidants in cancer prevention

An antioxidant is a molecule, which prevents the oxidation of other molecules. Oxidation is a chemical reaction containing the loss of electrons which can give free radicals. In sequence, these radicals can commence chain reactions. At what time the chain reaction occurs in a cell, it can make destruction or death to the cell. In brief, antioxidants are biochemical compounds, inhibiting oxidation, a procedure which could be destructive to the human body (Selvaduray et al., 2005).

ROS are considered as secondary messengers in cell signalings and they are required for many biological processes in normal cells. Under physiological conditions, ROS are continuously produced by ROS producers and removed through ROS scavenging systems in order to continue redox homeostasis (Glasauer and Chandel, 2014). If alterations occur in redox equilibrium, which are endogenously or exogenously produced, they can either lead to a rise in ROS levels or rate of creation, resulting in cell harmful oxidative stress and irregular cell signaling, or a reduction in ROS, leading to a distraction of cell signaling and thus distraction of cellular homeostasis. Thus, excessive generation of ROS damage to cells, especially the harm to DNA, may play a role in the growth of cancer and other health conditions (Ahmed, 2016).

A popular complementary therapies used by patients with cancer is antioxidants that can be administered through dietary interventions, intravenous infusion or most commonly, dietary supplementation. In addition to their anticancer effects, antioxidants can prevent or delay cellular damage, notably by scavenging free radicals and reducing oxidative stress. Commonly used antioxidants include vitamins, phytochemicals, minerals, natural products and other related substances (Yasueda et al., 2016).

Fruits, legumes, vegetables, nuts, and seeds are sources of varieties of antioxidant bioactive compounds, such as carotenoids (including beta-carotene and lycopene), vitamin C, vitamin E, quercetin, and selenium. Experimental evidences indicate a strong connection between oxidative damage, cancer, and aging. Epidemiological observations depict that a diet rich in fruits and vegetables is associated with lower incidence of some cancers and longer life expectancy; since vegetables and fruits contain natural antioxidants, a considerable efforts have been dedicated for understanding their efficacies in experimental studies and in human trials (Dolara et al., 2012; Somannavar and Kodliwadmath, 2012).

Antioxidant supplementations reduce adverse effects and toxicities from chemotherapy, though the authors noted inconsistencies in the past literature (Yasueda et al., 2016). The most studied oral antioxidant supplement may be melatonin, shown in vitro to have antitumor activity when used with irradiation (Farhood et al., 2019).

The role of vitamin C in cancer prevention

Vitamin C or ascorbic acid is a water-soluble antioxidant associated with the prevention against the common cold and is also a cofactor of hydrolase enzymes that participate in the synthesis of collagen and catecholamine neurotransmitter and hormones, and in the regulation of gene expression. In cancer, ascorbic acid is associated with prevention, progression, and treatment, due to its general properties or its role as a pro-oxidant at high concentration (Villagran et al., 2021).

The effects of ascorbic acid on cancer progression depend on the route of supplementation (oral or intravenous), as well as on the expression and compartmentalization of ascorbic acid transporters in tumor cells. For the expression of transporters of ascorbic acid in tumor cells, it has been documented that some tumor cells show increases in the expression of sodium–ascorbic acid transporter2 (SVCT2) and/or glucose transporter1 (GLUT1) and absorbs more ascorbic acid than normal cells (Vissers and Das, 2018).

Breast cancer prevention

Breast tumors incidence remains a major public health problem. The incidence is rising in most countries and is projected to rise further over the next 20 years in site of current efforts to prevent the disease (Rahib et al., 2014; Colditz and Bohlke, 2014). The high incidence is not surprising as there has been, in most countries, an elevation in numbers of women with major breast cancer risk factors, including lower age of menarche, late age of first pregnancy, fewer pregnancies, shorter or no periods of breastfeeding, and a later menopause. Another cancer risk factors which add to the burden of breast cancer are the increase in obesity, alcohol consumption, inactivity, and hormone replacement therapy (HRT) (Colditz and Bohlke, 2014).

Models and scoring systems have been established either to predict the probability that a person carries a mutation in the BRCA1/2 genes, which is relevant to relatively small numbers of women with strong family histories, or to predict breast cancer risk over time (Amir et al., 2010; Meads et al., 2012). Computer models such as "Breast and Ovarian Analysis of Disease Incidence and Carrier Estimation Algorithm" (BOADICEA) and "risk estimator for breast and ovarian cancer" (BRCAPRO) (Meads et al., 2012). The scoring systems perform well for predicting BRCA1/2 mutation carrier probabilities, which are important in deciding whether to perform a genetic test (Evans et al., 2009; Kast et al., 2014).

There is great interest in determining whether components of diets such as saturated fat contents or the amounts of fruits and vegetables are related to the risk of breast cancer. A randomized trial study performed by the WHI of reduction of the proportion of fat in the diet resulted in a nonsignificant 8% reduction in the risk of breast cancer, but there was some confounding with weight loss (Prentice et al., 2006).

The World Cancer Research Fund (WCRF) has concluded that physical activity probably protects against breast cancer. Independent of changes in adiposity, mechanisms that may rationalize for this protection include physical activity effects on estrogen metabolism, insulin sensitivity, chronic low-level inflammation, oxidative stress and immune function (World Cancer Research Fund/American Institute for Cancer Research, 2013; Wu et al., 2013; Neilson et al., 2017).

Experimental studies have also directly addressed why exercise is beneficial. For example, the colony-forming ability of non–small cell lung cancer (NSCLC) cells is reduced by 80% after preincubation with conditioned serum from exercised individuals (Kurgan et al., 2017).

The mechanism by which alcohol (now considered a class I carcinogen by the International Agency for Research on Cancer (IARC)) increases breast cancer risk is an active area of study. Ethanol is known to stimulate cell proliferation and the transcriptional activity of ligand-activated ER, which in turn increases levels of circulating estrogen levels (Singletary and Gapstur, 2001; Dorgan et al., 2001). Ethanol metabolism takes place mainly in the liver, where it is oxidized to acetaldehyde by the alcohol dehydrogenase (ADH) enzymes; however, ADH enzymes are also expressed in the breast (Triano et al., 2003). Acetaldehyde can induce DNA strand deletions, DNA strand breaks, DNA mutations, chromosome aberrations and DNA adducts, and is considered mutagenic and carcinogenic (Seitz and Stickel, 2010).

WCRF and AICR (the American Institute for Cancer Research) reports recommend that if alcoholic drinks are to be consumed, this is limited to no more than two drinks a day for men and one drink a day for women.

Lung cancer prevention

Prevention of lung cancer is based on primary, secondary and tertiary preventions. Primary prevention methods aimed at tobacco smoking cessation and noninitiation campaigns, which rely mainly on tobacco control policies. Globally, tobacco control foundations are set on WHO Framework Convention on Tobacco Control, which came into force in 2005, and the MPOWER measures proposed thereafter. The acronym MPOWER refers to six key measures for tobacco control (Monitor the use and prevention policies; Protect the population from tobacco smoke; Offer help for smoking cessation; Warn of the dangers of tobacco; Enforce bans on advertising, promotion, and sponsorship; Raise taxes on tobacco). The implementation of tobacco control policies is associated with different health outcomes (Gallus et al., 2014; Feliu et al., 2019) included negatively with the high risk of lung cancer in the European Union (EU) (González-Marrón et al., 2019).

At the secondary level, preventive approaches correspond to lung cancer screening programs. While chest X-ray with or without sputum cytology was found in the past to be ineffective in the reduction of lung cancer mortality, multiple trials have been conducted worldwide in the last decades, and others are still on course, to assess the efficacy of the low-dose computed tomography (LDCT) as screening tools. Results from the NLST trial published in 2011, showed a 20.0% reduction in lung cancer mortality and a 6.7% reduction in all-cause mortality in the arm screened with LDCT in comparison to the arm screened with chest X-Ray. These results prompted a positive recommendation from the United Nations (US) Preventive Services Task Force for the implementation of lung cancer screening programs in the US for adult current and former smokers with a high cumulative history of tobacco consumption. As a result, lung-cancer screenings in community settings are ongoing in the US, although uptake is so far low (National Lung Screening Trial Research Team, 2011).

In early 2020, the results of the NELSON trial also showed a significant reduction of 24.0% in lung cancer mortality in the screening group versus the control group, in which no interventions were performed (de Koning et al., 2020).

The most important risk factor for lung cancer is tobacco smoking, which is estimated to account for about 90% of all lung cancer cases (Alberg et al., 2013).

Cessation of tobacco smoking is crucial for the prevention of lung cancer. Public health measures aimed at quitting smoking have contributed to the reduced incidence of lung cancer (Jemal et al., 2010; Ng et al., 2014). Smoking cessation is also important in the treatment of lung cancer (Cataldo et al., 2010). After establishing a lung cancer diagnosis, cessation of tobacco smoking is linked to increased survival time, decreased postoperative complications, improved response to systemic therapies, improved response to radiation and improved quality of life. Cessation of tobacco is encouraged for all active smokers and especially individuals undergoing lung cancer screening or therapy (Fares et al., 2020).

Liver cancer prevention

Liver cancer is globally still the second most common cause of deaths from cancer, and is estimated to be responsible for nearly 746,000 deaths in 2012. Chronic liver diseases are the most significant risk factor for HCC development. The incidences vary among geographical regions mostly and are influenced by the distribution of the major etiological factors (Schütte et al., 2009).

The majority of cases develops in the setting of chronic hepatitis that progressed to liver fibrosis or cirrhosis which is the major risk factor in 70%–90% of patients (Schütte et al., 2009). About 75% of cases are related to chronic virus induced hepatitis, with HBV (hepatitis B virus) infection being the predominant risk factor worldwide. Other leading risk factors for HCC include, among others, HCV (hepatitis C virus) infection, contamination of food with aflatoxin, ALD (alcohol-induced liver disease), and NASH (nonalcoholic steatohepatitis). The interventions on the prevalence of some of these risk factors, including HBV immunization programs, successful treatments of HCV infection, and reduction of aflatoxin food contamination, have already resulted in significant changes in the epidemiology of HCC. Notably, there is a decrease of infection-related cases but an increase in cases related to other risk factors, with NASH being the predominant factor (Goh et al., 2015).

Primary preventions focus on risk factors for HCC and their treatments at an early stage, secondary preventions concentrate on the treatment of underlying liver diseases in patients with HCC aiming at a prevention of disease progression, and tertiary preventions aim at a reduction of recurrence after successful curative treatment of HCC (Fig. 2) (Singal and El-Serag, 2015).

Prevention of viral hepatitis includes blocking the transmission routes and vaccination. Hepatitis B vaccination is the most important approach to prevent HBV infection. The HBV vaccine is a purified hepatitis B surface antigen. After vaccination, it stimulates the immune system to produce protective antibodies. Preventing chronic HBV infection through vaccination can reduce the risk of HCC by 85% (Chiang et al., 2013).

Lifestyle plays a key role in HCC, including weight control and the maintenance of a healthy diet, especially comprising vegetables and fruits that can reduce the incidence of HCC. It is necessary to avoid alcohol drinking and tobacco smoking, to control hypertension and diabetes through medication, and to maintain normal circulating blood glucose and cholesterol levels (Simon and Chan, 2020).

Therapy of viral hepatitis does not only reduce the occurrence of HCC but also prevents the recurrence of HCC. Antihepatitis drug therapies are the most basic treatment for HBV/HCV infection, and they play important roles in preventing the onset and development of HCC. Anti-HBV drugs include entecavir, adefovir, tenofovir, lamivudine, telmivudine, and other nucleotide analogs (NAs). The 2013 Asia–Pacific Association for the Study of Liver Diseases (APASL) reported that nucleotide drug therapy can significantly reduce viral titer and reduces the risk of HCC. The application of antihepatitis drugs to patients with HCC can also significantly improve survival. At present, many studies have compared five types of NAs to reduce the risks of HCC (Singal et al., 2013).

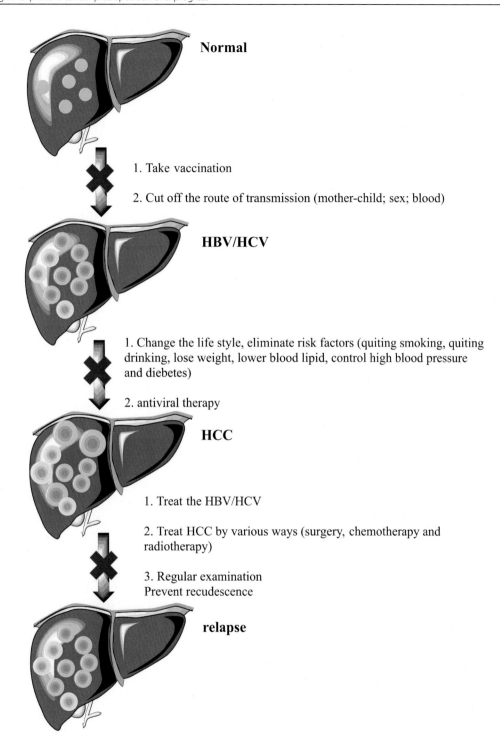

Fig. 2 Flow diagram of HCC prevention (Zhang et al., 2021).

Colorectal cancer prevention

Among all types of cancers, colorectal cancer is third in incidence and cause of cancer deaths (Siegel Rebecca et al., 2020).

Most cases (95%) of colorectal cancer occur in elders (>50 years) who commonly have other lifestyle-related conditions including type two diabetes mellitus and cardiovascular diseases (Klabunde et al., 2007; De Bruijn et al., 2013). These diseases share common risk factors related to obesity, impaired insulin sensitivity, and abnormal cholesterol and triglyceride levels (Jacobs et al., 2007; Sedjo et al., 2007). Meta-analysis studies have demonstrated a consistent association between obesity and colorectal cancer (notably in men) and with colorectal adenomas (Lee et al., 2011; Ben et al., 2012).

Dietary folate or vitamin B9 (from dietary supplements and food fortification) is necessary to synthesize, repair and methylate DNA. It is especially important during periods of rapid cell division and growth such as pregnancy and infancy. Vitamin B9 is also thought to help prevent changes to DNA that may lead to cancer, and its rule in colorectal cancer carcinogenesis has been extensively studied. Humans cannot synthesize colorectal cancer de novo, and therefore folate has to be supplied through diet to meet their daily requirements, with fresh fruits and vegetables being the major sources. There are growing data and a continuing controversy over the effect of vitamin B9 supplementation on cancer risk. Both the Nurse's Health Study (NHS) and secondary analysis from the Wheat Bran Fiber randomized trial reported that high dietary vitamin B9 was associated with 40% reduced risk of colorectal adenoma (highest vs. lowest quartile) (Martínez et al., 2004).

Pyridoxine (vitamin B6) is widely distributed in foods, with good sources including meats, vegetables, whole grain products, nuts and bananas. Pyridoxine is involved in almost 100 enzymatic reactions, among which one function involves transferring 1-carbon groups for DNA biosynthesis and methylations (Selhub, 2002). Therefore, pyridoxine deficiency may increase colorectal cancer risk through aberrations in DNA synthesis, repair, and methylations. Pyridoxine may also suppress colorectal carcinogenesis by reducing cell proliferation, angiogenesis, oxidative stress, inflammation, and nitric oxide (NO) synthesis (Matsubara et al., 2003; Shen et al., 2010).

Aspirin is considered the most established agent for chemoprevention of colorectal cancer (Drew et al., 2016; Drew and Chan, 2021). Previous publications have found that regular use of aspirin is associated with a lower risk of colorectal cancer in the Nurses' NHS and the Health Professionals Follow-up Study (HPFS) (Chan et al., 2005, 2007, 2008).

Skin cancer prevention

United States of America have the highest incidence of skin cancer. It is an abnormal growth of cells that starts in the outer most (epidermal) layer of the skin and is broadly classified as melanoma and nonmelanoma skin cancer. The incidence of melanoma, the most severe form of skin cancer, has been increasing, but overall melanoma mortality rates have not increased significantly (Guy Jr et al., 2015; Linos et al., 2009).

Because exposure to ultraviolet (UV) radiation is determined to be associated with 80% to 90% of skin cancers, the use of sunscreen which blocks ultraviolet radiation is promoted as an important means of preventing skin cancers (Koh et al., 1996; Parkin et al., 2011). Use of sunscreen has been shown to reduce the incidence of both melanoma and nonmelanoma skin cancers (Green et al., 1999, 2011).

Plant constituents are biologically active compounds that may have potential health benefits, especially in the chemoprevention of cancers. Many plant constituents have polyphenol groups consisting of multiple hydrophilic hydroxyl groups which act as scavengers for free radicals and ROS, thereby protecting the cells from the damaging effects of oxidative stress on DNA, protein, and lipids. Other plant constituents exert antiinflammatory properties by inhibiting cytokine formation or the release of inflammatory mediators, which in turn prevent the host cells from inflammation-induced damage. In addition, plant constituents also affect multiple cell signaling pathways and inhibit cell proliferation and angiogenesis (Kelloff et al., 2000; Afaq and Katiyar, 2011).

Plant constituents have been found in a variety of fresh fruits, vegetables, roots, and herbs such as silymarin, curcumin, apigenin, resveratrol, epigallocatechin-3-gallate, proanthocyanidins, genistein, luteolin, indole-3 carbinol, and capsaicin; these Plant constituents have been considered as a means to enhance cancer chemoprevention and treatment via multiple mechanisms of actions (Ng et al., 2018).

4. Conclusions and recommendations

The prognosis of cancer is crucial to avoid the risks of cancer onset and progress as well as to develop strategies for cancer prevention. Such cancer prevention strategies include primary, secondary and tertiary preventions. Based on the results of the prognostic tests, course, type and outcome of the cancer can be predicted and the promising cancer preventive and treatment strategy could be determined for reducing the prevalence, morbidity and the mortality of this disease. Clinical trials in previous publications have informed the development of lifestyle and medical approaches to cancer prevention. These include selective estrogen receptor modulators and aromatase inhibitors for breast cancer and the development of vaccines for viruses that are associated with specific tumors. For liver cancer, educating hospital administrators to remove structural barriers to good practice may help the control of transmission of viral hepatitis and thereby reducing the onset and development of related liver cancers. For lung cancer, controlling tobacco smoking, beginning with physicians, could be very effective in Egypt and other countries with increasing rates of smoking between the young so as to prevent the expected epidemics of lung cancers. For colorectal cancer, more attention to physician and public education about the importance of interviewing colorectal cancer patients about a family history of cancer and the screening of at-risk families could be very effective in early detection of colorectal cancer and thereby preventing its onset and development.

Thus, prevention of cancer, especially primary cancer prevention, remains the most promising strategy for reducing both its incidence and the mortality due to this disease.

References

Afaq, F., Katiyar, S.K., 2011. Polyphenols: skin photoprotection and inhibition of photocarcinogenesis. Mini-Rev. Med. Chem. 11 (14), 1200–1215.

Ahmed, O.M., 2016. Relationships between oxidative stress, cancer development and therapeutic interventions. J. Can. Sci. Res. 1, 1000e104.

Alberg, A.J., et al., 2013. Epidemiology of lung cancer: diagnosis and management of lung cancer: American College of Chest Physicians evidence-based clinical practice guidelines. Chest 143 (5), e1S–e29S.

Alves dos Santos, K., et al., 2020. Circulating exosomal miRNAs as biomarkers for the diagnosis and prognosis of colorectal cancer. Int. J. Mol. Sci. 22 (1), 346.

American Cancer Society, 2006. Cancer Facts and Figures, 2006. Author, Atlanta, GA.

American Cancer Society, 2008. Cancer Facts and Figures, 2008. Author, Atlanta, GA.

Amir, E., Freedman, O.C., Seruga, B., Evans, D.G., 2010. Assessing women at high risk of breast cancer: a review of risk assessment models. J. Natl. Cancer Inst. 102, 680–691.

Anand, P., et al., 2008. Cancer is a preventable disease that requires major lifestyle changes. Pharm. Res. 25 (9), 2097–2116. https://doi.org/10.1007/s11095-008-9661-9 (Epub 2008 Jul 15. Erratum in: Pharm Res. 2008; 25(9):2200. Kunnumakara, Ajaikumar B [corrected to Kunnumakkara, Ajaikumar B]) 18626751. PMC2515569.

Ascierto, P.A., et al., 2012. The role of BRAF V600 mutation in melanoma. J. Transl. Med. 10, 1–9.

Ben, Q., et al., 2012. Body mass index increases risk for colorectal adenomas based on meta-analysis. Gastroenterology 142 (4), 762–772.

Bjartell, A., et al., 2011. Tumour markers in prostate cancer II: diagnostic and prognostic cellular biomarkers. Acta Oncol. 50 (sup1), 76–84.

Bray, F., et al., 2013. Global estimates of cancer prevalence for 27 sites in the adult population in 2008. Int. J. Cancer. https://doi.org/10.1002/ijc.27711.

Cataldo, J.K., Dubey, S., Prochaska, J.J., 2010. Smoking cessation: an integral part of lung cancer treatment. Oncology 78, 289–301.

Cedrés, S., et al., 2011. Serum tumor markers CEA, CYFRA21-1, and CA-125 are associated with worse prognosis in advanced non-small-cell lung cancer (NSCLC). Clin. Lung Cancer 12 (3), 172–179.

Chan, A.T., Giovannucci, E.L., Meyerhardt, J.A., Schernhammer, E.S., Curhan, G.C., Fuchs, C.S., 2005. Long-term use of aspirin and nonsteroidal anti-inflammatory drugs and risk of colorectal cancer. JAMA 294 (8), 914–923. https://doi.org/10.1001/jama.294.8.914.

Chan, A.T., et al., 2007. Aspirin and the risk of colorectal cancer in relation to the expression of COX-2. N. Engl. J. Med. 356 (21), 2131–2142.

Chan, A.T., Giovannucci, E.L., Meyerhardt, J.A., Schernhammer, E.S., Wu, K., Fuchs, C.S., 2008. Aspirin dose and duration of use and risk of colorectal cancer in men. Gastroenterology 134 (1), 21–28.

Chen, H., et al., 2021. The prognostic value of preoperative serum tumor markers in non-small cell lung cancer varies with radiological features and histological types. Front. Oncol. 11, 2253.

Chiang, C.J., et al., 2013. Thirty-year outcomes of the national hepatitis B immunization program in Taiwan. JAMA 310 (9), 974–976.

Colditz, G.A., Bohlke, K., 2014. Priorities for the primary prevention of breast cancer. CA Cancer J. Clin. 64 (3), 186–194.

Colditz, G.A., et al., 2012. Applying what we know to accelerate cancer prevention. Sci. Transl. Med. 4 (127), 127rv4.

Crowe, F.L., et al., 2013. Risk of hospitalization or death from ischemic heart disease among British vegetarians and nonvegetarians: results from the EPIC-Oxford cohort study. Am. J. Clin. Nutr. 97 (3), 597–603.

De Bruijn, K., et al., 2013. Systematic review and meta-analysis of the association between diabetes mellitus and incidence and mortality in breast and colorectal cancer. Br. J. Surg. 100 (11), 1421–1429.

de Koning, H.J., et al., 2020. Reduced lung-cancer mortality with volume CT screening in a randomized trial. N. Engl. J. Med. 382 (6), 503–513.

de Martel, C., et al., 2012. Global burden of cancers attributable to infections in 2008: a review and synthetic analysis. Lancet Oncol. 13 (6), 607–615.

de Martel, C., et al., 2020. Global burden of cancer attributable to infections in 2018: a worldwide incidence analysis. Lancet Glob. Health 8 (2), e180–e190.

Denduluri, N., et al., 2016. Selection of optimal adjuvant chemotherapy regimens for human epidermal growth factor receptor 2 (HER2)–negative and adjuvant targeted therapy for HER2-positive breast cancers: an American Society of Clinical Oncology guideline adaptation of the Cancer Care Ontario clinical practice guideline. J. Clin. Oncol. 34 (20), 2416–2427.

Dolara, P., et al., 2012. Antioxidant vitamins and mineral supplementation, life span expansion and cancer incidence: a critical commentary. Eur. J. Nutr. 51 (7), 769–781.

Dorgan, J.F., et al., 2001. Serum hormones and the alcohol–breast cancer association in postmenopausal women. J. Natl. Cancer Inst. 93 (9), 710–715.

Drew, D.A., Chan, A.T., 2021. Aspirin in the prevention of colorectal neoplasia. Annu. Rev. Med. 72, 415–430.

Drew, D.A., et al., 2016. Aspirin and colorectal cancer: the promise of precision chemoprevention. Nat. Rev. Cancer 16 (3), 173–186.

Edge, S.B., Compton, C.C., 2010. The American joint committee on Cancer: the 7th edition of the AJCC cancer staging manual and the future of TNM. Ann. Surg. Oncol. 17 (6), 1471–1474.

El Gharras, H., 2009. Polyphenols: food sources, properties and applications–a review. Int. J. Food Sci. Technol. 44 (12), 2512–2518.

Emmons, K.M., Colditz, G.A., 2017. Realizing the potential of cancer prevention—the role of implementation science. N. Engl. J. Med. 376 (10), 986.

Evans, D.G.R., et al., 2009. Addition of pathology and biomarker information significantly improves the performance of the Manchester scoring system for BRCA1 and BRCA2 testing. J. Med. Genet. 46 (12), 811–817.

Ezzati, M., et al., 2002. Selected major risk factors and global and regional burden of disease. Lancet 360 (9343), 1347–1360.

Fares, A.F., et al., 2020. Smoking Cessation (SC) and Lung cancer (LC) Outcomes: A Survival Benefit for Recent-Quitters? A Pooled Analysis of 34,649 International Lung Cancer Consortium (ILCCO) Patients.

Farhood, B., et al., 2019. Melatonin as an adjuvant in radiotherapy for radioprotection and radiosensitization. Clin. Transl. Oncol. 21 (3), 268–279.

Feliu, A., et al., 2019. Impact of tobacco control policies on smoking prevalence and quit ratios in 27 European Union countries from 2006 to 2014. Tob. Control. 28 (1), 101–109.

Ferlay, J., et al., 2020. Global Cancer Observatory: Cancer Today. International Agency for Research on Cancer, Lyon. https://gco.iarc.fr/today. (Accessed February 2021).

Gallus, S., et al., 2014. Pricing policies and control of tobacco in Europe (PPACTE) project. Eur. J. Cancer Prev. 23 (3), 177–185.

Glasauer, A., Chandel, N.S., 2014. Targeting antioxidants for cancer therapy. Biochem. Pharmacol. 92 (1), 90–101.

Goh, G.B.B., et al., 2015. Changing epidemiology of hepatocellular carcinoma in Asia. Best Pract. Res. Clin. Gastroenterol. 29 (6), 919–928.

González-Marrón, A., et al., 2019. Relation between tobacco control policies and population at high risk of lung cancer in the European Union. Environ. Res. 179, 108594.

Green, A., et al., 1999. Daily sunscreen application and betacarotene supplementation in prevention of basal-cell and squamous-cell carcinomas of the skin: a randomised controlled trial. Lancet 354 (9180), 723–729.

Green, A.C., et al., 2011. Reduced melanoma after regular sunscreen use: randomized trial follow-up. J. Clin. Oncol. 29 (3), 257–263.

Greenwald, P., Dunn, B.K., 2009. Landmarks in the history of cancer epidemiology. Cancer Res. 69 (6), 2151–2162.

Guy Jr., G.P., et al., 2015. Vital signs: melanoma incidence and mortality trends and projections—United States, 1982–2030. MMWR Morb. Mortal. Wkly Rep. 64 (21), 591.

Hall, C., et al., 2019. A review of the role of carcinoembryonic antigen in clinical practice. Ann. Coloproctol. 35 (6), 294.

Halliwell, B., Gutteridge, J.M.C., 1990. The antioxidants of human extracellular fluids. Arch. Biochem. Biophys. 280 (1), 1–8.

Halliwell, B., Gutteridge, J.M.C., Cross, C.E., 1992. Free radicals, antioxidants, and human disease: where are we now? J. Lab. Clin. Med. 119 (6), 598–620.

Hussein, A.A., et al., 2018. A review of the most promising biomarkers for early diagnosis and prognosis prediction of tongue squamous cell carcinoma. Br. J. Cancer 119 (6), 724–736.

Institute of Medicine [US] and National Research Council [US] National Cancer Policy, 2003. 3, Lifestyle Behaviors Contributing to the Burden of Cancer. In: Curry, S.J., et al. (Eds.), Fulfilling the Potential of Cancer Prevention and Early Detection. National Academies Press, Washington, DC. Available from: https://www.ncbi.nlm.nih.gov/books/NBK223925/.

Irigaray, P., Newby, J.A., Clapp, R., Hardell, L., Howard, V., Montagnier, L., Epstein, S., Belpomme, D., 2007. Lifestyle-related factors and environmental agents causing cancer: an overview. Biomed. Pharmacother. 61, 640–658. https://doi.org/10.1016/j.bio pha.2007.10.006.

Irshad, M., Chaudhuri, P.S., 2002b. Oxidant-antioxidant system: role and signifcance in human body. Indian J. Exp. Biol. 40 (11), 1233–1239.

Jacobs, E.T., Martínez, M.E., Alberts, D.S., Jiang, R., Lance, P., Lowe, K.A., Thompson, P.A., 2007. Association between body size and colorectal adenoma recurrence. Clin. Gastroenterol. Hepatol. 5 (8), 982–990.

Jemal, A., et al., 2010. Global patterns of cancer incidence and mortality rates and trends. Cancer Epidemiol. Biomark. Prev. 19 (8), 1893–1907.

Jemal, A., et al., 2011. Global cancer statistics. CA Cancer J. Clin. 61, 69–90.

Kast, K., et al., 2014. Validation of the Manchester scoring system for predicting BRCA1/2 mutations in 9,390 families suspected of having hereditary breast and ovarian cancer. Int. J. Cancer 135 (10), 2352–2361.

Kelloff, G.J., et al., 2000. (2000). Progress in cancer chemoprevention: development of diet-derived chemopreventive agents. J. Nutr. 130 (2S Suppl), 467S–471S.

Khlebnikov, A.I., et al., 2007. Improved quantitative structure–activity relationship models to predict antioxidant activity of flavonoids in chemical, enzymatic, and cellular systems. Bioorg. Med. Chem. 15 (4), 1749–1770.

Klabunde, C.N., et al., 2007. A refined comorbidity measurement algorithm for claims-based studies of breast, prostate, colorectal, and lung cancer patients. Ann. Epidemiol. 17 (8), 584–590.

Koh, H.K., et al., 1996. Prevention and early detection strategies for melanoma and skin cancer: current status. Arch. Dermatol. 132 (4), 436–443.

Kohler, C., et al., 2011. Cell-free DNA in the circulation as a potential cancer biomarker. Anticancer Res. 31 (8), 2623–2628.

Krop, I., et al., 2017. Use of biomarkers to guide decisions on adjuvant systemic therapy for women with early-stage invasive breast cancer: American Society of Clinical Onoclogy clinical practice guideline focused update. J. Clin. Oncol. 35, 2838–2847.

Kurgan, N., et al., 2017. Inhibition of human lung cancer cell proliferation and survival by post-exercise serum is associated with the inhibition of Akt, mTOR, p70 S6K, and Erk1/2. Cancer 9 (5), 46.

Lee, Y.J., et al., 2011. Adiposity and the risk of colorectal adenomatous polyps: a meta-analysis. Cancer Causes Control 22 (7), 1021–1035.

Liao, R., et al., 2013. High expression of IL-17 and IL-17RE associate with poor prognosis of hepatocellular carcinoma. J. Exp. Clin. Cancer Res. 32 (1), 1–11.

Lichtenstein, P., et al., 2000. Environmental and heritable factors in the causation of cancer—analyses of cohorts of twins from Sweden, Denmark, and Finland. N. Engl. J. Med. 343 (2), 78–85.

Linos, E., et al., 2009. Increasing burden of melanoma in the United States. J. Invest. Dermatol. 129 (7), 1666–1674.

Lippman, S.M., Hawk, E.T., 2009. Cancer prevention: from 1727 to milestones of the past 100 years. Cancer Res 69 (13), 5269–5284.

Loomans-Kropp, H.A., Umar, A., 2019. Cancer prevention and screening: the next step in the era of precision medicine. npj Precis. Oncol. 3, 1–8. https://doi.org/10.1038/s41698-018-0075-9.

Ludwig, J.A., Weinstein, J.N., 2005. Biomarkers in cancer staging, prognosis and treatment selection. Nat. Rev. Cancer 5 (11), 845–856.

Mahon, S.M., 2000. Principles of cancer prevention and early detection. Clin. J. Oncol. Nurs. 4 (4), 169–176.

Mandal, M., 2019. In: Cashin-Garbutt, M.A. (Ed.), Cancer Prognosis. https://www.news-medical.net/health/Cancer-Prognosis.aspx.

Martínez, M.E., et al., 2004. Folate and colorectal neoplasia: relation between plasma and dietary markers of folate and adenoma recurrence. Am. J. Clin. Nutr. 2004 (79), 691–697. 15051616.

Matsubara, K., et al., 2003. Vitamin B6-mediated suppression of colon tumorigenesis, cell proliferation, and angiogenesis (review). J. Nutr. Biochem. 2003 (14), 246–250.

Meads, C., et al., 2012. A systematic review of breast cancer incidence risk prediction models with meta-analysis of their performance. Breast Cancer Res. Treat. 132, 365–377.

Miller, S.M., et al., 2008. Primary prevention, aging, and cancer: overview and future perspectives. Cancer 113 (S12), 3484–3492.

Montagnana, M., et al., 2011. HE4 in ovarian cancer: from discovery to clinical application. Adv. Clin. Chem. 55, 2.

Morris, V., Kopetz, S., 2013. BRAF inhibitors in clinical oncology. F1000Prime Rep. 5, 11. https://doi.org/10.12703/P5-11.

Muinao, T., et al., 2018. Diagnostic and prognostic biomarkers in ovarian cancer and the potential roles of cancer stem cells–an updated review. Exp. Cell Res. 362 (1), 1–10.

National Lung Screening Trial Research Team, 2011. Reduced lung-cancer mortality with low-dose computed tomographic screening. N. Engl. J. Med. 365 (5), 395–409.

Neilson, H.K., et al., 2017. Moderate–vigorous recreational physical activity and breast cancer risk, stratified by menopause status: a systematic review and meta-analysis. Menopause 24, 322–344.

Ng, M., et al., 2014. Smoking prevalence and cigarette consumption in 187 countries, 1980-2012. JAMA 311 (2), 183–192.

Ng, C.Y., et al., 2018. Phytochemicals in skin cancer prevention and treatment: an updated review. Int. J. Mol. Sci. 19 (4), 941. https://doi.org/10.3390/ijms19040941.

Nicolini, A., et al., 2018. Prognostic and predictive biomarkers in breast cancer: past, present and future. Semin. Cancer Biol. 52, 56–73 (Elsevier).

Oh, H.-H., Joo, Y.-E., 2020. Novel biomarkers for the diagnosis and prognosis of colorectal cancer. Intest. Res. 18 (2), 168.

ONS, 2002. Prevention and Early Detection of cancer in the United States [Position Statement]. Author, Pittsburgh, PA.

Parkin, D.M., et al., 2011. Cancers attributable to solar (ultraviolet) radiation exposure in the UK in 2010. Br. J. Cancer 105 (Suppl 2), S66–S69.

PATO/WHO, 2022. World Cancer Day 2022: Close the care gap. https://www.paho.org/en/campaigns/world-cancer-day-2022-close-care-gap.

Personeni, N., et al., 2012. Usefulness of alpha-fetoprotein response in patients treated with sorafenib for advanced hepatocellular carcinoma. J. Hepatol. 57 (1), 101–107.

Prentice, R.L., et al., 2006. Low-fat dietary pattern and risk of invasive breast cancer: the Women's health initiative randomized controlled dietary modification trial. JAMA 295, 629–642.

Rahib, L., et al., 2014. Projecting cancer incidence and deaths to 2030: the unexpected burden of thyroid, liver, and pancreas cancers in the United States. Cancer Res. 74, 2913–2921.

Sardana, G., et al., 2008. Emerging biomarkers for the diagnosis and prognosis of prostate cancer. Clin. Chem. 54 (12), 1951–1960.

Schulz, M., et al., 2008. Identification of a dietary pattern characterized by high-fat food choices associated with increased risk of breast cancer: the European prospective investigation into Cancer and nutrition (EPIC)-Potsdam study. Br. J. Nutr. 100 (5), 942–946.

Schütte, K., et al., 2009. Hepatocellular carcinoma–epidemiological trends and risk factors. Dig. Dis. 27, 80–92.

Sedjo, R.L., et al., 2007. Change in body size and the risk of colorectal adenomas. Cancer Epidemiol. Bio-markers Prev. 16 (3), 526–531.

Seitz, H.K., Stickel, F., 2010. Acetaldehyde as an underestimated risk factor for cancer development: role of genetics in ethanol metabolism. Genes Nutr. 5, 121–128.

Selhub, J., 2002. Folate, vitamin B12 and vitamin B6 and one carbon metabolism. J. Nutr. Health Aging 2002 (6), 39–42.

Selvaduray, K.R., et al., 2005. Antioxidants and prostate cancer. J. Oil Technol. Assoc. India 2005 (37), 19.

Shen, J., et al., 2010. Association of vitamin B-6 status with inflammation, oxidative stress, and chronic inflammatory conditions: the Boston Puerto Rican health study. Am. J. Clin. Nutr. 91, 337–342.

Shetti, A., et al., 2009. Antioxidants: enhancing oral and general health. J. Indian Acad. Oral Med. Radiol. 21 (1), 1.

Siegel Rebecca, L., et al., 2020. Colorectal cancer statistics 2020. CA Cancer J. Clin. 70 (3), 145–164.

Siegel, R.L., et al., 2018. Cancer statistics, 2018. CA Cancer J. Clin. 68, 7–30.

Simon, T.G., Chan, A.T., 2020. Lifestyle and environmental approaches for the primary prevention of hepa-tocellular carcinoma. Clin. Liver Dis. 24 (4), 549–576.

Sindhi, V., et al., 2013. Potential applications of antioxidants—a review. J. Pharm. Res. 7 (9), 828–835.

Singal, A.G., El-Serag, H.B., 2015. Hepatocellular carcinoma from epidemiology to prevention: translating knowledge into practice. Clin. Gastroenterol. Hepatol. 13, 2140–2151.

Singal, A.K., et al., 2013. Meta-analysis: the impact of Oral anti-viral agents on the incidence of hepatocel-lular carcinoma in chronic hepatitis B. Aliment. Pharmacol. Ther. 38 (2), 98–106.

Singletary, K.W., Gapstur, S.M., 2001. Alcohol and breast cancer: review of epidemiologic and experimen-tal evidence and potential mechanisms. JAMA 286, 2143–2151.

Somannavar, M.S., Kodliwadmath, M.V., 2012. Correlation between oxidative stress and antioxidant defence in south Indian urban vegetarians and non-vegetarians. Eur. Rev. Med. Pharmacol. Sci. 16 (3), 351–354.

Stewart, B.W., et al., 2016. Cancer prevention as part of precision medicine: 'plenty to be done'. Carcino-genesis 37 (1), 2–9.

Trevisani, F., et al., 2019. Alpha-fetoprotein for diagnosis, prognosis, and transplant selection. In: Seminars in Liver Disease. Thieme Medical Publishers.

Triano, E.A., et al., 2003. Class I alcohol dehydrogenase is highly expressed in normal human mammary epithelium but not in invasive breast cancer: implications for breast carcinogenesis. Cancer Res. 63 (12), 3092–3100.

Turini, M., DuBois, R., 2002. Primary prevention: phytoprevention and chemoprevention of colorectal cancer. Hematol. Oncol. Clin. North Am. 16, 811–840.

Uehara, M., et al., 2008. Long-term prognostic study of carcinoembryonic antigen (CEA) and carbohydrate antigen 15-3 (CA 15-3) in breast cancer. Int. J. Clin. Oncol. 13 (5), 447–451.

Villagran, M., et al., 2021. The role of vitamin C in cancer prevention and therapy: a literature review. Anti-oxidants 10 (12), 1894.

Virji, M.A., et al., 1988. Tumor markers in cancer diagnosis and prognosis. CA Cancer J. Clin. 38 (2), 104–126.

Vissers, M.C.M., Das, A.B., 2018. Potential mechanisms of action for vitamin C in cancer: reviewing the evidence. Front. Physiol. 9, 809.

WHO, 2007. The World Health Organization's Fight Against Cancer: Strategies that Prevent, Cure and Care. World Health Organization, Geneva. https://apps.who.int/iris/handle/10665/43665.

WHO, 2009. Strategy for cancer prevention and control in the Eastern Mediterranean Region. Regional Committee for the EM/RC56/4 Eastern Mediterranean. https://apps.who.int/iris/handle/10665/122801.

WHO, 2022. Health Topics. Cancer. WHO, Geneva. https://www.who.int/news-room/fact-sheets/detail/cancer.

World Cancer Research Fund (WCRF)/American Institute for Cancer Research, 2013. Cancer Prevent-ability Estimates for Body Fatness. WCRF International. http://www.wcrf-uk.org/uk/preventing-cancer/cancer-preventability-statistics/bowel-cancer.

Wu, Y., et al., 2013. Physical activity and risk of breast cancer: a meta-analysis of prospective studies. Breast Cancer Res. Treat. 137, 869–882.

Yasueda, A., et al., 2016. Efficacy and interaction of antioxidant supplements as adjuvant therapy in cancer treatment: a systematic review. Integr. Cancer Ther. 15 (1), 17–39.

Yu, L., et al., 2022. Novel prognostic Indicator combining inflammatory indicators and tumor markers for gastric cancer. Research Square. https://doi.org/10.21203/rs.3.rs-1268760/v1. Preprint.

Zhang, X., et al., 2021. Risk factors and prevention of viral hepatitis-related hepatocellular carcinoma. Front. Oncol. 11, 686962.

Further reading

Al-Dahshan, A., et al., 2020. Colorectal cancer awareness and its predictors among adults aged 50–74 years attending primary healthcare in the State of Qatar: a cross-sectional study. BMJ Open 10 (7), e035651.

Arnold, M., et al., 2013. Recent trends in incidence of five common cancers in 26 European countries since 1988: analysis of the European Cancer observatory. Eur. J. Cancer 51, 1164–1187.

Chapelle, N., et al., 2020. Recent advances in clinical practice: colorectal cancer chemoprevention in the average-risk population. Gut 69 (12), 2244–2255.

Clinton, S.K., et al., 2020. The world cancer research fund/American institute for cancer research third expert report on diet, nutrition, physical activity, and cancer: impact and future directions. J. Nutr. 150 (4), 663–671.

Czene, K., Hemminki, K., 2002. Kidney cancer in the Swedish family cancer database: familial risks and second primary malignancies. Kidney Int. 61, 1806–1813. https://doi.org/10.1046/j.1523-1755.2002.00304.x.

Dilley, R.J., et al., 2014. Vascularisation to improve translational potential of tissue engineering systems for cardiac repair. Int. J. Biochem. Cell Biol. 56, 38–46.

Dreher, D., Junod, A.F., 1996. Role of oxygen free radicals in cancer development. Eur. J. Cancer 32 (1), 30–38.

Eccles, S.A., et al., 2013. Critical research gaps and translational priorities for the successful prevention and treatment of breast cancer. Breast Cancer Res. 15 (5), 1–37.

Erm, A., et al., 2001. Optical and biological properties of Lake Ülemiste, a water reservoir of the city of Tallinn I: water transparency and optically active substances in the water. Lakes Reservoir 6 (1), 63–74.

Wu, Y, et al., 2013. Physical activity and risk of breast cancer: a meta-analysis of prospective studies. Breast Cancer Res. Treat. 137 (3), 869–882.

Ferlay, J. and Colombet, M. (2012). Soerjomataram I. Ervik M. Dikshit R. Eser S. Mathers C. et al. GLOBOCAN, v1.

Fischer, C., et al., 2013. Evaluating the performance of the breast cancer genetic risk models BOADICEA, IBIS, BRCAPRO and Claus for predicting BRCA1/2 mutation carrier probabilities: a study based on 7352 families from the German hereditary breast and ovarian Cancer consortium. J. Med. Genet. 50 (6), 360–367.

Hahn, W.C., Weinberg, R.A., 2002. Modelling the molecular circuitry of cancer. Nat. Rev. Cancer 2, 331–341. https://doi.org/10.1038/nrc795.

Irshad, M., Chaudhuri, P., 2002a. Oxidant-antioxidant system: role and significance in human body. Indian J. Exp. Biol. 40, 1233–1239.

Kohler, B.A., Sherman, R.L., Howlader, N., et al., 2015a. Annual Report to the Nation on the Status of Cancer, 1975–2011, Featuring Incidence of Breast Cancer Subtypes by Race/Ethnicity, Poverty, and State [published correction appears in J Natl Cancer Inst. 2015 May;107(5). pii: djv121. https://doi.org/10.1093/jnci/djv121] [published correction appears in J Natl Cancer Inst. 2015 Jul;107(7). pii: djv177. https://doi.org/10.1093/jnci/djv177]. J. Natl. Cancer Inst. 107 (6), djv048. Published 2015 Mar 30 https://doi.org/10.1093/jnci/djv048.

Kohler, B.A., et al., 2015b. Annual report to the nation on the status of cancer, 1975–2011, featuring incidence of breast cancer subtypes by race/ethnicity, poverty, and state. J. Natl. Cancer Inst. 107 (6), djv048.

Mucci, L.A., et al., 2001. The role of gene-environment interaction in the aetiology of human cancer: examples from cancers of the large bowel, lung and breast. J. Intern. Med. 249, 477–493.

ONS, 2007. Prevention and early detection of cancer in the United States. Oncol. Nurs. Forum 34 (4), 759–760.

Qin, F.A., et al., 2007. Lead and copper levels in tea samples marketed in Beijing, China. Bull. Environ. Contam. Toxicol. 78 (2), 128–131.

Vinson, J.A., Dabbagh, Y.A., 1998. Tea phenols: antioxidant effectiveness of teas, tea components, tea fractions and their binding with lipoproteins. Nutr. Res. 18, 1067–1075.

World Cancer Research Fund/American Institute for Cancer Research, 2007. Food, Nutrition, Physical Activity, and the Prevention of Cancer: A Global Perspective. American Institute for Cancer Research.

World Cancer Research Fund/American Institute for Cancer Research, 2018. Diet, Nutrition, Physical Activity and Breast Cancer. https://www.wcrf.org/sites/default/files/Summary-of-Third-Expert Report-2018.pdf.

CHAPTER NINE

Cytogenetics to multiomics in biology of cancer

Sikander S. Gill[a], Rajwant K. Gill[a], and R.C. Sobti[b]
[a]Freelancer Scientist, Vancouver, BC, Canada
[b]Department of Biotechnology, Panjab University, Chandigarh, India

1. Introduction

Cancer, a consolidated name for thousands of different diseases has taken an investment of sustained development of decades for our understanding of its biology. Cytogenetics and molecular genetics that embrace a common field, but individually with different focus have contributed tremendously toward the understanding of cancer biology. The former studied chromosomal abnormalities displaying big changes with large fragments broken off, missing or moving or sticking to another chromosome and the latter included the study of genes and their rearrangements at the DNA level in cancer cells, tissues and tumors.

Cytogenetics as a tool to determine number of chromosomes of an organism emerged in 1900. However, human cytogenetics was introduced in 1956 with accurate determination of the number of chromosomes as 46 in a diploid human cell was (Tjio and Levan, 1956). Ever since, our knowledge and ability to understand and diagnose human diseases, and to utilize cytogenetic data has increased by leaps and bounds. The emergence of the field of human cytogenetics led to development of new methods to visualize chromosome structure and organization. Numerous studies were embarked on determining the co relation between human disease and chromosomes.

Basically, the novel techniques explained that cancer happens when DNA control and repair mechanisms get disabled my mutations allowing cells to proliferate unnaturally (Gijsbers and CAL, 2011). These techniques have designated cancer as a disease of cellular evolution since the cells in a tumor follow Darwinian evolution and diverge genetically and phenotypically into distinct populations as clones or stem-lines that coexist in the same tumor (Baudoin and Bloomfield, 2021). This diversity of the cancer cells is the basic challenge in the task of understanding its biology since each type of cancer is a cluster of different subtypes or subclones. This heterogeneity of cancer tissue not only makes the disease more complex but also makes every cancer unique in its composition that the

Biomarkers in Cancer Detection and Monitoring of Therapeutics
https://doi.org/10.1016/B978-0-323-95116-6.00019-0

151

conventional karyotyping to next-gen karyotyping has understood (Biswas and Khan, 2020; Sha et al., 2017; Mareschal et al., 2021).

However, this knowledge has driven our understanding and uncovered new approaches toward its prevention, screening, diagnosis, and treatment of cancer. Many of these approaches have directly benefitted medical fields far beyond cancer.

But still despite the intensive efforts over a century and the promise from "War on Cancer" nearly 50 years ago has not materialized as much (Sonnenschein and Soto, 2020). Currently, one of the biggest challenges remain to be solved, is drug resistance in cancer therapy since cancers have multiple mechanisms of evading drugs to survive and grow that vary with tumor to tumor and patient to patient. Over this span of time, the evolution of techniques and strategies is aimed at solving this puzzle of drug resistance and offer therapy in preventing drug resistance.

Similarly, some techniques and approaches like precision medicine based on the genomic information about a patient's cancer has brought a revolution in cancer diagnosis and treatment as tailor-made customized therapies (Nath and Bild, 2021). In the development of biomarkers for prognostic and drug response normally rely on bulk "omics" data, which however, fails to capture intra-tumor heterogeneity and differentiation of normal versus tumor cells. The evolution of techniques encompassing integration and fusion of genomic and proteomic information will present a clear picture of patient's cancer for better treatment.

The contributions made by these techniques and strategies in the understanding of cancer biology, the number of cancer survivors has grown dramatically all over the world. These interventions will improve the quality of life of the cancer survivors. Eventually, all these early to latest advances in cancer prevention have contributed to a continuous decline in cancer death rate from 1991 to 2017 by a total of 29% (Elmore et al., 2020). However, despite this progress from classical cytogenetic karyotyping to molecular karyotyping, as much as we have learnt, much important gaps remain in our understanding. Therefore, omics are expected to improve understanding of cancer from different biological angels rather than single parameter model since the acquisition of cancer hallmarks reflect molecular alterations at multiple levels including genome, epigenome, transcriptome, proteome, and metabolome (Menyhartab and Győrffy, 2021). Therefore, the evolution of classical cytogenetic karyotyping through transitional techniques to "omics" displays an interesting path.

2. Karyotyping

Early cytogenetic studies revealed that an extra copy of chromosome 21 could lead to disease called Down syndrome or trisomy 21 (Lejeune et al., 1959). In the same year, changes in sex chromosome number were linked to several health abnormalities. In particular, the presence of a single X chromosome and absence of Y chromosome

(45,X) was associated with Turner's syndrome (Ford et al., 1959). Similarly, the presence of two copies of the X chromosome and one copy of the Y chromosome (47,XXY) determined Klinefelter's syndrome (Jacobs and Strong, 1959). Both these syndromes affect sexual differentiation in affected individuals that can be easily reflected by karyotyping.

The karyotyping is the process of pairing and ordering all the chromosomes of an organism. Eventually, since the 1970s, it was applied to detect chromosomal aberrations and clinical syndromes. As such, karyotyping was the first cytogenetics tool to analyze characteristics of chromosomes that could be applied to characterize and diagnose cancer cells, tissues and tumors. With time various methodologies evolved along the line and finally the evolution of these techniques lead to next-generation karyotyping that helped in these investigations (Mareschal et al., 2021).

2.1 Classical cytogenetic karyotyping

Cytogenetics, a field of study that deals with chromosomes and related abnormalities is also known as karyotyping that involves the pairing of homologous chromosomes. Karyotyping is basically chromosome analysis and involves the process of pairing and ordering all the chromosomes of an organism or tumor or normal or cancer cell. In other words, it provides a genome-wide snapshot of chromosomes of an individual or tumor or cell conveying gross structural changes in terms of deletions and inversions.

With a classical approach for diagnostic information from a chromosome preparation, images of the individual chromosomes are arranged into a standardized international format of karyotype also known as karyogram. In this process, out of 24 human chromosomes (22 autosomal pairs and X-Y sex chromosomes), the autosomes are arranged and numbered from 1 to 22 in descending size except chromosomes 21 and 22, while the sex chromosomes are placed at the end of the karyotype. In determining changes in the karyotype, the chromosomal abnormalities include both numerical and structural changes. The numeral changes involve any changes other than a complete set of 46 chromosomes while structural changes involve structural alterations in chromosomes. The type and degree of the abnormality may vary from patient to patient even though the same chromosome abnormality is manifested by the karyotype.

The process of karyotype involves taking tissue for example bone marrow or short-term cultured cells obtained from a specimen. The addition of colchicine that disrupts mitotic spindle formation, arrests dividing cells in metaphase of the cell division. The treatment of these cells with a hypotonic solution swells up their nuclei and makes the cells to burst followed by dropping a drop of the suspension onto a glass slide and eventually fixes the slide by treatment with a chemical fixative. The chemically fixed slides are processed through staining to reveal structural features of the chromosomes (O'Connor, 2008).

The karyotyping thus prepared involves aligning photographed chromosomes from microscopy along a horizontal axis with aligned centromere of each chromosome while the short p (petite in French) arm is at the top, and the long q (queue) arm at the bottom. The centromere location identifies the gross morphology, or shape of chromosomes: Metacentric chromosomes (p and q arms of nearly equal lengths, chromosomes 1, 3, and 16). Submetacentric chromosomes (slightly displaced centromere from the center, chromosomes 2, 6, and 10), acrocentric chromosomes (centromeres located near their ends, chromosomes 14, 15, and 21).

However, basic karyotyping in cancer cells remains challenging since numerous changes are acquired by cancer cell DNA that range from point mutations to complex DNA rearrangements ultimately leading to a complex cancer-associated genome (Lee and Lee, 2021). Annotation of such structural variations (SVs) and basic karyotyping in cancer cells poses another layer of challenges. In cancer biology, the first contribution of cytogenetic karyotyping was the chromosomal abnormality in 1959 when David Hungerford, and Peter Nowell discovered an abnormally mini chromosome known as Philadelphia chromosome or derivative chromosome 22 in samples from patients with chronic myeloid leukemia.

In addition to associating chromosomal abnormalities with disease, these cytogenetic approaches also advanced to map genes on the chromosomes. For example, Roger Dona-hue in 1968, studied metaphase chromosomes from his own blood cells, and discovered a loosely structured and uncoiled region near the centromere of one of his copies of chro-mosome 1. Extending these observations to his family pedigree along with conducting biochemical tests, he applied cytogenetic method to map the Duffy blood group locus to chromosome 1 (Donahue et al., 1968).

A decade After the application of cytogenetic karyotyping of cancer cells, Janet Rowley using quinacrine fluorescence and Giemsa staining reported a translocation between chromosomes 22 and 9 (Rowley, 1973). Ever since, the cytogenetic karyotyping has played a great role in understanding the biology of tumor cells displaying chromosomal aberrations both in structure and number of autosomes and sex chromo-some deviation from the paired order (Solomon et al., 1992).

Banded karyotyping

The normal karyotypes were grouped according to their size and the placement of their individual centromeres thus suffered from limitation in showing characteristic structural fea-tures of chromosomes. Shortly after the mapping of the Duffy blood group locus by Dona-hue, cytologists Maximo Drets and Margery Shaw, stained metaphase chromosomes using a dye called Giemsa producing signature banding pattern named G-bands, of all the 24 human chromosomes (Drets and Shaw, 1971). Later the DNA binding dye made the analysis more effective and efficient that generated characteristic banding patterns known as Q-banding for each chromosome. The banding is basically lengthwise variation in staining properties along a chromosome and refers to alternating light and dark regions along the length of a chromosome. With the display of banding pattern, each chromosome pair appears to have its own signatory "bar code" of bands (Table 1).

The fluorescent dye quinacrine used in Q-banding, alkylates DNA and was found to generate reproducible banding patterns for individual chromosomes. Eventually, quinacrine was replaced with Giemsa dye for better resolution of individual bands and

Table 1 Chromosome banding.

Banding	Image	Stain	Attributes	Introduction
Q-banding		Quinacrine staining	• Euchromatin bands • DNA rich in the bases A-T • Useful for chromosomal translocations, especially involving the Y chromosome • The first method for 46 chromosome identifications under UV light	1968
G-banding		Giemsa staining	• Euchromatin bands (guanine and cytosine and transcriptionally active) • Chromatin and deeper DNA patterns • 400 to 800 bands among the 23 pairs of human chromosomes. • Heterochromatic regions (AT-rich DNA) and relatively gene-poor, stain more darkly in G-banding • Less condensed chromatin (GC-rich) and more transcriptionally active incorporates less Giemsa stain and appear as light bands in G-banding. • Can be equated with Q-banding	1971

Continued

Table 1 Chromosome banding—cont'd

Banding	Image	Stain	Attributes	Introduction
C-banding		Giemsa staining	• Heterochromatin • Differentially stained centromeres • Stained constitutive heterochromatin, or genetically inactive DNA • Primarily stains chromosomes at the centromeres (AT-rich satellite DNA)	1971
R-banding		Reverse Giemsa staining	• Euchromatin bands • Involves Giemsa stain • Generates the reverse pattern from G-banding • The chromosomes are pre heated Giemsa staining that melts the DNA helix in the AT-rich regions and stains most strong • Comparatively GC-rich regions take up less stain • Provides critical details about gene-rich regions near the telomeres	1971
S-banding		Silver staining Ag–NOR staining	• Genes for ribosomal RNA • For nucleolus organizing regions(NORs) was	1975
T-banding		• Giemsa or acridine orange dye • Hoechst 33258	• Telomeric regions	1973
FISH		• Which uses fluorescently labeled DNA probes	• Staining of specific sequences within the chromosomes	Mid-1980s

analyzed with ordinary bright-field microscopy. The Q-banding displayed the staining differences along the length of a chromosome based on the base composition of the DNA and local chromatin structure. However, the G-banding variant of Giemsa staining involved brief pretreatment of chromosomes with trypsin that partly digested proteins allowing the Giemsa dye access to the DNA (O'Connor, 2008).

All the banding methodologies shared a common objective of accurately identifying chromosomes and their segments. The banding patterns presented insight into chromosome organization reflecting many features including native or aberrated molecular biology and cytogenetics. Thus, the banding pattern offered chromosome research a new and wider importance.

Prior to Q-banding, the 24 human chromosomes were divided on the basis of size and position of the centromere and thus divided into seven different groups (A to G). Now, these chromosomes could not only be undisputedly identified but specific regions and bands in the chromosomes could be easily identified. In 1976, an International Standing Committee on Human Cytogenetic Nomenclature was established to improve chromosome nomenclature. The introduction of Q-banding encouraged several other staining methods that generated different patterns that were steps forward in determining cancer biology in reference to changes in the genetic materials reflected by chromosomal aberrations (Schreck and Distèche, 2001; Kosyakova et al., 2013).

Normally, the banding patterns between the homologues chromosomes of any autosome are nearly identical except some artifacts attributed to natural structural variability among individuals and to technical processing artifacts. However, an average of few karyotypes can rule out such artifacts. Therefore, the banding patterns are recognized and linked to different disease phenotypes. The gross genetic anomalies detected in clinical human karyotypes include more subtle structural changes, such as chromosomal deletions, duplications, translocations, or inversions that involve several megabases or more of DNA or even chromosome numbers such as reporting trisomy 21 (Down syndrome). Typically, a G-band represents resolution of several megabases to 10 million base pairs of DNA spanning hundreds of genes (O'Connor, 2008). However, this can be sufficient to diagnose certain categories of abnormalities. Another chromosome number related anomaly, aneuploidy for example is often caused by the absence or addition of a chromosome which is very simple to detect by karyotyping. With staining procedures, cytogeneticists could also identify subtle deletions or inversions, or insertions as deviations from normal banding patterns. Similarly, translocations are also readily visible on karyotypes. Eventually, with the progress of medical genetics, karyotypes became a diagnostic tool for determining specific birth defects, genetic disorders, and cancers.

Despite better resolution offered by staining methods, the analysis from solid tumors was challenging due to various reasons including low mitotic index, the quality of metaphase chromosomes, and the cytogenetic abnormalities (Heim and Mitelman, 1995). However, the G- or R-banding karyotype analysis has widely contributed to the characterization of cytogenetic abnormalities in tumor cells.

The generation of chromosomal aneuploidies has profound genetic consequences of oncogenes due to increased copy number and loss of tumor suppressor genes. However, peri- or paracentric inversions and reciprocal translocations reflected by karyotyping can balance the net change while translocations (duplications, deletions, and nonreciprocal translocations) unbalance net gains or loss of DNA. In hematopoietic malignancies, however, the balanced chromosomal translocations have been regularly observed and linked to pathogenetic events (Knutsen and Ried, 2000). On the other hand, translocation findings have revealed the impact of the re-positioning of an oncogene in proximity to a strong enhancer from another gene leading to oncogene overexpression and become a reason of cellular transformation. An example is c-myc in human Burkitt's lymphoma where oncogene gets juxtaposed to the enhancer for the immunoglobulin heavy chain gene (Boxer and Dang, 2001).

The simple chromosomal structural variations including tandem duplications, deletions, inversions and insertions have also been reported tumorigenic (Yi and Ju, 2018). Similarly, the more complex structural variations that include translocations, fold-back inversions, chromothripsis, homogeneously staining regions and double minutes are also linked to cancer (Garsed et al., 2014; Storlazzi et al., 2010). The standard karyotyping techniques including banding display complex structural variations in derivative chromosomes or marker chromosomes (Knutsen et al., 2005). Thus, the benefits of karyotyping include: It can view the entire genome and it can visualize individual cells and individual chromosomes (Table 2). However, the standard karyotyping techniques suffered from the limitation of resolution of about 5 Mb and thus complex structural variations cannot be accurately identified. Additionally, an actively growing source of cells is required for this analysis. The classic karyotyping is time consuming due to several days

Table 2 The karyotyping analysis reveal following abnormalities.

Chromosomal abnormalities	Abbreviation	Description

Trisomy	tri	• Presence of an extra chromosome instead of a pair
		• Diseases:
		  ○ Down syndrome (Trisomy 21)
		  ○ Patau syndrome (Trisomy 13)
		  ○ Edward syndrome (Trisomy 18)
		  ○ Klinefelter syndrome (XXY versus XY)

Monosomy	mon	• Absence of one chromosome from a pair
		• Diseases:
		  ○ Turner syndrome (a female with a single X chromosome versus normal XX)
		  ○ Most other monosomies are mortal

Table 2 The karyotyping analysis reveal following abnormalities—cont'd

Chromosomal abnormalities	Abbreviation	Description
Deletion	del	• Missing pieces of chromosomes • Some segments too small to be detected

Insertion	ins	• Addition of one or more nucleotide base pairs (chromosome fragment) into a chromosome or larger DNA sequence
		  ○ This can often happen in microsatellite regions due to the DNA polymerase slipping.
		  ○ Can happen due to unequal meiotic crossover during meiosis.

Inversion	inv	• A chromosome segment is clipped out then turned 180°, and reinserted back into the chromosome • Can be inherited from one or both parents • Can occur in an individual
Duplication	dup	• Extra genetic material • May be present on any chromosome • In banding karyotype ○ Example: Presence of two bands instead of one on a location

Translocations	t	• Piece of chromosome translocates one to another chromosome
		• Disease outcome:
		  ○ Balanced translocation. As one-to-one switch total genetic material is present but at the wrong place
		  ○ Unbalanced translocation-to different chromosome

Genetic rearrangement		• Genetic material is present on a chromosome but at unusual location • Disease outcome: ○ Chromothripsis includes tens to thousands of chromosomal rearrangements

Derivative chromosome	(der)	• A structurally rearranged chromosome with an intact centromere
		  ○ Generated by:
		    ■ Involvement of two or more chromosomes
		    ■ Involvement of multiple chromosome aberrations within a single chromosome

involving preparation of cells and live lymphocytes are required for culture within a maximum of 48 h or sooner.

The karyotype of patient generally accompanies a cytogenetic notation decoded by the cytogeneticist (Table 3).

Table 3 Cytogenetic nomenclature: An example for interpretation of cytogenetic notation: 47, XY, del(7)(q21q34),+,t(8,9)(q13;q34) (6)/46,XY (3).

Notation	Description
47	Number of chromosomes detected
XY	Sex chromosomes
del(7)(q21q34),	Deletion of chromosomal material on the long arm of chromosome 7 between regions 21 and 34
+8	Trisomy 8 (extra chromosome 8)
t(8,9)(q13;q34)	Translocation of chromosomal material on the long arm of chromosome 8 and the long arm of chromosome 9
(6)	Number of cells (metaphases) examined with these abnormalities
/	Separates information about differing karyotypes
46	Differing karyotype chromosome number
XY	Sex chromosomes
(3)	Number of cells examined with this normal karyotype

Micronucleus

Micronuclei were first discovered by Henry Howell and Justin Marie Jolly in erythro-cytes about a century ago (Sears and Udden, 2012). These are formed when a broken chromosome fragment or rarely an entire chromosome or a few chromosomes fail to join a daughter nucleus and eventually form their own nuclear envelope from abnormal cell divisions (Frenech et al., 2016). Micronuclei are structurally comparable to primary nucleus but lack full functionality in transcription, replication and DNA damage repair due to impaired micronuclear trafficking as a consequence of reduced nuclear pore pro-tein levels (Terradas et al., 2012). Micronuclei formed can be of various sizes but typically vary from 1/10th to 1/100th the size of original nucleus. It is a well-known fact that during the past years, the DNA damage accumulates in micronuclei (Zhang et al., 2015). The DNA in the chromosomes in micronuclei undergoes damage at faster rates than the chromosomes in the main nucleus leading to chromothripsis—a process of com-plex structural re-arrangements of chromosomes in a short time period of a single cata-strophic event (Zhang et al., 2015; Baudoin and Bloomfield, 2021).

The micronuclei are frequently found in cancer pathologies and thus the presence of micronuclei is a hallmark of chromosome instability. Therefore, chromothripsis is com-monly observed in cancer and associated with poor prognosis (Ly and Cleveland, 2017; Rode et al., 2016). Among several different assays for the use of micronuclei including the cytokinesis-block, peripheral lymphocytic, and buccal assays, the peripheral lympho-cytic micronuclei assay as a biomarker (Sommer et al., 2020; Heng et al., 2021). Recently, micronuclei studies have re-emerged as a potential potent biomarker linked to chromosomal instability, cancer, and other aging-related diseases (Heng et al., 2021; Mirzayans et al., 2018).

2.2 Molecular karyotyping

The karyotyping of chromosomal rearrangements was proven an important tool to perform a distinctive and recognizable tool for clinical phenotypes. However, for the reason of its limited resolution of 5 to 10 Mb, and to identify candidate genes linked to the symptoms in patients, the development of new high-resolution techniques was felt.

Later in the 1980s, to address these limitations of the classical cytogenetics, molecular cytogenetic techniques were introduced. Interestingly, the molecular techniques dawned a different era of studying chromosomes with differential sequence specific colors. Eventually, down the road, the novel techniques upon implementation in the diagnostic clinic have enables the leap from karyotype to gene to bases to omics with increasing efficiency (O'Connor, 2008; Lewis et al., 2021). This process was eventually greatly facilitated by the completion of the Human Genome Project in correlating the cytogenetic bands with DNA sequence information.

Nucleic acid hybridization

Hybridization of nucleic acids is one of the most widely used tools in molecular biology and therefore, applied in several techniques in diagnostics and research. This technique was involved in the first introduction of "*in situ* hybridization" concept that boosted the chromosome mapping strategies and enabled the identification of complex chromosome rearrangements including translocation, deletion, insertion, and inversion. Eventually, a diversity of following advanced molecular techniques evolved that proved novel tools for understanding tumor stage-specific chromosome aberrations:

Fish

In the mid–1980s to early 1990s, the technique of fluorescence *in situ* hybridization (FISH) made it possible to stain specific sequences within the chromosomes. Thus, the use of fluorescence *in situ* FISH technique enabled microscopic visualization of the location of individual sequences on metaphase chromosomes opening an avenue of molecular cytogenetics. This technique was first introduced in 1986 by Pinkel using fluorescently labeled specific DNA sequences called probes while seeking the genomic DNA/RNA region for any abnormalities (Pinkel et al., 1986). Thereafter, the molecular cytogenetics paved the way for clinical and research developments by introducing FISH technique to diagnose and treat abnormalities. The labeled probes used in this technique bind their complementary regions on the chromosome and glow that can be observed under fluorescent microscope. Thus, the probes function as fluorescent reporter molecules targeting the specific genomic area or sequences of interest in the patient DNA. This, specificity leads to subsequent detection of pathological location of a given fluorescence signal indicating the presence, absence, or abnormal copy number.

In this way, FISH replaced specialized staining of chromosome regions and could apply a wide variety of probe types. The probes can be specific to unique regions or genes or repetitive sequences (telomeres and centromeres) or chromosome bands or chromosome arms or entire chromosomes or as large as entire genome in the case of comparative genomic hybridization (CGH). FISH probes can also be specifically designed for unique pan-genomic segments for example probes specific for all telomeres, or for all centromeres. It has also been used for studying the positions of genes during interphase (O'Connor, 2008). Technically, FISH was a link between the conventional cytogenetics and the human genome sequencing.

FISH offers following advantages over classical cytogenetic karyotyping:

(1) Higher resolution compared to G-banding in detecting abnormalities of about 100 kb to 1 Mb in contrast to the 5 Mb limit of classical cytogenetic karyotyping.

(2) The availability of probes specific to locus for many genetic defects enhanced the accuracy of microdeletion and duplication syndrome detection.

(3) It can almost use any DNA as a probe

(4) Can use cells in any stage of the cell cycle and fresh tissue is not required.

(5) Advances in stability, fluorochrome chemistry, and photodetectors enhanced its sensitivity and multiplicity of FISH (O'Connor, 2008).

(6) The following advanced techniques involving combinatorial labeling and FISH hybridization reflected higher sensitivity.

FISH has potentially identified abnormalities at gene level of patients. It was routinely used detecting BCR-ABL1 rearrangement for diagnosing acute myeloid leukemia or acute lymphocytic leukemia patients where the ABL1 gene fragment of chromosomes 9 joins the BCR gene of chromosome 22 (Kohla et al., 2021). The BCR-ABL test is used to diagnose or rule out chronic myeloid leukemia or a specific form of acute lymphoblastic leukemia called Ph (Philadelphia chromosome)-positive ALL. This test is not meant to diagnose other types of leukemia (https://medlineplus.gov/lab-tests/bcr-abl-genetic-test/).

However, FISH also suffered from some limitations: The main limitation was the specificity itself and accordingly it can only detect specific complimentary DNA sequences to which it can hybridize. Thus, the cytogeneticist could see only the region of the genome complementary to the probe used (https://www.eurofins-biomnis.com/wp-content/uploads/2016/04/56-INTGB-Focus_Karyotyping_SNP_array.pdf).

Modified FISH techniques

With the objective of addressing limitations and enhancing resolution of FISH technique, following modified FISH were developed over the years:

1. **Spectral karyotyping (SKY):** This technique involves the hybridization of differentially labeled probes to identify both numerical and chromosomal structural aberrations in the genome (Lauriola et al., 2020).

2. **m-FISH**: Just like SKY, this technique also involves the hybridization of differentially labeled probes to identify both numerical and chromosomal structural aberrations in the genome (Veselinyová et al., 2021)
3. **Comparative genomic hybridization (CGH):** This technique being quantitative, compares the copy number of genomic regions between a test sample of a tumor DNA and a normal cell DNA as control (Wijesiriwardhana et al., 2021).

Comparative genomic array or microarray

In the last few years, cytogenetics has moved from the microscope to genomic array or gene chip technology commonly known as DNA chip or biochip that addresses limitations associated with traditional CGH by combining the principles of CGH and microarrays (Schena et al., 1995). It comprises a collection of microscopic DNA spots immobilized to a solid surface and used to measure the gene expression of large numbers of genes simultaneously, thus genotyping multiple regions of a genome. The computer-based chip or array analysis involving testing with array-based test systems: Comparative genomic hybridization (CGH) or chromosome microarray analysis (CMA), also known as chromosome genomic array testing (CGAT). Both the CMA/CGAT can detect aberrations >1 Mb at low resolution or 10 Kb at high resolution.

This technique involves fragmenting the whole genome into many small regions and arrayed on slides or chips so that the exact location of each fragment within the whole genome can be identified. The array is then treated with thousands or millions of FISH custom-designed probes and uses a computer for analysis known as Multiplex-ligation dependent probe amplification (MLPA). Thus, it can be used to detect specific small chromosomal abnormalities. Thus, these arrays can simultaneously perform genome-wide analysis of cytogenetic abnormalities at high resolution.

The arrays can also be compared with a reference or normal control or standard genome to identify differences to locate regions of genomic imbalance like copy number variations (CNVs) in the patient. A CNV is detected as a segment of about 1000 DNA bases present in a variable number of copies in comparison to standard DNA. In principle, the tumor sample and reference DNA are labeled with differential fluorescent probes (red and green). The two samples with the appropriate labels are applied to immobilized DNA array that allows hybridization of complementary sequences. Upon scanning the array, the color and intensity reveal the CNV (Fig. 1):

1. No change in test patient sample versus reference sample = Yellow emission from red equal to green
2. Duplication in the test sample = red emission from more red than green
3. Deletions in the test sample = green emission from less red than green sample, and a net emission of green light.

Overall, in the diagnostic field, the molecular karyotyping has been the high-resolution whole-genome array techniques that can detect chromosomal aberrations at a resolution

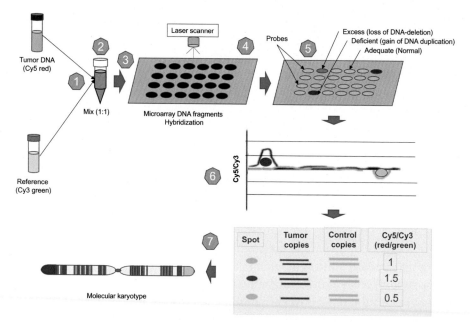

Fig. 1 Molecular karyotype, tumor heterogeneity, copy number variations through modified FISH as comparative genomic hybridization (CGH array). Steps 1–3: Tumor DNA and control DNA labeled with fluorescent dyes applied to the microarray, Step 4: Tumor DNA and control DNA compete hybridize to the microarray, Step 5: Signals is measured, Step 6: Software calculates log2 (Cy5/Cy3)—deletions or duplications, Step 7: Interpretation: +1 (*red*)=Duplication 3 copies, +2 (*red*)=Duplication 4 copies −1 (*green*)=Homozygous deletion, −2 (*green*)=Heterozygous deletion.

beyond conventional karyotyping. This technique has identified many new micro-deletion and microduplication syndromes (Gijsbers and Ruivenkamp, 2011).

As an example, CGH array can detect genetic malformations in prenatal genetic testing involving microduplications and microdeletions that are less than 10 Mb, and the microscope "does not see" with conventional karyotyping. Otherwise, these small mistakes can only be detected before childbirth or seen through a CGH array or molecular karyotype. However, both the old and the new methods share a commonality: 1. The material is procured by amniocentesis or chorionic villus sampling. 2. Display changes in total number of chromosomes and major alterations.

Single-nucleotide polymorphism (SNP) array

It represents an array to detect a variation at a single-nucleotide site in DNA. For example, in base sequence AACGAT of an SNP is the substitution of a C for a G producing the sequence AACCAT. The location of these SNPs in or near genes in the genome affects the function of these genes and thus, profoundly impacts gene expression, gene regulation, control of cell cycle, genome stability, and signal transduction pathways (Savas and Liu, 2009).

The basic principle and technique of SNP array are similar to CGH array, but the SNP enables genotyping in addition, and in comparison to CGH array that collects intensity data. Thus, the SNP array can determine both CNVs and loss of heterozygosity (LOH) that accounts for loss of genetic material of one of the two parents in addition to detecting aneuploidy. The SNP technique primarily differs from CGH in resolution from 10 kb (10 thousand base pairs) to 1 Mb (one million base pairs) in comparison to standard G-banded karyotype having a resolution of around 5 Mb.

This means that modern arrays detected both benign CNVs and pathogenic CNVs than karyotyping, and FISH. However, in view of the differences in benefits and limitations of each technique, before ordering the test, informed decision must be taken that should involve the clinical syndrome and genetic disease history of the patient. Karyotyping however stood as first line testing to detect or assess the followings:

(1) Typical aneuploidy (trisomy 21, 18 or aneuploidy of sex chromosome)
(2) Indeterminate gender
(3) Inappropriate secondary sexual development
(4) Amenorrhea in females
(5) Cleft lip or heart diseases
(6) Syndromes associated with chromosome breakage.
(7) Infertility

To the date, the most frequently diagnosed malignances by these techniques is prostate cancer although prostate-specific antigen (PSA) testing is also very popular. However, the lack of specificity of PSA test between benign and malignant forms is a major concern (Allemailem et al., 2021). In colorectal cancer, three SNPs as cancer biomarkers to predict long-term recurrence or metastasis risk have been reported (Yu et al., 2021).

In terms of evolution of the techniques from karyotype analysis to chromosome to FISH to CGH, the epithelial ovarian tumors studies relate how this evolution addressed the limitation of the older technique in cytogenetic characterization of ovarian carcinomas that eventually lead to the development of well-defined chromosome markers. Tibiletti et al. (2000) proposed that detection of chromosome band 6q27 supports early events in ovarian tumor development. The use of CGH displayed chromosomal loss of 16q and 17p and gain of 3q and 8q with various ovarian carcinomas (Iwabuchi et al., 1995). Whereas, FISH displayed the gain of chromosome band 20q13.2 leading to overexpression of oncogenes HER-2/neu on chromosome 17q21. Similarly, amplification of oncogene myc at 8q24 was an indicator of poor survival of patients (Grisanzio and Freedman, 2010).

Potential limitation of arrays is, however, its dependency on nucleic acid hybridization which displays fluctuations leading to background experimental noise affecting accuracy (Cohen et al., 2017).

In summary, both karyotyping and arrays are genome-wide technologies and the both can be used to assess the presence of genomic imbalance like copy number variations (CNVs).

RFLP

The technique of Restriction fragment length polymorphism (RFLP) originally known as DNA fingerprinting **or** DNA typing was invented in 1984 by the English scientist Alec John Jeffreys while working on hereditary diseases (Jeffreys et al., 1985). It is a molecular biology tool that can differentiate samples of homologous DNA molecules at restriction enzyme sites. This method involves a multistep process started with extraction of DNA from a sample like blood, saliva, and semen.

In this method, the purified DNA is treated with a restriction enzyme that cuts the DNA at specific sites. The resulting fragments of DNA thus generated are resolved according to their size using gel electrophoresis. In other words, the DNA fragments and their length variations can act as differentiating markers, or "fingerprints," for genetic identification rather than depending upon phenotypic characteristics. The length of restriction fragments of a restriction enzyme differs among individuals that help to identify a person or a cell. Additionally, the RFLP can be used to study genetic polymorphism along with inter-and intra-specific variations. The specific fragment(s) can be detected with the help of restriction probes.

The RFLP offering direct detection of DNA sequence polymorphism with restriction enzymes enabled novel approach for the identification of human tumors using tumor markers. Thus, the RFLP is also a DNA marker (molecular marker) defined by a different pattern of restriction fragments displayed in Southern blots using DNA probes with genomic DNA. The RFLP molecular marker is highly locus-specific to a single or combination of restriction enzymes. These markers called codominant markers displaying their codominance can detect both alleles in heterozygous sample (Pierotti and Porta, 1987).

The RFLP molecular probes can be derived from genomic sequences of known genetic loci free from repetitive sequences and thus can be from protein coding or noncoding sequences called anonymous DNA sequences. The applications of genetic human tumor markers through RFLPs have revealed DNA level differences between the normal and the transformed cell. Thus, such markers have identified cellular genes involved in tumor induction and progression converting into dominant oncogenes or by recessive mutations.

The neoplastic disease specific molecular markers improved the diagnostic cytology while minimizing delay in prognosis of patient treatment. For example, two RFLP markers have helped in pancreatic cancer treatment since mutations in the *Kras* oncogene and the p53 tumor suppressor gene can be detected relatively early in the initiation and progressive development of pancreatic cancer. The *Kras* gene mutations, however, can be detected with a smaller number of probes since these mutations are limited to one codon (van Es et al., 1995).

QF-PCR-RFLP

For determination of fetal genetic anomalies and to replace invasive testing, quantitative PCR (qPCR) was introduced. Therefore, during the evaluation of patient risk stratification informed by PCR-RFLP, this technique identified the HPV with high sensitivity and also displayed that it can classify samples as healthy, low, and high-risk samples (Melo et al., 2021).

Quantitative fluorescent PCR (QF-PCR) has also been involved in prenatal diagnosis by many laboratories to identify aneuploidies. It turned out to be a rapid, cost-effective, and amenable to automation for being able to detect abnormalities diagnosed by conventional karyotyping. Accordingly, the PCR can be reliably used in determining aneuploidy of chromosomes 13, 18, and 21 except sex chromosome aneuploidy where it lends support from a complete karyotype for performing less reliably at prenatal diagnosis (Nicolini et al., 2004; Finnegan et al., 2021; Alessandro et al., 2021).

Next-generation karyotyping

The advent of next-generation sequencing (NGS) technologies has revolutionized the understanding of genetic variation not only in the human genome but also in cancers (Supplitt et al., 2021). The technology offers an alternative sequencing-based karyotyping as next-gen karyotype (NGK) that has challenged conventional karyotyping (Mareschal et al., 2021). For example, targeted NGS panels can detect micro-deletions, micro-duplications, and the translocations and reliably offer sensitivity and specificity like routine FISH with the advantage of single-nucleotide resolution and precision (Fig. 2). The NGK, therefore, offered greater insight into the prognosis of acute myeloid leukemia patients due to its ability of better detecting copy number alterations in comparison to conventional cytogenetic analysis.

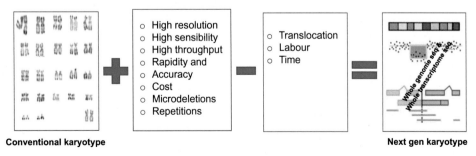

Conventional karyotype   **Next gen karyotype**

Fig. 2 Difference between conventional karyotyping and next-gen karyotyping (whole-genome sequencing and whole transcriptome sequences.

What is next-gen sequencing (NGS)

The nucleotide sequencing is the process of determining the order of the four bases in nucleic acids. The technology determines the order of nucleotides in the entire genomes or targeted regions of DNA or RNA. It is a massively parallel sequencing technology that offers high accuracy, ultra-high throughput, scalability, speed, and low cost and thus has revolutionized not only the cancer biology but also the biological sciences. The NGS has a relatively high resolution across the genome and the ability to precisely quantitate copy number variations (CNVs), single-nucleotide variations (SNVs), and inversions/deletions (Indels).

Therefore, sequence variants generated in the diseased cells or tissues and mutations detected by NGS are widely applied in comparing healthy and mutated DNA sequences for diagnosis of various disease including cancers (Chmielecki and Meyerson, 2014; Biswas and Khan, 2020). In this endeavor of correlating cytogenetic bands with 3.055 billion letters of DNA sequence information across 23 human chromosomes has been greatly supported by Human Genome Project (Zhang, 2021; Logsdon et al., 2021). In addition to the applications in diverse fields, the NGS offers fast turnaround of sequencing DNA that allows for faster and more personalized medical care.

Technical advances in NGS have moved rapidly from pure cancer genomics and it is the platform of choice for genomic profiling. Gone are the days of running multiple single gene tests, having long waits, and facing depletion of tissue. The NGS allows to run multiple biomarkers in a single test simultaneously to provide a comprehensive molecular profile. The technical advances have thus paved the way for personalized cancer patient therapy based on molecular profiles of the patients. However, several limitations need to be addressed to fully introduce NGS into routine clinical decision-making (Shamrikova et al., 2021).

The NGS suffers from accessory costs since it requires sophisticated bioinformatics systems, fast data processing and large data storage capabilities. Additionally, it is at still an unsolved issue to ensure when and how to apply NGS testing in the clinic. However, clinical research is experiencing fast evolution from basket tests (evaluating a targeted therapy on multiple diseases having commonality) and umbrella tests (evaluating multiple targeted therapies for a single disease) to an adaptive design. Moreover, before ordering the tests, the physicians must be aware with a critical point of view of the new biomarkers and NGS tests available (Colomer et al., 2020).

Generations of NGS In 1977, the first-generation DNA sequencing method also known as chemical sequencing was introduced by Frederick Sanger at the MRC Centre in Cambridge. It was based on chemical modification of DNA and subsequently cleaving the DNA at specific bases. It was basically a gel-based method that combined a DNA polymerase with a mixture of standard and chain-terminating nucleotides, known as ddNTPs (Maxam and Gilbert, 1977). This method known as the Sanger sequencing methods or chain-termination method soon became the method of choice because of its relative ease, reliability, and automation (Sanger et al., 1977). This technology, under continual improvement over the years, served as work horse of the Human Genome Project. To address some of the limitations of this method, the Sanger method was automated to achieve speed in sequencing, and it is still in use for sequencing short DNA pieces. Even today, despite low throughput, higher per-sample costs, and sequencing reads 500 to 1000 bp in length, the automated version of Sanger sequencing is primarily used in clinical labs. This method prevailed from the 1980s to the mid-2000s and continues while sequencing 1000 to 30,000 bases long fragments. Since DNA sequencing machines cannot sequence the whole genome in one go, the DNA is sequenced in short pieces or fragments of about 150 bases called a "read." However, to sequence human genome it may take a few years. But despite these limitations, Sanger sequencing due to its advantages, is still the "gold standard" with 99.99% accuracy (Table 4).

To address the limitations of Sanger's method, eventually, several new methods for DNA sequencing collectively known as NGS were developed in the mid to late 1990s. By the year 2000, the NGS were implemented in commercial settings for DNA sequencing in diverse fields. The sequencing by synthesis (SBS) was the first NGS technology to be commercialized that evolved from massively parallel signature sequencing (MPSS) developed by Lynx Therapeutics in the 1990s to identify and quantify mRNA transcripts (Richards, 2015). The NGS in contrast to the first generation of sequencing is typically scalable to the entire genome to be sequenced at once. Major NGS platforms/technologies are presented in Table 5.

Table 4 Benefits and limitations of Sanger sequencing and NGS.

Sanger sequencing	Targeted NGS
• Slow and costly • Fast and cost-effective sequencing for 1–20 targets • Simple workflow • Low sensitivity • Low ability to identify novel variants • Not cost-effective for >20 targets • Low scalability • Short-read sequencing 50–500 base pairs • Draft genomes (sequence gaps and incomplete assemblies)	• Massively fast • Cost effective • Higher sequencing depth enables higher sensitivity (down to 1%) • Higher discovery power • Higher mutation resolution • Efficient-more data/input DNA • Higher sample throughput • Mutation-resolution–single-nucleotide variants to large chromosomal rearrangements • Less cost-effective for 1–20 targets • Time-consuming for 1–20 targets • Long-read sequencing reads tens of kilobases in length • Create overlaps that complete genome assemblies

Table 5 Major next-gen sequencing platform/techniques.

Platform/ technique	Manufacturer	Gen	Reads Maximum kb length	Throughput (M/run)	Operation duration (h)	Accuracy
Sanger sequencing	• Caltec • Microchip Biotechnol Inc.	1st	0.5–1	1 DNA fragment	4	99.9
SOLEXA Seq by synthesis	Illumina	2nd	0.075–0.3	1–300	24–264	99.9
SOLiD	ABI	2nd	0.050	120–140	168–336	99.9
Pyrosequencing 454	Roche	2nd	0.7	1	24	99.9
Ion semiconductor	Ion Torrent	2nd	0.6	80	2	99.6
Nanopore Seq	Oxford Nanopore Technologies	3rd	500	Length dependent	0.01–48	92–97[a]
Single-molecule real-time seq	Pacific Biosciences	3rd	30	1000–2000	0.5–20	87[a]

[a]High accuracy offered by multiple-times-reading ability.

The NGS has sped up the process in taking weeks to days and from days to hours to sequence a human genome while making it cost effective by reducing the cost. With the advance NGS technologies developed so far, one human genome can be sequenced in about a day, though the analysis takes much longer. The first sequencing of the human genome by the Human Genome Project (HGP) had a cost of over $3 billion about 20 years ago while currently, the Whole-Genome Sequencing is offered for about $299 (https://nebula.org/whole-genome-sequencing-dna-test/).

Applications of NGS The major applications of the NGS are as blow:
- Rapid sequence of whole genomes
- Deep sequence of target regions
- RNA-Seq for discovering novel RNA variants/splice sites/mRNAs
- Analysis of the epigenetic factors
- Sequence cancer samples for diagnosis
- Sequence the human microbiome
- Identify pathogens

Types of NGS
The advent of NGS technologies has revolutionized the analysis of genetic variation in the genome. Cancer sequencing with NGS provides more information in less time compared to traditional single-gene and array-based approaches. Therefore, different types or

formats of NGS are used depending upon the application and each type involves different steps of sample prep. The cost of analysis can also be minimized by selecting adequate type of NGS:

Whole-genome sequencing Currently, the most comprehensive strategy for mutation detection in the entire genome is the whole-genome sequencing (WGS). It is also known as full genome sequencing, complete genome sequencing, or entire genome sequencing. Normal genome sequencing presents genetic picture of the patient for inherited genetic predisposition for cancer risk and drug metabolism. The WGS has been widely applied in the identification of Mendelian disorders, in various cancers and in neurodevelopmental disorders. The WGS has been applied to diagnosis and responsive feedback on treatment of the breast cancers thus improving the development of oncologic therapies. WGS is the currently most powerful form of DNA sequencing and look at all the DNA (both genes and outside of genes). Thus, it can determine every SNPs in 6 billion bases of human genome and determine as tumor mutational burden.

However, for selected sets of genes or genomic regions or for rapid and cost-effective sequencing, targeted sequencing is performed. It is also known as target analysis sequencing or target amplicon sequencing (TAS) focusing on amplicons. The upfront selection or isolation of genes or regions of interest is normally carried by PCR amplification or hybridization-based capture methods. To offer mutational characterization, diagnosis, and personalized treatment, it is typically applied in clinical oncology, carcinomas, colorectal cancer, and breast cancer (Dongre et al., 2021; Lee et al., 2021; Saied et al., 2021).

Additionally, the epigenetics sequencing is also performed on the genomic regions that include heritable genetic modifications not attributable to alterations in the primary DNA sequence. For the reason, the epigenetic modifications influence gene expression involving development, regulation, and maintenance of the normal cell, sequencing has made it feasible to genome-wide map epigenetic regions. It has revolutionized the DNA-protein interactions, DNA methylation, and chromosome conformation (Campagna et al., 2022; Morrison et al., 2021).

Exome sequencing Exons in the genome have code information for proteins, therefore, any mutation in the exons reflect in the structure and function of protein it codes for. To determine changes or variants in the gene of the corresponding protein, sequencing of exon is performed. Sequencing all the protein-coding regions (exons) of genes in a genome is called exome sequencing also known as whole exome sequencing (WES). Among the 30 million base pairs in human genome about 1% of the genome contains about 180,000 exons constitute about 1% of the genome (Ng et al., 2021).

Being exons and having the ability of sequencing to identify alterations in the coding regions of the genes, the exome sequencing does not cover the structural and noncoding variants associated with the disease that is determined by WGS (Ng et al., 2021; Réda et al., 2020; Rotunno et al., 2020; Dongre et al., 2021). But WGS being costly for large sample sizes while WES can offer better resolution free from noncoding regions. However, WES having focus on the exome (the entire set of exons in the genome), it requires exome-enrichment steps in comparison to WGS that has been made technically feasible by the availability of exome-enrichment kits though adding cost to the process.

The sample enrichment step involves selection of the subset of protein coding DNA (exomes) from the test sample which is eventually fed to any high-throughput DNA sequencing technology (Rotunno et al., 2020; Dongre et al., 2021). The enrichment of exome can be achieved by capturing exome through array-based enrichment using probes bound to high-density microarrays. The alternative method of *In-solute* capturing is based on magnetic bead nanoparticles that bind to target exome sequences. This approach offers an advantage since magnetic beads allow the reaction to be more effective by shaking or heating the system. Since most known mutations that cause disease occur in exons, and the exome sequencing allows assessment of only coding regions, offer better resolution of tumor progression (Shamrikova et al., 2021; Dongre et al., 2021). The WGS in contrast, studies mutations in the whole genome looking at all the genes in the patient.

Whole transcriptome sequencing   The limitations and cost of WGS and WES, has led to the emergence of the whole transcriptome sequencing (WTS) or RNA. The transcriptome of a given cell or tissue encompass a quasi-complete set of transcribed genes—mRNAs and noncoding RNAs. Thus, the WTS is an alternative approach to variant detection within protein coding regions. In other words, this approach bypasses the requirement of exome enrichment as an advantage over WES.

Transcriptomics is performed by two key contemporary techniques: quantifies predefined set of sequences called microarrays while the other uses high-throughput sequencing to capture all sequences called RNA-seq or RNA-Sequencing (Nazarov et al., 2017). The RNA-Seq provides far higher coverage and greater resolution of the dynamic nature of the transcriptome. RNA-Seq offers advantage over the microarrays allowing single base pair resolution with less background noise and providing unbiased analysis of the transcriptome in comparison to the expression arrays.

As a diagnostic tool, transcriptome sequencing in the form of gene expression arrays and some forms of cancers is quite established (Rao et al., 2019; Walter et al., 2021). The future advancement on transcriptomics may advance on the next step that may allow standardization and cost reduction of transcriptomics analysis and offer a solution of contemporary cancer medicine (Supplitt et al., 2021).

While the emergence of these molecular technologies has encouraged rapid sequencing and studying cancer genomes and epigenomes, revealing genetic alterations (Biswas and Khan, 2020). However, molecular cytogenetics cannot detect balanced translocations. Thus, molecular cytogenetics cannot replace the traditional karyotype analysis, and the G-banding can be used in the clinical cytogenetic diagnosis (Jing et al., 2017). Therefore, it needs to be learnt how and when to use the molecular cytogenetics or traditional karyotype analysis. However, when standard cancer treatments turn ineffective or to determine where a patient's cancer originated, NGS can be helpful in pinpointing mutations in a tumor that may be matched with undergoing treatments targeting those specific alterations (Demsky, 2021; Duncavage et al., 2021).

Multiomics

In the past decade, the attempts were aimed at untangling the molecular mechanisms of carcinogenesis applying single Omic approaches at a time. Such approaches have identified cancer-specific mutations, epigenetic alterations, gene and protein-expression based molecular subtyping of tumors. But these strategies failed to resolve relationship between molecular and phenotypic signatures that lead to manifestation of cancer hallmarks. Therefore, the hallmarks of cancer transformations such as metastasis and angiogenesis require information of molecular alterations at diverse molecular levels including sequencing the genome for cancer-specific mutations and identification of resultant epigenetic-landscapes within cancer cells. Additionally, the differential gene expression through transcriptomics, and structure & function of resulting proteins through proteomics is required (Chakraborty et al., 2018; Menyhartab and Győrffy, 2021; Kane et al., 2021).

Thus, the multiomics include the data sets from the genome (pangenomics), proteome, transcriptome, epigenome, metabolome, and microbiome (Tarazona et al., 2018). Such approaches involving multiple dimensions of the cancer cells or tissues, or tumors hold the potential to resolve the intricate underlying molecular mechanism (Fig. 3). Additionally, the multiomics, in other words studying cancer in a concerted way approaches can be instrumental in determining therapeutic approaches, diagnostic & prognostic markers for an earlier cancer diagnosis, more efficient personalized therapeutic approaches, and better patient stratification (Bock et al., 2016; Vilanova and Porcar, 2016). Therefore, the multiomics have offered advantages over simple correlations of single omics for translational cancer research by revealing valuable interactions and for delivering highly specific multiomic biomarkers in comparison to previous monogenic markers (Menyhartab and Győrffy, 2021).

Cancer initiation and metastasis are complicated processes that involve multiple pathways leading to tumor heterogeneity, extensive genetic aberrations, and diversity between tumors of the same cancer types (Burrell et al., 2013). Typically, there are 2 to 8 gene pathogenic or driver genomic mutations that drive cancer progression in comparison to passenger mutations that NGS can be helpful in identifying with increased computing capacity (Vogelstein et al., 2013).

The data fusion and analysis of multiomics has been successful. For example, Similarity network fusion (SNF) based on the inter-patient similarities constructs of individual networks per omic (Wang et al., 2014). Analysis of DNA methylation, mRNA and miRNA expression patterns with SNF helps in identifying cancer subtypes.

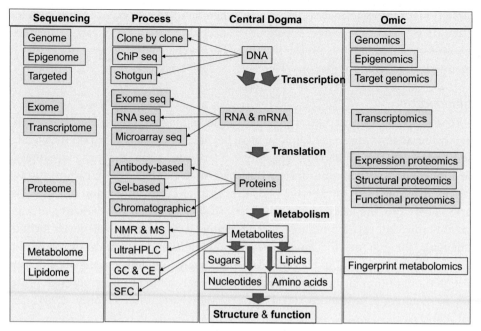

Fig. 3 Correlation of multiomics, methodologies, and central dogma of life.

The technological advances have enabled studying the whole proteome and/or metabolome interactions with other proteins and effects on cellular behavior (Biswas and Khan, 2020). Proteomics encompass the applications of technologies involved in identification and quantification of overall protein content of a cell, tissue or an organism. It involves protein expression proteomics, posttranslational modifications, structural proteomics, and about the proteome's temporal and spatial organization (Uzozie and Aebersold, 2018). Additionally, the use of proteomics is promising in diagnosis and precision cancer medicine ever since the early-stage breast cancer diagnostic protein microarray tests were introduced that significantly cut down the number of unnecessary breast biopsies (Lourenco et al., 2017). Similarly, proteomic profiling has played a promising role in molecular subclassification of early-stage hepatocellular carcinomas (Jiang et al., 2019).

Cells respond to environmental changes through the integrated network of signaling, transcriptomic, and metabolic actions and therefore metabolites represent the progression from the genome, to proteome, to metabolome, to the phenotype. It indicates actual state of the underlying biochemical processes related to internal (genetic) and external (environmental) factors. It involves analysis of hundreds to thousand metabolites present in the sample known as metabolome. Among omics technologies, the unique aspect of metabolomics reflects a retrospective and wide-ranging information of the underlying biological processes that have occurred within a biological fluid or cell or tissue or in an individual relevant to health. In cancer cells, metabolism is dysregulated to meet the demands of uncontrolled proliferation and the metabolome provides a direct readout of the upstream physiological changes (Schmidt et al., 2021). The metabolomic profiling of cancer cells can be used as noninvasive tool for discriminating cancerous tissue and has discovered key oncometabolites (Yang et al., 2013).

Cancer proteogenomics integrating proteomics with whole-exome sequencing, copy number variations (CNVs), RNA-seq, and miRNA-seq data revealed deeper insight into cancer biology and therapeutic vulncrabilities (Satpathy et al., 2020). Similarly, integration of genomic, transcriptomic, and proteome data from lung cancer tumor samples, uncovered alterations not known before by genomics and transcriptomics alone.

Future scope and limitation of multiomics approach

The move of multiomics technologies getting translated into accessible tools in routine daily medical diagnosis and therapy is unexpectedly slow (Menyhartab and Győrffy, 2021). Therefore, these technical hindrances need to be mitigated before the routine usage of the multiomics in clinical settings. Although data generation is becoming cost effective with increasingly affordable for single omics approaches, but each "omics" approach has its own limitations (Wang et al., 2019). While offering its unparalleled advantages, the multiomics approach is also not free from its drawbacks since it suffers from the following limitations:

1. Even though high-throughput technologies are cost-effective but increasing amount of data provided is highly complex from strategies including genomes, epigenomes, transcriptomes, proteomes, metabolomes, and microbiomes for multilayer analysis to get meaningful outcome

2. Data being very complex from diverse aspects of biology, its integration is slow to enter everyday clinics. However, systems biology approach is promising to understand biological interactions holistically and can integrate multidisciplinary information (Yan et al., 2018).

3. Technical challenges are presented from each omics platform in terms of sample treatment and coordinated sample processing.

4. Most of the time, the data from different omics platforms does not mature at the same time for each sample. Thus, the uneven maturity of different omics is another hurdle that does not match the data processing capacity and thus delays the translatability of theoretical findings.

5. An enormous diversity among data approaches for integrating multidimensional omics makes it more complex (Graw et al., 2021).

6. Multidisciplinary training of experts for data analysis, interpretation, and correlation is the basis of this approach. There are more than 100 analysis software in OmicTools service that add complexity to decision to choose and apply to the data sets. (https://www.re3data.org/search?contentTypes%5B0%5D=Software%20applications&page=6

Single-cell multiomics

The complexity of biological and heterogeneity of tumor cells complicates the processing and analysis of differentiating morphological and phenotypic profiles distinctively. To minimize some of the limitation of multiomics approach on a tumor or tissue, or patient, the analysis of multilevel single-cell data is a novel approach offering an unprecedent resolution at multilevel transitions in a single cancer cell (Hu et al., 2018; Biswas and Khan, 2020). Single-cell technology has, therefore, emerged as a powerful tool in addressing these difficulties. This technology offering an edge over the bulk analysis minimizing bulk interferences due to cell-to-cell variation, allows resolution of heterogeneity of tissue architectures (Hu et al., 2018).

Heterogeneity of tumor being a challenge, understanding intratumoral (within a tumor) molecular variation among cells can address prominent concerns in cancer biology. This understanding offers a promise in improving the diagnosis and intervention of specific cancer subtypes that normally exist in the tumors (Lewis et al., 2021). Therefore, RNA sequencing and other genomics performed under single-cell analyses, have contributed in determining molecular regulators, and novel biomarkers associated with tumor growth, metastasis and drug resistance. However, these approaches are far from providing complete understanding of tumor biology especially on locating cellular subtypes within the tumor micro-environment.

Since RNA omics data do not contain introns (noncoding genomic regions) and information regarding copy-number variation, therefore some methods of analysis using parallel single-cell genomics and transcriptomics allow insights that cannot be obtained solely from transcriptomic analysis (Kester et al., 2015). There are some methods that are based on either physical separation of RNA and genomic DNA or simultaneous amplification (Macaulay et al., 2016). Another method involves the integration of single-cell transcriptomes to single-cell methylomes, combining single-cell bi-sulfite sequencing (Mattia and Joseph, 2011; Gavin et al., 2014) to single cell RNA-Sequencing (Angermueller et al., 2016). Other techniques to analyze the epigenome, as single-cell ATAC-Seq (Greenleaf et al., 2015) and single-cell Hi-C have also been in use (Fraser et al., 2013).

Like the genomics and transcriptomics, the data integration was another challenge involving integration of proteomic and transcriptomic data. Therefore, like DNA and RNA separation, the approach to perform these analyses was to physically separate single-cell lysates in RNA, and into proteins (Darmanis et al., 2016). The proximity extension assays (PEA) that involve DNA-barcoded antibodies or a combination of heavy-metal RNA probes and protein antibodies for multiomic analysis, were employed (Gherardini et al., 2016).

3. Recent advances

In view of the limitation of conventional cytogenetic karyotyping, the multiomics approaches in cancer biology have their own limitations that are being addressed with new innovations including data integration and processing. Therefore, to impart and accelerate translatability of theoretical findings, apart from additional efforts including collaborations, standardization of sample processing, setting up analytical pipelines, multidisciplinary training, strategies on data analysis and interpretation, some recent strides taken forward are as below:

3.1 Multiomics and artificial intelligence

While high throughput cancer biology is on its rise, in parallel, machine learning with artificial intelligence applications to cancer biomedical data analysis are flourishing. This integrative approach of multiomics data analysis and machine learning has discovered new biomarkers as one of the methods of the mixOmics project employing sparse Partial Least Squares regression for selection of putative biomarkers (Lin and Lane, 2017; Rohart et al., 2017).

3.2 Cancer biomarkers

To offer a timely treatment of cancer and to prevent cancer deaths, an early cancer detection is imperative. Cancer treatment for many tumor types has been revolutionized by testing with biomarkers, the biological molecules produced by the body or tumor in a person suffering from cancer. These indicators are used to characterize alterations in the tumor over time. Diagnostic, prognostic, or predictive biomarkers address the inherent complexity of the tumors and dynamic genetic landscape of cancer. These markers can be DNA, RNA, protein or metabolomic profiles specific to the tumor (Biswas and Khan, 2020). The test includes genomic test detecting gene fusions at the DNA sequence or to measure RNA or protein levels.

Biomarkers can be applied for several purposes including assessment of individual's risk of developing cancer, and predicting the success of a given therapy for a specific patient (Chen et al., 2019; Kimmons, 2021). In recent years, novel biomarkers to detect tumor growth, metastasis and drug resistance have been revealed by single-cell analyses like RNA sequencing and other genomics information (Lewis et al., 2021). The circulating tumor DNA (ctDNA) from dying tumor cells released into the bloodstream are promising to determine tumor-associated mutations despite its limitation being detectable in low amount to detect tumor type and stage-dependent tumor burden and applied therapy (Zhang et al., 2018).

3.3 Multiplexed fluorescence, DNA, RNA, and isotope labeling

New approaches based on multiplexed fluorescence, DNA, RNA and isotope labeling have been successful in the detection of tens to thousands of cancer subtypes or molecular biomarkers within their native spatial domain. The promising and expeditious growth in these approaches, supported by accessory techniques for multiomics data integration, are bound to yield a comprehensive understanding of cell-to-cell variation of intratumor and intertumor (Lewis et al., 2021).

3.4 InfoGenomeR

In view of the limitations on resolving power of cytogenetic karyotyping and FISH, global reconstruction of genome karyotypes in cancers may contribute to understanding the underlying cancer development and evolution. The sequencing technology has resolved the genomic alterations at the single-nucleotide level and thus advanced our understanding of chromosomal structural variations. These early-stage sequencing methods could detect structural variations using discordant, integrated paired-end and split-read analysis from sequencing data (Wang et al., 2011; Lee and Lee, 2021). However, these methods suffered from limitation in the detection ability of identifying structural variations at breakpoint genomic windows. To address these limitations, several methods have been developed to integrate the genomic information including copy number alterations, ploidy, and haplotype information using graph-based rearranged cancer genomes. Therefore, do not analyze the actual karyotype chromosomes with karyotypic topologies like homogeneously staining region, double minute chromosomes, or chromothripsis.

A graph-based framework known as Integrative Framework for Genome Reconstruction (InfoGenomeR) can reconstruct cancer genome karyotypes. It translates data from whole-genome sequencing, structural variations, total copy number alterations, allele-specific copy numbers, and haplotype information into karyotypes. Analytical potential of the technique was demonstrated with whole-genome sequencing data from breast cancer, glioblastoma multiforme, and ovarian cancer patients. It also identified recurrent derivative chromosomes and genome karyotypes derived from chromosomes (Lee and Lee, 2021). The workflow involves DELLY26, Manta7, and novoBreak8 tools that evaluate whole-genome sequences in generating initial structural variations and then applies BIC-seq224 tool to perform copy number change detection and segmentation.

The workflow involves: After aligning whole-genome sequencing data, a breakpoint graph is constructed. It is followed by the construction of allele-specific graph and then through haplotype graph construction, the karyotype gets constructed. This potential of the technique is highly promising in guiding targeted therapies based on cancer-specific genome-wide structural variations.

4. Conclusion

The field of cancer diagnosis has evolved through conventional cytogenetic karyotyping to the next-gen karyotyping with the evolution of new tools and techniques that have contributed toward increasing sensitivity with higher resolution (Fig. 4). The cytogenetic karyotyping lacks the ability to detect microdeletions and repetitions that can

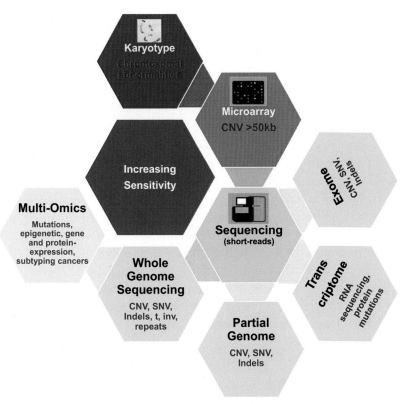

Fig. 4 Evolution of major technologies with increasing resolution in determinations of copy number variation (CNV), single-nucleotide variants (SNV), insertion/deletion (Indels), translocations (t), and tandem repeats.

be achieved by molecular karyotype techniques involving high-throughput DNA sequencing or gene chip technology. However, molecular karyotype can be used as a complement to conventional analysis techniques for cell genetic diagnosis.

Despite effective strides have been taken up in the cancer diagnostic field, still today, in clinical setting, a wider selection of cytogenetic tests is available. However, it is a million–dollar question to decide which test to choose & use. Despite standard built-in guidance, the question is still very complicated. The standard testing pathway includes, receiving a sample from the clinic for testing with suspected diagnosis. It is followed by taking a decision by the pathologists and the cytogeneticists on the appropriate test considering factors like clinical condition suspected, sample type, sample volume available, and family history (https://dermnetnz.org/topics/cytogenetic-testing). For example, acute promyelocytic leukemia sample with translocation (t(15;17)) will be tested with FISH for the reason of this disease being typically very acute, and time sensitive since there is no time for culturing and diagnosis to be faster. Similarly, FISH must be for malignancies including chronic lymphocytic leukemia or multiple myeloma since the karyotype analysis normally does not show abnormalities. Moreover, the FISH panel can pinpoint the disease since it specifically detects the genes and chromosomes normally aberrated in these disorders.

Another example is Burkitt lymphoma, an aggressive and rapidly growing lymphoma for which cytogenetic testing detects the classic t(8;14)(q14;q32) chromosomal translocation between the MYC gene on chromosome 8 and the IGH gene on chromosome 14. Karyotyping can quickly confirm this diagnosis allowing immediate therapy. Similarly, myelofibrosis that involves del7 or inv3 for which cytogenetics plays a factor in its prognosis said (Collinge et al., 2021).

Early detection of cancers and precancerous lesions is a proven strategy for the fight against cancers. Unfortunately, effective prescreening tests for early detection are not available for many cancers. However, diagnostic tools that identify specific molecular abnormalities in tumors do have the importance in precision medicine. Hopefully in future, development of innovations coupled with artificial intelligence that would happen allow detection, diagnosis, and monitoring of many types of cancers as *point of care* technologies reflecting details on type, stage, and major genetic features of the cancers without the need for an invasive biopsy.

References

Alessandro, A.V., Ammari, S., Dercle, L., Arnedos, M., 2021. Optimizing the management of cancer patients treated with systemic therapies during the COVID-19 pandemic: the new role of PCR and CT scan. Front. Oncol. https://doi.org/10.3389/fonc.2021.560585.

Allemailem, K.S., Almatroudi, A., Alrumaihi, F., Almansour, N.M., Aldakheel, F.H., Rather, R.A., Afroze, D., Rah, B., 2021. Single nucleotide polymorphisms (SNPs) in prostate cancer: its implications in diagnostics and therapeutics. Am. J. Transl. Res. 13 (4), 3868–3889. https://doi.org/10.1002/1878-0261.13067.

Angermueller, C., Clark, S.J., Lee, H.J., Macaulay, I.C., Teng, M.J., Hu, T.X., Krueger, F., Smallwood, S.-A., Ponting, C.P., 2016. Parallel single-cell sequencing links transcriptional and epigenetic heterogeneity. Nat. Methods 13 (3), 229–232. https://doi.org/10.1038/nmeth.3728. ISSN 1548-7091. PMC4770512 26752769.

Baudoin, N.C., Bloomfield, M., 2021. Genomes and the tumor microenvironment. Genes 12 (558), 1–32. https://doi.org/10.3390/genes12040558.

Biswas, D., Khan, M.W., 2020. New techniques in understanding cancer biology and metabolism. Technol. Cancer Res. Treat. 19, 1533033820943248. https://doi.org/10.1177/1533033820943248. 32672097. PMC7366405.

Bock, C., Farlik, M., Sheffield, N.C., 2016. Multi-omics of single cells: strategies and applications. Trends Biotechnol. 34 (8), 605–608. https://doi.org/10.1016/j.tibtech.2016.04.004. PMC4959511 27212022.

Boxer, L., Dang, C., 2001. Translocations involving c-myc and c-myc function. Oncogene 20, 5595–5610. https://doi.org/10.1038/sj.onc.1204595.

Burrell, R.A., McGranahan, N., Bartek, J., Swanton, C., 2013. The causes and consequences of genetic heterogeneity in cancer evolution. Nature 501 (7467), 338–345. https://doi.org/10.1038/nature12625.

Campagna, M.P., Xavier, A., Stankovich, J., Maltby, V., Slee, M., Kilpatrick, T., Scott, R.J., Butzkueven, H., Scott, J.L., Lea, R., Jokubaitis, V., 2022. Birth history is associated with whole-blood and T-cell methylation patterns in relapse 2 onset multiple sclerosis. medRxiv. https://doi.org/10.1101/2022.03.24.22272917.

Chakraborty, S., Hosen, M.I., Ahmed, H., Shekhar, H.U., 2018. Onco-multi-OMICS approach: a new frontier in cancer research. Biomed. Res. Int., 9836256. https://doi.org/10.1155/2018/9836256.

Chen, Y., Yang, Z., Wang, Y., 2019. Karyotyping of circulating tumor cells for predicting chemotherapeutic sensitivity and efficacy in patients with esophageal cancer. BMC Cancer 19, 651. https://doi.org/10.1186/s12885-019-5850-7.

Chmielecki, J., Meyerson, M., 2014. DNA sequencing of cancer: what have we learned? Annu. Rev. Med. 65 (1), 63–79. https://doi.org/10.1146/annurev-med-060712-200152. 24274178.

Cohen, K.E., Morgan, J., Wood, H., Tsika, A., Berri, S., Mason, G.C., Sheridan, E., Taylor, G.R., 2017. Molecular Karyotyping Using Massively Parallel Sequencing – A Next Generation Approach to Prenatal Diagnosis? BMFMS Fetal Medicine Posters.

Collinge, B., Ben-Neriah, S., Chong, I., Boyle, M., Jiang, A., Miyata-Takata, T., Farinha, P., Craig, J.W., Slack, G.W., Ennishi, D., 2021. The impact of MYC and BCL2 structural variants in tumors of DLBCL morphology and mechanisms of false-negative MYC IHC. Blood 37 (16), 2196–2208. https://doi.org/10.1182/blood.2020007193.

Colomer, R., Mondejar, R., Romero-Laorden, N., Alfranca, A., Sanchez-Madrid, F., Quintela-Fandino, M., 2020. When should we order a next generation sequencing test in a patient with cancer? Lancet 25, 100487. https://doi.org/10.1016/j.eclinm.2020.100487.

Darmanis, S., Spyros, G., Caroline, J., Marinescu, V.D., Niklasson, M., Segerman, A., Flamourakis, G., Fredriksson, S., Assarsson, E., Lundberg, M., 2016. Simultaneous multiplexed measurement of RNA and proteins in single cells. Cell Rep. 14 (2), 380–389. https://doi.org/10.1016/j.celrep.2015.12.021. ISSN 2211-1247. PMC4713867 26748716.

Demsky, I., 2021. How Useful is Next-Generation Sequencing for Patients with Advanced Cancer? M Health Lab. 11 March 2021.

Donahue, R.P., Bias, W.B., Renwick, J.H., McKusick, V.A., 1968. Probable assignment of the Duffy blood group locus to chromosome 1 in man. Proc. Natl. Acad. Sci. 61, 949–955. https://doi.org/10.1073/pnas.61.3.949.

Dongre, H.N., Have, H., Fromreide, S., Erland, F.A., Emblem, S.E., Dhayalan, S.M., Riis, R.K., Sapkota, D., Costea, D.E., Aarstad, H.J., Vintermyr, 2021. Targeted next-generation sequencing of cancer-related genes in a Norwegian patient cohort with head and neck squamous cell carcinoma reveals novel actionable mutations and correlations with pathological parameters. Front. Oncol. https://doi.org/10.3389/fonc.2021.734134. 24 September 2021.

Drets, M.E., Shaw, M.W., 1971. Specific banding patterns of human chromosomes. Proc. Natl. Acad. Sci. 68, 2073–2077. https://doi.org/10.1073/pnas.68.9.2073.

Duncavage, E.J., Schroeder, M.C., O'Laughlin, M., Wilson, R., MacMillan, S., Bohannon, A., Kruchowski, S., Garza, J., Du, F., Hughes, A.E.O., Robinson, J., Hughes, E., Heath, S.E., Baty, J.D., Neidich, J., Christopher, M.J., Jacoby, M.A., Uy, G.L., Fulton, R.S., Miller, C.A., Payton, J.E., Link, D.C., Walter, M.J., Westervelt, P., DiPersio, J.F., Ley, T.J., Spencer, D.H., 2021. Genome sequencing as an alternative to cytogenetic analysis in myeloid cancers. N. Engl. J. Med. 384 (10), 924–935. https://doi.org/10.1056/NEJMoa2024534. 33704937. PMC8130455.

Elmore, L.E., Greer, S.F., Daniels, E.C., Saxe, C.C., Melner, M.H., Krawiec, G.M., Cance, W.G., Phelps, W.C., 2020. Blueprint for cancer research: critical gaps and opportunities. CA Cancer J. Clin. 71 (2), 107–139. https://doi.org/10.3322/caac.21652C.

Finnegan, C., Smyth, S., Smith, O., Flood, K., Malone, F.D., 2021. PCR vs karyotype for CVS and amniocentesis—the experience at one tertiary fetal medicine unit. Ir. J. Med. Sci. 2021. https://doi.org/10.1007/s11845-021-02715-y.

Ford, C.E., Jones, K.W., Polani, P.E., De Almeida, J.C., Bridges, J.H., 1959. A sex-chromosome anomaly in a case of gonadal dysgenesis (Turner's syndrome). Lancet 1 (7075), 711–713. https://doi.org/10.1016/s0140-6736(59)91893-8.

Fraser, P., Tanay, A., Laue, E.D., Dean, W., Yaffe, E., Schoenfelder, S., Stevens, T.J., Lubling, Y., Nagano, T., 2013. Single-cell hi-C reveals cell-to-cell variability in chromosome structure. Nature 502 (7469), 59–64. https://doi.org/10.1038/nature12593. Bibcode:2013Natur.502...59N. ISSN 1476-4687. PMC3869051 24067610.

Frenech, M., Knasmueller, S., Bolognesi, C., Bonassi, S., Holland, N., Migliore, L., 2016. Molecular mechanisms by which in vivo exposure to exogenous chemical genotoxic agents can lead to micronucleus formation in lymphocytes in vivo and ex vivo in humans. Mutat. Res. 770, 12–25. https://doi.org/10.1016/j.mrrev.2016.04.008.

Garsed, D.W., Marshall, O.J., Corbin, V.D., Hsu, A., Di Stefano, L., Schröder, J., Li, J., Feng, Z.P., Kim, B.-W., Kowarsky, M., Lansdell, B., Brookwell, R., Myklebost, O., Meza-Zepeda, L., Holloway, A.J., Pedeutour, F., 2014. The architecture and evolution of cancer neochromosomes. Cancer Cell 26 (5), 653–667. https://doi.org/10.1016/j.ccell.2014.09.010.

Gavin, K., Wolf, R., Oliver, S., Andrews, S.R., Julian, P., Saadeh, H., Krueger, F., Angermueller, C., Lee, H.J., 2014. Single-cell genome-wide bisulfite sequencing for assessing epigenetic heterogeneity. Nat. Methods 11 (8), 817–820. https://doi.org/10.1038/nmeth.3035. ISSN 1548-7105. PMC4117646 25042786.

Gherardini, P.F., Nolan, G.P., Chen, S.-Y., Hsieh, E.W., Elena, W.Y., Zunder, E.R., Bava, F., Frei, A.P., 2016. Highly multiplexed simultaneous detection of RNAs and proteins in single cells. Nat. Methods 13 (3), 269–275. https://doi.org/10.1038/nmeth.3742. ISSN 1548-7105. PMC4767631 26808670.

Gijsbers, A.C.J., Ruivenkamp, C.A.L., 2011. Molecular karyotyping: from microscope to SNP arrays. Horm. Res. Paediatr. 76, 208–213. https://doi.org/10.1159/000330406.

Graw, S., Chappell, K., Washam, C.L., Gies, A., Bird, J., Robeson, M.S., Byrum, S.D., 2021. Multi-omics data integration considerations and study design for biological systems and disease. Mol. Omics 2021 (17), 170–185. https://doi.org/10.1039/D0MO00041H.

Greenleaf, W.J., Chang, H.Y., Snyder, M.P., Michael, L.G., Ruff, D., Litzenburger, U.M., Wu, B., Buenrostro, J.D., 2015. Single-cell chromatin accessibility reveals principles of regulatory variation. Nature 523 (7561), 486–490.

Grisanzio, C., Freedman, M.L., 2010. Chromosome 8q24-associated cancers and MYC. Genes Cancer 1 (6), 555–559. https://doi.org/10.1177/1947601910381380.

Heim, S., Mitelman, F., 1995. Cancer Cytogenetics: Chromosomal and Molecular Genetic Aberrations of Tumor Cells, second ed. Wiley-Liss, Inc., New York.

Heng, E., Moy, A., Liu, G., Heng, H.H., Zhang, K., 2021. ER stress and micronuclei cluster: stress response contributes to genome Chaos in Cancer. Front. Cell Dev. Biol. https://doi.org/10.3389/fcell.2021.673188. 04 August 2021.

Hu, Y., Qin, A., Sheu, K., Trejo, B., Fan, S., Ying, G., 2018. Single cell multi-omics technology: methodology and application. Front. Cell Dev. Biol. 6, 28. https://doi.org/10.3389/fcell.2018.00028. ISSN 2296-634X. PMC5919954 29732369.

Iwabuchi, H., Sakamoto, M., Sakunaga, H., Ma, Y.Y., Carcangiu, M.L., Pinkel, D., Yang-Feng, T.L., Gra, J.W., 1995. Genetic analysis of benign, low-grade, and high-grade ovarian tumors. Cancer Res. 155, 6172–6180.

Jacobs, P., Strong, J., 1959. A case of human intersexuality having a possible XXY sex-determining mechanism. Nature 183, 302–303. https://doi.org/10.1038/183302a0.

Jeffreys, A., Wilson, V., Thein, S., 1985. Individual-specific 'fingerprints' of human DNA. Nature 316, 76–79. https://doi.org/10.1038/316076a0.

Jiang, Y., Sun, A., Zhao, Y., Ying, W., Sun, H., Yang, X., 2019. Proteomics identifies new therapeutic targets of early-stage hepatocellular carcinoma. Nature 567 (7747), 257–261. https://doi.org/10.1038/s41586-019-0987-8.

Jing, S.J., Liu, F., Zhang, F., Huang, Y., Zhang, Q., Juan, G., Zhai, J., 2017. Next-generation sequencing and karyotype analysis for the diagnosis of Robertsonian translocation type trisomy 13: a case report. Iran. J. Public Health 46 (6), 848–851. PMC5558080 28828329.

Kane, L.E., Mellotte, G.S., Conlon, K.C., Ryan, B.M., Maher, S.G., 2021. Multi-Omic biomarkers as potential tools for the characterisation of pancreatic cystic lesions and cancer: innovative patient data integration. Cancers 13, 769. https://doi.org/10.3390/cancers13040769.

Kester, L., Bienko, S.B., van Oudenaarden, M., Dey, A., Siddharth, S., 2015. Integrated genome and transcriptome sequencing of the same cell. Nat. Biotechnol. 33 (3), 285–289. https://doi.org/10.1038/nbt.3129. OCLC 931063996. PMC4374170 25599178.

Kimmons, L., 2021. How Are Biomarkers Used to Treat cancer? MD Anderson Cancer Centre (April 5, 2021).

Knutsen, T., Gobu, V., Knaus, R., Padilla-Nash, H., Augustus, M., Strausberg, R.L., Kirsch, I.R., Sirotkin, K., Ried, T., 2005. The interactive online SKY/M-FISH & CGH database and the Entrez cancer chromosomes search database: linkage of chromosomal aberrations with the genome sequence. Genes Chromosomes Cancer 44 (1), 52–64. https://doi.org/10.1002/gcc.20224.

Knutsen, T., Ried, T., 2000. A comprehensive diagnostic and research tool. A review of the first 300 published cases. J. Assoc. Genet. Technol. 26, 3–15.

Kohla, S., Kourashy, S., Nawaz, Z., Youssef, R., Al-Sabbagh, A., Ibrahim, F., 2021. P190BCR-ABL1 in a patient with Philadelphia chromosome positive T-cell acute lymphoblastic leukemia: a rare case report and review of literature. Case Rep Oncol 14, 1040–1050. https://doi.org/10.1159/000516270.

Kosyakova, N., Hamid, A.B., Chaveerach, A., 2013. Generation of multicolor banding probes for chromosomes of different species. Mol. Cytogenet. 6, 6. https://doi.org/10.1186/1755-8166-6-6.

Lauriola, A., Martello, A., Fantini, S., Marverti, G., Zanocco-Marani, T., Davalli, O.P., Guardavaccaro, D., Mai, S., Caporali, A., D'Arca, D., 2020. Depletion of trichoplein (TpMs) causes chromosome missegregation, dna damage and chromosome instability in cancer cells. Cancers 12 (4), 993. https://doi.org/10.3390/cancers12040993.

Lee, Y., Lee, H., 2021. Integrative reconstruction of cancer genome karyotypes using InfoGenomeR. Nat. Commun. 12, 2467. https://doi.org/10.1038/s41467-021-22671-6.

Lee, J., Choi, S., Jung, D., Jung, Y., Kim, J.H., Jung, S., Lee, W.S., 2021. Mutational characterization of colorectal cancer from Korean patients with targeted sequencing. J. Cancer 12 (24), 7300–7310. https://doi.org/10.7150/jca.61324. Available from: https://www.jcancer.org/v12p7300.htm.

Lejeune, J., Turpin, R., Gautier, M., 1959. Le mongolisme, maladie chromosomique. Bull. Acad. Natl Med. 143, 256–265.

Lewis, S.M., Asselin-Labat, M.L., Nguyen, Q., Berthelet, J., Tan, X., Wimmer, V.C., Merino, D., Rogers, K.L., Naik, S.H., 2021. Spatial omics and multiplexed imaging to explore cancer biology. Nat. Methods. https://doi.org/10.1038/s41592-021-01203-6.

Lin, E., Lane, H.-Y., 2017. Machine learning and systems genomics approaches for multi-omics data. Biomarker Res. 5 (1), 2. https://doi.org/10.1186/s40364-017-0082-y. ISSN 2050-7771. PMC5251341 28127429.

Logsdon, G.A., Vollger, M.R., Hsieh, P., 2021. The structure, function and evolution of a complete human chromosome 8. Nature 593, 101–107. https://doi.org/10.1038/s41586-021-03420-7.

Lourenco, A., Benson, K.L., Henderson, M.C., Silver, M., Letsios, E., 2017. A non-invasive blood-based combinatorial proteomic biomarker assay to detect breast cancer in women under the age of 50 years. Clin. Breast Cancer 17 (2017), 516–525.e516. https://doi.org/10.1016/j.clbc.2017.05.004.

Ly, P., Cleveland, D.W., 2017. Rebuilding chromosomes after catastrophe: emerging mechanisms of chromothripsis. Trends Cell Biol. 27 (12), 917–930. https://doi.org/10.1016/j.tcb.2017.08.005.

Macaulay, L.C., Teng, M.J., Haerty, W., Kumar, P., Ponting, C.P., Voet, T., 2016. Separation and parallel sequencing of the genomes and transcriptomes of single cells using G&T-seq. Nat. Protoc. 11 (11), 2081–2103. https://doi.org/10.1038/nprot.2016.138. 27685099. hdl:20.500.11820/015ce29d-7e2d-42c8-82fa-cb1290b761c0. ISSN 1754-2189. PMID. S2CID 24351548.

Mareschal, S., Palau, A., Lindberg, J., Ruminy, P., Nilsson, C., Bengtzén, S., Engvall, M., Eriksson, A., Neddermeyer, A., Marchand, V., Jansson, M., Jardin, F., Rantalainen, M., Lennartsson, A., Cavelier, L., Grönberg, H., Lehmann, C., 2021. Challenging conventional karyotyping by next-generation karyotyping in 281 intensively treated patients with AML. Blood Adv. 5 (4), 1003–1016. https://doi.org/10.1182/bloodadvances.2020002517. PMCID: PMC7903223 33591326.

Mattia, P., Joseph, R.E., 2011. The DNA methylome. FEBS Lett. 585 (13), 1994–2000. https://doi.org/10.1016/j.febslet.2010.10.061. PMC3129437. NIHMSID: NIHMS252724 21056564.

Maxam, A.M., Gilbert, W., 1977. A new method for sequencing DNA. Proc. Natl. Acad. Sci. U. S. A. 74 (2), 560–564. https://doi.org/10.1073/pnas.74.2.560. PMC392330 265521. (Bibcode:1977PNAS...74..560M).

Melo, I.M.A., Viana, M.R.P., Pupin, B., Bhattacharjee, T.T., Canevari, A.R., 2021. PCR-RFLP and FTIR-based detection of high-risk human papilloma virus for cervical cancer screening and prevention. Biochem. Biophys. Rep. 26, 100993. https://doi.org/10.1016/j.bbrep.2021.100993.

Menyhartab, O., Győrffy, B., 2021. Multi-omics approaches in cancer research with applications in tumor subtyping, prognosis, and diagnosis. Comput. Struct. Biotechnol. J. 19, 949–960. https://doi.org/10.1016/j.csbj.2021.01.009.

Mirzayans, R., Andrais, B., Murray, D., 2018. Roles of polyploid/multinucleated giant cancer cells in metastasis and disease relapse following anticancer treatment. Cancers 10, 118. https://doi.org/10.3390/cancers10040118.

Morrison, J., Koeman, J.M., Johnson, B.K., 2021. Evaluation of whole-genome DNA methylation sequencing library preparation protocols. Epigenetics Chromatin 14, 28. https://doi.org/10.1186/s13072-021-00401-y.

Nath, A., Bild, A.H., 2021. Leveraging single-cell approaches in cancer precision medicine. Trends Cancer 7 (4), 359–372. https://doi.org/10.1016/j.trecan.2021.01.007. Epub 2021 Feb 6. PMID: 33563578; PMCID: PMC7969443.

Nazarov, P.V., Muller, A., Kaoma, T., 2017. RNA sequencing and transcriptome arrays analyses show opposing results for alternative splicing in patient derived samples. BMC Genomics 18, 443. https://doi.org/10.1186/s12864-017-3819-y.

Ng, S., Turner, E., Robertson, P., Steven, D.F., Abigail, W.B., Lee, C., Shaffer, T., Wong, M., Bhattacharjee, A., Eichler, E.E., Bamshad, M., Nickerson, D.A., Shendure, J., 2021. Targeted capture and massively parallel sequencing of 12 human exomes. Nature 461, 272–276. https://doi.org/10.1038/nature08250.

Nicolini, U., Lalatta, F., Natacci, F., Curcio, C., 2004. The introduction of QF-PCR in prenatal diagnosis of fetal aneuploidies: time for reconsideration. Hum. Reprod. Update 10 (6), 541–548. https://doi.org/10.1093/humupd/dmh046.

O'Connor, C., 2008. Karyotyping for chromosomal abnormalities. Nat. Educ. 1 (1), 27.

Pierotti, M.A., Porta, G.D., 1987. Restriction fragment length polymorphism (RFLPs)p as genetic tumor marker. In: Human Tumor Markers. De Gruyter, https://doi.org/10.1515/9783110846515-007.

Pinkel, D., Straume, T., Gray, J.W., 1986. Cytogenetic analysis using quantitative, high-sensitivity, fluorescence hybridization. Proc. Natl. Acad. Sci. U. S. A. 83 (9), 2934–2938. https://doi.org/10.1073/pnas.83.9.2934.

Rao, M.S., Ciurlionis, V.V.R., Buck, W.R., Mittelstadt, S.W., Blomme, E.A.G., Liguori, M.J., 2019. Comparison of RNA-Seq and microarray gene expression platforms for the toxicogenomic evaluation of liver from short-term rat toxicity studies. Front. Genet. https://doi.org/10.3389/fgene.2018.00636.

Réda, M., Richard, C., Bertaut, A., Niogret, J., Collot, T., Fumet, J.D., Blanc, J., Truntzer, C., Desmoulins, I., Ladoire, S., Hennequin, A., Favier, L., Bengrine, L., Vincent, J., Hervieu, A., Dusserre, J.G., Lepage, C., Foucher, P., Borg, C., Albuisson, J., Arnould, L., Nambot, S., Faivre, L., Boidot, R., Ghiringhelli, F., 2020. Implementation and use of whole exome sequencing for metastatic solid cancer. EBioMedicine 51, 102624. https://doi.org/10.1016/j.ebiom.2019.102624. Epub 2020 Jan 7 31923800. PMC7000332.

Richards, C., 2015. How next-generation sequencing came to be: a brief history. Drug Target Rev. (31 January 2015).

Rode, A., Maass, K.K., Willmund, K.V., Lichter, P., Ernst, A., 2016. Chromothripsis in cancer cells: an update. Int. J. Cancer 138 (10), 2322–2333. https://doi.org/10.1002/ijc.29888.

Rohart, F., Gautier, B., Singh, A., Lê, C., 2017. mixOmics: an R package for 'omics feature selection and multiple data integration. PLoS Comput. Biol. 13 (11), e1005752. bioRxiv 10.1101/108597 https://doi.org/10.1371/journal.pcbi.1005752. PMC5687754 29099853.

Rotunno, M., Barajas, R., Clyne, M., Hoover, E., Simonds, N.I., Lam, T.K., Mechanic, L.E., Goldstein, A.-M., Gillanders, E.M., 2020. A systematic literature review of whole exome and genome sequencing population studies of genetic susceptibility to Cancer. Cancer Epidemiol. Biomark. Prev. https://doi.org/10.1158/1055-9965.EPI-19-1551 (Published August 2020).

Rowley, J.D., 1973. A new consistent chromosomal abnormality in chronic myelogenous leukaemia identified by quinacrine fluorescence and Giemsa staining. Nature 243, 290–293.

Saied, M.H., Elkaffash, D., Fadl, R., Haleem, R.A., Refeat, A., Ibrahim, I., Tahoun, M., Elkayal, A., Tayae, E., 2021. Preliminary results of targeted sequencing of BRCA1 and BRCA2 in a cohort of breast cancer families: new insight into pathogenic variants in patients and at-risk relatives. Mol. Med. Rep. 24 (3), 678. https://doi.org/10.3892/mmr.2021.12317. Epub 2021 Jul 23 34296289.

Sanger, F., Nicklen, S., Coulson, A.R., 1977. DNA sequencing with chain-terminating inhibitors. Proc. Natl. Acad. Sci. U. S. A. 74 (12), 5463–5477. Bibcode:1977PNAS...74.5463S https://doi.org/10.1073/pnas.74.12.5463. PMC431765 271968.

Satpathy, S., Jaehnig, E.J., Krug, K., Kim, B.J., Saltzman, A.B., Chan, D.W., 2020. Microscaled proteogenomic methods for precision oncology. Nat. Commun. 11 (1). https://doi.org/10.1038/s41467-020-14381-2.

Savas, S., Liu, G., 2009. Studying genetic variations in cancer prognosis (and risk): a primer for clinicians. Oncologist 14 (7), 657–666. https://doi.org/10.1634/theoncologist.2009-0042.

Schena, M., Shalon, D., Davis, R.W., Brown, P.O., 1995. Quantitative monitoring of gene expression patterns with a complementary DNA microarray. Science 270, 467–470. https://doi.org/10.1126/science.270.5235.467.

Schmidt, D.R., Patel, R.K., Kirsch, D.G., Lewis, C.R., 2021. Metabolomics in cancer research and emerging applications in clinical oncology. CA Cancer J. Clin. 71 (4), 333–358. https://doi.org/10.3322/caac.21670Citations.

Schreck, R.R., Distèche, C.C., 2001. Chromosome banding techniques. Curr. Protoc. Hum. Genet. https://doi.org/10.1002/0471142905.hg0402s00 (Chapter 4, Unit 4.2).

Sears, D.A., Udden, M.M., 2012. Howell-Jolly bodies: a brief historical review. Am J Med Sci 343, 407–409. https://doi.org/10.1097/MAJ.0b013e31823020d1.

Sha, J., Liu, F., Zhang, B., Huang, Y., Zhang, Q., Juan, G., Zha, H., 2017. Next-generation sequencing and karyotype analysis for the diagnosis of Robertsonian translocation type trisomy 13: a case report. Iran. J. Public Health 46 (6), 848–851.

Shamrikova, V., Shilo, P., Stepanova, M., Dekhanova, K., Ledin, E., 2021. Clinical application of next-generation sequencing in cancer patients. J. Clin. Oncol. 39 (15), 50.

Solomon, E., Borrow, J., Goddard, A.D., 1992. Chromosome aberrations and cancer. Science 254, 1153–1160.

Sommer, S., Buraczewska, I., Kruszewski, M., 2020. Micronucleus assay: the state of art, and future directions. Int. J. Mol. Sci. 21, 1534. https://doi.org/10.3390/ijms21041534.

Sonnenschein, C., Soto, A.M., 2020. Over a century of cancer research: inconvenient truths and promising leads. PLoS Biol. https://doi.org/10.1371/journal.pbio.3000670.

Storlazzi, C.T., Lonoce, A., Guastadisegni, M.C., Trombetta, D., D'Addabbo, P., Daniele, G., L'Abbate, A., Macchia, G., Surace, C., Kok, K., Ullmann, R., Purgato, S., Palumbo, O., Carella, M., Ambros, P.-F., Rocchi, M., 2010. Gene amplification as double minutes or homogeneously staining regions in solid tumors: origin and structure. Genome Res. 20 (9), 1198–1206. https://doi.org/10.1101/gr.106252.110. Epub 2010 Jul 14 20631050. PMC2928498.

Supplitt, S., Karpinski, P., Sasiadek, M., Laczmanska, I., 2021. Current achievements and applications of transcriptomics in personalized Cancer medicine. Int. J. Mol. Sci. 22 (3), 1422. https://doi.org/10.3390/ijms22031422. PMC7866970 33572595.

Tarazona, S., Balzano-Nogueira, L., Cones, A., 2018. Multiomics data integration in time series experiments. Compr. Anal. Chem. https://doi.org/10.1016/bs.coac.2018.06.005.

Terradas, M., Martin, M., Hernandez, L., Tusell, L., Genesca, A., 2012. Nuclear envelope defects impede a proper response to micronuclear DNA lesions. Mutat. Res. 729, 35–40. https://doi.org/10.1016/j.mrfmmm.2011.09.003.

Tibiletti, M.G., Sessa, F., Bernasconi, B., Cerutti, R., Broggi, B., 2000. A large 6q deletion is a common cytogenetic alteration in fibroadenomas, pre-malignant lesions, and carcinomas of the breast. Clin. Cancer Res. 6, 1422–1431.

Tjio, J.G., Levan, A., 1956. The chromosome numbers of man. Hereditas 42, 1–6.

Uzozie, A.C., Aebersold, R., 2018. Advancing translational research and precision medicine with targeted proteomics. J. Proteome 189, 1–10. https://doi.org/10.1016/j.jprot.2018.02.021.

van Es, J.M., Polak, M.M., van den Berg, F.M., Ramsoekh, T.B., Craanen, M.E., Hruban, R.H., Offerhaus, G.J.A., 1995. Molecular markers for diagnostic cytology of neoplasms in the head region of the pancreas: mutation of K-ras and overexpression of the p53 protein product. Clin. Pathol. 48, 218–222.

Veselinyová, D., Mašlanková, J., Kalinová, K., Mareková, M., Rabajdová, M., 2021. Selected in situ hybridization methods: principles and application. Molecules 26, 3874. https://doi.org/10.3390/molecules26133874.

Vilanova, C., Porcar, M., 2016. Are multi-omics enough? Nat. Microbiol. 1 (8), 16101. https://doi.org/10.1038/nmicrobiol.2016.101. 27573112. (S2CID 3835720).

Vogelstein, B., Papadopoulos, N., Velculescu, V.E., Zhou, S., Diaz, L.A., Kinzler, K.W., 2013. Cancer genome landscapes. Science 339 (6127), 1546–1558. https://doi.org/10.1126/science.1235122.

Walter, W., Shahswar, R., Stengel, A., 2021. Clinical application of whole transcriptome sequencing for the classification of patients with acute lymphoblastic leukemia. BMC Cancer 21, 886. https://doi.org/10.1186/s12885-021-08635-5.

Wang, J., Mulligan, C.G., Easton, J., Roberts, S., Heatley, S.L., Ma, J., Rusch, M.C., Chen, K., Harris, C.-C., Ding, L., Holmfeldt, L., Payne-Turner, D., Fan, X., Wei, L., Zhao, D., Obenauer, J.C., Naeve, C., Mardis, E.R., Wilson, R.K., Downing, J.R., Zhang, J., 2011. CREST maps somatic structural variation in cancer genomes with base-pair resolution. Nat. Methods 8 (8), 652–654. https://doi.org/10.1038/nmeth.1628. 21666668. PMC3527068.

Wang, B.O., Mezlini, M., Demir, F., Fiume, F., Tu, Z., Brudno, M., 2014. Similarity network fusion for aggregating data types on a genomic scale. Nat. Methods 11 (3), 333–337. https://doi.org/10.1038/nmeth.2810.

Wang, Q.I., Peng, W.X., Wang, L.U., Ye, L., 2019. Toward multiomics-based next-generation diagnostics for precision medicine. Perinat. Med. 16 (2), 157–170. https://doi.org/10.2217/pme-2018-0085.

Wijesiriwardhana, P., Wettasinghe, K., Dissanayeke, V.H.W., 2021. Copy number variants captured by the array comparative genomic hybridization in a cohort of patients affected with hereditary colorectal cancer in Sri Lanka. Asian Pac. J. Cancer Prev. 22 (6), 1957–1966. https://doi.org/10.31557/APJCP.2021.22.6.1957.

Yan, J., Risacher, S.L., Shen, Saykin, A.J., 2018. Network approaches to systems biology analysis of complex disease: integrative methods for multi-omics data. Brief. Bioinform. 19, 1370–1381.

Yang, M., Soga, T., Pollard, P.J., 2013. Oncometabolites: linking altered metabolism with cancer. J. Clin. Invest. 123 (9), 3652–3658. https://doi.org/10.1172/JCI67228.

Yi, J., Ju, Y.S., 2018. Patterns and mechanisms of structural variations in human cancer. Exp. Mol. Med. 50, 1–11. https://doi.org/10.1038/s12276-018-0112-3.

Yu, Y., Werdyani, S., Carey, M., Parfrey, P., Yilmaz, Y.E., Savas, S., 2021. A comprehensive analysis of SNPs and CNVs identifies novel markers associated with disease outcomes in colorectal cancer. Mol. Oncol. https://doi.org/10.1002/1878-0261.13067.

Zhang, S., 2021. The Human Genome Is—Finally!—Complete. The Atlantic (11 June 2021).

Zhang, C.Z., Spektor, A., Cornils, H., Francis, J.M., Jackson, E.K., Liu, S., Meyerson, M., Pellman, D., 2015. Chromothripsis from DNA damage in micronuclei. Nature 522, 179–184. https://doi.org/10.1038/nature14493.

Zhang, J., Shi, H., Shi, H., Jiang, T., 2018. Circulating tumor cells with karyotyping as a novel biomarker for diagnosis and treatment of nasopharyngeal carcinoma. Cancer 18 (1). https://doi.org/10.1186/s12885-018-5034-x.

CHAPTER TEN

Role of noncoding RNA as biomarkers for cancer

Deepti Malik[a], Manisha Prajapat[b], Gurjeet Kaur[b], Gajendra Choudhary[b], Ajay Prakash[b], and Bikash Medhi[b]
[a]Department of Biochemistry, All India Institute of Medical Sciences, Bilaspur, India
[b]Department of Pharmacology, Postgraduate Institute of Medical Education and Research, Chandigarh, India

1. Introduction

Gene expression regulates the growth and the maintenance of cellular and tissue homeostasis. Genomic DNA in the nucleus plays a crucial role in this process, which is used to create messenger RNAs, which then go into the cytoplasm and translate proteins. These processes need the use of a variety of non-protein-coding RNAs (ncRNAs). Splicing of messenger RNA is regulated by small nuclear RNAs (snRNAs) that have the capability to detect three-nucleotide mRNA sequences and subsequently guiding amino acids to ribosome. Ribosomes are the structures that are most numerous and help with protein translation. They play a major role in housekeeping and keeping a check on regular cell activity. Small nuclear RNAs are also said to contribute to chemical changes to a major part of these housekeeping RNAs. (Matera et al., 2007). In experiments, "Andrew Fire" was able to demonstrate that double-stranded RNAs have the ability to shut down corresponding messenger RNAs posttranscriptionally in Caenorhabditis worms. siRNAs and microRNAs typically called endogenous dsRNAs are commonly found in plants, flies, and humans. siRNAs, miRNAs, and Piwi-associated RNAs are few of the most well sequenced classes of regulatory short RNAs (Farazi et al., 2008; Carthew and Sontheimer, 2009; Bartel, 2009; Czech and Hannon, 2011; Dueck and Meister, 2014; Mendell and Olson, 2012; Siomi et al., 2011).

With the advances in transcriptome sequencing technology our knowledge on the mammalian transcriptome's protein-coding/noncoding components has grown exponentially. We now have the detailed insight into components which are a result of protein-coding/noncoding sites. We now know that approximately 66% of the mammalian genome is actively transcribed, while only 9% encodes for proteins (Mattick, 2001; Djebali et al., 2012). lncRNAs are the major component of transcriptional activity. The defining characteristic of these RNA molecules is presence of poly-A tail which can be truncated like mRNAs. In humans it is estimated that there are somewhere between 5400 and more than 10,000 lncRNA transcripts. We still do not have a clear idea on the functional importance of lncRNA transcripts (Cabili et al., 2011; Djebali et al., 2012). Even it's surmised that lncRNAs play critical part in multiple processes such as epigenetic regulation of gene expression (Bond et al., 2009), X-chromosome inactivation (Lee and Bartolomei, 2013), imprinting (Tian et al., 2010), and nuclear architecture preservation (Hacisuleyman et al., 2014). In our chapter, we will focus on various types of noncoding RNAs and the role they play as biomarkers for cancer.

2. Micro RNA

microRNAs are 19–23-nucleotide-long RNA sequences defined by short and single strands and ability to bind to 3′-UTR sequences of target genes consequential in dilapidation of mRNA further resulting in reduced expression of genes (Malik and Kaul, 2015). In cancer cells, miRNAs are heavily dysregulated. miRNAs have huge influence on diverse molecular pathways which in turn controls cell cycle regulation hematopoiesis, differentiation, apoptosis, proliferation, apoptosis, and multiple other cellular processes specifically in mammals. Ambros and his team identified that a tiny non-protein-coding RNA in *Caenorhabditis elegans* (*C. elegans*) that regulates the expression of the protein lin-14 affecting the RNA development. miRNA are widely postulated to control the expression of significant number of human genes making them one of the significant classes of genomic regulators (Calin et al., 2004). The most current estimate is that we have 1872 human miRNA precursor genes resulting in approximately 2000 developed miRNA sequences (http://www.mirbase.org). miRNAs biogenesis typically originates with transcription by RNA polymerase, resulting in an extended primary transcript (pri-miRNA) with a cap5′ start and a poly A tail characterized by alternative structure, and while it's still in nucleus, it is sliced by RNase III and Drosha and their cofactor DGCR8 (Di George Syndrome critical region gene 8) resulting in the generation of a predecessor molecule with approx. Size of 70 nucleotides. pre-miRNA is quickly shifted to cytoplasm via exportina-5 (Exp5), a nuclear exportation protein that makes use of Ran-GTP as a cofactor. After been transferred to cytoplasm, it is treated by RNase III creating a double strand of miRNA, 22 nucleotides in length. This product binds to the RISC complex (an induction complex for RNA silencing) and directs sequence-specific cleavage of target mRNAs (Fig. 1).

Studies in the past have made it clear that microRNA is extremely deregulated in human malignancies and the core reason for the same is chromosomal abnormalities, abnormal transcriptional control of miRNAs, amplification or deletion of miRNA genes, epigenetic changes which are dysregulated and flaws in the miRNA biogenesis apparatus.

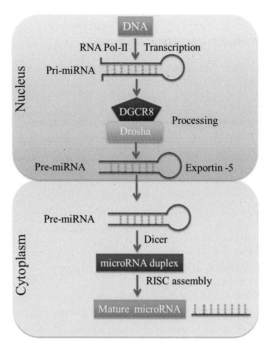

Fig. 1 The biogenesis and function of miRNAs.

3. Amplification or deletion of miRNA genes

Research in last 10 years have clearly shown that miRNA expression is highly discontrolled in cancer cells and acts like protein-coding genes it is easily prone to epigenetic modulation. Also research has clearly shown that altered expression of microRNAs (miRNAs) has a major role in activating cancer development (Peng and Croce, 2016). microRNAs are typically characterized by RNA sequences between (18–22 nucleotides) which are typically short and single stranded, with capability to bind to 3′-UTR sequences which results in specific genes degradation of mRNA causing reduced gene levels (Malik and Kaul, 2015). Mutations in miRNAs potentially can cause overexpression of an oncogene and/or the reduction of a tumor suppressor gene (Wahida et al., 2010; Kaur et al., 2022; Sharma et al., 2015). Breast cancer is characterized by overexpression of miR-21, miR-155, miR-23, miR-191, and miR-196b (Yan et al., 2008; Kaul and Malik, 2012), and AML by miR-191, miR-199a, and miR-155 (Ramamurthy et al., 2016). miR-2909 seems to play a role in immunomodulation (Kaul et al., 2019), and energy metabolism (Malik and Kaul, 2018; Kaushik et al., 2019). Its changed expression can lead to many diseases including rheumatoid arthritis (Malik et al., 2015) and pediatric acute lymphoblastic leukemia (Malik et al., 2014).

4. Dysregulated epigenetic changes

Epigenetic alteration is typically present in cancer and these alternations can include global genomic DNA hypomethylation, aberrant DNA hypermethylation of tumor suppressor genes, and disruption of the histone modification patterns (Sharma et al., 2010). miRNAs are also prone to epigenetic modulation (Sharma et al., 2010). miR-34b/c are found to be silenced in cancer cells because of hypermethylation and if we restore these miRNAs in cancer it can lead to inhibition of motility, reduced tumor growth and inhibited metastasis formation in vivo (Lujambio et al., 2008). Similarly, reduced expressions of miR-9-1, miR-124a, and miR-145-5p are attributed to DNA hypermethylation in breast, lung and colon carcinomas, respectively (Lujambio et al., 2008).

5. Defects in miRNA biogenesis machinery

Enzymes and proteins play a crucial role in controlling miRNA biogenesis. Typical examples been Drosha, Dicer, argonaute proteins, and exportin 5 resulting in maturation in miRNA precursors hence any kind of aberrant expression in any microRNA biogenesis component can result in abnormal expression of miRNAs. Drosha and Dicer are dysregulated in certain tumors (Bartel, 2009). Like Dicer and Drosha, argonaute proteins also dysregulated in cancer. For example, Wilms' tumor of the kidney is characterized by absence of *EIF2C1/hAgo1* gene (Peng and Croce, 2016).

Genome profiling provides clear clues that miRNA expression signatures have a clear correlation with tumor type, tumor grade and clinical outcomes proving without a doubt that miRNAs are very useful candidates for diagnostic biomarkers, prognostic biomarkers, therapeutic targets, or tools. However further research is required to screen miRNA candidates by utilizing the advanced sequencing techniques and create the validation of miRNA candidates as diagnostic and prognostic biomarkers.

5.1 siRNA

RNAi (RNA interference) is involved in post transcriptional process which able to inhibits the expression of gene by cleavage on a specific target location of messenger RNA. Hence this method has demonstrated hopeful treatment effects for a variety of disorders, including cancer (Mahmoodi Chalbatani et al., 2019). siRNA is a potential therapeutic reagent which can inhibit specific gene function both in vivo and in vitro studies. siRNA is a double-strand RNA that contains 20–23 nucleotide base pair in length and prevents the translation process by degradation of messenger RNA (mRNA). In terms of function, siRNA (small interfering RNA) is comparable to microRNA, except that microRNA may encourage the expression of various genes via imperfect base pairing, but siRNA shows more specificity for a binding with single gene. Both siRNA and miRNA show common role in gene regulation and gene silencing, but clinical potential is different. One important difference, miRNA has numerous mRNA targets, but siRNA has just single mRNA target (Charbe et al., 2020). siRNAs, protect genome integrity in the face of invading nucleic acids like as transgenes, transposons, viruses, and miRNAs regulate endogenous genes (Dana et al., 2017). However, siRNA technology confronts several challenges in terms of efficient transfer and effectiveness. Now different method used to deliver siRNA into in vivo such as ultrasound method, electroporation method, tail vein injection in mice, use of gene gun delivers. In addition, it can inject directly through subcutaneous, intraperitoneal, intravenous injection and other approach, chemical-based method such as by polymer, cationic lipid, and peptide (Mahmoodi Chalbatani et al., 2019). To increase the siRNA stability for cancer therapy, some chemical modifications at sugar and phosphate group are been done to improve efficient siRNA delivery system into cytoplasm of target cell (Mahmoodi Chalbatani et al., 2019).

Many additional RNAi pathways employ Dicer cleavage to make mature regulatory short RNAs. Endogenous siRNAs (*endo*-siRNAs) may generate dsRNA structures by combining sense and antisense transcripts from bidirectional or complementary loci. They're generated from dsRNAs taken in by the cell. In plants and drosophila, viral dsRNA is transformed into siRNAs that target viral mRNAs (Billy et al., 2001; García-Sastre, 2011; Li et al., 2013; Maillard et al., 2013; Nayak et al., 2013; Szittya and Burgyán, 2013). In 1999, plant siRNAs were identified, and their ability to direct sequence-dependent endonucleolytic cleavage of the messenger RNA they can control in mammalian cells was also established.

5.2 piRNA

piRNA (known as a PIWI-interacting RNA) is a short noncoding RNAs which are found in somatic and germ cells. It has 24–31-base nucleotide sequence with uridine at $5'$ terminal. piRNA firstly identified in Drosophila test, which is involved to maintain male fertility through silence transcripts. To convert into the functional mature piRNA, biogenesis typically based on RNase type III enzyme (Czech and Hannon, 2016).

The biogenesis mechanism of piRNA involves two pathways: primary and secondary amplification pathways which represent the ping pong mechanism. First is primary amplification-based pathway in which the piwi protein make complex with piRNA further is cleavage by Zuc to producer $3'$ end and follow the methylation process in cytoplasm, the mature piRNA-piwi complex is produced. Which influenced rearrangement of genes, silencing of transposon, and spermiogenesis, regulated epigenetics, and also maintained germ stem cells (Liu et al., 2019). Other one is ping pong-based pathway, in which piRNA bind with AUB protein or AGO protein to form complex for further generates new piRNA (Liu et al., 2019). piRNAs seem to work in the germline, targeting and suppressing transposable and repetitive sequences to maintain genomic integrity, unlike miRNAs. piRNAs are considered to arise from gene clusters rich in mobile repeating elements. Using transgenic model systems, mature piRNAs have been demonstrated to protect genomic integrity by targeting and inhibiting RTE (repetitive transposable elements). Manipulating retrotransposons in the male germline stopped gametogenesis and resulted in male infertility in mice. That piRNAs are required for maintain male germline genomic integrity. Endogenous siRNAs (endo-siRNAs) regulate transposable element silencing in the female genome of mammals (Luteijn and Ketting, 2013; Siomi et al., 2011).

5.3 SnoRNA

Small nucleolar RNA (snoRNA) was one of the first noncoding RNA classes identified but it was generally overlooked by cancer researchers owing to the misconception that its activities were limited to the nucleolus. Now full genomic sequence of SnoRNA is available and identified many of new snoRNAs. Previous study showed that snoRNA has diverse functionality. The current agreement is that several snoRNAs are dysregulate in cancer disease. The expression of snoRNA is different according to cancer type, cancer stage, metastases. The mTOR pathway is implicated to promote snoRNA expression in cancer cells. snoRNA involved in the production of ribosome. Some species may express snoRNA which is able to alter splicing process and function of mRNA, and they may have role in antitumor immune response.

In other cases, snoRNA may act as a therapeutic target of the immune proteins. Therefore, snoRNA have a potential as a drug targets in the context of immunotherapies. Many snoRNAs have recently been related to cancer And SNOR50A/B snoRNA loss in cancer. SNORD50A/B deficiency enhances K-Ras activation, resulting to ERK1/2 MAPK pathway hyperactivation.

tRNA-derived fragments (tRFs) have been shown to have biological activities which independent of complete full-length tRNA function. tRNA glycine GCC fragment may silence retroelement-driven transcripts. This decreased pro-oncogene transcript stability and metastasis. It is conceivable but not yet shown that rRNA or snoRNA fragments influence RNA-binding proteins (Röther and Meister, 2011; Siprashvili et al., 2016).

6. Long noncoding RNAs

They are a diverse group of regulatory noncoding RNAs in terms of structure, function, and location. Mammalian lncRNAs have little structural, functional, or molecular similarities. There are hundreds of predicted mammalian lncRNAs, but only a few are known to operate in vivo. On the other hand, other reviews aggregate functionally investigated lncRNAs based on shared mechanisms of action (Batista and Chang, 2013; Guttman and Rinn, 2012; Mercer and Mattick, 2013; Morris and Mattick, 2014; Wang and Chang, 2011). Subcellular lncRNA localization may help limit action pathways. Many nuclear lncRNAs regulate genes. These include promoter-specific transcription suppression or activation.

7. Regulatory functions of housekeeping ncRNAs

Recent research shows that some housekeeping small ncRNAs may be transformed into regulatory ncRNAs. While snoRNAs are often employed to regulate the chemistry of other small housekeeping RNAs, some have been shown to be processed into miRNA-like molecules (Ender et al., 2008).

Many snoRNAs have recently been related to cancer and SNOR50A/B snoRNA loss in cancer. SNORD50A/B deficiency enhances K-Ras activation, resulting to ERK1/2 MAPK pathway hyperactivation. tRNA-derived fragments (tRFs) have recently been shown to have biological activities independent of full-length tRNA function. tRNA-glycine-GCC fragments may silence retroelement-driven transcripts. This decreased pro-oncogene transcript stability and metastasis. It is conceivable but not yet shown that rRNA or snoRNA fragments influence RNA-binding proteins. (Röther and Meister, 2011; Siprashvili et al., 2016).

8. LncRNA modes of action in the nucleus

Subcellular lncRNA localization may help limit action pathways. Many nuclear lncRNAs regulate genes. These include promoter-specific transcription suppression or activation.

9. Characteristics and functions of long noncoding RNAs

They are a diverse group of regulatory ncRNAs in terms of structure, function, and location. Mammalian lncRNAs have little structural, functional, or molecular similarities. There are hundreds of predicted mammalian lncRNAs, but only a few are known to operate in vivo. On the other hand, other reviews aggregate functionally investigated lncRNAs based on shared mechanisms of action (Batista and Chang, 2013; Guttman and Rinn, 2012; Mercer and Mattick, 2013; Morris and Mattick, 2014; Wang and Chang, 2011).

10. ncRNAs in clinical practice

Multiple studies have clearly shown that ncRNAs play a major role in tumorigenesis and currently the world researchers are widely studying their role for therapeutic, prognostic and diagnostic uses (Le et al., 2021) and after them researchers are focusing on lncRNAs which are also keenly looked into within clinical setting (Vicentini et al., 2019).

Currently as per https://clinicaltrials.gov around 300+ studies involving miRNA are been conducted out of which 100+ studies are interventional in nature. Phase I clinical trial of NCT02369198 are focused on introduction of TargomiRs as second and third line of therapy for patients suffering with recurrent malignant pleural mesothelioma and NSCLC (Reid et al., 2013). Close to 13 studies are focusing on lncRNAs, with 11 studies been observational and 3 been interventional (Grillone et al., 2020). The major shortcoming of the current studies is that all the studies are focused on checking the role of miRNAs and lncRNAs in terms of checking their expressions as biomarkers and missing out on evaluating their roles as RNA-based therapeutics (Grillone et al., 2020; Malik et al., 2021). This provides clear pointers that we need to focus on checking the role of ncRNAs as targeting method (ASOs, SMs, etc.) for multiple clinical applications. Multiple challenges such as what kind of delivery strategy can be deployed, the underlying stability of the treatment and we also need to make sure that there is no toxicity in the developed treatments. Further research efforts in the future are expected to overcome all the current challenges.

References

Bartel, D.P., 2009. MicroRNAs: target recognition and regulatory functions. Cell 136, 215–233. https://doi.org/10.1016/j.cell.2009.01.002.

Batista, P.J., Chang, H.Y., 2013. Long noncoding RNAs: cellular address codes in development and disease. Cell 152, 1298–1307. https://doi.org/10.1016/j.cell.2013.02.012.

Billy, E., Brondani, V., Zhang, H., Müller, U., Filipowicz, W., 2001. Specific interference with gene expression induced by long, double-stranded RNA in mouse embryonal teratocarcinoma cell lines. Proc. Natl. Acad. Sci. U. S. A. 98, 14428–14433. https://doi.org/10.1073/pnas.261562698.

Bond, A.M., VanGompel, M.J.W., Sametsky, E.A., Clark, M.F., Savage, J.C., Disterhoft, J.F., Kohtz, J.D., 2009. Balanced gene regulation by an embryonic brain ncRNA is critical for adult hippocampal GABA circuitry. Nat. Neurosci. 12, 1020–1027. https://doi.org/10.1038/nn.2371.

Cabili, M.N., Trapnell, C., Goff, L., Koziol, M., Tazon-Vega, B., Regev, A., Rinn, J.L., 2011. Integrative annotation of human large intergenic noncoding RNAs reveals global properties and specific subclasses. Genes Dev. 25, 1915–1927. https://doi.org/10.1101/gad.17446611.

Calin, G.A., Sevignani, C., Dumitru, C.D., Hyslop, T., Noch, E., Yendamuri, S., Shimizu, M., Rattan, S., Bullrich, F., Negrini, M., Croce, C.M., 2004. Human microRNA genes are frequently located at fragile sites and genomic regions involved in cancers. Proc. Natl. Acad. Sci. U. S. A. 101 (9), 2999–3004.

Carthew, R.W., Sontheimer, E.J., 2009. Origins and mechanisms of miRNAs and siRNAs. Cell 136, 642–655. https://doi.org/10.1016/j.cell.2009.01.035.

Charbe, N.B., et al., 2020. Small interfering RNA for cancer treatment: overcoming hurdles in delivery. Acta Pharm. Sin. B 10, 2075–2109. https://doi.org/10.1016/j.apsb.2020.10.005.

Czech, B., Hannon, G.J., 2011. Small RNA sorting: matchmaking for argonautes. Nat. Rev. Genet. 12, 19–31. https://doi.org/10.1038/nrg2916.

Czech, B., Hannon, G.J., 2016. One loop to rule them all: the ping-pong cycle and piRNA-guided silencing. Trends Biochem. Sci. 41, 324–337. https://doi.org/10.1016/j.tibs.2015.12.008.

Dana, H., Chalbatani, G.M., Mahmoodzadeh, H., Karimloo, R., Rezaian, O., Moradzadeh, A., et al., 2017. Molecular mechanisms and biological functions of siRNA. Int. J. Biomed. Sci. 13, 48–57.

Djebali, S., Davis, C.A., Merkel, A., Dobin, A., Lassmann, T., Mortazavi, A., et al., 2012. Landscape of transcription in human cells. Nature 489, 101–108. https://doi.org/10.1038/nature11233.

Dueck, A., Meister, G., 2014. Assembly and function of small RNA—argonaute protein complexes. Biol. Chem. 395, 611–629. https://doi.org/10.1515/hsz-2014-0116.

Ender, C., Krek, A., Friedländer, M.R., Beitzinger, M., Weinmann, L., Chen, W., et al., 2008. A human snoRNA with microRNA-like functions. Mol. Cell 32, 519–528. https://doi.org/10.1016/j.molcel.2008.10.017.

Farazi, T.A., Juranek, S.A., Tuschl, T., 2008. The growing catalog of small RNAs and their association with distinct Argonaute/Piwi family members. Development 135, 1201–1214. https://doi.org/10.1242/dev.005629.

García-Sastre, A., 2011. Induction and evasion of type I interferon responses by influenza viruses. Virus Res. 162, 12–18. https://doi.org/10.1016/j.virusres.2011.10.017.

Grillone, K., Riillo, C., Scionti, F., Rocca, R., Tradigo, G., Guzzi, P.H., Alcaro, S., Di Martino, M.T., Tagliaferri, P., Tassone, P., 2020. Non-coding RNAs in cancer: platforms and strategies for investigating the genomic "dark matter". J. Exp. Clin. Cancer Res. 39 (1), 117. https://doi.org/10.1186/s13046-020-01622-x.

Guttman, M., Rinn, J.L., 2012. Modular regulatory principles of large non-coding RNAs. Nature 482, 339–346. https://doi.org/10.1038/nature10887.

Hacisuleyman, E., Goff, L.A., Trapnell, C., Williams, A., Henao-Mejia, J., Sun, L., et al., 2014. Topological organization of multichromosomal regions by the long intergenic noncoding RNA firre. Nat. Struct. Mol. Biol. 21, 198–206. https://doi.org/10.1038/nsmb.2764.

Kaul, D., Malik, D., 2012. MIR196B (microRNA 196b). Atlas Genet. Cytogenet. Oncol. Haematol. 16 (5), 357–360.

Kaul, D., Malik, D., Wani, S., 2019. Cellular miR-2909 RNomics governs the genes that ensure immune checkpoint regulation. Mol. Cell. Biochem. 451 (1–2), 37–42.

Kaur, G., Bhadada, S.K., Santra, M., Pal, R., Sarma, P., Sachdeva, N., Dhiman, V., Dahiya, D., Saikia, U.N., Chakraborty, A., Sood, A., Prakash, M., Behera, A., Rao, S.D., 2022. Multilevel annotation of germline MEN1 variants of synonymous, nonsynonymous, and uncertain significance in Indian patients with sporadic primary hyperparathyroidism. J. Bone Miner. Res. 37 (10), 1860–1875. https://doi.org/10.1002/jbmr.4653.

Kaushik, H., Malik, D., Parsad, D., Kaul, D., 2019. Mitochondrial respiration is restricted by miR-2909 within human melanocytes. Pigment Cell Melanoma Res. 32 (4), 584–587.

Le, P., Romano, G., Nana-Sinkam, P., Acunzo, M., 2021. Non-coding RNAs in cancer diagnosis and therapy: focus on lung cancer. Cancers 13 (6), 1372. https://doi.org/10.3390/cancers13061372.

Lee, J.T., Bartolomei, M.S., 2013. X-inactivation, imprinting, and long noncoding RNAs in health and disease. Cell 152, 1308–1323. https://doi.org/10.1016/j.cell.2013.02.016.

Li, Y., Lu, J., Han, Y., Fan, X., Ding, S.-W., 2013. RNA interference functions as an antiviral immunity mechanism in mammals. Science 342. https://doi.org/10.1126/science.1241911.

Liu, Y., Dou, M., Song, X., Dong, Y., Liu, S., Liu, H., Tao, J., Li, W., Yin, X., Xu, W., 2019. The emerging role of the piRNA/piwi complex in cancer. Mol. Cancer 18, 123. https://doi.org/10.1186/s12943-019-1052-9.

Lujambio, A., et al., 2008. microRNA DNA methylation signature for human cancer metastasis. Proc. Natl. Acad. Sci. 105, 13556–13561.

Luteijn, M.J., Ketting, R.F., 2013. PIWI-interacting RNAs: from generation to transgenerational epigenetics. Nat. Rev. Genet. 14, 523–534. https://doi.org/10.1038/nrg3495.

Mahmoodi Chalbatani, G., Dana, H., Gharagouzloo, E., Grijalvo, S., Eritja, R., Logsdon, C.D., et al., 2019. Small interfering RNAs (siRNAs) in cancer therapy: a nano-based approach. Int. J. Nanomedicine 14, 3111–3128.

Maillard, P.V., Ciaudo, C., Marchais, A., Li, Y., Jay, F., Ding, S.W., Voinnet, O., 2013. Antiviral RNA interference in mammalian cells. Science 342. https://doi.org/10.1126/science.1241930.

Malik, D., Kaul, D., 2015. KLF4 genome: a double edged sword. J. Solid Tumors 5, 49–64.

Malik, D., Kaul, D., 2018. Human cellular mitochondrial remodelling is governed by miR-2909 RNomics. PLoS One 13 (9), e0203614.

Malik, D., Kaul, D., Chauhan, N., Marwaha, R.K., 2014. miR-2909-mediated regulation of KLF4: a novel molecular mechanism for differentiating between B-cell and T-cell pediatric acute lymphoblastic leukemias. Mol. Cancer 13 (1), 175.

Malik, D., Sharma, A., Raina, A., Kaul, D., 2015. Deregulated blood cellular miR-2909 RNomics observed in rhematoid arthritis patients. Arch. Med. 7 (1), 1.

Malik, D., Mahendiratta, S., Kaur, H., Medhi, B., 2021. Fututristic approach to cancer treatment. Gene 2021 (805), 145906. https://doi.org/10.1016/j.gene.2021.145906.

Matera, A.G., Terns, R.M., Terns, M.P., 2007. Non-coding RNAs: lessons from the small nuclear and small nucleolar RNAs. Nat. Rev. Mol. Cell Biol. 8, 209–220. https://doi.org/10.1038/nrm2124.

Mattick, J.S., 2001. Non-coding RNAs: the architects of eukaryotic complexity. EMBO Rep. 2, 986–991. https://doi.org/10.1093/embo-reports/kve230.

Mendell, J.T., Olson, E.N., 2012. MicroRNAs in stress signaling and human disease. Cell 148, 1172–1187. https://doi.org/10.1016/j.cell.2012.02.005.

Mercer, T.R., Mattick, J.S., 2013. Structure and function of long noncoding RNAs in epigenetic regulation. Nat. Struct. Mol. Biol. 20, 300–307. https://doi.org/10.1038/nsmb.2480.

Morris, K.V., Mattick, J.S., 2014. The rise of regulatory RNA. Nat. Rev. Genet. 15, 423–437. https://doi.org/10.1038/nrg3722.

Nayak, A., Tassetto, M., Kunitomi, M., Andino, R., 2013. RNA interference-mediated intrinsic antiviral immunity in invertebrates. Curr. Top. Microbiol. Immunol. 371, 183–200. https://doi.org/10.1007/978-3-642-37765-5_7.

Peng, Y., Croce, C., 2016. The role of MicroRNAs in human cancer. Signal Transduct. Target. Ther. 1, 15004. https://doi.org/10.1038/sigtrans.2015.4.

Ramamurthy, R., Hughes, M., Morris, V., Bolouri, H., Gerbing, R.B., Wang, Y.C., et al., 2016. miR-155 expression and correlation with clinical outcome in pediatric AML: a report from children's oncology group. Pediatr. Blood Cancer 63 (12), 2096–2103.

Reid, G., Pel, M.E., Kirschner, M.B., Cheng, Y.Y., Mugridge, N., Weiss, J., Williams, M., Wright, C., Edelman, J.J., Vallely, M.P., McCaughan, B.C., Klebe, S., Brahmbhatt, H., MacDiarmid, J.A., van Zandwijk, N., 2013. Restoring expression of miR-16: a novel approach to therapy for malignant pleural mesothelioma. Ann. Oncol. 24 (12), 3128–3135. https://doi.org/10.1093/annonc/mdt412 (Epub 2013 Oct 22).

Röther, S., Meister, G., 2011. Small RNAs derived from longer non-coding RNAs. Biochimie 93, 1905–1915. https://doi.org/10.1016/j.biochi.2011.07.032.

Sharma, S., Kelly, T.K., Jones, P.A., 2010. Epigenetics in cancer. Carcinogenesis 31 (1), 27–36. https://doi.org/10.1093/carcin/bgp220.

Sharma, S., Kaul, D., Arora, M., Malik, D., 2015. Oncogenic nature of a novel mutant AATF and its interactome existing within human cancer cells. Cell Biol. Int. 39 (3), 326–333.

Siomi, M.C., Sato, K., Pezic, D., Aravin, A.A., 2011. PIWI-interacting small RNAs: the vanguard of genome defence. Nat. Rev. Mol. Cell Biol. 12, 246–258. https://doi.org/10.1038/nrm3089.

Siprashvili, Z., Webster, D.E., Johnston, D., Shenoy, R.M., Ungewickell, A.J., Bhaduri, A., et al., 2016. The noncoding RNAs SNORD50A and SNORD50B bind K-Ras and are recurrently deleted in human cancer. Nat. Genet. 48, 53–58. https://doi.org/10.1038/ng.3452.

Szittya, G., Burgyán, J., 2013. RNA interference-mediated intrinsic antiviral immunity in plants. Curr. Top. Microbiol. Immunol. 371, 153–181. https://doi.org/10.1007/978-3-642-37765-5_6.

Tian, D., Sun, S., Lee, J.T., 2010. The long noncoding RNA, Jpx, is a molecular switch for X-chromosome inactivation. Cell 143, 390–403. https://doi.org/10.1016/j.cell.2010.09.049.

Vicentini, C., Galuppini, F., Corbo, V., Fassan, M., 2019. Current role of non-coding RNAs in the clinical setting. Non Coding RNA Res. 3 (4), 82–85.

Wahida, F., Shehzada, A., Khanb, T., Kima, Y.Y., 2010. MicroRNAs: synthesis, mechanism, function, and recent clinical trials. Biochim. Biophys. Acta Mol. Cell Res. 1803 (11), 1231–1243.

Wang, K.C., Chang, H.Y., 2011. Molecular mechanisms of long noncoding RNAs. Mol. Cell 43, 904–914. https://doi.org/10.1016/j.molcel.2011.08.018.

Yan, L.X., Huang, X.F., Shao, Q., Huang, M.Y., Deng, L., Wu, Q.L., et al., 2008. MicroRNA miR-21 overexpression in human breast cancer is associated with advanced clinical stage, lymph node metastasis and patient poor prognosis. RNA 14 (11), 2348–2360.

Further reading

Charbe, N.B., Amnerkar, N.D., Ramesh, B., Tambuwala, M.M., Bakshi, H.A., Aljabali, A.A.A., et al., 2014. Ancient endo-siRNA pathways reveal new tricks. Curr. Biol. 24, R703–R715. https://doi.org/10.1016/j.cub.2014.06.009.

Fire, A., Xu, S., Montgomery, M.K., Kostas, S.A., Driver, S.E., Mello, C.C., 1998. Potent and specific genetic interference by double-stranded RNA in Caenorhabditis elegans. Nature 391, 806–811. https://doi.org/10.1038/35888.

Siomi, H., Siomi, M.C., 2009. On the road to reading the RNA-interference code. Nature 457, 396–404. https://doi.org/10.1038/nature07754.

Treiber, T., Treiber, N., Meister, G., 2012. Regulation of microRNA biogenesis and function. Thromb. Haemost. 107, 605–610. https://doi.org/10.1160/TH11-12-0836.

CHAPTER ELEVEN

Viral miRNAs role as diagnostic, prognostic biomarkers for cancer and infectious diseases

Sneha Kumari[a], Abhishek Pandeya[a], Raj Kumar Khalko[a], Ulkarsha[a], R.C. Sobti[b], and Sunil Babu Gosipatala[a]
[a]Department of Biotechnology, Babasaheb Bhimrao Ambedkar University, Lucknow, India
[b]Department of Biotechnology, Panjab University, Chandigarh, India

1. Introduction

In the quest of diagnostic tests for infectious diseases and/or cancer, several molecules derived from the host or pathogen have been scrutinized as prospective biomarkers by quite a few research groups. Out of which, the differential expression of microRNA(miRNA) profiles has taken the central stage as prospective biomarkers due to its variation in different stages of cancer as well as in the infectious diseases and their progression with in the individual. Some of the cellular miRNA panels are used in the detection of viral diseases, for example in HIV infections (Biswas et al., 2019). Keeping this view, several studies attempted to identify viral miRNA(s) profiles as diagnostic/prognostic markers in viral-induced carcinogenesis and infections, in determining the endpoints in cancer therapy and infectious diseases; predict the clinical outcome of therapy; and to develop new drugs.

Since the discovery of v-miRNAs first time in Epstein-Barr virus (EBV) (Pfeffer et al., 2004), more than 250 v-miRNAs have been identified till date and their biological functions revealed the regulation of both cellular as well as viral gene expressions paving the conducive environment for viral latency and virulence (Plaisance-Bonstaff and Renne, 2011). As per the miRbase, release 22.1 (the miRNA repository) a total of 34 viruses reported to encode miRNAs, among them 9 human viruses are also present. The list of virus encoding miRNAs will expand in near future, because of the advent of different techniques which can recognize the small RNA sequences from whole genome even in very small concentrations. Recent studies also indicate the possibility of miRNAs in the SARS CoV-2 genome (small RNA like). The cellular as well as v-miRNAs are reported to be stable under unfavorable conditions which would typically degrade most RNAs, such as very low or high pH levels, extended storage, boiling, and up to 10 freeze-thaw cycles (Chen et al., 2008). These miRNA profiles are influenced by the pathogen and are

Biomarkers in Cancer Detection and Monitoring of Therapeutics
https://doi.org/10.1016/B978-0-323-95116-6.00001-3
199

secreted in the fluid through the infected cells (Mishra, 2014; Turchinovich et al., 2012). Further, the miRNAs are reported to be present in body fluids such as serum, blood, urine, sweat, microvescicles, exosomes, apoptotic bodies, lipoproteins, and large microparticles which increases their possibility as biomarkers, as well as their alterations in various conditions during disease progression could make them ideal biomarkers (Dieckmann et al., 2012; Mo et al., 2012; Russo et al., 2012; Sun et al., 2012; Zhao et al., 2013). The ultimate challenge is identifying the candidate miRNA profiles for the particular disease that can give distinct results with a large group of patients with every environmental and physiological condition.

The possibility of miRNAs as diagnostic markers first came by the studies of Calin et al., where the human miRNAs, i.e., hsa-miR-15 and hsa-miR-16 downregulations were speculated as a diagnostic marker in chronic lymphocytic leukemia (Calin et al., 2002). Lawrie et al. demonstrated that cellular miRNAs, miR-155, 210, 20 were upregulated in diffuse large B cell lymphoma compared to control samples, pointing out that the miRNAs could be good biomarker (Lawrie et al., 2008). Later on, multiple studies reported the impact of miRNAs in neoplastic transformation, progression and patient outcomes (Chan et al., 2011; Guttilla and White, 2009; Kefas et al., 2008; Schultz et al., 2008; Van Der Heide et al., 2004; Wurz et al., 2010). For example, the study of Michael et al. shows that the change in miRNA expressions during tumorigenesis and reduced accumulation of specific miRNAs in colorectal neoplasia (Michael et al., 2003), diabetes, Alzheimer's (Lugli et al., 2015; Michael et al., 2003), hendra virus infection (Stewart et al., 2013), HIV infection (Biswas et al., 2019), influenza (Scheller et al., 2019), and Ebola infection (Duy et al., 2016) could be a possible biomarker. All these studies support the view of v-miRNAs as a diagnostic marker (Calin and Croce, 2006; Vojtechova and Tachezy, 2018).

The human infecting viruses coevolved with their human hosts and advanced their miRNAs accordingly, the evolutionary conservation of these viral miRNAs (no viral miRNA exhibit sequence homology with other viral miRNAs) made them unique biomarkers in viral induced diseases (Skalsky and Cullen, 2010). The v-miRNAs are slowly adapting to regulate both innate and adaptive immunity, establishing latency and sometimes inducing carcinogenesis (Naqvi et al., 2018; Weng et al., 2018). These viral miRNAs are capable to enter even in the distant cells when exported through exosomal route, thus allowing the virus to manipulate host immunity (Naqvi et al., 2018). The viral miRNAs play a dual role; one way in tumor progression by enhancing the cell proliferation and metastasis, on the other, by downregulating cell differentiation, apoptosis and immune signaling, suggesting that the outcome of the viral miRNA mediated regulation should ultimately benefit the virus. The detailed diagram showing how the viral miRNAs are isolated and detected as possible biomarkers in various conditions are shown in Fig. 1.

In this chapter, we are discussing the prospects of v-miRNA profiles as a potential biomarker with reference to the cancer and infectious diseases caused due to various viral infections. The possibility of known human oncoviruses such as human papilloma virus

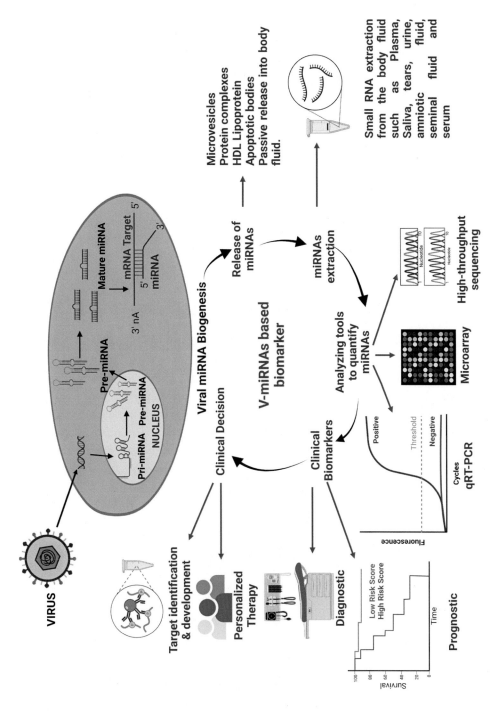

Fig. 1 Viral miRNAs used as a biomarker (Generated through Biorender).

(HPV), Epstein-Barr virus (EBV), human herpes virus-8 (KSHV), and hepatitis B virus (HBV) with their miRNAs as possible diagnostic markers. In addition, we added a note on human polyoma virus also known as John Cunningham virus (JCV), herpes simplex virus (HSV), and human cytomegaloviruses (HCMV) miRNAs role as a biomarker. The advent of techniques in identifying/quantifying the miRNAs in body fluids and the standardization protocols could make v-miRNAs as future diagnostic and prognostic markers with clinical significance.

2. Prospects of viral microRNA as potential biomarkers in cancer

Multiple studies have proven that viruses play an imperative role in causing cancers in humans, in fact 12% human cancers are attributed to viral infections (de Martel et al., 2020). Both DNA and RNA viruses cause cancer and encode miRNAs through canonical and noncanonical pathways (Drosha-independent pathway) (Tycowski et al., 2015). The existence of v-miRNAs came into light by the studies of Pfeffer et al. in the EBV (Pfeffer et al., 2004) and later on in many viruses. The miRNAs encoded by herpes virus group are most numerous and best studied. The association of v-miRNA in developing cancer has been reported in many studies, and human oncoviruses like EBV, KSHV, HCMV, HSV, HBV, and MCPyV also encode miRNAs (Moens, 2009; Navari et al., 2018; Qin et al., 2012; Wang et al., 2017; Yao et al., 2019). Though hepatitis C virus (HCV) and human T-lymphotropic virus (HTLV) cause cancer in humans, however, they have not been reported to encode miRNAs. The relative abundance of v-miRNA in the human oncoviruses has been summarized in Fig. 2.

As we know that v-miRNA expression profile changes during the progression of a disease, these changes can be helpful in identifying the initiation, progression, and/or different stages of the disease. Both host and viral miRNAs can be detected at the site of infection and in diseased tissue as well as in various body fluids such as serum, saliva,

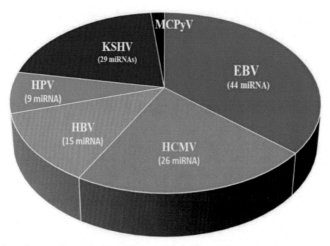

Fig. 2 Relative abundance of miRNAs in different oncoviruses as per miRbase.

plasma, cerebrospinal fluid, or urine. Circulating miRNAs and exosomal derived miRNAs are released in the body fluid through the infected cells by cytolysis, tissue injury, or within apoptotic bodies (Mi et al., 2013).

Majority of known v-miRNAs are encoded by herpesviruses, out of which most of their functions are associated with viral latency and subverting the immune response helping the survival of virus in the host (Piedade and Azevedo-Pereira, 2016; Stern-Ginossar et al., 2007). The members of herpesvirus group are majorly categorized into alpha, beta, and gamma subfamilies.

Herpes simplex virus (HSV) belonging to the subfamily of α-herpes virus is usually involved in forming oral and genital lesions and consists two members, HSV-1 and HSV-2. The miRNAs encoded by both HSV-1 and HSV-2 are connected with latency-mediated transcript and are expressed during the latent phase of infection (Boss et al., 2009). The higher expression of HSV-encoded miRNAs, i.e., hsv1-miR-H18, hsv2-miR-H9-5p in all sample types including biopsy, blood, and urine samples of prostate hyperplasia (BPH) makes them as a biomarker in HSV associated prostate malignancy (Yun et al., 2015).

Human cytomegalovirus (HCMV) or Human herpes virus-5 belongs to subfamily *β-herpes virus* and encodes 26 mature miRNAs, targeting various cellular pathways. Recent studies attribute the carcinogenic potential to this virus as the oncomodulatory properties were observed in glioblastoma multiform (Mitchell et al., 2008). The higher expressions of hcmv-miR-UL112-3p and miR-UL70-3p in the glioblastoma advocates the potentiality of these v-miRNA as biomarkers in HCMV induced glioblastoma (Liang et al., 2017b; Ulasov et al., 2017).

The *Epstein-Barr virus* (EBV) or HHV4 is the first identified oncovirus of humans as well as the first reported virus to contain miRNAs (Do Nyun et al., 2007; Pfeffer et al., 2004); belongs to subfamily of *γ-herpes viruses* and is etiologically connected to many carcinomas and malignancies including nasopharyngeal carcinoma (NPC), gastric cancer (GC), extranodal NK/T-cell lymphoma, Hodgkin's lymphoma, nasal type, and lymphoproliferative disorders of immunocompromised hosts. Over expression of EBV miRNAs such as ebv-miR-BART-3p,2-5p,5,6-5p,6-3p,7,8,9,14,17-5p,18-5p and 19-3p in NPC (Navari et al., 2018; Wong et al., 2012), and their correlations related to recurrence free survival (Cosmopoulos et al., 2009) makes them a potential biomarker in NPC. Further, the ebv-miR-BART11 overexpressed in NPC and GC, exhibits oncogenic potential by targeting the transcription factor, FOXP1, resulting in inhibition of TAM (tumor-associated macrophage differentiation) (Song et al., 2016). In addition, the oncogenic potential to ebv-miR BART-5 (Babu et al., 2011); and ebv-miR-BART-3 (Lei et al., 2013) was also reported. Several EBV-associated miRNAs have been detected in the serum of nasal natural killer/T-cell lymphoma; ebv-miR-BART2-5p, miR-BART-7-3p, miR-BART-13-3p, and miR-BART-1-5p were expressed in high concentration compared to the controls. Many studies reported the use of miR-BART-2-5p, miR-BART-7-3p, miR-BART-13-3p, and miR-BART-1 as a diagnostic marker for NPC (Jiang et al., 2015; Lu et al., 2020;

Shen et al., 2014). Another EBV encoded miRNA, ebv-miR-BHRF1-1, directly inhibits TSG p53 through its 3′UTR and enhances cell proliferation (Do Nyun et al., 2007).

Kaposi sarcoma herpes virus (KSHV), a *γ-subfamily herpesvirus*, also known as human herpesvirus 8 (HHV8), encodes 18–25 mature miRNAs processed from 12 different miRNAs and also reported to cause cancer. Chugh et al. noticed the elevated levels of detectable KSHV miRNAs such as miRs K12-4-3p, K12-4-5p, K12-5, K12-6-5p, K12-10a, and K12-11 in pleural fluids (Chugh et al., 2013), suggesting the probability of these miRNAs as potential biomarkers in KSHV positive tumors.

Similarly, the miRNAs encoded by human polyoma virus 2, commonly referred as *John Cunningham virus* (JCV), also have the potential as a biomarker in JCV infections. JCV encodes two miRNAs, viz., Jcv-miR-J1-5p and miR-J1-3p is used as a biomarker in colorectal cancer samples of JCV infection (Link et al., 2014).

Merkel cell polyoma virus (McPV) encoded miRNA, mcpv-miR-M1-5p is predicted to affect many cellular targets involved in transformation, and is expressed in 50% of MCPyV-positive MCC tumors (Lee et al., 2011).

Hepatitis B virus (HBV) is a small enveloped DNA virus belonging to the *Hepadnaviridae* family (Seeger and Mason, 2015) encoding miRNA HBV-miR-3 (Yang et al., 2017) which is highly expressed during HBV related hepatocellular carcinoma (HCC) and is secreted in serum of patients. The most common oncoviral miRNAs and their expression in the tissues/fluids which can be used as a marker for carcinogenesis are summarized below in Table 1.

Table 1 Expression profile of viral miRNAs in different cancers.

Virus	Viral miRNA	Expression	Cancer type
EBV	miR-BART2-5p miR-BART7-3p miR-BART13-3p miR-BART1-5p	Overexpressed	Nasal NK and T cell lymphoma
	miR-BART-19-5p miR-BART-20-3p&5p miR-BART-17-3p miR-BART-11-3p	Overexpressed	Nasopharyngeal carcinoma
JCV	miR-J1-5p	Under expressed	Colorectal cancer
HSV	hsv1-miR-H18 hsv2-miR-H9-5p	High expression	Prostate cancer
HCMV	miR-UL112-3p hcmv-miR-UL70-3p	High expression	Glioblastoma multiform
KSHV	miR-K12-4-3p&5p miR-K-12-5 miR-K-12-6-5p miR-K-12-10a	Expression	KSHV-associated lymphomagenesis

3. Antiapoptotic viral miRNAs

Numerous regulatory mechanisms that effect miRNA activity are found to be associated with carcinogenic processes. Apoptosis is one such process, which is dysregulated in many tumors culminating to the tumorigenesis. Many of the miRNAs originated from the viruses are antiapoptotic, effect the cell cycle and various cellular process thereby promoting the carcinogenesis. Hence, profiling of such antiapoptotic/cell cycle regulatory/immunoregulatory v-miRNA expressions can be useful as diagnostic, prognostic markers as well as, relevance to the cancer initiation, progression, and metastasis (Anfossi et al., 2018; Graveel et al., 2015; Peng and Croce, 2016).

Many of the EBV encoded miRNAs are reported to be antiapoptotic targeting several proapoptotic genes, thus favoring the tumorigenesis. The ebv-miR-BART-5/16, and ebv-miR-BART's in cluster 1 targets the pro-apoptotic genes PUMA, TOMM22, and BIM to downregulate apoptosis (Bellot et al., 2007; Choy et al., 2008). In EBV associated malignancies, the ebv-miR-BART1/2/3/4/7/8 and 22 expression seen in the samples and they reported to target effector caspases such as caspase 3 and regulate the apoptosis (Harold et al., 2016). These, studies show that if we can detect these v-mRNAs in the suspected tumor samples, we can get some information related the initiation and progression of the tumorigenesis in EBV-positive tumors. Similarly the KSHV/HHV-8 encoded miRNA, i.e., kshv-miR-K12-10 reported to be antiapoptotic (Abend et al., 2010) affecting cell cycle regulation and tumor suppressive mechanisms (Vojtechova and Tachezy, 2018). The HCMV miRNAs, i.e., hcmv-miR-UL148D (Wang et al., 2014), miR-UL70-3p (Babu et al., 2014; Pandeya et al., 2021), miR-UL36-5p (Guo et al., 2015) miR US5-1 and miR UL-112-3p (Hancock et al., 2021); miR UL36-3p, miR US25-1-3p, miR US-5-1, 5-2-3p, miR-US25-2-3p, miR-UL112, miR-UL22A-5p miR-UL33-5p (Kim et al., 2016) were also reported to be antiapoptotic. The regulation of apoptosis by HCMV miRNAs is dual in nature as few HCMV miRNAs also aggravates apoptosis (Shao et al., 2016, 2017). If we exploit these v-miRNAs in the patients and able to find their differential expressions; could lead to a diagnostic marker.

4. Viral miRNAs in tumor progression

Few v-miRNAs are reported to affect cell adhesion and thereby influences the metastasis process. The hcmv-miR-US25-1 acts as an oncogene targeting 20 different cellular transcripts involved in cell cycle control by binding to their 5′UTR. The most common targets are the collagenase stimulatory factor (CD147), cyclin E2 (CCNE2), the BRCA1/BRCA2-containing complex, the EP300 interacting inhibitor of differentiation 1 (EID1), subunit 3 (BRCC3), histone proteins (H3F3B), and microtubule-associated proteins, the RP/EB family member 2 (MAPRE2) (Grey et al., 2010). The KSHV-miR-K12-11 is reported to associate with KSHV-associated lymphomagenesis and splenic B-cell expansion by targeting the C/EBPβ thereby hampering the immune recognition of infected cells by suppressing the cytokines (Boss et al., 2009). The mcpv-miR-M1-5p decreases the migration of neutrophils at the site of infection by reducing the secretion of CXCL8 (a neutrophil chemoattractant and activator that modulates neutrophil migration) which may result in the host-cell immune evasion strategy of MCPV and leads to the development of carcinoma (Akhbari et al., 2018). The HPV miRNAs, i.e., HPV6-miR-H1, HPV16-miR-H1, HPV16-miR-H2, HPV16-miR-H3, HPV16-miR-H5, HPV16-miR-H6, HPV38-miR-H1, HPV45-miR-H1, and HPV68-miR-H1 are also reported to interfere with immune responses, cell cycle regulation, and cell adhesion/migration in the cervical lesion of humans (Qian et al., 2013). Particularly HPV16-mir-H1-1 and H2-1 inhibits the T-cell activation and immune development wherein, HPV16-mir-H1-1 targets CHD7, ITGAM, BCL11A, RAG1, and TCEA1 genes, while HPV16-mir-H2-1 targets SP3, PKNOX1, XRCC4, FOXP1, and JAK2 proteins. This regulation acts as an indirect pathway for tumorigenesis by HPV encoded miRNAs. HBV miRNA, miR-3 enhances IFN production, activates JAK/STAT signaling, affects macrophages polymerization/depolarization, and induces the production of interferons and IL-6 by repressing SOCS5/STAT1 pathway (Zhao et al., 2020). Moreover, HBV-miR-3 interacts directly with the protein phosphatase 1A (PPM1A) and phosphatase and TENs in homolog (PTEN), silencing these human genes, enhances cell invasion and proliferation in HCC development (Tang et al., 2020).

The altered expression of miRNAs (viral and human) in different carcinomas, targeting and regulating the cellular responses which could make v-miRNAs as possible diagnostic tool are briefed in Table 2.

Table 2 Cellular targets and biological roles of viral miRNAs.

Virus name	Viral miRNAs	Cellular targets	Biological roles	References
EBV	ebv-miR-BART-1,3,9,11,12	BIM	Antiapoptotic	Marquitz et al. (2011)
	ebv-miR-BART4-5p	BID		Kim et al. (2015) and Shinozaki-Ushiku et al. (2015)
	ebv-miR-BART-4	PUMA		Navari et al. (2018)
	ebv-miR-BART4-16	TOMM22		Bellot et al. (2007) and Choy et al. (2008)

Table 2 Cellular targets and biological roles of viral miRNAs—cont'd

Virus name	Viral miRNAs	Cellular targets	Biological roles	References
	ebv-miR-BART-1,2,3,4,7&8 ebv-miR-BART22	CASP3		Harold et al. (2016)
	ebv-miR-BART5	NR3C1, UBE2Z, GAB2	Tumorigenesis	Babu et al. (2011)
HHV-8/KSHV	kshv-miR-K1 kshv-miR-K12-1	P21	Cell cycle inhibition	Gottwein and Cullen (2010)
	kshv-miR-K12-1&3	CASP3	Antiapoptotic	Suffert et al. (2011)
	kshv-miR-K12-4-5P	CASP3		Catrina et al. (2014)
	kshv-miR-K12-10A/B	TWEAKR BCLAF1	Antiapoptotic	Abend et al. (2010)
	kshv-miR-K12-11 (identical to hsa-miR-155)	NFIB	Cell cycle control	
HCMV	hcmv-miR-UL148D	IEX1 ERN1	Antiapoptotic	Wang et al. (2014) Babu et al. (2014)
	hcmv-miR-UL112	FOXO3a		Hancock et al. (2021)
	hcmv-miR-UL70-3p	MOAP1		Babu et al. (2014) and Pandeya et al. (2021)
	hcmv-miR-UL36-5p	ANT3		Guo et al. (2015)
	hcmv-miR-US4	QARS	Aggravates apoptosis	Shao et al. (2016)
	hcmv-miR-US4-5p	PAK1		Shao et al. (2017)
HSV	hsv2-miR-H9-5p	SOCS2	Metastasis	Wang et al. (2017)
	hsv-miR-H1	TGF-β1 SMAD3	Antiapoptotic	Shojaei Jeshvaghani et al. (2021)
HBV	hbv-miR-3	PTEN	Cell cycle control	Tang et al. (2020)
HPV	hpv-16-miR-H1	BCL11A CHD7 ITGAM RAG1	Inhibit T-cell activation and immune development	Qian et al. (2013)
	hpv-miR-H2-1	SP3, JAK2 XRCC4 PKNOX1 FOXP1 CEA1		

5. Prospects of viral microRNAs as potential biomarkers in infectious diseases

The disease and illness caused by pathogens are known as infectious diseases; these pathogens can be any bacteria, viruses, fungi etc. All infectious diseases contribute to a considerable amount to total morbidity and around 15% of the total mortality as per the WHO data (*WHO Reveals Leading Causes of Death and Disability Worldwide: 2000–2019, n.d.*). Among all infectious diseases, malaria, HIV, and tuberculosis are the leading causes of death globally. Other than the mentioned ones, varied tropical diseases, such as dengue, Chagas disease, yellow fever, chikungunya, West Nile, and Japanese encephalitis have also contributed to global mortality. Recently, the world has witnessed the pandemic infection of SARS-CoV-2, which necessitates the need of early diagnosis to break the chain of infection. The landscape for clinical diagnostic is diverse and looks either for the pathogen or host's response to pathogen in the detection of infectious diseases.

The HCMV infections leads to the activation of proinflammatory signals which means higher cell proliferation that causes Atherosclerotic plaque formation (Zhu and Liu, 2020), and two HCMV miRNAs, i.e., hcmv-miR-UL112 and hcmv-miR-US25-1 expressions were correlated with atherosclerosis (Li et al., 2011). Even in cardiovascular diseases the hcmv-miR-US33-5p was 22-fold increased and can be used a marker in AAD (Dong et al., 2017). During the hepatitis B virus (HBV) infections, the HBVmiR-2 and HBV-miR-3 are overexpressed during liver related infections and can be used as diagnostic markers (Yang et al., 2017). Even in the Ebola virus (EBOV) infections, the EBOV encoded miRNAs are reported to present in the samples suggesting the potentiality of EBOV miRNAs as diagnostic biomarkers. The HIV-1 encoded miRNA, i.e., hiv 1-mir-H1 selectively suppresses apoptosis antagonizing transcription factor (AATF) protein expression which significantly down regulates (anti-apoptotic genes) genes coding for C-myc, Bcl-2, β-amyloid at translational level as well as genes coding for Par-4 and dicer at transcriptional level leading to cell death and spread of infection (Kaul et al., 2009). During the HSV infections the overexpression of HSV-miR-H1 is reported during active infection (Cui et al., 2006) while miR-H2-6 expressed during latency (Umbach et al., 2008). They are actively exported and packaged into exosomes to infect the normal cells (Kalamvoki et al., 2014), giving a clue that these miRNAs could be useful in identifying the active and latent infections of HSV.

6. Viral miRNA detection platforms

The studies with the intent of diagnostic potential of altered v-miRNA profiles have often reported divergent results. The detection methods (e.g., RNA seq, microarray chips, and RT-qPCR), normalization and analytical tools, sample preparation (e.g., fresh, frozen, or fixed), source and quality of sample (e.g., bulk tissue vs sorted cells, serum vs plasma), patient characteristics (e.g., sex, age, ethnicity, stage, treatment history), sample size, study design (e.g., single cohort, vs training and validation set), and statistical tools can affect the miRNA expression data. Thus, it is important to understand the influence of these variables in experimental design and scrutiny of miRNA analysis.

It is expected that v-miRNA profile varies from one cancer to the other and even if in the same cancer, one stage to the next stage which could make miRNAs as an effective diagnostic marker in viral pathophysiology. The advent of miRNA detection platforms made it possible to detect the minute quantity of miRNA (viral as well as host; circulating as well as exosomal miRNAs) in various samples. The hybridization-based detection method(s) such as northern blotting and RNA protection assays, require large amounts of total RNA ($>1\,\mu g$) for analysis with low throughput. The qRT-PCR ($>25\,pg$) (Chen et al., 2005) and next-generation RNA sequencing (RNA seq) are the recent additions with some advantages like deep expression analysis of well annotated miRNAs and their variants (e.g., isomers) as well as unknown miRNAs. Recent techniques like capture-probe microarray and bead platforms comes with high throughput miRNA analysis in bulk tissue samples (Liu et al., 2004; Nelson et al., 2004). The advances in spatial transcriptomics, single cell RNA seq, and microfluidic sorting will soon enable the detection at an unprecedented level of single cell and even single extracellular vesicle. We will discuss the different techniques used in the detection of miRNAs in general.

Northern blot is the standard and most widely used miRNA detection method, and is used for detecting both mature and precursor miRNAs. The isolated RNA is first digested with the restriction endonucleases, and then separated by agarose gel electrophoresis. These resolved RNA molecules will be denatured and transferred onto the nitrocellulose/nylon membrane followed by the hybridization through probes/markers labeled with the isotopes (Pall et al., 2007; Torres et al., 2011). The hybridized miRNA can be observed by autoradiography or any other technique based on the tagging molecule.

qRT-PCR is another technique used in the detection of miRNA in the samples, where the isolated total RNA from the samples is reverse transcribed into complementary DNA (cDNA) and then amplified by using specific primers/probes keeping the reference/housekeeping genes as controls. Then the miRNAs are detected through the sequence-specific probes containing a fluorophore and quencher that binds to the cDNA template, DNA polymerase cleaves the quencher releasing fluorophore during amplification, subsequent fluorescence is measured (Wong et al., 2015).

Next-generation sequencing (NGS) also involves reverse transcription and amplification, but it does not require primers/probes specific to miRNAs, and is of high through put in nature. This technique is used to quantify all the miRNAs present in the sample, even novel ones. Despite this, it is used for preliminary screening of miRNAs followed by qRT-PCR.

Microarray is the most rapid and high throughput method for detection of miRNAs (Calin and Croce, 2006; Li and Ruan, 2009; Wang et al., 2019), where the total RNA isolated from the cells infected with virus are reverse transcribed using the labeled probe. The fluorophores or biotin-labeled cDNAs are detected using solid-phase oligonucleotides having the same sequence as the target miRNAs. The labeled cDNA samples are added to each well of the microarray plate, followed by a series of procedure. The fluorescence intensity of each well is used to determine the expression level of the identified biomarker miRNA. Although this technique gives fast results, it suffers with high processing costs (Cissell et al., 2009), and too short or low copy number miRNA cannot be detected. This may pose a major challenge in analyzing the v-miRNAs with similar sequences.

Recently, **nanomaterials** are being applied in miRNA analysis/recognition in vivo, for example, gold nanoparticles (AuNPs) (Alhasan et al., 2012) magnetic nanoparticles (Hosseinzadeh et al., 2018), silver nanoclusters (AgNCs) (Pan et al., 2018), graphene oxidase nanoparticles (Wang et al., 2019), and quantum dots (QDs) (Foda et al., 2014) were used, because of their large surface area, tremendous electrical conductivity, and notable chemical stability. In addition, the flexibility of cell transfection, photostability, and lower immunogenicity made them considered to be in in vivo imaging. However, their innate cytotoxicity and self-clustering inside the cells are still issues for the steady application.

To improve the sensitivity of miRNA detection, as their lower concentrations in the samples, the nucleic acid amplification techniques were usually utilized. The simplicity, specificity, and high sensitivity of **rolling circle amplification (RCA)** method made it a popular technique in miRNA recognition based on nucleic acid amplification. The miRNA template hybridizes with padlock probe and ligates with T4 RNA ligase or SplintR enzyme, framing a round ssDNA, trailed likewise around the circle with an outer primer or itself miRNA as a primer (Ye et al., 2019). At last, the conjoined miRNA is displaced and a long chain nucleic acid cascade is produced which is detected by signal generating techniques, like colorimetry, fluorescence, electrochemistry, SERS, LAMP, and electrochemiluminescence. Strangely, the produced concatemers are so enormous that they can accumulate on surfaces be detected as a single molecule.

The key advantage of **DSN**-based amplification is that it hydrolyzes DNA either in DNA/RNA duplex or specific length double-stranded DNA (dsDNA), and does not cleave RNA or ssDNA (Qiu et al., 2015). This distinctive character of DSN makes it possible to yield only RNA during thermal amplification. This method can also be coupled with fluorescent, colorimetric, and electrochemical platforms. Le et al. (2018) developed a selectivity and sensitivity (one base mismatch discrimination) miRNA-21 detection method with DSN-based amplification.

LAMP is an isothermal reaction assay based on exponential amplification of RNAs and DNAs targeting 6–8 different template sequences by 4–6 different primers at the same time, due to which selectivity is improved. Usually, the presence of miRNAs trigger the reaction for hybridizing with probe followed by extension with DNA polymerase and nucleic acid synthesis by strand displacement method. One of the drawbacks of this technique is synergistic hybridization of multiple primers at the template strand as the template region contains 4–6 stem-loop formation sequences, due to which its sensitivity decreases.

SDA is another isothermal reaction assay based on polymerase extension and strand displacement of template miRNAs. The major difference between LAMP and SDA is that it is a linear amplification technique while the other one is exponential.

In the **enzyme-free amplification** reaction, miRNA usually acts as a trigger to initiate the strand displacement process by opening up one or more DNA hairpins driven by the negative free energy change of base pair formation. Hybridization chain reaction (HCR) (Nie et al., 2019; Zhou et al., 2019), catalytic hairpin assembly (CHA) (Bao et al., 2019), and entropy-driven catalysis (Liang et al., 2017a; Zhang et al., 2018) are some of the developed enzyme free assays designed for miRNA detection and imaging.

All of the above-mentioned techniques are summarized in the form of a chart in Fig. 3.

Apart from these detection technologies, a few more methods can identify v-miRNAs in patient samples were developed with the intent to develop portable, safe, fast, specific, sensitive, low-cost, user-friendly detection kits. This may help the lab-based methods for point of care (PoC) benefit in identifying and controlling infectious illnesses. Using lateral flow devices (strip test), significant advances have been made, which meet all emerging detection and diagnostic requirements. In 2018, Zheng et al. developed a lateral flow assay for the simultaneous detection of two or more miRNAs (Deng et al.,

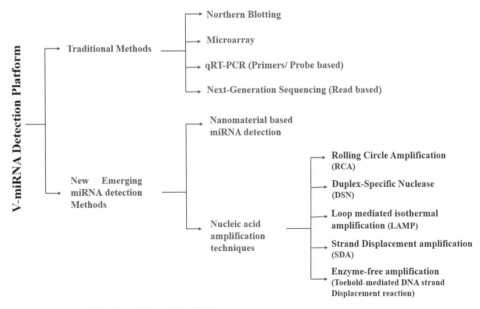

Fig. 3 Detection techniques for viral miRNAs.

2017b; Gao et al., 2014; Hou et al., 2012). In addition to the electrochemical biosensors, a fourth detection kit was developed to identify miRNAs using the four-way junction formation. Another μpad was developed to spot microRNAs (miRNAs) (Deng et al., 2017a). A miRNA extraction device and a miRNA detection device were developed by this group using paper-based technologies. With the help of the magnetic sheet, this may be interfaced quite effortlessly. To accomplish this, only a heating block was required for isothermal amplification. This showed a low odds ratio (LOD) of the miRNA copies from the tumor cell lysate and was also used in the diagnosis of infectious diseases. The colorimetric analysis provided an additional platform for the identification of the miRNAs. It was established in 2017 by Feng et al., who were motivated by the pH strips in their study (Feng et al., 2017). During the process of developing the analysis kit, they made use of three separate pH indicators, each of which could be seen by the naked eye. Either this can be used for the quantitative analysis. It will need to be analyzed using a UV–vis spectrophotometer, or it may be used for the qualitative analysis.

7. Advantages of viral miRNAs as biomarkers

The early detection of cancer as well as any other infectious disease is often momentous to improve the patient prognosis as well as limit the spread of disease in case of cancer, and essential in controlling the emerging/re-emerging infectious diseases. Early detection benefits in the control of the disease, aids in quarantine, surveillance and biocontainment. In Fig. 4, we have outlined the advantages of miRNAs as a biomarker. The reported v-miRNA profiles vary within an individual at different stages of disease, making them ideal biomarker for defining each stage of the disease.

In addition, the clinical manifestations for most of the viral diseases often appears nonspecifically such as headache, fever, lethargy, body pains, etc., and provide least information about the causative organism, which can lead to misdiagnosis. Using v-miRNA biomarkers, specific and exact diagnosis of causal agent plays an effective role in the treatment of concerning disease.

The clinical significance of miRNA encoded by viruses has been demonstrated in many cancers including gastric cancer, nasopharyngeal carcinoma, prostate cancer, head, and neck cancer as well as in noncancerous diseases including acute aortic dissection, and liver disease, etc. The major advantage of using the virally encoded miRNA as a biomarker is their specificity in viral oncogenesis or pathogenesis.

It is pertinent that sometimes, the patient's genotype effects response to the therapeutic intervention, which actually impacts the clinician's ability in providing the accurate prognosis. The altering v-miRNAs profiles in the disease prognosis will certainly

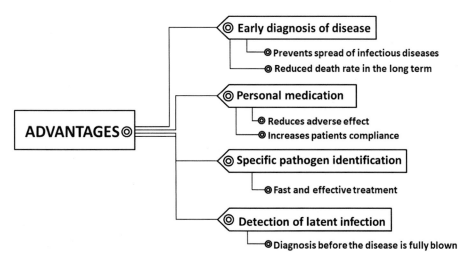

Fig. 4 Advantages of V-miRNA as biomarkers.

help in providing with personalized medicines to the individuals with different genotypes.

8. Future challenges

The use of v-miRNAs as diagnostic markers is quite exciting and significant progress has been made in the evaluation of circulating miRNAs as a potential biomarker in various pathological conditions. Though the field of miRNAs as biomarkers moves beyond the simple differential expression analysis to apprehend the spectrum of alterations in expression of these molecules, utilizing a statistical cut off to justify the selection, which suffers sometimes in identifying the diagnostically relevant miRNAs.

Despite of the progress in this area, none of the v-miRNA panels has entered in clinical practice so far, this may be mostly due to the lack of protocol standardizations, small sample size, and discrepancies in the measurement techniques. Further, several challenges involved in the use of v-miRNAs as a biomarker for in vitro diagnosis. All the mentioned markers need to be validated for consistent result over varying conditions and stimulations. A cohort study is necessary to support the preliminary outcomes from case-control literature that have proposed the role of miRNAs as novel biomarkers for cancer and other infectious diseases.

Future studies are required to establish v-miRNA expression pattern in identifying and characterizing the diseases. The development of v-miRNAs as diagnostic and prognostic biomarkers will entail the diligent eradication of several hurdles.

Acknowledgments

The authors would like to acknowledge Babasaheb Bhimrao Ambedkar University, Lucknow, India for providing the necessary infrastructure facilities.

Consent for publication

The authors give consent for publication.

Conflict of interest

The author declares that there is no conflict of interest.

References

Abend, J.R., Uldrick, T., Ziegelbauer, J.M., 2010. Regulation of tumor necrosis factor-like weak inducer of apoptosis receptor protein (TWEAKR) expression by Kaposi's sarcoma-associated herpesvirus micro-RNA prevents TWEAK-induced apoptosis and inflammatory cytokine expression. J. Virol. 84 (23), 12139–12151. https://doi.org/10.1128/JVI.00884-10.

Akhbari, P., Tobin, D., Poterlowicz, K., Roberts, W., Boyne, J.R., 2018. MCV-miR-M1 targets the host-cell immune response resulting in the attenuation of neutrophil chemotaxis. J. Invest. Dermatol. 138 (11), 2343–2354. https://doi.org/10.1016/j.jid.2018.03.1527.

Alhasan, A.H., Kim, D.Y., Daniel, W.L., Watson, E., Meeks, J.J., Thaxton, C.S., Mirkin, C.A., 2012. Scanometric microRNA array profiling of prostate cancer markers using spherical nucleic acid-gold nanoparticle conjugates. Anal. Chem. 84 (9), 4153–4160. https://doi.org/10.1021/ac3004055.

Anfossi, S., Babayan, A., Pantel, K., Calin, G.A., 2018. Clinical utility of circulating non-coding RNAs—an update. Nat. Rev. Clin. Oncol. 15 (9), 541–563. https://doi.org/10.1038/s41571-018-0035-x.

Babu, S.G., Ponia, S.S., Kumar, D., Saxena, S., 2011. Cellular oncomiR orthologue in EBV oncogenesis. Comput. Biol. Med. 41 (10), 891–898. https://doi.org/10.1016/j.compbiomed.2011.07.007.

Babu, S.G., Pandeya, A., Verma, N., Shukla, N., Kumar, R.V., Saxena, S., 2014. Role of HCMV miR-UL70-3p and miR-UL148D in overcoming the cellular apoptosis. Mol. Cell. Biochem. 393 (1–2), 89–98. https://doi.org/10.1007/s11010-014-2049-8.

Bao, J., Hou, C., Zhao, Y., Geng, X., Samalo, M., Yang, H., Bian, M., Huo, D., 2019. An enzyme-free sensitive electrochemical microRNA-16 biosensor by applying a multiple signal amplification strategy based on Au/PPy-rGO nanocomposite as a substrate. Talanta 196, 329–336. https://doi.org/10.1016/j.talanta.2018.12.082.

Bellot, G., Cartron, P.-F., Er, E., Oliver, L., Juin, P., Armstrong, L.C., Bornstein, P., Mihara, K., Manon, S., Vallette, F.M., 2007. TOM22, a core component of the mitochondria outer membrane protein translocation pore, is a mitochondrial receptor for the proapoptotic protein Bax. Cell Death Differ. 14 (4), 785–794. https://doi.org/10.1038/sj.cdd.4402055.

Biswas, S., Haleyurgirisetty, M., Lee, S., Hewlett, I., Devadas, K., 2019. Development and validation of plasma miRNA biomarker signature panel for the detection of early HIV-1 infection. EBioMedicine 43, 307–316. https://doi.org/10.1016/j.ebiom.2019.04.023.

Boss, I.W., Plaisance, K.B., Renne, R., 2009. Role of virus-encoded microRNAs in herpesvirus biology. Trends Microbiol. 17 (12), 544–553. https://doi.org/10.1016/j.tim.2009.09.002.

Calin, G.A., Croce, C.M., 2006. MicroRNA signatures in human cancers. Nat. Rev. Cancer 6 (11), 857–866. https://doi.org/10.1038/nrc1997.

Calin, G.A., Dumitru, C.D., Shimizu, M., Bichi, R., Zupo, S., Noch, E., Aldler, H., Rattan, S., Keating, M., Rai, K., Rassenti, L., Kipps, T., Negrini, M., Bullrich, F., Croce, C.M., 2002. Frequent deletions and down-regulation of micro-RNA genes miR15 and miR16 at 13q14 in chronic lymphocytic leukemia. Proc. Natl. Acad. Sci. U. S. A. 99 (24), 15524–15529. https://doi.org/10.1073/pnas.242606799.

Catrina, A.M., Borze, I., Guled, M., Costache, M., Leen, G., Sajin, M., Ionica, E., Chitu, A., Knuutila, S., 2014. MicroRNA expression profiles in Kaposi's sarcoma. Pathol. Oncol. Res. 20 (1), 153–159. https://doi.org/10.1007/s12253-013-9678-1.

Chan, E., Patel, R., Nallur, S., Ratner, E., Bacchiocchi, A., Hoyt, K., Szpakowski, S., Godshalk, S., Ariyan, S., Sznol, M., Halaban, R., Krauthammer, M., Tuck, D., Slack, F.J., Weidhaas, J.B., 2011. MicroRNA signatures differentiate melanoma subtypes. Cell Cycle (Georgetown, Tex.) 10 (11), 1845–1852. https://doi.org/10.4161/cc.10.11.15777.

Chen, C., Ridzon, D.A., Broomer, A.J., Zhou, Z., Lee, D.H., Nguyen, J.T., Barbisin, M., Xu, N.L., Mahuvakar, V.R., Andersen, M.R., Lao, K.Q., Livak, K.J., Guegler, K.J., 2005. Real-time quantification of microRNAs by stem-loop RT-PCR. Nucleic Acids Res. 33 (20), e179. https://doi.org/10.1093/nar/gni178.

Chen, X., Ba, Y., Ma, L., Cai, X., Yin, Y., Wang, K., Guo, J., Zhang, Y., Chen, J., Guo, X., Li, Q., Li, X., Wang, W., Zhang, Y., Wang, J., Jiang, X., Xiang, Y., Xu, C., Zheng, P., Zhang, C.-Y., 2008. Characterization of microRNAs in serum: a novel class of biomarkers for diagnosis of cancer and other diseases. Cell Res. 18 (10), 997–1006. https://doi.org/10.1038/cr.2008.282.

Choy, E.Y.-W., Siu, K.-L., Kok, K.-H., Lung, R.W.-M., Tsang, C.M., To, K.-F., Kwong, D.L.-W., Tsao, S.W., Jin, D.-Y., 2008. An Epstein-Barr virus-encoded microRNA targets PUMA to promote host cell survival. J. Exp. Med. 205 (11), 2551–2560. https://doi.org/10.1084/jem.20072581.

Chugh, P.E., Sin, S.-H., Ozgur, S., Henry, D.H., Menezes, P., Griffith, J., Eron, J.J., Damania, B., Dittmer, D.P., 2013. Systemically circulating viral and tumor-derived microRNAs in KSHV-associated malignancies. PLoS Pathog. 9 (7), e1003484. https://doi.org/10.1371/journal.ppat.1003484.

Cissell, K.A., Rahimi, Y., Shrestha, S., Deo, S.K., 2009. Reassembly of a bioluminescent protein Renilla luciferase directed through DNA hybridization. Bioconjug. Chem. 20 (1), 15–19. https://doi.org/10.1021/bc8003099.

Cosmopoulos, K., Pegtel, M., Hawkins, J., Moffett, H., Novina, C., Middeldorp, J., Thorley-Lawson, D.A., 2009. Comprehensive profiling of Epstein-Barr virus microRNAs in nasopharyngeal carcinoma. J. Virol. 83 (5), 2357–2367. https://doi.org/10.1128/JVI.02104-08.

Cui, C., Griffiths, A., Li, G., Silva, L.M., Kramer, M.F., Gaasterland, T., Wang, X.-J., Coen, D.M., 2006. Prediction and identification of herpes simplex virus 1-encoded microRNAs. J. Virol. 80 (11), 5499–5508. https://doi.org/10.1128/JVI.00200-06.

de Martel, C., Georges, D., Bray, F., Ferlay, J., Clifford, G.M., 2020. Global burden of cancer attributable to infections in 2018: a worldwide incidence analysis. Lancet Glob. Health 8 (2), e180–e190. https://doi.org/10.1016/S2214-109X(19)30488-7.

Deng, H., Liu, Q., Wang, X., Huang, R., Liu, H., Lin, Q., Zhou, X., Xing, D., 2017a. Quantum dots-labeled strip biosensor for rapid and sensitive detection of microRNA based on target-recycled non-enzymatic amplification strategy. Biosens. Bioelectron. 87, 931–940. https://doi.org/10.1016/j.bios.2016.09.043.

Deng, H., Zhou, X., Liu, Q., Li, B., Liu, H., Huang, R., Xing, D., 2017b. Paperfluidic chip device for small RNA extraction, amplification, and multiplexed analysis. ACS Appl. Mater. Interfaces 9 (47), 41151–41158. https://doi.org/10.1021/acsami.7b12637.

Dieckmann, K.-P., Spiekermann, M., Balks, T., Flor, I., Löning, T., Bullerdiek, J., Belge, G., 2012. MicroRNAs miR-371-3 in serum as diagnostic tools in the management of testicular germ cell tumours. Br. J. Cancer 107 (10), 1754–1760. https://doi.org/10.1038/bjc.2012.469.

Do Nyun, K., Hiun-Suk, C., Taek, O.S., Jin-Hyoung, K., Hyun, P.C., Sang, P.W., Kenzo, T., Myun, L.J., Won-Keun, L., Kyeong, L.S., 2007. Expression of viral MicroRNAs in Epstein-Barr virus-associated gastric carcinoma. J. Virol. 81 (2), 1033–1036. https://doi.org/10.1128/JVI.02271-06.

Dong, J., Bao, J., Feng, R., Zhao, Z., Lu, Q., Wang, G., Li, H., Su, D., Zhou, J., Jing, Q., Jing, Z., 2017. Circulating microRNAs: a novel potential biomarker for diagnosing acute aortic dissection. Sci. Rep. 7 (1), 12784. https://doi.org/10.1038/s41598-017-13104-w.

Duy, J., Koehler, J.W., Honko, A.N., Schoepp, R.J., Wauquier, N., Gonzalez, J.-P., Pitt, M.L., Mucker, E.M., Johnson, J.C., O'Hearn, A., Bangura, J., Coomber, M., Minogue, T.D., 2016. Circulating microRNA profiles of Ebola virus infection. Sci. Rep. 6, 24496. https://doi.org/10.1038/srep24496.

Feng, C., Mao, X., Shi, H., Bo, B., Chen, X., Chen, T., Zhu, X., Li, G., 2017. Detection of microRNA: a point-of-care testing method based on a pH-responsive and highly efficient isothermal amplification. Anal. Chem. 89 (12), 6631–6636. https://doi.org/10.1021/acs.analchem.7b00850.

Foda, M.F., Huang, L., Shao, F., Han, H.-Y., 2014. Biocompatible and highly luminescent near-infrared $CuInS_2/ZnS$ quantum dots embedded silica beads for cancer cell imaging. ACS Appl. Mater. Interfaces 6 (3), 2011–2017. https://doi.org/10.1021/am4050772.

Gao, X., Xu, H., Baloda, M., Gurung, A.S., Xu, L.-P., Wang, T., Zhang, X., Liu, G., 2014. Visual detection of microRNA with lateral flow nucleic acid biosensor. Biosens. Bioelectron. 54, 578–584. https://doi.org/10.1016/j.bios.2013.10.055.

Gottwein, E., Cullen, B.R., 2010. A human herpesvirus microRNA inhibits p21 expression and attenuates p21-mediated cell cycle arrest. J. Virol. 84 (10), 5229–5237. https://doi.org/10.1128/JVI.00202-10.

Graveel, C.R., Calderone, H.M., Westerhuis, J.J., Winn, M.E., Sempere, L.F., 2015. Critical analysis of the potential for microRNA biomarkers in breast cancer management. Breast Cancer (Dove Medical Press) 7, 59–79. https://doi.org/10.2147/BCTT.S43799.

Grey, F., Tirabassi, R., Meyers, H., Wu, G., McWeeney, S., Hook, L., Nelson, J.A., 2010. A viral micro-RNA down-regulates multiple cell cycle genes through mRNA 5'UTRs. PLoS Pathog. 6 (6). https://doi.org/10.1371/JOURNAL.PPAT.1000967.

Guo, X., Huang, Y., Qi, Y., Liu, Z., Ma, Y., Shao, Y., Jiang, S., Sun, Z., Ruan, Q., 2015. Human cytomegalovirus miR-UL36-5p inhibits apoptosis via downregulation of adenine nucleotide translocator 3 in cultured cells. Arch. Virol. 160 (10), 2483–2490. https://doi.org/10.1007/s00705-015-2498-8.

Guttilla, I.K., White, B.A., 2009. Coordinate regulation of FOXO1 by miR-27a, miR-96, and miR-182 in breast cancer cells. J. Biol. Chem. 284 (35), 23204–23216. https://doi.org/10.1074/jbc.M109.031427.

Hancock, M.H., Crawford, L.B., Perez, W., Struthers, H.M., Mitchell, J., Caposio, P., 2021. Human cytomegalovirus UL7, miR-US5-1, and miR-UL112-3p inactivation of FOXO3a protects CD34 + hematopoietic progenitor cells from apoptosis. mSphere 6 (1). https://doi.org/10.1128/msphere.00986-20.

Harold, C., Cox, D., Riley, K.J., 2016. Epstein-Barr viral microRNAs target caspase 3. Virol. J. 13 (1), 1–8. https://doi.org/10.1186/s12985-016-0602-7.

Hosseinzadeh, S., Hosseinzadeh, H., Pashaei, S., Khodaparast, Z., 2018. Synthesis of magnetic functionalized MWCNT nanocomposite through surface RAFT co-polymerization of acrylic acid and N-isopropyl acrylamide for removal of cationic dyes from aqueous solutions. Ecotoxicol. Environ. Saf. 161, 34–44. https://doi.org/10.1016/j.ecoenv.2018.05.063.

Hou, S.-Y., Hsiao, Y.-L., Lin, M.-S., Yen, C.-C., Chang, C.-S., 2012. MicroRNA detection using lateral flow nucleic acid strips with gold nanoparticles. Talanta 99, 375–379. https://doi.org/10.1016/j.talanta.2012.05.067.

Jiang, S., Qi, Y., He, R., Huang, Y., Liu, Z., Ma, Y., Guo, X., Shao, Y., Sun, Z., Ruan, Q., 2015. Human cytomegalovirus microRNA miR-US25-1-5p inhibits viral replication by targeting multiple cellular genes during infection. Gene 570 (1), 108–114. https://doi.org/10.1016/j.gene.2015.06.009.

Kalamvoki, M., Du, T., Roizman, B., 2014. Cells infected with herpes simplex virus 1 export to uninfected cells exosomes containing STING, viral mRNAs, and microRNAs. Proc. Natl. Acad. Sci. U. S. A. 111 (46), E4991–E4996. https://doi.org/10.1073/pnas.1419338111.

Kaul, D., Ahlawat, A., Gupta, S.D., 2009. HIV-1 genome-encoded hiv1-mir-H1 impairs cellular responses to infection. Mol. Cell. Biochem. 323 (1–2), 143–148. https://doi.org/10.1007/s11010-008-9973-4.

Kefas, B., Godlewski, J., Comeau, L., Li, Y., Abounader, R., Hawkinson, M., Lee, J., Fine, H., Chiocca, E.A., Lawler, S., Purow, B., 2008. microRNA-7 inhibits the epidermal growth factor receptor and the Akt pathway and is down-regulated in glioblastoma. Cancer Res. 68 (10), 3566–3572. https://doi.org/10.1158/0008-5472.CAN-07-6639.

Kim, S., Seo, D., Kim, D., Hong, Y., Chang, H., Baek, D., Kim, V.N., Lee, S., Ahn, K., 2015. Temporal landscape of microRNA-mediated host-virus crosstalk during productive human cytomegalovirus infection. Cell Host Microbe 17 (6), 838–851.

Kim, E.S., Choi, Y.E., Hwang, S.J., Han, Y.-H., Park, M.-J., Bae, I.H., 2016. IL-4, a direct target of miR-340/429, is involved in radiation-induced aggressive tumor behavior in human carcinoma cells. Oncotarget 7 (52), 86836–86856. https://doi.org/10.18632/oncotarget.13561.

Lawrie, C.H., Gal, S., Dunlop, H.M., Pushkaran, B., Liggins, A.P., Pulford, K., Banham, A.H., Pezzella, F., Boultwood, J., Wainscoat, J.S., Hatton, C.S.R., Harris, A.L., 2008. Detection of elevated levels of tumour-associated microRNAs in serum of patients with diffuse large B-cell lymphoma. Br. J. Haematol. 141 (5), 672–675. https://doi.org/10.1111/j.1365-2141.2008.07077.x.

Le, B.H., Nguyen, T.-V.T., Joo, H.N., Seo, Y.J., 2018. Large-Stokes-shift-based folded DNA probing systems targeting DNA and miRNA 21 with signal amplification. Bioorg. Med. Chem. 26 (17), 4881–4885. https://doi.org/10.1016/j.bmc.2018.08.027.

Lee, S., Paulson, K.G., Murchison, E.P., Afanasiev, O.K., Alkan, C., Leonard, J.H., Byrd, D.R., Hannon, G.J., Nghiem, P., 2011. Identification and validation of a novel mature microRNA encoded by the Merkel cell polyomavirus in human Merkel cell carcinomas. J. Clin. Virol. 52 (3), 272–275. https://doi.org/10.1016/j.jcv.2011.08.012.

Lei, T., Yuen, K.-S., Xu, R., Tsao, S.W., Chen, H., Li, M., Kok, K.-H., Jin, D.-Y., 2013. Targeting of DICE1 tumor suppressor by Epstein-Barr virus-encoded miR-BART3* microRNA in nasopharyngeal carcinoma. Int. J. Cancer 133 (1), 79–87. https://doi.org/10.1002/ijc.28007.

Li, W., Ruan, K., 2009. MicroRNA detection by microarray. Anal. Bioanal. Chem. 394 (4), 1117–1124. https://doi.org/10.1007/s00216-008-2570-2.

Li, S., Zhu, J., Zhang, W., Chen, Y., Zhang, K., Popescu, L.M., Ma, X., Lau, W.B., Rong, R., Yu, X., Wang, B., Li, Y., Xiao, C., Zhang, M., Wang, S., Yu, L., Chen, A.F., Yang, X., Cai, J., 2011. Signature microRNA expression profile of essential hypertension and its novel link to human cytomegalovirus infection. Circulation 124 (2), 175–184. https://doi.org/10.1161/CIRCULATIONAHA.110.012237.

Liang, C.-P., Ma, P.-Q., Liu, H., Guo, X., Yin, B.-C., Ye, B.-C., 2017a. Rational engineering of a dynamic, entropy-driven DNA nanomachine for intracellular MicroRNA imaging. Angew. Chem. Int. Ed. 56 (31), 9077–9081. https://doi.org/10.1002/anie.201704147.

Liang, Q., Wang, K., Wang, B., Cai, Q., 2017b. HCMV-encoded MIR-UL112-3p promotes glioblastoma progression via tumour suppressor candidate 3. Sci. Rep. 7 (October 2016), 1–12. https://doi.org/10.1038/srep44705.

Link, A., Balaguer, F., Nagasaka, T., Boland, C.R., Goel, A., 2014. MicroRNA miR-J1-5p as a potential biomarker for JC virus infection in the gastrointestinal tract. PLoS One 9 (6), e100036. https://doi.org/10.1371/journal.pone.0100036.

Liu, C.-G., Calin, G.A., Meloon, B., Gamliel, N., Sevignani, C., Ferracin, M., Dumitru, C.D., Shimizu, M., Zupo, S., Dono, M., Alder, H., Bullrich, F., Negrini, M., Croce, C.M., 2004. An oligonucleotide microchip for genome-wide microRNA profiling in human and mouse tissues. Proc. Natl. Acad. Sci. U. S. A. 101 (26), 9740–9744. https://doi.org/10.1073/pnas.0403293101.

Lu, R., Zhao, X., Li, J., Niu, P., Yang, B., Wu, H., Wang, W., Song, H., Huang, B., Zhu, N., Bi, Y., Ma, X., Zhan, F., Wang, L., Hu, T., Zhou, H., Hu, Z., Zhou, W., Zhao, L., et al., 2020. Genomic characterisation and epidemiology of 2019 novel coronavirus: implications for virus origins and receptor binding. Lancet 395 (10224), 565–574. https://doi.org/10.1016/S0140-6736(20)30251-8.

Lugli, G., Cohen, A.M., Bennett, D.A., Shah, R.C., Fields, C.J., Hernandez, A.G., Smalheiser, N.R., 2015. Plasma exosomal miRNAs in persons with and without Alzheimer disease: altered expression and prospects for biomarkers. PLoS One 10 (10), e0139233. https://doi.org/10.1371/journal.pone.0139233.

Marquitz, A.R., Mathur, A., Nam, C.S., Raab-Traub, N., 2011. The Epstein-Barr virus BART microRNAs target the pro-apoptotic protein Bim. Virology 412 (2), 392–400. https://doi.org/10.1016/j.virol.2011.01.028.

Mi, S., Zhang, J., Zhang, W., Huang, R.S., 2013. Circulating microRNAs as biomarkers for inflammatory diseases. MicroRNA (Shariqah, United Arab Emirates) 2 (1), 63–71. https://doi.org/10.2174/2211536611302010007.

Michael, M.Z., O'Connor, S.M., van Holst Pellekaan, N.G., Young, G.P., James, R.J., 2003. Reduced accumulation of specific microRNAs in colorectal neoplasia. Mol. Cancer Res. 1 (12), 882–891.

Mishra, P.J., 2014. Non-coding RNAs as clinical biomarkers for cancer diagnosis and prognosis. Expert Rev. Mol. Diagn. 14 (8), 917–919. https://doi.org/10.1586/14737159.2014.971761.

Mitchell, D.A., Xie, W., Schmittling, R., Learn, C., Friedman, A., McLendon, R.E., Sampson, J.H., 2008. Sensitive detection of human cytomegalovirus in tumors and peripheral blood of patients diagnosed with glioblastoma. Neuro Oncol. 10 (1), 10–18. https://doi.org/10.1215/15228517-2007-035.

Mo, M.-H., Chen, L., Fu, Y., Wang, W., Fu, S.W., 2012. Cell-free circulating miRNA biomarkers in cancer. J. Cancer 3, 432–448. https://doi.org/10.7150/jca.4919.

Moens, U., 2009. Silencing viral MicroRNA as a novel antiviral therapy? J. Biomed. Biotechnol. 2009. https://doi.org/10.1155/2009/419539.

Naqvi, A.R., Shango, J., Seal, A., Shukla, D., Nares, S., 2018. Viral miRNAs Alter host cell miRNA profiles and modulate innate immune responses. Front. Immunol. 9, 433. https://doi.org/10.3389/fimmu.2018.00433.

Navari, M., Etebari, M., Ibrahimi, M., Leoncini, L., Piccaluga, P.P., 2018. Pathobiologic roles of Epstein-Barr virus-encoded MicroRNAs in human lymphomas. Int. J. Mol. Sci. 19 (4). https://doi.org/10.3390/ijms19041168.

Nelson, P.T., Baldwin, D.A., Scearce, L.M., Oberholtzer, J.C., Tobias, J.W., Mourelatos, Z., 2004. Microarray-based, high-throughput gene expression profiling of microRNAs. Nat. Methods 1 (2), 155–161. https://doi.org/10.1038/nmeth717.

Nie, Y., Yuan, X., Zhang, P., Chai, Y., Yuan, R., 2019. Versatile and ultrasensitive electrochemiluminescence biosensor for biomarker detection based on nonenzymatic amplification and aptamer-triggered emitter release. Anal. Chem. 91 (5), 3452–3458. https://doi.org/10.1021/acs.analchem.8b05001.

Pall, G.S., Codony-Servat, C., Byrne, J., Ritchie, L., Hamilton, A., 2007. Carbodiimide-mediated cross-linking of RNA to nylon membranes improves the detection of siRNA, miRNA and piRNA by northern blot. Nucleic Acids Res. 35 (8), e60. https://doi.org/10.1093/nar/gkm112.

Pan, S., Liu, W., Tang, J., Yang, Y., Feng, H., Qian, Z., Zhou, J., 2018. Hydrophobicity-guided self-assembled particles of silver nanoclusters with aggregation-induced emission and their use in sensing and bioimaging. J. Mater. Chem. B 6 (23), 3927–3933. https://doi.org/10.1039/C8TB00463C.

Pandeya, A., Khalko, R.K., Mishra, A., Singh, N., Singh, S., Saha, S., Yadav, S., Saxena, S., Gosipatala, S.B., 2021. Human cytomegalovirus miR-UL70-3p downregulates the H2O2-induced apoptosis by targeting the modulator of apoptosis-1 (MOAP1). Int. J. Mol. Sci. 23 (1). https://doi.org/10.3390/ijms23010018.

Peng, Y., Croce, C.M., 2016. The role of MicroRNAs in human cancer. Signal Transduct. Target. Ther. 1, 15004. https://doi.org/10.1038/sigtrans.2015.4.

Pfeffer, S., Zavolan, M., Grässer, F.A., Chien, H., Russo, J.J., Ju, J., John, B., Enright, A.J., Marks, D., Sander, C., Tuschl, T., 2004. Identification of virus-encoded microRNAs. Science (New York, N.Y.) 304 (5671), 734–736. https://doi.org/10.1126/SCIENCE.1096781.

Piedade, D., Azevedo-Pereira, J.M., 2016. The role of microRNAs in the pathogenesis of herpesvirus infection. Viruses 8 (6). https://doi.org/10.3390/v8060156.

Plaisance-Bonstaff, K., Renne, R., 2011. Viral miRNAs. Methods Mol. Biol. (Clifton, N.J.) 721, 43–66. https://doi.org/10.1007/978-1-61779-037-9_3.

Qian, K., Pietilä, T., Rönty, M., Michon, F., Frilander, M.J., Ritari, J., Tarkkanen, J., Paulín, L., Auvinen, P., Auvinen, E., 2013. Identification and validation of human papillomavirus encoded micro-RNAs. PLoS One 8 (7). https://doi.org/10.1371/journal.pone.0070202.

Qin, Z., Jakymiw, A., Findlay, V., Parsons, C., 2012. KSHV-encoded MicroRNAs: lessons for viral cancer pathogenesis and emerging concepts. Int. J. Cell Biol. 2012, 603961. https://doi.org/10.1155/2012/603961.

Qiu, W.-R., Xiao, X., Lin, W.-Z., Chou, K.-C., 2015. iUbiq-Lys: prediction of lysine ubiquitination sites in proteins by extracting sequence evolution information via a gray system model. J. Biomol. Struct. Dyn. 33 (8), 1731–1742. https://doi.org/10.1080/07391102.2014.968875.

Russo, F., Di Bella, S., Nigita, G., Macca, V., Laganà, A., Giugno, R., Pulvirenti, A., Ferro, A., 2012. miRandola: extracellular circulating microRNAs database. PLoS One 7 (10), e47786. https://doi.org/10.1371/journal.pone.0047786.

Scheller, N., Herold, S., Kellner, R., Bertrams, W., Jung, A.L., Janga, H., Greulich, T., Schulte, L.N., Vogelmeier, C.F., Lohmeyer, J., Schmeck, B., 2019. Proviral MicroRNAs detected in extracellular vesicles from bronchoalveolar lavage fluid of patients with influenza virus-induced acute respiratory distress syndrome. J Infect Dis 219 (4), 540–543. https://doi.org/10.1093/infdis/jiy554.

Schultz, J., Lorenz, P., Gross, G., Ibrahim, S., Kunz, M., 2008. MicroRNA let-7b targets important cell cycle molecules in malignant melanoma cells and interferes with anchorage-independent growth. Cell Res. 18 (5), 549–557. https://doi.org/10.1038/cr.2008.45.

Seeger, C., Mason, W.S., 2015. Molecular biology of hepatitis B virus infection. Virology 479–480, 672–686. https://doi.org/10.1016/j.virol.2015.02.031.

Shao, Y., Qi, Y., Huang, Y., Liu, Z., Ma, Y., Guo, X., Jiang, S., Sun, Z., Ruan, Q., 2016. Human cytomegalovirus-encoded miR-US4-1 promotes cell apoptosis and benefits discharge of infectious virus particles by targeting QARS. J. Biosci. 41 (2), 183–192. https://doi.org/10.1007/s12038-016-9605-1.

Shao, Y., Qi, Y., Huang, Y., Liu, Z., Ma, Y., Guo, X., Jiang, S., Sun, Z., Ruan, Q., 2017. Human cytomegalovirus miR-US4-5p promotes apoptosis via downregulation of p21-activated kinase 2 in cultured cells. Mol. Med. Rep. 16 (4). https://doi.org/10.3892/mmr.2017.7108.

Shen, Z.-Z., Pan, X., Miao, L.-F., Ye, H.-Q., Chavanas, S., Davrinche, C., McVoy, M., Luo, M.-H., 2014. Comprehensive analysis of human cytomegalovirus MicroRNA expression during lytic and quiescent infection. PLoS One 9 (2), e88531. https://doi.org/10.1371/journal.pone.0088531.

Shinozaki-Ushiku, A., Kunita, A., Isogai, M., Hibiya, T., Ushiku, T., Takada, K., Fukayama, M., 2015. Profiling of virus-encoded MicroRNAs in Epstein-Barr virus-associated gastric carcinoma and their roles in gastric carcinogenesis. J. Virol. 89 (10), 5581–5591. https://doi.org/10.1128/JVI.03639-14.

Shojaei Jeshvaghani, Z., Arefian, E., Asgharpour, S., Soleimani, M., 2021. Latency-associated transcript-derived MicroRNAs in herpes simplex virus type 1 target SMAD3 and SMAD4 in TGF-β/SMAD signaling pathway. Iran. Biomed. J. 25 (3), 169–179. https://doi.org/10.29252/ibj.25.3.169.

Skalsky, R.L., Cullen, B.R., 2010. Viruses, microRNAs, and host interactions. Annu. Rev. Microbiol. 64, 123–141. https://doi.org/10.1146/annurev.micro.112408.134243.

Song, Y., Li, X., Zeng, Z., Li, Q., Gong, Z., Liao, Q., Li, X., Chen, P., Xiang, B., Zhang, W., Xiong, F., Zhou, Y., Zhou, M., Ma, J., Li, Y., Chen, X., Li, G., Xiong, W., 2016. Epstein-Barr virus encoded miR-BART11 promotes inflammation-induced carcinogenesis by targeting FOXP1. Oncotarget 7 (24), 36783–36799. https://doi.org/10.18632/oncotarget.9170.

Stern-Ginossar, N., Elefant, N., Zimmermann, A., Wolf, D.G., Saleh, N., Biton, M., Horwitz, E., Prokocimer, Z., Prichard, M., Hahn, G., Goldman-Wohl, D., Greenfield, C., Yagel, S., Hengel, H., Altuvia, Y., Margalit, H., Mandelboim, O., 2007. Host immune system gene targeting by a viral miRNA. Science (New York, N.Y.) 317 (5836), 376–381. https://doi.org/10.1126/SCIENCE.1140956.

Stewart, C.R., Marsh, G.A., Jenkins, K.A., Gantier, M.P., Tizard, M.L., Middleton, D., Lowenthal, J.W., Haining, J., Izzard, L., Gough, T.J., Deffrasnes, C., Stambas, J., Robinson, R., Heine, H.G., Pallister, J.-A., Foord, A.J., Bean, A.G., Wang, L.-F., 2013. Promotion of Hendra virus replication by microRNA 146a. J. Virol. 87 (7), 3782–3791. https://doi.org/10.1128/JVI.01342-12.

Suffert, G., Malterer, G., Hausser, J., Viiliäinen, J., Fender, A., Contrant, M., Ivacevic, T., Benes, V., Gros, F., Voinnet, O., Zavolan, M., Ojala, P.M., Haas, J.G., Pfeffer, S., 2011. Kaposi's sarcoma herpesvirus microRNAs target caspase 3 and regulate apoptosis. PLoS Pathog. 7 (12), e1002405. https://doi.org/10.1371/journal.ppat.1002405.

Sun, Y., Wang, M., Lin, G., Sun, S., Li, X., Qi, J., Li, J., 2012. Serum microRNA-155 as a potential biomarker to track disease in breast cancer. PLoS One 7 (10), e47003. https://doi.org/10.1371/journal.pone.0047003.

Tang, J., Xiao, X., Jiang, Y., Tian, Y., Peng, Z., Yang, M., Xu, Z., Gong, G., 2020. miR-3 encoded by hepatitis B virus downregulates PTEN protein expression and promotes cell proliferation. J. Hepatocell. Carcinoma 7, 257–269. https://doi.org/10.2147/JHC.S271091.

Torres, A.G., Fabani, M.M., Vigorito, E., Gait, M.J., 2011. MicroRNA fate upon targeting with anti-miRNA oligonucleotides as revealed by an improved Northern-blot-based method for miRNA detection. RNA (New York, N.Y.) 17 (5), 933–943. https://doi.org/10.1261/rna.2533811.

Turchinovich, A., Weiz, L., Burwinkel, B., 2012. Extracellular miRNAs: the mystery of their origin and function. Trends Biochem. Sci. 37 (11), 460–465. https://doi.org/10.1016/j.tibs.2012.08.003.

Tycowski, K.T., Guo, Y.E., Lee, N., Moss, W.N., Vallery, T.K., Xie, M., Steitz, J.A., 2015. Viral noncoding RNAs: more surprises. Genes Dev. 29 (6), 567–584. https://doi.org/10.1101/gad.259077.115.

Ulasov, I.V., Kaverina, N.V., Ghosh, D., Baryshnikova, M.A., Kadagidze, Z.G., Karseladze, A.I., Baryshnikov, A.Y., Cobbs, C.S., 2017. CMV70-3P miRNA contributes to the CMV mediated glioma stemness and represents a target for glioma experimental therapy. Oncotarget 8 (16), 25989–25999. https://doi.org/10.18632/oncotarget.11175.

Umbach, J.L., Kramer, M.F., Jurak, I., Karnowski, H.W., Coen, D.M., Cullen, B.R., 2008. MicroRNAs expressed by herpes simplex virus 1 during latent infection regulate viral mRNAs. Nature 454 (7205), 780–783. https://doi.org/10.1038/nature07103.

Van Der Heide, L.P., Hoekman, M.F.M., Smidt, M.P., 2004. The ins and outs of FoxO shuttling: mechanisms of FoxO translocation and transcriptional regulation. Biochem. J. 380 (Pt 2), 297–309. https://doi.org/10.1042/BJ20040167.

Vojtechova, Z., Tachezy, R., 2018. The role of miRNAs in virus-mediated oncogenesis. Int. J. Mol. Sci. 19 (4). https://doi.org/10.3390/ijms19041217.

Wang, Y., Tang, Q., Li, M., Jiang, S., Wang, X., 2014. MicroRNA-375 inhibits colorectal cancer growth by targeting PIK3CA. Biochem. Biophys. Res. Commun. 444 (2), 199–204. https://doi.org/10.1016/j.bbrc.2014.01.028.

Wang, X., Liu, S., Zhou, Z., Yan, H., Xiao, J., 2017. A herpes simplex virus type 2-encoded microRNA promotes tumor cell metastasis by targeting suppressor of cytokine signaling 2 in lung cancer. Tumor Biol. 39 (5). https://doi.org/10.1177/1010428317701633. 1010428317701633.

Wang, Y., Zou, L., Wu, T., Xiong, L., Zhang, T., Kong, L., Xue, Y., Tang, M., 2019. Identification of mRNA-miRNA crosstalk in human endothelial cells after exposure of PM2.5 through integrative transcriptome analysis. Ecotoxicol. Environ. Saf. 169, 863–873. https://doi.org/10.1016/j.ecoenv.2018.11.114.

Weng, S.-L., Huang, K.-Y., Weng, J.T.-Y., Hung, F.-Y., Chang, T.-H., Lee, T.-Y., 2018. Genome-wide discovery of viral microRNAs based on phylogenetic analysis and structural evolution of various human papillomavirus subtypes. Brief. Bioinform. 19 (6), 1102–1114. https://doi.org/10.1093/bib/bbx046.

WHO Reveals Leading Causes of Death and Disability Worldwide: 2000–2019. (n.d.).

Wong, A.M.G., Kong, K.L., Tsang, J.W.H., Kwong, D.L.W., Guan, X.-Y., 2012. Profiling of Epstein-Barr virus-encoded microRNAs in nasopharyngeal carcinoma reveals potential biomarkers and oncomirs. Cancer 118 (3), 698–710. https://doi.org/10.1002/cncr.26309.

Wong, W., Farr, R., Joglekar, M., Januszewski, A., Hardikar, A., 2015. Probe-based real-time PCR approaches for quantitative measurement of microRNAs. J. Vis. Exp. 98. https://doi.org/10.3791/52586.

Wurz, K., Garcia, R.L., Goff, B.A., Mitchell, P.S., Lee, J.H., Tewari, M., Swisher, E.M., 2010. MiR-221 and MiR-222 alterations in sporadic ovarian carcinoma: relationship to CDKN1B, CDKNIC and overall survival. Genes Chromosomes Cancer 49 (7), 577–584. https://doi.org/10.1002/gcc.20768.

Yang, Y., Liu, Y., Xue, J., Yang, Z., Shi, Y., Shi, Y., Lou, G., Wu, S., Qi, J., Liu, W., Wang, J., Chen, Z., 2017. MicroRNA-141 targets Sirt1 and inhibits autophagy to reduce HBV replication. Cell. Physiol. Biochem. 41 (1), 310–322. https://doi.org/10.1159/000456162.

Yao, L., Zhou, Y., Sui, Z., Zhang, Y., Liu, Y., Xie, H., Gao, H., Fan, H., Zhang, Y., Liu, M., Li, S., Tang, H., 2019. RETRACTED: HBV-encoded miR-2 functions as an oncogene by downregulating TRIM35 but upregulating RAN in liver cancer cells. EBioMedicine 48, 117–129. https://doi.org/10.1016/j.ebiom.2019.09.012.

Ye, J., Xu, M., Tian, X., Cai, S., Zeng, S., 2019. Research advances in the detection of miRNA. J. Pharm. Anal. 9 (4), 217–226. https://doi.org/10.1016/j.jpha.2019.05.004.

Yun, S.J., Jeong, P., Kang, H.W., Kim, Y.-H., Kim, E.-A., Yan, C., Choi, Y.-K., Kim, D., Kim, J.M., Kim, S.-K., Kim, S.-Y., Kim, S.T., Kim, W.T., Lee, O.-J., Koh, G.-Y., Moon, S.-K., Kim, I.Y., Kim, J., Choi, Y.-H., Kim, W.-J., 2015. Urinary MicroRNAs of prostate cancer: virus-encoded hsv1-miRH18 and hsv2-miR-H9-5p could be valuable diagnostic markers. Int. Neurourol. J. 19 (2), 74–84. https://doi.org/10.5213/inj.2015.19.2.74.

Zhang, N., Shi, X.-M., Guo, H.-Q., Zhao, X.-Z., Zhao, W.-W., Xu, J.-J., Chen, H.-Y., 2018. Gold nanoparticle couples with entropy-driven toehold-mediated DNA strand displacement reaction on magnetic beads: toward ultrasensitive energy-transfer-based photoelectrochemical detection of miRNA-141 in real blood sample. Anal. Chem. 90 (20), 11892–11898. https://doi.org/10.1021/acs.analchem.8b01966.

Zhao, A., Li, G., Péoc'h, M., Genin, C., Gigante, M., 2013. Serum miR-210 as a novel biomarker for molecular diagnosis of clear cell renal cell carcinoma. Exp. Mol. Pathol. 94 (1), 115–120. https://doi.org/10.1016/j.yexmp.2012.10.005.

Zhao, X., Sun, L., Mu, T., Yi, J., Ma, C., Xie, H., Liu, M., Tang, H., 2020. An HBV-encoded miRNA activates innate immunity to restrict HBV replication. J. Mol. Cell Biol. 12 (4), 263–276. https://doi.org/10.1093/jmcb/mjz104.

Zhou, L., Wang, Y., Yang, C., Xu, H., Luo, J., Zhang, W., Tang, X., Yang, S., Fu, W., Chang, K., Chen, M., 2019. A label-free electrochemical biosensor for microRNAs detection based on DNA nanomaterial by coupling with Y-shaped DNA structure and non-linear hybridization chain reaction. Biosens. Bioelectron. 126, 657–663. https://doi.org/10.1016/j.bios.2018.11.028.

Zhu, W., Liu, S., 2020. The role of human cytomegalovirus in atherosclerosis: a systematic review. Acta Biochim. Biophys. Sin. 52 (4), 339–353. https://doi.org/10.1093/abbs/gmaa005.

CHAPTER TWELVE

Pharmacogenomics and oncology: A therapeutic approach for cancer treatment

Neetu Saini[a], Monika Kadian[b], and Anil Kumar[b]
[a]Dolphin PG College of Science and Agriculture, Chunni Kalan, Punjab, India
[b]Pharmacology Division, University Institute of Pharmaceutical Sciences (UIPS), UGC Centre of Advanced Study, Panjab University, Chandigarh, India

1. Introduction

Pharmacogenomics, sometimes known as "personalized medicine," is a branch of genetics that focuses on predicting a person's reaction to specific therapeutic medications (Carr et al., 2021). Pharmacogenetics is a phrase that has been around for a long time. Friedrich Vogel, a German scientist, was the first to employ it in 1959 (Vogel, 1959). Pharmacogenetics was previously defined as "phenotypic variation in metabolism and drug response." Due to the discovery that most medication reactions are complex, pharmacogenetics has evolved into the discipline of pharmacogenomics throughout time (Lindpaintner, 2002). Advances in analytical technologies and gene cloning led to a better understanding of the genetic underpinnings of this variance later on. In the late 1990s, the cloning and sequencing of the entire human genome gave rise to a new term: pharmacogenomics. These two concepts are now interchangeable, though pharmacogenomics incorporates the production of novel medications that target specific disease-causing genes as well (Durmaz et al., 2015; Ventola, 2011).

Pharmacogenetics and pharmacogenomics are multidisciplinary research efforts aimed at understanding the relationship between genotype (i.e., polymorphisms and genetic mutations), gene expression profiles (the level of gene expression of all genes in the genome), and phenotype (as expressed in individual variability in drug response or toxicity) (Wang, 2010). Pharmacogenetics is the study of complicated multigene patterns throughout the genome, whereas pharmacogenomics is the study of effects involving a restricted number of genes, generally involving drug metabolism. Individual genome polymorphisms are variations that remain stable throughout a person's lifespan (Ahmed et al., 2016; Slagboom et al., 2011).

The human genome has an estimated 1.4 million single nucleotide polymorphisms, many of which contribute to medication pharmacokinetic and pharmacodynamic variability (Lee, 2010). Genetic mutations are changes in gene sequences that only occur in specific cells. When compared to host tissues, tumor cells may acquire mutations at a faster rate (Testa et al., 2018). Drug transport and metabolism, cellular targets, signaling pathways, and cellular responses to treatment are all affected by these genetic variations (Li et al., 2019). Gene expression profiling uses microarray analysis of messenger RNA (mRNA) to discover gene expression patterns, which may then be defined and categorized using a variety of statistical techniques (Ontario, 2020).

The ultimate goal of pharmacogenetics and pharmacogenomics is to develop personalized medicine by defining the population diversity of polymorphisms, genetic mutations, and gene expression profiles of clinical interest, allowing for drug prescription based on a patient's unique genetic or biological profile, or the unique genetic profile of tumors (Horgan et al., 2020; Krzyszczyk et al., 2018). Oncologists have previously used pharmacogenetics and pharmacogenomics to predict cancer susceptibility, tumor development and recurrence, patient survival, and the responsiveness to the toxicity of standard chemotherapy regimens. With the rising success of targeted anticancer drugs, such as monoclonal antibody therapy, it's critical to assess the role of pharmacogenetics and pharmacogenomics in clinical efficacy and toxicity of these novel treatments (Wheeler et al., 2013; Dressler, 2012).

From a research implementation approach, this book chapter summarizes conceptual understanding of targeting biomarkers with drug target into cancer therapy.

2. Targeting biomarkers in cancer therapy

2.1 Thiopurine methyltransferase (TPMT)

Prokaryotes and eukaryotes both have a cytoplasmic transmethylase called thiopurine methyltransferase (TPMT). Mercaptopurine, thioguanine, thiopurine nucleotides, and nucleosides are all methylated by TPMT. Because TPMT catalyzes the primary inactivation mechanism for thiopurines, people with TPMT deficiency accrue high levels of active thioguanine nucleotides even when taking conventional thiopurine doses (Lennard et al., 2015). It inhibits the production and synthesis of purine ribonucleotides and promotes apoptosis by including thioguanine nucleotide analogues. Patients with excess thioguanine nucleotides due to defective TPMT activity are at a considerably higher risk of myelosuppression, which is a dose–limiting danger of thiopurine therapy (Asadov et al., 2017).

2.2 BCR-ABL

The Philadelphia chromosome, which is formed by a translocation between chromosomes 9 and 22 fusing the breakpoint cluster region (BCR) with the abelson gene (ABL) oncogene and is ultimately responsible for the development of chronic myeloid leukemia (CML), has made drug development of highly potent targeted therapies in hematologic malignancies. In 95% of CML cases, the BCR–ABL translocation occurs, resulting in constitutive activation of signal transduction pathways linked to cell proliferation and tumor formation (Kang et al., 2016). Tyrosine kinase inhibitors (TKIs) including imatinib, nilotinib, dasatinib, and bosutinib discovered in a high-throughput screening assay for agents that inhibit the translocation, approved by the FDA (United States Food and Drug Administration) for first-line treatment to treat BCR–ABL-positive CML (Quintas-Cardama and Cortes, 2009).

2.3 UGT1A1

Topoisomerase I inhibitors, has anticancer therapy in various type of cancer, including gastrointestinal and lung carcinomas. Topoisomerase I and II are normal host enzymes found in mammalian cells' nuclei and are necessary for normal DNA replication and cellular division. Single-stranded nicks in cellular DNA are created and later repaired by the enzymes. These inhibitors must be bioactivated to the active metabolite, SN-38, via carboxylesterase enzymes, and subsequently glucuronidated and inactivated to SN-38G by uridine diphosphate glucuronosyl transferase 1A1 (UGT1A1). Polymorphic UGT1A1 variations reduce gene expression and enzyme activity, resulting in supratherapeutic SN-38 levels and a higher risk of severe toxicity, including neutropenia (Nelson et al., 2021; Atasilp et al., 2016).

2.4 DPYD and 5-FU

The antimetabolite chemotherapeutic drug 5-fluorouracil (5-FU) has been the standard of care for various cancers, including gastrointestinal colon, rectal, and stomach tumors. The rate-limiting enzyme dihydropyrimidine dehydrogenase (DPD) is responsible for the conversion of roughly 80%–85% of 5-FU to the inert 5,6-dihydrofluorouracil. Over 30 genetic variations in DPYD, the gene that codes for DPD, have been shown to cause decreased DPD enzyme activity, potentially raising the risk of 5-FU-induced toxicity (Miura et al., 2010; Pallet et al., 2020).

The FDA label carries a warning about an increased risk of toxicity in patients with deficient DPD activity; however, the FDA does not define "deficient," and genetic testing for DPYD is not required prior to 5-FU therapy (White et al., 2021).

2.5 BRAF

A BRAF mutation is an alteration in the BRAF gene (a human gene that encodes a protein called B-Raf) that causes cancer. This mutation in the gene can cause a change in a protein that controls cell development, allowing the melanoma to grow more aggressively. Approximately half of all melanomas have this mutation, which is referred to as BRAF positive or mutant. Wild-type or BRAF-negative melanomas are melanomas that do not have the BRAF mutation. Activating BRAF mutations cause the MAPK pathway to be activated and signal indefinitely, encouraging cell proliferation and tumor's development (Alqathama, 2020; van Staveren et al., 2011).

2.6 Estrogen receptor (ESR)

Estrogen and other steroid hormones work through receptors called estrogen receptor alfa (ER) and estrogen receptor beta (ER). The nuclear receptor superfamily includes ERs, which function as transcription factors in homo- or heterodimers. Estrogen binding to nuclear receptors causes nuclear translocation, which activates genomic pathways and causes many target genes to be transcribed (Yasar et al., 2017). The activation of a "nongenomic route" causes steroid hormones to have a faster effect. In this situation, membrane-bound estrogen receptors are responsible for cytosolic signaling changes, resulting in enhanced RAS/BRAF/MEK axis activity (Bozovic et al., 2021).

2.7 ERBB2 (HER2)

Through different processes, mutations in ERBB2, the gene that encodes the HER2 receptor tyrosine kinase, can lead to uncontrolled cellular proliferation and oncogenesis. ERBB2 amplifications are well understood in breast adenocarcinomas, where they predict clinical benefit from HER2-directed monoclonal antibodies (trastuzumab and pertuzumab), antibody-drug conjugates (trastuzumab emtansine), and HER2 kinase inhibitors (lapatinib). In gastroesophageal junction adenocarcinoma, ERBB2 amplifications are also predictive of trastuzumab response. Furthermore, rather than amplification of the wild-type gene, it is now known that some malignancies activate ERBB2 through mutation (Gottesdiener et al., 2018).

2.8 Anaplastic lymphoma kinase (ALK)

ALK is a tyrosine kinase receptor that is frequently altered, mutated, or amplified in neoplastic disorders such as lymphoma, neuroblastoma, nonsmall cell lung cancer, and, to a lesser extent, melanoma. ALK-specific mRNA and protein have also been found in various cell lines derived from ectodermal solid tumors, including melanoma. ALK is found in about 5% of all instances of nonsmall cell lung cancer (NSCLC). The RAS-MEK-ERK, janus kinase 3 (JAK3)-STAT3, and PI3K-AKT signaling pathways are all activated as a result of the translocation. ALK is competitively inhibited by treatment with a targeted TKI therapy (Holla et al., 2017).

2.9 HLA

HLA-I expression on cancer cell surfaces is required for T-cell activation to be successful. As a result, tumor cells that lack HLA-I expression have a significant impact on tumors detection and the activation of T-cells, which remain unstimulated and incapable of detecting cancer cells. Anti–CTLA-4, -PD1, and -PDL1 medications would not work in this situation. To identify the suitability of an immunotherapy treatment based on T-cell activation, the HLA status on the tumors cell surface must first be established.

2.10 PIK3CA

Phosphatidylinositol 3-kinases (PI3Ks) are a family of lipid kinases that govern cell proliferation, adhesion, survival, and motility through signaling pathways. The PI3K pathway is thought to play a key role in tumors development. Activating mutations of the PI3K p110 subunit (PIK3CA) have been found in a wide range of malignancies. PIK3CA mutations boost the PI3K signal, stimulate downstream Akt signaling, promote growth factor-independent growth, and promote cell invasion and metastasis, according to studies. Rapamycin inhibits cellular transformation produced by PI3K mutants, implying that mTOR and its downstream targets are critical components in the transformation process (Ippen et al., 2019a, b).

2.11 Gene signature (T-effector)

The gene signature encompasses genes associated to T-cell activation, cytotoxicity, and IFN-γ downstream regulation, suggesting that this signature may influence CD8$^+$ T cells in melanoma via IFN-γ activation. Coexpression of genes linked to CD8$^+$ T-cell infiltration include CCL5, GBP5, GZMA, GZMH, IRF1, LAG3, NKG7, PRF1, and PSMB10. Immunotherapy for solid tumors, particularly in melanoma, has been hampered by a lack of CD8+ T lymphocytes in central tumors regions. Therefore, treatment strategies that increase the accumulation of CD8+ T lymphocytes in core tumors areas are urgently required (Yan et al., 2021).

2.12 CD274

This gene codes an immune inhibitory receptor ligand that is expressed by both hematopoietic and nonhematopoietic cells, including T and B cells, as well as tumors cells. The encoded protein has immunoglobulin V-like and C-like domains and is a type I transmembrane protein. T-cell activation and cytokine production are inhibited when this ligand interacts with its receptor (Masugi et al., 2017). This relationship is critical for preventing autoimmunity by maintaining immunological homeostasis during infection or inflammation of normal tissue. Through cytotoxic T-cell inactivation, this relationship allows tumors cells to escape the immune system in tumors microenvironments. Many forms of human cancers, including colon cancer and renal cell carcinoma, are thought to be prognostic when this gene is expressed in tumors cells. Multiple transcripts are produced as a result of alternative splicing (Gonzalez et al., 2018).

2.13 PML-RARA

Although acute promyelocytic leukemia (APL) is one of the most well-studied forms of acute myeloid leukemia (AML), the molecular processes underlying its genesis and progression remain unknown. As a result of the translocation, the PML-RARA rearrangement defines APL.

PML-RARA inhibits the transcription of multiple genes involved in myeloid differentiation, including those involved in granulocyte differentiation, in a way that is unaffected by normal levels of retinoic ligands. PML-RARA, on the other hand, gives leukemic cells a survival and proliferation advantage, resulting in the increasing accumulation of promyelocytes in APL patients' bone marrow.

The use of two medications, ATRA and ATO, which are routinely used in clinical practice, can restore PML-RARA functions. These bind to the RARA and PML portions of the fusion protein, respectively, to cause PML-RARA breakdown. As a result of the release of many corepressors, including epigenetic enzymes (e.g., HDACs and DNA methyltransferases) and the interaction with a series of coactivators, ATRA transforms PML-RARA into a transcriptional activator, resulting in more accessible chromatin. ATO, on the other hand, causes various posttranscriptional alterations to the PML moiety's second B-box domain, resulting in a shift in the PML-RARA organization (Liquori et al., 2020; Hattori et al., 2018).

2.14 ROS1

ROS1 protein shows substantial homology to ALK (both belong to insulin receptor superfamily), particularly within the ATP binding site (84% homology) and the kinase domains (64% homology) (D'Angelo et al., 2020). Genomic alteration of *ROS1* is well known and normally leads to gene fusion with several fusion partners, resulting fusion proteins are robust oncogenic drivers. As a consequence, ROS1 kinase activity is constitutively activated, leading to increased cell proliferation, survival and migration due to the upregulation of JAK/STAT, PI3K/AKT, and MAPK/ERK signaling pathways. ROS1 has shown tumorigenic potential in vitro and in vivo, with glioblastoma the first human cancer shown to harbor ROS1 rearrangements (Drilon et al., 2021).

Specific somatic mutations are predictive of treatment success for various targeted medicines, and the US Food and Drug Administration (FDA) highlights these connections in drug labeling, as shown in Table 1.

Table 1 Oncology pharmacogenomics biomarkers and FDA approved drug.

Drug	Biomarker	Drug target
Abemaciclib	ESR (Hormone Receptor), ERBB2 (HER2)	Abemaciclib reduces retinoblastoma (Rb) protein phosphorylation in early G1 by specifically inhibiting CDK4 and 6. Rb phosphorylation inhibition limits CDK-mediated G1-S phase transitions, halting the cell cycle in the G1 phase, decreasing DNA synthesis, and slowing cancer cell development (Naz et al., 2018)
Ado-Trastuzumab Emtansine	ERBB2 (HER2)	Trastuzumab emtansine interacts to subdomain IV of the HER2 receptor and enters the cell via receptor-mediated endocytosis. Trastuzumab emtansine is degraded by lysosomes, releasing DM1. DM1 binds to tubulin in microtubules, preventing microtubule function and causing cell death (Li et al., 2018)
Alectinib	ALK	Alectinib is a tyrosine kinase inhibitor that prevents NSCLC cells from growing and spreading by inhibiting the function of the protein produced by the mutant ALK gene. The RET protein, a receptor tyrosine kinase involved in cell proliferation and differentiation, is similarly targeted by Alectinib (Tomasini et al., 2019)
Allopurinol	HLA-B	High amounts of uric acid in the body produced by certain cancer medicines, and kidney stones are all treated with allopurinol. Allopurinol belongs to the xanthine oxidase inhibitor class of drugs. It works by lowering uric acid production in the body (Somkrua et al., 2011)
Alpelisib	ERBB2 (HER2), ESR (hormone receptor), PIK3CA	Alpelisib suppresses the activation of the PI3K signaling pathway by inhibiting PI3K in the PI3K/AKT kinase (or protein kinase B) signaling pathway. In vulnerable tumor cell populations, this could result in tumor cell growth and survival being inhibited (Wang et al., 2020)
Anastrozole	ESR	Anastrozole is a nonsteroidal AI that binds reversibly to the heme ion of the aromatase enzyme and inhibits it. Anastrozole reduces the levels of E2, E1, and E1S in the peripheral and mammary tissue by blocking the action of aromatase (Ingle et al., 2015)

Continued

Table 1 Oncology pharmacogenomics biomarkers and FDA approved drug—cont'd

Drug	Biomarker	Drug target
Arsenic trioxide	PML-RARA	Arsenic appears to disrupt a variety of intracellular signal transduction pathways and alter cellular function. Arsenic's activities may cause apoptosis to be induced, growth and angiogenesis to be inhibited, and differentiation to be promoted (Burnett et al., 2015)
Atezolizumab	CD274 (PD-L1), gene signature (T-effector), ALK, BRAF	Atezolizumab is a humanized monoclonal antibody immune checkpoint inhibitor that binds to PD-L1 and prevents PD-1 from interacting with B7. a (i.e., CD80 receptors). The antibody still permits PD-L2 and PD-1 to interact (Shah et al., 2018)
Avelumab	CD274 (PD-L1)	Avelumab is a complete monoclonal antibody of the isotype IgG1 that binds to the programmed death-ligand 1 (PD-L1) and thereby prevents the receptor programmed cell death 1 from binding to it (PD-1) (Julia et al., 2018)
Binimetinib	BRAF, UGT1A1	Binimetinib binds to MEK1/2 and suppresses its activity in a noncompetitive manner with ATP. MEK1/2 inhibition prevents MEK1/2-dependent effector proteins and transcription factors from being activated. Growth factor-mediated cell signaling can be inhibited as a result of this mechanism (Woodfield et al., 2016)
Brigatinib	ALK	Brigatinib binds to ALK kinase and ALK fusion proteins, as well as EGFR and mutant versions, and inhibits them. This inhibits ALK kinase and EGFR kinase, impairs their signaling pathways, and ultimately stops tumor cells from growing in vulnerable tumor cells (Lin et al., 2018)
Cemiplimab-rwlc	ALK, CD274 (PD-L1), EGFR, ROS1	Cemiplimab-rwlc interacts to the PD-1 receptor on T-cells, reducing T-cell proliferation and cytokine production by blocking its interaction with PD ligand 1 (PD-L1) and PD-L2 (Yang et al., 2021)
Ceritinib	ALK	Ceritinib works by preventing autophosphorylation of ALK, phosphorylation of the downstream signaling molecule STAT3 by ALK, and proliferation of ALK-dependent cancer cells (Subbiah et al., 2021)

Table 1 Oncology pharmacogenomics biomarkers and FDA approved drug—cont'd

Drug	Biomarker	Drug target
Cisplatin	TPMT	The capacity of cisplatin to crosslink with the urinary bases on DNA to produce DNA adducts has been linked to its ability to impede DNA repair, resulting in DNA damage and inducing death in cancer cells (Tchounwou et al., 2021)
Cobimetinib	BRAF	Cobimetinib works by inhibiting the MEK1 and MEK2 proteins, which are part of the MAPK signaling system. The extracellular signal-related kinase pathway, which is important for cell proliferation, is regulated by these MEK proteins. Uncontrolled cell development and cancer can result from signaling system flaws (Cheng and Tian, 2017)
Crizotinib	ALK, ROS1	Crizotinib is a tyrosine kinase inhibitor that targets ALK, the Hepatocyte Growth Factor Receptor (HGFR, c-Met). Translocations can alter the ALK gene, causing oncogenic fusion proteins to be expressed (Chen et al., 2021)
Docetaxel	ESR	Docetaxel prevents the microtubular depolymerization and attenuated the bcl-2 and bcl-xL gene expression effects (Tymon-Rosario et al., 2021)
Durvalumab	CD274 (PD-L1)	Durvalumab is a human immunoglobulin G1 kappa monoclonal antibody that inhibits immunological responses by blocking the interaction of PD-L1 with PD-1 and CD80 (B7. 1) without causing antibody-dependent cell-mediated cytotoxicity (Arends et al., 2021)
Encorafenib	BRAF	Encorafenib is an ATP-competitive RAF kinase inhibitor that reduces ERK phosphorylation and CyclinD1 expression. This causes senescence without apoptosis by stopping the cell cycle at G1. As a result, it works exclusively in melanomas with a BRAF mutation, which account for half of all melanomas (Arends et al., 2021)
Entrectinib	ROS1	Entrectinib is a tyrosine kinase inhibitor that targets a number of different receptors. It inhibits tropomyosin receptor tyrosine kinases (TRK) TRKA, TRKB, and TRKC, as well as the proto-oncogene tyrosine-protein kinase ROS1 and anaplastic lymphoma kinase ALK (ALK) (Rolfo et al., 2015)

Continued

Table 1 Oncology pharmacogenomics biomarkers and FDA approved drug—cont'd

Drug	Biomarker	Drug target
Erdafitinib	CYP2C9	Erdafitinib is a targeted kinase inhibitor that works by attaching to and inhibiting the enzymatic activity of FGFR1, FGFR2, FGFR3, and FGFR4. Other proteins that erdafitinib binds to include FLT4, KIT, VEGFR2, RET, CSF1R, and PDGFRA (Loriot et al., 2019)
Eribulin	ERBB2 (HER2), ESR	Eribulin belongs to the halichondrin class of antineoplastic medicines. It is a microtubule dynamics inhibitor with a tubulin-based mechanism of action (MOA) that inhibits the growth phase of the microtubule without inhibiting the shortening phase (Cortes et al., 2011)
Everolimus	ERBB2 (HER2), ESR (hormone receptor)	Several human malignancies, as well as tuberous sclerosis complex, have dysregulated mTOR pathways (TSC). Everolimus binds to FKBP-12, an intracellular protein that forms an inhibitory complex with mTOR complex 1 (mTORC1), inhibiting mTOR kinase activity (Lee et al., 2018)
Exemestane	ESR	Exemestane inactivates aromatase by binding to it covalently as a pseudo-substrate (Yang et al., 2019)
Fulvestrant	ERBB2 (HER2), ESR	When fulvestrant binds to estrogen receptor monomers, it inhibits receptor dimerization, makes activating functions 1 and 2 inactive, reduces receptor translocation to the nucleus, and speeds up estrogen receptor degradation. As a result, the effects are purely antiestrogenic (Boer, 2017)
Gefitinib	CYP2D6	Several tyrosine kinases linked with transmembrane cell surface receptors, including those associated with the epidermal growth factor receptor, are phosphorylated intracellularly by gefitinib (EGFR-TK). Many normal and malignant cells express EGFR on their cell surfaces (Nurwidya et al., 2016)
Inotuzumab Ozogamicin	BCR-ABL1 (Philadelphia chromosome)	Inotuzumab is a humanized anti-CD22 monoclonal antibody linked to the calicheamicin, a poisonous natural substance. Endocytosis transports inotuzumab into the cytoplasm. Calicheamicin enters the nucleus, attaches to the minor DNA groove, breaks the double-stranded DNA, and brings the cell cycle to a halt in the G2/M phase (Stock et al., 2021)

Table 1 Oncology pharmacogenomics biomarkers and FDA approved drug—cont'd

Drug	Biomarker	Drug target
Ipilimumab	HLA-A, CD274 (PD-L1), ALK	Ipilimumab acts by preventing normal and malignant T-cells from expressing the CTLA-4 antigen. Ipilimumab binds to CTLA-4, causing T-cell activation and proliferation to increase. In patients with melanoma, the mechanism of action of ipilimumab is indirect, presumably through T-cell-driven antitumor immune responses (Rosskopf et al., 2019)
Irinotecan	UGT1A1	Topoisomerase I is inhibited by irinotecan. By attaching to the topoisomerase I-DNA complex, irinotecan blocks DNA strand relegation. The development of this ternary complex causes replication arrest and deadly double-stranded breaks in DNA by interfering with the moving replication fork (Fujita et al., 2015)
Lorlatinib	ALK, ROS1	Lorlatinib binds to both ALK and ROS1 kinases and inhibits them. Inhibition of the kinase causes ALK and ROS1-mediated signaling to be disrupted, which limits tumor cell proliferation in ALK- and ROS1-overexpressing tumor cells (Shaw et al., 2020)
Nilotinib	BCR-ABL1 (Philadelphia chromosome), UGT1A1	The BCR-ABL protein's tyrosine kinase activity is inhibited by nilotinib (Blay and von Mehren, 2011)
Niraparib	BRCA, genomic instability (homologous recombination deficiency)	Niraparib inhibits the PARP enzymes PARP-1 and PARP-2, which are involved in DNA repair. Niraparib causes DNA damage and cell death by inhibiting PARP enzymatic activity and promoting the formation of PARP-DNA complexes (Blay and von Mehren, 2011)
Nivolumab	BRAF, CD274 (PD-L1), EGFR, ALK, ERBB2 (HER2)	Nivolumab is a monoclonal antibody that binds to the PD-1 receptor and disrupts its association with PD-L1 and PD-L2, releasing PD-1 pathway-mediated suppression of the immune response, including the antitumor immune response, resulting in tumor growth inhibition (Sundar et al., 2015)

Continued

Table 1 Oncology pharmacogenomics biomarkers and FDA approved drug—cont'd

Drug	Biomarker	Drug target
Olaparib	BRCA, ERBB2 (HER2), ESR, PGR (hormone receptor)	Olaparib inhibits poly(ADPribose) polymerase, preventing single-strand DNA breaks from being repaired. Synthetic lethality occurs in BRCA-associated cancer cells, which have a defect in a different DNA repair pathway called homologous recombination (Montemorano et al., 2019)
Olaratumab	PDGFRA	Olaratumab is a human IgG1 antibody that binds to PDGFR and prevents receptor-activating ligands from triggering pathway activation (Davis and Chugh, 2017)
Omacetaxine	BCR-ABL1 (Philadelphia chromosome)	Omacetaxine competes with tRNA for binding to the A-site cleft in the large ribosomal subunit, preventing protein elongation. Protein synthesis is halted, resulting in a reduction in proteins, particularly those with short half-lives, and death in cells that rely on them (Wetzler and Segal, 2011)
Palbociclib	ESR (hormone receptor), ERBB2 (HER2)	Palbociclib inhibits cyclin-dependent kinases 4 (CDK4) and 6 (CDK6), preventing retinoblastoma (Rb) protein phosphorylation and cell cycle arrest early in the G1 phase. DNA replication is inhibited, and tumor cell proliferation is reduced (Serra et al., 2019)
Pembrolizumab	BRAF, CD274 (PD-L1), ALK, ERBB2 (HER2)	Pembrolizumab is a highly selective humanized monoclonal IgG4 antibody that targets the cell surface PD-1 receptor. The medication inhibits PD-L1 and PD-L2 binding and activation by blocking the PD-1 receptor. T-cell-mediated immune responses against tumor cells are activated as a result of this process (Allen et al., 2021)
Pertuzumab	ERBB2 (HER2), ESR	Pertuzumab is a humanized monoclonal antibody that binds to the extracellular domain II of the human epidermal growth factor receptor 2. It works in tandem with trastuzumab, blocking ligand-dependent HER2-HER3 dimerization and decreasing signaling through intracellular pathways such phosphatidylinositol 3-kinase (PI3K/Akt) (Tai et al., 2010)

Table 1 Oncology pharmacogenomics biomarkers and FDA approved drug—cont'd

Drug	Biomarker	Drug target
Ponatinib	BCR-ABL1 (Philadelphia chromosome)	BCR-ABL, an aberrant tyrosine kinase that is seen in CML, is the major target for ponatinib. Due to a genetic defect that produces the BCR-ABL protein, CML is characterized by an excessive and unregulated synthesis of white blood cells by the bone marrow (Tan et al., 2019)
Raloxifene	ESR (hormone receptor)	The activity of raloxifene is mediated by its ability to bind to estrogen receptors. In tissues that express estrogen receptors, this binding causes estrogenic pathways to be activated (estrogen-agonistic impact) or blocked (estrogen-antagonistic effect) (Raloxifene (Evista) for breast cancer prevention in postmenopausal women, 2006; Seeman, 2001)
Sacituzumab Govitecan-hziy	UGT1A1	Sacituzumab govitecan-hziy interacts to Trop-2-expressing cancer cells and is internalized, releasing SN-38 after the linker is hydrolyzed. SN-38 interacts with topoisomerase I and prevents topoisomerase I-induced single strand breaks from being re-ligated (Syed, 2020)
Talazoparib	BRCA, ERBB2 (HER2)	Talazoparib works by inhibiting PARP1/2 enzymes, which are important for detecting and repairing single-strand DNA damage; subsequent PARP entrapment, in which PARP proteins remain attached to a PARP inhibitor and to DNA, hinders DNA repair, replication, and transcription, and ultimately leads to death (Litton et al., 2018)
Thioguanine	TPMT	Thioguanine is an antimetabolite because it is a guanine analogue that affects DNA and RNA synthesis. Hypoxanthine-guanine phosphoribosyl transferase converts 6-thioguanine to 6-thioguanosine monophosphate, which is an analogue of purine guanine (Dreisig et al., 2021)
Toremifene	ESR (hormone receptor)	Toremifene has the ability to compete with estrogen for binding sites in the tumor, preventing estrogen's growth-stimulating actions (Song et al., 2021)

Continued

Table 1 Oncology pharmacogenomics biomarkers and FDA approved drug—cont'd

Drug	Biomarker	Drug target
Trastuzumab	ERBB2 (HER2), ESR	Trastuzumab suppresses the proliferation and survival of HER2-dependent cancers by binding to the extracellular juxtamembrane region of HER2. The Food and Drug Administration (FDA) has approved it for patients with aggressive breast cancer who overexpress HER2 (Li et al., 2022)
Tretinoin	PML-RARA	Tretinoin binds to the retinoic acid receptors alpha, beta, and gamma (RARs). Acute promyelocytic leukemia and squamous cell carcinoma have both been linked to RAR-alpha and RAR-beta, respectively. RAR-gamma is linked to the effects of retinoids on mucocutaneous tissues and bone (Yoham and Casadesus, 2022)
Tucatinib	ERBB2 (HER2)	Tucatinib is a HER2 tyrosine kinase inhibitor. In vivo and in vitro, it suppresses the growth of HER2-expressing tumor proteins. TUKYSA inhibits HER2 and HER3 protein phosphorylation, which inhibits downstream AKT and MAPK signaling and inhibits cell growth (Curigliano et al., 2022)
Vemurafenib	RAS	Vemurafenib is the first molecularly targeted medication to be approved for the treatment of advanced melanoma in the United States and Europe. It works by selectively inhibiting the mutant BRAF V600E kinase, resulting in decreased signaling via the abnormal mitogen-activated protein kinase (MAPK) pathway (Khaddour et al., 2022)
Vincristine	BCR–ABL1 (Philadelphia chromosome)	Vincristine is a chemotherapeutic medication that belongs to the vinca alkaloids family of medicines. Vincristine acts by preventing cancer cells from dividing and forming two new cells. As a result, the cancer's progress is halted (Skubnik et al., 2021)

3. Conclusion

Pharmacogenomics germline variation is frequent, and it can affect the efficacy and safety of anticancer treatments. There are a number of pharmacogenomics variations in particular that have been linked to an elevated risk of significant ADRs. Although few pharmacogenetics variants have been implemented into clinical practice, as genomics data becomes more widely available, there will be a growing need to consider pharmacogenetics variants, both common and rare, and whether they should be used to improve cancer treatment prescribing, including dose and drug choice. Obviously, this cannot be employed alone, but rather in conjunction with somatic genotypes and clinical variables (such as age, renal function, hepatic function, and concomitant drugs). Furthermore, certain medications may benefit from other technologies such as micro-biomics and therapeutic drug monitoring. This inevitably makes cancer treatment more complicated—though this may not be a problem in oncology because most doctors are already well-versed in sophisticated treatments. Nonetheless, computerized decision support systems will very certainly be required in the future to help with the reduction of prescribing errors and the integration of pharmacogenomics into clinical practice. While oncology is considered as the poster child for precision medicine, this is largely due to improved efficacy. In oncology, true precision medicine must include both efficacy and safety in the same patient.

Conflict of interest

Authors declare no conflict of interest.

References

Ahmed, S., Zhou, Z., Zhou, J., Chen, S.Q., 2016. Pharmacogenomics of drug metabolizing enzymes and transporters: relevance to precision medicine. Genomics Proteomics Bioinformatics 14, 298–313. https://doi.org/10.1016/j.gpb.2016.03.008.

Allen, P.B., Savas, H., Evens, A.M., Advani, R.H., Palmer, B., Pro, B., Karmali, R., Mou, E., Bearden, J., Dillehay, G., Bayer, R.A., Eisner, R.M., Chmiel, J.S., O'Shea, K., Gordon, L.I., Winter, J.N., 2021. Pembrolizumab followed by AVD in untreated early unfavorable and advanced-stage classical Hodgkin lymphoma. Blood 137, 1318–1326. https://doi.org/10.1182/blood.2020007400.

Alqathama, A., 2020. BRAF in malignant melanoma progression and metastasis: potentials and challenges. Am. J. Cancer Res. 10, 1103–1114.

Arends, R., Guo, X., Baverel, P.G., Gonzalez-Garcia, I., Xie, J., Morsli, N., Yovine, A., Roskos, L.K., 2021. Association of circulating protein biomarkers with clinical outcomes of durvalumab in head and neck squamous cell carcinoma. Oncoimmunology 10, 1898104. https://doi.org/10.1080/2162402X.2021.1898104.

Asadov, C., Aliyeva, G., Mustafayeva, K., 2017. Thiopurine S-methyltransferase as a pharmacogenetic biomarker: significance of testing and review of major methods. Cardiovasc. Hematol. Agents Med. Chem. 15, 23–30. https://doi.org/10.2174/1871525715666170529091921.

Atasilp, C., Chansriwong, P., Sirachainan, E., Reungwetwattana, T., Chamnanphon, M., Puangpetch, A., Wongwaisayawan, S., Sukasem, C., 2016. Correlation of UGT1A1(*)28 and (*)6 polymorphisms with irinotecan-induced neutropenia in Thai colorectal cancer patients. Drug Metab. Pharmacokinet. 31, 90–94. https://doi.org/10.1016/j.dmpk.2015.12.004.

Blay, J.Y., von Mehren, M., 2011. Nilotinib: a novel, selective tyrosine kinase inhibitor. Semin. Oncol. 38 (Suppl 1), S3–S9. https://doi.org/10.1053/j.seminoncol.2011.01.016.

Boer, K., 2017. Fulvestrant in advanced breast cancer: evidence to date and place in therapy. Ther. Adv. Med. Oncol. 9, 465–479. https://doi.org/10.1177/1758834017711097.

Bozovic, A., Mandusic, V., Todorovic, L., Krajnovic, M., 2021. Estrogen receptor beta: the promising bio-marker and potential target in metastases. Int. J. Mol. Sci. 22. https://doi.org/10.3390/ijms22041656.

Burnett, A.K., Russell, N.H., Hills, R.K., Bowen, D., Kell, J., Knapper, S., Morgan, Y.G., Lok, J., Grech, A., Jones, G., Khwaja, A., Friis, L., McMullin, M.F., Hunter, A., Clark, R.E., Grimwade, D., Group UKNCRIAMLW, 2015. Arsenic trioxide and all-trans retinoic acid treatment for acute promyelocytic leukaemia in all risk groups (AML17): results of a randomised, controlled, phase 3 trial. Lancet Oncol. 16, 1295–1305. https://doi.org/10.1016/S1470-2045(15)00193-X.

Carr, D.F., Turner, R.M., Pirmohamed, M., 2021. Pharmacogenomics of anticancer drugs: personalising the choice and dose to manage drug response. Br. J. Clin. Pharmacol. 87, 237–255. https://doi.org/10.1111/bcp.14407.

Chen, Y., Cai, C., Li, Y., 2021. The impact of baseline brain metastases on clinical benefits and progression patterns after first-line crizotinib in anaplastic lymphoma kinase-rearranged non-small cell lung cancer. Medicine (Baltimore) 100, e24784. https://doi.org/10.1097/MD.0000000000024784.

Cheng, Y., Tian, H., 2017. Current development status of MEK inhibitors. Molecules 22. https://doi.org/10.3390/molecules22101551.

Cortes, J., O'Shaughnessy, J., Loesch, D., Blum, J.L., Vahdat, L.T., Petrakova, K., Chollet, P., Manikas, A., Dieras, V., Delozier, T., Vladimirov, V., Cardoso, F., Koh, H., Bougnoux, P., Dutcus, C.E., Seegobin, S., Mir, D., Meneses, N., Wanders, J., Twelves, C., Investigators E, 2011. Eribulin mon-otherapy versus treatment of physician's choice in patients with metastatic breast cancer (EMBRACE): a phase 3 open-label randomised study. Lancet 377, 914–923. https://doi.org/10.1016/S0140-6736(11)60070-6.

Curigliano, G., Mueller, V., Borges, V., Hamilton, E., Hurvitz, S., Loi, S., Murthy, R., Okines, A., Paplomata, E., Cameron, D., Carey, L.A., Gelmon, K., Hortobagyi, G.N., Krop, I., Loibl, S., Pegram, M., Slamon, D., Ramos, J., Feng, W., Winer, E., 2022. Tucatinib versus placebo added to trastuzumab and capecitabine for patients with pretreated HER2+ metastatic breast cancer with and without brain metastases (HER2CLIMB): final overall survival analysis. Ann. Oncol. 33, 321–329. https://doi.org/10.1016/j.annonc.2021.12.005.

D'Angelo, A., Sobhani, N., Chapman, R., Bagby, S., Bortoletti, C., Traversini, M., Ferrari, K., Voltolini, L., Darlow, J., Roviello, G., 2020. Focus on ROS1-positive non-small cell lung cancer (NSCLC): crizotinib, resistance mechanisms and the newer generation of targeted therapies. Cancer 12. https://doi.org/10.3390/cancers12113293.

Davis, E.J., Chugh, R., 2017. Spotlight on olaratumab in the treatment of soft-tissue sarcoma: design, devel-opment, and place in therapy. Drug Des. Devel. Ther. 11, 3579–3587. https://doi.org/10.2147/DDDT.S121298.

Dreisig, K., Brunner, E.D., Marquart, H.V., Helt, L.R., Nersting, J., Frandsen, T.L., Jonsson, O.G., Taskinen, M., Vaitkeviciene, G., Lund, B., Abrahamsson, J., Lepik, K., Schmiegelow, K., 2021. TPMT polymorphisms and minimal residual disease after 6-mercaptopurine post-remission consolidation ther-apy of childhood acute lymphoblastic leukaemia. Pediatr. Hematol. Oncol. 38, 227–238. https://doi.org/10.1080/08880018.2020.1842570.

Dressler, L.G., 2012. Return of research results from pharmacogenomic versus disease susceptibility studies: what's drugs got to do with it? Pharmacogenomics 13, 935–949. https://doi.org/10.2217/pgs.12.59.

Drilon, A., Jenkins, C., Iyer, S., Schoenfeld, A., Keddy, C., Davare, M.A., 2021. ROS1-dependent cancers—biology, diagnostics and therapeutics. Nat. Rev. Clin. Oncol. 18, 35–55. https://doi.org/10.1038/s41571-020-0408-9.

Durmaz, A.A., Karaca, E., Demkow, U., Toruner, G., Schoumans, J., Cogulu, O., 2015. Evolution of genetic techniques: past, present, and beyond. Biomed. Res. Int. 2015, 461524. https://doi.org/10.1155/2015/461524.

Fujita, K., Kubota, Y., Ishida, H., Sasaki, Y., 2015. Irinotecan, a key chemotherapeutic drug for metastatic colorectal cancer. World J. Gastroenterol. 21, 12234–12248. https://doi.org/10.3748/wjg.v21.i43.12234.

Gonzalez, H., Hagerling, C., Werb, Z., 2018. Roles of the immune system in cancer: from tumor initiation to metastatic progression. Genes Dev. 32, 1267–1284. https://doi.org/10.1101/gad.314617.118.

Gottesdiener, L.S., O'Connor, S., Busam, K.J., Won, H., Solit, D.B., Hyman, D.M., Shoushtari, A.N., 2018. Rates of ERBB2 alterations across melanoma subtypes and a complete response to trastuzumab emtansine in an ERBB2-amplified acral melanoma. Clin. Cancer Res. 24, 5815–5819. https://doi.org/10.1158/1078-0432.CCR-18-1397.

Hattori, H., Ishikawa, Y., Kawashima, N., Akashi, A., Yamaguchi, Y., Harada, Y., Hirano, D., Adachi, Y., Miyao, K., Ushijima, Y., Terakura, S., Nishida, T., Matsushita, T., Kiyoi, H., 2018. Identification of the novel deletion-type PML-RARA mutation associated with the retinoic acid resistance in acute promyelocytic leukemia. PLoS One 13, e0204850. https://doi.org/10.1371/journal.pone.0204850.

Holla, V.R., Elamin, Y.Y., Bailey, A.M., Johnson, A.M., Litzenburger, B.C., Khotskaya, Y.B., Sanchez, N.S., Zeng, J., Shufean, M.A., Shaw, K.R., Mendelsohn, J., Mills, G.B., Meric-Bernstam, F., Simon, G.R., 2017. ALK: a tyrosine kinase target for cancer therapy. Cold Spring Harb. Mol. Case Stud. 3, a001115. https://doi.org/10.1101/mcs.a001115.

Horgan, D., Ciliberto, G., Conte, P., Baldwin, D., Seijo, L., Montuenga, L.M., Paz-Ares, L., Garassino, M., Penault-Llorca, F., Galli, F., Ray-Coquard, I., Querleu, D., Capoluongo, E., Banerjee, S., Riegman, P., Kerr, K., Horbach, B., Buttner, R., Van Poppel, H., Bjartell, A., Codacci-Pisanelli, G., Westphalen, B., Calvo, F., Koeva-Balabanova, J., Hall, S., Paradiso, A., Kalra, D., Cobbaert, C., Varea Menendez, R., Maravic, Z., Fotaki, V., Bennouna, J., Cauchin, E., Malats, N., Gutierrez-Ibarluzea, I., Gannon, B., Mastris, K., Bernini, C., Gallagher, W., Buglioni, S., Kent, A., Munzone, E., Belina, I., Van Meerbeeck, J., Duffy, M., Sarnowska, E., Jagielska, B., Mee, S., Curigliano, G., 2020. Bringing greater accuracy to Europe's healthcare systems: the unexploited potential of biomarker testing in oncology. Biomed. Hub 5, 182–223. https://doi.org/10.1159/000511209.

Ingle, J.N., Kalari, K.R., Buzdar, A.U., Robson, M.E., Goetz, M.P., Desta, Z., Barman, P., Dudenkov, T.T., Northfelt, D.W., Perez, E.A., Flockhart, D.A., Williard, C.V., Wang, L., Weinshilboum, R.M., 2015. Estrogens and their precursors in postmenopausal women with early breast cancer receiving anastrozole. Steroids 99, 32–38. https://doi.org/10.1016/j.steroids.2014.08.007.

Ippen, F.M., Alvarez-Breckenridge, C.A., Kuter, B.M., Fink, A.L., Bihun, I.V., Lastrapes, M., Penson, T., Schmidt, S.P., Wojtkiewicz, G.R., Ning, J., Subramanian, M., Giobbie-Hurder, A., Martinez-Lage, M., Carter, S.L., Cahill, D.P., Wakimoto, H., Brastianos, P.K., 2019a. The dual PI3K/mTOR pathway inhibitor GDC-0084 achieves antitumor activity in PIK3CA-mutant breast cancer brain metastases. Clin. Cancer Res. 25, 3374–3383. https://doi.org/10.1158/1078-0432.CCR-18-3049.

Ippen, F.M., Grosch, J.K., Subramanian, M., Kuter, B.M., Liederer, B.M., Plise, E.G., Mora, J.L., Nayyar, N., Schmidt, S.P., Giobbie-Hurder, A., Martinez-Lage, M., Carter, S.L., Cahill, D.P., Wakimoto, H., Brastianos, P.K., 2019b. Targeting the PI3K/Akt/mTOR pathway with the pan-Akt inhibitor GDC-0068 in PIK3CA-mutant breast cancer brain metastases. Neuro Oncol. 21, 1401–1411. https://doi.org/10.1093/neuonc/noz105.

Julia, E.P., Amante, A., Pampena, M.B., Mordoh, J., Levy, E.M., 2018. Avelumab, an IgG1 anti-PD-L1 immune checkpoint inhibitor, triggers NK cell-mediated cytotoxicity and cytokine production against triple negative breast cancer cells. Front. Immunol. 9, 2140. https://doi.org/10.3389/fimmu.2018.02140.

Kang, Z.J., Liu, Y.F., Xu, L.Z., Long, Z.J., Huang, D., Yang, Y., Liu, B., Feng, J.X., Pan, Y.J., Yan, J.S., Liu, Q., 2016. The Philadelphia chromosome in leukemogenesis. Chin. J. Cancer 35, 48. https://doi.org/10.1186/s40880-016-0108-0.

Khaddour, K., Kurn, H., Zito, P.M., 2022. Vemurafenib. StatPearls, Treasure Island, FL.

Krzyszczyk, P., Acevedo, A., Davidoff, E.J., Timmins, L.M., Marrero-Berrios, I., Patel, M., White, C., Lowe, C., Sherba, J.J., Hartmanshenn, C., O'Neill, K.M., Balter, M.L., Fritz, Z.R., Androulakis, I.P., Schloss, R.S., Yarmush, M.L., 2018. The growing role of precision and personalized medicine for cancer treatment. Technology (Singap. World Sci.) 6, 79–100. https://doi.org/10.1142/S2339547818300020.

Lee, N.H., 2010. Pharmacogenetics of drug metabolizing enzymes and transporters: effects on pharmacokinetics and pharmacodynamics of anticancer agents. Anticancer Agents Med Chem. 10, 583–592. https://doi.org/10.2174/187152010794474019.

Lee, L., Ito, T., Jensen, R.T., 2018. Everolimus in the treatment of neuroendocrine tumors: efficacy, side-effects, resistance, and factors affecting its place in the treatment sequence. Expert Opin. Pharmacother. 19, 909–928. https://doi.org/10.1080/14656566.2018.1476492.

Lennard, L., Cartwright, C.S., Wade, R., Vora, A., 2015. Thiopurine dose intensity and treatment outcome in childhood lymphoblastic leukaemia: the influence of thiopurine methyltransferase pharmacogenetics. Br. J. Haematol. 169, 228–240. https://doi.org/10.1111/bjh.13240.

Li, B.T., Shen, R., Buonocore, D., Olah, Z.T., Ni, A., Ginsberg, M.S., Ulaner, G.A., Offin, M., Feldman, D., Hembrough, T., Cecchi, F., Schwartz, S., Pavlakis, N., Clarke, S., Won, H.H., Brzostowski, E.B., Riely, G.J., Solit, D.B., Hyman, D.M., Drilon, A., Rudin, C.M., Berger, M.F., Baselga, J., Scaltriti, M., Arcila, M.E., Kris, M.G., 2018. Ado-trastuzumab emtansine for patients with HER2-mutant lung cancers: results from a phase II basket trial. J. Clin. Oncol. 36, 2532–2537. https://doi.org/10.1200/JCO.2018.77.9777.

Li, Y., Meng, Q., Yang, M., Liu, D., Hou, X., Tang, L., Wang, X., Lyu, Y., Chen, X., Liu, K., Yu, A.M., Zuo, Z., Bi, H., 2019. Current trends in drug metabolism and pharmacokinetics. Acta Pharm. Sin. B 9, 1113–1144. https://doi.org/10.1016/j.apsb.2019.10.001.

Li, B.T., Smit, E.F., Goto, Y., Nakagawa, K., Udagawa, H., Mazieres, J., Nagasaka, M., Bazhenova, L., Saltos, A.N., Felip, E., Pacheco, J.M., Perol, M., Paz-Ares, L., Saxena, K., Shiga, R., Cheng, Y., Acharyya, S., Vitazka, P., Shahidi, J., Planchard, D., Janne, P.A., Investigators, D.E.-L.T., 2022. Trastuzumab Deruxtecan in HER2-mutant non-small-cell lung cancer. N. Engl. J. Med. 386, 241–251. https://doi.org/10.1056/NEJMoa2112431.

Lin, J.J., Zhu, V.W., Schoenfeld, A.J., Yeap, B.Y., Saxena, A., Ferris, L.A., Dagogo-Jack, I., Farago, A.F., Taber, A., Traynor, A., Menon, S., Gainor, J.F., Lennerz, J.K., Plodkowski, A.J., Digumarthy, S.R., Ou, S.I., Shaw, A.T., Riely, G.J., 2018. Brigatinib in patients with Alectinib-refractory ALK-positive NSCLC. J. Thorac. Oncol. 13, 1530–1538. https://doi.org/10.1016/j.jtho.2018.06.005.

Lindpaintner, K., 2002. Pharmacogenetics and the future of medical practice. Br. J. Clin. Pharmacol. 54, 221–230. https://doi.org/10.1046/j.1365-2125.2002.01630.x.

Liquori, A., Ibanez, M., Sargas, C., Sanz, M.A., Barragan, E., Cervera, J., 2020. Acute promyelocytic leukemia: a constellation of molecular events around a single PML-RARA fusion gene. Cancer 12. https://doi.org/10.3390/cancers12030624.

Litton, J.K., Rugo, H.S., Ettl, J., Hurvitz, S.A., Goncalves, A., Lee, K.H., Fehrenbacher, L., Yerushalmi, R., Mina, L.A., Martin, M., Roche, H., Im, Y.H., Quek, R.G.W., Markova, D., Tudor, I.C., Hannah, A.L., Eiermann, W., Blum, J.L., 2018. Talazoparib in patients with advanced breast cancer and a germline BRCA mutation. N. Engl. J. Med. 379, 753–763. https://doi.org/10.1056/NEJMoa1802905.

Loriot, Y., Necchi, A., Park, S.H., Garcia-Donas, J., Huddart, R., Burgess, E., Fleming, M., Rezazadeh, A., Mellado, B., Varlamov, S., Joshi, M., Duran, I., Tagawa, S.T., Zakharia, Y., Zhong, B., Stuyckens, K., Santiago-Walker, A., De Porre, P., O'Hagan, A., Avadhani, A., Siefker-Radtke, A.O., Group BLCS, 2019. Erdafitinib in locally advanced or metastatic urothelial carcinoma. N. Engl. J. Med. 381, 338–348. https://doi.org/10.1056/NEJMoa1817323.

Masugi, Y., Nishihara, R., Yang, J., Mima, K., da Silva, A., Shi, Y., Inamura, K., Cao, Y., Song, M., Nowak, J.A., Liao, X., Nosho, K., Chan, A.T., Giannakis, M., Bass, A.J., Hodi, F.S., Freeman, G.J., Rodig, S., Fuchs, C.S., Qian, Z.R., Ogino, S., 2017. Tumour CD274 (PD-L1) expression and T cells in colorectal cancer. Gut 66, 1463–1473. https://doi.org/10.1136/gutjnl-2016-311421.

Anon., 2006. Raloxifene (Evista) for breast cancer prevention in postmenopausal women. Med. Lett. Drugs Ther. 48, 37.

Miura, K., Kinouchi, M., Ishida, K., Fujibuchi, W., Naitoh, T., Ogawa, H., Ando, T., Yazaki, N., Watanabe, K., Haneda, S., Shibata, C., Sasaki, I., 2010. 5-fu metabolism in cancer and orally-administrable 5-fu drugs. Cancer 2, 1717–1730. https://doi.org/10.3390/cancers2031717.

Montemorano, L., Lightfoot, M.D., Bixel, K., 2019. Role of Olaparib as maintenance treatment for ovarian cancer: the evidence to date. Onco. Targets. Ther. 12, 11497–11506. https://doi.org/10.2147/OTT.S195552.

Naz, S., Sowers, A., Choudhuri, R., Wissler, M., Gamson, J., Mathias, A., Cook, J.A., Mitchell, J.B., 2018. Abemaciclib, a selective CDK4/6 inhibitor, enhances the radiosensitivity of non-small cell lung cancer in vitro and in vivo. Clin. Cancer Res. 24, 3994–4005. https://doi.org/10.1158/1078-0432.CCR-17-3575.

Nelson, R.S., Seligson, N.D., Bottiglieri, S., Carballido, E., Cueto, A.D., Imanirad, I., Levine, R., Parker, A.S., Swain, S.M., Tillman, E.M., Hicks, J.K., 2021. UGT1A1 guided cancer therapy: review of the evidence and considerations for clinical implementation. Cancer 13. https://doi.org/10.3390/cancers13071566.

Nurwidya, F., Takahashi, F., Takahashi, K., 2016. Gefitinib in the treatment of nonsmall cell lung cancer with activating epidermal growth factor receptor mutation. J. Nat. Sci. Biol. Med. 7, 119–123. https://doi.org/10.4103/0976-9668.184695.

Ontario, H., 2020. Gene expression profiling tests for early-stage invasive breast cancer: a health technology assessment. Ont. Health Technol. Assess. Ser. 20, 1–234.

Pallet, N., Hamdane, S., Garinet, S., Blons, H., Zaanan, A., Paillaud, E., Taieb, J., Laprevote, O., Loriot, M.A., Narjoz, C., 2020. A comprehensive population-based study comparing the phenotype and genotype in a pretherapeutic screen of dihydropyrimidine dehydrogenase deficiency. Br. J. Cancer 123, 811–818. https://doi.org/10.1038/s41416-020-0962-z.

Quintas-Cardama, A., Cortes, J., 2009. Molecular biology of bcr-abl1-positive chronic myeloid leukemia. Blood 113, 1619–1630. https://doi.org/10.1182/blood-2008-03-144790.

Rolfo, C., Ruiz, R., Giovannetti, E., Gil-Bazo, I., Russo, A., Passiglia, F., Giallombardo, M., Peeters, M., Raez, L., 2015. Entrectinib: a potent new TRK, ROS1, and ALK inhibitor. Expert Opin. Investig. Drugs 24, 1493–1500. https://doi.org/10.1517/13543784.2015.1096344.

Rosskopf, S., Leitner, J., Zlabinger, G.J., Steinberger, P., 2019. CTLA-4 antibody ipilimumab negatively affects CD4(+) T-cell responses in vitro. Cancer Immunol. Immunother. 68, 1359–1368. https://doi.org/10.1007/s00262-019-02369-x.

Seeman, E., 2001. Raloxifene. J. Bone Miner. Metab. 19, 65–75. https://doi.org/10.1007/s007740170043.

Serra, F., Lapidari, P., Quaquarini, E., Tagliaferri, B., Sottotetti, F., Palumbo, R., 2019. Palbociclib in metastatic breast cancer: current evidence and real-life data. Drugs Context 8, 212579. https://doi.org/10.7573/dic.212579.

Shah, N.J., Kelly, W.J., Liu, S.V., Choquette, K., Spira, A., 2018. Product review on the anti-PD-L1 antibody atezolizumab. Hum. Vaccin. Immunother. 14, 269–276. https://doi.org/10.1080/21645515.2017.1403694.

Shaw, A.T., Bauer, T.M., de Marinis, F., Felip, E., Goto, Y., Liu, G., Mazieres, J., Kim, D.W., Mok, T., Polli, A., Thurm, H., Calella, A.M., Peltz, G., Solomon, B.J., Investigators, C.T., 2020. First-line Lorlatinib or Crizotinib in advanced ALK-positive lung cancer. N. Engl. J. Med. 383, 2018–2029. https://doi.org/10.1056/NEJMoa2027187.

Skubnik, J., Pavlickova, V.S., Ruml, T., Rimpelova, S., 2021. Vincristine in combination therapy of cancer: emerging trends in clinics. Biology 10. https://doi.org/10.3390/biology10090849.

Slagboom, P.E., Beekman, M., Passtoors, W.M., Deelen, J., Vaarhorst, A.A., Boer, J.M., van den Akker, E.B., van Heemst, D., de Craen, A.J., Maier, A.B., Rozing, M., Mooijaart, S.P., Heijmans, B.T., Westendorp, R.G., 2011. Genomics of human longevity. Philos. Trans. R. Soc. Lond. B Biol. Sci. 366, 35–42. https://doi.org/10.1098/rstb.2010.0284.

Somkrua, R., Eickman, E.E., Saokaew, S., Lohitnavy, M., Chaiyakunapruk, N., 2011. Association of HLA-B*5801 allele and allopurinol-induced stevens Johnson syndrome and toxic epidermal necrolysis: a systematic review and meta-analysis. BMC Med. Genet. 12, 118. https://doi.org/10.1186/1471-2350-12-118.

Song, D., Hu, Y., Diao, B., Miao, R., Zhang, B., Cai, Y., Zeng, H., Zhang, Y., Hu, X., 2021. Effects of tamoxifen vs. toremifene on fatty liver development and lipid profiles in breast cancer. BMC Cancer 21, 798. https://doi.org/10.1186/s12885-021-08538-5.

Stock, W., Martinelli, G., Stelljes, M., DeAngelo, D.J., Gokbuget, N., Advani, A.S., O'Brien, S., Liedtke, M., Merchant, A.A., Cassaday, R.D., Wang, T., Zhang, H., Vandendries, E., Jabbour, E., Marks, D.I., Kantarjian, H.M., 2021. Efficacy of inotuzumab ozogamicin in patients with Philadelphia chromosome-positive relapsed/refractory acute lymphoblastic leukemia. Cancer 127, 905–913. https://doi.org/10.1002/cncr.33321.

Subbiah, V., Kuravi, S., Ganguly, S., Welch, D.R., Vivian, C.J., Mushtaq, M.U., Hegde, A., Iyer, S., Behrang, A., Ali, S.M., Madison, R.W., Venstrom, J.M., Jensen, R.A., McGuirk, J.P., Amin, H.M., Balusu, R., 2021. Precision therapy with anaplastic lymphoma kinase inhibitor ceritinib in ALK-rearranged anaplastic large cell lymphoma. ESMO Open 6, 100172. https://doi.org/10.1016/j.esmoop.2021.100172.

Sundar, R., Cho, B.C., Brahmer, J.R., Soo, R.A., 2015. Nivolumab in NSCLC: latest evidence and clinical potential. Ther. Adv. Med. Oncol. 7, 85–96. https://doi.org/10.1177/1758834014567470.

Syed, Y.Y., 2020. Sacituzumab Govitecan: first approval. Drugs 80, 1019–1025. https://doi.org/10.1007/s40265-020-01337-5.

Tai, W., Mahato, R., Cheng, K., 2010. The role of HER2 in cancer therapy and targeted drug delivery. J. Control. Release 146, 264–275. https://doi.org/10.1016/j.jconrel.2010.04.009.

Tan, F.H., Putoczki, T.L., Stylli, S.S., Luwor, R.B., 2019. Ponatinib: a novel multi-tyrosine kinase inhibitor against human malignancies. Onco. Targets. Ther. 12, 635–645. https://doi.org/10.2147/OTT.S189391.

Tchounwou, P.B., Dasari, S., Noubissi, F.K., Ray, P., Kumar, S., 2021. Advances in our understanding of the molecular mechanisms of action of cisplatin in cancer therapy. J. Exp. Pharmacol. 13, 303–328. https://doi.org/10.2147/JEP.S267383.

Testa, U., Pelosi, E., Castelli, G., 2018. Colorectal cancer: genetic abnormalities, tumor progression, tumor heterogeneity, clonal evolution and tumor-initiating cells. Med. Sci. 6. https://doi.org/10.3390/medsci6020031.

Tomasini, P., Egea, J., Souquet-Bressand, M., Greillier, L., Barlesi, F., 2019. Alectinib in the treatment of ALK-positive metastatic non-small cell lung cancer: clinical trial evidence and experience with a focus on brain metastases. Ther. Adv. Respir. Dis. 13, 1753466619831906. https://doi.org/10.1177/1753466619831906.

Tymon-Rosario, J., Adjei, N.N., Roque, D.M., Santin, A.D., 2021. Microtubule-interfering drugs: current and future roles in epithelial ovarian cancer treatment. Cancer 13. https://doi.org/10.3390/cancers13246239.

van Staveren, M.C., Theeuwes-Oonk, B., Guchelaar, H.J., van Kuilenburg, A.B., Maring, J.G., 2011. Pharmacokinetics of orally administered uracil in healthy volunteers and in DPD-deficient patients, a possible tool for screening of DPD deficiency. Cancer Chemother. Pharmacol. 68, 1611–1617. https://doi.org/10.1007/s00280-011-1661-5.

Ventola, C.L., 2011. Pharmacogenomics in clinical practice: reality and expectations. PT 36, 412–450.

Vogel, F., 1959. Moderne problem der humangenetik. Ergeb. Inn. Med. U. Kinderheilk 12, 52–125. https://doi.org/10.2217/pgs-2017-0035.

Wang, L., 2010. Pharmacogenomics: a systems approach. Wiley Interdiscip. Rev. Syst. Biol. Med. 2, 3–22. https://doi.org/10.1002/wsbm.42.

Wang, D.G., Barrios, D.M., Blinder, V.S., Bromberg, J.F., Drullinsky, P.R., Funt, S.A., Jhaveri, K.L., Lake, D.E., Lyons, T., Modi, S., Razavi, P., Sidel, M., Traina, T.A., Vahdat, L.T., Lacouture, M.E., 2020. Dermatologic adverse events related to the PI3Kalpha inhibitor alpelisib (BYL719) in patients with breast cancer. Breast Cancer Res. Treat. 183, 227–237. https://doi.org/10.1007/s10549-020-05726-y.

Wetzler, M., Segal, D., 2011. Omacetaxine as an anticancer therapeutic: what is old is new again. Curr. Pharm. Des. 17, 59–64. https://doi.org/10.2174/138161211795049778.

Wheeler, H.E., Maitland, M.L., Dolan, M.E., Cox, N.J., Ratain, M.J., 2013. Cancer pharmacogenomics: strategies and challenges. Nat. Rev. Genet. 14, 23–34. https://doi.org/10.1038/nrg3352.

White, C., Scott, R.J., Paul, C., Ziolkowski, A., Mossman, D., Ackland, S., 2021. Ethnic diversity of DPD activity and the DPYD gene: review of the literature. Pharmgenomics Pers. Med. 14, 1603–1617. https://doi.org/10.2147/PGPM.S337147.

Woodfield, S.E., Zhang, L., Scorsone, K.A., Liu, Y., Zage, P.E., 2016. Binimetinib inhibits MEK and is effective against neuroblastoma tumor cells with low NF1 expression. BMC Cancer 16, 172. https://doi.org/10.1186/s12885-016-2199-z.

Yan, K., Lu, Y., Yan, Z., Wang, Y., 2021. 9-gene signature correlated with CD8(+) T cell infiltration activated by IFN-gamma: a biomarker of immune checkpoint therapy response in melanoma. Front. Immunol. 12, 622563. https://doi.org/10.3389/fimmu.2021.622563.

Yang, J.C., Chang, N., Wu, D.C., Cheng, W.C., Chung, W.M., Chang, W.C., Lei, F.J., Liu, C.J., Wu, I.C., Lai, H.C., Ma, W.L., 2019. Preclinical evaluation of exemestane as a novel chemotherapy for gastric cancer. J. Cell. Mol. Med. 23, 7417–7426. https://doi.org/10.1111/jcmm.14605.

Yang, F., Paccaly, A.J., Rippley, R.K., Davis, J.D., DiCioccio, A.T., 2021. Population pharmacokinetic characteristics of cemiplimab in patients with advanced malignancies. J. Pharmacokinet. Pharmacodyn. 48, 479–494. https://doi.org/10.1007/s10928-021-09739-y.

Yasar, P., Ayaz, G., User, S.D., Gupur, G., Muyan, M., 2017. Molecular mechanism of estrogen-estrogen receptor signaling. Reprod. Med. Biol. 16, 4–20. https://doi.org/10.1002/rmb2.12006.

Yoham, A.L., Casadesus, D., 2022. Tretinoin. StatPearls, Treasure Island, FL.

CHAPTER THIRTEEN

Obesity: Emerging risk factor for cancer beyond metabolic syndrome

Indu Sharma[a], Anuradha Sharma[a], Puneet Bhardwaj[a], and R.C. Sobti[b]
[a]Department of Zoology, Panjab University, Chandigarh, India
[b]Department of Biotechnology, Panjab University, Chandigarh, India

1. Introduction

Obesity, a situation characterized by a body mass index (BMI) ≥ 30, is the most blatantly visible—yet most neglected health challenge faced by the 21st century. It develops when exceeding energy consumption overtakes energy expenditure of body leading to increased fat accumulation. Earlier considered a high-income country problem, it is now prevailing in low- and middle-income countries also. In 2016, more than 1.9 billion adults, 18 years and older, were found to be overweight. Of these over 650 million were obese (World Health Organization, 2021). The health risks associated with obesity include many chronic diseases like hypertension, dyslipidemia, Mets, diabetes mellitus (DM) type 2, cardiovascular diseases (CVD), nonalcoholic fatty liver disease (NAFLD), and cancer (Upadhyay et al., 2018). The prevalence of overweight and obesity has been expanded dramatically in almost all developing and developed countries, reaching pandemic levels of 60%–70% in the adult population in industrialized countries and being more frequent in females of urban areas (Kelly et al., 2008). Not only being an established risk factor for various types of malignancies, obesity also leads to poor prognosis, delayed treatment outcome, and increased cancer-related mortality. The most commonly mutated PI3K/Akt/mTOR pathway involved in cancer progression is activated by obesity-associated factors like insulin, IGF-1, leptin, and adiponectin, and therefore acts as a bridge between the two diseases (Moore et al., 2008). The current therapeutic interventions mainly emphasize on chemotherapy and radiotherapy for obese cancer patients. However, doses of chemotherapeutic drugs to be administered are usually estimated according to the patient's actual body weight which raises the concern of relative overdosing in the obese cancer patients. Therefore, more elaborative understanding of the molecular players linking obesity to cancer, is needed to mitigate the damage. In this review, we will elucidate the link between obesity and cancer synopsizing the main biological mechanisms behind this association.

Biomarkers in Cancer Detection and Monitoring of Therapeutics
https://doi.org/10.1016/B978-0-323-95116-6.00020-7

2. Epidemiologic evidences supporting the link between obesity and cancer

Several studies have shown that obesity is associated with increased risk of several cancer types, including colon, endometrium, postmenopausal breast, kidney, esophagus, pancreas, gallbladder, liver, and hematological malignancy. On an average, 20% cancer cases are caused by excess body weight (Wolin et al., 2010). Potential routes guiding the obesity-related cancer risk include growth factors, modulation of energy balance and calorie restriction, multiple signaling pathways, and inflammatory processes. The profusely present fat tissue secretes two most abundant polypeptide hormones (adipokines), leptin and adiponectin which are known to be involved in cancer development (Kershaw and Flier, 2004). Leptin is considered to be protumorigenic and proangiogenic as it is known to promote proliferation in breast epithelial cells via estrogen and STAT3 signaling, MAPKs activation, and inhibition of apoptosis via AKT signaling (Delort et al., 2015).

Adiponectin, on the other hand, has negative correlation with adiposity, hyperinsulinemia, and inflammation. It activates 5 AMP-activated protein kinase (AMPK) and hence downregulates insulin/insulin-like growth factor (IGF)-1 and mTOR signaling. Further, anticancerous and antiinflammatory effects are exerted via the inhibition of nuclear factor kappa-light-chain-enhancer of activated B cells (NF-B) (Dalamaga et al., 2012).

Emerging data supports the presence of high body fat in late adolescence and early adulthood leading to malignancy risk at an older age. This is well established now that excess body weight leads to an increased risk for cancer of at least 13 anatomic sites, including endometrial, esophageal, renal, pancreatic, hepatocellular, gastric carcinoma, colorectal, postmenopausal breast, ovarian, gallbladder and thyroid cancers (Avgerinos et al., 2019) (Fig. 1).

3. Effect of weight gain and weight loss paradigm in regulating cancer risk

Weight gain and weight loss, both are crucial for regulating the risk of developing cancer as well as to monitor the survival among cancer patients. Weight gain comes with increased adiposity which leads to upregulated levels of proinflammatory cytokines, like prostaglandin E2, TNF-α, IL-2, IL-8, IL-10, and monocyte chemoattractant protein (MCP)-1 (Vucenik and Stains, 2012). Adult weight gain also elevates the cancer risk, particularly for esophageal, colorectal (especially in men), pancreatic, liver, gallbladder (in women), renal, postmenopausal breast, endometrial, ovarian, and advanced stage prostate cancers, based on data of the WCRF project (Keum et al., 2015). Intentionally losing weight and keeping it off has been related with lower risk of cancer, particularly

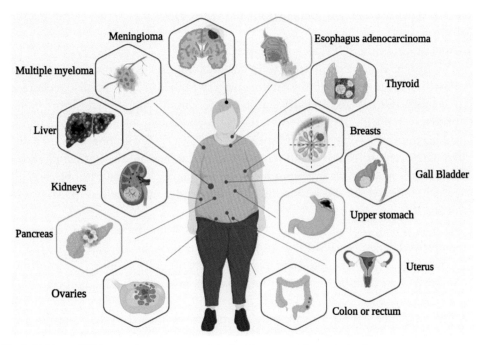

Fig. 1 Thirteen (13) types of cancers associated with overweight and obesity.

obesity associated cancers in women, highlighting the link between excess body weight and cancer risk (Luo et al., 2019). The inflammatory markers of cancer have been found to be reduced twofold to fourfold with weight loss. Similarly, estradiol, a causal mediator of cancer is also known to be substantially reduced in circulation following weight loss (Byers and Sedjo, 2011). The data obtained from randomized and nonrandomized control trials revealed that the risk of obesity associated cancers decreased significantly after bariatric surgery done for weight loss (Casagrande et al., 2014). Several observational studies conducted on humans have reported increased mortality in obese cancer and type 2 diabetes patients, which may be the result of either hyperinsulinemia or increased IGF-1. On the other hand, the patients having low insulin, IGF-1, and IGF-2 levels seem to be comparatively more protected from cancer risks than the former ones (Gallagher and LeRoith, 2011).

4. Pathophysiology of obesity mediated cancer

The triad comprising overweight/obesity, IR, and adipocytokines is regularly seen to be associated with increased cancer risk in numerous cohort studies. Although the correlation between obesity and cancer is significant, yet the underlying molecular and cellular mechanisms remain hidden from the light. However, some of the plausible mechanisms include:

(a) Aberrations in the IGF-I axis and hyperinsulinemia

The Insulin-like growth factor (IGF) system comprises growth factors: IGF-I and IGF-II, 6 specific high-affinity binding proteins: IGFBP-1 to IGFBP-6, cell surface receptors: IGF-IR and IGF-IIR, proteases for Insulin-like growth factor-binding proteins (IGFBP), and numerous IGFBP-interacting molecules which regulate IGF actions in several tissues (Chaves and Saif, 2011). IGFs along with their IGF-binding proteins (IGFBPs) and receptors not only regulate the normal physiology of growth, metabolism and reproduction but also play a crucial pathophysiological role in obesity, insulin resistance and type 2 diabetes mellitus (DM) (Lewitt et al., 2014).

Considering increased levels of IGF-2 in circulation in colorectal cancer and suppressed activity of IGFBP-5 in osteosarcoma, it becomes evident that the IGF axis serves as the key modulator to study mechanisms of neoplasia. Current non-surgical forms of cancer treatment including chemotherapy and radiotherapy show poor outcome in certain cases owing to the resistance developed by the tumor cells. This resistance has been recurrently deemed to be caused by IGF signaling. For example, the crosstalk between IGF-1R and estrogen receptor (ER) serves as the key player in progression of breast cancer in ER+ cases even after antiestrogen therapy (Massarweh et al., 2008).

High *IGF1R* mRNA levels were recorded in 21 tumor tissue samples examined in The Cancer Genome Atlas (TCGA), isolated from patients of breast, ovary, prostate, head and neck cancer; squamous-cell lung cancer (SCLC); and melanoma (Farabaugh et al., 2015). Insulin and IGF induce a multitude of tumor-promoting effects like proliferation, antiapoptosis, angiogenesis and lymph angiogenesis (Brahmkhatri et al., 2015) through the cascade of cellular events, including downstream transduction through the phosphatidylinositol 3-kinase (PI3K)–AKT– mammalian target of rapamycin (mTOR) pathway regulating cell growth and differentiation, and the Ras–Raf–MEK–Mitogen-Activated Protein Kinase (MAPK) pathway that induces proliferation (Yakar and Adamo, 2012) (Fig. 2).

In case of glioma which accounts for nearly 30% of all central nervous tumors, chemotherapy is not fruitful due to the immediate resistance developed by the tumor, while cancer stem cells hinder the radiotherapeutic treatment. This hindrance is further enhanced by the IGF signaling via upregulation of both IGF1 and IGF-1R (Osuka et al., 2013). Type 2 DM has been shown to cause a consistent elevation in the risk of pancreatic, biliary tract, and esophageal cancer in men; breast and endometrial cancer (EC) in women; and kidney, liver and colorectal cancer in both genders (Avgerinos et al., 2019).

IGF as well as IGF receptors are highly expressed in many types of cancers. Insulin receptor exists in two splice variants, Insulin Receptor-A (IR-A) and IR-B. In

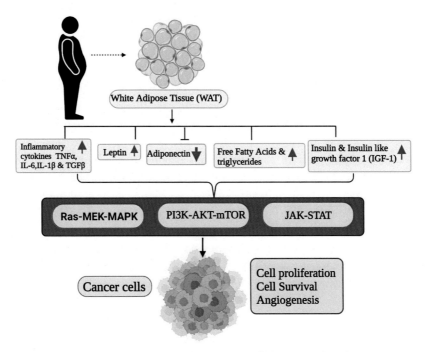

Fig. 2 The factors and pathways involved in progression of obesity mediated cancer.

tumors, aberrant signaling leads to an increase in *IRA:IRB* ratio which further imparts more aggressive characteristics to several cancer types (Nevado et al., 2006). The significance of insulin receptor has been demonstrated by a study where overexpressing IRA was found to enhance the growth of human RL95–2 endometrial cancer xenografts in nude mice through augmented activation of AKT signaling compared to control cell (Wang et al., 2013).

(b) Role of sex hormones in cancer development:

Biological sex impacts the trajectory of disease pathogenesis in many cases. Sex steroid hormones mainly comprise androgens and estrogen, the former having cholesterol as the precursor. Leptin levels are higher in females as compared to males before puberty. After puberty, estrogens and testosterone further enhance the leptin synthesis and secretion via sex steroid receptor-dependent transcriptional mechanisms (Machinal et al., 1999). In premenopausal women, the estradiol levels get slightly influenced by obesity which on the other hand deeply effects the menstrual cycles causing reduced progesterone levels. These alterations enhance the risk for endometrial cancer but decrease the risk for breast cancer. Later, in postmenopausal stage, when estradiol levels are not regulated by negative feedback, obesity leads to upregulation of serum levels of estradiol; which further increases in the risk for both endometrial cancer and breast cancer (Key et al., 2001). The crucial role of estrogen is strengthened by the fact that the risk of obesity-associated breast cancer is higher in hormone receptor positive (ER+/PR+) postmenopausal women having no history of hormone replacement (Gravena et al., 2018).

Similarly, the androgens regulate the progression of prostate cancer. The development of cancerous prostate from normal one depends on the balance between androgen induced cell proliferation and apoptosis. Normal prostate is characterized by steady balance between synthesis and inactivation of active androgens while increased synthesis or decreased inactivation of androgens can lead to excessive androgen influence and increased cell proliferation, hence prostate cancer (Soronen et al., 2004). Elevated blood concentrations of androgens have been associated with increased risk of breast cancer in women regardless of menopausal status (Dimitrakakis and Bondy, 2009).

The Endogenous Hormones and Breast Cancer Collaborative Group (EHBCCG) observed the decreased concentrations of sex hormone binding globulin (SHBG) associated with augmented risk of breast cancer in postmenopausal women (Hormones et al., 2013). Estrogen promotes tumorigenesis in endometrial tissue by stimulation of cell proliferation and inhibition of apoptosis. These effects are mediated by the induction of IGF1 production in endometrial tissue which acts on the endometrium in a paracrine manner (Shaw et al., 2016). Progesterone, on the other hand, opposes estrogen effects mainly by stimulating the production of IGF1 binding protein which, in turn, inhibits IGF1 (Christopoulos et al., 2015).

Testosterone exhibits a bimodal relationship as it is found to be elevated in obese women but decreased in obese men. The low testosterone environment in obese men seems to promote the development of a less differentiated but more aggressive cancer phenotype as seen in prostate cancer (Severi et al., 2006; Giovannucci and Michaud, 2007).

(c) Inflammation: a bridge between obesity and cancer

Chronic inflammation constitutes an established mediator of cancer development and progression as many inflammatory components are found abundantly in the tumor microenvironment and promote a cancerous phenotype (Coussens and Werb, 2002). When comparing obese subjects with or without adipose inflammation and metabolic dysfunction, the former exhibits elevated cancer and cardiovascular disease risk (Van Guilder et al., 2006). White adipose tissue (WAT), a major component of the adipose tissue is considered to be a metabolically active endocrine organ. It releases a variety of adipocytokines in the bloodstream, the more important being adiponectin and leptin. Visceral obesity and excessive ectopic fat distribution are strongly associated with hypoadiponectinemia (Chait and den Hartigh, 2020). Adiponectinemia has an inverse correlation with inflammatory cytokines such as tumor necrosis factor-α (TNF-α) and interleukin (IL)-6, usually elevated in obesity. Leptin levels positively correlate with BMI and adipose tissue mass (Makki et al., 2013). Contrary to adiponectin, leptin exerts proinflammatory actions by stimulating the production of IL-1, 6, 12, TNF-α, Leukotriene B4 (LTB-4) and COX-2 while enhancing the T cell proliferation and TH1 phenotype and suppressing regulatory T cells (Carbone et al., 2012).

Hypoadiponectinemia has been observed in a multitude of malignancies, confirming its tumor suppressive role (Dalamaga et al., 2012). Beside their direct effect on tissues, inflammatory adipocytokines influence the sex hormone mechanism of tumorigenesis via stimulation of estrogen production by aromatase. Tumor progression in obesity-related malignancies involves insulin resistance, which in turn produces chronic low-grade inflammation by generating inflammatory cytokines such as TNF-α, IL-6, leptin and MCP-1 which further stimulates cancer progression (Giovannucci et al., 2010). The inflammatory environment of obesity has been observed to be reduced after weight loss; as evidenced by reduction of subcutaneous adipose tissue inflammation observed in patients who undergo bariatric surgery to achieve decreased BMI (Hagman et al., 2017).

Hyperglycemia along with elevated free fatty acid levels induce reactive oxygen species (ROS) production and the secretion of proinflammatory cytokines that additively provoke mitochondrial and DNA damage (Dikalov and Nazarewicz, 2013). The effect of inflammation-combating medication on obesity-related cancer is an ongoing research question.

(d) Irregularity in adipocytokine levels

The adipocyte-rich tumor microenvironment offers an easily accessible and vast reservoir of lipids to support the high energy requirements of cancer cells. The extent of adipose tissue invasion serves as the marker for tumor aggressiveness in many cancer cases and higher value indicates poor prognosis. The obesity-related swift cell proliferation and growth of adipose tissue induces hypoxia which instigates the development of compensatory angiogenesis, in order to meet the nutrient and oxygen supply requirements. This condition disrupts the balance between normal leptin and adiponectin levels, which in combination with factors like infiltration of macrophages, mitochondrial dysfunction and increased endoplasmic reticulum (ER) stress response, may be associated with promotion of cancers such as colorectal cancer in obese individuals (Avgerinos et al., 2019). Another study by Uddin et al. (2009) demonstrated a direct role of leptin in the growth and survival of ovarian cancer cells in vitro; however, further in vivo studies are required to clearly understand the mechanism. Adiponectin was found to inhibit the leptin-induced proliferation of hepatocellular tumor cells through decreased activation of Stat3. This was further confirmed by significantly reduced leptin-induced tumor burden in a nude mice xenograft model after adiponectin treatment (Sharma et al., 2010).

5. Prevention and treatment

Obesity causes a lethal threat to cancer survivors also, depending on the tumor site, due to the presence of abundant insulin receptors. Recent research being carried out in case of colon cancer patients emphasizes on the interaction between obesity and oncoprotein-18 also known as Stathmin (STMN1). It has been seen that the adverse effect of BMI in colon cancer patients were confined to the STMN1$^+$ patients only (Ogino et al., 2009). This further necessitates the need to tackle the problem of obesity at initial stages so that one doesn't have to deal with the obesity-related malignancy problems in future.

Several studies have reported that T2DM patients undergoing metformin treatment had a lower chance of developing cancer than their counterparts taking other medications like insulin etc. (Evans et al., 2005). Metformin works by targeting the enzyme AMP-activated protein kinase (AMPK) which has an upstream regulator; a protein kinase known as LKB1. LKB1 is a well-known tumor suppressor (Lizcano et al., 2004). Other plausible mechanisms underlying the protective effects of metformin may include hindering cancer cell growth, downregulating the overexpression of ErbB-2 oncoprotein, and inhibition of mammalian target of rapamycin (Alimova et al., 2009).

For past several years, the effect of exercise and physical activity on tumor initiation and progression has been a topic of controversy. There is strong evidence that higher levels of physical activity are linked to lower risk of several types of cancer since the etiology of most cancers depend on the interaction between genetic, environmental and lifestyle factors. Therefore, lifestyle changes may help in improving survival chances in cancer patients. McTiernan and coworkers in their systematic review, analyzed the findings of Physical Activity Guidelines Advisory Committee (PAGAC), 2018 on individual cancers and reported strong or moderate association between increased physical activity and reduced cancer risk (McTiernan et al., 2019) (Fig. 3).

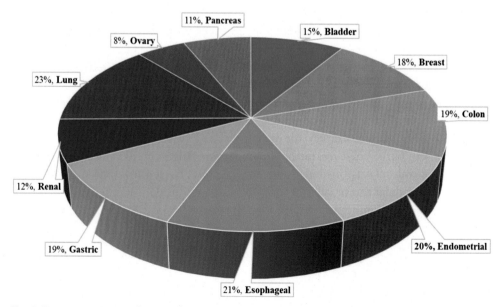

Fig. 3 Representative pie diagram showing approximate percent risk reduction of developing cancer relative to physical activity.

6. Conclusion

Obesity is one of the most important factors causing cancer mortality and is associated with a worse clinical outcome. From a public health aspect, tackling obesity offers the opportunity to prevent an important number of chronic noncommunicable diseases, including cardiovascular diseases, with the same panel of public health interventions. The most important preventive measures for obesity associated cancers are based on lifestyle modification, diets leading to weight loss, medical nutrition therapy and bariatric surgery. A significant percentage of cancer cases may become preventable through quitting smoking, maintaining a healthy weight, following a diet with nuts, fruits, vegetables and olive oil, increasing physical exercise and decreasing alcohol intake dietary patterns rich in vegetables, fruits, nuts, olive oil, fibers, wholegrains, and low in processed food are associated with decreased cancer incidence and mortality. In summary, there is evidence for a strong connection between obesity-driven chronic inflammation, insulin resistance, adipokines, altered microbiome and cancer. Further basic and translational research is essential to identify the causal mechanisms of obesity-associated cancers and to design new clinical regimens that reduce the ferocity of obesity-induced health damage.

References

Alimova, I.N., Liu, B., Fan, Z., Edgerton, S.M., Dillon, T., Lind, S.E., Thor, A.D., 2009. Metformin inhibits breast cancer cell growth, colony formation and induces cell cycle arrest in vitro. Cell Cycle 8 (6), 909–915.

Avgerinos, K.I., Spyrou, N., Mantzoros, C.S., Dalamaga, M., 2019. Obesity and cancer risk: emerging biological mechanisms and perspectives. Metabolism 92, 121–135.

Brahmkhatri, V.P., Prasanna, C., Hanudatta, S.A., 2015. Insulin-like growth factor system in cancer: novel targeted therapies. Biomed. Res. Int. 2015, 538019.

Byers, T., Sedjo, R.L., 2011. Does intentional weight loss reduce cancer risk? Diabetes Obes. Metab. 13 (12), 1063–1072.

Carbone, F., La Rocca, C., Matarese, G., 2012. Immunological functions of leptin and adiponectin. Biochimie 94 (10), 2082–2088.

Casagrande, D.S., Rosa, D.D., Umpierre, D., Sarmento, R.A., Rodrigues, C.G., Schaan, B.D., 2014. Incidence of cancer following bariatric surgery: systematic review and meta-analysis. Obes. Surg. 24 (9), 1499–1509.

Chait, A., den Hartigh, L.J., 2020. Adipose tissue distribution, inflammation and its metabolic consequences, including diabetes and cardiovascular disease. Front. Cardiovasc. Med. 7, 22.

Chaves, J., Saif, M.W., 2011. IGF system in cancer: from bench to clinic. Anti-Cancer Drugs 22 (3), 206–212.

Christopoulos, P.F., Msaouel, P., Koutsilieris, M., 2015. The role of the insulin-like growth factor-1 system in breast cancer. Mol. Cancer 14, 43.

Coussens, L.M., Werb, Z., 2002. Inflammation and cancer. Nature 420 (6917), 860–867. https://doi.org/10.1038/nature01322.

Dalamaga, M., Diakopoulos, K.N., Mantzoros, C.S., 2012. The role of adiponectin in cancer: a review of current evidence. Endocr. Rev. 33 (4), 547–594.

Delort, L., Rossary, A., Farges, M.C., Vasson, M.P., Caldefie-Chezet, F., 2015. Leptin, adipocytes and breast cancer: focus on inflammation and anti-tumor immunity. Life Sci. 140, 37–48.

Dikalov, S.I., Nazarewicz, R.R., 2013. Angiotensin II-induced production of mitochondrial reactive oxygen species: potential mechanisms and relevance for cardiovascular disease. Antioxid. Redox Signal. 19 (10), 1085–1094.

Dimitrakakis, C., Bondy, C., 2009. Androgens and the breast. Breast Cancer Res. 11 (5), 212.

Evans, J.M., Donnelly, L.A., Emslie-Smith, A.M., Alessi, D.R., Morris, A.D., 2005. Metformin and reduced risk of cancer in diabetic patients. BMJ 330 (7503), 1304–1305.

Farabaugh, S.M., Boone, D.N., Lee, A.V., 2015. Role of IGF1R in breast cancer subtypes, stemness, and lineage differentiation. Front. Endocrinol. 6, 59.

Gallagher, E.J., LeRoith, D., 2011. Minireview: IGF, insulin, and cancer. Endocrinology 152, 2546–2551.

Giovannucci, E., Michaud, D., 2007. The role of obesity and related metabolic disturbances in cancers of the colon, prostate, and pancreas. Gastroenterology 132 (6), 2208–2225.

Giovannucci, E., Harlan, D.M., Archer, M.C., Bergenstal, R.M., Gapstur, S.M., Habel, L.A., Pollak, M., Regensteiner, J.G., Yee, D., 2010. Diabetes and cancer: a consensus report. Diabetes Care 33, 1674–1685.

Gravena, A.A.F., Lopes, T.C.R., de Oliveira Demitto, M., Borghesan, D.H.P., Dell'Agnolo, C.M., Brischiliari, S.C.R., Pelloso, S.M., 2018. The obesity and the risk of breast cancer among pre and post-menopausal women. Asian Pac. J. Cancer Prev. 19 (9), 2429.

Hagman, D.K., Larson, I., Kuzma, J.N., Cromer, G., Makar, K., Rubinow, K.B., Foster-Schubert, K.E., van Yserlo, B., Billing, P.S., Landerholme, R.W., Crouthamel, M., Flum, D.R., Cummings, D.E., Kratz, M., 2017. The short-term and long-term effects of bariatric/metabolic surgery on subcutaneous adipose tissue inflammation in humans. Metabolism 70, 12–22.

Hormones, E., Key, T.J., Reeves, P.N.G.K., Travis, R.C., Alberg, A.J., Barricarte, A., et al., 2013. Sex hormones and risk of breast cancer in premenopausal women: a collaborative reanalysis of individual participant data from seven prospective studies. Lancet Oncol. 14, 1009–1019.

Kelly, T., Yang, W., Chen, C.S., Reynolds, K., He, J., 2008. Global burden of obesity in 2005 and projections to 2030. Int. J. Obes. 32 (9), 1431–1437.

Kershaw, E.E., Flier, J.S., 2004. Adipose tissue as an endocrine organ. J. Clin. Endocrinol. Metab. 89, 2548–2556.

Keum, N., Greenwood, D.C., Lee, D.H., Kim, R., Aune, D., Ju, W., Hu, F.B., Giovannucci, E.L., 2015. Adult weight gain and adiposity-related cancers: a dose-response meta-analysis of prospective observational studies. J. Natl. Cancer Inst. 107 (2), djv088.

Key, T., Allen, N., Verkasalo, P., Banks, E., 2001. Energy balance and cancer: the role of sex hormones. Proc. Nutr. Soc. 60 (1), 81–89.

Lewitt, M.S., Dent, M.S., Hall, K., 2014. The insulin-like growth factor system in obesity, insulin resistance and type 2 diabetes mellitus. J. Clin. Med. 3 (4), 1561–1574.

Lizcano, J.M., Göransson, O., Toth, R., Deak, M., Morrice, N.A., Boudeau, J., Hawley, S.A., Udd, L., Mäkelä, T.P., Hardie, D.G., Alessi, D.R., 2004. LKB1 is a master kinase that activates 13 kinases of the AMPK subfamily, including MARK/PAR-1. EMBO J. 23 (4), 833–843.

Luo, J., Hendryx, M., Manson, J.E., Figueiredo, J.C., LeBlanc, E.S., Barrington, W., Rohan, T.E., Howard, B.V., Reding, K., Ho, G.Y., Garcia, D.O., Chlebowski, R.T., 2019. Intentional weight loss and obesity-related cancer risk. JNCI Cancer Spectr. 3 (4), pkz054.

Machinal, F., Dieudonne, M.N., Leneveu, M.C., Pecquery, R., Giudicelli, Y., 1999. In vivo and in vitro ob gene expression and leptin secretion in rat adipocytes: evidence for a regional specific regulation by sex steroid hormones. Endocrinology 140 (4), 1567–1574.

Makki, K., Froguel, P., Wolowczuk, I., 2013. Adipose tissue in obesity-related inflammation and insulin resistance: cells, cytokines, and chemokines. ISRN Inflamm. 2013, 139239. https://doi.org/10.1155/2013/139239.

Massarweh, S., Osborne, C.K., Creighton, C.J., Qin, L., Tsimelzon, A., Huang, S., Weiss, H., Rimawi, M., Schiff, R., 2008. Tamoxifen resistance in breast tumors is driven by growth factor receptor signaling with repression of classic estrogen receptor genomic function. Cancer Res. 68 (3), 826–833.

McTiernan, A., Friedenreich, C.M., Katzmarzyk, P.T., Powell, K.E., Macko, R., Buchner, D., Pescatello, L.S., Bloodgood, B., Tennant, B., Vaux-Bjerke, A., George, S.M., Troiano, R.P., Piercy, K.L., 2018 PHYSICAL ACTIVITY GUIDELINES ADVISORY COMMITTEE*, 2019. Physical activity in cancer prevention and survival: a systematic review. Med. Sci. Sports Exerc. 51 (6), 1252–1261.

Moore, T., Beltran, L., Carbajal, S., Strom, S., Traag, J., Hursting, S.D., DiGiovanni, J., 2008. Dietary energy balance modulates signaling through the Akt/mammalian target of rapamycin pathways in multiple epithelial tissues. Cancer Prev. Res. 1 (1), 65–76.

Nevado, C., Valverde, A.M., Benito, M., 2006. Role of insulin receptor in the regulation of glucose uptake in neonatal hepatocytes. Endocrinology 147, 3709–3718.

Ogino, S., Nosho, K., Baba, Y., Kure, S., Shima, K., Irahara, N., Toyoda, S., Chen, L., Kirkner, G.J., Wolpin, B.M., Chan, A.T., Giovannucci, E.L., Fuchs, C.S., 2009. A cohort study of STMN1 expression in colorectal cancer: body mass index and prognosis. Am. J. Gastroenterol. 104 (8), 2047–2056.

Osuka, S., Sampetrean, O., Shimizu, T., Saga, I., Onishi, N., Sugihara, E., Okubo, J., Fujita, S., Takano, S., Matsumura, A., Saya, H., 2013. IGF1 receptor signaling regulates adaptive radioprotection in glioma stem cells. Stem Cells 31 (4), 627–640.

Severi, G., Morris, H.A., MacInnis, R.J., English, D.R., Tilley, W., Hopper, J.L., Boyle, P., Giles, G.G., 2006. Circulating steroid hormones and the risk of prostate cancer. Cancer Epidemiol. Biomark. Prev. 15 (1), 86–91.

Sharma, D., Wang, J., Fu, P.P., Sharma, S., Nagalingam, A., Mells, J., Handy, J., Page, A.J., Cohen, C., Anania, F.A., Saxena, N.K., 2010. Adiponectin antagonizes the oncogenic actions of leptin in hepatocellular carcinogenesis. Hepatology 52 (5), 1713–1722.

Shaw, E., Farris, M., McNeil, J., Friedenreich, C., 2016. Obesity and endometrial cancer. Recent Results Cancer Res. 208, 107–136.

Soronen, P., Laiti, M., Törn, S., Härkönen, P., Patrikainen, L., Li, Y., Pulkka, A., Kurkela, R., Herrala, A., Kaija, H., Isomaa, V., Vihko, P., 2004. Sex steroid hormone metabolism and prostate cancer. J. Steroid Biochem. Mol. Biol. 92 (4), 281–286.

Uddin, S., Bu, R., Ahmed, M., Abubaker, J., Al-Dayel, F., Bavi, P., Al-Kuraya, K.S., 2009. Overexpression of leptin receptor predicts an unfavorable outcome in middle eastern ovarian cancer. Mol. Cancer 8, 74.

Upadhyay, J., Farr, O., Perakakis, N., Ghaly, W., Mantzoros, C., 2018. Obesity as a disease. Med. Clin. 102 (1), 13–33.

Van Guilder, G.P., Hoetzer, G.L., Greiner, J.J., Stauffer, B.L., DeSouza, C.A., 2006. Influence of metabolic syndrome on biomarkers of oxidative stress and inflammation in obese adults. Obesity 14 (12), 2127–2131.

Vucenik, I., Stains, J.P., 2012. Obesity and cancer risk: evidence, mechanisms, and recommendations. Ann. N. Y. Acad. Sci. 1271 (1), 37–43.

Wang, C.F., Zhang, G., Zhao, L.J., Qi, W.J., Li, X.P., Wang, J.L., Wei, L.H., 2013. Overexpression of the insulin receptor isoform a promotes endometrial carcinoma cell growth. PLoS One 8 (8), e69001.

Wolin, K.Y., Carson, K., Colditz, G.A., 2010. Obesity and cancer. Oncologist 15 (6), 556–565.

World Health Organization, 2021. Obesity and Overweight. https://www.who.int/news-room/fact-sheets/detail/obesity-and-overweight.

Yakar, S., Adamo, L.M., 2012. Insulin-like growth factor-1 physiology: lessons from mouse models. Endocrinol. Metab. Clin. N. Am. 41 (2), 231–v.

CHAPTER FOURTEEN

Homologous repair deficiency and PARP inhibitors in cancer management

Peeyush Prasad[a], Shyam Aggarwal[b], and Shivani Arora Mittal[a]
[a]Department of Research, Sir Ganga Ram Hospital, New Delhi, India
[b]Department of Molecular Oncology, Sir Ganga Ram Hospital, New Delhi, India

Abbreviations

53BP1	the tumor suppressor p53-binding protein 1
Abl	Abelson tyrosine-protein kinase
ATM	Ataxia-telangiectasia mutated
ATR	Ataxia telangiectasia and Rad3 related
BCL2	B-cell CLL/lymphoma 2
BET	bromodomain and extraterminal domain
BLM syndrome	Bloom syndrome
BRCA1	breast cancer type 1
BRCA2	breast cancer type 2
BRD4	bromodomain containing 4
BRIP1	BRCA1 interacting protein
CDK12	cyclin-dependent kinase 12
CHK1/2	check point kinase ½
DNMT	DNA methyltransferase 1
HER2	human epidermal growth factor receptor 2
MLH1	MutL homolog 1
MSH2	MutS homolog 2
MSH6	MutS homolog 6
NBN	Nibrin
ORF	open reading frame
PALB2	partner and localizer of BRCA2
PDX	patient derived xenograft
PTEN	phosphatase and tensin homolog
PTIP	Pax transcription activation domain-interacting protein
RIF1	replication timing regulatory factor 1
SHLD1	Shieldin complex subunit 1
SHLD2	Shieldin complex subunit 2
SNPs	single nucleotide polymorphisms
TCGA	The Cancer Genome Atlas
TNBC	triple negative breast cancer
VEGF	vascular endothelial growth factor

Biomarkers in Cancer Detection and Monitoring of Therapeutics
https://doi.org/10.1016/B978-0-323-95116-6.00005-0

1. DNA damage and repair

DNA is considered highly stable as a chemical structure, with phosphodiester bonds linking the deoxyribose sugar. However, spontaneous changes in DNA are quite common, such as hydrolysis of adenine and guanine nucleotides (depurination, rate of 5000/day), conversion of cytosine to uracil (deamination, rate of 100 bases/cell/day). DNA damage also occurs due to reactions with reactive metabolites, like reactive oxygen species, ultraviolet radiation, or certain chemicals. If such changes are left uncorrected during DNA replication, it would lead to mutations in the daughter strands, by either copying of the mutated base or deletion of the missing base/s. Such mutations would be dangerous to the cells and hence nature provides for their repair using various mechanisms.

Most of the DNA damage is repaired using two mechanisms, base excision and nucleotide excision repair. The nomenclature is based upon whether a single defective base is removed or a stretch of nucleotides are removed and religated. Double-stranded breaks (DSBs) are repaired by either nonhomologous end joining (NHEJ) or homologous recombination repair (HRR) mechanisms. In nonhomologous end joining, the breaks are brought closer and resealed, generally accompanied by a loss of one/two nucleotides at the site of joining. HRR mechanism is a more accurate mechanism, requiring one of the sister chromatids as a template (Fig. 1).

2. Homologous recombination deficiency

HRR mechanism repairs DSBs, which could arise due to various reasons, such as replication occurring through a nick, ionizing radiation, and reactive oxygen species. This is an error-free repair mechanism, where first an exonuclease creates a single-strand overhang. A key protein involved here is BRCA1, which is part of a large complex of the sensor, involved in sensing DS DNA damage. This complex also includes MRN complex, mismatch repair proteins (MSH2, MSH6, and MLH1), BLM syndrome helices, and ATM. BRCA2 further helps in the loading of Rad51 on the ssDNA overhangs, which enables strand invasion and replication fork stabilization. The ssDNA overhang searches for a sister chromatid with homologous regions, which serves as a template for the repair. Since this repair mechanism requires a sister chromatid, it can only occur in the S and G2 phases of the cell cycle (Fig. 2).

Defects in DNA repair mechanisms are cancer enablers. The DNA repair defect is often an early event in tumor evolution. Most of the solid tumors are known to possess DNA repair deficiency. Tumors that have functional defects in HRR are termed as HR deficient (HRD). These deficiencies could be due to genetic or epigenetic mechanisms. Thus, HRD is a functional effect resulting from deficiencies in HRR. HRD cells would

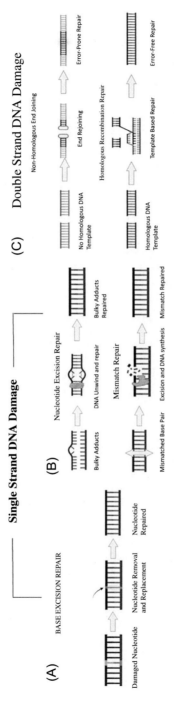

Fig. 1 DNA damage repair pathway. (A) Base excision repair. (B) Nucleotide excision repair. (C) Double-strand DNA break repair nonhomologous end joining and homologous recombination repair. *(Made in Biorender.com.)*

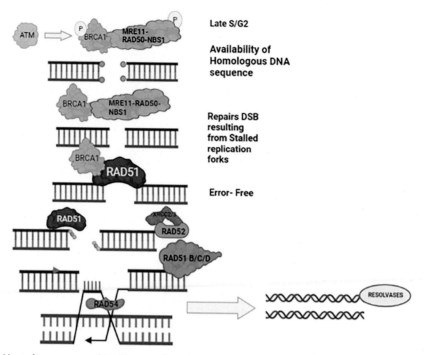

Fig. 2 Homologous recombination repair pathway. Key molecules like BRAC1 (breast cancer gene), MRE11 (meiotic recombination 11), RAD50 (double-strand break repair protein), NBS1 (Nijmegen breakage syndrome 1), RAD51, and resolvases are involved in DNA double-strand repair HRR pathway. *(Made in Biorender.com.)*

rely on other mechanisms of DSB repair, such as NHEJ, microhomology-mediated end joining, which represent low fidelity and are error-prone. With further cell divisions, inaccurately repaired mutations would keep on accumulating leading to genomic aberrations such as insertions, deletions, translocations, which drive carcinogenesis.

HRD was first observed in tumors with germline Brca1/Brca2 deficiency. However, genetic or epigenetic events in other HRR components can also lead to their deficiencies, resulting in sporadic cancers with HRD phenotype. Around 13% and 15% of HRD is present in ovarian and TNBC cancers, which is attributed to gBRCA1/2 mutation (Bell et al., 2011; Akashi-Tanaka et al., 2015). Further, 50% and 40% of ovarian and TNBC cancers also harbor HRD in absence of BRCA1/2 mutation. BRCA1 and BRCA2 are found to have a significant ability to protect against genomic instability. These not only help DSB repair in the HRR pathway but also protect stalled replication forks, protecting them against attack by various nucleases, thereby further protecting DNA damage. Germline mutation testing or panel testing for BRCA1/2 is relatively inexpensive but is limited in its ability to identify HRD, as it will overlook epigenetic modifications and other mutations in other HRR genes. Also, HRD contributions by somatic mutations and other non–BRCA events would be ignored. Mutations in other HRR pathway genes, such as Rad51B/C/D, PALB2, ATM, CHK1/2, CDK12, BRIP1, NBN, and Fanconi anemia genes, can also contribute to HRD status.

Epigenetic changes, such as aberrant methylation in CpG islands in promoter regions of genes, can lead to reduced transcription, causing deficiency of the gene products. The contribution of such silencing events has been reported in BRCA1 and RAD51C genes for high-grade ovarian carcinoma cells. However, it is important to note that biallelic BRCA1 methylation and the time point of sample collection are critical factors here. Single copies of demethylated BRCA1 do not correlate well with HRD response and also chemotherapy is shown to cause demethylation of previously methylated BRCA1 copies.

3. Biomarkers to evaluate HRD status

HRD is known to generate mutational signatures, structural chromosomal abnormalities, and copy number changes due to low fidelity repair pathways. These changes can be identified and present methods of evaluating HRD status. Assessing HRD is of clinical relevance because these tumors are more sensitive to DNA damaging drugs. According to data from TCGA, around 56% of ovarian cancers are HRD positive (Fig. 3). Such tumors have been recently approved for PARP inhibitor therapy in ovarian cancers.

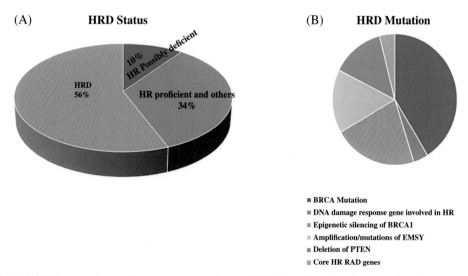

Fig. 3 (A) HRD status in ovarian cancers according to TCGA data. Mutational status of various genes in HRD positive tumors is shown (HR possibly deficient mutation: 10%, HR proficient and other genes: 34%, HRD: 56%). (B) HRD mutation (BRCA: 21%, DNA damage response genes involved in HR: 2%, epigenetic silencing of BRCA1: 11%, amplification/mutations of EMSY: 8%, deletion of PTEN: 7%, core HR RAD genes: 2%).

Some of the key biomarkers for assessing the HRD status of tumors are described below.

3.1 Germline or somatic BRCA mutation

Germline mutations are present in all cells of the body, normal or tumor, and require one inactivation event in the tumor cells to inactivate both copies of the gene. Somatic mutations are present only in the tumor cells and require a second hit event to inactivate both the copies of the gene. Both germline and somatic BRCA1/2 mutations are approved as biomarkers for PARPi therapy in ovarian cancer and have become routine testing in clinics.

3.2 BRCA LOH percentage

Loss of heterozygosity (LOH) refers to the permanent loss of one of the parent's copies of a specific allele. In the percent genomic LOH test, BRCA1/2 mutational status along with the percentage of loss of homozygosity in tumor DNA is detected. This test performs NGS of tumor samples for more than 315 genes, including BRCA1/2 and various other HRR genes. A high percentage of LOH (>16%) is associated with higher chances of response to drugs inducing DSBs. However, data from clinical trials (Coleman, 2017; Swisher et al., 2017) indicate that the discriminating power of percent LOH testing is suboptimal and hence more chromosomal aberrations should be taken into consideration for detecting HRD.

3.3 Genomic instability/HRD score

Genomic Instability reveals permanent genomic footprints of DNA damage. Three parameters are measured here using next-generation sequencing (NGS) of DNA sample isolated from tumor tissue, LOH (loss of heterozygosity), TAI (telomeric allelic imbalance), and LSTs (large-scale transitions). LOH is measured by the allele-specific copy number profile of SNPs. It indicates the loss of one of the parent's copies of the allele at a specific location, leading to homozygosity at that site. TAI indicates an imbalance in the alleles which extend up to the subtelomeric regions (>11 Mb size). LSTs are again allelic imbalance (>10 Mb) resulting due to either translocations or copy number alterations. The mean score of these three factors together is given a genomic instability (GIS) score. This reveals a permanent footprint of DNA damage during the history of the cells, irrespective of the etiology. This scoring has more prognostic value when combined than independently. Tumors with either GIS score ≥ 42 or with biallelic BRCA1/2 mutations are considered to be HRD positive. However, as this score reveals the history of DNA damage, it does not account for the possible activation of key DNA damage proteins during the treatment.

3.4 Mutation gene signatures

Germline and somatic mutations in not only BRCA1/2 but also other HR-related genes may affect response to platinum therapy. The extent of involvement of other HR genes is not very clear. The type of mutations can be quantified and patterns of nucleotide transitions created can be accounted for to create an HR mutation signature. Signature3 is an example based on single base substitutions and includes larger deletions with overlapping microhomology at breakpoint junctions. Signature3 has been shown to correlate with BRCA1/2 mutations in a variety of cancer types and also with response to platinum therapy in high-grade ovarian cancer (Alexandrov et al., 2013). Another signature, HRDetect, use whole-genome sequencing to take into account an average of six HRD associated signatures into one, microhomology-mediated deletions, base-substitution signature3, rearrangement signature3, rearrangement signature5, HRD index, base-substitution signature8. This has very high sensitivity, approaching 100% in ovarian cancers, to identify BRCA1/2 null cancers.

3.5 Functional HRD measurement

Platinum-sensitivity status

The ultimate way to assess HRD status would be through functional assays. Sensitivity to platinum drugs is considered as a surrogate marker for measuring HR proficiency. Screening through cell lines, organoids, and tissue sections for drug sensitivity can indicate the functional HRD status but are time-consuming. In resource limiting setups, evaluation of response to platinum drugs as a neoadjuvant can be used as a viable option to stratify patients who would respond to PARP inhibitors. However, the issue here is that HRD status can only be indicated after the initial cycles of chemotherapy. In recurrent tumors, platinum sensitivity has already shown to be a superior biomarker for response to PARP inhibitory therapy (Coleman, 2017; Pujade-lauraine et al., 2017; Del Campo et al., 2019) but is still not considered in the frontline setting.

Rad51 foci

Rad51 is a downstream effector protein of the HR pathway that is accumulated onto DSBs, where strand invasion takes place for repair. Preclinically, in case of DNA damage, Rad51 along with BRCA1/2 forms nuclear foci at sites of DSBs, and these foci can be visualized ex vivo using the Immunofluorescence technique. Hence, Rad51 foci formation on DSBs is an indicator of the current functional status of HRD. Rad51 foci can be compared using biopsy samples before and after chemotherapy. Another way would be to induce DSBs on the tumor tissue ex vivo before starting treatment, using ionizing radiation and then assessing Rad51 foci formation. Geminin is used to stain the S/G2 population. Many preclinical and clinical studies have shown the potential of this assay to evaluate the real-time response of HR restoration after therapy. However, translating this analysis into clinical practice remains a challenge.

4. PARP inhibitors

Poly ADP Ribose Polymerase (PARP) are nuclear proteins that recognize and bind to ssDNA breaks and are key for the functionality of other DNA damage repair pathways, like base excision repair and microhomology-mediated end joining repair (alternate pathway to HRR for DSBs). Various tumors, such as ovarian, breast, and prostate, have impaired HR pathway genes, such as BRCA1/2, causing genomic instability, thereby driving tumorigenesis. Such HRD positive tumors are found sensitive to PARP inhibitors (PARPi), by two suggested mechanisms. One is called synthetic lethality, which means selective targeting of cancer cells by simultaneous inactivation of two pathways when inactivation of either of them is nonlethal. An alternative mechanism of direct cell death is also suggested, where PARPi may trap PARP complexes on the DNA breaks, thereby obstructing replication forks, which would require additional BRCA-dependent repair pathways. In case of BRCA1/2 deficient tumors, HRR of DS breaks is nonfunctional. In addition, if PARPi is given, base excision repair and MEJ repair pathways are also blocked, leading to unrepaired breaks, causing further DNA damage with each cell division, generating genomic instability.

PARP inhibitors, first discovered in the 1980s, were used as chemosensitizers. In 2005, two scientific groups reported that BRCA1/2-deficient tumors displayed 100–1000-fold higher sensitivity to PARPi than BRCA1/2 heterozygous or wild-type cell lines. Various clinical trials have now studied the role of PARPi therapy in HR deficient tumors.

4.1 PARP inhibitors in cancer management
Ovarian cancer
Epithelial ovarian cancer (EOC) is one of the major causes of death and it is the 7th most common cancer among women (Momenimovahed et al., 2019). Around 70% of epithelial ovarian cancers are high-grade serous adenocarcinomas and around 50% of these have aberrations in the HR pathway (Ledermann et al., 2016). Two types of molecularly targeted therapies have been successfully employed in clinical trials: antiangiogenic agents and PARP inhibitors. Bevacizumab, a monoclonal antibody against VEGF, has been used extensively for ovarian cancer and has shown significant improvement in progression-free survival (Garcia et al., 2020). Three PARP inhibitors have been approved for ovarian cancer therapy: Olaparib, Rucaparib, and Niraparib (Gupta et al., 2019; Clovis Oncology, 2020; Indications and Usage Maintenance Treatment of Recurrent Ovarian Cancer, 2017). The key clinical trials leading to approval of PARPi as first-line maintenance therapy in high-grade ovarian cancers are given in Table 1.

Table 1 Summary of key phase 3 trials and their outcomes using PARPi in high-grade ovarian cancer.

Trial	Clinical context	Treatment group	BRCA status	HRD test	Significant outcome	References
SOLO1 (Phase 3)	Conducted in partial/ complete responders to first-line platinum therapy	Olaparib (maintenance therapy) vs placebo	Only patients with germline or somatic mutation were included	N/A	Olaparib vs placebo PFS: NA vs 13.8 months	Moore et al. (2018)
PRIMA (Phase 3)	Conducted in partial/ complete responders to first-line platinum therapy	Niraparib (maintenance therapy) vs placebo	Any	Myriad myChoice HRD ≥42	Niraparib vs placebo PFS: 13.8 vs 8.2 months	González-Martín et al. (2019)
PAOLA-1 (Phase 3)	Conducted in patients who responded partially/ completely to the combination of first-line platinum-based therapy and Bevacizumab	Bevacizumab (maintenance therapy) vs Olaparib + bevacizumab (maintenance therapy)	Any	Myriad myChoice HRD ≥42	Olaparib/Bevacizumab vs Bevacizumab maintenance PFS: 22.1 vs 16.6 months	Ray-Coquard et al. (2019)
VELIA (Phase 3)	Conducted on patients who were untreated at entry stage	1. Carboplatin/paclitaxel: control (placebo maintenance) 2. Carboplatin/paclitaxel + veliparib (placebo maintenance) 3. Carboplatin/paclitaxel + veliparib (veliparib maintenance)	Any	Myriad myChoice HRD ≥33	Veliparib vs control PFS: 23.5 vs 17.3 months	Coleman et al. (2019)

Randomized, phase III trials NOVA/ENGOT-OV16, SOLO-2/ENGOT-OV21, and ARIEL3 provided the evidence for regulatory approval of niraparib, olaparib, and rucaparib for maintenance therapy in recurrent ovarian cancer patients, who are also platinum-sensitive (Mirza et al., 2020). Olaparib was the first PARPi approved by US FDA with demonstrated efficacy in BRCA-associated tubal, peritoneal, and epithelial ovarian cancers. (Moore et al., 2020) Olaparib (formerly referred to as AZD2281 or KU0059436) binds to the catalytic domain of PARP1 and PARP2 and inhibits the process of poly-ADP ribosylation at nanomolar concentration. Further, it also shows an anticancer effect by trapping PARP enzymes on DNA which leads to the formation of toxic PARP-DNA complexes, further causing increased double-strand breaks (Bochum et al., 2018). Olaparib vs placebo as maintenance therapy has been evaluated in SOLO-1 trial for up to 2 years or beyond in newly diagnosed ovarian cancer patients (mtBRCA1/2) with a partial response at 2 years. After chemotherapy, most patients had no evidence of disease (NCT01844986, 2016). With respect to other interventions like placebo or chemotherapy, Olaparib is found to prolong progression-free survival (Ma et al., 2019). One of the studies showed that in patients who are newly diagnosed with advanced ovarian cancer with a BRCA1/2 mutation disease progression or death was reduced with Olaparib compared to placebo (DiSilvestro et al., 2020). The most common adverse events were fatigue, gastrointestinal toxicity, and anemia. Potentially fatal conditions, such as myelodysplastic syndrome/acute myeloid leukemia was seen in <1% of the cases (Ni et al., 2019).

Rucaparib is a small molecule PARP inhibitor that can act against PARP1, -2, and -3 (Clovis Oncology, 2020; Colombo et al., 2018). A randomized, double-blind, placebo-controlled phase 3, ARIEL3 study provided evidence for the efficacy of Rucaparib in the maintenance treatment of recurrent ovarian cancer. The United States and EU approved rucaparib for the treatment of patients with BRCA1/2 mutation in the epithelial ovarian, fallopian tube, or primary peritoneal cancer and in the relapsed adult cases of the aforementioned. These patients had shown complete or partial response to platinum-based therapy (Coleman, 2017). Adverse events associated with rucaparib are gastrointestinal events, fatigue, and myelosuppression–related events (Oza et al., 2017).

Niraparib is another FDA approved drug, which has been found to significantly increase progression-free survival among patients with recurrent ovarian cancer receiving platinum-based chemotherapy, irrespective of the HRD status. This study also found 84% overall survival in the niraparib treated group. The most common side effects were anemia, thrombocytopenia, and neutropenia (González-Martín et al., 2019).

Breast cancer

Breast cancer is the second most common malignancy in women. Approximately, 2.09 million new cases were diagnosed in 2018, which was 12% of all cancers. Around

627,000 deaths occurred in 2018 due to breast cancer (https://www.who.int/cancer/prevention/diagnosis-screening/breast-cancer/en/, n.d.). Germline mutations are found in less than 5% of breast cancers and account for approximately 30% of hereditary breast cancer which is responsible for genomic instability and high probability of disease during a lifetime (Wang et al., 2019). For germline BRCA-mutated, HER2-negative breast cancers, olaparib, and talazoparib have been approved as monotherapies. Olaparib and talazoparib monotherapies had shown significant progression-free survival benefits in phase 3 trials compared to other chemotherapy (Cortesi et al., 2021). In patients having germline BRCA mutation, HER2-negative metastatic breast cancers, efficacy, and safety of olaparib vs single-agent standard therapy (TPC; capecitabine, eribulin, or vinorelbine) was evaluated in OlympiAD, open-label, randomized, multicenter, international, phase 3 trial (Im et al., 2020). Similarly, the efficacy and safety of talazoparib vs single-agent standard TPC (capecitabine, eribulin, gemcitabine, or vinorelbine) were evaluated in EMBRACA trial (Wang et al., 2020). Based on published data from the OlympiAD and EMBARCA trials, an indirect treatment comparison was done using the Bayesian fixed-effect approach. The study found that olaparib and talazoparib were equally efficacious with respect to progression-free survival. They differed in their safety profiles, with olaparib having fewer adverse effects related to hematology (anemia, neutropenia, and thrombocytopenia). However, increased risk of nausea and vomiting were found associated with olaparib. In another phase 3 trial on patients with HER2 negative early breast cancer having BRCA1 or BRCA2 germline mutation, patients were treated with a year oral adjuvant olaparib or placebo. Compared to placebo, significantly longer survival of invasive or distant disease was observed in patients who were given adjuvant olaparib after completion of local treatment (Tutt et al., 2021). Another phase 3 trial (BrightNess) was conducted on triple-negative breast cancer patients (TNBC). Out of the total of 634 patients, a combination of paclitaxel, carboplatin, and veliparib was given to 316 patients, a combination of paclitaxel and carboplatin was given to 160 patients and 158 patients took only paclitaxel alone. Pathological complete response was higher in patients who received paclitaxel, carboplatin, and veliparib compared to those with only paclitaxel. In patients receiving carboplatin, grade 3 or 4 toxicities like neutropenia were more common. Further, toxicity did not increase substantially in the veliparib group. This study also reported that addition of veliparib to carboplatin and paclitaxel did achieve a complete pathological response (Loibl et al., 2018). One of the major challenges for the implementation of PARP inhibitors is identifying patients that would respond to PARPi. Identifying BRCA mutation along with mutation in genes associated with HRR is required. However, the cost of tests, lack of understanding, and knowledge about genetic counseling and testing by physicians and patients are a few potential barriers to BRCA testing. Providing free genetic counseling and creating awareness could increase BRCA testing and help in better patient stratification for PARP inhibitor therapy.

Prostate cancer

Worldwide, prostate cancer is the fifth most common cause of death among men (Villers and Grosclaude, 2008). Prostate cancer remains lethal at the metastatic castration-resistant stage (mCRPC) despite advancements in hormonal therapies, chemotherapies, and radionuclides. Genomic studies found not only changes in androgen-receptor signaling but also in DNA-damage response (DDR) pathways, which could be contributing factors to the development and progression of large numbers of advanced prostate cancers. A strong association between germline mutations in DDR genes and advanced prostate cancer has been reported (Virtanen et al., 2019). In nearly 23% of all metastatic castration-resistant prostate cancer, DDR alterations are present, such as BRCA1/2 and PTEN (Robinson et al., 2015). BRCA mutated cancers are found associated with higher grade and metastasis (Castro et al., 2013). Rucaparib has been approved for prostate cancer patients with BRCA mutation, who were previously treated by androgen receptor-directed and taxane-based chemotherapy (Abida et al., 2019). Olaparib has been approved for the treatment of metastatic castration-resistant prostate cancer with germline or somatic HRR gene mutations (Grewal et al., 2021). Niraparib is not yet approved for prostate cancer but significant progress has been seen as a potential treatment strategy.

4.2 Resistance to PARP inhibitors

Cancer cells often show resistance against chemotherapy due to various contributing factors like cancer stem cells, mutation in the targeted gene, hypoxic tumor microenvironment, and increased efflux of drugs. PARP inhibitor therapy resistance is universal in clinic. More than 40% of ovarian cancer patients who carry BRCA1/2 mutations fail to respond to PARP inhibitor therapy (Li et al., 2020). In most patients, prolonged oral administration of PARPi causes resistance and failure to respond. Two general mechanisms of resistance are proposed as either functional restoration of HRR pathway genes or protection of replication fork by alternative mechanisms. This is often due to induction of the ATR/CHK1 pathway which leads to phosphorylation and activation of multiple proteins involved in replication fork stability (Liao et al., 2018). Another mechanism is through the restoration of BRCA1/2 function through intragenic mutations (Edwards et al., 2008; Lakkaraju and Rodriguez-Boulan, 2008). Whole-genome characterization of chemoresistant ovarian cancer cells revealed reversion events in BRCA1/2 genes (Quigley et al., 2018). Functional restoration of BRCA1/2 is caused by genetic events that cancel frameshift, thereby restoring the open reading frame and hence the expression of full-length proteins (Swisher et al., 2009). Functional restoration can also be caused by reversion of inherited mutation which leads to the expression of the wild-type protein. Genetic events which restore

BRCA1/2 mutation are often seen in patients exposed to cisplatin or PARPi. Tumor-specific secondary mutations that restore ORF of BRCA1/2 are seen in 46% of patients receiving platinum therapy (D'Andrea, 2018). Restoration of BRCA1/2 is also often observed due to promoter demethylation. Extensive promoter methylation and low BRCA1 expression were observed in sensitive samples and relapsed samples were found to have demethylation and BRCA1 expression at comparable levels to HR proficient cancer cells (Kondrashova et al., 2018). Conserved N- and C-terminal domains of BRCA1 are most important for response to HR deficiency targeted therapies as revealed by analysis of BRCA1 missense mutations. The N-terminal RING domain is found to be disrupted due to BRCA1-C61G mutation, which causes cancer cells to respond poorly to PARP inhibitors (Drost et al., 2011). These tumor cells also rapidly develop resistance. BRCA mutation in the C-terminal (BRCT) domain of BRCA1 expresses the protein, which can be degraded by proteases due to improper folding (Johnson et al., 2013). However, the BRCT domain is found to be stabilized by HSP90 under the selection pressure of PARPi. The BRCT domain stabilized by HSP90 proteins interact efficiently with PALB2-BRCA2-RAD51 and form RAD51 foci, which can effectively repair the damage (Johnson et al., 2013). Several proteins such as 53BP1, REV7, PTIP, and RIF1 are involved in the suppression of end resection and inhibition of HRR. Loss of 53BP1 and increased requirement of BRCA1 have been found together in cancer cells (Bouwman et al., 2010). In BRCA-deleted mouse embryonic stem cells, loss of 53BP1 causes partial restoration of HR defect (Bouwman et al., 2010). This also causes the reversal of hypersensitivity to DNA-damaging agents.

Response or resistance to PARPi can also be affected by ATP-binding cassette (ABC) transporters. Expression of ABC transporters like P-glycoprotein (PgP) efflux pumps are found to be increased in drug-resistant cancer cells (Choi and Yu, 2014). Resistance to platinum-based therapy is a strong indicator of PARPi resistance which suggests that they share a common mechanism of resistance. In mouse models of mesenchymal carcinomas, PARPi resistant cells showed high expression of ABcb1a/b.

ABcb1a/b gene encodes for P-glycoprotein which is a drug efflux transporter. A study suggests that inhibition of P-glycoprotein could re-sensitize the sarcomatoid tumors to olaparib (Jaspers et al., 2015). In a patient with high-grade serous ovarian cancer with de novo PARPi resistance, a PARP1 mutation (R591C) that abolishes PARP trapping was found. Reduced mRNA expression of SHLD1, SHLD2, TP53BP1, and/or PARP1 is also reported in PARPi-resistant PDX models of BRCA1-deficient tumors (Dev et al., 2018). Various approaches have been suggested to overcome PARPi resistance such as ATR inhibition, DNMT inhibition for epigenetic re-sensitization, cell cycle checkpoint inhibition, BET inhibition (BRD4 inhibition), and combination therapy with antiangiogenic inhibitors. For patients with mutations in HR pathways, combination therapy with BET inhibitor along with Src/Abl kinase inhibitor, dasatinib, and navitoclax (BCL2 inhibitor) with rucaparib have been employed. Irrespective of clinical subtype or HRD status, BETi is found to enhance the effect of rucaparib. Further, the addition of dasatinib increased the effect of PARPi and BETi, suggesting that triple therapy is effective for high-grade serous (HGSC) and clear cell ovarian carcinomas (OCCC) (Lui et al., 2020). Poly (ADP-ribose) glycohydrolase (PARG) is an enzyme that removes PAR chains from target proteins and is one of the key factors in the development of resistance against PARPi. In genetically engineered mouse models having BRCA1/2 deficient mammary tumors, loss of PARG confers resistance to PARPi (Gogola et al., 2018). Fig. 4 represents the different mechanisms of how cancer cells acquire PARP inhibitor resistance.

5. Future perspectives

Genomic instability/scar assays for HRD have become a crucial biomarker for response to PARP inhibitors, as documented in recent clinical trials, for advanced ovarian cancers. Although HRD has been evaluated using TCGA pan-cancer data for most tumor types, its relevance as a clinical biomarker for PARP inhibitor in other solid tumors is yet to be determined. Also, the threshold score for the HRD tests would need to be optimized for different tumor types. BRCA1/2 mutation testing is still considered a viable option in the first line of testing as socio-economic challenges and lack of access to genome sequencing facilities are real-life obstacles for HRD testing. Some of the limitations of currently available HRD tests include the proportion of samples returned as "of unknown status," false negatives, high cost, and lack of access to testing. HRD-GIS biomarkers and dynamic functional assays like Rad51 should be compared for their diagnostic relevance, as functional biomarkers would indicate the current state of HRD status. Some discordance exists between HRD test results and clinical response to PARP inhibitors, and more understanding is required whether this is due to accuracy of testing or biological features of the tumor such as HRD mechanism of PARP inhibitor resistance. Various PARP inhibitors have been introduced in the clinical setup, however, their efficiency for PARP1/2 trapping may vary. Accordingly, their efficacy would vary in different tumor settings. Thus resistance to PARP inhibitor therapy is a concern and strategies to target it needs to be addressed in the future. Combination therapy with PARPi and other DNA damaging agents are also being explored and hold promise for the future. Further research is needed to help refine our ability to detect HRD and select patients who would receive the maximum benefit from PARP inhibitors, while sparing others from the toxicities, in different solid tumors.

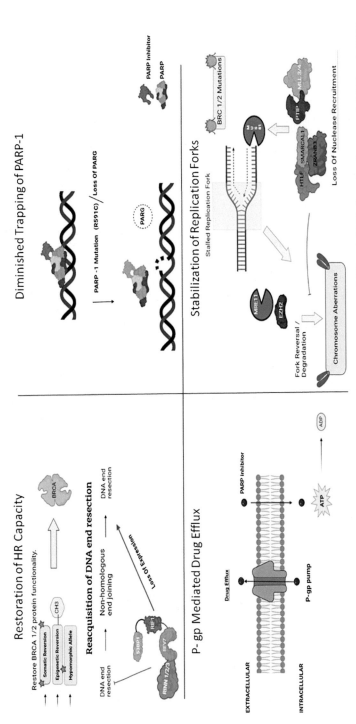

Fig. 4 Mechanism of PARP inhibitor resistance. Abbreviations: *BRCA*, breast cancer genes; *PARP*, poly(ADP-ribose) polymerase 1; *PARG*, poly (ADP-ribose) glycohydrolase; *P-gp*, P-glycoprotein. (*Made in Biorender.com.*)

Acknowledgment

We are grateful to Ms Surbhi, CSIR JRF, for helping with referencing of this chapter. We would like to thank Mr Mrinal Singh for helping with modification of the figures.

References

Abida, W., et al., 2019. Preliminary results from the TRITON2 study of rucaparib in patients (pts) with DNA damage repair (DDR)-deficient metastatic castration-resistant prostate cancer (mCRPC): updated analyses. Ann. Oncol. 30 (October), v327–v328. https://doi.org/10.1093/annonc/mdz248.003.

Akashi-Tanaka, S., et al., 2015. BRCAness predicts resistance to taxane-containing regimens in triple negative breast cancer during neoadjuvant chemotherapy. Clin. Breast Cancer 15 (1), 80–85. https://doi.org/10.1016/j.clbc.2014.08.003.

Alexandrov, L.B., et al., 2013. Signatures of mutational processes in human cancer. Nature 500 (7463), 415–421. https://doi.org/10.1038/nature12477.

Bell, D., et al., 2011. Integrated genomic analyses of ovarian carcinoma. Nature 474 (7353), 609–615. https://doi.org/10.1038/nature10166.

Bochum, S., Berger, S., Martens, U.M., 2018. Olaparib. Recent Results Cancer Res. 211, 217–233. https://doi.org/10.1007/978-3-319-91442-8_15.

Bouwman, P., et al., 2010. 53BP1 loss rescues BRCA1 deficiency and is associated with triple-negative and BRCA-mutated breast cancers. Nat. Struct. Mol. Biol. 17 (6), 688–695. https://doi.org/10.1038/nsmb.1831.

Castro, E., et al., 2013. Germline BRCA mutations are associated with higher risk of nodal involvement, distant metastasis, and poor survival outcomes in prostate cancer. J. Clin. Oncol. 31 (14), 1748–1757. https://doi.org/10.1200/JCO.2012.43.1882.

Choi, Y., Yu, A.M., 2014. ABC transporters in multidrug resistance and pharmacokinetics, and strategies for drug development. Curr. Pharm. Des. 20 (5), 793–807. https://doi.org/10.2174/13816128005140214165212.

Clovis Oncology, 2020. Rubraca® (rucaparib) [package insert]. pp. 1–22. (Online). Available from: https://www.accessdata.fda.gov/drugsatfda_docs/label/2018/209115s003lbl.pdf.

Coleman, R.L., et al., 2017. Rucaparib maintenance treatment for recurrent ovarian carcinoma after response to platinum therapy (ARIEL3): a randomised, double-blind, placebo-controlled, phase 3 trial. Lancet 390 (10106), 1949–1961. https://doi.org/10.1016/S0140-6736(17)32440-6.

Coleman, R.L., et al., 2019. Veliparib with first-line chemotherapy and as maintenance therapy in ovarian cancer. N. Engl. J. Med. 381 (25), 2403–2415. https://doi.org/10.1056/nejmoa1909707.

Colombo, I., Lheureux, S., Oza, A.M., 2018. Rucaparib: a novel PARP inhibitor for BRCA advanced ovarian cancer. Drug Des. Devel. Ther. 12, 605–617. Published 2018 Mar 21 https://doi.org/10.2147/DDDT.S130809.

Cortesi, L., Rugo, H.S., Jackisch, C., 2021. An overview of PARP inhibitors for the treatment of breast cancer. Target. Oncol. 16 (3), 255–282. https://doi.org/10.1007/s11523-021-00796-4.

D'Andrea, A.D., 2018. Mechanisms of PARP inhibitor sensitivity and resistance. DNA Repair 71, 172–176. https://doi.org/10.1016/j.dnarep.2018.08.021.

Del Campo, J.M., et al., 2019. Niraparib maintenance therapy in patients with recurrent ovarian cancer after a partial response to the last platinum-based chemotherapy in the ENGOT-OV16/NOVA trial. J. Clin. Oncol. 37 (32), 2968–2973. https://doi.org/10.1200/JCO.18.02238.

Dev, H., et al., 2018. Shieldin complex promotes DNA end-joining and counters homologous recombination in BRCA1-null cells. Nat. Cell Biol. 20 (8), 954–965. https://doi.org/10.1038/s41556-018-0140-1.

DiSilvestro, P., et al., 2020. Efficacy of maintenance Olaparib for patients with newly diagnosed advanced ovarian cancer with a BRCA mutation: subgroup analysis findings from the SOLO1 trial. J. Clin. Oncol. 38 (30), 3528–3537. https://doi.org/10.1200/JCO.20.00799.

Drost, R., et al., 2011. BRCA1 RING function is essential for tumor suppression but dispensable for therapy resistance. Cancer Cell 20 (6), 797–809. https://doi.org/10.1016/j.ccr.2011.11.014.

Edwards, S.L., et al., 2008. Resistance to therapy caused by intragenic deletion in BRCA2. Nature 451 (7182), 1111–1115. https://doi.org/10.1038/nature06548.

Garcia, J., et al., 2020. Bevacizumab (Avastin®) in cancer treatment: a review of 15 years of clinical experience and future outlook. Cancer Treat. Rev. 86 (December 2019), 102017. https://doi.org/10.1016/j.ctrv.2020.102017.

Gogola, E., et al., 2018. Selective loss of PARG restores PARylation and counteracts PARP inhibitor-mediated synthetic lethality. Cancer Cell 33 (6), 1078–1093.e12. https://doi.org/10.1016/j.ccell.2018.05.008.

González-Martín, A., et al., 2019. Niraparib in patients with newly diagnosed advanced ovarian cancer. N. Engl. J. Med. 381 (25), 2391–2402. https://doi.org/10.1056/nejmoa1910962.

Grewal, K., Grewal, K., Tabbara, I.A., 2021. PARP inhibitors in prostate cancer. Anticancer Res. 41 (2), 551–556. https://doi.org/10.21873/ANTICANRES.14807.

Gupta, et al., 2019. Maintenance therapy for recurrent epithelial ovarian cancer: current therapies and future perspectives—a review. J. Ovarian Res. 12, 103. https://doi.org/10.1186/s13048-019-0579-0.

https://www.who.int/cancer/prevention/diagnosis-screening/breast-cancer/en/.

Im, S.A., et al., 2020. Olaparib monotherapy for Asian patients with a germline BRCA mutation and HER2-negative metastatic breast cancer: OlympiAD randomized trial subgroup analysis. Sci. Rep. 10 (1), 1–8. https://doi.org/10.1038/s41598-020-63033-4.

Indications and Usage Maintenance Treatment of Recurrent Ovarian Cancer, 2017. ZEJULA® is indicated for the maintenance treatment of adult patients with recurrent epithelial ovarian, fallopian tube, or primary peritoneal cancer who are in a complete or part.

Jaspers, J.E., et al., 2015. BRCA2-deficient sarcomatoid mammary tumors exhibit multidrug resistance. Cancer Res. 75 (4), 732–741. https://doi.org/10.1158/0008-5472.CAN-14-0839.

Johnson, N., et al., 2013. Stabilization of mutant BRCA1 protein confers PARP inhibitor and platinum resistance. Proc. Natl. Acad. Sci. U. S. A. 110 (42), 17041–17046. https://doi.org/10.1073/pnas.1305170110.

Kondrashova, O., et al., 2018. Methylation of all BRCA1 copies predicts response to the PARP inhibitor rucaparib in ovarian carcinoma. Nat. Commun. 9 (1). https://doi.org/10.1038/s41467-018-05564-z.

Lakkaraju, A., Rodriguez-Boulan, E., 2008. Secondary mutation as a mechanism of cisplatin resistance in BRCA-2 mutated cancer, NIH public access. Trends Cell Biol. 18 (5), 199–209. https://doi.org/10.1038/nature06633.Secondary.

Ledermann, J.A., Drew, Y., Kristeleit, R.S., 2016. Homologous recombination deficiency and ovarian cancer. Eur. J. Cancer 60, 49–58. https://doi.org/10.1016/j.ejca.2016.03.005.

Li, H., Liu, Z.Y., Wu, N., Chen, Y.C., Cheng, Q., Wang, J., 2020. PARP inhibitor resistance: the underlying mechanisms and clinical implications. Mol. Cancer 19 (1), 1–16. https://doi.org/10.1186/s12943-020-01227-0.

Liao, H., Ji, F., Helleday, T., Ying, S., 2018. Mechanisms for stalled replication fork stabilization: new targets for synthetic lethality strategies in cancer treatments. EMBO Rep. 19 (9), 1–18. https://doi.org/10.15252/embr.201846263.

Loibl, S., et al., 2018. Addition of the PARP inhibitor veliparib plus carboplatin or carboplatin alone to standard neoadjuvant chemotherapy in triple-negative breast cancer (BrighTNess): a randomised, phase 3 trial. Lancet Oncol. 19 (4), 497–509. https://doi.org/10.1016/S1470-2045(18)30111-6.

Lui, G.Y.L., et al., 2020. BET, SRC, and BCL2 family inhibitors are synergistic drug combinations with PARP inhibitors in ovarian cancer. eBioMedicine 60, 1–12. https://doi.org/10.1016/j.ebiom.2020.102988.

Ma, J., et al., 2019. Efficacy and safety of olaparib maintenance therapy in platinum-sensitive ovarian cancer patients with BRCA mutations: a meta-analysis on randomized controlled trials. Cancer Manag. Res. 11, 3061–3078. https://doi.org/10.2147/CMAR.S191107.

Mirza, M.R., et al., 2020. The forefront of ovarian cancer therapy: update on PARP inhibitors. Ann. Oncol. 31 (9), 1148–1159. https://doi.org/10.1016/j.annonc.2020.06.004.

Momenimovahed, Z., Tiznobaik, A., Taheri, S., Salehiniya, H., 2019. Ovarian cancer in the world: epidemiology and risk factors. Int. J. Women's Health 11, 287–299. https://doi.org/10.2147/IJWH.S197604.

Moore, K., et al., 2018. Maintenance Olaparib in patients with newly diagnosed advanced ovarian cancer. N. Engl. J. Med. 379 (26), 2495–2505. https://doi.org/10.1056/nejmoa1810858.

Moore, K.N., Pothuri, B., Monk, B., Coleman, R.L., 2020. PARP inhibition as frontline therapy in ovarian cancer. Clin. Adv. Hematol. Oncol. 18 (9), 550–556.

NCT01844986, 2016. Olaparib Maintenance Monotherapy in Patients With BRCA Mutated Ovarian Cancer Following First Line Platinum Based Chemotherapy. (Online). Available from: https://clinicaltrials.gov/show/NCT01844986.

Ni, J., Cheng, X., Zhou, R., Xu, X., Guo, W., Chen, X., 2019. Olaparib in the therapy of advanced ovarian cancer: first real world experiences in safety and efficacy from China. J. Ovarian Res. 12, 1–9.

Oza, A.M., et al., 2017. Antitumor activity and safety of the PARP inhibitor rucaparib in patients with high-grade ovarian carcinoma and a germline or somatic BRCA1 or BRCA2 mutation: integrated analysis of data from study 10 and ARIEL2. Gynecol. Oncol. 147 (2), 267–275. https://doi.org/10.1016/j.ygyno.2017.08.022.

Pujade-lauraine, E., et al., 2017. SOLO2/ENGOT-Ov21: a phase 3, randomised, double-blind, placebo-controlled trial of olaparib tablets as maintenance therapy in platinum-sensitive, relapsed ovarian cancer. Lancet Oncol. 18 (9), 1274–1284.

Quigley, D., et al., 2018. Cancer Discov. 7 (9), 999–1005. https://doi.org/10.1158/2159-8290.CD-17-0146 (HHS Public Access).

Ray-Coquard, I., et al., 2019. Olaparib plus bevacizumab as first-line maintenance in ovarian cancer. N. Engl. J. Med. 381 (25), 2416–2428. https://doi.org/10.1056/nejmoa1911361.

Robinson, D., Van Allen, E.M., Wu, Y.M., et al., 2015. Integrative clinical genomics of advanced prostate cancer. Cell 161 (5), 1215–1228.

Swisher, E.M., Sakai, W., Karlan, B.Y., Wurz, K., Taniguchi, T., 2009. Carcinomas with platinum resistance. 68 (8), 2581–2586. https://doi.org/10.1158/0008-5472.CAN-08-0088.Secondary.

Swisher, E.M., et al., 2017. Rucaparib in relapsed, platinum-sensitive high-grade ovarian carcinoma (ARIEL2 part 1): an international, multicentre, open-label, phase 2 trial. Lancet Oncol. 18 (1), 75–87. https://doi.org/10.1016/S1470-2045(16)30559-9.

Tutt, A.N.J., Garber, J.E., Kaufman, B., Viale, G., et al., 2021. OlympiA clinical trial steering committee and investigators. Adjuvant Olaparib for patients with BRCA1- or BRCA2-mutated breast cancer. N. Engl. J. Med. 384 (25), 2394–2405.

Villers, A., Grosclaude, P., 2008. Epidemiology of prostate cancer. Med. Nucl. 32 (1), 2–4. https://doi.org/10.1016/j.mednuc.2007.11.003.

Virtanen, V., Paunu, K., Ahlskog, J.K., Varnai, R., Sipeky, C., Sundvall, M., 2019. PARP inhibitors in prostate cancer—the preclinical rationale and current clinical development. Genes (Basel) 10 (8), 1–19. https://doi.org/10.3390/genes10080565.

Wang, X., et al., 2019. Prevalence of BRCA1 and BRCA2 gene mutations in Chinese patients with high-risk breast cancer. Mol. Genet. Genomic Med. 7 (6), 943–949. https://doi.org/10.1002/mgg3.677.

Wang, J., Zhang, Y., Yuan, L., et al., 2020. Comparative efficacy, safety, and acceptability of single-agent poly (ADP-ribose) polymerase (PARP) inhibitors in BRCA-mutated HER2-negative metastatic or advanced breast cancer: a network meta-analysis. Aging (Albany NY) 13 (1), 450–459. https://doi.org/10.18632/aging.202152.

CHAPTER FIFTEEN

Molecular prospects of transcription activator-like effector nucleases (TALENs) in cancer management: Challenges and adaptations

Sweety Mehra[a], Madhu Sharma[a], R.C. Sobti[b], and Mani Chopra[a]
[a]Department of Zoology, Panjab University, Chandigarh, India
[b]Department of Biotechnology, Panjab University, Chandigarh, India

1. Introduction

Specific genome editing is a broadly applicable approach for effectively modifying any concerned sequence in specific cells or organisms. This technique uses engineered nucleases, i.e., synthetic proteins comprised of a customized sequence-specific DNA-binding motif fused to a nuclease that cleaves DNA in a non-sequence-specific manner. These nucleases are utilized to induce targeted double-strand breaks (DSBs) into DNA sites. These breaks are then restored by processes that can be manipulated to create alterations at the cleavage site sequence (Joung and Sander, 2013). This Nuclease based genome editing allows genetic studies that were challenging or impossible to perform in the past. This technology might also offer therapeutic approaches for genetic disorders, including monogenic diseases such as sickle cell anemia, cystic fibrosis or specific mutations like in cancer.

Most of the targeted genome editing has been accomplished using zinc-finger nucleases (ZFNs) and recently by transcription activator-like effector nucleases (TALENs). TALENs have quickly emerged for genome editing as an alternative to ZFNs and inducing targeted DSBs. TALENs are like ZFNs and consist of a nonspecific nuclease domain *Fok*I fused to a customized DNA-binding domain(Boch and Bonas, 2010). This DNA-binding *Fok*I domain is composed of highly preserved repeats, derivatives of transcription activator-like effectors (TALEs), which are secreted proteins of *Xanthomonas* bacteria to modify the transcription of genes in host cells (Römer et al., 2007) (Fig. 1B).

TALENs are of high interest and effectiveness because they can be designed rapidly by investigators using a simple "protein-DNA code" that relates repeated DNA-binding TALE domains to specific bases in a target-binding location. Over the past years, leveraging techniques and practices have advanced to use TALENs to modify endogenous genes

Biomarkers in Cancer Detection and Monitoring of Therapeutics
https://doi.org/10.1016/B978-0-323-95116-6.00017-7

275

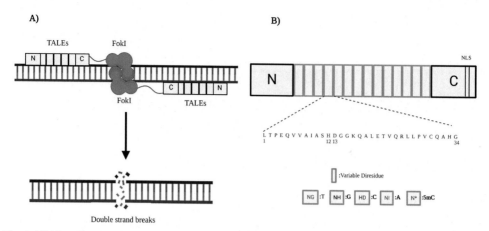

Fig. 1 (A) Identification and attachment of TALE protein to target sites at opposed DNA strands; dimer *Fok*I containing specific variable diresidue precisely cleaves target DNA and form double strand breaks (B) Pictorial representation of a transcription-activator-like effector. The DNA binding domain of the TALE protein includes several repeat modules of 34 residues flanked by an N and C-terminus, which may include mammalian NLS or other functional domains. The corresponding repeat variable diresidues like NG, NH, HD, NI, N* for each letter of DNA, including 5-methylcytosine are also shown at the bottom of the figure (Amino acid letter codes N, G, H, D, I correspond to asparagine, glycine, histidine, aspartic acid and isoleucine, respectively). *A*: adenine; *5mC*: 5-methyl cytosine; *C*: carboxy terminal; *C*: cytosine; *G*: guanine; *N*: amino terminal; *NLS*: nuclear localization signal; *TALEs*: transcription activator-like effectors attached with endonuclease *Fok*I; *T*: thymine.

in yeast, fruit fly, zebrafish, rat, pig, cow, and human somatic, and pluripotent stem cells (Huang et al., 2011; Miller et al., 2011; Tesson et al., 2011). Furthermore, a study validated the high success rate of TALENs to target any DNA sequence of concern in human cells effectively (Miller et al., 2011). Thus, the comfort of design, high rates of cleavage action, and the effective inexhaustible targeting range of TALENs make them appropriate for the use by researchers for their beneficial use in cancer.

2. Emergence and principles of technique

Transcription activator-like effector (TALEs) proteins are secreted by plant pathogenic bacteria *Xanthomonas* and have been developed for the swift and efficient targeting of any DNA sequence of preference. Emerging attempts in TALE technology have taken the lead in applications like activation, repression, deletion, and insertion of a preferred DNA sequence in wide range of cell types and model organisms (Pérez–Quintero et al., 2013). The C-terminus of TALE protein is ligated to a domain with endonuclease catalytic activity of *Fok*I. When two different TALENs bind to adjacent targeted DNA sequence, then site specific DSBs are created on opposite strands. So, due to their activity to act in dimer form, they are designed in pairs for a specific targeted site (Ousterout and Gersbach, 2016) (Fig. 1A).

TALEs have an integrated DNA-binding domain (DBD) consisting of repetitive sequences of residues and each region of repeat comprises of 34 amino acids. A couple of residues present at the 12th and 13th positions of each TALE repeats defines the nucleotide targeting and are defined as the repeat variable diresidue (RVD) (Streubel et al., 2012). The half-repeat, i.e. the last repeat is typically shortened to 20 amino acids. Combining these repeat regions allows the production of sequence-targeted synthetic TALEs. The C-terminus usually includes a nuclear localization signal (NLS), which helps the movement of a TALE to the nucleus, including a functional domain that modulates transcription (Forsyth et al., 2016) (Fig. 1B).

Till date, all custom made TALE repeat arrays use four domains with RVDs, i.e., HD (histidine aspartic acid), NG (asparagine glycine), NI (asparagine isoleucine), and NN (asparagine asparagine) for the recognition of nucleotides C, T, A, and G/A, respectively. Studies also suggest that NH (asparagine histidine) has a higher specificity for G than NN and results in stronger TALE binding. This basic code enables DNA targeting to generate an array of programmable enzymes to manipulate genes in targeted sites (Miller et al., 2011). So, TALE repeats with desirable specificities can be engineered using RVD codes. It would be of more interest to investigate whether different RVD combinations will have more or different affinities for nucleotides or not.

2.1 Assembly of TALE proteins

The construction of customized TALE repeats arrays can be difficult due to the necessity to engineer various identical repeat sequence and thorough selection of sites for the specific introduction of a double-strand break is a critical part of working with the TALEN systems. The necessity for a preliminary bioinformatic analysis is described by the possibility of off-target effects—introducing nonspecific double-strand breaks into the genome. For selection of targeted sites, regions of repetitive sequences, and regions with higher homology to other regions of the genome, should not be considered (Nemudryi et al., 2014). Moreover, different platforms like high-throughput FLASH assembly method, "Golden Gate" cloning method, Solid based cloning method and commercially available kits allow rapid and custom assemblage of TALE repeat regions among the N- and C-terminus of the protein. These platforms vary in their cloning methods used, requirement of plasmids, the usage of PCR, length of arrays to be engineered, and web-based software. These techniques can be used to assemble custom DNA binding domains, which are then cloned into an expression vector containing a functional domain. Most options for de novo synthesis of TALENs in the laboratory combine digestion and ligation steps in a reaction with type II restriction enzymes (Cermak et al., 2011).

TALE nucleases utilize a C-terminal fusion with the type II restriction enzyme *Fok*I to create a heterodimer which produces a double-stranded break (DSB) in DNA.

Nuclease-induced DSBs are repaired by nonhomologous end joining (NHEJ) or homologous directed repair (HDR). Using this technique, two TALEN proteins must bind to the sense and antisense strand of DNA to create a FokI heterodimer and form a double-stranded break (Zhang et al., 2013).

A considerable body of literature validates the normal cellular repair of TALENs-induced DSBs by NHEJ or HDR can be developed to introduce targeted genome alterations in a broad range of organisms and cell types. NHEJ-mediated repair of a nuclease-induced DSB results in the effective introduction of variable length insertion/deletion (indel) mutations that arise at the site of the break. Thus, NHEJ-facilitated repair of DSBs introduced into gene coding sequences will often generate frameshift mutations that can result in knockout of gene function (Chen et al., 2011). Moreover, if a double-stranded DNA "donor template" is supplied, HDR of a nuclease-induced DSB can be employed to introduce precise nucleotide substitutions or insertions of up to 7.6 kb at or near the site of the break (Fig. 2). Latest work has also shown that oligonucleotides can be utilized with TALENs to introduce particular insertions in human somatic and pluripotent stem cells using double-stranded donor templates (Moehle et al., 2007). Therefore, researchers found it relevant to use the TALEN-based genome editing tool as an alternative therapeutic approach in case of cancer (Shankar et al., 2017).

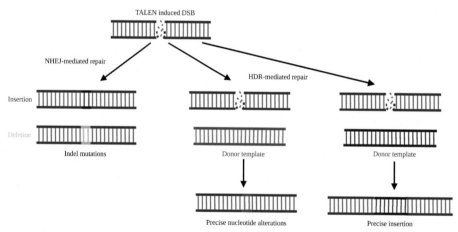

Fig. 2 TALEN-induced genome editing. TALEN-induced targeted double-strand breaks in a gene locus can be repaired by either nonhomologous end-joining (NHEJ) or homologous directed repair (HDR). NHEJ-mediated repair introduces the insertion and deletion (indel) mutations. HDR with double-stranded DNA "donor templates" can help in the introduction of the precise nucleotide substitutions or precise insertions. *DSB*: double-strand break, *HDR*: homologous directed repair, *indel mutations*: insertion and deletion mutations, *NHEJ*: nonhomologous end-joining.

3. TALENs in cancer management

3.1 Need of TALENs in cancer research

In cancer, somatic mutagenesis within the genome leading to activation of oncogene or inactivation of tumor suppressor gene is more common than germline mutations (Rivlin et al., 2011). Over time, various carcinogenic agents have been used to initiate random somatic mutations but the targeted mutations are striking and comparable difficult to generate (Zhang et al., 2014). In the past, many genome editing techniques like short hairpin RNAs, transposition, and zinc finger nucleases (ZFNs) have been used to eliminate the targeted mutation in cancer. But these techniques came with drawbacks in which off-targeting is the most common (Gupta and Musunuru, 2014; Sander et al., 2011; Weir et al., 2004). These uncontrolled off-targeting conditions produced due to the engineered proteins themselves contribute to tumorigenesis which makes these techniques highly unsuccessful in cancer management (Carroll, 2011; Beer et al., 2010: Grimm et al., 2006).

Overpassing these limitations, theoretically, TALENs have appeared as effective genome editing technology that assesses the functionality of genes and initiates precise manipulation of cellular behavior. The clinical potential of TALENs empowered researchers to use genetically engineered animals to investigate the etiology behind cancer further to clarify molecular aspects that can be targeted for better therapeutic strategies. But its accuracy and clarity, especially in vivo *models*, need to be explored (Zhang et al., 2014).

3.2 Clinical potentials of TALENs in cancer management

Over the last few years, the revolutionary research related to genome editing in the field of cancer enabled scientists to better understand the contribution of a single-gene product to in occurrence and development of cancer. Targeted gene modification in oncogenes and mutant tumor suppressor genes via TALENs provides outstanding genome modulating approaches and helps in designing therapeutics for cancer treatment (Li et al., 2020). This engineered TALEN technology pledges to facilitate and enhance genetic manipulations in cancerous cells. The TALEN-based genome-editing tool has been used to distort oncogenes and tumor suppressor genes in the genome, as an alternative therapeutic approach. In cancer, genetic engineered TALENs were experimentally used for activation of B cells, allogenic t-cell editing (Ashmore-Harris and Fruhwirth, 2020), targeting of E7 gene of Human papillomavirus in SiHa cells (Shankar et al., 2017), create translocations t(11;22)(q24;q12) and t(2;5)(p23;q35) translocations in human cells (Piganeau et al., 2013), prostate-specific androgen receptor gene rearrangements (Nyquist et al., 2013), and targeting mutated genes in Human myeloma cell lines HMCLs

(Wu et al., 2014). These experiments highlight the clinical potentials of TALENs as genome editing in cancer research and strongly believe in their success when applied as a therapeutic approach.

4. Executing challenges, limitations, and adaptations in TALENs

Genome editing via TALENs is an advanced technology that identifies the relevant and TALENs' sequence-specific area of the genome to be modified, thereby augmenting the accuracy of insertion, preventing cell toxicity, and enhancing the reproducibility. The technique is cheaper and its efficiency and capabilities make it more pronounced over other genome editing tools. But over the year, researchers face some obstacles in the execution of this genome editing tool which makes its implications difficult especially in the case of cancer.

(a) Time consumption

The reaction products in the particular technique need purification and the confirmation of correct orientation. This process enhances the reproducibility of the technique but makes the technique tedious and time-consuming (Nemudryi et al., 2014).

Adaptations

Over time, researchers modify these genome editing tools and reported that the simultaneous ligation and hydrolysis by restriction endonucleases in the same reaction mixture could reduce the overall time required for completion of the process. A reduction in the total time required would make this technique more efficient and striking (Reyon et al., 2012).

(b) Difficulty in generating the genetic construct

Reliable and accurate genetic constructs of this editing tool are the most crucial factors which should be kept in the mind for the successful implication of the technique. As the genome is widely diverse and evolutionary, the genetic constructs' specificity and nonspecific binding are of major concern. Therefore, the construction of precise and effective TALENs constructs is the most common difficulty faced by researchers (Nemudryi et al., 2014).

Adaptations

To overcome the problems associated with the genetic constructs of the technique following adaptations are recommended.

- *Enhancement of TALENs specificity*

  It is prescribed that long TALENs constructs must be generated for the successful implication of the technique. Longer TALENs would be more tolerant of mismatches, yet are more specific in a genomic context. This would enhance the specificity of the TALENs which in turn would enhance the reproducibility of the technique (Guilinger et al., 2014).

- *Reduction of nonspecific binding*

  Identification and mutation of residues that directly or indirectly contribute to nonspecific DNA binding is the prime substitute for the incorrect binding of the TALENs (Joung and Sander, 2013).

(c) Delivery associated issues:

TALENs have large size and repetitive characteristics which increased the specificity of reaction but made the in vivo delivery difficult, especially in targeted cells. These properties cause unwanted recombination events while packaging of TALENs (Nemudryi et al., 2014; Wang et al., 2016).

Adaptations

TALENs delivery-associated issues can be resolved by using high-capacity Adeno Viruses (HCAdVs), cationic polymers, and cell-penetrating peptides (CPPs)-TAT, but clinical trials are still needed to investigate its proper delivery (Wang et al., 2016).

Although the TALEN technology has advanced rapidly in recent years, still many important questions must be answered before these proteins can be used routinely in cancer research and cancer therapeutic applications. Therefore, the proper exploration of this technique is well needed. Investigating the blueprints to overcome the limitations and compensating methods for the drawbacks of this technique would be fruitful in achieving milestones in cancer management and could make this technique more pronounced for future use in cancer therapeutics.

5. Concluding remarks

Cancer is a leading disease-causing high rate of mortalities worldwide. Accumulation of tumor suppressor genes (TSGs) and proto-oncogenes are the important factors behind the etiology of cancer. In the past few years, TALENs appeared as a remarkable genome editing tool in cancer and their use in therapeutic design is considerable. This therapeutic genome editing tool is mediated by sequence-specific targeting nucleases, also known as programmable nucleases. But its proper delivery and implications of the technique are long overdue and need more investigations along with adaptations.

6. Future prospects

TALENs is a considerable genome editing tool that has emerged as a rewarding technique in cancer management due to its simple design, precision, flexibility, and lower off-target sites. TALENs offer new opportunities to mitigate cancer but some important queries remain to be addressed if TALENs are to be used usually, for research and therapeutic applications in cancer. First, although the TALENs produce lower off-target sites still it is a major concern that decreases its specificity in therapeutic application in cancer. Second, optimization of accurate methods for efficiently delivering TALENs and encoding them into cells will also be crucial for future cancer research. While increasingly genome editing approaches are also beginning to emerge, with certain modifications TALENs could prove to be of great biological importance in the field of cancer if explored and investigated well.

References

Ashmore-Harris, C., Fruhwirth, G.O., 2020. The clinical potential of gene editing as a tool to engineer cell-based therapeutics. Clin. Transl. Med. 9 (1). https://doi.org/10.1186/s40169-020-0268-z.

Beer, S., Bellovin, D.I., Lee, J.S., Komatsubara, K., Wang, L.S., Koh, H., Börner, K., Storm, T.A., Davis, C.R., Kay, M.A., Felsher, D.W., Grimm, D., 2010. Low-level shRNA cytotoxicity can contribute to MYC-induced hepatocellular carcinoma in adult mice. Mol. Ther. 18 (1). https://doi.org/10.1038/mt.2009.222.

Boch, J., Bonas, U., 2010. Xanthomonas AvrBs3 family-type III effectors: discovery and function. Annu. Rev. Phytopathol. 48. https://doi.org/10.1146/annurev-phyto-080508-081936.

Carroll, D., 2011. Genome engineering with zinc-finger nucleases. Genetics 188 (4). https://doi.org/10.1534/genetics.111.131433.

Cermak, T., Doyle, E.L., Christian, M., Wang, L., Zhang, Y., Schmidt, C., Baller, J.A., Somia, N.v., Bogdanove, A.J., Voytas, D.F., 2011. Efficient design and assembly of custom TALEN and other TAL effector-based constructs for DNA targeting. Nucleic Acids Res. 39 (12). https://doi.org/10.1093/nar/gkr218.

Chen, F., Pruett-Miller, S.M., Huang, Y., Gjoka, M., Duda, K., Taunton, J., Collingwood, T.N., Frodin, M., Davis, G.D., 2011. High-frequency genome editing using ssDNA oligonucleotides with zinc-finger nucleases. Nat. Methods 8 (9). https://doi.org/10.1038/nmeth.1653.

Forsyth, A., Weeks, T., Richael, C., Duan, H., 2016. Transcription activator-like effector nucleases (TALEN)-mediated targeted DNA insertion in potato plants. Front. Plant Sci. 7 (OCTOBER2016). https://doi.org/10.3389/fpls.2016.01572.

Grimm, D., Streetz, K.L., Jopling, C.L., Storm, T.A., Pandey, K., Davis, C.R., Marion, P., Salazar, F., Kay, M.A., 2006. Fatality in mice due to oversaturation of cellular microRNA/short hairpin RNA pathways. Nature 441 (7092). https://doi.org/10.1038/nature04791.

Guilinger, J.P., Pattanayak, V., Reyon, D., Tsai, S.Q., Sander, J.D., Joung, J.K., Liu, D.R., 2014. Broad specificity profiling of TALENs results in engineered nucleases with improved DNA-cleavage specificity. Nat. Methods 11 (4). https://doi.org/10.1038/nmeth.2845.

Gupta, R.M., Musunuru, K., 2014. Expanding the genetic editing tool kit: ZFNs, TALENs, and CRISPR-Cas9. J. Clin. Investig. 124 (10). https://doi.org/10.1172/JCI72992.

Huang, P., Xiao, A., Zhou, M., Zhu, Z., Lin, S., Zhang, B., 2011. Heritable gene targeting in zebrafish using customized TALENs. Nat. Biotechnol. 29 (8). https://doi.org/10.1038/nbt.1939.

Joung, J.K., Sander, J.D., 2013. TALENs: a widely applicable technology for targeted genome editing. Nat. Rev. Mol. Cell Biol. 14 (1). https://doi.org/10.1038/nrm3486.

Li, H., Yang, Y., Hong, W., Huang, M., Wu, M., Zhao, X., 2020. Applications of genome editing technology in the targeted therapy of human diseases: mechanisms, advances and prospects. Signal Transduct. Target. Ther. 5 (1). https://doi.org/10.1038/s41392-019-0089-y.

Miller, J.C., Tan, S., Qiao, G., Barlow, K.A., Wang, J., Xia, D.F., Meng, X., Paschon, D.E., Leung, E., Hinkley, S.J., Dulay, G.P., Hua, K.L., Ankoudinova, I., Cost, G.J., Urnov, F.D., Zhang, H.S., Holmes, M.C., Zhang, L., Gregory, P.D., Rebar, E.J., 2011. A TALE nuclease architecture for efficient genome editing. Nat. Biotechnol. 29 (2). https://doi.org/10.1038/nbt.1755.

Moehle, E.A., Rock, J.M., Lee, Y.L., Jouvenot, Y., DeKelver, R.C., Gregory, P.D., Urnov, F.D., Holmes, M.C., 2007. Targeted gene addition into a specified location in the human genome using designed zinc finger nucleases. Proc. Natl. Acad. Sci. U. S. A. 104 (9). https://doi.org/10.1073/pnas.0611478104.

Nemudryi, A.A., Valetdinova, K.R., Medvedev, S.P., Zakian, S.M., 2014. TALEN and CRISPR/Cas genome editing systems: tools of discovery. Acta Nat. 6 (22). https://doi.org/10.32607/20758251-2014-6-3-19-40.

Nyquist, M.D., Li, Y., Hwang, T.H., Manlove, L.S., Vessella, R.L., Silverstein, K.A.T., Voytas, D.F., Dehm, S.M., 2013. TALEN-engineered AR gene rearrangements reveal endocrine uncoupling of androgen receptor in prostate cancer. Proc. Natl. Acad. Sci. U. S. A. 110 (43). https://doi.org/10.1073/pnas.1308587110.

Ousterout, D.G., Gersbach, C.A., 2016. The development of TALE nucleases for biotechnology. Methods Mol. Biol. 1338. https://doi.org/10.1007/978-1-4939-2932-0_3.

Pérez-Quintero, A.L., Rodriguez-R, L.M., Dereeper, A., López, C., Koebnik, R., Szurek, B., Cunnac, S., 2013. An improved method for TAL effectors DNA-binding sites prediction reveals functional convergence in TAL repertoires of Xanthomonas oryzae strains. PLoS One 8 (7). https://doi.org/10.1371/journal.pone.0068464.

Piganeau, M., Ghezraoui, H., de Cian, A., Guittat, L., Tomishima, M., Perrouault, L., René, O., Katibah, G.E., Zhang, L., Holmes, M.C., Doyon, Y., Concordet, J.P., Giovannangeli, C., Jasin, M., Brunet, E., 2013. Cancer translocations in human cells induced by zinc finger and TALE nucleases. Genome Res. 23 (7). https://doi.org/10.1101/gr.147314.112.

Reyon, D., Khayter, C., Regan, M.R., Keith Joung, J., Sander, J.D., 2012. Engineering designer transcription activator-like effector nucleases (TALENs) by REAL or REAL-fast assembly. Curr. Protoc. Mol. Biol. Suppl. 100. https://doi.org/10.1002/0471142727.mb1215s100.

Rivlin, N., Brosh, R., Oren, M., Rotter, V., 2011. Mutations in the p53 tumor suppressor gene: important milestones at the various steps of tumorigenesis. Genes Cancer 2 (4). https://doi.org/10.1177/1947601911408889.

Römer, P., Hahn, S., Jordan, T., Strauß, T., Bonas, U., Lahaye, T., 2007. Plant pathogen recognition mediated by promoter activation of the pepper Bs3 resistance gene. Science 318 (5850). https://doi.org/10.1126/science.1144958.

Sander, J.D., Dahlborg, E.J., Goodwin, M.J., Cade, L., Zhang, F., Cifuentes, D., Curtin, S.J., Blackburn, J.-S., Thibodeau-Beganny, S., Qi, Y., Pierick, C.J., Hoffman, E., Maeder, M.L., Khayter, C., Reyon, D., Dobbs, D., Langenau, D.M., Stupar, R.M., Giraldez, A.J., Joung, J.K., 2011. Selection-free zinc-finger-nuclease engineering by context-dependent assembly (CoDA). Nat. Methods 8 (1). https://doi.org/10.1038/nmeth.1542.

Shankar, S., Prasad, D., Sanawar, R., Das, A.v., Pillai, M.R., 2017. TALEN based HPV-E7 editing triggers necrotic cell death in cervical cancer cells. Sci. Rep. 7 (1). https://doi.org/10.1038/s41598-017-05696-0.

Streubel, J., Blücher, C., Landgraf, A., Boch, J., 2012. TAL effector RVD specificities and efficiencies. Nat. Biotechnol. 30 (7). https://doi.org/10.1038/nbt.2304.

Tesson, L., Usal, C., Meq´noret, S., Leung, E., Niles, B.J., Remy, S., Santiago, Y., Vincent, A.I., Meng, X., Zhang, L., Gregory, P.D., Anegon, I., Cost, G.J., 2011. Knockout rats generated by embryo microinjection of TALENs. Nat. Biotechnol. 29 (8). https://doi.org/10.1038/nbt.1940.

Wang, L., Li, F., Dang, L., Liang, C., Wang, C., He, B., Liu, J., Li, D., Wu, X., Xu, X., Lu, A., Zhang, G., 2016. In vivo delivery systems for therapeutic genome editing. Int. J. Mol. Sci. 17 (5). https://doi.org/10.3390/ijms17050626.

Weir, B., Zhao, X., Meyerson, M., 2004. Somatic alterations in the human cancer genome. Cancer Cell 6 (5). https://doi.org/10.1016/j.ccr.2004.11.004.

Wu, X., Blackburn, P.R., Tschumper, R.C., Ekker, S.C., Jelinek, D.F., 2014. TALEN-mediated genetic tailoring as a tool to analyze the function of acquired mutations in multiple myeloma cells. Blood Cancer J. 4 (5). https://doi.org/10.1038/bcj.2014.32.

Zhang, Y., Zhang, F., Li, X., Baller, J.A., Qi, Y., Starker, C.G., Bogdanove, A.J., Voytas, D.F., 2013. Transcription activator-like effector nucleases enable efficient plant genome engineering. Plant Physiol. 161 (1). https://doi.org/10.1104/pp.112.205179.

Zhang, S., Li, L., Kendrick, S.L., Gerard, R.D., Zhu, H., 2014. TALEN-mediated somatic mutagenesis in murine models of cancer. Cancer Res. 74 (18). https://doi.org/10.1158/0008-5472.CAN-14-0529.

CHAPTER SIXTEEN

Immunopeptidomic approaches for management of cancer

Gurjeet Kaur[a], Gitika Batra[b], Praisy K. Prabha[a], Ajay Prakash[a], and Bikash Medhi[a]
[a]Department of Pharmacology, Postgraduate Institute of Medical Education and Research, Chandigarh, India
[b]Department of Neurology, Post Graduate Institute of Medical Education, Chandigarh, India

1. Introduction to immunopeptidomics

The specific identification of workable tumor antigens is requisite for development of multiple cancer immunotherapies, including T-cell receptor–activated T cells and patient-specific mRNA. Majority of tumor antigen were considered to be canonical, when they were derived from protein-coding regions of genome. These immune peptides or their specific antigens were identified through extensive molecular characterization using different molecular techniques. Using the breakthrough technology of T-cell–based immunotherapy, including CAR T cells, immune checkpoint inhibitor, adoptive T-cell transfer, and bispecific antibodies, has provided new hope for the treatment of multiple solid tumors and many hematological malignancies. An immunopeptide-based method usually depends on the specific immune recognition of tumor-associated human leukocyte antigen (HLA)–presented peptides, representing the favorable alternatives of the treatments with minimum side effects. Also targeting the mutation-derived neoepitopes, using vaccination in melanoma—a high-mutational burden tumor entity—has demonstrated immunogenicity and first clinical efficacy. Whereas in sporadic or on-mutated tumor-associated antigens, that originated through differential gene expression or protein processing in tumor cells, might supplement neoepitope targeting in low-mutational burden malignancies (Schmitt et al., 2008).

Cancer immunopeptidome plays a crucial role while identifying tumor specific or tumor-associated antigens (TAA) mainly displayed by cancer cells. Personalized immunotherapy or neoantigen-based therapies involves the exploration of generated CD4[+] and CD8[+] cells against tumor-specific neoantigen or immunopeptidome. Neoantigen or immunopeptide epitope presented by cancer T cells helps in the early diagnosis of cancer as well as the individual patient-oriented tissue-specific treatment approaches. Peptide epitopes have also been utilized for the development of neoantigen/immunopeptide-based vaccines (Bassani-Sternberg, 2018).

Biomarkers in Cancer Detection and Monitoring of Therapeutics
https://doi.org/10.1016/B978-0-323-95116-6.00003-/

285

Major application of cancer immunopeptidomics is:

2. Identification of peptide-HLA antigen

Major histocompatibility complex (MHC) is encoded by a polymorphic genetic cluster, i.e., human leukocyte antigen (HLA). MHC-I and MHC-II bound peptides are presented against CD8$^+$ and CD4$^+$ cells, respectively (Kote et al., 2020). In case of cancer biology, tumor specific or tumor associated antigens/peptides are derived mainly from overexpressed or mutated tumor peptides/proteins, endogenous retroviral transposable elements in human DNA, oncogenic viruses, self/nonself proteins (Solleder et al., 2020).

2.1 Biomarker discovery and treatment targets

Currently, mass spectrometry (MS) based techniques are the most explored and useful methodology for the identification and discovery of immunopeptidome such as HLA or MHC binding proteins/peptides or neoantigens or tumor associated antigens (TAA) (Solleder et al., 2020). Moreover, it is quite difficult to identify various tissue specific posttranslationally modified or mutated peptides, so modified MS based methodology provides significant insight in the identification of an array of tumor associated antigens landscape (Kwon et al., 2021). One such example is a study by Gao et al. (2019), where they explored the phosphoproteomics-based approach and identified tissue specific PYCR2 and ADH1A tumor antigen via in-solution digestion and LC–MS/MS for the early prognosis of liver cancer (HCC). Moreover, Zhang et al. (2021) explored MS based phosphoproteomics in EGFR-mutant cell lines and identified PI3K/AKT targets for the treatment of resistant lung cancer.

2.2 Biomarkers/target for immunotherapy

Tumor antigens or peptides are presented by the immune cells against the tumor cells that determine the adaptive immune response, and this also determines the clinical response toward the personalized immunotherapy (Hayes et al., 2018). Therefore, predicting the accurate clinical response is the most important aspect of immunotherapy. Hence, advanced immunoproteomics is required to identify as well as quantify the whole comprehensive antigenic landscape of different types of tumor. Harel et al. (2019) used the melanoma patient tissue samples and identified MHC as a biomarker for the personalized immunotherapy which provides the mechanistic link between the tumor mitochondria dependent metabolism with tumor specific immunogenicity.

2.3 Utility of various samples

MS-based immunoproteomics aids in the identification and quantification of various proteins and integrated proteomics such as proteogenomics helps in the identification of DNA, RNA, and miRNA-based biomarker discovery. In integrated MS-based approach various types of clinical samples such as tissue, blood, plasma, urine, saliva, extracellular fluid, circulating tumor cells, cancer stem cells and others (Huang et al., 2017). For the early prognosis of invasive ductal pancreatic adenocarcinoma, Yoneyama et al. (2016) identified IGFBP2 and IGFBP3 using plasma samples of patients with pancreatic cancer.

Hence, integrated MS-based immunoproteomics provides insight into the vast antigenic landscape of tumor specific or associated antigens for future biomarker discovery and personalized neoantigen based therapy or immunotherapy. Various types of modified techniques are used for the sample preparation, antigen identification and further clinical validation. It mainly includes LC–MS/MS, MEA, AND PROTEOGENOMICS (Gould et al., 2018).

2.4 Importance of immunopeptidomics in cancer

Cancer immunopeptidome plays a crucial role while identifying tumor specific or tumor associated antigens (TAA) mainly displayed by cancer cells. Personalized immunotherapy or neoantigen based therapies involves the exploration of generated $CD4^+$ and $CD8^+$ cells against tumor specific neoantigen or immunopeptidome. Neoantigen or immunopeptide epitope presented by cancer T cells helps in the early diagnosis of cancer as well as the individual patient oriented tissue specific treatment approaches. Peptide epitopes have also been utilized for the development of neoantigen/immunopeptide based vaccines (Bassani–Sternberg, 2018).

Major application of cancer immunopeptidomics is:

2.5 Identification of peptide-HLA antigen

Major histocompatibility complex (MHC) is encoded by a polymorphic genetic cluster i.e. human leukocyte antigen (HLA). MHC-I and MHC-II bound peptides are presented against $CD8^+$ and $CD4^+$ cells, respectively (Kote et al., 2020). In case of cancer biology, tumor specific or tumor associated antigens/peptides are derived mainly from overexpressed or mutated tumor peptides/proteins, endogenous retroviral transposable elements in human DNA, oncogenic viruses, and self/nonself proteins (Solleder et al., 2020).

2.6 Biomarker discovery and treatment targets

Currently, mass spectrometry (MS) based techniques are the most explored and useful methodology for the identification and discovery of immunopeptidome such as HLA or MHC binding proteins/peptides or neoantigens or tumor associated antigens (TAA) (Solleder et al., 2020). Moreover, it is quite difficult to identify various tissue specific post-translationally modified or mutated peptides, so modified MS based methodology provides significant insight in the identification of an array of tumor associated antigens landscape (Kwon et al., 2021). One such example is, Gao et al., 2019 explored the phosphoproteomics based approach and identified tissue specific PYCR2 and ADH1A tumor antigen via in-solution digestion and LC–MS/MS for the early prognosis of liver cancer (HCC). Moreover, Zhang et al., 2021 explored MS based phosphoproteomics in EGFR-mutant cell lines and identified PI3K/AKT targets for the treatment of resistant lung cancer.

2.7 Biomarkers/target for immunotherapy

Tumor antigens or peptides are presented by the immune cells against the tumor cells that determine the adaptive immune response and this also determines the clinical response toward the personalized immunotherapy (Hayes et al., 2018). Therefore, predicting the accurate clinical response is the most important aspect of immunotherapy. Hence, advanced immunoproteomics is required to identify as well as quantify the whole comprehensive antigenic landscape of different types of tumor. Harel et al. (2019) used the melanoma patient tissue samples and identified MHC as a biomarker for the personalized immunotherapy which provides the mechanistic link between the tumor mitochondria dependent metabolism with tumor specific immunogenicity.

2.8 Utility of various samples

MS-based immunoproteomics aids in the identification and quantification of various proteins and integrated proteomics such as proteogenomics helps in the identification of DNA, RNA, and miRNA-based biomarker discovery. In integrated MS-based approach various types of clinical samples such as tissue, blood, plasma, urine, saliva, extracellular fluid, circulating tumor cells, cancer stem cells and others (Huang et al., 2017). For the early prognosis of invasive ductal pancreatic adenocarcinoma, Yoneyama et al. (2016) identified IGFBP2 and IGFBP3 using plasma samples of patients with pancreatic cancer.

Hence, integrated MS-based immunoproteomics provides insight into the vast antigenic landscape of tumor specific or associated antigens for future biomarker discovery and personalized neoantigen based therapy or immunotherapy. Various types of modified techniques are used for the sample preparation, antigen identification and further clinical validation. It mainly includes LC–MS/MS, MEA, AND PROTEOGENOMICS (Gould et al., 2018).

2.9 Different approaches for identification of tumor-specific immunopeptidome

Identification of tumor-specific immunopeptidome is the first step for development of vaccines and drugs against different kinds of tumors. There are three main approaches available to identify tumor-specific immunopeptidome. These can be broadly classified as:
  i. cDNA Expression profiling based approach
  ii. Next generation sequencing based approach
  iii. Mass spectrometry based approach

i. **cDNA expression profiling based approach:** This approach was the first one to be used for the identification of tumor antigens (Kawakami et al., 1994). In this approach, both tumor cells and tumor reactive T-cells are isolated from patient tumor sample. The T-cells can also be isolated from peripheral blood lymphocytes (PBL). The tumor cells are then processed for total RNA extraction followed by cDNA preparation to prepare pools of cDNA plasmid. These are then cotransfected with plasmid encoding specific MHC molecules into the recipient cells. The cells with successful cotransfection are then cocultured with the tumor reactive T-cells isolated from the patient. The cells, harboring cDNA plasmids, that are able to demonstrate T-cell recognition are then used to define the specific encoded epitope for peptide synthesis. These epitopes are then further validated by testing for immunogenicity. However, the time-consuming and tedious procedures involved in this approach make it less suitable for high throughput screening (HTS) of tumor-specific immunopeptidome (Fritsche et al., 2018; Leko and Rosenberg, 2020) (Fig. 1).

ii. **Next generation sequencing based approach:** This approach is less laborious and cost-effective compared to cDNA expression profiling based method. In this approach, the most important mutations are identified among all the mutations in the site-of-tumor, usually by genomic sequencing of peripheral blood mononuclear cells (PBMCs) (Kaur et al., 2022). Based on the preference, one can either go for whole-exome sequencing (WES) or RNA sequencing (RNA-seq) (Brohl et al., 2021; Chong et al., 2020; Dong et al., 2020; Fritsche et al., 2018; Qi et al., 2021). The identified mutations are then provided into specific T-cell epitope algorithms in order to predict the binding affinities of the peptides derived from these mutations to specific HLA alleles. The results of these prediction algorithms are based on the data conditioned to them previously from in-vitro binding assays or immunopeptidomics data. The "Good binders" or the mutations exhibiting good binding affinity by passing an already specified consensus threshold, are cloned to form Tandem minigene (TMG) libraries. These TMG constructs are then transfected into antigen-presenting cells (APCs) to test for immunogenicity with the T-cells. The constructs demonstrating T-cell recognition are then further used to identify the specific mutations in them. These mutations are then separately transfected into the APCs to test their immunogenicity individually against T-cells (Leko and Rosenberg, 2020; Zhang et al., 2019) (Fig. 2).

Usually mutations are identified using tools like HaplotypeCaller (Broad Institute), GATK framework v3.7, SnpEff (Microsoft Genomics), edgeR package, and Picard Tools v2.9.0 (DePristo et al., 2011).

Similarly different softwares (NetMHCpan-4.0, MixMHCpred.v2) and databases (Immune Epitope Database and Analysis Resource) can be accessed for the prediction of the binding affinities of the peptides derived from these mutations to specific HLA alleles.

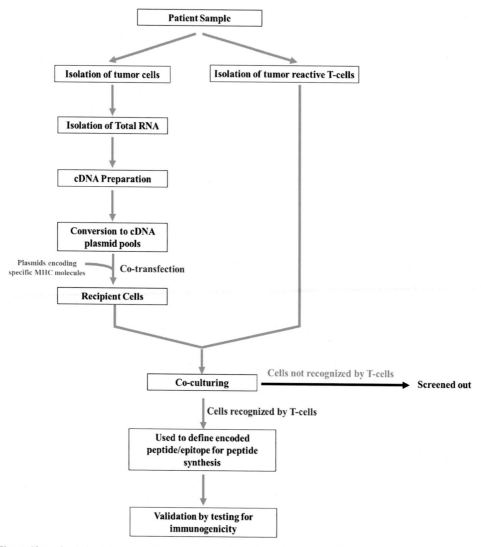

Fig. 1 Flow chart depicting cDNA expression profiling based approach for the identification of tumor-specific immunopeptidome.

iii. **Mass spectrometry based approach:** This is the most direct approach to identify tumor specific immunopeptidomes. In this approach, the HLA complexes are directly isolated from the patient sample either by immunoprecipitation (IP) or by mild acid elution (MAE). The bound antigen peptides that are eluted out along with the HLA molecules are then dissociated from the latter and subjected to epitope purification, followed by mass spectrometry based analysis of the purified peptides. The analyzed data is then validated by comparing to MS raw files after extensive

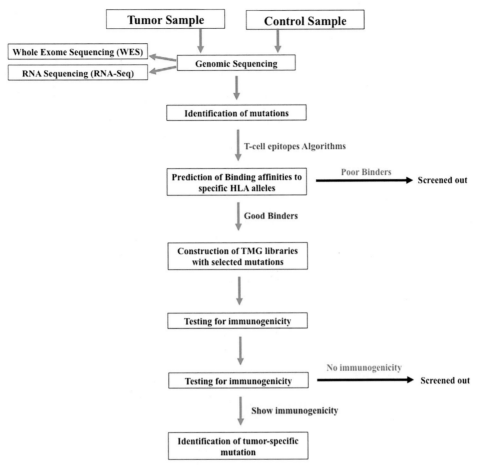

Fig. 2 Flow chart depicting next-generation sequencing-based approach for the identification of tumor-specific immunopeptidome.

database or library search for similar peptides. This is followed by matching to corresponding HLA alleles using prediction algorithms. The matched peptide–HLA complex is then tested for immunogenicity to identify and validate the specific mutation (Leko and Rosenberg, 2020; Zhang et al., 2019) (Fig. 3).

Different mass spectrometry based methods are being used for the identification of tumor-specific antigens. However, most commonly used MS methods are liquid chromatography/mass spectrometry or LC–MS (Chow and Rardin, 2021; Fritsche et al., 2018; Ghosh et al., 2020), and tandem mass spectrometry or TMS (Ghosh et al., 2020; Park et al., 2017; Pfammatter et al., 2020).

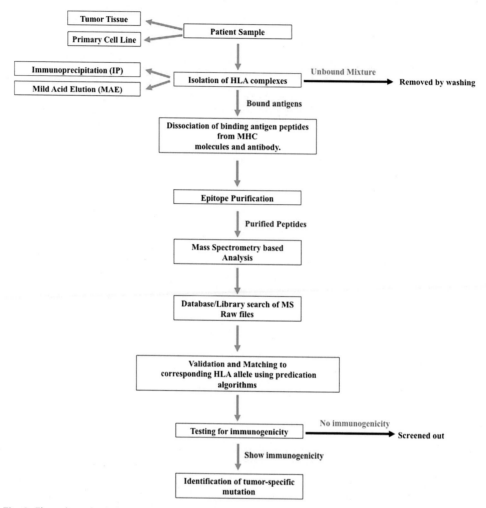

Fig. 3 Flow chart depicting mass spectrometry based approach for the identification of tumor-specific immunopeptidome.

3. Translating immunopeptidomics to immunotherapy

Mass spectrometry-based proteomics technology has not only started to contribute directly to immunotherapy but has also already aided to elucidate the signal and protein interaction mechanisms to improve the understanding of multiple cancer diagnosis and molecular mechanism to assist the application of immunotherapy.

Still now, for many types of tumors, the induction mechanism still needs to be clearly explained. Proteomics particularly the identification of specific immune peptides can cover a larger number of proteins and subsequently solidify the final drivers of multiple tumor type. Whole-genome sequencing and transcriptome sequencing only provide a hint of what is leading to the occurrence of the tumor; thus, the identification and quantification of specific proteins by proteomics could finally verify what is arising in the tumor to transfer the cells. Many high-throughput proteomics studies have revealed that there are more possible candidate proteins to elucidate these mechanisms. For successful designing of immunotherapy, integration of next generation sequencing data and insights of antigen selection, interaction of tumor cells with the immune system and rational selection of combination therapies, we can aim to develop clinically effective peptide vaccination. These approaches can enable us to design different immune peptides that could provide the foundation for the development of time- and cost-effective personalized T-cell–based immunotherapy approaches.

References

Bassani-Sternberg, M., 2018. Mass spectrometry based immunopeptidomics for the discovery of cancer neoantigens. Methods Mol. Biol. 1719, 209–221. https://doi.org/10.1007/978-1-4939-7537-2_14.

Brohl, A.S., Sindiri, S., Wei, J.S., Milewski, D., Chou, H.-C., Song, Y.K., Wen, X., Kumar, J., Reardon, H.V., Mudunuri, U.S., Collins, J.R., Nagaraj, S., Gangalapudi, V., Tyagi, M., Zhu, Y.J., Masih, K.E., Yohe, M.E., Shern, J.F., Qi, Y., Khan, J., 2021. Immuno-transcriptomic profiling of extracranial pediatric solid malignancies. Cell Rep. 37 (8), 110047. https://doi.org/10.1016/j.celrep.2021.110047.

Chong, C., Müller, M., Pak, H., Harnett, D., Huber, F., Grun, D., Leleu, M., Auger, A., Arnaud, M., Stevenson, B.J., Michaux, J., Bilic, I., Hirsekorn, A., Calviello, L., Simó-Riudalbas, L., Planet, E., Lubiński, J., Bryśkiewicz, M., Wiznerowicz, M., Bassani-Sternberg, M., 2020. Integrated proteogenomic deep sequencing and analytics accurately identify non-canonical peptides in tumor immunopeptidomes. Nat. Commun. 11 (1), 1293. https://doi.org/10.1038/s41467-020-14968-9.

Chow, D.T., Rardin, M.J., 2021. Identification and mitigation of defensins in the immunopurification of peptide MHC-I antigens from lung tissue. J. Am. Soc. Mass Spectrom. https://doi.org/10.1021/jasms.1c00024.

DePristo, M.A., Banks, E., Poplin, R.E., Garimella, K.V., Maguire, J.R., Hartl, C., Philippakis, A.A., del Angel, G., Rivas, M.A., Hanna, M., McKenna, A., Fennell, T.J., Kernytsky, A.M., Sivachenko, A.Y., Cibulskis, K., Gabriel, S.B., Altshuler, D., Daly, M.J., 2011. A framework for variation discovery and genotyping using next-generation DNA sequencing data. Nat. Genet. 43 (5), 491–498. https://doi.org/10.1038/ng.806.

Dong, L.-Q., Peng, L.-H., Ma, L.-J., Liu, D.-B., Zhang, S., Luo, S.-Z., Rao, J.-H., Zhu, H.-W., Yang, S.-X., Xi, S.-J., Chen, M., Xie, F.-F., Li, F.-Q., Li, W.-H., Ye, C., Lin, L.-Y., Wang, Y.-J., Wang, X.-Y., Gao, D.-M., Gao, Q., 2020. Heterogeneous immunogenomic features and distinct escape mechanisms in multifocal hepatocellular carcinoma. J. Hepatol. 72 (5), 896–908. https://doi.org/10.1016/j.jhep.2019.12.014.

Fritsche, J., Rakitsch, B., Hoffgaard, F., Römer, M., Schuster, H., Kowalewski, D.J., Priemer, M., Stos-Zweifel, V., Hörzer, H., Satelli, A., Sonntag, A., Goldfinger, V., Song, C., Mahr, A., Ott, M., Schoor, O., Weinschenk, T., 2018. Translating immunopeptidomics to immunotherapy-decision-making for patient and personalized target selection. Proteomics 18 (12), e1700284. https://doi.org/10.1002/pmic.201700284.

Gao, Q., Zhu, H., Dong, L., Shi, W., Chen, R., Song, Z., Huang, C., Li, J., Dong, X., Zhou, Y., Liu, Q., Ma, L., Wang, X., Zhou, J., Liu, Y., Boja, E., Robles, A.I., Ma, W., Wang, P., Li, Y., Fan, J., 2019. Integrated proteogenomic characterization of HBV-related hepatocellular carcinoma. Cell 179 (5), 1240. https://doi.org/10.1016/j.cell.2019.10.038.

Ghosh, M., Gauger, M., Marcu, A., Nelde, A., Denk, M., Schuster, H., Rammensee, H.-G., Stevanović, S., 2020. Guidance document: validation of a high-performance liquid chromatography-tandem mass spectrometry immunopeptidomics assay for the identification of HLA class I ligands suitable for pharmaceutical therapies. Mol. Cell. Proteomics 19 (3), 432–443. https://doi.org/10.1074/mcp.C119.001652.

Gould, T., Jamaluddin, M.F.B., Petit, J., King, S.J., Nixon, B., Scott, R., Dun, M.D., 2018. Finding needles in haystacks: the use of quantitative proteomics for the early detection of colorectal cancer. In: Segelov, E. (Ed.), Advances in the Molecular Understanding of Colorectal Cancer. IntechOpen. Chapter 7.

Harel, M., Ortenberg, R., Varanasi, S.K., Mangalhara, K.C., Mardamshina, M., Markovits, E., Baruch, E.N., Tripple, V., Arama-Chayoth, M., Greenberg, E., Shenoy, A., Ayasun, R., Knafo, N., Xu, S., Anafi, L., Yanovich-Arad, G., Barnabas, G.D., Ashkenazi, S., Besser, M.J., Schachter, J., Geiger, T., 2019. Proteomics of melanoma response to immunotherapy reveals mitochondrial dependence. Cell 179 (1), 236–250.e18. https://doi.org/10.1016/j.cell.2019.08.012.

Hayes, S.A., Clarke, S., Pavlakis, N., Howell, V.M., 2018. The role of proteomics in the age of immunotherapies. Mamm. Genome 29 (11–12), 757–769. https://doi.org/10.1007/s00335-018-9763-6.

Huang, R., Chen, Z., He, L., He, N., Xi, Z., Li, Z., Deng, Y., Zeng, X., 2017. Mass spectrometry-assisted gel-based proteomics in cancer biomarker discovery: approaches and application. Theranostics 7 (14), 3559–3572. https://doi.org/10.7150/thno.20797.

Kaur, G., Bhadada, S.K., Santra, M., Pal, R., Sarma, P., Sachdeva, N., Dhiman, V., Dahiya, D., Saikia, U.N., Chakraborty, A., Sood, A., Prakash, M., Behera, A., Rao, S.D., 2022. Multilevel annotation of germline MEN1 variants of synonymous, nonsynonymous, and uncertain significance in Indian patients with sporadic primary hyperparathyroidism. J. Bone Miner. Res. 37 (10), 1860–1875. https://doi.org/10.1002/jbmr.4653.

Kawakami, Y., Eliyahu, S., Sakaguchi, K., Robbins, P.F., Rivoltini, L., Yannelli, J.R., Appella, E., Rosenberg, S.A., 1994. Identification of the immunodominant peptides of the MART-1 human melanoma antigen recognized by the majority of HLA-A2-restricted tumor infiltrating lymphocytes. J. Exp. Med. 180 (1), 347–352. https://doi.org/10.1084/jem.180.1.347.

Kote, S., Pirog, A., Bedran, G., Alfaro, J., Dapic, I., 2020. Mass spectrometry-based identification of MHC-associated peptides. Cancers 12 (3), 535. https://doi.org/10.3390/cancers12030535.

Kwon, Y.W., Jo, H.S., Bae, S., Seo, Y., Song, P., Song, M., Yoon, J.H., 2021. Application of proteomics in cancer: recent trends and approaches for biomarkers discovery. Front. Med. 8, 747333. https://doi.org/10.3389/fmed.2021.747333.

Leko, V., Rosenberg, S.A., 2020. Identifying and targeting human tumor antigens for T cell-based immunotherapy of solid tumors. Cancer Cell 38 (4), 454–472. https://doi.org/10.1016/j.ccell.2020.07.013.

Park, J., Talukder, A.H., Lim, S.A., Kim, K., Pan, K., Melendez, B., Bradley, S.D., Jackson, K.R., Khalili, J.-S., Wang, J., Creasy, C., Pan, B.-F., Woodman, S.E., Bernatchez, C., Hawke, D., Hwu, P., Lee, K.-M., Roszik, J., Lizée, G., Yee, C., 2017. SLC45A2: a melanoma antigen with high tumor selectivity and reduced potential for autoimmune toxicity. Cancer Immunol. Res. 5 (8), 618–629. https://doi.org/10.1158/2326-6066.CIR-17-0051.

Pfammatter, S., Bonneil, E., Lanoix, J., Vincent, K., Hardy, M.-P., Courcelles, M., Perreault, C., Thibault, P., 2020. Extending the comprehensiveness of immunopeptidome analyses using isobaric peptide labeling. Anal. Chem. 92 (13), 9194–9204. https://doi.org/10.1021/acs.analchem.0c01545.

Qi, Y.A., Maity, T.K., Cultraro, C.M., Misra, V., Zhang, X., Ade, C., Gao, S., Milewski, D., Nguyen, K.D., Ebrahimabadi, M.H., Hanada, K.-I., Khan, J., Sahinalp, C., Yang, J.C., Guha, U., 2021. Proteogenomic analysis unveils the HLA class I-presented immunopeptidome in melanoma and EGFR-mutant lung adenocarcinoma. Mol. Cell. Proteomics 20, 100136. https://doi.org/10.1016/j.mcpro.2021.100136.

Schmitt, M., Schmitt, A., Rojewski, M.T., Chen, J., Giannopoulos, K., Fei, F., et al., 2008. RHAMM-R3 peptide vaccination in patients with acute myeloid leukemia, myelodysplastic syndrome, and multiple myeloma elicits immunologic and clinical responses. Blood 111 (3), 1357–1365. https://doi.org/10.1182/blood-2007-07-099366.

Solleder, M., Guillaume, P., Racle, J., Michaux, J., Pak, H.S., Müller, M., Coukos, G., Bassani-Sternberg, M., Gfeller, D., 2020. Mass spectrometry based immunopeptidomics leads to robust predictions of phosphorylated HLA class I ligands. Mol. Cell. Proteomics 19 (2), 390–404. https://doi.org/10.1074/mcp.TIR119.001641.

Yoneyama, T., Ohtsuki, S., Honda, K., Kobayashi, M., Iwasaki, M., Uchida, Y., Okusaka, T., Nakamori, S., Shimahara, M., Ueno, T., Tsuchida, A., Sata, N., Ioka, T., Yasunami, Y., Kosuge, T., Kaneda, T., Kato, T., Yagihara, K., Fujita, S., Huang, W., Terasaki, T., 2016. Identification of IGFBP2 and IGFBP3 as compensatory biomarkers for CA19-9 in early-stage pancreatic cancer using a combination of antibody-based and LC-MS/MS-based proteomics. PLoS One 11 (8), e0161009. https://doi.org/10.1371/journal.pone.0161009.

Zhang, X., Qi, Y., Zhang, Q., Liu, W., 2019. Application of mass spectrometry-based MHC immunopeptidome profiling in neoantigen identification for tumor immunotherapy. Biomed. Pharmacother. 120, 109542. https://doi.org/10.1016/j.biopha.2019.109542.

Zhang, X., Maity, T.K., Ross, K.E., Qi, Y., Cultraro, C.M., Bahta, M., Pitts, S., Keswani, M., Gao, S., Nguyen, K., Cowart, J., Kirkali, F., Wu, C., Guha, U., 2021. Alterations in the global proteome and phosphoproteome in third generation EGFR TKI resistance reveal drug targets to circumvent resistance. Cancer Res. 81 (11), 3051–3066. https://doi.org/10.1158/0008-5472.CAN-20-2435.

CHAPTER SEVENTEEN

Regulation of tumor microenvironment by nutrient trafficking

Subodh Kumar[a,b], Gitika Batra[b], Seema Bansal[b], Praisy K. Prabha[b], Hardeep Kaur[b], Ajay Prakash[b], Anurag Kuhad[a], and Bikash Medhi[b]

[a]UIPS, Panjab University, Chandigarh, India
[b]Department of Pharmacology, Postgraduate Institute of Medical Education and Research, Chandigarh, India

1. Introduction

Cancer remains leader to dwell a noteworthy financial, social, and mental burden worldwide. As per WHO report, worldwide in 2020, around 1.93 billion new cancer cases were diagnosed with a death rate of approximately half of these reported cases (WHO, 2020), and it is likely to increase every year. Therefore, due to increased mortality and high healthcare cost, it is vital to understand the molecular and cellular dynamics of the tumor formation and progression so that appropriate interventions can be taken place. Tumors consisted of malignant cells as a result of altered/mutated function of essential cellular components and corrupt the functional mechanism of other cells in the body. Tumor tissues create a tumor microenvironment (TME) through expending and building a vascular network as well as through mutual and dynamic crosstalk in order to survive. Tumor cells of TME control the function of nonmalignant cells and induce them to work for their own benefit using micronutrients and complex signaling networks. With the advancement of molecular and biochemical tools, knowledge underlying TME of cancerous cells have deeply expanded our understanding of the mechanisms of altered metabolic impression at various phases of tumorigenesis such as (1) ability to acquire the necessary nutrients by affecting the metabolite influx, (2) ensuring that acquired nutrients are routed through altered metabolic influx and reaching efficiently to malignant cells, and (3) exerting in differentiation of TME constituents and themselves. Therefore, understanding the tumor microenvironment (TME), micronutrient trafficking, and decoding metabolic alterations among tumor cells will improve the understanding of cancer and efforts are going on. In this chapter, we highlighted the components of tumor microenvironment, alteration in tumorigenic metabolism, importance of micronutrients in cancer therapies that target cancer cells Metabolism.

Biomarkers in Cancer Detection and Monitoring of Therapeutics
https://doi.org/10.1016/B978-0-323-95116-6.00016-5

2. TME and changes in tumor cells metabolism

The tumor microenvironment role is crucial in the process of tumorigenesis including progression and metastasis. TME in itself is a separate entity with its own characteristic features in different types of cancers. One can easily differentiate different types of tumors based on the composition of the TME of the particular tumor. TME comprises of both cellular and noncellular components. However, some of these components are constant in all the tumors (Arneth, 2019; Nm and Mc, 2020). Fig. 1 depicts different components and subcomponents of the tumor microenvironment. Each and every component is crucial due to their individual role in progression and/or inhibition of tumor growth (pro- and antitumorigenic function, respectively) depending upon certain chemical cues they receive within the tumor microenvironment.

2.1 Components of the tumor microenvironment

Immune cells: These include T cells, B cells, natural killer cells, macrophages, neutrophils, and dendritic cells. While T cells, B cells, and natural killer cells form the part of adaptive immunity, innate immunity comprises of macrophages, neutrophils, and dendritic cells.

T cells: A heterogeneous population of different subsets of T cells can be found influencing the tumor cells in different ways. While cytotoxic and help T cells are antitumorigenic in their effect, regulatory T cells can turn as the tumor promoters due to their role in suppression of previously generated immune response.

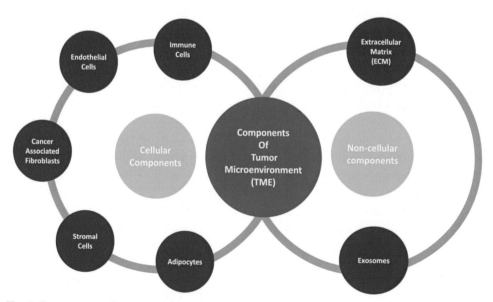

Fig. 1 Components of tumor microenvironment (TME).

B cells: These are usually present at the periphery of the tumors in the lymph nodes found in close proximity to the TME. B cells show antitumorigenic effect as antigen presenting cells (APCs), antitumor antibody producing cells, and cytokine releasers for the promotion of cytotoxic immune response. However, regulatory B cells are pro-tumorigenic in nature due to their immunosuppressive role in the body.

Natural killer cells: These are present in the blood stream and are very efficient in killing the tumors cells found in circulation, thereby, playing an important role in blocking metastasis. These cells can either directly participate in killing of tumor cells or indirectly by the secretion of inflammatory cytokines.

Macrophages: Both M1 and M2 macrophages are found in the TME. While M1 phenotype of macrophages is antitumorigenic and have a role in phagocytosis of tumor cells, M2 phenotype is immune-suppressive and promote tumor development. The TME specifically promote the M2 phenotype for tumor growth and progression. Macrophages also play a critical part in angiogenesis by secreting vascular endothelial growth factor-A (VEGF-A) (Vitale et al., 2019).

Neutrophils: Neutrophils can act both as tumor suppressors and promoters, depending upon the type of tumor and the stage of tumor development. In the early stages of tumor development, neutrophils in the TME generate an inflammatory response by the release of cytokines to promote tumor cell death. On the other hand, same neutrophils can turn out to be protumorigenic in later stages of tumor development by serving as modulators of extracellular matrix as well as promoters of angiogenesis.

Dendritic cells: Even though dendritic cells play a critical role in generation of an immune response and killing of tumor cells by serving as antigen presenting cells, this effect can be blocked by certain cytokines present in the TME that may prompt the dendritic cells to become tolerant to the tumor cells.

Endothelial cells: Endothelial cells play a major role in angiogenesis. VEGF induces EC migration to generate lumens of new blood vessels in both autocrine and paracrine manner. Following that, ECs secrete proteins in order to create new basement membranes. The tumor microenvironment usually has leaky vasculature due to the presence of immature blood vessels. ECs are important in cancer cell migration, invasion, and metastasis, in addition to angiogenesis. In nature, ECs are very malleable and have the ability to change cell fate. Endothelial-mesenchymal transition occurs during tumor growth, causing ECs to become cancer related.

Cancer-associated fibroblasts (CAFs): CAFs are one of the most important components of the tumor stroma, having critical role in aiding the crosstalk among tumor cells and TME. CAFs can be considered as manufacturing units that secrete most of the extracellular components required in the TME, such as extracellular matrix, growth factors, and cytokines. CAFs have the ability to modify TME by different ways like neoangiogenesis, immunosuppression, ECM remodeling, etc. Epithelial–mesenchymal transition (EMT) is a pivotal phase in metastasis in epithelial malignancies, in which epithelial cells lose their polarized and adhesive properties to acquire migratory and invasive mesenchymal behaviors.

Stromal cells: To encourage essential phases in tumor growth, cancer cells attract supportive cells from adjacent endogenous tissue stroma. These might include but are not limited to vessel endothelial cells, adipocytes, fibroblasts, and stellate cells. The fraction of these cells in total stromal cell composition may vary greatly between tumor types. Stromal cells release a variety of factors on being recruited to the TME that promote proliferation, angiogenesis, metastasis, and invasion.

Adipocytes: Adipocytes in the TME secrete metabolites, cytokines, growth factors, hormones, and enzymes to facilitate the progression of tumor cells. Their role is reported to be crucial in the modification of the extracellular matrix by secreting certain metalloproteases.

Extracellular matrix: Extracellular matrix (ECM) constitute as the major components of the TME, especially in case of solid tumors. They provide a physical scaffold for cells, as well as promote the dissemination of the tumor cells. ECM is composed of collagen, laminin, fibronectin, and elastin and serves as a reservoir cytokines and growth factors required for tumor growth and progression.

Exosomes: These are microvesicles produced by tumor cells in the TME. They have a critical role in initiating the stromal cells' transition into cancer-associated fibroblasts. They are also involved in inflammation, angiogenesis, metastasis, and tumor progression.

3. Nutrients and cancer cell metabolism

It is well known now that that various environmental factors plays crucial role in cancer cell metabolism. One of them most important is nutrition. Studies have reported that alteration in nutrient uptake influence the cancer cell metabolism. Type of diet uptake tremendously affects the health. Intake of Mediterranean diet leads to enhancement of lifespan while western diet intake leads to different chronic diseases. Plant based diet reduces the risks of cancer. Metabolism of lipids, proteins and carbohydrates provides a golden opportunity to modulate cancer cell metabolism. Apart from this nutrition can cause gene alteration hence plays an important role in diseases pathologies including cancer via epigenetic changes. Main mechanisms via which nutrients can influence epigenetic status include DNA methylation, histone modifications, and miRNA-dependent gene silencing. Alteration in these mechanisms may result either increase or decrease risk of cancer development (Andreescu et al., 2018). Different molecular links via which diet influence cell metabolism are described as following.

3.1 Influence of restriction of calorie on cancer cell metabolism

Large numbers of in vivo studies have reported that calorie restriction can prevent cancer from different tissues lungs, prostate, pancreatic, hepatic, skin, etc. It involves multiple mechanisms such as via reducing circulating levels of different growth factors such as IGF-1. It also modulates different signaling pathways such as PI3K/AKT/mTOR, activity of which have been dysregulated during cancers. Study by O'Flanagan et al. (2017) reported that calorie restriction in diet showed proapoptotic and antiangiogenic effect in mice. Further, study by Redman et al. (2018) reported that calorie restriction slows metabolic rate in humans resulting in decrease of age related diseases via decreasing release of reactive oxygenated species.

3.2 Influence of fasting on cancer cell metabolism

Fasting regimens such as fasting on alternate days or restrict diet according to time influence the health. Short-term fast results decrease of growth factors. Study by Lee et al. (2012) reported that nutrient restriction in yeast and mammalian cells showed antitumor genic effect due decline of oxidative stress. Main mechanism behind protective effect of fasting is that fasting directs normal cells toward the stress resistant state; however cancer cells are not able to adopt stress resistance.

3.3 Influence of epigenetic changes occurring due to nutrition on cancer cell metabolism

Micronutrients involved in one-carbon metabolism such as folate, cobalamine, and riboflavin result in DNA methylation in cancer. Studies have reported folic acid intake reduce incidence of cervical dysplasia and cervical cancer via modulation of DNA methylation. Another study reported that low dietary intake of cobalamine, niacin, and pyridoxine enhances breast cancer chances. Different phytoestrogens such as genistein and resveratrol interact with estrogen receptors. In in vitro study, it is reported that genistein inhibits various epigenetic modifications which are accountable for the proliferation of esophageal squamous carcinoma and prostate cancer (Fang et al., 2005). Study reported that genistein showed equivalent effect as that of 5-aza-cytidine in renal carcinoma cell lines via decrease promoter methylation of cell lines. An in vitro study reported that curcumin inhibited DNMT activity and thus induced DNA hypomethylation and showed anticancer effect (Liu et al., 2009). Various in vitro and in vivo studies have reported the importance of the nutrients in epigenetic changes especially in histone proteins as enhancement of histone deacetylation (HDAC) has been found in many cancers which affects cell cycle kinetics and apoptosis. Dietary constituents like EGCG, organosulfur compounds, and genistein have been reported to show anticancer effect via inhibition of HDAC activity. Sodium butyrate, peppermint, celery, and parsley inhibit growth of tumor cells via inhibition of HDACs and enhancement of histone acetylation. Anticancer effect of genistein is via increase of histone acetylation, while curcumin shows anticancer effect via inhibition of histone deacetylation. Administration of vitamin D inhibits prostate cancer cell proliferation. EGCG showed anticancer effect via alteration of histone acetylation and methylation while inhibition of histone deacetylation. Various noncoding RNAs such as miRNA, siRNA, and pi RNAs regulate the gene expression. Kutay et al. (2006) reported that miRNA alterations can be prevented by folate intake. Curcumin showed anticancer effect via enhancement of miRNA 22 tumor suppressor gene. Along-with this, curcumin also influences the expression of miR-15 and miR-16 in breast and prostate cancer.

4. Strategies adopted by cancer cells to alter the tumor microenvironment via metabolic reprogramming

Metabolic reprogramming is widely acknowledged as one of the signatures of cancer that regulates the cellular plasticity of tumor cells. Anaerobic glycolysis or Warburg effect majorly regulates cancer cell growth while utilizing high glucose ultimately reprograms cellular metabolism. Other than this the major contributors of nutrient trafficking in tumor microenvironment includes autophagy and macropinocytosis (Choi et al., 2017).

4.1 Autophagy

Autophagy is a phenomenon in which unwanted organelles (damaged or nonfunctional) and macromolecules (nucleic acids, proteins, and carbohydrates) are trapped and transported to lysosomes for their degradation (Neufeld, 2012). Under metabolic stress situations such as food restriction, numerous cargo molecules regulating the autophagy are destroyed and reprocessed to support metabolic activities while maintaining cellular bioenergy equilibrium or homeostasis. Autophagy, a common catabolic mechanism, is adversely regulated by many growth-signaling pathways (Choi et al., 2017). PI3K/AKT/mTOR signaling pathway is the major signaling axis that regulates the autophagy. mTOR (mammalian target of rapamycin) is a serine/threonine protein kinase that senses extracellular nutrients which leads to cell differentiation, growth and suppression of autophagy, whereas in nutrient deprived condition, mTOR gets inactivated and induces autophagy (Zoncu et al., 2011). Therefore, stress induced activation of autophagy utilizes lysosomes for the efficient degradation of various cargo molecules via multiple trafficking routes, both dependent on and independent of the autophagy pathway. Moreover, lysosomes have recently gotten a lot of interest as a means to control the mTORC1 pathway. mTORC1 activity has a significant impact on lysosomal function and localization. The intracellular nutritional status of mTOR, notably amino acid levels, influences its subcellular location. The active state of mTOR is found at the lysosomal membrane in nutrient-complete conditions. During food deprivation, mTOR is no longer localized at the membrane of lysosomes in its inactive state, but is instead widely disseminated all over the cytoplasm (Efeyan et al., 2012). Choi et al. (2017) have shown that REP1 regulates the activation of mTORC1 and autophagy. Other than mTOR, K-Ras also regulates the autophagy in nutrient deprived conditions and alters the malignant cancer cell transformation (Kim et al., 2011).

4.2 Macropinocytosis

Macropinocytosis cellular pathway that scavenges the nutrients to modulate the cancer tumor microenvironment via the endocytic uptake of fluid in macropinosomes for the lysosomal degradation of various molecules such as serum albumin. This provides the cancer cells with all the necessary nutrients required for their growth and survival especially in stressed conditions. Macropinocytosis is more common in Ras-driven cancer cells, which aids in the internalization of extracellular proteins (ECPs). Amino acid shortage causes extracellular protein (e.g., albumin) macropinocytosis, followed by breakdown in the lysosomes and production of amino acid in Ras-driven cancer cells. Therefore, inhibiting the mTORC1 signaling pathway activates the macropinocytosis in order to utilize the extracellular proteins (Kamphorst et al., 2015). Cell death occurs at the tumor's core due to a lack of nutrition and oxygen delivery. Kim et al. (2018) showed that in Ras-driven PTEN deficient prostate cancer cells, nutrient starvation condition activates AMPK and inhibits mTORC1 which aids in cell proliferation by triggering cell debris scavenging. Amino acids derived from cell debris have been found to aid in the formation of cell biomass. Under glucose deprivation, PDAC cells can absorb collagen I and IV by macropinocytosis, and under low glutamine circumstances, they can do so via receptor-dependent endocytosis. One study highlights the degradation of collagen via lysosomes that yields proline. This proline is used for the generation of energy/ATP through TCA cycle. Therefore, amino acids generated energy activates ERK1/2 signaling pathway that leads to cell proliferation and survival of PDAC cells. In the starvation of amino acid and glucose, AMPK activation and mTORC1 inhibition aid cell proliferation by triggering cell debris scavenging in prostate cancer cell lines and KRas-driven pancreatic cancer cells (Olivares et al., 2017). It's unclear whether other collagen amino acids play a role in cancer cell survival as well. Although Ras has been recognized for its role in producing macropinocytosis under stress conditions, its activity in the presence of various growth factors may be redundant. PI3K-dependent macropinocytosis via growth factors leads to enhanced extracellular protein absorption in murine embryonic fibroblasts (MEF). As glucose and amino acids promotes the activation of AKT/mTORC1 signaling, in the absence of amino acids, stimulation of Rac1 and PLCγ as a potent PI3K effector promote ECP macropinocytosis. This permits cells to absorb macromolecules by using free amino acids from transporters rather than macropinocytosis (Palm et al., 2017). EGFR signaling is potentiated by glutamine deficiency, resulting in the Ras/Pak-activated signaling pathway. Activated Pak1 also regulates the treatment modalities such as BCG entry in bladder cancer cells (Redelman-Sidi et al., 2013).

Therefore, in cancer cells various signaling pathways regulate the metabolic reprogramming under nutrient deprived or starved conditions that modulates the extracellular matrix protein such as collagen or albumin. Further, detailed studies are required to understand the nutrient trafficking pathways utilized by the cancer cells to facilitate their growth and survival one such phenomenon is angiogenesis which forms blood vessels for cancer cells for more uptake of amino acids such as glutamine and glucose. Nutritional adaptation also regulates the immune surveillance which leads to more of TILs (tumor-infiltrating cells) in the tumor microenvironment (Cantelmo et al., 2016). Therefore, with given knowledge we have accumulated over more than a decade regarding the nutrient demands and signaling used by cancer cells, researchers can develop new advanced therapies to cut off the nutritional fuel of the cancer cells in order to hamper their growth and survival (Ngwa et al., 2019).

5. Cancer metabolism based therapies

It is well evident that targeting metabolic dependency in tumor microenvironment provides an opportunity to tumor metabolism specialists for proficient therapeutic interventions. In this chapter we focused on metabolic enzymes based drugs and agents that interfere with DNA replication. Among earliest drugs, methotrexate was used as an anti-cancer which is an antifolate drug that inhibits thymidine synthesis (Sun et al., 2017). Similarly, aminopterin, another folate analog, has shown effectiveness in children with acute lymphoblastic leukemia (Farber and Diamond, 1948). Success with these clinical outcomes opened the doors for using these small molecule inhibitors of nucleotide synthesis enzymes and became the backbone of multi agent hemotherapy regimens. These include inhibitors of purine and pyrimidine synthesis as well as salvage such as dihydrofolate reductase and other folate using enzymes, thymidylate synthase, phosphoribosyl pyrophosphate amido transferase, and ribonucleotide reductase. Another cancer targeting approach discovered include that exogenous asparagine is essential to acute lymphoblastic leukemia cells for their growth so the use of the L-asparaginase limited the availability of asparagine for leukemic cells and found very efficient in arresting of these cells growth. In recent times, efforts are in progress to target the central metabolic pathways which are aberrantly regulated in cancer cells such as TCA cycle and glycolysis and some of the agents are already at clinical stage. The main challenge about targeting central metabolic pathways is the use of therapeutic window as these molecules are involved in the normal systemic metabolism and abnormal alteration can have harmful effects. Example include targeting glycolysis metabolic pathway shown low therapeutic index of 2-deoxyglucose which is a glucose uptake inhibitors, affected glucose uptake in both type of cells. However, later on researcher's interest arose again with the finding that central metabolic pathways have altered regulation in tumor cells for example targeting pyruvate kinase (PK). Pyruvate kinases have differential expression in different tissues and expresses PKM2 isoform in cancer cells while it is differentially expressed in liver (PKL), erythrocytes (PKR), brain (PKM1), and myocytes (PKM1). Targeting PKM2 has shown its effectiveness and safety in preclinical and clinical trial studies (Anastasiou et al., 2012; Parnell et al., 2013; Kung et al., 2017; Grace et al., 2019). Another targeting approach is lactate because in cancer cells most of the glucose is metabolized to lactate which is secreted by monocarboxylate transporters present on the plasma membrane. Lactate dehydrogenase A inhibitors which are under preclinical investigations include quinoline, 3-sulfonamides, FX11, and PSTMB (Qian et al., 2014; Kim et al., 2019). While AZD3965 which is an inhibitor of mono carboxylate transporter 1, is in clinical trials for Burkitt lymphoma diffuse large B-cell lymphoma, and solid tumors. Another metabolic target is GAPDH of glycolysis whose therapeutic window is determined by the extent of the Warburg effect (Shestov et al., 2014; Liberti et al., 2017). Another metabolism based approach is targeting amino acids. In cancer cells amino acids induces anabolic metabolism such as glutamine dependence has been observed in in vitro experimental studies of cancer cell lines and its antagonist, JHU083, proven to be have antitumor response in combinational therapy with immune checkpoint blockade (Leone et al., 2019). Drugs targeting glutaminase, such as IPN60090, and CB-839, have shown effectiveness and now are in clinical trials for various malignancies with the advantage that these can work in combinational chimeric antigen receptor T-cell-based immune therapies. In several in vitro studies upregulated expression of lipogenic enzymes has been observed in cancer cells, and three lipogenic enzymes such as fatty acid synthase, ATP-citrate lyase, and acetyl-CoA carboxylase have been in attention for drug development but limited to tumor types because of the requirement of increased de novo fatty acid synthesis for their survival. While most of the drugs target both types of cells but in case of IDH-mutant cancers, drug development has been done in such a way that they target mutated enzyme selectively such as treating IDH-mutated AML and are in clinical trials (Stein et al., 2017; DiNardo et al., 2018; Heuser et al., 2020). Despite all these targeted therapies, it is worth pointing out that these drugs against metabolic enzymes are effective in reducing tumor growth but rarely eradicate completely which indicates that these agents work as maintenance therapy till date, and efforts are in progress for metabolic target-based complete eradication of tumors.

6. Conclusion and future directions

Tumor microenvironment (TME) plays pivotal role in tumorigenesis process, and efforts are going on worldwide in the direction of identifying tumor microenvironment, role of micronutrients, and metabolism-based therapeutic targeting. One of the challenges with these approaches is the variety and chemical complexity of metabolites that exist. The major challenge is to learn about how to interpret the therapeutic metabolic window for targeting cancer metabolism from these measurements and using hypothesis-driven investigations, we can discover functional and diagnostic relevant alterations in cancer cells. We propose that, by identifying all the components/micronutrients of tumor microenvironment, role of each component as well as decoding crosstalk between these metabolic components will give us better platform for arresting the tumor growth completely in the clinic and at the bedside.

References

Anastasiou, D., Yu, Y., Israelsen, W.J., et al., 2012. Pyruvate kinase M2 activators promote tetramer formation and suppress tumorigenesis. Nat. Chem. Biol. 8, 839–847. 115,159-161.

Andreescu, N., Puiu, M., Niculescu, M., 2018. Effects of dietary nutrients on epigenetic changes in cancer. Methods Mol. Biol., 121–139. https://doi.org/10.1007/978-1-4939-8751-1_7.

Arneth, B., 2019. Tumor microenvironment. Medicina 56 (1). https://doi.org/10.3390/medicina56010015.

Cantelmo, A.R., Conradi, L.C., Brajic, A., Goveia, J., Kalucka, J., Pircher, A., Chaturvedi, P., Hol, J., Thienpont, B., Teuwen, L.A., Schoors, S., Boeckx, B., Vriens, J., Kuchnio, A., Veys, K., Cruys, B., Finotto, L., Treps, L., Stav-Noraas, T.E., Bifari, F., Carmeliet, P., 2016. Inhibition of the glycolytic activator PFKFB3 in endothelium induces tumor vessel normalization, impairs metastasis, and improves chemotherapy. Cancer Cell 30 (6), 968–985. https://doi.org/10.1016/j.ccell.2016.10.006.

Choi, J., Kim, H., Bae, Y.K., Cheong, H., 2017. REP1 modulates autophagy and macropinocytosis to enhance cancer cell survival. Int. J. Mol. Sci. 18 (9), 1866. https://doi.org/10.3390/ijms18091866.

DiNardo, C.D., Stein, E.M., de Botton, S., et al., 2018. Durable remissions with ivosidenib in IDH1-mutated relapsed or refractory AML. N. Engl. J. Med. 378, 2386–2398.

Efeyan, A., Zoncu, R., Sabatini, D.M., 2012. Amino acids and mTORC1: from lysosomes to disease. Trends Mol. Med. 18 (9), 524–533. https://doi.org/10.1016/j.molmed.2012.05.007.

Fang, M.Z., Chen, D., Sun, Y., Jin, Z., Christman, J.K., Yang, C.S., 2005. Reversal of hypermethylation and reactivation of p16INK4a, RARβ, and MGMT genes by genistein and other isoflavones from soy. Clin. Cancer Res. 11, 7033–7041. https://doi.org/10.1158/1078-0432.CCR-05-0406.

Farber, S., Diamond, L.K., 1948. Temporary remissions in acute leukemia in children produced by folic acid antagonist, 4-aminopteroyl-glutamic acid. N. Engl. J. Med. 238, 787–793.

Grace, R.F., Rose, C., Layton, D.M., et al., 2019. Safety and efficacy of mitapivat in pyruvate kinase deficiency. N. Engl. J. Med. 381, 933–944.

Heuser, M., Palisiano, N., Mantzaris, I., et al., 2020. Safety and efficacy of BAY1436032 in IDH1-mutant AML: phase I study results. Leukemia 34, 2903–2913.

Kamphorst, J.J., Nofal, M., Commisso, C., Hackett, S.R., Lu, W., Grabocka, E., Vander Heiden, M.G., Miller, G., Drebin, J.A., Bar-Sagi, D., Thompson, C.B., Rabinowitz, J.D., 2015. Human pancreatic cancer tumors are nutrient poor and tumor cells actively scavenge extracellular protein. Cancer Res. 75 (3), 544–553. https://doi.org/10.1158/0008-5472.CAN-14-2211.

Kim, M.J., Woo, S.J., Yoon, C.H., Lee, J.S., An, S., Choi, Y.H., Hwang, S.G., Yoon, G., Lee, S.J., 2011. Involvement of autophagy in oncogenic K-Ras-induced malignant cell transformation. J. Biol. Chem. 286 (15), 12924–12932. https://doi.org/10.1074/jbc.M110.138958.

Kim, S.M., Nguyen, T.T., Ravi, A., Kubiniok, P., Finicle, B.T., Jayashankar, V., Malacrida, L., Hou, J., Robertson, J., Gao, D., Chernoff, J., Digman, M.A., Potma, E.O., Tromberg, B.J., Thibault, P., Edinger, A.L., 2018. PTEN deficiency and AMPK activation promote nutrient scavenging and anabolism in prostate cancer cells. Cancer Discov. 8 (7), 866–883. https://doi.org/10.1158/2159-8290.CD-17-1215.

Kim, E.Y., Chung, T.W., Han, C.W., et al., 2019. A novel lactate dehydrogenase inhibitor, 1-(phenylseleno)-4-(trifluoromethyl) benzene, suppresses tumor growth through apoptotic cell death. Sci. Rep. 9, 3969.

Kung, C., Hixon, J., Kosinski, P.A., et al., 2017. AG-348 enhances pyruvate kinase activity in red blood cells from patients with pyruvate kinase deficiency. Blood 130, 1347–1356.

Kutay, H., Bai, S., Datta, J., Motiwala, T., Pogribny, I., Frankel, W., Jacob, S.T., Ghoshal, K., 2006. Down-regulation of miR-122 in the rodent and human hepatocellular carcinomas. J. Cell. Biochem. 99, 671–678. https://doi.org/10.1002/jcb.20982.

Lee, C., Raffaghello, L., Brandhorst, S., Safdie, F.M., Bianchi, G., Martin-Montalvo, A., Pistoia, V., Wei, M., Hwang, S., Merlino, A., Emionite, L., de Cabo, R., Longo, V.D., 2012. Fasting cycles retard growth of tumors and sensitize a range of cancer cell types to chemotherapy. Sci. Transl. Med. 4. https://doi.org/10.1126/scitranslmed.3003293.

Leone, R.D., Zhao, L., Englert, J.M., et al., 2019. Glutamine blockade induces divergent metabolic programs to overcome tumor immune evasion. Science 366, 1013–1021.

Liberti, M.V., Dai, Z., Wardell, S.E., et al., 2017. A predictive model for selective targeting of the Warburg effect through GAPDH inhibition with a natural product. Cell Metab. 26, 648–659.e8.

Liu, R.T., Zou, L.B., Lu, Q.J., 2009. Liquiritigenin inhibits Abeta(25-35)-induced neurotoxicity and secretion of Abeta(1-40) in rat hippocampal neurons. Acta Pharmacol. Sin. 30, 899–906. https://doi.org/10.1038/aps.2009.74.

Neufeld, T.P., 2012. Autophagy and cell growth—the yin and yang of nutrient responses. J. Cell Sci. 125 (Pt. 10), 2359–2368. https://doi.org/10.1242/jcs.103333.

Ngwa, V.M., Edwards, D.N., Philip, M., Chen, J., 2019. Microenvironmental metabolism regulates antitumor immunity. Cancer Res. 79 (16), 4003–4008. https://doi.org/10.1158/0008-5472.CAN-19-0617.

Nm, A., Mc, S., 2020. The tumor microenvironment. Curr. Biol. 30 (16). https://doi.org/10.1016/j.cub.2020.06.081.

O'Flanagan, C.H., Smith, L.A., McDonell, S.B., Hursting, S.D., 2017. When less may be more: calorie restriction and response to cancer therapy. BMC Med. 15, 106. https://doi.org/10.1186/s12916-017-0873-x.

Olivares, O., Mayers, J.R., Gouirand, V., Torrence, M.E., Gicquel, T., Borge, L., Lac, S., Roques, J., Lavaut, M.N., Berthezène, P., Rubis, M., Secq, V., Garcia, S., Moutardier, V., Lombardo, D., Iovanna, J.L., Tomasini, R., Guillaumond, F., Vander Heiden, M.G., Vasseur, S., 2017. Collagen-derived proline promotes pancreatic ductal adenocarcinoma cell survival under nutrient limited conditions. Nat. Commun. 8, 16031. https://doi.org/10.1038/ncomms16031.

Palm, W., Araki, J., King, B., DeMatteo, R.G., Thompson, C.B., 2017. Critical role for PI3-kinase in regulating the use of proteins as an amino acid source. Proc. Natl. Acad. Sci. U. S. A. 114 (41), E8628–E8636. https://doi.org/10.1073/pnas.1712726114.

Parnell, K.M., Foulks, J.M., Nix, R.N., et al., 2013. Pharmacologic activation of PKM2 slows lung tumor xenograft growth. Mol. Cancer Ther. 12, 1453–1460.

Qian, Y., Wang, X., Chen, X., 2014. Inhibitors of glucose transport and glycolysis as novel anticancer therapeutics. World J. Transl. Med. 3, 37–57.

Redelman-Sidi, G., Iyer, G., Solit, D.B., Glickman, M.S., 2013. Oncogenic activation of Pak1-dependent pathway of macropinocytosis determines BCG entry into bladder cancer cells. Cancer Res. 73 (3), 1156–1167. https://doi.org/10.1158/0008-5472.CAN-12-1882.

Redman, L.M., Smith, S.R., Burton, J.H., Martin, C.K., Il'yasova, D., Ravussin, E., 2018. Metabolic slowing and reduced oxidative damage with sustained caloric restriction support the rate of living and oxidative damage theories of aging. Cell Metab. 27, 805–815.e4. https://doi.org/10.1016/j.cmet.2018.02.019.

Shestov, A.A., Liu, X., Ser, Z., et al., 2014. Quantitative determinants of aerobic glycolysis identify flux through the enzyme GAPDH as a limiting step. elife 3, e03342.

Stein, E.M., DiNardo, C.D., Pollyea, D.A., et al., 2017. Enasidenib in mutant IDH2 relapsed or refractory acute myeloid leukemia. Blood 130, 722–731.

Sun, J., Wei, Q., Zhou, Y., Wang, J., Liu, Q., Xu, H., 2017. A systematic analysis of FDA-approved anticancer drugs. BMC Syst. Biol. 11 (suppl 5), 87.

Vitale, I., Manic, G., Coussens, L.M., Kroemer, G., Galluzzi, L., 2019. Macrophages and metabolism in the tumor microenvironment. Cell Metab. 30 (1), 36–50. https://doi.org/10.1016/j.cmet.2019.06.001.

World Health Organization (WHO), 2020. Global Health Estimates 2020: Deaths by Cause, Age, Sex, by Country and by Region, 2000–2019. WHO. Accessed December 11, 2020 who.int/data/gho/data/themes/mortality-and-global-health-estimates/ghe-leading-causes-of-death.

Zoncu, R., Bar-Peled, L., Efeyan, A., Wang, S., Sancak, Y., Sabatini, D.M., 2011. mTORC1 senses lysosomal amino acids through an inside-out mechanism that requires the vacuolar H(+)-ATPase. Science 334 (6056), 678–683. https://doi.org/10.1126/science.1207056.

CHAPTER EIGHTEEN

Environmental factors influencing epigenetic changes initiating neoplastic changes

Rupa Joshi, Seema Bansal, Ashish Jain, Shweta Jain, Ajay Prakash, and Bikash Medhi
Department of Pharmacology, Postgraduate Institute of Medical Education and Research, Chandigarh, India

1. Introduction

The term epigenetics can be explained by the interconnection between genotype and phenotype and found to be inherited without change in DNA sequence. It is a broad phenomenon covering an extensive range of cellular mechanisms like cell growth, differentiation, disease development, progression, etc. Most commonly, DNA methylation, histone deacetylation, chromatin posttranslational changes, noncoding RNAs, etc. are involved in epigenetics. It is influenced by both intracellular signaling pathways and extracellular stimuli. Thus, the better understanding of these influences would act as potential treatment options for various diseases like cancer and so on.

Environmental epigenetics defines as the process of interaction between the environment and epigenome which may alter the phenotype and affects the disease susceptibility like initiation of neoplastic changes. In the presence of harmful environmental factors, genetic mutations are considered as an important initiative factor in cancer pathology. Therefore, epigenetic modifications have vital role in expression and regulation of different genes. Moreover, epigenetic incongruities encourage carcinogenesis and its progression. By contrast, environmental influences like nutritional, behavioral, etc. can trigger the protective epigenetic modifications to modify the disease risk. This chapter explores the different environmental factors involved in developing potential preventive or treatment strategies for cancer. Furthermore, environmental epigenetic changes can also be beneficial for developing personalized health programs for treating different types of cancer.

Biomarkers in Cancer Detection and Monitoring of Therapeutics
https://doi.org/10.1016/B978-0-323-95116-6.00014-1

2. Epigenetic mechanisms influencing gene expression

Cancer is an alter gene expression disease controlled by epigenetic processes. Epigenetic refers to heritable and stable gene expression alteration that does not change DNA sequence. Still, they are strong enough to influence the dynamic of gene expression pattern in a cell. The key processes involved are DNA methylation, histone and chromatin posttranslational modifications (PTMs) and RNA-based mechanisms (Gibney and Nolan, 2010). Several studies revealed that epigenetic alterations leading to oncogene activation, chromosomal instability, tumor-suppressor genes (TSGs) and DNA repair system inactivation resulting in oncogenic phenotype (Jones and Baylin, 2002).

DNA methylation causes gene silencing in mammals using DNA methyltransferase (DNMT) (Li and Zhang, 2014). They predominantly occur at the carbon-5 position of CpG dinucleotides (5mC) in the proximal promoter region. It is postulated that the methylation in the major groove hinder the binding of transcription factors that might influence the gene expression. DNA methylation is a normal process that are associated with the retention of genomic integrity by methylating the repetitive regions of genome however, in cancer cells, deregulated methylation occur that potentially contributes to genomic instability, increases aneuploidy, activate transcription of repeat sequences, transposable elements (TEs), and oncogenes (Hur et al., 2014).

CpG islands retain about 50%–60% of gene promoters that are generally unmethylated in normal cells. However, in almost every type of human neoplasm, promoter hypermethylation occurs owing to inappropriate transcriptional silencing of TSGs. There are several TSGs including VHL, E-cadherin, P16Ink4a, MLH1, APC, Stk4, and Rb, and when mutated, it results in inherited forms of cancer. In addition to these, many more also found to be frequently hypermethylated on one or both alleles of TSGs (Baylin and Jones, 2016). Studies revealed that promoters methylation not alone silence transcription until chromatin proteins are recruited to that region. These chromatin protein include methyl binding domain (MBD) family comprising MeCP2, MBD1, MBD2, MBD3, and MBD4 that recognize methylated CpG and inhibit gene expression (Bird and Wolffe, 1999). Most studied MBD is MeCP2 that associate with transcription corepressor Sin3A that recruit histone deacetylase (HDAC) leading to transcriptional silencing (Nan et al., 1998).

Chromatin borders that normally separate inactive chromatin from active genome are found to be disrupted in cancer phenotype. These borders are maintained by specific PTMs to histone tails having covalent modifications. PTMs may be methylation, acetylation, phosphorylation, ubiquitination, sumoylation, ADP ribosylation, and proline isomerization. The addition or removal of these chemical groups by various enzymes such as histone acetyltransferase (HAT) and deacetylase (HDAC), histone methyltransferase (HMTs) and demethylase (HDM), kinase, phosphatases, ubiquitin ligases and deubiquitinases, etc. (Kouzarides, 2007). These modifications decide the condensation and decondensation of chromatin thereby gene expression. Various combinations of altered histone modifications such as acetylation of H3 (H3K9ac and H3K14ac) along with abnormal DNA methylation are associated with cancer (Shen and Laird, 2013).

Epigenetic control also involves noncoding RNA (ncRNA) and long noncoding RNAs (lncRNAs). ncRNA such as small interfering RNA (siRNAs), microRNAs (miRNAs), and Piwi-interacting RNA (piRNAs) are involved in the gene regulation. siRNAs are double-stranded, 19–24 nt exogenous RNA which can repress transcription by activating RNA-induced transcriptional Silencing (RITS) complex. RITS attract DNMTs and HMTs that eventually causes gene silencing. miRNAs are single-stranded, 19–24 nt endogenous RNAs that play important role in gene regulation by manipulating mRNA translation. They can be classified as tumor-promoting (miR-155, miR-21, and miR-17-92) found usually overexpressed and tumor-suppressing miRNAs (miR-15-16) that are downregulated (Kasinski and Slack, 2011). piRNAs are typically 24–31 nt long and play major role in limiting transposition through an RNA interference pathway. Transposon limitation is important because they may integrate to coding sequence and interfere with gene function. piRNAs are strongly associated with DNA methylation and chromatin regulation by efficiently recruiting the heterochromatin protein 1 (HP1) (Huang et al., 2013). LncRNAs are generally >200 nt in length that play a vital role in tumorigenesis. PEG3 are maternally imprinted and known to function in tumor suppression by activating p53 TSGs. Dysregulation of Hox transcript antisense RNA (HOTAIR) has been reported in colorectal, pancreatic, and lung cancer (Kogo et al., 2011; Kim et al., 2013; Nakagawa et al., 2013). In conclusion, epigenetic modifications can bring alteration at gene and chromosome level that can influence the gene expression pattern in a cell thereby initiating or progressing cancer phenotype.

3. Environmental influences on epigenetic changes

3.1 Nutrients causing epigenetic changes in cancer

Nutrition can cause gene alteration hence plays an important role in diseases pathologies including cancer via epigenetic changes. Main mechanisms via which nutrients can influence epigenetic status include DNA methylation, histone modifications, and miRNA-dependent gene silencing. Alteration in these mechanisms may result either increase or decrease risk of cancer development (Andreescu et al., 2018). Studies have reported that daily intake of nutrients present in food plays protective role in cancer treatment either directly inhibition of cancer progression or via modification of cancer microenvironment (Bishop and Ferguson, 2015). Nutrients effecting epigenetics of human genome and showing promising effect in the treatment of cancer has been summarized in Table 1.

Table 1 Summary epigenetic mechanisms via which nutrients show anticancer effect.

Nutrients	Epigenetic modifications	Anticancer effect	References
Folic acid		Decrease risk for pancreatic and lungs cancer	Supic et al. (2013)
Vitamin B12		Colorectal carcinoma	Supic et al. (2013)
Vitamin B6	DNA methylation	Decrease risk for breast cancer and colorectal cancer	Wei et al. (2005)
Vitamin D		Decrease risk for colorectal and prostate cancer	Trump and Aragon-Ching (2018)
Resveratrol		Decrease risk for breast cancer	Chen et al. (2014)
Genistein		Decrease risk for esophageal squamous carcinoma cell, prostate and breast cancer	Fang et al. (2005)
EGCG		Prostate cancer	Khanim et al. (2004)
Curcumin		Pancreatic cancer, Prostate cancer	Goel and Aggarwal (2010)
Lycopene		Prostate cancer	Bishop and Ferguson (2015)
Organosulfur compounds	Histone modifications	Colon cancer	Mariadason (2008)
Sodium butyrate		Human epithelioid cancer cells	Attoub et al. (2011)
Genistein		Breast cancer	Cheng and Blumenthal (2010)
Resveratrol		Breast cancer	Chung et al. (2010)
Vitamin D		Prostate cancer	Khanim et al. (2004)
EGCG		Skin and prostate cancer	Khanim et al. (2004)
Curcumin	Influence on small noncoding RNAs	Breast and prostate cancer	Saini et al. (2010)
Folic acid		Hepatocarcinoma cells	Kutay et al. (2006)
Genistein		Prostate cancer	Sun et al. (2009a, b)

Nutrients affecting DNA methylation in cancer: Nutrients involved in one-carbon metabolism such as folate, cobalamine, and riboflavin are associated with DNA methylation in cancer. Studies have reported folic acid intake reduce incidence of cervical dysplasia and cervical cancer via modulation of DNA methylation. Another study reported that low dietary intake of cobalamine, niacin, pyridoxine enhance chances of breast cancer, however intake of folate reduces the chances of breast cancer risk in premenopausal women especially estrogen receptor negative cancer. In contrary, study by Supic et al. (2013) reported that intake of folic acid and vitamin B12 causes misincorporation of uracil in to DNA, and hence, it promotes methylation in rectal mucosa of patients having colorectal adenomas. Pyridoxine act as cofactor for the serine hydroxymethyltransferase involved in 5,10 MTHF synthesis hence plays an important role in glutathione hence deficiency of pyridoxine causes enhancement of risk for cancer progression. Different phytoestrogens such as genistein, resveratrol interacts with estrogen receptors. In-vitro study by Fang et al. (2005) reported that genistein inhibit various epigenetic mechanisms responsible for the proliferation of esophageal squamous carcinoma and prostate cancer. Study reported that genistein showed equivalent effect as that of 5-aza-cytidine in renal carcinoma cell lines via decrease promoter methylation of cell lines. Bioflavonoids such as quercetin, tea catechins are also been reported to inhibit DNA methyltransferase activity by interfering with the catechol-O-methyltransferase (COMT) substrate for methyl reactions. Curcumin is a polyphenol. In vitro study also reported that curcumin showed anticancer effect via inhibition of DNMT activity and thus inducing DNA hypomethylation.

Nutrients affecting histone modification in cancer: Various in vitro and in vivo studies have reported that nutrients play a role in the epigenetic modifications of histones especially via inhibition of histone acetyltransferase, demethylation, and deacetylation. Studies have reported that enhancement of histone deacetylation (HDAC) has been found in many cancers which affects cell cycle kinetics and apoptosis. Dietary components such as EGCG, organosulfur compounds, and genistein have been reported to show anticancer effect via inhibition of HDAC activity. Diallyl disulfide is a competitive inhibitor of HDAC which induces histone hyperacetylation. Sodium butyrate, peppermint, celery, and parsley inhibit HDACs and enhance histone acetylation resulting in inhibition of cancer cell growth. Anticancer effect of genistein is via increase of histone acetylation while curcumin show anticancer effect via inhibition of histone deacetylation. Administration of vitamin D enhances the expression of antiproliferative target genes and apoptosis and inhibits prostate cancer cell proliferation. EGCG showed anticancer effect via alteration of histone acetylation and methylation while inhibition of histone deacetylation.

Nutrients affecting small non coding RNAs in cancer: Various noncoding RNAs such as miRNA, siRNA, and pi RNAs regulate the gene expression. Studies have reported that western diet alters the miRNA expression, while Mediterranean diets were

Table 2 Nutrients enhance risk of cancer.

Nutrient	Cancer site	Reference
Red/processed meat	Colorectal cancer	Aykan (2015)
Arsenic and beta carotene supplements	Lungs and urothelial cancer	Di Giovanni et al. (2020)
Alcohol	Mouth, esophagus, breast cancer, colorectal cancer	Rumgay et al. (2021)
Salted and salty foods	Stomach cancer	Umesawa et al. (2016)
Aflatoxin B1	Hepatic cancer	Sugimura (2000)
Tomatoes and pepper	Thyroid neoplasia	Frentzel-Beyme and Helmert (2000)

reported to reduce the risk for cancer development. Kutay et al. (2006) reported that miRNA alterations can be prevented by folate intake. Curcumin showed anticancer effect via enhancement of miRNA 22 tumor suppressor gene. Along-with this curcumin also influences the expression of miR-15a in breast and miR-16 species in prostate cancer. Studies have reported that genistein downregulates oncogenic miRNA-27a in cancer cells resulting in inhibition of cell proliferation.

Nutrients increasing risk of cancer: Apart from beneficial foods, some of the foods also contain ingredients use, which enhances cancer risk. Food treatment after heat can also generate various compounds alone or some environmental factors which can modify epigenetics of human genome and can be debilitating reason for cancer. Some of the foods which increased risk of cancer have been summarized in Table 2.

4. Chemically influenced epigenetic changes

Heavy metals are common environmental pollutants linked to cancer, cardiovascular illness, neurological problems, and autoimmune diseases. Several findings have shown a link among DNA methylation and metals found in the environment, such as nickel, cadmium, lead, and especially arsenic. Through redox cycling, metals are known to catalytically promote the formation of reactive oxygen species (ROS). The capacity of methyltransferases to bind with DNA can be hampered by oxidative DNA damage, resulting in a generalized change in cytosine methylation at CpG sites. Contact to air pollens/pollution, cyclohexatriene (benzene), organic contaminations, and radio-waves disrupts epigenetic markers. Other potential environmental stresses such as chemical and xenobiotic substances can change epigenetic states. Environmental contaminants portray more significant effect during embryonic development, increasing the likelihood of disease development in the different generations. It is always focused at how specific

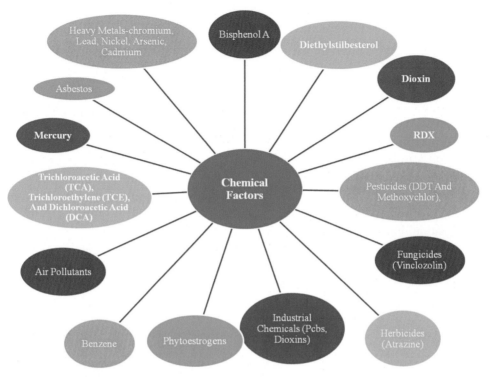

Fig. 1 Number of chemical factors influencing epigenetics.

stressors, like metals and air contaminants be able to influence the epigenetic changes, linked to the onset of numerous diseases (Fig. 1) (Hou et al., 2012; Toraño et al., 2016).

4.1 Cadmium (Cd)

Cadmium is a well-known carcinogen with minimal mutagenesis potential. It is found in abundance in the atmosphere because of industrialized operations, polluted water, or soil. It has a broad range of industrial applications, including as a component in battery manufacturing. Many different mechanisms for cadmium carcinogenesis have been proposed, but the generation of reactive oxygen species (ROS) (free radical) and changes in DNA methylation appear to be the most important biological factors. Also, cadmium exposure is primarily caused by our foods, particularly grains and vegetables and tobacco use. It contributes to many health issues, including cancer, a higher chance of bone fractures, renal damage, and likely delayed development in children. During embryonic development and throughout life, epigenetic changes could be linked to cadmium toxicity pathways. In in-vitro, Cd obstructs DNMTs and causes total DNA hypomethylation (TRL1215 rat liver cells). Additionally, long-term exposure causes

DNA hypermethylation resulting in increased DNMT activity. Cadmium can also prevent proto-oncogene DNA methylation, which leads to oncogene production and cell proliferation (Toraño et al., 2016).

4.2 Arsenic (As)

The most prevalent metal in the environment is arsenic (As). It can be found in various places, including stones, mud, water, pesticides, and airborne elements. Chronic arsenic exposure has been linked to various health issues, including skin lesions, neuropathy, depression, cardiac disease, and malignancies of several types and can result in histone modification alterations. DNA methylation alterations, both total and specific to gene, have been discovered in experimental studies following arsenic exposure. In several population-based studies, arsenic levels in adults have been linked to LINE-1 DNA hypomethylation. Furthermore, it has been discovered that it can result DNA methylation alterations at specific-site. For example, high arsenic exposure has been associated to DNA hypermethylation of the tumor suppressor genes p16 and RASSF1A. Arsenic in drinking water has been linked to hypermethylation in a dose–response relationship (Tajuddin et al., 2013).

4.3 Nickel (Ni)

Nickel (Ni) is a common metal that has been demonstrated to generate de novo DNA methylation of critical tumor suppressors or senescence genes, as well as enhance chromatin condensation. It is found in various products, including jewelry, coins, batteries, and medical gadgets. Although the International Agency for Research on Cancer (IARC) has established that some compounds (nickel) are oncogenic to humans (mostly connected to lung malignancies), information on the molecular pathways involved is limited, and more research is needed. The processes underlying nickel's negative health effects, such as carcinogenicity and circulatory diseases, are still not clear. Nickel has been suggested as a possible replacement for magnesium in DNA interactions thereby enhancing chromatin condensation, and triggers de novo DNA methylation. Moreover, nickel-induced hypermethylation has been found in G12 cells (Chinese hamster) transfected with gtp gene (*E. coli*), silencing the transfected gene's expression (Toraño et al., 2016; Wilhelm et al., 2010).

4.4 Lead (Pb)

Lead is one of the most dangerous metals in the environment employed in various applications, including building construction, batteries, and consumer goods. It has a lot of oxidative qualities. Long-term lead exposure has been found to change epigenetic markers. Pb treatment of hESCs in vitro resulted in altered gene methylation in neuronal signaling pathways. Maternal exposure resulted in neurodevelopmental deficits and lower intelligence in the child. By K-X-Ray fluorescence, in patella and tibia LINE-1 methylation lead levels were investigated in the Normative Aging Study. Reduced LINE-1 DNA methylation was linked to patella lead levels. The relationship among exposure to lead and LINE-1 DNA methylation could have implications for how lead affects health. According to the researchers, changes in DNA methylation could also be utilized as a diagnostic for earlier lead exposure (Wright et al., 2010).

4.5 Chromium (Cr)

Using PCR (methylation-specific), chromium was revealed to produce p16 methylation in lung cancer patients ($n = 30$) associated to chromate and nonchromate-exposed lung tumors ($n = 38$). Furthermore, when chromate exposure was compared to nonchromate lung cancer tissues, p16 hypermethylation was affected. Chromium diminishes H3 phosphorylation, trimethylation, and acetylation marks in H3 and H4, in in vitro.

In human lung A549 cells, chromium treatment raised di- and trimethylated histone H3 lysine 9 (H3K9) and lysine 4 (H3K4), but lowered tri-methylated histone H3 lysine 27 (H3K27) and dimethylated histone H3 arginine 2 (H3K2) (H3R2). After chromate exposure, H3K9 dimethylation was shown to be more frequent in the human MLH1 gene promoter, which was linked to reduced MLH1 mRNA expression. After being exposed to chromium, the protein and mRNA levels of G9a, a histone methyltransferase that preferentially methylates H3K9, increased. The total rise in H3K9 dimethylation could be attributed to this Cr(VI)-induced increase in G9a. The H3K9 dimethylation produced by chromate was largely reversed by supplementing with ascorbate, a significant reductant of Cr(VI), and important for histone demethylase activity (Toraño et al., 2016; Sun et al., 2009a, b).

4.6 Methylmercury/mercury

Mercury (Hg) is a poisonous element that has unknown physiological consequences. A few examples of mercury-containing products are batteries, medical devices, fluorescent bulbs, thermometers, dental amalgams, and thermostats. The polar bear's brain tissue DNA has been hypomethylated because of Hg exposure. Humans are exposed to mercury through fish and shellfish, which contain high levels of mercury in their bodies. Immunotoxic effects, cancer, cardiac and kidney disease are some of the health outcomes associated with mercury exposure. In rats', prenatal mercury exposure reduces brain cell proliferation, and it is linked to DNA hypomethylation. A recent study in humans found that even low mercury exposure in utero caused DNA methylation alterations. Additionally, prenatal mercury exposure in cord blood has also been linked to alterations in the immune cells. In adult women, DNA methylation of the tumor suppressor gene GSTM1's promoter region increases after high amounts of mercury exposure. A link between hair mercury levels and SEPP1 DNA hypomethylation was discovered in a study of male dental workers. In addition, mouse embryonic stem cells exposed to mercury for 48–96 h revealed hypermethylation of the Rnd2 gene (Goodrich et al., 2013).

4.7 Asbestos

Asbestos comprises six minerals—chrysotile, amosite, crocidolite, anthophyllite, tremolite, and actinolite. Chrysotile is the most common kind of asbestos (white asbestos). It is found in the roofs, ceilings, walls, and flooring of homes and businesses. Earlier it was used in hardware appliances such as pipes, ducts, and household appliances such as gaskets, boiler seals, & in cars as brake linings and for insulation applications.

Amosite (brown asbestos) is used in pipes and cement sheets. Apart from this, it is used in electric boards, ceiling tiles, and thermal insulation for household purposes.

Anthophyllite was used in small amounts in insulation and construction products. As a contaminant, it can be found in vermiculite, talc and in chrysotile asbestos. The appearance and its visibility are in white, gray, or dull green.

Elements like tremolite and actinolite aren't used in industry. However, their availability is like anthophyllite as impurities. Tremolite and actinolite come in various colors such as gray, brown, green, white, and translucent.

Asbestos can change the epigenome. Adults exposed develop malignant pleural mesothelioma (MPM), although the pathogenic processes involved in tumor reformation remain unknown. "APC, CCND2, CDKN2A, CDKN2B, ESR1, HPPBP1, RASSF1, SLC6A20, SYK, and ZIC1" have all been related to promoter DNA methylation in MPM because of asbestos exposure (Tsou et al., 2005; Christensen et al., 2008; Cheng et al., 2013).

5. Trichloroacetic acid (TCA), trichloroethylene (TCE), and dichloroacetic acid (DCA)

Peroxisome proliferators and carcinogens in mouse liver include trichloroethylene (TCE), dichloroacetic acid (DCA), and trichloroacetic acid (TCA). These three carcinogens, chloroform, DCA, and TCA, are present in drinking water and are chlorine disinfection by-products. Mice liver exposed to these carcinogens, results in lowered promoter region methylation at the c-jun and c-myc genes. Additionally, reduced methylation and elevated proto-oncogenes' mRNAs and proteins were prevented by methionine supplementation. This depicts that carcinogens can cause DNA hypomethylation by reducing the availability of SAM (S'-adenosyl-L-methionine), however DNA hypomethylation is prevented by sustaining enough SAM levels, through methionine (Toraño et al., 2016).

5.1 Air pollution

Elevated risk of cardiorespiratory disease morbidity, lung cancer risk, and death has been associated with air pollution/particulate matter (PM). In elderly males, 1097 of blood DNA samples in Boston area, black carbon, a constituent of PM produced from traffic vehicles, was associated to lower DNA methylation in LINE-1 repetitive sequences. Moreover, examined workers in the steel industry with well-characterized exposure to PM with diameters of 10 m provided more evidence for PM impacts on DNA methylation (PM10). Compared to baseline, methylation of the inducible nitric oxide synthase gene promoter region was reduced in blood samples of workers exposed to PM10. In Alu and LINE-1, PM10 continuous exposure was inversely linked with methylation. Because global DNA hypomethylation has been discovered in cancer and cardiac diseases, these alterations may recapitulate epigenetic processes linked to disease development and indicate methods by which human health is affected by particle air pollution.

The sperm DNA of mice exposed to steel plant air was hypermethylated relative to control mice, and this modification lasted after the animals were removed from the environmental exposure. This study necessitates more investigation to see if air pollution causes DNA methylation alterations passed down through generations (Toraño et al., 2016; Tarantini et al., 2009).

5.2 Benzene

Benzene is a chemical found in the environment linked to an increased incidence of hematological cancers, especially in acute myeloid and nonlymphocytic leukemia. Benzene is one of the top 20 compounds produced in the United States. Benzene is a potent immunosuppressant. Low levels of benzene can cause DNA methylation modifications in the peripheral blood, including diminished LINE-1, AluI, and MAGE-1 methylation, as well as p15 hypermethylation. Acute myelogenous leukemia could become more common because of these alterations. AML is portrayed by abnormal global hypomethylation and gene-specific hypermethylation/hypomethylation, and high-level benzene exposure has been linked to elevated disease risk (Toraño et al., 2016).

5.3 RDX (hexahydro-1,3,5-trinitro-1,3,5-triazine)

RDX (Royal Demolition Explosive—British code) is a usual explosive component used in army and civil actions. The explosive and its metabolites are discovered in water sources, even though the conservational hazard is in soils. Both of these can cause neurotoxicity, immunotoxicity, and an increased risk of cancer. RDX exposed mice showed distinct miRNA expression profiles in cancer, toxicant-metabolizing enzymes, and neurotoxicity gene pathways (Zhang and Pan, 2009).

6. Reproductive toxicants and chemicals disrupting endocrine mechanisms

Endocrine disruptors are chemical pollutants that can influence the endocrine system and have negative developmental, neurological, reproductive, and immunological consequences at specific concentrations. A few examples that can cause these problems are pesticides (DDT and methoxychlor), fungicides (vinclozolin), herbicides (atrazine), industrial chemicals (PCBs, dioxins), and plant hormones (phytoestrogens) are only a few examples. However, plastics, notably bisphenol A (BPA) and phthalates, most commonly harm mammalian creatures. The National Toxicology Program-Center has extensively researched and reported the effects of exposure to both polymers on human health for the Evaluation of Risks to Human Reproduction. Because of their ubiquitous use in the production of polycarbonate plastics, exposure to these two chemicals poses an ever-increasing health risk. Female fertility is reduced, and cancer susceptibility is increased because of exposure. BPA is a synthetic carbon-based chemical found in CDs, DVDs, plastic bottles and containers, and epoxy resins used to line metal food and beverage cans (Toraño et al., 2016).

6.1 Diethylstilbesterol (DES)

Synthetic estrogen diethylstilbesterol (DES) was used in pregnant women in the early 1940s, to prevent miscarriages. During pregnancy, DES exposure possesses hazardous breast cancer in both mother and their offspring. Furthermore, when epithelial breast cells were DES exposed, 82 miRNAs expression (9.1% of the 898 miRNAs tested) were transformed. Similarly, epithelial cells showed decreased expression of miR-9-3 and were associated by promoter hypermethylation of the respective coding gene.

Prenatal and neonatal DES exposure produces a broad spectrum of gene expression alterations in animal models. Exogenous estrogen causes gene expression like lactoferrin, epidermal growth factor (EGF), and proto-oncogenes like c-fos, c-jun, and c-myc to persist. Exogenous estrogen suppressed catechol-O-methyltransferase (COMT) gene transcription, indicating an indirect link between methylation alterations and estrogen. In the presence of Mg^{2+}, COMT catalyzes the relocation of the methyl groups from SAM to catechol hydroxyl groups. The methylation process is inhibited when this enzyme is inhibited (Toraño et al., 2016).

6.2 Bisphenol A (BPA)

BPA is an estrogenic chemical found in a variety of everyday commodities like food and drinks containers, infant bottles, and dental composites. The methylation of the metastable loci Avy and CapbIAP in rats was altered by maternal BPA exposure. Surprisingly, maternal food diet with methyl group (e.g., folic acid, phytoestrogen genistein), blocked DNA methylation. This resulted in altered color of exposed mice skin.

Hoxa10, a uterine organogenesis regulating gene resulted in reduced methylation and elevated Hoxa10 expression, when CD-1 pregnant mice were BPA treated. Low-dose BPA revealed 170 genes that changed expression in breast epithelial cells in response to BPA. Moreover, due to promoter region DNA hypermethylation, the LAMP3 protein (lysosomal-associated membrane protein 3) was repressed (Dolinoy et al., 2007).

6.3 Dioxin

Dioxin is a human carcinogen classified by the "International Agency for Research on Cancer" (IARC). Dioxin being a mild mutagen, researchers have spent much time figuring out how it causes cancer. One suggested mechanism to carcinogenesis is the activation of microsomal enzymes (CYP1B1) by dioxin, which could stimulate additional procarcinogen chemicals to active carcinogens. According to new research, the capacity of dioxin to stimulate CYP1B1 in vitro depends on the methylation of the CYP1B1 promoter. In rat liver, dioxin has also been demonstrated to diminish Igf2 DNA methylation. Dioxin-treated mice's splenocytes showed changes in DNA methylation across numerous genomic regions, a discovery that could be linked to dioxin immunotoxicity. Dioxin was found to upregulate miR-191 in a xenograft mice model of hepatocellular cancer. Inhibition of miR-191 also reduced cell proliferation and prevented apoptosis, implying that elevated miR-191 expression can result in dioxin-induced carcinogenicity. The aryl-hydrocarbon receptor (AhR) is involved in dioxin toxicity, necessitating changes in target gene transcription. Furthermore, miRNAs may be accountable for mRNA downregulation in dioxin/AhR-associated mechanisms. Nevertheless, a few minor changes in miRNA levels were identified utilizing two distinctive miRNA array platforms and Real-time PCR, showing a limited miRNA function in dioxin toxicity (Toraño et al., 2016; Moffat et al., 2007).

7. Epigenetic drugs

Although there was great development in recent decades in treatment of different neoplasms, however, promising drug therapies are still lacking. In the presence of harmful environmental factors, genetic mutations are considered as an important initiative factor in cancer pathology (Kaur et al., 2022). Therefore, epigenetic modifications have vital role in expression and regulation of different genes. Moreover, epigenetic incongruities encourage carcinogenesis and its progression. Epithelial to mesenchymal transition induced by epigenetic plasticity generates stem cell like properties and promotes the metastasis and therapeutic resistance in cancer cells. Thus, epigenetic has become the focused area for the treatment of cancers. Since last decade, many epigenetic drugs have been approved by US FDA for hematological malignancies.

8. DNMT inhibitors

Two epigenetic drugs targeting DNMT1, i.e., azacytidine and decitabine, are approved by the US FDA for the treatment of acute and chronic myeloid leukemias and myelodysplastic syndrome (MDS). DNMT1 inhibitors stimulate re-expression of tumor suppressor genes and downregulates DNA methylation. Newer molecular mechanisms are involved in reactivation of the endogenous retroviral elements in cancer cells and trigger an anticancer immune response.

9. HDAC inhibitors

Vorinostat, romidepsin, belinostat, panobinostat, and chidamide are some of the epigenetic drugs acting through inhibition of the enzyme histone deacetylase. These drugs induce cell differentiation, augment cell cycle arrest and endorse apoptosis of cancer cells. The list of various epigenetic drugs approved by US-FDA as well as under clinical investigation is given in Table 3.

10. Innovative epigenetic targets as research hotspots

A key regulator in demethylation of histone H3, i.e., G9a and polycomb repressive complex 2 (PRC2) component EZH2 causes histone methylation at lysine 27 were considered as novel druggable epigenetic targets. Another is DOT1L enzyme which catalyzes the methylation of H3 at lysine 79. LSD1 demethylates mono and dimethylated lysines and plays significant role in embryogenesis and tissue differentiation.

Noncoding RNAs act as main component in progression of cancer cells. miRNA and long noncoding RNAs are identified as important therapeutic targets in oncogenesis.

Table 3 Epigenetic drugs for solid tumors.

Epigenetic targets	Examples of epigenetic drugs	Applications
DNMT	5-Azacitidine, Decitabine, Mocetinostat, Guadecitabine, Hydralazine	AML, CML, MDS
HDAC	Vorinostat, Belinostat, Pracinostat, Quisinostat, Panobinostat, Abexinostat, Chidamide, CHR-3996	CTCL, MM, PTCL
Benzamides	Entinostat, Guadeciatbine	AML, ALL
Fatty acids	Valproic acid, Pivanex, Phenylbutyric acid	CLL, NSCLC, AML
Cyclic peptides	Romidepsin	CTCL

For example, p38 MAPK, AKT2, STAT3, etc. have been targeted by miR-124 and downregulates EGFR signaling pathway. Thus, studies have shown promising results in clinical trials conducted on MRX34, a liposome-based miR-34 for treatment of patients with refractory advanced solid tumors (Beg et al., 2017).

Earlier, there were concerns about the safety of epigenetic drugs being affecting entire genome unselectively and regulates the transcriptions of all genes. But nowadays both academias as well as industries are focusing epigenetic drugs as new hotspots for research in therapeutics of cancers as promising results have been obtained in terms of efficacy and safety.

11. Combination of epigenetic drugs with other treatment options for cancer

The promising results are always obtained by combining two different treatment modalities. Similarly, in treatment of different types of cancers, epigenetic drugs are being combined with conventional antineoplastic agents. It proves to be an attractive concept of combining drugs with multiple mechanisms in a single therapy by exploring various epigenetic inhibitors or drugs, epigenetic drugs. Furthermore, the combination of treatment modalities should be scientifically rational to be efficacious in treatment. The synergism caused by these molecules should guarantee the synergistic effect with minimum toxicity profile. There are many examples of combining multiple epigenetic drugs in combination with chemotherapy, molecular targeting drugs, radiotherapy, immunotherapy and hormonal therapy given in Table 4.

Table 4 Epigenetic drugs as adjuvant therapy.

S. No.	Description	Examples	Inference
1.	Combination with chemotherapy	Decitabine and carboplatin	Reduced toxicity of carboplatin (Phase II) (Appleton et al., 2007)
		Decitabline and temozolomide	Safe and effective in metastatic melanoma (Tawbi et al., 2013)
		Vorinostat and carboplatin/paclitaxel	Enhanced the efficacy of carboplatin in advance NSCLC (Ramalingam et al., 2010.
2.	Combination with radiotherapy (Groselj et al., 2013)	Vorinostat with short-term palliative pelvic radiotherapy	Gastrointestinal tract carcinoma (Phase II)
		VPA, temozolomide, and radiotherapy	High-grade glioma (Phase II)
		Vorinostat with palliative radiation	NSCLC (Phase I)
		Panobinostat and radiotherapy	Multiple types of solid cancers (Phase I)

Continued

Table 4 Epigenetic drugs as adjuvant therapy—cont'd

S. No.	Description	Examples	Inference
3.	Combination with immunotherapy	Entinostat reduced the interferon response Atezolizumab (PD-L1 mAb) with Azacytidine/ Guadecitabine Pembrolizumab (PD-1 mAb) and entinostat/ romidepsin/vorinostat	
4.	Combination with hormonal therapy	Vorinostat and Biclutamide (androgen receptor antagonist)	Synergistic effect in prostate cancer (Phase II) (Marrocco et al., 2007, Marrocco-Tallarigo et al., 2009)
		TSA with Biclutamide and finasteride (5α-reductase inhibitor)	Prostate cancer (Pfeiffer et al., 2010)
		Azacytidine with TSA and diarylpropionitrile (ERβ agonist)	Prostate cancer (Marchini et al., 2016)
5.	Combination with other epigenetic drugs	BET inhibitor and DOT1L inhibitor	Exhibit functional collaboration
6.	Combination with Molecular targeting agents	Entinostat (HDAC inhibitor) and Erlotinib (EGFR-TK inhibitor)	Increased the efficacy of erlotinib in NSCLC (Witta et al., 2012)
		Guadecitabine and Talazoparib (PARP inhibitor)	Reduces the resistance in breast and ovarian cancer (Pulliam et al., 2018)
		Entinostat and Vidaza	Suppress tumor growth and reprograms the epigenome (Belinsky et al., 2011)
		Decitabine and vemuraferib with cobimetinib	Metastatic melanoma and BRAF-mutated metastatic melanoma (Phase I/II)
		Vorinostat and Olaparib (PARP inhibitor)	Refractory lymphoma patients (Phase I/II)

12. Conclusion and future perspectives

Environmental epigenetics plays an important role in vicinity of cancer treatment. There are number of environmental factors like nutrients, chemicals, etc. which affects the epigenetics and involves in cancer development. Although a number of epigenetic drugs have proved to be beneficial as adjuvant to anticancer drugs, however, many are in pipeline, in different phases of clinical trials. There are many off target problems of epigenetic drugs like acquired resistance, toxicity profile, etc. But, the advent of technologies like high-throughput epigenome mapping and the whole genome is available for drug screening, and thus, personalized treatment options with high efficacy and safety profile would be available for individual patients throughout the globe.

References

Andreescu, N., Puiu, M., Niculescu, M., 2018. Effects of dietary nutrients on epigenetic changes in cancer. Methods Mol. Biol., 121–139. https://doi.org/10.1007/978-1-4939-8751-1_7.

Appleton, K., Mackay, H.J., Judson, I., et al., 2007. Phase I and pharmacodynamic trial of the DNA methyltransferase inhibitor decitabine and carboplatin in solid tumors. J. Clin. Oncol. 25 (29), 4603–4609.

Attoub, S., Hassan, A.H., Vanhoecke, B., Iratni, R., Takahashi, T., Gaben, A.M., Bracke, M., Awad, S., John, A., Kamalboor, H.A., Al Sultan, M.A., Arafat, K., Gespach, C., Petroianu, G., 2011. Inhibition of cell survival, invasion, tumor growth and histone deacetylase activity by the dietary flavonoid luteolin in human epithelioid cancer cells. Eur. J. Pharmacol. 651, 18–25. https://doi.org/10.1016/j.ejphar.2010.10.063.

Aykan, N.F., 2015. Red meat and colorectal cancer. Oncol. Rev. https://doi.org/10.4081/oncol.2015.288.

Baylin, S.B., Jones, P.A., 2016. Epigenetic determinants of Cancer. Cold Spring Harb. Perspect. Biol. 8, a019505.

Beg, M.S., Brenner, A.J., Sachdev, J., et al., 2017. Phase I study of MRX34, a liposomal miR-34a mimic, administered twice weekly in patients with advanced solid tumors. Investig. New Drugs 35 (2), 180–188.

Belinsky, S.A., Grimes, M.J., Picchi, M.A., et al., 2011. Combination therapy with vidaza and entinostat suppresses tumor growth and reprograms the epigenome in an orthotopic lung cancer model. Cancer Res. 71 (2), 454–462.

Bird, A., Wolffe, A.P., 1999. Methylation-induced repression—belts, braces and chromatin. Cell 99, 451–454.

Bishop, K.S., Ferguson, L.R., 2015. The interaction between epigenetics, nutrition and the development of cancer. Nutrients. https://doi.org/10.3390/nu7020922.

Chen, M., Rao, Y., Zheng, Y., Wei, S., Li, Y., Guo, T., Yin, P., 2014. Association between soy isoflavone intake and breast cancer risk for pre- and post-menopausal women: a meta-analysis of epidemiological studies. PLoS One 9. https://doi.org/10.1371/journal.pone.0089288.

Cheng, X., Blumenthal, R.M., 2010. Coordinated chromatin control: structural and functional linkage of DNA and histone methylation. Biochemistry. https://doi.org/10.1021/bi100213t.

Cheng, Y.Y., Kirschner, M.B., Cheng, N.C., Gattani, S., Klebe, S., Edelman, J.J., Vallely, M.P., McCaughan, B.C., Jin, H.C., van Zandwijk, N., Reid, G., 2013. ZIC1 is silenced and has tumor suppressor function in malignant pleural mesothelioma. J. Thorac. Oncol. 8 (10), 1317–1328.

Christensen, B.C., Godleski, J.J., Marsit, C.J., Houseman, E.A., Lopez-Fagundo, C.Y., Longacker, J.L., Bueno, R., Sugarbaker, D.J., Nelson, H.H., Kelsey, K.T., 2008. Asbestos exposure predicts cell cycle control gene promoter methylation in pleural mesothelioma. Carcinogenesis 29 (8), 1555–1559.

Chung, S., Yao, H., Caito, S., Hwang, J.W., Arunachalam, G., Rahman, I., 2010. Regulation of SIRT1 in cellular functions: role of polyphenols. Arch. Biochem. Biophys. https://doi.org/10.1016/j.abb.2010.05.003.

Di Giovanni, P., Di Martino, G., Scampoli, P., Cedrone, F., Meo, F., Lucisano, G., Romano, F., Staniscia, T., 2020. Arsenic exposure and risk of urothelial cancer: systematic review and meta-analysis. Int. J. Environ. Res. Public Health 17, 3105. https://doi.org/10.3390/ijerph17093105.

Dolinoy, D.C., Huang, D., Jirtle, R.L., 2007. Maternal nutrient supplementation counteracts bisphenol A-induced DNA hypomethylation in early development. Proc. Natl. Acad. Sci. 104 (32), 13056–13061.

Fang, M.Z., Chen, D., Sun, Y., Jin, Z., Christman, J.K., Yang, C.S., 2005. Reversal of hypermethylation and reactivation of p16INK4a, RARβ, and MGMT genes by genistein and other isoflavones from soy. Clin. Cancer Res. 11, 7033–7041. https://doi.org/10.1158/1078-0432.CCR-05-0406.

Frentzel-Beyme, R., Helmert, U., 2000. Association between malignant tumors of the thyroid gland and exposure to environmental protective and risk factors. Rev. Environ. Health. https://doi.org/10.1515/REVEH.2000.15.3.337.

Gibney, E.R., Nolan, C.M., 2010. Epigenetics and gene expression. Heredity 105, 4–13.

Goel, A., Aggarwal, B.B., 2010. Curcumin, the golden spice from Indian saffron, is a chemosensitizer and radiosensitizer for tumors and chemoprotector and radioprotector for normal organs. Nutr. Cancer. https://doi.org/10.1080/01635581.2010.509835.

Goodrich, J.M., Basu, N., Franzblau, A., Dolinoy, D.C., 2013. Mercury biomarkers and DNA methylation among Michigan dental professionals. Environ. Mol. Mutagen. 54 (3), 195–203.

Groselj, B., Sharma, N.L., Hamdy, F.C., et al., 2013. Histone deacetylase inhibitors as radiosensitisers: effects on DNA damage signalling and repair. Br. J. Cancer 108 (4), 748–754.

Hou, L., Zhang, X., Wang, D., Baccarelli, A., 2012. Environmental chemical exposures and human epigenetics. Int. J. Epidemiol. 41 (1), 79–105.

Huang, X.A., Yin, H., Sweeney, S., Raha, D., Snyder, M., Lin, H., 2013. A major epigenetic programming mechanism guided by piRNAs. Dev. Cell 24, 502–516.

Hur, K., Cejas, P., Feliu, J., Moreno-Rubio, J., Burgos, E., Boland, C.R., Goel, A., 2014. Hypomethylation of long interspersed nuclear element-1 (LINE-1) leads to activation of proto-oncogenes in human colorectal cancer metastasis. Gut 63, 635–646.

Jones, P.A., Baylin, S.B., 2002. The fundamental role of epigenetic events in cancer. Nat. Rev. Genet. 3, 415–428.

Kasinski, A.L., Slack, F.J., 2011. Epigenetics and genetics. MicroRNAs en route to the clinic: progress in validating and targeting microRNAs for cancer therapy. Nat. Rev. Cancer 11, 849–864.

Kaur, G., Bhadada, S.K., Santra, M., Pal, R., Sarma, P., Sachdeva, N., Dhiman, V., Dahiya, D., Saikia, U.N., Chakraborty, A., Sood, A., Prakash, M., Behera, A., Rao, S.D., 2022. Multilevel annotation of germline MEN1 variants of synonymous, nonsynonymous, and uncertain significance in Indian patients with sporadic primary hyperparathyroidism. J. Bone Miner. Res. 37 (10), 1860–1875. https://doi.org/10.1002/jbmr.4653.

Khanim, F.L., Gommersall, L.M., Wood, V.H.J., Smith, K.L., Montalvo, L., O'Neill, L.P., Xu, Y., Peehl, D.M., Stewart, P.M., Turner, B.M., Campbell, M.J., 2004. Altered SMRT levels disrupt vitamin D3 receptor signalling in prostate cancer cells. Oncogene 23, 6712–6725. https://doi.org/10.1038/sj.onc.1207772.

Kim, K., et al., 2013. HOTAIR is a negative prognostic factor and exhibits pro-oncogenic activity in pancreatic cancer. Oncogene 32, 1616–1625.

Kogo, R., et al., 2011. Long noncoding RNA HOTAIR regulates polycomb-dependent chromatin modification and is associated with poor prognosis in colorectal cancers. Cancer Res. 71, 6320–6326.

Kouzarides, T., 2007. Chromatin modifications and their function. Cell 128, 693–705.

Kutay, H., Bai, S., Datta, J., Motiwala, T., Pogribny, I., Frankel, W., Jacob, S.T., Ghoshal, K., 2006. Downregulation of miR-122 in the rodent and human hepatocellular carcinomas. J. Cell. Biochem. 99, 671–678. https://doi.org/10.1002/jcb.20982.

Li, E., Zhang, Y., 2014. DNA methylation in mammals. Cold Spring Harb. Perspect. Biol. 6, a019133.

Marchini, A., Scott, E.M., Rommelaere, J., 2016. Overcoming barriers in oncolytic virotherapy with HDAC inhibitors and immune checkpoint blockade. Viruses 8 (1).

Mariadason, J.M., 2008. HDACs and HDAC inhibitors in colon cancer. Epigenetics. https://doi.org/10.4161/epi.3.1.5736.

Marrocco, D.L., Tilley, W.D., Bianco-Miotto, T., et al., 2007. Suberoylanilide hydroxamic acid (vorinostat) represses androgen receptor expression and acts synergistically with an androgen receptor antagonist to inhibit prostate cancer cell proliferation. Mol. Cancer Ther. 6 (1), 51–60. 100.

Marrocco-Tallarigo, D.L., Centenera, M.M., Scher, H.I., et al., 2009. Finding the place of histone deacetylase inhibitors in prostate cancer therapy. Expert. Rev. Clin. Pharmacol. 2 (6), 619–630.

Moffat, I.D., Boutros, P.C., Celius, T., Lindén, J., Pohjanvirta, R., Okey, A.B., 2007. microRNAs in adult rodent liver are refractory to dioxin treatment. Toxicol. Sci. 99 (2), 470–487.

Nakagawa, T., et al., 2013. Large noncoding RNA HOTAIR enhances aggressive biological behavior and is associated with short disease-free survival in human non-small cell lung cancer. Biochem. Biophys. Res. Commun. 436, 319–324.

Nan, X., Ng, H.-H., Johnson, C.A., Laherty, C.D., Turner, B.M., Eisenman, R.N., Bird, A., 1998. Transcriptional repression by the methyl-CpG-binding protein MeCP2 involves a histone deacetylase complex. Nature 393, 386–389.

Pfeiffer, M.J., Mulders, P.F., Schalken, J.A., 2010. An in vitro model for preclinical testing of endocrine therapy combinations for prostate cancer. Prostate 70 (14), 1524–1532.

Pulliam, N., Fang, F., Ozes, A.R., et al., 2018. An effective epigenetic-PARP inhibitor combination therapy for breast and ovarian cancers independent of BRCA mutations. Clin. Cancer Res. 24 (13), 3163–3175.

Ramalingam, S.S., Maitland, M.L., Frankel, P., et al., 2010. Carboplatin and paclitaxel in combination with either vorinostat or placebo for first-line therapy of advanced non-small-cell lung cancer. J. Clin. Oncol. 28 (1), 56–62.

Rumgay, H., Murphy, N., Ferrari, P., Soerjomataram, I., 2021. Alcohol and cancer: epidemiology and biological mechanisms. Nutrients 13, 3173. https://doi.org/10.3390/nu13093173.

Saini, S., Majid, S., Dahiya, R., 2010. Diet, MicroRNAs and prostate cancer. Pharm. Res. https://doi.org/10.1007/s11095-010-0086-x.

Shen, H., Laird, P.W., 2013. Interplay between the cancer genome and epigenome. Cell 153, 38–55.

Sugimura, T., 2000. Nutrition and dietary carcinogens. Carcinogenesis. https://doi.org/10.1093/carcin/21.3.387.

Sun, Q., Cong, R., Yan, H., Gu, H., Zeng, Y., Liu, N., Chen, J., Wang, B., 2009a. Genistein inhibits growth of human uveal melanoma cells and affects microRNA-27a and target gene expression. Oncol. Rep. 22, 563–567. https://doi.org/10.3892/or_00000472.

Sun, H., Zhou, X., Chen, H., Li, Q., Costa, M., 2009b. Modulation of histone methylation and MLH1 gene silencing by hexavalent chromium. Toxicol. Appl. Pharmacol. 237 (3), 258–266.

Supic, G., Jagodic, M., Magic, Z., 2013. Epigenetics: a new link between nutrition and cancer. Nutr. Cancer 65, 781–792. https://doi.org/10.1080/01635581.2013.805794.

Tajuddin, S.M., Amaral, A.F., Fernández, A.F., Rodríguez-Rodero, S., Rodríguez, R.M., Moore, L.E., Tardón, A., Carrato, A., García-Closas, M., Silverman, D.T., Jackson, B.P., 2013. Genetic and non-genetic predictors of LINE-1 methylation in leukocyte DNA. Environ. Health Perspect. 121 (6), 650–656.

Tarantini, L., Bonzini, M., Apostoli, P., Pegoraro, V., Bollati, V., Marinelli, B., Cantone, L., Rizzo, G., Hou, L., Schwartz, J., Bertazzi, P.A., 2009. Effects of particulate matter on genomic DNA methylation content and iNOS promoter methylation. Environ. Health Perspect. 117 (2), 217–222.

Tawbi, H.A., Beumer, J.H., Tarhini, A.A., et al., 2013. Safety and efficacy of decitabine in combination with temozolomide in metastatic melanoma: a phase I/II study and pharmacokinetic analysis. Ann. Oncol. 24 (4), 1112–1119.

Toraño, E.G., García, M.G., Fernández-Morera, J.L., Niño-García, P., Fernández, A.F., 2016. The impact of external factors on the epigenome: in utero and over lifetime. Biomed. Res. Int. 2016.

Trump, D., Aragon-Ching, J., 2018. Vitamin D in prostate cancer. Asian J. Androl. https://doi.org/10.4103/aja.aja_14_18.

Tsou, J.A., Shen, L.Y., Siegmund, K.D., Long, T.I., Laird, P.W., Seneviratne, C.K., Koss, M.N., Pass, H.I., Hagen, J.A., Laird-Offringa, I.A., 2005. Distinct DNA methylation profiles in malignant mesothelioma, lung adenocarcinoma, and non-tumor lung. Lung Cancer 47 (2), 193–204.

Umesawa, M., Iso, H., Fujino, Y., Kikuchi, S., Tamakoshi, A., 2016. Salty food preference and intake and risk of gastric cancer: the JACC study. J. Epidemiol. 26, 92–97. https://doi.org/10.2188/jea.JE20150023.

Wei, E.K., Giovannucci, E., Selhub, J., Fuchs, C.S., Hankinson, S.E., Ma, J., 2005. Plasma vitamin B6 and the risk of colorectal cancer and adenoma in women. J. Natl. Cancer Inst. 97, 684–692. https://doi.org/10.1093/jnci/dji116.

Wilhelm, C.S., Kelsey, K.T., Butler, R., Plaza, S., Gagne, L., Zens, M.S., Andrew, A.S., Morris, S., Nelson, H.H., Schned, A.R., Karagas, M.R., 2010. Implications of LINE1 methylation for bladder cancer risk in women. Clin. Cancer Res. 16 (5), 1682–1689.

Witta, S.E., Jotte, R.M., Konduri, K., et al., 2012. Randomized phase II trial of erlotinib with and without entinostat in patients with advanced non–small-cell lung cancer who progressed on prior chemotherapy. J. Clin. Oncol. 30 (18), 2248–2255.

Wright, R.O., Schwartz, J., Wright, R.J., Bollati, V., Tarantini, L., Park, S.K., Hu, H., Sparrow, D., Vokonas, P., Baccarelli, A., 2010. Biomarkers of lead exposure and DNA methylation within retrotransposons. Environ. Health Perspect. 118 (6), 790–795.

Zhang, B., Pan, X., 2009. RDX induces aberrant expression of microRNAs in mouse brain and liver. Environ. Health Perspect. 117 (2), 231–240. https://doi.org/10.1289/ehp.11841.

CHAPTER NINETEEN

Somatic mutation: Pharmacogenomics in oncology care

Satyabrata Kundu, Shriyansh Srivastava, and Shamsher Singh
Department of Pharmacology, ISF College of Pharmacy, Moga, Punjab, India

Abbreviations

AI	aromatase inhibitor
ALK	anaplastic lymphoma kinase
ALL	acute lymphoblastic leukemia
BRAF	v-raf murine sarcoma viral oncogene homolog B1
CDK	cyclin-dependent kinase
CML	chronic myeloid lymphoma
CPIC	clinical pharmacogenetics implementation consortium
EGFR	epidermal growth factor receptor
FISH	fluorescence in situ hybridization
GIST	gastrointestinal stromal tumor
GTP	guanine nucleotide-binding protein
HOXB9	homeobox transcription factor gene
IHC	immunohistochemistry
ISH	in situ hybridization
JAK	Janus kinase
KRAS	Kirsten rat sarcoma virus
MAPK	mitogen-activated protein kinase
MEK	mitogen-activated extracellular signal-regulated kinase
MET	mesenchymal-epithelial transition factor
mTOR	mammalian target of rapamycin
NGS	next-generation sequencing
NSCLC	nonsmall cell lung cancer
OS	overall survival
PDGFR	platelet-derived growth factor receptors
PFS	progression-free survival
pI3K	phosphoinositide 3-kinase
PTEN	phosphatase and tensin homolog
ROS1	ROS proto-oncogene 1
SNP	single-nucleotide polymorphisms
TCGA	The Cancer Genome Atlas
TKI	tyrosine kinase inhibitor
VEGF	vascular endothelial growth factor
VEGFR	vascular endothelial growth factor receptor
WT	wild-type

1. Introduction

Over the past few years, the development of cancer pharmacogenomics has gained a lot of attention, providing insights into the pattern of gene expression in both normal and tumor cells. Recent studies showed the role of cancer pharmacogenomics in the optimization of cancer treatments. Around the globe, approximately, 1000 Genomes project has demonstrated the variations among the human population. Phase 3 considered 2504 individual from 26 populations, and introduced phased over 88 million variants sites (84.7 million single-nucleotide polymorphisms [SNPs], 3.6 million insertions/deletions, also 60,000 structural variants) (Purcell et al., 2007). Basically, in a typical genome, 4.1 million to 5.0 million sites differ from the reference genome and most of these variations are short indels and SNPs (Purcell et al., 2007). Cancer Pharmacogenomics studies are critical for determining the association between genetic changes and their impact on anticancer drug pharmacokinetics and pharmacodynamics. The human genome's genetic changes can be split into two categories: germline and somatic mutations. Highly penetrant susceptibility mutations and some other genetic variants that pass from generations after generations are the examples of germline changes. These changes, especially single-nucleotide polymorphisms (SNPs), might be used as biomarkers to predict drug-induced adverse events and therapeutic responses. Somatic mutations, on the other hand, are acquired at random after exposure to substances that have the ability to harm DNA in cells. Accumulation of somatic mutation in cancer cells is frequently utilized as therapeutic targets in the context of cancer. Genomic technology has progressed over the last 2 decades from examining a single gene mutation to a genome-wide perspective via large-scale genotyping and next-generation sequencing (NGS). Large-scale research targeted at verifying genomic sequencing and expression data to find harmful germline mutations that predispose to cancer are now possible thanks to the emergence of massive NGS data (Huang et al., 2018).

Pharmacogenomics of antineoplastic drugs has focused on the right dosage regimen, due to its narrow therapeutic index, which is the range of efficacious and toxic dosages. On the other hand, inter- and intraindividual variability in oncotherapy, and also some toxicity effects in the normal cells are another major problem. This concern has needed searching of appropriate biomarkers for individual treatments with correct dose in the right patients (McLeod, 2013; Crews et al., 2012; Paugh et al., 2011). The Clinical Pharmacogenetics Implementation Consortium (CPIC) clinical guidelines have suggested five antineoplastic drugs including mercaptopurine, tamoxifen, thioguanine, and capecitabine/5-fluorouracil (Relling et al., 2011). Also, tegafur and irinotecan have been added to that list by the Royal Dutch Association for the Advancement of Pharmacy Pharmacogenetics Working Group (DPWG) (O'neill and Temple, 2012). The Food and Drug Administration has noted down more than 100 approved drugs with pharmacogenomic biomarkers in drug labeling data, for potency and lethality (Emtansines et al., 2019) (Table 1).

Table 1 Somatic biomarkers in FDA approved targeted drugs.

Targets	Drugs	Cancer type	Somatic alteration	Detection method	References
ALK	Alectinib	Nonsmall cell line cancer (NSCLC)	Mutation, fusion	FISH, IHC, NGS	Peters et al. (2017)
	Certinib	NSCLC	Mutation, fusion	FISH, IHC, NGS	Soria et al. (2017a)
	Brigatinib	NSCLC	Mutation		Camidge et al. (2018)
ALK, MET, ROS1	Crizotinib	NSCLC	Fusion and ROS1 gene fusion	FISH, IHC, NGS	Kazandjian et al. (2014)
BCR–ABL1	Bosutinib	CML	Fusion	Cytogenetics, FISH, RT-PCR	Cortes et al. (2018)
	Dasatinib	CML, ALL	Fusion	Cytogenetics, FISH, RT-PCR	Müller et al. (2009)
	Imatinib	ALL, CML, GIST	Fusion	Cytogenetics, FISH, RT-PCR	Johnson et al. (2003) and Schultz et al. (2009)
	Nilotinib	CML	Fusion	Cytogenetics, FISH, RT-PCR	Kantarjian et al. (2011)
BCR–ABL1, BCR–ABL1 T315I	Ponatinib	CML	Fusion	Cytogenetics, FISH, RT-PCR	Cortes et al. (2013)
BRAFV600E, V600K	Dabrafenib	NSCLC, melanoma, thyroid cancer (anaplastic)	Mutation in BRAF V600E/K	RT-PCR, NGS	Long et al. (2017), Planchard et al. (2017), and Subbiah et al. (2018)
CDK 4/6	Abemaciclib	ER+ HER2− breast cancer		FISH	Goetz et al. (2017)
	Palbociclib	HR+ HER2− breast cancer		FISH	Turner et al. (2015)
	Ribociclib	HR+ HER2− breast cancer		FISH	

Continued

Table 1 Somatic biomarkers in FDA approved targeted drugs—cont'd

Targets	Drugs	Cancer type	Somatic alteration	Detection method	References
EGFR	Cetuximab	Head and neck cancer, colorectal cancer	KRAS wt/EGFR	RT-PCR, NGS	Hortobagyi et al. (2018) and Janni et al. (2018)
	Erlotinib	NSCLC, pancreatic cancer	EGFR exon 19 del, EGFR exon 21 (L858R)	RT-PCR, NGS	Licitra et al. (2013)
	Gefitinib	NSCLC	EGFR exon 19 del, EGFR exon 21 (L858R)	RT-PCR, NGS	Cicènas et al. (2016), Shin et al. (2016), and Wang et al. (2015)
	Necitumumab	Squamous NSCLC			Douillard et al. (2014a)
	Osimertinib	NSCLC	EGFR T790M	NGS	Reck et al. (2016) Akamatsu et al. (2018), Mok et al. (2017), and Soria et al. (2018)
	Panitumumab		KRAS wt/EGFR	RT-PCR, IHC	Douillard et al. (2014b) and Price et al. (2014)
EGFR/ERBB2	Afatinib	NSCLC	EGFR exon 19 del, EGFR exon 21 (L858R)	RT-PCR, NGS	Yang et al. (2015)
ERBB2	Ado-Trastuzumab Ado-Emtansine	HER2+ breast cancer			Krop et al. (2014) and Diéras et al. (2017)
	Trastuzumab	HER2+ breast cancer, HER2+ gastric cancer		ISH, IHC, NGS	Cameron et al. (2017), Gianni et al. (2011), and Bang et al. (2010)

Target	Drug	Indication	Biomarker	Method	Reference
	Pertuzumab	HER2+ breast cancer		ISH, IHC, NGS	Von Minckwitz et al. (2017)
	Lapatinib	HER2+ breast cancer		ISH, IHC, NGS	Ryan et al. (2008)
	Neratinib	HER2+ breast cancer		ISH, IHC, NGS	Chan et al. (2016) and Martin et al. (2017)
JAK1/2	Ruxolitinib	Acute lymphoblastic leukemia	Mutation		Downes et al. (2021)
KIT	Imatinib	Gastrointestinal stromal tumor	Kit (CD117) +	IHC	Dagher et al. (2002)
		Aggressive systemic mastrocytosis	KIT D816V negative	PCR	Droogendijk et al. (2006)
MEK	Trametinib	Melanoma, thyroid cancer (anaplastic), NSCLC	BRAFV600E, V600K	RT-PCR, NGS	Long et al. (2017) and Planchard et al. (2016)
mTOR	Everolimus	Metastatic renal cell cancer, gastrointestinal, pancreatic and lung neuroendocrine tumors, subependymal giant cell astrocytoma, HR + HER2− breast cancer		ISH, IHC, FISH	Yardley et al. (2013), Yao et al. (2011, 2016), Motzer et al. (2010), and Franz et al. (2013)
PDGFR	Imatinib	Myelodysplastic/myeloproliferative neoplasm	PDGFR gene rearrangements	FISH	Apperley et al. (2002)
		Dermatofibrosarcoma protuberans	COL1A1-PDGFB fusion	FISH	Rutkowski et al. (2010)
		Chronic myelogenous leukemia	FIP1L1-PDFGRA fusion	NGS, FISH	Pardanani et al. (2003)

Continued

Table 1 Somatic biomarkers in FDA approved targeted drugs—cont'd

Targets	Drugs	Cancer type	Somatic alteration	Detection method	References
VEGF	Bevacizumab	Colorectal cancer, glioblastoma, renal cell carcinoma, cervical cancer, nonsmall cell line cancer	Mutation		Sandler et al. (2006) and Monk et al. (2013)
VEGFR2	Ramucirumab	Advanced gastric cancer, colorectal cancer, nonsmall cell carcinoma	Mutation		Garon et al. (2014)

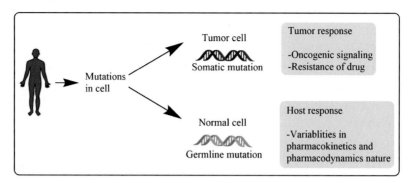

Fig. 1 Outline of cancer pharmacogenomics.

2. Cancer pharmacogenomics

In healthcare research studies, the interindividual variability in drug response is still a matter of concern. In 1959, Fredrick Vogel first looked at this problem. He coined the term "pharmacogenetics" to demonstrate the role of a genomic factor in drug response (Vogel, 1959). The genes identification related to drug response consisted of information of relevant genes from the perspective of pharmacokinetics and pharmacodynamic role. The pharmacogenomic study optimizes drug therapy, maximum efficacy with minimal toxicity individually (Zhang and Nebert, 2017) (Fig. 1).

Pharmacogenomics has been defined as a branch of pharmacology that deals with the role of genetic variability on drug response in the individual by connecting the expression of genes or SNPs with drug efficacy and toxicity including somatic and germline variation (Zhang and Nebert, 2017; Burki, 2017; Scott et al., 2019).

The Cancer Genome Atlas (TCGA) and the International Cancer Genome Consortium have aided in the detection of somatic mutations in cancer genomes using next-generation sequencing (NGS). One of the important components that have activated the integration of genomic data into clinical practice is a next-generation sequencing (NGS). NGS generates a massive pool of genomic sequence data by sequencing millions of DNA fragments at the same time. The approach can be used to sequence a specific number of genes (gene panel), the entire exome, or the entire genome. With the advent of technology and bioinformatic pipelines, this technique may now be completed at a low cost and in a reasonable amount of time (Hui, 2012; Kamps et al., 2017). As a result of the availability of large-scale genome sequencing using NGS, numerous studies have been done to study the mutational profile of various cancer types. To improve our understanding of the mutational landscape in cancer, large consortia and networks (COSMIC and GENIE), assemble and combine somatic mutation data from multiple sources (Forbes et al., 2016; Consortium, 2017). These databases can help researchers learn more about the probable links between genomic data and cancer subtypes, metastasis, and prognosis. More critically, advances in cancer genomics have enabled the discovery of molecular targets that may allow cancer patients to begin treatment with an established targeted medication or be enrolled in clinical trials. Cancer pharmacogenomics is the science of analyzing genetic changes and their implications on the pharmacokinetics and pharmacodynamics of anticancer medications, with the goal of providing cancer patients with the exact treatment that will achieve a favorable response while causing low/no adverse events. Genomic research has progressed from single-gene analysis to whole-genome investigations employing large-scale genotyping and next-generation sequencing techniques, thanks to advancements in biotechnology and bioinformatics. International collaboration has led to the creation of databases to curate clinically significant genetic changes, which are now used in clinical sequencing and liquid biopsy screening/monitoring. Furthermore, a large number of clinical studies have amassed enough evidence to match cancer patients to medicines based on clinically significant changes (Kaur et al., 2019).

Pharmacogenomics research is producing tools for molecular diagnostics that can be used to select the drug and dose for each patient. In light of the narrow therapeutic index of most anticancer drugs and the implications of undertreatment, pharmacogenomics holds great promise for translating into cancer chemotherapy. This study looks at how inherited (germline) and acquired (somatic) sources of genomic diversity can affect cancer treatment efficacy and toxicity (Paugh et al., 2011).

The precision medicine on drug response needs searching of right biomarkers to find out the best therapeutic agent. Biological markers are the variables (mutation, altered protein levels) that are linked with disease outcome (progression of the disease). Comparatively, predictive biomarkers are changeable related to drug's effects, where the outcome relies upon the biomarker's presence (Ballman, 2015).

3. Somatic mutation

Somatic mutation highlights the genetic variations of malignant cells (drug resistance, tumorigenesis, microenvironment, etc.). Somatic mutations have represented the importance of understanding the biological attribution of carcinoma with discoveries explaining the genetic alteration driving the gain of malignant properties of normal cells delivering molecular drug targets. From the past few years, tumor sequencing is being increased prospectively, changing the type of cancer treatment from site-specific treatment to molecularly targeted therapy (MacConaill et al., 2011; Ong et al., 2012). Uses of genomic data for the development of targeted therapy molecularly were first described

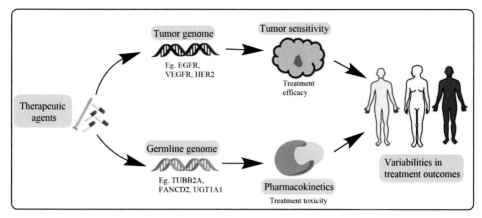

Fig. 2 Schematic diagram of treatment variabilities in somatic and germline mutation.

in the use of imatinib in chronic myeloid lymphoma (CML) patients. An important characteristic of CML is the presence of the fused BCR-ABL gene, which leads to the active form of tyrosine kinase, which results in the uncontrollable proliferation of cells. Imatinib, is a first-generation ABL tyrosine kinase inhibitor approved by USFDA for newly diagnosed as well as failed interferon-alpha response patients (Westin and Kurzrock, 2012). Soon, imatinib recognized as a first-line treatment for CML due to its better efficacy and low toxicity among patients who were failed to give a response with IFα.

Various drugs are in the queue being developed based on molecular targets (Simon, 2013), such as the role of crizotinib in anaplastic lymphoma kinase (ALK)[+] nonsmall cell lung cancer. The DNA sequencing of the tumor selected two patients with nonsmall cell lung cancer (NSCLC) bearing rearrangement of ALK as tyrosine kinase inhibitor (crizotinib), moved into early Phase I clinical trial. Both patients showed response to this tyrosine kinase inhibitor prompting protocol revision to prospectively test for rearrangement of ALK throughout clinical trials (Ou et al., 2012; Ou, 2011). Targeted therapy via molecular alteration, like crizotinib, has replaced ongoing treatments in various cancer types including melanoma, colorectal cancer, breast cancer, lung cancer (Ou et al., 2012; Gillis et al., 2014). Treatment response variabilities are seen among patients treated with cancer therapies (Fig. 2). Recently, next-generation sequencing has taken a major role in the in-depth identification of genomic biomarkers that could help in targeting by FDA-approved treatments. However, the jump from cytotoxic treatments to molecularly designed treatment is new to cancer drug design, and will be discussed in a later part.

4. Biomarkers

The two most common forms are predictive and prognostic biomarkers. A biomarker with a predictive value may give information about the prognosis and severity of cancer regardless of the therapy utilized. BRAF mutations are a poor prognostic sign for colorectal cancer, however BRAF inhibitors are more helpful in other disorders, such as melanoma. A predictive biomarker may be used to predict whether a patient will react well to treatment or is more likely to have adverse effects. "However, some biomarkers are both prognostic and predictive within the same tumor type, such as HER2 overexpression in breast cancer, which is a poor prognostic marker in the absence of chemotherapy because it results in an aggressive phenotype; however, with the development of therapies targeting HER2 (e.g., trastuzumab), this biomarker is now considered a positive predictive biomarker for therapy response" (Patel, 2016).

4.1. Epidermal growth factor receptor (EGFR)

EGFR inhibitors in NSCLC patients are the suitable and personalized genomic-based targeted therapy till now. Since somatic mutations of EGFR account for 15%–50% of all NSCLCs, they are among the most extensively studied targets. Ninety percent of total EGFR mutations are based on exon 20 substitution (−L858R) and exon 19 deletions. Alterations in these genes result in tyrosine kinase mutation with constant phosphorylation, which further activates various signaling pathways (RAS/MAPK and PI3K/Akt), leading to the development of tumors. Mostly, these mutations are act as sensitizing mutations, were observed to assume the response rate of tyrosine kinase inhibitors in NSCLC patients (Russo et al., 2015; Ahmadzada et al., 2018). Various clinical trials data have demonstrated that not more than 67% of NSCLC patients linked with sensitizing mutation showed objective response from some FDA-approved first-generation tyrosine kinase inhibitors (TKIs) (Jackman et al., 2009). Also, TKIs have shown a better response rate and PFS compared to standard chemotherapy in patients who harbor sensitizing mutation (Yang et al., 2014; Rosell et al., 2012). These positive outcomes made TKIs as a first-line treatment option for patients with NSCLC who harbor sensitizing mutation of EGFR. Although most of the cases, up to 50% of patients have undergone resistance within 12 months of treatments, with secondary mutation in −T90M gene (Ma et al., 2011). Moreover, dacomitinib and afatinib (second-generation TKIs) were intended to defeat resistance by increasing inhibition potency but, unfortunately, they are not able to defeat resistance due to −T90M mutation (Liao et al., 2015); rather, afatinib showed its efficacy against other EGFR-mutated genes, including S768I/L861Q/G719X with maximum patients who harbor any of these aforementioned mutations (Yang et al., 2015). Recently, one-third generation TKI (osimertinib) has been approved for patients with NSCLC linked to T790M mutation. This approval was addressed from a phase II clinical trial which showed clinical efficacy of Osimertinib in patients who were linked to either acquired or intrinsic mutation in EGFR-T790M. Less than 70% of patients showed objective response with controlled side effects (Goss et al., 2016). Combination therapy of erlotinib and gemcitabine is now approved for patients with pancreatic neoplasms based on the achievement of increased PFS and disease controlling rate (Wang et al., 2015).

Apart from EGFR inhibitors, anti-EGFR monoclonal antibodies have been designed for inhibition of downstream signaling and auto-phosphorylation of EGFR. These agents are mostly used for the treatment of colorectal cancers (Martinelli et al., 2009). Combination of cetuximab, panitumumab, and irinotecan or as monotherapy against EGFR (+) colorectal cancer patients are approved due to its great clinical efficacy, disease controlling the rate and improved progression-free survival (PFS) compared to standard chemotherapy (Cunningham et al., 2004; Wilke et al., 2008; Van Cutsem et al., 2007). Currently, the combination of necitumumab (second-generation anti-EGFR monoclonal antibody), cisplatin, and gemcitabine has got its approval as first-line therapy for metastatic NSCLC. This result was acquired from a multicenter study that involved squamous NSCLC ($N=1093$) patients across 26 countries (Fala, 2016). These patients were separated by two treatment arms: cisplatin and gemcitabine with or without necitumumab; and Improvement in the PFS and overall survival (OS) rates was shown by the patients treated with necitumumab (Fala, 2016). Anti-EGFR monoclonal antibodies have a role in showing more clinical efficacy compared to existing standard chemotherapy. Various clinical trials have shown that patients with EGFR (+), identified by immunohistochemistry or in situ hybridization, have shown positive outcomes from cetuximab and necitumumab compared to EGFR negative patients (Pirker et al., 2012; Paz-Ares et al., 2016). Although the specificity from immunohistochemistry or in situ hybridization in predicting EGFR expression is still questionable. For maintaining higher sensitivity, NGS is essential for verification and quantification (Martinelli et al., 2009). On the other hand, KRAS mutation status has a role in the prediction of response to panitumumab and cetuximab. KRAS mutation has a role in the activation of guanine nucleotide-binding protein (GTP) protein that allows the tumor to bypass the inhibition effect of EGFR related therapies. These effects have been observed in various studies where a good response rate and increased PFS of EGFR targeted therapies were observed in KRAS wild-type groups (Lievre et al., 2006; Amado et al., 2008). Currently, in colorectal cancer patients, BRAF and NRAS mutations were found to check the response rate of panitumumab and cetuximab. Anti-EGFR targeted therapies are unlikely to act on the patients whose tumor is linked with mutations in BRAF V600E and NRAS exons 2, 3, and 4 (van Brummelen et al., 2017). Various research studies have developed the relation of cetuximab/panitumumab and KRAS mutation (Lievre et al., 2006; Karapetis et al., 2008). KRAS is a membrane GTPase that has a role in the activation of various proteins in EGFR signaling pathways including PI3K and c-Raf. Abnormal activation of these proteins may lead to the development of cancer (Kranenburg, 2005). Although, KRAS-induced cancer cannot be cured by inactivating EGFR with cetuximab or panitumumab if it is actively mutated. Pharmacogenomics research demonstrated that mutation in exon 2 at G13 and G12 caused abnormal activation of KRAS and results development of cancer (Amado et al., 2008). It was described that approximately 40% of patients with colon cancer have these mutations (Lievre et al., 2006). So that, pharmacogenomics test on the KRAS gene has been required before administrating cetuximab and panitumumab for lung, head and neck and colon cancers. Only patients with colon cancer who expressed EGFR mutation and negative KRAS mutation (WT) are supposed to take these drugs according to mentioned drug label. Testing of RAS mutation is very essential before the administration of panitumumab and cetuximab therapy as these are not listed for patients whose tumor is linked to somatic mutations in the exon of NRAS or KRAS.

Recently, researchers have explored the possibility of targeting EGFR in NSCLC patients with immunotherapy in in-vitro studies. Moreover, in a pre-clinical study, researchers developed a T-cell treatment linked with the chimeric antigen receptor which is directed against EGFR. Human lung cancer xenografts expressing EGFR showed significant regression through the use of T-cell treatment linked with chimeric antigen receptor cells modified for anticancer efficacy (Li et al., 2018). A further clinical study is needed for the confirmation of their efficacy. Currently, one clinical trial (Clinical trial number: NCT03152435) is undergoing (phase I/II) to check the efficacy of chimeric antigen mediated T cell targeting EGFR in metastatic colorectal cancer patients.

4.2. Vascular endothelial growth factor (VEGF)

Despite substantial efforts over the past decade to discover predictive biomarkers for anti-angiogenic treatments, no such marker is useful in clinical practice (Cidon et al., 2016). Developing pharmacogenetics biomarkers is difficult due to the complexity of the angiogenesis signal pathway and the overlap of distinct angiogenesis components. Bates et al. looked examined CRC tumor samples from the phase III bevacizumab E3200 study in 2012 to investigate whether VEGF165b, a VEGF splice variant, had any bearing on treatment results. Patients having a lower level of VEGF165b tended to benefit better from bevacizumab therapy, despite the lack of statistical significance. According to a recent study, patients whose tumors were negative for the gene HOXB9 had significantly higher PFS when treated with first-line bevacizumab-containing regimens than patients whose patients' tumors were positive for that gene (Bates et al., 2012). The homeobox transcription factor gene (HOXB9) is highly conserved in a wide variety of cells and is involved in promoting tumor cell invasion, neoplastic transformation, and tumor progression through apoptosis inhibition (Carbone et al., 2017). These positive results will probably certainly be verified in the future. mCRC patients treated with chemotherapy and bevacizumab have been depicted to have NOTCH1 expression as a negative predictive factor (Paiva et al., 2015). A phase Ib study in mCRC is ongoing to assess the clinical effectiveness data of VEGF and the NOTCH ligand DLL4 (OMP-305B83) in conjunction with FOLFIRI as second-line therapy. Finally, the protein apelin is a novel player in the angiogenesis regulatory pathways (APLN). APLN signaling is engaged in some physiological processes, including angiogenesis, and interacts with important pathways that regulate cell growth, survival, and death at different levels. APLN mRNA levels are correlated significantly with response to treatment in preclinical data based on tissue samples from patients receiving bevacizumab. Nonresponders showed higher levels of APLN, while bevacizumab-treated patients had lower levels (Zuurbier et al., 2017). All of these possible symptoms, however, must be validated. Since the introduction of new antiangiogenic drugs into clinical practice in recent years, researchers have been looking for particular biomarkers for each chemical. CtDNA from liquid biopsies obtained from about 350 patients treated with regorafenib in the CORRECT study was used to determine the impact of the mutations KRAS, PIK3CA, and BRAF on regorafenib effectiveness. According to the findings, regorafenib increases survival and treatment results independent of KRAS and PIK3CA mutation status (Tabernero et al., 2015). A mutational status investigation was not clinically evaluable due to the minimal number of BRAF-mutated individuals. Aflibercept-treated patients recently had their biomarkers RAS, BRAF, and sidedness measured in the VELOUR study. Although there was a tendency toward better outcomes for BRAF-mutated tumors treated with aflibercept compared to the control arm, this analysis found no significant interactions between RAS and BRAF status. The RAISE trial participants who were administered ramucirumab showed comparable results. Ramucirumab exhibited the same beneficial therapeutic impact in RAS-mutated and all RAS/RAF WT cancers; however, the advantage in terms of OS and PFS was greater in BRAF-mutated tumors. Tabernero et al. looked studied the relationship between some baseline marker levels (including VEGFR-2 immunohistochemistry in tumor tissue) and clinical outcomes in RAISE patients (Yoshino et al., 2018). Only circulating blood levels of VEGF-D were shown to be statistically significant, with larger levels of this soluble factor (115 pg/mL) linked to greater ramucirumab efficiency than placebo. Over time, many SNPs in genes linked to the VEGF signaling pathway have been studied. According to a comprehensive meta-analysis including 158 SNPs and 1348 patients from five phase III randomized trials, VEGFA and VEGFR-2 polymorphisms were connected to improved PFS in bevacizumab-treated patients (Tabernero et al., 2018).

4.3. Anaplastic lymphoma kinase

Targeted therapies have been approved for patients with NSCLC who harbor genetic anaplastic lymphoma kinase (ALK). In patients with NSCLC, approximately 3%–7% of patients are linked with ALK mutation including point mutation and amplification, and gene fusion. Most of the fusion partners of ALK have been described, and the gene that includes EML4 has been demonstrated in NSCLC patients. A number of other partners are involved in fusion, including HIP1, CRIM1, STRN, PTPN3, FBX036, CLTC, KLC1, DCTN1, and KIF5B (Wu et al., 2017). Rearrangements of ALK result formation of an oncogenic fusion protein which directly activates the JAK-STAT pathway or mitogen-activated protein kinase (MAPK) (Garinet et al., 2018). For NSCLC patients linked with ALK mutation, various ALK inhibitors have been approved for good clinical efficacy and considered as the best treatment for NSCLC patients. One phase III randomized clinical trial showed that the median PFS in NSCLC patients treated with the standard chemotherapeutic agent was less as compared to NSCLC patients treated with first-generation ALK/ROS1/MET inhibitor (crizotinib) (3.0 vs 7.7 months, respectively) (Kazandjian et al., 2014). Also, in comparison to the chemotherapy arm, the objective response rate was 46% higher in ALK/ROS1/MET inhibitor treatment arm (Kazandjian et al., 2014). Unluckily, the treatment with crizotinib arm showed relapse within 1–2 years, with resistance in either ALK independent or ALK dependent (Wilson et al., 2015). Secondary mutation in the tyrosine kinase domain of ALK (fusion protein reactivation) is the main reason behind resistance (30% cases) (Wilson et al., 2015). Some examples of reported secondary point mutations include F1174V, L1196M, C1156Y, and F1174L (Schrank et al., 2018). The resistance process has been overcome by designing second- and third-generation ALK inhibitors (brigatinib, alectinib, and ceritinib) with improved clinical efficacy and ALK fusion protein selectivity (Sharma et al., 2018). In two clinical trials, alectinib and ceritinib showed a better overall response rate (more than 50%) in patients intolerant to crizotinib (Yang et al., 2017a; Kim et al., 2016). Moreover, these agents have shown good clinical efficacy in ALK inhibitor-naive patients in comparison to standard chemotherapy; ALK-mutant NSCLC patients were recently approved for first-line treatment with these drugs due to their good efficacy (Peters et al., 2017; Soria et al., 2017b). One pre-clinical study on FDA-approved ALK inhibitor (brigatinib) showed inhibitory effect against various ALK acquired resistance mutations (E1210K, G1269A, L1196M, V1180L, C1156Y, and I1171S/T) (Sabari et al., 2017). This result was found in a clinical trial (phase II), where ALK-positive and crizotinib-treated NSCLC patients showed more than 53% of the overall response rate to brigatinib (Camidge et al., 2018).

4.4. Breakpoint cluster region protein (BCR-ABL)

Chronic myeloid leukemia (CML) results when the Philadelphia chromosome combines the BCR with the c-ABL oncogene from chromosomes 9 and 22 resulting in the Philadelphia chromosome (Nowell and Hungerford, 1960). "The discovery of the Philadelphia chromosome, which is produced by a translocation between chromosomes 9 and 10, has raised the prospect of developing extremely effective targeted medicines for hematologic malignancies." In 95% of CML patients, the BCR-ABL translocation occurs, resulting in "constant activation of signal transduction pathways associated to cell proliferation and tumor growth" (Klein et al., 1982). The first translocation inhibitor to be found through a high-throughput screening assay for translocation inhibitors was imatinib, which was approved by the FDA in 2001 for the treatment of CML with

BCR–ABL positivity. Because of the advent of imatinib resistance, other TKIs including dasatinib, nilotinib, bosutinib, and ponatinib have been developed in recent years. Second- and third-generation TKIs may be used following progression on previous TKI treatment because of minor differences in the mechanism. Dasatinib inhibits the c-ABL kinase in both active and inactive forms. Imatinib, nilotinib, and ponatinib bind to the c-ABL kinase's inactive form and block it from transitioning to the active form. Nilotinib binds to c-ABL kinase with a greater affinity than imatinib, leading to better selectivity and potency (Bixby and Talpaz, 2009). At the time of diagnosis, 10%–15% of CML patients may acquire imatinib resistance, and 20%–25% may develop resistance over time (e.g., 1–5 years) (Zhang et al., 2009). The T315I point mutation in the c-ABL oncogene that produces steric hindrance has the largest magnitude of resistance because existing TKIs need threonine at position 315 to bind to their targets (Gorre et al., 2001). Ponatinib features a triple carbon bond, which helps the drug overcome early resistance by reducing steric hindrance (Lierman et al., 2012). Imatinib, the first small-molecule kinase inhibitor authorized for clinical usage to treat chronic myeloid leukemia by targeting the BCR–ABL protein tyrosine kinase, is the first illustration of the effectiveness of small-molecule targeted medicines in cancer therapy (CML). A shortened chromosome 22, known as the Philadelphia (pH) chromosome, is generated when the BCR and the non-receptor protein tyrosine kinase ABL merge as a consequence of a reciprocal chromosomal translocation $t(9;22)$. The fusion protein that results possesses constitutive tyrosine kinase activity, which allows for the activation of numerous signaling pathways including Ras, PI3K-Akt, and Jak-STAT, which leads to cell proliferation and survival. Both CML and acute lymphoblastic leukemia have been related to the BCR–ABL protein. Imatinib inhibits the BCR–ABL protein kinase by attaching to it and keeping it inactive. As it is selective for certain proteins, it is utilized to treat malignancies caused by dysregulated forms of the platelet-derived growth factor receptor, a-polypeptide (PDGFRA), and the KIT protein kinases (Michor et al., 2005). A mutation at the T315 location (T315V) has also been reported to provide constitutive kinase activity to ABL and diminish its responsiveness to imatinib when compared to wild-type ABL (Corbin et al., 2002). Imatinib binding is impaired by the T315I point mutation, which reduces imatinib's inhibitory action on ABL. Imatinib resistance has been related to more than 50 different point mutations in the ABL gene. The majority, on the other hand, are rare, with six amino-acid residues (Gly250, Tyr253, Glu255, Thr315, Met351, and Phe359) accounting for 60%–70% of imatinib-resistant mutations found thus far. In vitro transforming potential has been shown in two of the most prevalent ABL mutants, Y253F and E255K (Weisberg et al., 2007). This in vitro discovery is in line with clinical data that P-loop mutations such Y253F and E255K are linked to a higher incidence of blast crisis and shorter overall survival in imatinib-treated patients (Soverini et al., 2005). Another ABL variation, T315I, is typically identified in patients with advanced CML and predicts a lower overall survival in patients on imatinib treatment when compared to other ABL mutations.

4.5. Serine-threonine protein kinase and mitogen-activated protein kinase

A mutation of serine-threonine protein kinases BRAF along with V600E (half of the advanced melanomas) is the most prevalent mutation (BRAF mutations account for 90% of all mutations). The MEK proteins are phosphorylated and activated through BRAF mutation, which leads to activation of the MAPK pathway, resulting uncontrolled cell division and proliferation (Cheng et al., 2018). The higher number of mutated BRAF in melanomas acts as the perfect candidate for targeted treatment against melanoma. BRAF inhibitors (dabrafenib and vemurafenib) were showed increased PFS and OS compared to dacarbazine in BRAF-V600 metastatic melanoma patients (Falchook et al., 2012; Colllins et al., 2005) (Fig. 3).

Unluckily, most of the patients with BRAF inhibitor monotherapy developed resistance within 6–7 months of treatment (Manzano et al., 2016). The appearance of resistance melanoma cells is either by having pre-existing resistant clones present in biopsy sample or by having secondary mutations occur (Seluanov et al., 2018). Alternative splicing of BRAF, NRAS mutations (Q61, Q13 on codon 12 or 61), amplification of BRAF copy number, and PI3K alteration are the commonly known BRAF inhibitors mutation. Melanoma cells are able to escape BRAF inhibition through secondary mutations that reactivate the MAPK pathway (Arozarena and Wellbrock, 2017). Apart from BRAF inhibitors, trametinib (MEK inhibitor) has been selected to interfere in MAPK pathway in BRAF-V600 mutated melanoma patients. One study reported that trametinib improved OS in 6 months compared to other established chemotherapeutic agents (81% vs 67%, respectively); although resistance was approached quickly with 4.8 months of median PFS (Arozarena and Wellbrock, 2017). The combined therapy of trametinib and dabrafenib has shown good clinical efficacy with advanced benefits which beats the resistance noticed in approved monotherapies (Long et al., 2017). 3-Year of PFS and OS has shown significant improvement with combined targeted therapy compared to dabrafenib monotherapy, (22% vs 12%) and (44% vs 32%), respectively (Long et al., 2017). For advanced melanomas that are linked with BRAF V600E/K mutation, combined therapies of dabrafenib + trametinib or cobimetinib + vemurafenib have been currently approved. Moreover, combined treatment of trametinib + dabrafenib has shown clinical efficacy in anaplastic thyroid cancer and NSCLC with a mutation in BRAF V600 (Planchard et al., 2017; Subbiah et al., 2018).

4.6. ERBB2 kinase

The drug trastuzumab, a monoclonal antibody developed to treat breast cancer patients with tumors that overexpress the ERBB2 protein, is another example of how targeted drugs are successful in treating cancer. The ERBB2 protein tyrosine kinase overexpression and amplification in metastatic breast tumors cause aberrant signaling via

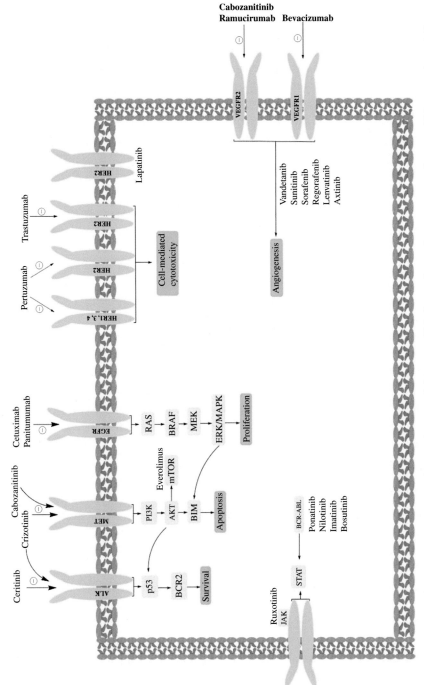

Fig. 3 An overview of somatic cancer biomarkers and targeted therapies. This figure shows downstream pathways within somatic mutation and their targeted therapies.

the PI3K and MAPK pathways which eventually lead to cell proliferation and apoptosis (Slamon et al., 1989). Elevated ERBB2 has been associated with an early recurrence and shorter overall survival in breast cancer. As a consequence, trastuzumab, a drug that targets the ERBB2 protein in some cancers, might help patients live longer. Trastuzumab was the first genetically-based cancer drug to get FDA approval (Roskoski Jr, 2004). Trastuzumab, a monoclonal antibody, is given intravenously rather than orally, as is the case with small-molecule kinase inhibitors. Trastuzumab is efficacious as a single treatment after the failure of several chemotherapy regimens. Understanding the molecular mechanisms behind primary or acquired trastuzumab resistance in individuals with metastatic breast cancer whose tumors overexpress ERBB2 is critical (Nahta et al., 2006). In addition to activating PI3K signaling, ERBB2 signaling also activates the Ras pathway. Constitutive PI3K/AKT activation has been shown to impede Trastuzumab-induced cell-cycle arrest and death. Trastuzumab therapy was less effective for patients whose tumors overexpress ERBB2 and have phosphatase and tensin homolog (PTEN) defects. In vitro and in vivo, trastuzumab resistance reportedly reversed by PI3K inhibitors in phosphatase and tensin homolog (PTEN)-deficient cells (Nagata et al., 2004). As a consequence, PTEN deletion might be utilized to predict trastuzumab resistance, and PI3K inhibitors could be used to treat trastuzumab-resistant cancers in PTEN-null mice. Intragenic mutations in the ERBB2 gene's conserved kinase region have also been found in certain lung cancers (Stephens et al., 2004). ERBB2 mutations tend to occur mostly in nonsmall cell lung cancer (NSCLC) with adenocarcinoma histology, are more prevalent in female patients, and are never smokers, similar to the clinicopathological presentation of EGFR mutations. At the time, for the treatment of ERBB2 mutant NSCLC patients, trastuzumab was thought to be beneficial. Trastuzumab monotherapy or the combination of cancer chemotherapeutics has not yet been shown to be effective against NSCLCs with overexpressed ERBB2 (Gatzemeier et al., 2004).

4.7. c-Met tyrosine kinase and cyclin-dependent kinases 4/6

Apart from approved biomarkers mentioned earlier, some other targets also have been exposed to showcase the treatment potential for cancer patients. Although, further studies are noted to specify genomic markers for certain severe patients. Dysregulations of c-Met tyrosine kinase (MET), particularly MET exon 14 splice site mutations, are seen in 3%–4% of lung adenocarcinoma (Garinet et al., 2018). Amplification of MET has also appeared in NSCLC patients with acquired resistance to EGFR inhibitors (Bean et al., 2007). In clinical trials, several studies have described the effective role of MET inhibition as a treatment option. A combination of cabozantinib, onartuzumab, and erlotinib (EGFR TKI) showed significant restoration of progression-free survival (PFS) in comparison to monotherapy with erlotinib (Neal et al., 2016; Spigel et al., 2013). Unfortunately, the promising results from these studies could not be forwarded after the phase III clinical trial, where the benefits from MET inhibitors were not observed in patients with NSCLC who sheltered the MET mutation (Spigel et al., 2017). Moreover, the patients who participated in these trials were chosen based on the overexpression of MET in tumors, determined by immunohisto-chemistry. Till now, it is not clear whether IHC selectively identifies MET-positive patients. More studies with prominent molecular profiling using genome sequencing are needed for the validation of MET in NSCLC patients.

Several studies demonstrated the role of cyclin-dependent kinases 4/6 (CDK4 and CDK6, respectively) in cell division and hyperactivation in various tumors. Scientists have been engaged in developing drugs that can directly target CDK activity, and three of those are now approved for estrogen receptor-positive advanced or metastatic breast cancer in combination with aromatase inhibitor (AI). The combination of CDK 4/6 inhibitors (Palbociclib, abemaciclib, and ribociclib) and hormone therapy has successfully improved PFS compared to AI alone (Goetz et al., 2017; Hortobagyi et al., 2018; Rugo et al., 2018). The sensitivity of CDK4/6 inhibitors is still unexplored despite having their great efficacy in cancer treatments. Both pre-clinical and clinical trials have been performed to check the association of cyclin D1 amplification and response to CDK4/6. Mantle cell lymphoma patients whose tumors linked with cyclin D1 dysregulation were observed to be CDK4/6 inhibitors sensitive, although this response was not noticed in breast cancer patients (Leonard et al., 2012; Finn et al., 2015). Cyclin D1 dependent genetic alteration is directly linked to disease specificity; so CDK4/6 inhibitors are mostly sensitive toward tumors (Knudsen and Witkiewicz, 2017). The clinical trial (phase II) of Palbociclib was found to be sensitive in CDK4 amplified liposarcoma patients (Dickson et al., 2013); although due to the lack of a control arm, this study was not able to assess whether CDK4 amplification can be act as a biomarker for identification of sensitive patients. Moreover, multiple contradicting results have been observed in animal studies where CDK4/6 amplification was linked to CDK4/6 inhibitors resistance in renal and breast cancers (Yang et al., 2017b; Olanich et al., 2015). Various clinical trials have been addressed to confirm the link between those genetic biomarkers with CDK4/6 inhibitors efficacy (Clinical trial number: NCT02187783, NCT03310879).

4.8. KIT and platelet-derived growth factor receptors (PDGFR) kinase

Dasatinib has also been authorized for the treatment of Ph-positive ALL patients who have developed resistance to or intolerance to imatinib (Talpaz et al., 2006). Because imatinib is selective for the proteins KIT and PDGFRA, it is used to treat gastrointestinal cancers (GISTs) that have mutant versions of those proteins. Majority of the GISTs are associated with oncogenic KIT or PDGFRA receptor tyrosine kinase mutations (Fletcher and Rubin, 2007). Mutations of KIT or PDGFRA are linked to GIST oncogenesis at an early stage, activating the upstream signaling networks mediated by signal transducer and activator of transcription (STAT) and mitogen-activated protein kinase (MAPK) (Corless et al., 2002).

Imatinib, a powerful inhibitor of KIT signaling, was recently approved as the first-line therapy for metastatic GIST after in vitro studies revealed that it had therapeutic promise in a human GIST cell line (Tuveson et al., 2001). Surgical excision of primary localized GIST was the sole option for a cure before imatinib. Standard chemotherapy and radiation were ineffective against GISTs. With a projected 5-year survival rate of 30% (DeMatteo et al., 2000), illness recurrence was a certain conclusion. In metastatic GISTs, prospective studies of imatinib have indicated that around 80% of patients react to the drug and attain stable disease. Exon 11 mutations in the KIT kinase cause the juxtamembrane autoinhibition of the KIT kinase to be lost in 75% of GISTs (Tarn et al., 2005). The number of patients who responded to imatinib therapy was higher for patients with exon 11 KIT mutations compared to those with other KIT/PDGFRA mutations (Ikediobi, 2008). When compared to exon 11 KIT mutants, patients lacking a detectable KIT or PDGFRA mutation react less often to imatinib therapy. 38 patients lacking KIT or PDGFRA mutations, on the other hand, react to imatinib in up to 39% of cases (Heinrich et al., 2006). These findings imply that imatinib therapy should be investigated for all GIST patients, regardless of whether or not they have a KIT or PDGFRA mutation. 40 patients with a primary imatinib-resistant mutation of PDGFRA may be the lone exception (D842V). Imatinib resistance will develop in the majority of metastatic GIST patients. It is most prevalent when secondary exon 13, 14, or 17 of KIT are mutated, preventing imatinib binding. Some of these secondary mutations, such as the common V654A change, are innately imatinib-resistant. Other mutations, such as those containing the N822 residue, are inherently imatinib sensitive but are linked to clinical imatinib resistance when they occur in the same exon as a KIT mutation in exon 11 (Joensuu, 2006). To possibly overcome imatinib resistance, new powerful inhibitors of KIT and PDGFRA must be developed. In November, Shutinib was licensed to treat patients with imatinib-resistant GISTs and those who were unable to take imatinib therapy. Shutinib is an inhibitor of the KIT, PDGFRA, FLT3, and VEGFR2. In a randomized phase III study of patients whose tumors had progressed while on imatinib, sunitinib extended the median time to tumor progression relative to placebo (Demetri et al., 2006). Sunitinib, on the other hand, only gives a brief benefit to imatinib-resistant GIST patients, necessitating the development of other treatment alternatives. In preclinical trials, treatment with heat-shock protein 90 inhibitors led to degradation of the KIT oncoprotein in GIST cell lines, suggesting it is a potential treatment option for GIST with imatinib resistance.

5. Future direction

Identification of a somatic mutation in recent days is easily achieved through the development of NGS in genomic profiling. Moreover, various factors should be taken into consideration in the selection of these targeted-based therapies. One of the major problems associated with somatic mutation identification using biopsy specimens is the clonal heterogeneity of cancer. A sampling of biomarkers in the tumor region may not be detectable or under detect which may be important for some targeted-based therapies. As a result of a better understanding of clonal heterogeneity, combination target therapies may be developed to reduce the incidence of resistance. Combining targeted therapies may help prevent the recurrence of melanoma, as evidenced by the success of the combination therapy using BRAF and MEK inhibitors. However, in the future, there is a need for more research to confirm whether the mutation profile obtained through liquid biopsy and tumor tissue are concordant.

Till now, some studies have been showing variability frequency across different groups. One study from Nagahashi et al. demonstrated that NRAS, TP53, APC, and ERBB2 mutations were seen in Japanese colorectal patients than the data received from The Cancer Genome Atlas that were linked to the population of the United States (Nagahashi et al., 2016). This study also showed that 50% of BRAF mutations occurred outside of V600E in the Western population. Also, the mutation in EGFR is directly linked to the nonsmoking Asian population compared to the Western population (Hudson et al., 2015; Mitsudomi, 2014).

Recently, detection of circulating tumor cells or tumor DNA from the blood samples of patients by liquid biopsy has been improved the patient outcome. Liquid biopsy in combination with NGS shows monitorization of disease alteration and development of resistance (Hench et al., 2018). Globally, NGS has enabled genomic information translation in clinical practices and the development of targeted based cancer therapies.

6. Conclusion

The inclusion and development of genomics have changed the period from one-size-fits-all to specific and targeted therapy for cancer patients that are linked to the administration of the precise dose of the drug to the right patients. Recently, clinical trials also pre-screened patients for checking individual genetic alteration before enrolment, increasing the role of genetic mutation in the clinical approach. Also, basket trial involvement in cancer types showed drug repurposing possibility for the treatment of cancer patients which could be beneficial in the coming years. Hopefully, cancer patients should be benefitted from the incorporation of genetic information since it could improve treatment precision and increased quality of life.

References

Ahmadzada, T., et al., 2018. An update on predictive biomarkers for treatment selection in non-small cell lung cancer. J. Clin. Med. 7 (6), 153.

Akamatsu, H., et al., 2018. Osimertinib in Japanese patients with EGFR T790M mutation-positive advanced non-small-cell lung cancer: AURA 3 trial. Cancer Sci. 109 (6), 1930–1938.

Amado, R.G., et al., 2008. Wild-type KRAS is required for panitumumab efficacy in patients with metastatic colorectal cancer. J. Clin. Oncol. 26, 1626–1634.

Apperley, J.F., et al., 2002. Response to imatinib mesylate in patients with chronic myeloproliferative diseases with rearrangements of the platelet-derived growth factor receptor beta. N. Engl. J. Med. 347 (7), 481–487.

Arozarena, I., Wellbrock, C., 2017. Overcoming resistance to BRAF inhibitors. Ann. Transl. Med. 5 (19).

Ballman, K.V., 2015. Biomarker: predictive or prognostic? J. Clin. Oncol. Off. J. Am. Soc. Clin. Oncol. 33 (33), 3968–3971.

Bang, Y.-J., et al., 2010. Trastuzumab in combination with chemotherapy versus chemotherapy alone for treatment of HER2-positive advanced gastric or gastro-oesophageal junction cancer (ToGA): a phase 3, open-label, randomised controlled trial. Lancet 376 (9742), 687–697.

Bates, D.O., et al., 2012. Association between VEGF splice isoforms and progression-free survival in metastatic colorectal cancer patients treated with bevacizumab. Clin. Cancer Res. 18 (22), 6384–6391.

Bean, J., et al., 2007. MET amplification occurs with or without T790M mutations in EGFR mutant lung tumors with acquired resistance to gefitinib or erlotinib. Proc. Natl. Acad. Sci. 104 (52), 20932–20937.

Bixby, D., Talpaz, M., 2009. Mechanisms of resistance to tyrosine kinase inhibitors in chronic myeloid leukemia and recent therapeutic strategies to overcome resistance. Hematology Am. Soc. Hematol. Educ. Program 2009 (1), 461–476. ASH Education Program Book.

Burki, T.K., 2017. Defining precision medicine. Lancet Oncol. 18 (12), e719.

Cameron, D., et al., 2017. 11 years' follow-up of trastuzumab after adjuvant chemotherapy in HER2-positive early breast cancer: final analysis of the HERceptin adjuvant (HERA) trial. Lancet 389 (10075), 1195–1205.

Camidge, D.R., et al., 2018. Exploratory analysis of brigatinib activity in patients with anaplastic lymphoma kinase-positive non–small-cell lung cancer and brain metastases in two clinical trials. J. Clin. Oncol. 36 (26), 2693–2701.

Carbone, C., et al., 2017. Homeobox B9 mediates resistance to anti-VEGF therapy in colorectal cancer patients. Clin. Cancer Res. 23 (15), 4312–4322.

Chan, A., et al., 2016. Neratinib after trastuzumab-based adjuvant therapy in patients with HER2-positive breast cancer (ExteNET): a multicentre, randomised, double-blind, placebo-controlled, phase 3 trial. Lancet Oncol. 17 (3), 367–377.

Cheng, L., et al., 2018. Molecular testing for BRAF mutations to inform melanoma treatment decisions: a move toward precision medicine. Mod. Pathol. 31 (1), 24–38.

Cicènas, S., et al., 2016. Maintenance erlotinib versus erlotinib at disease progression in patients with advanced non-small-cell lung cancer who have not progressed following platinum-based chemotherapy (IUNO study). Lung Cancer 102, 30–37.

Cidon, E.U., Alonso, P., Masters, B., 2016. Markers of response to antiangiogenic therapies in colorectal cancer: where are we now and what should be next? Clin. Med. Insights Oncol. 10, CMO.S34542.

Colllins, B., LeonBarnes Jr., E., Abernethy, J., 2005. Oral malignant melanoma. J. Clin. Oncol. 55, 74–108.

Consortium, A.P.G., 2017. AACR project GENIE: powering precision medicine through an international consortium. Cancer Discov. 7 (8), 818–831.

Corbin, A.S., et al., 2002. Analysis of the structural basis of specificity of inhibition of the Abl kinase by STI571. J. Biol. Chem. 277 (35), 32214–32219.

Corless, C.L., et al., 2002. KIT mutations are common in incidental gastrointestinal stromal tumors one centimeter or less in size. Am. J. Pathol. 160 (5), 1567–1572.

Cortes, J.E., et al., 2013. A phase 2 trial of ponatinib in Philadelphia chromosome–positive leukemias. N. Engl. J. Med. 369 (19), 1783–1796.

Cortes, J.E., et al., 2018. Bosutinib versus imatinib for newly diagnosed chronic myeloid leukemia: results from the randomized BFORE trial. J. Clin. Oncol. 36 (3), 231.

Crews, K.R., et al., 2012. Pharmacogenomics and individualized medicine: translating science into practice. Clin. Pharmacol. Ther. 92 (4), 467–475.

Cunningham, D., et al., 2004. Cetuximab monotherapy and cetuximab plus irinotecan in irinotecan-refractory metastatic colorectal cancer. N. Engl. J. Med. 351 (4), 337–345.

Dagher, R., et al., 2002. Approval summary: imatinib mesylate in the treatment of metastatic and/or unresectable malignant gastrointestinal stromal tumors. Clin. Cancer Res. 8 (10), 3034–3038.

DeMatteo, R.P., et al., 2000. Two hundred gastrointestinal stromal tumors: recurrence patterns and prognostic factors for survival. Ann. Surg. 231 (1), 51.

Demetri, G.D., et al., 2006. Efficacy and safety of sunitinib in patients with advanced gastrointestinal stromal tumour after failure of imatinib: a randomised controlled trial. Lancet 368 (9544), 1329–1338.

Dickson, M.A., et al., 2013. Phase II trial of the CDK4 inhibitor PD0332991 in patients with advanced CDK4-amplified well-differentiated or dedifferentiated liposarcoma. J. Clin. Oncol. 31 (16), 2024.

Diéras, V., et al., 2017. Trastuzumab emtansine versus capecitabine plus lapatinib in patients with previously treated HER2-positive advanced breast cancer (EMILIA): a descriptive analysis of final overall survival results from a randomised, open-label, phase 3 trial. Lancet Oncol. 18 (6), 732–742.

Douillard, J., et al., 2014a. First-line gefitinib in Caucasian EGFR mutation-positive NSCLC patients: a phase-IV, open-label, single-arm study. Br. J. Cancer 110 (1), 55–62.

Douillard, J.-Y., et al., 2014b. Final results from PRIME: randomized phase III study of panitumumab with FOLFOX4 for first-line treatment of metastatic colorectal cancer. Ann. Oncol. 25 (7), 1346–1355.

Downes, C.E., et al., 2021. Acquired JAK2 mutations confer resistance to JAK inhibitors in cell models of acute lymphoblastic leukemia. NPJ Precis. Oncol. 5 (1), 1–13.

Droogendijk, H.J., et al., 2006. Imatinib mesylate in the treatment of systemic mastocytosis: a phase II trial. Cancer 107 (2), 345–351.

Emtansines, A.T., Afatinib, Ì., Trioxider, A., 2019. Table of Pharmacogenomic Biomarkers in Drug Labeling. US Food and Drug Administration.

Fala, L., 2016. Portrazza (Necitumumab), an IgG1 monoclonal antibody, FDA approved for advanced squamous non–small-cell lung cancer. Am. Health Drug Benefits 9 (Spec Feature), 119.

Falchook, G.S., et al., 2012. Dabrafenib in patients with melanoma, untreated brain metastases, and other solid tumours: a phase 1 dose-escalation trial. Lancet 379 (9829), 1893–1901.

Finn, R.S., et al., 2015. The cyclin-dependent kinase 4/6 inhibitor palbociclib in combination with letrozole versus letrozole alone as first-line treatment of oestrogen receptor-positive, HER2-negative, advanced breast cancer (PALOMA-1/TRIO-18): a randomised phase 2 study. Lancet Oncol. 16 (1), 25–35.

Fletcher, J.A., Rubin, B.P., 2007. KIT mutations in GIST. Curr. Opin. Genet. Dev. 17 (1), 3–7.

Forbes, S., et al., 2016. COSMIC: high-resolution cancer genetics using the catalogue of somatic mutations in cancer. Curr. Protoc. Hum. Genet. 91 (1), 10.11.1–10.11.37.

Franz, D.N., et al., 2013. Efficacy and safety of everolimus for subependymal giant cell astrocytomas associated with tuberous sclerosis complex (EXIST-1): a multicentre, randomised, placebo-controlled phase 3 trial. Lancet 381 (9861), 125–132.

Garinet, S., et al., 2018. Current and future molecular testing in NSCLC, what can we expect from new sequencing technologies? J. Clin. Med. 7 (6), 144.

Garon, E.B., et al., 2014. Ramucirumab plus docetaxel versus placebo plus docetaxel for second-line treatment of stage IV non-small-cell lung cancer after disease progression on platinum-based therapy (REVEL): a multicentre, double-blind, randomised phase 3 trial. Lancet 384 (9944), 665–673.

Gatzemeier, U., et al., 2004. Randomized phase II trial of gemcitabine–cisplatin with or without trastuzumab in HER2-positive non-small-cell lung cancer. Ann. Oncol. 15 (1), 19–27.

Gianni, L., et al., 2011. Treatment with trastuzumab for 1 year after adjuvant chemotherapy in patients with HER2-positive early breast cancer: a 4-year follow-up of a randomised controlled trial. Lancet Oncol. 12 (3), 236–244.

Gillis, N.K., Patel, J.N., Innocenti, F., 2014. Clinical implementation of germ line cancer pharmacogenetic variants during the next-generation sequencing era. Clin. Pharmacol. Ther. 95 (3), 269–280.

Goetz, M.P., et al., 2017. MONARCH 3: abemaciclib as initial therapy for advanced breast cancer. J. Clin. Oncol. 35 (32).

Gorre, M.E., et al., 2001. Clinical resistance to STI-571 cancer therapy caused by BCR-ABL gene mutation or amplification. Science 293 (5531), 876–880.

Goss, G., et al., 2016. Osimertinib for pretreated EGFR Thr790Met-positive advanced non-small-cell lung cancer (AURA2): a multicentre, open-label, single-arm, phase 2 study. Lancet Oncol. 17 (12), 1643–1652.

Heinrich, M.C., et al., 2006. Molecular correlates of imatinib resistance in gastrointestinal stromal tumors. J. Clin. Oncol. 24 (29), 4764–4774.

Hench, I.B., Hench, J., Tolnay, M., 2018. Liquid biopsy in clinical management of breast, lung, and colorectal cancer. Front. Med. 5, 9.

Hortobagyi, G.N., et al., 2018. Updated results from MONALEESA-2, a phase III trial of first-line ribociclib plus letrozole versus placebo plus letrozole in hormone receptor-positive, HER2-negative advanced breast cancer. Ann. Oncol. 29 (7), 1541–1547.

Huang, K.-L., et al., 2018. Pathogenic germline variants in 10,389 adult cancers. Cell 173 (2), 355–370.e14.

Hudson, A.M., et al., 2015. Using large-scale genomics data to identify driver mutations in lung cancer: methods and challenges. Pharmacogenomics 16 (10), 1149–1160.

Hui, P., 2012. Next generation sequencing: chemistry, technology and applications. Chem. Diagn., 1–18.

Ikediobi, O., 2008. Somatic pharmacogenomics in cancer. Pharmacogenomics J. 8 (5), 305–314.

Jackman, D.M., et al., 2009. Impact of epidermal growth factor receptor and KRAS mutations on clinical outcomes in previously untreated non–small cell lung cancer patients: results of an online tumor registry of clinical trials. Clin. Cancer Res. 15 (16), 5267–5273.

Janni, W., et al., 2018. First-line ribociclib plus letrozole in postmenopausal women with HR+, HER2− advanced breast cancer: tumor response and pain reduction in the phase 3 MONALEESA-2 trial. Breast Cancer Res. Treat. 169 (3), 469–479.

Joensuu, H., 2006. Sunitinib for imatinib-resistant GIST:[comment]. Lancet 368 (9544), 1303–1304.

Johnson, J.R., et al., 2003. Approval summary: imatinib mesylate capsules for treatment of adult patients with newly diagnosed Philadelphia chromosome-positive chronic myelogenous leukemia in chronic phase. Clin. Cancer Res. 9 (6), 1972–1979.

Kamps, R., et al., 2017. Next-generation sequencing in oncology: genetic diagnosis, risk prediction and cancer classification. Int. J. Mol. Sci. 18 (2), 308.

Kantarjian, H.M., et al., 2011. Nilotinib versus imatinib for the treatment of patients with newly diagnosed chronic phase, Philadelphia chromosome-positive, chronic myeloid leukaemia: 24-month minimum follow-up of the phase 3 randomised ENESTnd trial. Lancet Oncol. 12 (9), 841–851.

Karapetis, C.S., et al., 2008. K-ras mutations and benefit from cetuximab in advanced colorectal cancer. N. Engl. J. Med. 359 (17), 1757–1765.

Kaur, P., et al., 2019. Comparison of TCGA and GENIE genomic datasets for the detection of clinically actionable alterations in breast cancer. Sci. Rep. 9 (1), 1–15.

Kazandjian, D., et al., 2014. FDA approval summary: crizotinib for the treatment of metastatic non-small cell lung cancer with anaplastic lymphoma kinase rearrangements. Oncologist 19 (10), e5–e11.

Kim, D.-W., et al., 2016. Activity and safety of ceritinib in patients with ALK-rearranged non-small-cell lung cancer (ASCEND-1): updated results from the multicentre, open-label, phase 1 trial. Lancet Oncol. 17 (4), 452–463.

Klein, A.d., et al., 1982. A cellular oncogene is translocated to the Philadelphia chromosome in chronic myelocytic leukaemia. Nature 300 (5894), 765–767.

Knudsen, E.S., Witkiewicz, A.K., 2017. The strange case of CDK4/6 inhibitors: mechanisms, resistance, and combination strategies. Trends Cancer 3 (1), 39–55.

Kranenburg, O., 2005. The KRAS oncogene: past, present, and future. Biochim. Biophys. Acta 1756 (2), 81–82.

Krop, I.E., et al., 2014. Trastuzumab emtansine versus treatment of physician's choice for pretreated HER2-positive advanced breast cancer (TH3RESA): a randomised, open-label, phase 3 trial. Lancet Oncol. 15 (7), 689–699.

Leonard, J.P., et al., 2012. Selective CDK4/6 inhibition with tumor responses by PD0332991 in patients with mantle cell lymphoma. Blood 119 (20), 4597–4607.

Li, H., et al., 2018. Antitumor activity of EGFR-specific CAR T cells against non-small-cell lung cancer cells in vitro and in mice. Cell Death Dis. 9 (2), 1–11.

Liao, B.-C., Lin, C.-C., Yang, J.C.-H., 2015. Second and third-generation epidermal growth factor receptor tyrosine kinase inhibitors in advanced nonsmall cell lung cancer. Curr. Opin. Oncol. 27 (2), 94–101.

Licitra, L., et al., 2013. Predictive value of epidermal growth factor receptor expression for first-line chemotherapy plus cetuximab in patients with head and neck and colorectal cancer: analysis of data from the EXTREME and CRYSTAL studies. Eur. J. Cancer 49 (6), 1161–1168.

Lierman, E., et al., 2012. Ponatinib is active against imatinib-resistant mutants of FIP1L1-PDGFRA and KIT, and against FGFR1-derived fusion kinases. Leukemia 26 (7), 1693–1695.

Lievre, A., et al., 2006. KRAS mutation status is predictive of response to cetuximab therapy in colorectal cancer. Cancer Res. 66 (8), 3992–3995.

Long, G., et al., 2017. Dabrafenib plus trametinib versus dabrafenib monotherapy in patients with metastatic BRAF V600E/K-mutant melanoma: long-term survival and safety analysis of a phase 3 study. Ann. Oncol. 28 (7), 1631–1639.

Ma, C., Wei, S., Song, Y., 2011. T790M and acquired resistance of EGFR TKI: a literature review of clinical reports. J. Thorac. Dis. 3 (1), 10.

MacConaill, L.E., et al., 2011. Clinical implementation of comprehensive strategies to characterize cancer genomes: opportunities and challenges. Cancer Discov. 1 (4), 297–311.

Manzano, J.L., et al., 2016. Resistant mechanisms to BRAF inhibitors in melanoma. Ann. Transl. Med. 4 (12).

Martin, M., et al., 2017. Neratinib after trastuzumab-based adjuvant therapy in HER2-positive breast cancer (ExteNET): 5-year analysis of a randomised, double-blind, placebo-controlled, phase 3 trial. Lancet Oncol. 18 (12), 1688–1700.

Martinelli, E., et al., 2009. Anti-epidermal growth factor receptor monoclonal antibodies in cancer therapy. Clin. Exp. Immunol. 158 (1), 1–9.

McLeod, H.L., 2013. Cancer pharmacogenomics: early promise, but concerted effort needed. Science 339 (6127), 1563–1566.

Michor, F., et al., 2005. Dynamics of chronic myeloid leukaemia. Nature 435 (7046), 1267–1270.

Mitsudomi, T., 2014. Molecular epidemiology of lung cancer and geographic variations with special reference to EGFR mutations. Transl. Lung Cancer Res. 3 (4), 205.

Mok, T.S., et al., 2017. Osimertinib or platinum–pemetrexed in EGFR T790M–positive lung cancer. N. Engl. J. Med. 376 (7), 629–640.

Monk, B.J., et al., 2013. Patient reported outcomes of a randomized, placebo-controlled trial of bevacizumab in the front-line treatment of ovarian cancer: a gynecologic oncology group study. Gynecol. Oncol. 128 (3), 573–578.

Motzer, R.J., et al., 2010. Phase 3 trial of everolimus for metastatic renal cell carcinoma: final results and analysis of prognostic factors. Cancer 116 (18), 4256–4265.

Müller, M.C., et al., 2009. Dasatinib treatment of chronic-phase chronic myeloid leukemia: analysis of responses according to preexisting BCR-ABL mutations. Blood 114 (24), 4944–4953.

Nagahashi, M., et al., 2016. Genomic landscape of colorectal cancer in Japan: clinical implications of comprehensive genomic sequencing for precision medicine. Genome Med. 8 (1), 1–13.

Nagata, Y., et al., 2004. PTEN activation contributes to tumor inhibition by trastuzumab, and loss of PTEN predicts trastuzumab resistance in patients. Cancer Cell 6 (2), 117–127.

Nahta, R., et al., 2006. Mechanisms of disease: understanding resistance to HER2-targeted therapy in human breast cancer. Nat. Clin. Pract. Oncol. 3 (5), 269–280.

Neal, J.W., et al., 2016. Erlotinib, cabozantinib, or erlotinib plus cabozantinib as second-line or third-line treatment of patients with EGFR wild-type advanced non-small-cell lung cancer (ECOG-ACRIN 1512): a randomised, controlled, open-label, multicentre, phase 2 trial. Lancet Oncol. 17 (12), 1661–1671.

Nowell, P.C., Hungerford, D.A., 1960. Chromosome studies on normal and leukemic human leukocytes. J. Natl. Cancer Inst. 25 (1), 85–109.

Olanich, M.E., et al., 2015. CDK4 amplification reduces sensitivity to CDK4/6 inhibition in fusion-positive rhabdomyosarcoma. Clin. Cancer Res. 21 (21), 4947–4959.

O'neill, R., Temple, R., 2012. The prevention and treatment of missing data in clinical trials: an FDA perspective on the importance of dealing with it. Clin. Pharmacol. Ther. 91 (3), 550–554.

Ong, F., et al., 2012. Personalized medicine and pharmacogenetic biomarkers: progress in molecular oncology testing. Expert Rev. Mol. Diagn. 12, 593–602.

Ou, S.-H.I., 2011. Crizotinib: a novel and first-in-class multitargeted tyrosine kinase inhibitor for the treatment of anaplastic lymphoma kinase rearranged non-small cell lung cancer and beyond. Drug Des. Devel. Ther. 5, 471.

Ou, S.H.I., et al., 2012. Crizotinib for the treatment of ALK-rearranged non-small cell lung cancer: a success story to usher in the second decade of molecular targeted therapy in oncology. Oncologist 17 (11), 1351–1375.

Paiva, T.F., et al., 2015. Angiogenesis-related protein expression in bevacizumab-treated metastatic colorectal cancer: NOTCH1 detrimental to overall survival. BMC Cancer 15 (1), 1–12.

Pardanani, A., et al., 2003. Imatinib therapy for hypereosinophilic syndrome and other eosinophilic disorders. Blood 101 (9), 3391–3397.

Patel, J.N., 2016. Cancer pharmacogenomics, challenges in implementation, and patient-focused perspectives. Pharmgenomics Pers. Med. 9, 65.

Paugh, S., et al., 2011. Cancer pharmacogenomics. Clin. Pharmacol. Ther. 90 (3), 461–466.

Paz-Ares, L., et al., 2016. Correlation of EGFR-expression with safety and efficacy outcomes in SQUIRE: a randomized, multicenter, open-label, phase III study of gemcitabine–cisplatin plus necitumumab versus gemcitabine–cisplatin alone in the first-line treatment of patients with stage IV squamous non-small-cell lung cancer. Ann. Oncol. 27 (8), 1573–1579.

Peters, S., et al., 2017. Alectinib versus crizotinib in untreated ALK-positive non–small-cell lung cancer. N. Engl. J. Med. 377 (9), 829–838.

Pirker, R., et al., 2012. EGFR expression as a predictor of survival for first-line chemotherapy plus cetuximab in patients with advanced non-small-cell lung cancer: analysis of data from the phase 3 FLEX study. Lancet Oncol. 13 (1), 33–42.

Planchard, D., et al., 2016. Dabrafenib plus trametinib in patients with previously treated BRAFV600E-mutant metastatic non-small cell lung cancer: an open-label, multicentre phase 2 trial. Lancet Oncol. 17 (7), 984–993.

Planchard, D., et al., 2017. Dabrafenib plus trametinib in patients with previously untreated BRAFV600E-mutant metastatic non-small-cell lung cancer: an open-label, phase 2 trial. Lancet Oncol. 18 (10), 1307–1316.

Price, T.J., et al., 2014. Panitumumab versus cetuximab in patients with chemotherapy-refractory wild-type KRAS exon 2 metastatic colorectal cancer (ASPECCT): a randomised, multicentre, open-label, non-inferiority phase 3 study. Lancet Oncol. 15 (6), 569–579.

Purcell, S., et al., 2007. PLINK: a tool set for whole-genome association and population-based linkage analyses. Am. J. Hum. Genet. 81 (3), 559–575.

Reck, M., et al., 2016. The effect of necitumumab in combination with gemcitabine plus cisplatin on tolerability and on quality of life: results from the phase 3 SQUIRE trial. J. Thorac. Oncol. 11 (6), 808–818.

Relling, M., et al., 2011. Clinical pharmacogenetics implementation consortium guidelines for thiopurine methyltransferase genotype and thiopurine dosing. Clin. Pharmacol. Ther. 89 (3), 387–391.

Rosell, R., et al., 2012. Erlotinib versus standard chemotherapy as first-line treatment for European patients with advanced EGFR mutation-positive non-small-cell lung cancer (EURTAC): a multicentre, open-label, randomised phase 3 trial. Lancet Oncol. 13 (3), 239–246.

Roskoski Jr., R., 2004. The ErbB/HER receptor protein-tyrosine kinases and cancer. Biochem. Biophys. Res. Commun. 319 (1), 1–11.

Rugo, H., et al., 2018. Impact of palbociclib plus letrozole on patient-reported health-related quality of life: results from the PALOMA-2 trial. Ann. Oncol. 29 (4), 888–894.

Russo, A., et al., 2015. A decade of EGFR inhibition in EGFR-mutated non small cell lung cancer (NSCLC): old successes and future perspectives. Oncotarget 6 (29), 26814.

Rutkowski, P., et al., 2010. Imatinib mesylate in advanced dermatofibrosarcoma protuberans: pooled analysis of two phase II clinical trials. J. Clin. Oncol. 28 (10), 1772.

Ryan, Q., et al., 2008. FDA drug approval summary: lapatinib in combination with capecitabine for previously treated metastatic breast cancer that overexpresses HER-2. Oncologist 13 (10), 1114–1119.

Sabari, J.K., et al., 2017. The activity, safety, and evolving role of brigatinib in patients with ALK-rearranged non-small cell lung cancers. Onco. Targets. Ther. 10, 1983.

Sandler, A., et al., 2006. Paclitaxel–carboplatin alone or with bevacizumab for non–small-cell lung cancer. N. Engl. J. Med. 355 (24), 2542–2550.

Schrank, Z., et al., 2018. Current molecular-targeted therapies in NSCLC and their mechanism of resistance. Cancers 10 (7), 224.

Schultz, K.R., et al., 2009. Improved early event-free survival with imatinib in Philadelphia chromosome–positive acute lymphoblastic leukemia: a children's oncology group study. J. Clin. Oncol. 27 (31), 5175.

Scott, R.H., Fowler, T.A., Caulfield, M., 2019. Genomic medicine: time for health-care transformation. Lancet 394 (10197), 454–456.

Seluanov, A., et al., 2018. Mechanisms of cancer resistance in long-lived mammals. Nat. Rev. Cancer 18 (7), 433–441.

Sharma, G.G., et al., 2018. Tumor resistance against ALK targeted therapy—where it comes from and where it goes. Cancers 10 (3), 62.

Shin, S., et al., 2016. Erlotinib plus gemcitabine versus gemcitabine for pancreatic cancer: real-world analysis of Korean national database. BMC Cancer 16 (1), 1–7.

Simon, R., 2013. Drug-diagnostics co-development in oncology. Front. Oncol. 3, 315.

Slamon, D.J., et al., 1989. Studies of the HER-2/neu proto-oncogene in human breast and ovarian cancer. Science 244 (4905), 707–712.

Soria, J.-C., et al., 2017a. First-line ceritinib versus platinum-based chemotherapy in advanced ALK-rearranged non-small-cell lung cancer (ASCEND-4): a randomised, open-label, phase 3 study. Lancet 389 (10072), 917–929.

Soria, J., Tan, D., Chiari, R., 2017b. First-line ceritinib versus platinum-based chemotherapy in advanced ALK-rearranged non-small-cell lung cancer (ASCEND-4): a randomised, open-label, phase 3 study (vol. 389, p. 917, 2017). Lancet 389 (10072), 908.

Soria, J.-C., et al., 2018. Osimertinib in untreated EGFR-mutated advanced non–small-cell lung cancer. N. Engl. J. Med. 378 (2), 113–125.

Soverini, S., et al., 2005. ABL mutations in late chronic phase chronic myeloid leukemia patients with up-front cytogenetic resistance to imatinib are associated with a greater likelihood of progression to blast crisis and shorter survival: a study by the GIMEMA Working Party on Chronic Myeloid Leukemia. J. Clin. Oncol. 23 (18), 4100–4109.

Spigel, D.R., et al., 2013. Randomized phase II trial of onartuzumab in combination with erlotinib in patients with advanced non–small-cell lung cancer. J. Clin. Oncol. 31 (32), 4105.

Spigel, D.R., et al., 2017. Results from the phase III randomized trial of onartuzumab plus erlotinib versus erlotinib in previously treated stage IIIB or IV non-small-cell lung cancer: METLung. J. Clin. Oncol. 35, 412–420.

Stephens, P., et al., 2004. Intragenic ERBB2 kinase mutations in tumours. Nature 431 (7008), 525–526.

Subbiah, V., et al., 2018. Dabrafenib and trametinib treatment in patients with locally advanced or metastatic BRAF V600–mutant anaplastic thyroid cancer. J. Clin. Oncol. 36 (1), 7.

Tabernero, J., et al., 2015. Analysis of circulating DNA and protein biomarkers to predict the clinical activity of regorafenib and assess prognosis in patients with metastatic colorectal cancer: a retrospective, exploratory analysis of the CORRECT trial. Lancet Oncol. 16 (8), 937–948.

Tabernero, J., et al., 2018. Analysis of angiogenesis biomarkers for ramucirumab efficacy in patients with metastatic colorectal cancer from RAISE, a global, randomized, double-blind, phase III study. Ann. Oncol. 29 (3), 602–609.

Talpaz, M., et al., 2006. Dasatinib in imatinib-resistant Philadelphia chromosome–positive leukemias. N. Engl. J. Med. 354 (24), 2531–2541.

Tarn, C., et al., 2005. Analysis of KIT mutations in sporadic and familial gastrointestinal stromal tumors: therapeutic implications through protein modeling. Clin. Cancer Res. 11 (10), 3668–3677.

Turner, N.C., et al., 2015. Palbociclib in hormone-receptor–positive advanced breast cancer. N. Engl. J. Med. 373 (3), 209–219.

Tuveson, D.A., et al., 2001. STI571 inactivation of the gastrointestinal stromal tumor c-KIT oncoprotein: biological and clinical implications. Oncogene 20 (36), 5054–5058.

van Brummelen, E.M., et al., 2017. BRAF mutations as predictive biomarker for response to anti-EGFR monoclonal antibodies. Oncologist 22 (7), 864–872.

Van Cutsem, E., et al., 2007. Open-label phase III trial of panitumumab plus best supportive care compared with best supportive care alone in patients with chemotherapy-refractory metastatic colorectal cancer. J. Clin. Oncol. 25 (13), 1658–1664.

Vogel, F., 1959. Moderne probleme der humangenetik. In: Ergebnisse der inneren medizin und kinderheilkunde. Springer, pp. 52–125.

Von Minckwitz, G., et al., 2017. Adjuvant pertuzumab and trastuzumab in early HER2-positive breast cancer. N. Engl. J. Med. 377 (2), 122–131.

Wang, J.P., et al., 2015. Erlotinib is effective in pancreatic cancer with epidermal growth factor receptor mutations: a randomized, open-label, prospective trial. Oncotarget 6 (20), 18162.

Weisberg, E., et al., 2007. Second generation inhibitors of BCR-ABL for the treatment of imatinib-resistant chronic myeloid leukaemia. Nat. Rev. Cancer 7 (5), 345–356.

Westin, J.R., Kurzrock, R., 2012. It's about time: lessons for solid tumors from chronic myelogenous leukemia therapy. Mol. Cancer Ther. 11 (12), 2549–2555.

Wilke, H., et al., 2008. Cetuximab plus irinotecan in heavily pretreated metastatic colorectal cancer progressing on irinotecan: MABEL study. J. Clin. Oncol. 26 (33), 5335–5343.

Wilson, F.H., et al., 2015. A functional landscape of resistance to ALK inhibition in lung cancer. Cancer Cell 27 (3), 397–408.

Wu, W., Haderk, F., Bivona, T.G., 2017. Non-canonical thinking for targeting ALK-fusion onco-proteins in lung cancer. Cancers 9 (12), 164.

Yang, J.C.-H., et al., 2014. Epidermal growth factor receptor mutation analysis in previously unanalyzed histology samples and cytology samples from the phase III Iressa Pan-ASia Study (IPASS). Lung Cancer 83 (2), 174–181.

Yang, J.C., et al., 2015. Clinical activity of afatinib in patients with advanced non-small-cell lung cancer harbouring uncommon EGFR mutations: a combined post-hoc analysis of LUX-Lung 2, LUX-Lung 3, and LUX-Lung 6. Lancet Oncol. 16 (7), 830–838.

Yang, J.C.-H., et al., 2017a. Pooled systemic efficacy and safety data from the pivotal phase II studies (NP28673 and NP28761) of alectinib in ALK-positive non-small cell lung cancer. J. Thorac. Oncol. 12 (10), 1552–1560.

Yang, C., et al., 2017b. Acquired CDK6 amplification promotes breast cancer resistance to CDK4/6 inhibitors and loss of ER signaling and dependence. Oncogene 36 (16), 2255–2264.

Yao, J.C., et al., 2011. Everolimus for advanced pancreatic neuroendocrine tumors. N. Engl. J. Med. 364 (6), 514–523.

Yao, J.C., et al., 2016. Everolimus for the treatment of advanced, non-functional neuroendocrine tumours of the lung or gastrointestinal tract (RADIANT-4): a randomised, placebo-controlled, phase 3 study. Lancet 387 (10022), 968–977.

Yardley, D.A., et al., 2013. Everolimus plus exemestane in postmenopausal patients with HR+ breast cancer: BOLERO-2 final progression-free survival analysis. Adv. Ther. 30 (10), 870–884.

Yoshino, T., et al., 2018. Are BRAF mutated metastatic colorectal cancer (mCRC) tumors more responsive to VEGFR-2 blockage? Analysis of patient outcomes by RAS/RAF mutation status in the RAISE study—a global, randomized, double-blind, phase III study. J. Clin. Oncol. 36, 622. American Society of Clinical Oncology.

Zhang, G., Nebert, D.W., 2017. Personalized medicine: genetic risk prediction of drug response. Pharmacol. Ther. 175, 75–90.

Zhang, W.W., et al., 2009. Predictors of primary imatinib resistance in chronic myelogenous leukemia are distinct from those in secondary imatinib resistance. J. Clin. Oncol. 27 (22), 3642.

Zuurbier, L., et al., 2017. Apelin: a putative novel predictive biomarker for bevacizumab response in colorectal cancer. Oncotarget 8 (26), 42949.

Precision medicine: Dose for anticancer therapy

Shiva Tushir[a], Monu Yadav[b], Sudha Bansal[c], and Anil Kumar[d]
[a]Department of Pharmacy, Panipat Institute of Engineering and Technology (PIET), Samalkha, Panipat, Haryana, India
[b]Department of Pharmacy, School of Medical & Allied Sciences, GD Goenka University, Gurgaon, India
[c]Department of Pharmaceutical Sciences, Guru Jambeshwar University of Science and Technology, Hissar, India
[d]Pharmacology Division, University Institute of Pharmaceutical Sciences (UIPS), UGC Centre of Advanced Study, Panjab University, Chandigarh, India

1. Introduction

Precision medicine is the way of providing specific care to the individual patient based on its genetic profile. Cancer is an extremely harmful disease-causing loss in the life of thousands of people throughout the world. Standard therapy selected for a large population may fail or produce variable responses due to polymorphism in genes encoding for drug metabolism enzymes and transporters leading to increased variation for response to standard therapy, this increased the scope of precision medicine in cancer (Krzyszczyk et al., 2018). In the traditional methods of cancer therapy, some issues can be resolved by the application of pharmacogenomics as there is a very high need of increasing the safety of anticancer therapy and reductions in associated toxicity.

2. Pathophysiology of cancer

Cancer has a complex Pathophysiology because mutations in the tumor cells are produced due to mutations in the normal cells at the gene level causing uncontrolled tumor masses growing with altered physiology (Parks et al., 2017). There are some latest techniques like MSVM for correct identification and accurate classification of cancer type based on its genetic expression profiles (Lee and Lee, 2003). One property of cancer cells that have been successfully utilized in the past for the development of anticancer medicines is the inhibition of cellular reproduction. The majority of cancer-killing medications now on the market hinder DNA synthesis or interfere with its function in some way. A cell must reproduce all components, including its genome, to split into two cells, and unlike the synthesis of other main macromolecules (protein, RNA, lipid, etc.), DNA synthesis does not occur to a considerable extent in quiescent cells. Because the majority of cells in an adult organism are dormant and not repeating their genome directing DNA

Biomarkers in Cancer Detection and Monitoring of Therapeutics
https://doi.org/10.1016/B978-0-323-95116-6.00002-5

Copyright © 2024 Elsevier Inc.
All rights reserved.

replication allows for some selection. Of course, certain organs (bone marrow, gastrointestinal tract, hair follicles, and so on) are replicative, and all cells must repair their DNA regularly. As a result, inhibiting DNA replication in normal tissues causes significant toxicity, limiting the quantity of medicine that a patient may take. Despite this issue, very effective anticancer medications have been discovered that improve survival and, in some situations, cure the patient's condition. Purines and pyrimidines are salvaged by human cells for the manufacture of deoxyribonucleotides, which are used to make DNA, and analogs of these nucleotide precursors have shown to be significant class of anticancer drugs. The FDA has authorized a total of 14 antimetabolites for purines and pyrimidines (Parker, 2009).

3. Pharmacogenetics in cancer

Any kind of Genetic modification like mutation or polymorphism in genes encoding specifically for drug-metabolizing enzymes can influence strongly the pharmacokinetics of anticancer drugs. Any changes in the pharmacokinetics of anticancer drugs, e.g., absorption, metabolism, distribution, etc., influence further effects produced along with its toxicity. There will be a great help in the identification of either response or resistance for any proposed anticancer drugs in those patients who are eligible for chemotherapy by the technique of pharmacogenetics screening (Bertholee et al., 2017). Significant improvements in the field of cancer research have happened in the last 10 years. Only a few cancer therapies were approved by FDA in the last decade and now huge progress is seen as thousands of drugs are under clinical trial investigation (Aggarwal, 2010). Immunotherapy has been identified as one of the promising therapy for cancer has the advantage of targeting to host immune system for the killing of cancerous cells (Couzin-Frankel, 2013). Tumor cells possess inherent complex biology and due to the impact of multiple oncogenic driver mutations, most of the agents to be targeted for therapy produced initial response but are not able to control diseases over a long period. So major challenge faced by cancer research is resistance to chemotherapy and resistance to therapy designed for specific molecular targets (Holohan et al., 2013). There is a need for personalized medicine and the successful completion of human genome project in the past decade give insights to scientist and clinicians working in cancer research that pharmacogenomics has the potential of affecting pharmacokinetics and pharmacodynamics of any drug therapy which further lead to the concept of individualized or personalized medicine for cancer (Green and Guyer, 2011). Two types of mutations are very important for the selection of anticancer therapy dosing play an important role in the selection for precision medicine for cancer. Somatic mutations decide the pharmacodynamics of any drug which further may help in the selection of anticancer therapy but germline mutations play a very important role in the pharmacokinetics like absorption metabolism, etc., of drug and possible drug response of any crude drug (Patel, 2014).

The dose of anticancer therapy can be personalized by two methods one is TDM-Therapeutic drug monitoring second is pharmacokinetic guided dosing to improve patient access to the medicine and increase the quality and safety of patient care. Method of TDM-therapeutic drug monitoring is best favorable for the dose selection of drugs that possess narrow therapeutic index, severe toxicity, and predictable relationship of dose and response and traditional method of chemotherapy possess all these qualities. Due to the proven relationship between pharmacokinetics and pharmacodynamics along with a narrow therapeutic index of traditional therapies like 5 fluorouracil, methotrexate, topotecan, etc. Therapeutic drug monitoring is not adopted in routine (Gao et al., 2012). Any drug can be metabolized by three phases consist of modification in the drug in phase one, conjugation in the second phase and its elimination in urine or bile in the third phase. In phase 1 metabolism, hydrolysis, reduction, and oxidation of individual drugs take place and the majority of that belongs to the family of cytochrome P_{450} (Lamb et al., 2007). Conjugation makes most drugs more soluble and easily excreted by the kidneys. Glucuronidation is the most common phase II reaction and specific phase II drug-metabolizing enzymes, such as glutathione S-transferases (GSTs) play a very important role in this (Jancova et al., 2010). Polymorphism in the genes encoding for enzymes responsible for phase 2 reactions may influence the pharmacokinetics of anticancer drugs. Genes encoding for the enzymes which are responsible for phase 2 reactions in purine and pyrimidine analogs have been known to possess more mutations and polymorphism affecting the activity of respective enzymes (McLeod et al., 2000). Similarly, absorption and excretion of anticancer drugs can be affected by any kind of polymorphism in genes encoding for drug efflux transporters like P-glycoprotein (Leiri, 2012). Monoclonal antibodies are utilized nowadays and pharmacokinetics of monoclonal antibodies impart a severe impact on the therapeutic response of an individual patient. For example, polymorphism in the FCGRT gene responsible for FcRn protein expression act as an important pharmacogenetic biomarker affecting the pharmacokinetics of monoclonal antibodies like cetuximab for metastatic colorectal cancer (Passot et al., 2013).

4. Types of enzymes and transporters responsible for pharmacokinetics of anticancer drugs

4.1 Enzymes for phase 1 metabolism

Cytochrome enzymes belonging to a family of membrane-bound proteins located in the endoplasmic reticulum are responsible for Phase 1 reactions. Cytochrome enzymes are very important for the pathophysiology of cancer and its intervention for treatment. Some can mediate metabolic activation of precarcinogens and lead to its effect on the activity of anticancer drugs (Rodriguez-Antona and Ingelman-Sundberg, 2006). About 57 active genes in humans and 58 pseudogenes are known till now (Nelson et al., 2004). Mutations in the genes encoding for cytochrome enzymes may lead to a complete absence of enzyme, it may increase or decrease the expression of a specific enzyme, or may lead to alteration in substrate specificity. The affected people may be classified into four primary phenotypes based on the allele composition: poor metabolizers (PMs), who have two alleles; poor metabolizers (PMs), who have one allele; poor metabolizers (PMs), who have two alleles; and poor metabolizers (PMs), who have the metabolism of cancer drugs affected by cytochrome CYP1A2 enzyme. Polymorphic enzymes of phase 1 metabolism are classified further into two types. Class 1 consists of CYP2E1, CYP3A4, CYP1A1, and CYP1A2, and these all are very active in the metabolism of carcinogens and hence are important for pharmacokinetic of anticancer drugs, but many of its polymorphism are not clinically important. Class II consists of CYP2B6, CYP2C9, CYP2D6, and CYP2C19 which are very active in the metabolism of drugs other than precarcinogens and are highly polymorphic (Rodriguez-Antona and Ingelman-Sundberg, 2006). Cancer drug metabolism is affected by only one member, i.e., CYP1A2 out of the CYP1 family. This enzyme is responsible for the metabolism of 20 drugs which are very useful in the clinical setting and contribute to 15% in human liver out of total cytochrome CYP450 amount (van Schaik, 2005). CYP2 family is very important as the majority of enzymes responsible for polymorphism are members of this, e.g., CYP2A6, CYP2B6, CYP2C9, CYP2C19, and CYP2D6. Tegafur is the prodrug of 5-fluorouracil and is activated by the CYP2A6 enzyme. In a study on Chinese livers, the CYP2A6*4 allele caused the reduction of in vitro microsomal conversion of 5 fluorouracil from its prodrug tegafur whereas the CYP2A6*1B variant of allele caused increases in the in vitro formation of 5 fluorouracil (Wang et al., 2011). Metabolism of more than 50% of clinically useful drugs like cyclophosphamide, etoposide, vinblastine, vincristine, and paclitaxel are caused by CYP3A subfamily. The activity of this enzyme range covers a broad range of subjects. Enzymatic activity is affected based on nongenetic factors like the age of the subject, its hormone level, the health of any person along environmental stimulus. CYP3A is responsible for a wide range of activities that cannot be justified by its genetic variations even though it possesses 40 allele variants and is not practiced clinically (Deenen et al., 2011).

4.2 Non-CYP phase II-metabolizing enzymes

There are various reports in the literature for the polymorphism in genes associated with Phase II metabolism and anticancer drugs pharmacokinetics. Four families of glutathione S-transferase (GST) are found which are named GSTA, GSTM, GSTP, and GSTT. Detoxification of several anticancer drugs like melphalan, busulfan, and chlorambucil is caused by GSTA1. Allele GSTA1*B have clinical significance in the therapeutic monitoring and dose calculation of busulfan especially in the pediatric population as a 30% reduction in the clearance of this medicine has been reported due to the presence of the mutation in this particular GSTA1*B allele (Johnson et al., 2013; Gaziev et al., 2010).

4.3 Uridine diphosphate glucuronosyltransferases

This enzyme belongs to the superfamily of enzymes that are responsible for the glucuronidation of any xenobiotics. The process of glucuronidation of any xenobiotics involves its binding with glucuronic acid and this helps in the elimination of any drug by bile or kidney as any substance originated due to cellular metabolism would be water-soluble whenever combined with glucuronic acid. Gilbert syndrome or Crigler-Najjar syndrome caused by the absence or defect in the enzyme responsible for conjugation of bilirubin and named as uridine diphosphate glucuronosyltransferase-1A1 (UGT1A1) was found to be associated with polymorphism in the UGT1A1*28 variant of this enzyme (Strassburg, 2008). At present, 113 different variants of this enzyme has been reported throughout the genes and these lead to change in activity which may be either increases or decreases in the activity of enzyme along with expression of normal or defective characteristics of any organism.

4.4 Enzymes of purine and pyrimidine metabolism

The compound having a structure similar to the structure of nucleosides and nucleobases are utilized in the drugs for management of viral infections, inflammatory condition and cancer management of viral infections, inflammatory condition, and cancer. These structural analogs are inactive which are further activated to their triphosphate form by intracellular phosphorylation once taken up by the specific transporters of nucleosides and nucleobases. Few structural analogs may cause inhibition of enzymes responsible for the purine and pyrimidine nucleotides production for the synthesis of DNA and RNA. Some enzymes do not support the activation of purine and pyrimidine analogs and may cause either inactivation or degradation of product or parent compound or any of its synthetic products, Hence deficiency of any enzyme plays a very important role either in the metabolic pathways for breaking down of molecule into smaller units or biosynthetic pathways for synthesis of a larger compound by purine and pyrimidine analogs can strongly affect the pharmacokinetics of drug to be selected for anticancer therapy. Based on the pharmacokinetics study, 5-fluorouracil is prescribed in cancer patients either as adjuvant therapy or as palliative treatment in cancer of GIT, head, neck, and breast along with its prodrug Capecitabine to be consumed by oral route (Meyerhardt and Mayer, 2005; Twelves et al., 2005). However, 5-fluorouracil and its prodrug can express its anticancer effect after enzyme activation to fluoropyrimidines nucleotides. Dihydropyrimidine dehydrogenase enzymes involved in the breakdown of uracil and thymine is responsible for the catabolism of maximum amount (about 80%) of 5-fluorouracil (Heggie et al., 1987). Cancer patients can face lethal toxicities if they consume the constant dose of this drug and activity of dihydropyrimidine dehydrogenase enzyme is reduced as the therapeutic index of 5-fluorouracil is narrow (van Kuilenburg, 2004). Cancer patients having partial or complete deficiency of dihydropyrimidine dehydrogenase enzyme are at potential risk of lethal toxicities associated with 5-fluorouracil taken as part of anticancer therapy because the deficiency of dihydro-pyrimidine dehydrogenase enzyme leads to reduction in the enzymatic activity (Maring et al., 2002). Mutations occurring in the gene encoding for dihydropyrimidine dehydrogenase enzyme creates deficiency of this enzyme in any individual. In a pharma-cokinetic study by van Kuilenburg 40% lower mean Vmax value of drugs was reported by two compartmental models for Michaelis–Menten elimination in patients having two different alleles (c.1905 + 1G > A) for the mutations in the gene encoding for dihydropyrimidine dehydrogenase and mean terminal half-life was increased two times as compared to control group. The second enzyme in the catabolism of 5-fluorouracil (5FU) is dihydropyrimidinase (DHP), and it has been proposed that people with a deficit of this enzyme are at risk of severe 5-fluorouracil 5FU-related toxicity (van Kuilenburg et al., 2012). Complete deficiency of dihydropyrimidinase in any person reduces the activity of the enzyme and also the metabolism of dihydropyrimidine which further lead to the increased level of dihydropyrimidine along with uracil and thymine (patients with a partial DHP deficit have a decreased flux through the pyrimidine degradation pathway and are more likely to experience severe toxicity when given 5-fluorouracil, van Kuilenburg et al., 2010). Deoxycytidine kinase (CK) enzyme is very important in the metabolism of anticancer drugs because activation of various anticancer drugs like cytarabine, gemcitabine, decitabine, fludarabine, and clofarabine at the initial level is car-ried out by deoxycytidine kinase (dCK), any impairment in the expression of this enzyme leads to resistance to these drugs and overexpression in the cells with deficiency of this enzyme increased sensitivity of its analogs (Sumi et al., 1998).

4.5 Drug transporters

Variations in the pharmacokinetics of anticancer drugs and individual patient. Response can be caused by the polymorphism in genes encoding for drug transporters like P-glycoprotein and BCRP (van Rompay et al., 2003). P-gp is a membrane transporter that is part of the ABC superfamily transporter. It is involved in the active transport of lipophilic and phospholipids across lipid membranes (Leiri, 2012). Although BCRP carries bile salts, regulatory authorities consider BCRP a therapeutically relevant drug transporter because of its function in the pharmacokinetics of key medicines like rosuvastatin and the resulting drug–drug interactions (DDI). BCRP is a 72-kDa "half transporter" that is encoded by the ABCG2 gene and operates as a homodimer or homo-tetramer. The colon, small intestine, blood–brain barrier (BBB), placenta, and liver can-alicular membrane are all abundant in this. Multidrug-resistant gene MDR1 gene present at chromosome 7q21 encodes for P-gp transporters and number of polymorphism in this particular genes significantly affect the pharmacokinetics of various anticancer drugs (Cascorbi et al., 2001; Ekhart et al., 2009). Doxorubicin is the best example being a substrate of P-gp and BCRP and widely used either singly or in combination cancer therapy in the treatment of solid tumors like breast cancer (Lal et al., 2008).

4.6 Immunoglobulin-metabolizing enzymes

Monoclonal antibodies (mAbs or mobs) are antibodies created by cloning a single white blood cell. Monoclonal antibodies can only attach to the same epitope and have a monovalent affinity (the part of an antigen that is recognized by the antibody). Monoclonal antibodies may be made to precisely attach to practically any acceptable material, and then used to detect or purify it. Biochemistry, molecular biology, and medicine have all benefited from this potential. On a clinical level, monoclonal antibodies are used to diagnose and treat a variety of disorders. Several countries have approved the use of monoclonal antibodies for the treatment of mild COVID-19 symptoms. Monoclonal antibodies can be produced by recombinant DNA technology (Breedveld, 2000). There is an increase in the trend for use of monoclonal antibodies due to their specificity for tumor target and good activity (Wold et al., 2016). It is very difficult to predict the response of any cancer patient toward monoclonal antibodies based on different kinds of variability altering individual pharmacokinetic Pharmacokinetics of monoclonal antibodies selected for any cancer therapy possess similarity with immunoglobulin (IgG) in various properties because these are derived from human immunoglobulin G (IgG) (Ternant and Paintaud, 2005). Any structure of IgG possesses two portions for binding which are identical in structure (Fab) along with another portion able to crystallize (Fc). Neonatal Fc receptor on the phagocytic cells of reticuloendothelial system responsible for the protection of immunoglobulin G (IgG) from destructive metabolism (Keizer et al., 2010) will bind with the Fc portion of immunoglobulin G. Intracellular catabolism or destructive metabolism is the main pathway for the immunoglobulin G and monoclonal antibodies elimination with its Fc portion (Ternant et al., 2015). FCGRT gene located on chromosome no 19 encodes for neonatal Fc receptor (FcRn) (Mikulska et al., 2000), and very little information is available about the reported polymorphism in this gene affecting the pharmacokinetics of anticancer drugs. Metastatic colorectal cancer can be treated by the administration of Cetuximab either as single or in combination chemotherapy. It is a chimeric immunoglobulin monoclonal antibody targeting epidermal growth factor receptors (van Cutsem et al., 2008). The various number of studies reported the role of polymorphism in the FCGR gene affecting the anticancer effect of Cetuximab as a part of therapy.

4.7 Clinical trials

A budget of 215 million US dollars was released under the heading of "National precision medicine initiative" in the United States for the establishment of a natural database of genetics of 1 million population in the country. A clinical trial involves data collection

Basket trial

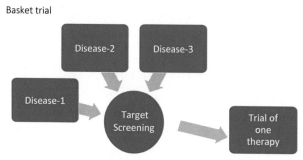

Fig. 1 About basket trial in precision medicine.

Umbrella trial

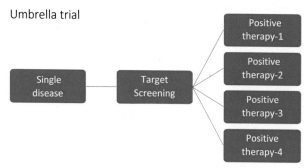

Fig. 2 About umbrella trial in precision medicine.

from thousands of people in its classical model but precision medicine testing involves testing of interventions in a different manner. Clinical study focusing on a single person or individual is known as N of −1 trials. Trials are designed in various ways one is the umbrella trial (Fig. 1) in which the effect of multiple drugs are tested for a single disease and in basket trial (Fig. 2) participants sharing certain genetic anomalies are considered as a basket and assigned with different treatments. Any clinician may prescribe only one drug at a time and study its effect on different biochemical parameters of any person before trying different therapy (Schork, 2015). Imatinib has shown the survival rate of leukemia patients to be doubled with Philadelphia translocation a kind of chromosomal abnormality (Druker and Sherbenou, 2007). Similarly, cetuximab increases the chances of survival in colorectal cancer patients with a mutation in the EGFR gene (Karapetis et al., 2008).

5. Future perspectives

P450s, which are expressed at greater levels in tumor cells than in surrounding normal tissue, provide therapeutic alternatives by activating prodrugs only in cancer cells and minimizing unwanted systemic effects associated with this. Recent progress in exploiting polymorphic P450 as a therapeutic target in cancer therapy is encouraging, and it might give a unique and effective cancer treatment option in the future (Rodriguez-Antona and Ingelman-Sundberg, 2006).

For molecular profiling, a necessary part of precision medicine, specific informed permission for testing in the context of clinical decision making is usually not necessary. The general permission form for testing and treatment at a cancer clinic should include molecular testing as a part of medical practice (Schwartzberg et al., 2017). Precision medicine-based dose selection of anticancer therapy possess a different kind of advantages but therapy can be very expensive for those patients who require any specific therapy or immunotherapy treatment because of the genetic profile of the tumor to be treated.

6. Concluding remarks

Nowadays, researchers are focusing on precision medicine also known as personalized medicine to reduce cancer therapy-related adverse effects and to enhance the efficacy of prescribed medicines. Screening of cancer patients eligible for combination chemotherapy according to its pharmacogenetics before the treatment initiation helps in the correct identification of responsive or resistant patients for the proposed anticancer therapy along with chances of toxicity produced if any. The purpose of precision medicine is to provide the right cancer therapy for the right patients at the appropriate time with an accurate dose. Precision oncology involves profiling of tumors at a molecular level and interpretation of genomic data with multidisciplinary inputs Oncologists should understand the concept of precision medicine to help patients in dose selection and to reduce cancer therapy-associated toxicities.

References

Aggarwal, S., 2010. Targeted cancer therapies. Nat. Rev. Drug Discov. 9 (6), 427.

Bertholee, D., Maring, J.G., van Kuilenburg, A.B., 2017. Genotypes affecting the pharmacokinetics of anticancer drugs. Clin. Pharmacokinet. 56 (4), 317–337.

Breedveld, F., 2000. Therapeutic monoclonal antibodies. Lancet 355 (9205), 735–740. https://doi.org/10.1016/S0140-6736(00)01034-5.

Cascorbi, I., Gerloff, T., Johne, A., 2001. Frequency of single nucleotide polymorphisms in the P-glycoprotein drug transporter MDR1 gene in white subjects. Clin. Pharmacol. Ther. 69 (3), 169–174. pii: S0009-9236(01)37416-7.

Couzin-Frankel, J., 2013. Cancer immunotherapy. Sci. Mag. 342, 1432–1433.

Deenen, M.J., Cats, A., Beijnen, J.H., Schellens, J.H., 2011. Part 2: pharmacogenetic variability in drug transport and phase I anticancer drug metabolism. Oncologist 16 (6), 820–834. https://doi.org/10.1634/theoncologist.2010-0259.

Druker, B.J., Sherbenou, D.W., 2007. Applying the discovery of the Philadelphia chromosome. J. Clin. Investig. 117 (8), 2067–2074. https://doi.org/10.1172/JCI31988.

Ekhart, C., Rodenhuis, S., Smits, P.H.M., 2009. An overview of the relations between polymorphisms in drug metabolising enzymes and drug transporters and survival after cancer drug treatment. Cancer Treat. Rev. 35 (1), 18–31. https://doi.org/10.1016/j.ctrv.2008.07.003.

Gao, B., Yeap, S., Clements, A., Balakrishnar, B., Wong, M., Gurney, H., 2012. Evidence for therapeutic drug monitoring of targeted anticancer therapies. J. Clin. Oncol. 30, 4017–4025. https://doi.org/10.1200/JCO.2012.43.5362.

Gaziev, J., Nguyen, L., Puozzo, C., 2010. Novel pharmacokinetic behaviour of intravenous busulfan in children with thalassemia undergoing hematopoietic stem cell transplantation: a prospective evaluation of pharmacokinetic and pharmacodynamic profile with therapeutic drug monitoring. Blood 115 (22), 4597–4604. https://doi.org/10.1182/blood-2010-01-265405.

Green, E.D., Guyer, M.S., 2011. Charting a course for genomic medicine from base pairs to bedside. Nature 470 (7333), 204–213.

Heggie, G.D., Sommadossi, J.P., Cross, D.S., 1987. Clinical pharmacokinetics of 5-fluorouracil and its metabolites in plasma, urine and bile. Cancer Res. 47, 2203–2206.

Holohan, C., van Schaeybroeck, S., Longley, D.B., Johnston, P.G., 2013. Cancer drug resistance: an evolving paradigm. Nat. Rev. Cancer 13, 714–726.

Jancova, P., Anzenbacher, P., Anzenbacherova, E., 2010. Phase II drug metabolizing enzymes. Biomed. Pap. Med. Fac. Univ. Palacky Olomouc Czech Repub. 154 (2), 103–116.

Johnson, G.G., Lin, K., Cox, T.F., 2013. CYP2B6*6 is an independent determinant of inferior response to fludarabine plus cyclophosphamide in chronic lymphocytic leukemia. Blood 122 (26), 4253–4258. https://doi.org/10.1182/blood-2013-07-516666.

Karapetis, C.S., Khambata-Ford, S., Jonker, D.J., O'Callaghan, C.J., Tu, D., Tebbutt, N.C., Zalcberg, J.R., 2008. K-ras mutations and benefit from cetuximab in advanced colorectal cancer. N. Engl. J. Med. 359 (17), 1757–1765.

Keizer, R.J., Huitema, A.D., Schellens, J.H., Beijnen, J.H., 2010. Clinical pharmacokinetics of therapeutic monoclonal antibodies. Clin. Pharmacokinet. 49 (8), 493–507. https://doi.org/10.2165/11531280-000000000-00000.

Krzyszczyk, P., Acevedo, A., Davidoff, E.J., Timmins, L.M., Marrero-Berrios, I., Patel, M., White, C., Lowe, C., Sherba, J.J., Hartmanshenn, C., O'Neill, K.M., 2018. The growing role of precision and personalized medicine for cancer treatment. Technology 6 (04), 79–100.

Lal, S., Wong, Z.W., Sandanaraj, E., 2008. Influence of ABCB1 and ABCG2 polymorphisms on doxorubicin disposition in Asian breast cancer patients. Cancer Sci. 99 (4), 816–823. https://doi.org/10.1111/j.1349-7006.2008.00744.x.

Lamb, D.C., Waterman, M.R., Kelly, S.L., Guengerich, F.P., 2007. Cytochromes P450 and drug discovery. Curr. Opin. Biotechnol. 18 (6), 504–512. pii: S0958-1669(07)00122-X.

Lee, Y., Lee, C.K., 2003. Classification of multiple cancer types by multicategory support vector machines using gene expression data. Bioinformatics 19 (9), 1132–1139.

Leiri, I., 2012. Functional significance of genetic polymorphisms in P-glycoprotein (MDR1, ABCB1) and breast cancer resistance protein (BCRP, ABCG2). Drug Metab. Pharmacokinet. 27 (1), 85–105. pii: JST.JSTAGE/dmpk/DMPK-11-RV-098.

Maring, J.G., van Kuilenburg, A.B.P., Haasjes, J., 2002. Reduced 5-FU clearance in a patient with low DPD activity due to heterozygosity for a mutant allele of the DPYD gene. Br. J. Cancer 86, 1028–1033.

McLeod, H.L., Krynetski, E.Y., Relling, M.V., Evans, W.E., 2000. Genetic polymorphism of thiopurine methyltransferase and its clinical relevance for childhood acute lymphoblastic leukemia. Leukemia 14, 567–572.

Meyerhardt, J.A., Mayer, R.J., 2005. Systemic therapy for colorectal cancer. N. Engl. J. Med. 352, 476–487.

Mikulska, J.E., Pablo, L., Canel, J., Simister, N.., 2000. Cloning and analysis of the gene encoding the human neonatal Fc receptor. Eur. J. Immunogenet. 27 (4), 231–240. https://doi.org/10.1046/j.1365-2370.2000.00225.x.

Nelson, D.R., Zeldin, D.C., Hoffman, S.M., Maltais, L.J., Wain, H.M., Nebert, D.W., 2004. Comparison of cytochrome P450 (CYP) genes from the mouse and human genomes, including nomenclature recommendations for genes, pseudogenes and alternative-splice variants. Pharmacogenetics 14, 1–18.

Parker, W.B., 2009. Enzymology of purine and pyrimidine antimetabolites used in the treatment of cancer. Chem. Rev. 109 (7), 2880–2893. https://doi.org/10.1021/cr900028p.

Parks, S.K., Cormerais, Y., Pouysségur, J., 2017. Hypoxia and cellular metabolism in tumour pathophysiology. J. Physiol. 595 (8), 2439–2450.

Passot, C., Azzopardi, N., Renault, S., 2013. Influence of FCGRT gene polymorphisms on pharmacokinetics of therapeutic antibodies. mAbs 5 (4), 614–619. https://doi.org/10.4161/mabs.24815.

Patel, J.N., 2014. Application of genotype-guided cancer therapy in solid tumors. Pharmacogenomics 15, 79–93. https://doi.org/10.2217/pgs.13.227.

Rodriguez-Antona, C., Ingelman-Sundberg, M., 2006. Cytochrome P_{450} pharmacogenetics and cancer. Oncogene 25 (11), 1679–1691.

Schork, N.J., 2015. Personalized medicine: time for one-person trials. Nature 520 (7549), 609–611.

Schwartzberg, L., Kim, E.S., Liu, D., Schrag, D., 2017. Precision oncology: who, how, what, when, and when not? Am. Soc. Clin. Oncol. Educ. Book 37, 160–169.

Strassburg, C.P., 2008. Pharmacogenetics of Gilbert's syndrome. Pharmacogenomics 9 (6), 703–715. https://doi.org/10.2217/14622416.9.6.703.

Sumi, S., Imaeda, M., Kidouchi, K., 1998. Population and family studies of dihydropyrimidinuria: prevalence, inheritance mode, and risk of fluorouracil toxicity. Am. J. Med. Genet. 78, 336–340.

Ternant, D., Paintaud, G., 2005. Pharmacokinetics and concentration effect relationships of therapeutic monoclonal antibodies and fusion proteins. Exp. Opin. Biol. Ther. 5, S37–S47. https://doi.org/10.1517/14712598.5.1.S37.

Ternant, D., Bejan-Angoulvant, T., Passot, C., 2015. Clinical pharmacokinetics and pharmacodynamics of monoclonal antibodies approved to treat rheumatoid arthritis. Clin. Pharmacokinet. 54 (11), 1107–1123. https://doi.org/10.1007/s40262-015-0296-9.

Twelves, C., Wong, A., Nowacki, M.P., 2005. Capecitabine as adjuvant treatment for stage III colon cancer. N. Engl. J. Med. 352, 2696–2704.

van Cutsem, E., Lang, I., D'haens, G., Moiseyenko, V., Zaluski, J., Folprecht, G., Rougier, P., 2008. KRAS status and efficacy in the first-line treatment of patients with metastatic colorectal cancer (mCRC) treated with FOLFIRI with or without cetuximab: the CRYSTAL experience. J. Clin. Oncol. 26 (15), 2.

van Kuilenburg, A.B.P., 2004. Dihydropyrimidine dehydrogenase and the efficacy and toxicity of 5-fluorouracil. Eur. J. Cancer 40, 939–950.

van Kuilenburg, A.B.P., Dobritzsch, D., Meijer, J., 2010. Dihydropyrimidinase deficiency: phenotype, genotype and structural consequences in 17 patients. Biochim. Biophys. Acta 1802, 639–648.

van Kuilenburg, A.B.P., Hausler, P., Schalhorn, A., 2012. Evaluation of 5-fluorouracil pharmacokinetics in cancer patients with ac.1905?1G[A mutation in DPYD by means of a Bayesian limited sampling strategy]. Clin. Pharmacokinet. 51, 163–174.

van Rompay, A.R., Johansson, M., Karlsson, A., 2003. Substrate specificity and phosphorylation of antiviral and anticancer nucleoside analogues by human deoxyribonucleoside kinases and ribonucleoside kinases. Pharmacol. Ther. 100, 119–139.

van Schaik, R.H., 2005. Cancer treatment and pharmacogenetics of cytochrome P450 enzymes. Investig. New Drugs 23 (6), 513–522. https://doi.org/10.1007/s10637-005-4019-1.

Wang, H., Bian, T., Liu, D., 2011. Association analysis of CYP2A6 genotypes and haplotypes with 5-fluorouracil formation from tegafur in human liver microsomes. Pharmacogenomics 12 (4), 481–492. https://doi.org/10.2217/pgs.10.202.

Wold, E.D., Smider, V., Felding, B.H., 2016. Antibody therapeutics in oncology. Immunotherapy 2 (108). https://doi.org/10.4172/imt.1000108.

Index

Note: Page numbers followed by *f* indicate figures, *t* indicate tables, and *b* indicate boxes.

Printed in the United States
by Baker & Taylor Publisher Services